HOUSING DESIGN AND SOCIETY IN AMSTERDAM

Nancy Stieber

HOUSING DESIGN AND SOCIETY IN AMSTERDAM

Reconfiguring Urban Order and Identity, 1900–1920

The University of Chicago Press

Chicago & London

NANCY STIEBER is associate professor of art at the University of Massachusetts, Boston.

The University of Chicago Press, Chicago 60637
The University of Chicago Press, Ltd., London

Printed in the United States of America
07 06 05 04 03 02 01 00 99 98   1 2 3 4 5
CLOTH ISBN 0-226-77417-1

Library of Congress Cataloging-in-Publication Data

Stieber, Nancy.
Housing design and society in Amsterdam : reconfiguring urban order and identity, 1900–1920 / Nancy Stieber.
p. cm.
Includes bibliographical references and index.
ISBN 0-226-77417-1 (alk. paper)
1. Working class—Dwellings—Netherlands—Amsterdam—History —20th century. 2. International style (Architecture)—Netherlands—Amsterdam. 3. Architecture and state—Netherlands—Amsterdam. 4. Amsterdam (Netherlands)—Buildings, structures, etc. I. Title.
NA7555.N4S75 1998
363.5'9623'09492352—dc21   97-50001
CIP

♾ The paper used in this publication meets the minimum requirements of the American National Standard for Information Sciences—Permanence of Paper for Printed Library Materials, ANSI Z39.48-1992

CONTENTS

ACKNOWLEDGMENTS

This book grew from research carried out in preparation for a doctoral dissertation in the history, theory, and criticism section of the MIT Department of Architecture. I owe a great debt of gratitude to my dissertation adviser Stanford Anderson, whose probing inquiry into historiography inspired my methodology and whose intellectual integrity set a standard to emulate. I am also grateful to the two other members of my dissertation committee: Helen Searing, eloquent, pioneering historian of the Amsterdam School, and John Habraken, a continuing model of the thoughtful commitment to housing design engendered in the Netherlands.

My investigation into Dutch housing and urbanism could not have been carried out without the continuing support and stimulation from others pursuing parallel issues. I benefited particularly from discussions with Ed Taverne and Maristella Casciato. Especially in the early days of my research I was helped by a number of gifted scholars, including Wim de Wit, Wessel Reinink, Manfred Bock, the late Peter de Ruyter, Frank Smit, Clara Brinkgreve, Selma Leydesdorf, Ali de Regt, Richter Roegholt, Egbert Hoogenberk, Donald Grinberg, and Wim Denslagen. I am thankful as well to those who read this draft in whole or in part and gave me the benefit of their critical comments: the late Richard Pommer, Mardges Bacon, Francesco Passanti, Joseph Siry, and two anonymous readers.

The hulking brick edifice called Ceres, which once housed a bread factory, was demolished in 1988, but the memory of the labyrinthine path that led through several doors and along dark flights of stairs to the floors of stacked portfolios is indelible to anyone who ever made use of the archives stored in this temporary branch of the Amsterdam Municipal Archives. Much of the material for this study was ferreted out from the Ceres depository through the patient and thorough persistence of archivist E. O. van der Goot. At the main Amsteldijk branch of the Municipal Archives I was assisted by a team of capable archivists; the personnel at the Topographical Atlas, the Press Collection, and the Library all provided invaluable assistance. Several departments of municipal government in Amsterdam graciously allowed me to consult their archives; I am indebted to Mr. Weyerstrass of the Publieke Werken, Ernst Klijzing of the Bouw- en Woningtoezicht, and Egbert Ottens of Volkshuisvesting. Fons Asselbergs and the late Dick van Woerkum made me welcome at the Nederlands Documentatiecentrum voor de Bouwkunst, and Mariet Willinge continued that hospitality at the successor organization, the Nederlands Architectuurinstituut. At the International Institute of Social History in Amsterdam, I was ably assisted by Johanna M. Welcker. I am especially grateful to J. H. Stork of the Algemene Woningbouw Vereniging for making available to me the archives of the Amsterdamsch Bouwfonds.

The staffs of many libraries repeatedly demonstrated their competence and professionalism: the library of the University of Amsterdam, the library of the Technical University of Delft, the Royal Library in the Hague, the library of NIROV in the Hague, the Amsterdam Public Library, the Amsterdam City Hall Library, Widener Library at Harvard University, the Avery Library at Columbia University, and Rotch Library at MIT.

The research for this study was undertaken with support from a number of sources: the Columbia Center for European Studies, the Social Science Research Council, the J. Paul Getty Foundation, the Harvard-MIT Joint Center for Urban Studies, the Technical University of Delft, and the University of Massachusetts in Boston. I am deeply grateful to the anonymous reviewers who saw fit to fund this research.

Without the patient encouragement of my editors at the University of Chicago Press, this manuscript would not have taken its final form. Christina O'Sullivan made a significant contribution to the manuscript by painstakingly drafting the floor plans. I am grateful to Eugène Dabekaussen for kindly reviewing the Dutch in the text.

When Richard D. Duke of the University of Michigan invited me to join him as his research assistant during a sabbatical at the Netherlands Institute for Advanced Studies, neither he nor I had any way of predicting the determining impact that encounter with Dutch culture would have on my subsequent career. I am indebted to him for giving me the opportunity to experience that sane society firsthand. My life has been enriched by the hospitality and assistance of the many friends in the Netherlands who so generously opened their doors to a peripatetic American: Bertil Geerts, Marion Smit, Paul Geerts, Geertje Buxtehude, Jan van Paradijs, Madeleine Godard, Maria Moesman, Prasuna Hoogenberk, Ellen Datloff, Maarten Schalekamp, and many others. In the United States, Francis Bone and Elizabeth Campbell never failed to come through at those terrible moments when only gargantuan effort would see the project to its finish. This book is dedicated to all these friends.

INTRODUCTION

During the first decades of the twentieth century, when an invigorating era of urban reform gave rise to a new ring of residential neighborhoods encircling the city's dispirited nineteenth-century districts, Amsterdam developed an international reputation as the mecca for social housing. The recently constructed housing, built primarily with government subsidy, was not only affordable to the general populace but also met rigorous standards of urban planning and architectural design. The city had effectively intervened in the real estate market; under its progressive patronage, housing that met the newly established standards was viewed as a right guaranteed for all citizens.

Many of the new housing blocks were distinguished by a fresh architectural style so closely associated with the city that it came to be called the Amsterdam School. The dramatic, sometimes extravagant, aestheticism of these projects drew worldwide attention to Amsterdam between the wars, attracted as much by the innovative architectural style as by the city's enlightened municipal policies. These colorful brick blocks of undulating walls, imaginatively textured surfaces, and playful decoration expressed modern aspirations for the city and its inhabitants. Although most of the new housing construction in Amsterdam was tamer, many of the new districts arose with an unusually consistent application of the style. The most fantastic projects of the Amsterdam School permeated their neighborhoods with a utopian aura that generated a mixture of excitement and curiosity among visitors and inhabitants alike. In parallel experiments elsewhere in the city, garden suburb planning and concrete housing construction demonstrated Amsterdam's commitment to finding new solutions to the problem of urban growth. Thus the city played a leading role during the early, formative years of publicly sponsored housing in the Netherlands, its institutions creating what Helen Searing has aptly described as a laboratory for experimentation in housing.[1]

Architectural commentators have invariably considered Amsterdam alongside nearly contemporaneous projects of housing reform in London, Berlin, Frankfurt, and Vienna. Its aesthetic achievements have drawn the most sustained criticism. The Amsterdam School offered an expressionism considered more modern than the Arts and Crafts vernacular being built by the London county council. But Amsterdam's housing has been chastised for failing to achieve the modernist breakthrough of Frankfurt or Berlin. This assessment according to a fixed trajectory leading inexorably to functional forms placed Amsterdam's housing design outside the mainstream of modernism. Dutch functionalists of the 1920s abhorred the decorative treatment of the facade as an entity divorced from the spatial implications of the interior, a practice they associated with the Amsterdam School. Their criticism was echoed in the deterministic teleology of architectural critics who posited modernism as the triumph of rationalism and deemed expressionist styles irrational and therefore irrelevant.

Attention was first refocused on Amsterdam's housing history when the postwar reassessment of modern architecture prompted revision of the propagandistic histories that had identified the International Style as the culmination of twentieth-century architectural achievement. As a counterbalance to this approach, scholars began research into styles that did not belong to the orthodox modernist canon. Analysis of the Amsterdam School's expressionism resulted in a greater appreciation for the inventive style and formed an important corrective to the rhetoric of earlier histories.[2] In addition to investigation into the formal genesis of the style, the utopian character of the Amsterdam School was studied. It has been interpreted both as a visual translation of the hopes and aspirations of social democratic workers and as an example of the social engagement of twentieth-century architects.

This study emerges from different considerations. It has been inspired by the attempt of social historians to use cultural artifacts to study social processes and the attempt of social theorists to describe cultural production. It begins from the notion that the movement for improved mass urban housing in Europe catalyzed new patterns of public architectural patronage, and that this experiment in creating architecture for the public good is illustrative of issues central to both the modern welfare state and architectural modernism. Accordingly, this study does not approach architecture from the view internal to the discipline, that is, an object-oriented view trying to explain the genesis of particular forms. This is not a book about style; the development of the Amsterdam School has been ably described and its forms analyzed elsewhere.[3] Instead, the aim has been to provide the social history of a particular struggle to define architecture as knowledge, art, profession, and social service.

From its inception as a field of scientific study, art history has been driven by attempts to theorize the development and evolution of form. Such theories have run the gamut from the autonomous development of Riegl's *Kunstwollen* to Marxist theories of reflection, that is, from the genealogy of pure form to the hypothesis that aesthetic decisions reflect economic, class, or ideological position.[4] This study attempts to avoid the false methodological dilemma posed by a choice between the internal, autonomous and the external, contextual explanation of form. It adopts instead an approach based in part on the analysis of the social dynamics of cultural production introduced by Pierre Bourdieu.[5] Bourdieu puts forward the notion of a field of cultural production whose constitutive tensions are engendered by a structured set of forces between the institutions and agents operating in the field. For Bourdieu, the "artistic field is a field of forces, but it is also a field of struggles tending to transform or conserve this field of forces."[6] Such struggles and the forces that produce them become the object of study. Approached from this theoretical perspective, housing design in Amsterdam ceases to be viewed purely as an issue of modern aesthetics and instead can be analyzed as a product of modern social practices, that is, as the product of tensions within modernity. This shifts the inquiry away from explaining the generation of form to describing the field of cultural production. Form is no longer presented as the reflection, representation, or embodiment of some factor external to the aesthetic, be it zeitgeist, race, class, region, ideology, regime, or means of production. Rather, form emerges as a semiautonomous factor within a dynamic theater of social relations.[7]

The theater of social interaction under investigation here took shape as housing reform moved to the public stage. That transition gave rise to relationships that enabled and restrained architectural practice, defined new openings and limits for action by politicians, extended and contracted the range of choices for citizens. The advent of a public forum on housing quality opened new fields of contention, a new institutional setting in which the forces of politics, class, and the cultural domain operated in constitutive tensions. With the introduction of housing reform into the public realm, the disciplines of urban planning and architecture participated in this new social theater, transforming it and being transformed in turn.

Within this social domain, the nature of everyday life became a matter of public debate and the regulation of everyday life became a government function. Giles Deleuze has described the social domain as a recently formed landscape not precisely coterminous with the public or the private sector that nevertheless renegotiates the boundaries between public and private realms.[8] Areas previously dominated by individual choice, by the marketplace, or by the church were now introduced into this new domain, where players developed visions of civic order, institutions arose to serve those visions, and disciplines of knowledge emerged to legitimate and develop tools to realize them. Housing reform occupied one section of this new arena for social interaction as the problem of regulating daily life was translated into a program for shaping urban order.

The model of a social landscape as the basis for the study of housing design may appear to omit the architect's role as creative agent. However, although this theoretical framework subordinates analysis of the artist's process of decision making to the description of the landscape within which agents act, it by no means dismisses such analysis. Agents are present, but in situations not entirely of their own making. It is important to distinguish this approach from contextual analyses, in which autonomous actors are viewed as conditioned by their circumstances, or from reflection models, in which art is viewed as the direct expression of some external factor. Gombrich correctly objected to reflection models because they neglect the autonomous development of art as knowledge. With science as the exemplar of the growth of knowledge, Gombrich argued for a history of art that would permit the study of the internal, rational development of aesthetic understanding and technique.[9] Bourdieu rejects reflection theories on a similar basis: they overlook the relative autonomy of any field.[10] However, he does not posit a model of autonomous disciplinary development as the alternative to reflection or contextual theories. For Bourdieu, the artistic field is contained within, yet still relatively independent of, the field of power.[11] It cannot be reduced either to an autonomous world of art or to a mere reflection of the external political world.[12] One may acknowledge the independent histories of discourses, while recognizing that these discourses operate in a condition of reciprocity with other fields: they participate in the fields of power, of social class, and in the institutional environment. The model of a field of cultural production thus offers no deterministic hypotheses, but rather acknowledges the possibility for autonomous form development and permits the laying out of limits and openings for artistic freedom. Over time, the internal dynamics of a social environment are manifested in different ways, delineating the constraints and potentials for action created by and through its tensions. Those tensions are what the historian can and must try to describe.

IN ENGLAND, FRANCE, GERMANY, and other industrialized countries, inadequate housing had been identified as one of a number of problems arising from the rapid urbanization of the nineteenth century. Along with the modernization of water supply, utilities, urban transportation, and sanitation, the improvement of housing was viewed as an opportunity to fashion and maintain urban order by controlling the physical environment.[13] An international movement to contain the worst effects of capitalist development on daily lives made urban infrastructure the object of reform alongside other, less material issues such as education and labor relations.

Amsterdam's housing reform paralleled efforts elsewhere in Europe both in scope and aim. Through the nineteenth century, the European urban reform movement spawned campaigns that varied in political complexion but shared a similar genesis. Housing reform was initially a phenomenon of middle-class charity, in which individual doctors and amateur philanthropists attempted to ameliorate conditions piecemeal through the documentation of ills and the construction of model housing projects.

New housing types that incorporated hygienic measures were meant to demonstrate the feasibility of improved housing quality to the private housing market. Not until the turn of the century did the movement for housing reform intensify in recognition of the futility of such isolated achievements. A major transformation ensued. From the 1890s, a wave of housing and urban planning legislation was passed throughout Europe, introducing various national measures to regulate housing construction and urban development and to authorize government sponsorship of low-cost dwellings. State-sponsored housing projects arose next to the model dwellings erected by private philanthropists, introducing a challenge to the private housing market. This creation of a "substitution market" was resisted by property owners but supported both by progressives who intended it to serve as model and spur to the private construction industry and by socialists who hoped that state-controlled housing provision would eventually supplant the free market.[14] The transformation of the housing reform campaign from philanthropy to welfare, from privately sponsored to state sponsored, was also characterized by a change in the chief proponents of reform from individual amateurs to organized professionals. This was one of several strands in the campaign to regulate the urban environment that gave rise to the planning professions and altered the profession of architecture. There was a corresponding change in the definition of the dwellers, no longer paupers and the worthy poor, but the masses, the people, the citizenry. As Bullock and Read have put it: "With the introduction of programmes of State finance, housing reform as demonstration finally gave way to housing reform as execution. The contract which had been written in the mid-nineteenth century, between the individual, generous philanthropist and the individual, worthy worker was now finally presented as a contract between society as a whole and the individual who was entitled to a home as a member of that society."[15] As government became involved in the regulation and provision of housing, a modern institutional environment for housing reform was created, a stage on which the various players, the politicians, professionals, and dwellers, would assume new roles and new relationships.

The European urban reform movement was rooted in the Enlightenment project for social amelioration, a recurring subject of sociological, philosophical, and historical analysis during the twentieth century. The aim of that project was emancipatory: to release mankind from the shackles of oppressive regimes, whether political or dogmatic. The struggle for democracy and against superstition depended on the application of reason to the rule of law and doctrine. The underlying, and problematic, assumption was that through the application of reason, society might be improved.

Max Weber was one of the first to view with skepticism the emancipatory potential of the shift to social rationalism in its late-nineteenth-century manifestations. His work has been followed by a continuous series of critiques of this aspect of modernity, variously defined as increasing bureaucratization, societal rationalization, or instrumental rationalism.[16] Theodor Adorno and Max Horkheimer problematized the "transition to the world of the administered life" by raising the larger question of whether the Enlightenment had achieved emancipation from premodern regimes of political and epistemological domination only to create new forms of domination.[17] Their negative assessment has shaped further discussion.

One of the most extensive and provocative discussions of the Enlightenment project has appeared in the works of Michel Foucault, who associates it with the emergence of a power distinct from the sovereign power of government: the power constituted by normalization. According to Foucault, modernity is characterized by the advent of a society in which the space of administered welfare, with its systematic construction of "public spheres," is regulated by scientifically legitimated social norms derived for the public good. In the wake of Foucault, Paul Rabinow writes of the period in which this social landscape was invented: "For an array of interested parties, the problem was becoming one of constructing and regulating a new social field of everyday relations in an industrial, scientific, and democratic—i.e. modern—world, of regulating the normal."[18] Foucault examines the emergence of the human sciences as the disciplines that serve the project of "regulating the normal." The relationship of power to knowledge has been one of the most suggestive aspects of his work on normalization. In *The Order of Things*, he charted the construction and rise of the human sciences as the discourses of the social.[19] In subsequent work, in particular, *Discipline and Punish*, he has argued that the modern era is characterized by a reciprocal configuration of power and knowledge through which knowledge generates power and power engenders knowledge. Foucault not only views disciplinary discourses as coercive forces, but believes that these discourses invade the area of sovereignty and thus colonize the rule of law. In a society of normalization, the coercive forces of the new discourses of disciplinary power overwhelm and dominate whatever discourse of right invests sovereignty. It is through this process that the power of the human sciences is ultimately manifested.[20]

Many have criticized Foucault's formulation for its absolute negation of freedom, its claim that social rationalization has offered only the illusion of liberation, and its argument that the new disciplines generated by the Enlightenment project of social amelioration can act only as instruments of domination.[21] Charles Taylor accuses Foucault of viewing the rise of humanitarianism one-sidedly in terms of new technologies of control, missing "the ambivalence of these new disciplines," which can also permit "new kinds of collective action characterized by more egalitarian forms of participation." Taylor's point is that disciplines can function either as structures of domination or as bases for collective action.[22] This position rejects both the self-congratulatory triumphalism of rationalism's champions and the pessimistic paranoia of the Enlightenment's most extreme critics. It suggests that the practice of the human sciences is marked by inherent conflicts and tensions that can shape, constrain, limit, or enable the emancipatory impulse.

The critique of the Enlightenment has compelled confrontation and appraisal of the dual liberative and repressive character of the welfare state, a duality intrinsic to the engineered modernization that attempts to improve society. Its rationalistic and democratic basis provides liberation from the arbitrary rule of dogma and despot, but imposes another, nonconspiratorial and incomplete, form of coercion, the natural result of the attempt to control behavior through the derivation and application of norms.

As one of the means for reshaping society generated within the Enlightenment project, housing reform encompassed the contradictory aims of emancipation and social control. It might bring material improvement and spiritual uplift, but only through the imposition of a set of values. Whatever gain in autonomy housing improvements might offer the individual was countered by the controlling tendencies of the norms applied by the forces of reform. Those norms always reflected an agenda claiming to represent the interests of the community. Whether the claim was legitimized by religious revelation, historiographical teleology, or the supposed laws of the marketplace, the order to be imposed was made to appear both natural and beneficial, codified by a discourse and rules of fair public debate.

Housing design was thus assimilated into the paradoxical, double-edged condition that characterizes the tools of the modern welfare state. Within the social landscape of the welfare state, institutions and agents contended and through their struggles created conditions for liberation and control, for resistance and conformity. Liberative and controlling impulses coexisted in the campaign for social improvement, generating unavoidable tensions and producing space for individual and institutional action that both expanded and contracted opportunity.

The regulation of everyday life to create and maintain civic order generated a contingent set of issues: how to define civic order, how to organize a public forum for that definition and the nature of participation in such a forum, the creation of an institutional apparatus for the setting and application of norms, and the development of expertise that might legitimize norms. Once the Dutch Housing Act had wrested the control of housing provision from speculative developers and vested it in the public interest, the struggle began to define the public interest, to delimit the power that could be exerted in the name of that public interest, and to identify the norms of control. Shaping civic order introduced the problem of determining whose views and what values, what means and what criteria would be used to establish norms. Existing power relations, social and political, influenced the relative power of the various constituencies with an interest in housing reform. As a result, conflicting visions of civic order and conflicting attitudes toward the normalizing process emerged among modernists and traditionalists, the bourgeoisie and the working class, experts and laymen. The social landscape of housing reform was constituted through the resulting tensions.

IN AMSTERDAM, three linked aspects of modernity were primarily responsible for catalyzing the transformation of housing reform from philanthropic amateurism to welfare professionalism at the turn of the century: the introduction of government intervention, the new role of professional expertise, and the rise of mass political representation, especially of the working class. Each influenced the newly opened zone of social interaction that conditioned housing design and each produced specific tensions within that zone.

The first, government intervention, was the outcome of a long history of political reform, part of a general European development brilliantly described by Karl Polanyi as a self-imposed check on laissez-faire economics to contain those social consequences of the free market most disadvantageous to the status quo.[23] A wave of social legislation in the Netherlands at the turn of the century addressed issues such as child labor, workman's compensation, and old age pensions. In particular, the Dutch Housing Act of 1902 enabled municipalities to initiate housing improvement and required them to undertake urban planning, thus creating a new arena of activities for municipalities prepared to exploit its provisions. A high degree of municipal autonomy meant that local politics could play an important role in determining housing standards. In Amsterdam, the partisans of intervention were the Progressive Liberals and the Social Democrats, who made common cause in their espousal of governmental means to improve living conditions in opposition to the conservative defenders of private real estate interests. However, the split of class interests between liberals and socialists led to disagreements on the extent and ambition of housing reform.

The government thus became an active participant in a public discussion about establishing criteria and setting standards for the quality of housing. The legitimization of new housing standards required the authority of expertise, that is, the application of appropriate disciplines to determine or guide the setting and meeting of standards. The need of the government for such "scientific" legitimization stimulated the professionalization of several new reform disciplines, and the creation of that network of authority then set in motion a number of ancillary processes: the turf fights between disciplines for areas in which to exercise expertise, the fights within disciplines to define expertise, and the institutionalization of expertise in advisory bodies.

Second, in the wake of the new opportunities opened by commissions for large-scale housing projects, the architectural profession reorganized itself. New public standards of urban aesthetics led to a campaign to define architectural competence that split the ranks of architects. Public patronage for large-scale urban housing projects fueled the polarization of stylistic historicists and modernists, raising the question of how matters of taste should be resolved in a democracy. As the design of government-sponsored housing was made the subject of public debate, competing interests vied as legitimate determinants of taste: the "community," popular opinion, the housing societies constructing housing, the civil servants administering housing reform, and the architects themselves. Public and private rights and interests were disputed as the government attempted to establish standards for aesthetics in its own housing and that built by others. Tensions arose as architects debated ideals of aesthetic freedom versus the imposition of public standards of excellence.

Finally, setting public standards for housing design, which in effect regulated choices of lifestyle and taste for the community as a whole, was made more complex by increasing political representation in a society defined along class and religious lines. With wider suffrage, those previously underrepresented, such as workers and certain religious groups, strengthened their organization in a process the Dutch call *verzuiling:* the creation of parallel "pillars," each with its own schools, trade unions, newspapers, sports clubs, and housing associations. The secular parties, socialists and liberals, formed subcultures endorsing modernization in its many forms. Against them aligned the antimodernist confessionals: the Roman Catholic and the Orthodox Protestant pillars. Housing societies empowered to receive state financing under the Housing Act divided along these lines and became the institutional avenues for competing views on housing design.

Government intervention, increased professionalization, and the processes of political democratization in turn generated three pivotal conflicts in the field of housing reform and design. First, the conflict over the dimensions of the public realm: What should be the extent of its intervention into everyday life and the methods and aims of such intervention? What powers were to be granted government authorized institutions, and what would be their purview: to maintain civic order or foster a utopian order? The second conflict involved authority: By what criteria were norms to be legitimated? This issue involved the relative perspectives of the expert and the layperson, the former defending the rationalized representations of space projected by professionals, what Lefebvre calls "conceptualized space," the latter asserting the experienced perceptions of space, what Lefebvre calls "space as directly lived."[24] This conflict was complicated by the overlay of class meanings ascribed to norms, since the authority of the expert was often a translation of reform values. The conflict between expert and layperson could thus become a dispute between progressive bourgeois values and traditional working-class values, which might in turn be interpreted as the tension between progressive and conservative values.[25] Third, the conflict resulting from the attempt to establish universal standards of housing in a deeply segmented society: At what level of collectivity should norms be formed? For the individual, group, city, region, or nation? What definition describes the public realm: the liberal's notion of public interest, the socialist's class struggle, the conservative's rooted community? Each of these three areas of conflict, the roles of government, expertise, and the segmented public, exposed the complex nature of housing reform's social landscape.

Amsterdam's pioneer period of public housing reform thus reveals a theater of social interaction in which various facets of modernity contended: the preservation of individual property rights, the protection of the public interest, the rise of living standards, the freedom of expression, and the autonomy accorded disciplines of knowledge. Through the acts of individual agents and institutions whose decisions were conditioned by the new social environment of the modern reform movement, Amsterdam's housing took shape. The institutional environment modernized as a whole, encompassing not only those who supported the Enlightenment ideal of the rational improvement of society implicated in the urban reform movement, but also those who resisted it; both progressives and conservatives took on modern roles in this theater.

Amsterdam was also a pioneer in confronting a series of problems constitutive of the modern architectural project. In assuming housing commissions, architects had to adjust their professional identity to the conditions of public service. Public patronage problematized the identity of the architectural patron: was it the anonymous masses, the elected representative, the bureaucrat, the individual dweller? Architecture enlisted to improve daily life confronted the dilemma that popular taste was generated according to processes different from and often at odds with the autonomous development of the high culture endorsed by architects. At the end of the nineteenth century, architects were starting to argue for a reform of their discipline. When that internal agenda was called upon to serve modern urban reform through the design of housing and cities, the architectural profession was transformed. This institutional transformation tells us as much about architectural modernism as do disputes over style, if by architecture we mean not only the discipline itself, but also its social practice. The tensions between architects and laymen, between conservatives and progressives, between modernists and traditionalists illustrate a central dilemma of the modern architectural profession: the tension between its dual commitment to serve society and to further the progress of the architectural discipline.

In Amsterdam, the housing reform movement passed through a phase in which aesthetic reform was as important as technical improvements, when housing hygiene and architectural style became parallel tools in the project to bring order to the city. Housing design was to be the means of creating higher living standards, better citizens, and social integration; both sociotechnical and aesthetic knowledge were to be used to regulate and normalize aspects of daily life on behalf of the community.

Historians of housing reform tend to give short shrift to aesthetics, privileging instead the economic and demographic as determining realities. Architectural historians, on the other hand, generally focus on the formal development of high style, which even placed in social and political context defines architecture too narrowly as art. Analysis of the urban reform movement manifested in Amsterdam's pioneering housing projects must acknowledge the belief placed by reformers in the efficacy of the visual, as well as the hygienic, as a technique of amelioration. This phase of the reform movement endowed aesthetic knowledge with social power, assuming its potential to convey community, to create collectivity, to impose harmony, to express emancipatory desires, group identity, or empowerment. Reformers may have disagreed about the messages to be communicated through housing design, but they did not dispute the capacity of design to serve social reform. Indeed, arguments focused on design's assumed power and the purposes for which it might be exploited.

The design of reform housing in Amsterdam, particularly the development and application of the Amsterdam School, occurred within a conceptual and institutional context that separated the design of the street facade from that of the plan for housing units. This split was the result of a historical division of tasks so naturalized into design practice that it was not a subject of discussion. On the one hand, the genesis of the housing problem from within the social reform movement privileged the perspectives of hygiene and social work, which appropriated the floor plan as a tool to promote health and proper family life. On the other hand, housing design could be interpreted as an aesthetic issue like any other design problem, which the architect would approach in the capacity of artist. The separation of facade and plan was facilitated by the traditional building pattern of row houses in a perimeter block, where the continuous street facade could be solved as an aesthetic design problem and the floor plan as a functional problem. The split between facade and plan and their respective identification with the discourses of aesthetics and social hygiene were integral to the conceptualization of design solutions during the initial years of regulated housing design in Amsterdam and constituted the framework within which solutions evolved.

Accordingly, the institutions developed in Amsterdam to administer and review housing design identified the facade as a purely aesthetic issue, within the purview of the architects alone. The floor plan, on the other hand, was claimed by urban planners, social workers, and medical experts as well as by architects. The governmental review of housing proposals was carried out by different committees whose composition reflected the professional division of the turf. Public discourse was similarly divided. While the debates around the design of the housing facade raised issues of style, design control, and taste, debates on plan typology addressed lifestyles and ideological convictions. But in both cases, the problem of setting norms and of establishing public standards engendered tensions over the extent and nature of government control, the troubled relationship between the values of experts and of those to be regulated, and the question of collective or plural standards.

The division between the treatment of plans and facades in the theater of social reform has determined the organization of this book. The first two chapters map the field of housing reform, charting the political and disciplinary forces that defined it. In the first chapter, the nature of the housing problem as an aspect of the politics of daily life is described and the constellation of political groups participating in Amsterdam's urban reform outlined. The segmented nature of Amsterdam society is also discussed. The second chapter examines both the response of professions to the new tasks opened by the urban reform movement and the organization of housing expertise in the Amsterdam municipal government. It explains the emergence of the system for reviewing housing proposals that separated consideration of the plan and the facade, which in essence created separate locations for the discourses of hygiene and aesthetics. The remaining chapters then take up those two discourses in turn, examining for each the three issues of normalization outlined above: the extent and nature of government intervention in setting housing standards, the professional role in shaping working-class behavior, and the codification of normalized housing solutions for the community as a whole.

This account attempts to elucidate for one particular time, place, and field of endeavor the theater of relationships engendered by the contradictory controlling and liberative impulses of normalization. The consequent tensions between layman and professional, bourgeois and working class, political conservative and progressive, aesthetic modernist and traditionalist are constitutive of that space. Within this theater of social conflict, then, we can watch how social practices and relationships conditioned cognitive discourses as two fields of knowledge that impinged on the shaping of the city, hygiene and aesthetics, were caught in those tensions. The space of cultural production is seen to enable and constrain the cultural production of space.

This study is therefore less concerned with describing the development of the realm of housing reform in Amsterdam as a simple trajectory of success, either as social policy or aesthetic progress, than in identifying the inherent contradictions that conditioned design decisions. Rather than defining the direction of change, emphasis is placed on describing those tensions. The aim is to examine architectural design as a social practice implicated in the fields of political and cultural practice.[26] While acknowledging the autonomous history of the architectural discipline and the predispositions of its individual agents, it is possible to observe the simultaneous interaction of architecture with other fields, each dynamic, each reshaping the others. Henri Lefebvre suggests a history of the "social realm of spatial production" in which spatial production is viewed as a social process, and the interactions and relations of those using space, creating space, and controlling space can be studied.[27] The advent of the social welfare state gave rise to a new social realm of spatial production in which architecture was practiced both as social service and as autonomous discipline. By demonstrating the particular tensions created when Amsterdam made housing design a public issue, the disparate and contradictory nature of the project to reconfigure urban order and identity may be revealed.

PART ONE

THE POLITICS OF DAILY LIFE

By the end of the nineteenth century, housing conditions in Amsterdam had so deteriorated that official housing surveys, usually couched in a language of clinical objectivity, occasionally abandoned cold numerical analysis to express the poignancy of inhabitants' lives. A passage from an 1899 statistical report by the Amsterdam Building Inspector's Office conveys the sense of horror and outrage evoked by the worst neighborhoods:

> Mention must also be made of houses where the wood floor is in such bad condition that in places it is worn through and the ground is visible, while an unpleasant odor pervades the dwelling; where the outer walls are cracked through to the room inside; where the walls are so damp that the wallpaper, half fallen away, is covered with mold; of living rooms so dark that the inspector had to make his notes by candlelight although the day was bright and clear; of particularly neglected and dirty houses, crawling with insects; of overcrowded houses where the children sleep in the same drafty corner as the chamber pot used by all the family; or of parents who sleep with one or more of the younger children, while the older children, boys and girls together, sleep on the floor.[1]

Pervasive dampness, lack of sanitation, dark steep stairways, and vermin characterized the conditions under which many people lived, and in some instances worked, in the poorest districts of Amsterdam.

Overcrowding in inadequate housing was the unanticipated result of the dramatic changes the city had experienced during the last decades of the nineteenth century, when recovery from more than a century of economic decline produced rapid urban growth. Emerging from its early-nineteenth-century position as a backwater of Europe, Amsterdam's shipbuilding and financial sectors benefited from German industrial strength.[2] Amsterdam improved the infrastructure of its harbor and warehouse facilities and revived its traditional role as a trading and shipping center, bolstering its banking, insurance, and financial activities. Light industries such as diamond cutting and sugar manufacture also flourished; modern factories coexisted with traditional craft workshops. In the Dutch countryside, however, there was a depression, driven by the competition of lower-priced American grain. The rural poor streamed to the large cities, and in the 1880s and 1890s Amsterdam's population swelled with families seeking work in its harbors, stores, workshops, offices, and factories.[3] While Amsterdam did not keep pace with the faster-growing Rotterdam, it consistently maintained its position as the largest Dutch city. Inevitably, as demand for industrial sites, offices, and housing grew, Amsterdam expanded over the surrounding countryside in a pat-

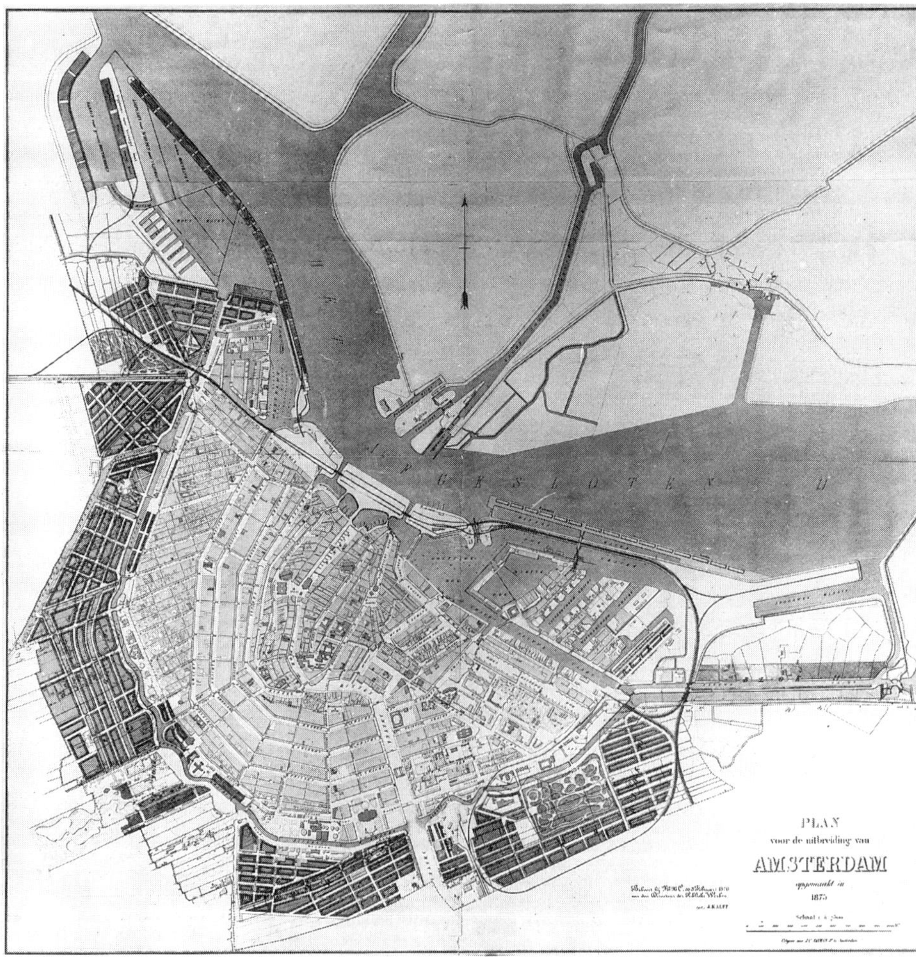

FIGURE 1.1 Jan Kalff, extension plan of Amsterdam, 1877. Gemeentearchief Amsterdam, negative E3762.

tern not atypical for European cities. Following the 1877 plan of city engineer Jan Kalff, vast districts of dense rental housing arose in a half circle around the seventeenth-century core of the city (fig. 1.1).[4] Within that core, as the wealthy streamed out to commuter suburbs in the Gooi and Haarlem, housing stock was transformed for commercial and administrative use, while traditional worker's districts near the harbors and within the city center absorbed families into already overpopulated neighborhoods. It was here, in the Jordaan, the Eastern Islands, and the Jewish Quarter, that the most egregious housing conditions could be found.[5]

FIGURE 1.2 Groot Hemelrijk, alley in the center of Amsterdam. Gemeentearchief Amsterdam, negative D26896.

FIGURE 1.3 Blankenstraat, Funen. Gemeentearchief Amsterdam, negative D26527.

Under the pressure of overpopulation, every conceivable building site in these districts had been constructed with housing. Parts of the old urban fabric had become a warren of alleys; dwellings were reached from narrow passages connected to the street only by other alleys (fig. 1.2). The density of construction meant houses had little natural light or ventilation, and the absence or insufficiency of sewage, drains, or plumbing of any description made living conditions extremely insalubrious. The threat to health was compounded for families living in damp cellars or cramped into one or two rooms with many children. That these dwellings also frequently had to serve as the

SCALE OF ALL FLOOR PLANS:

0 5 M

KEY:

A	Alcove
BR	Bedroom
K	Kitchen
K-LR	Kitchen-living room
LR	Living room
N	Built-in bed niche
P	Parlor
s	Sink
S	Storage
WC	Water closet

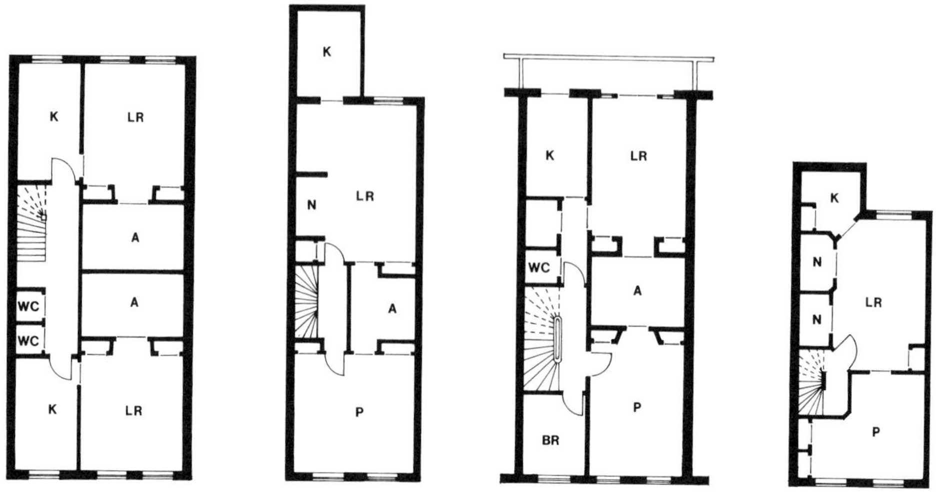

FIGURE 1.4 Speculative dwelling plans in Amsterdam, circa 1900. From Amsterdamsche Woningraad, *De Verbetering der volkshuisvesting te Amsterdam* (Amsterdam, 1913).

workplace for the sweated labor that supported the family only worsened already insufferable conditions.

Newly constructed housing in the outlying neighborhoods of the Kalff plan, which housed an increasing percentage of the city's population, often provided only minimal improvement.[6] The ring of districts around the half moon of Amsterdam's historic core consisted of poorly constructed speculative housing hastily erected for quick profit.[7] In the Dapperbuurt, Pijp, Kinkerbuurt, Staatsliedenbuurt, and Funen, monotonous rows of densely packed four-story housing arose along street grids uninterrupted by greenery or architectural monuments (fig. 1.3). Planning provisions and municipal building standards were not adequate to prevent the rapid degeneration of these new areas. The sad, gray neighborhoods gave little indication of the economic boom that had attracted their inhabitants to the city. Inside, the individual flats offered some improvement in amenity over their decrepit inner-city counterparts, but cut-rate construction methods and uninspired design recreated some of the abuses of the slums. Steep stairs lit poorly or not at all led to small flats, usually only one or two rooms per family, with enclosed alcoves instead of bedrooms. Toilets might be shared between families or placed in the kitchen. The arrangement of sleeping alcoves and back-to-back construction made cross-ventilation impossible (fig. 1.4).[8]

The inadequacies of Amsterdam's new districts meant that the housing problem was not restricted only to the poorest segment of the population, that is, to the indigent, charity cases or casual laborers who inhabited the inner-city slums. All segments of the labor force were affected by a real estate market in which rents were forced up by the high price of land and by speculative builders given free rein to exploit the rising demand for housing. White-collar workers such as clerks, low-level bureaucrats, and teachers were as adversely affected as longshoremen, construction workers, and diamond workers. Rents increased sharply in the late nineteenth century. A family that could afford to rent two upper rooms in a cross street favorably located off one of the main canals in the 1860s had to pay just as much rent for a back-alley slum dwelling in the 1890s.[9] Wages failed to keep pace with rents, especially in the 1880s when there was an acute crisis in the housing supply. As a family grew larger, it might be forced to move into a smaller flat in order to save money to feed the new mouths. Even families with a steady income, who could afford to live in the new districts, nonetheless had to accept conditions insufficient to their needs.

At the turn of the century, the fact that a broad segment of Amsterdam's population was so poorly housed made evident the need for reform. Reformers publicized their cause by stressing the conditions of the hardest hit. The slums of the inner city provided the material for their propaganda: images of struggling widows and disabled workers forced to eke out livelihoods in meager dwellings elicited concern for the housing problem from those not directly affected by it. A typical account of slum life, a 1901 study sponsored by the Amsterdam Labor League, describes the misery and decay of the city's slums through text and illustrations assembled by socialist journalists.[10] The outrage that underlay such clinical descriptions fueled a growing movement to redress the contemporary neglect of urban planning and to deepen government intervention in the design and production of housing. During the first decades of the new century, the images of those pitiful slum dwellings continued to haunt reformers and shape their assumptions about housing improvement, spurring condemnation and urban renewal, as well as the construction of better replacement housing.

The socialists' 1901 study belonged to a tradition of Dutch investigation into urban housing. From the middle of the nineteenth century, bourgeois reformers in Amsterdam, as in other European cities, had turned their attention to deplorable slum conditions and begun gathering statistics on occupancy, health, cellar dwellings, and other aspects of the housing problem, which they identified as a hygienic and moral issue. Engagement in reform work followed: the construction of philanthropic model homes, an 1874 municipal housing project, and further investigations carried out under private and public auspices.[11] Activity was sporadic and uncoordinated; individual philanthropists and private societies working for the benefit of the community carried out well-intentioned, but isolated efforts to deal with this aspect of the "social question."

The ineffectiveness of such piecemeal and superficial efforts eventually became apparent. By 1901, the socialist journalists were using their account of wretched housing conditions to argue for comprehensive government intervention in the housing market. Their arguments were not that different from those of progressive circles of bourgeois reformers in favor of national housing legislation.[12] One of the most compelling arguments for such legislation was the hard evidence that Amsterdam reformers had failed to turn a profit on dwellings that were both affordable and met hygienic standards.[13] It was also apparent that the number of rental units provided by privately endowed philanthropic societies was insufficient to answer the need for housing at low cost. Frustration with these solutions contributed to growing support for housing legislation in Amsterdam and elsewhere. In 1901, as one of the last initiatives of the Liberal cabinet of Prime Minister N. G. Pierson, a housing act was proposed as part of a larger package of social reforms. The following year the act was approved by Parliament, supported by members across the political spectrum.[14]

The new legislation gave municipalities the power to act on housing and urban planning issues. It permitted local councils to apply for loans from the national government to support housing projects to be built by a municipality itself or by officially recognized societies founded exclusively for the purpose of improving housing conditions. These housing societies would provide models of excellent design to the commercial builders, who presumably would be forced to improve their construction to meet the competition of raised standards. The new housing act was accordingly conceived within the ideology of free market competition; government-supported housing would correct, not displace, the real estate market. Offering a range of additional corrective measures, the act indicated what could be regulated by local building ordinances. Most significant, it required every municipality with a population of more than 10,000 to draw up a comprehensive urban plan.

By granting these powers to the local authorities, the Housing Act of 1902 created new, extensive opportunities for control of housing and urban planning while essentially preserving the free market system. Like the municipal administration of such utilities as gas and water, local government intervention was introduced to rectify the worst aspects of an unregulated housing market, but it stopped far short of replacing private with public control. This reflected the ambivalence of liberal reformers, who supported government intervention but believed it should not compete with private construction. They could justify intervention only when the unregulated market created conditions detrimental to social and civic order. Thus, although the government might build for the low-cost market neglected by the private sector, government-sponsored housing might serve only as a model for the private construction industry. The hope and expectation was that the free market would continue to be the main provider of housing.[15]

In Amsterdam, even before passage of the Housing Act, the municipality had already initiated several changes conducive to better urban planning. In 1896, under the influence of a radical minority, the city had introduced a policy of land management that ended sales of municipal land to developers. Instead, through new long-term leases of its extensive holdings, the city could exert continuous influence on land use. In 1899, after several scandalous building collapses, the Building Inspector's Office was reorganized and modernized. And in 1898, the city took the first steps toward planning a large urban extension to the south.

After 1902, the newly reorganized Building and Housing Inspection Office (Bouw- en Woningtoezicht) had primary responsibility for execution of the Housing Act in Amsterdam. The engineer J. W. C. Tellegen, head of the new office, drafted an extensive, modern building ordinance, which was debated and approved by the municipal council in 1905. The provisions of that ordinance were used to condemn substandard housing in the Jordaan and the Jewish Quarter. However, condemnation was slowed because of pressure to refrain from depleting the already insufficient housing stock. Only in 1914, after repeated resistance from the right, did the Amsterdam City Council approve a proposal to build municipal housing put forth by the Social Democrats. Liberal approval was won on the basis that the city should shoulder responsibility for those displaced by municipal condemnations and urban renewal since the housing market would not. An alderman and advisory committee for housing were instituted by the municipal council, and a housing authority (Woningdienst) was established to oversee construction of municipal housing and to supervise the activities of the newly constituted housing societies. From 1909, these societies had slowly begun to win council approval for their proposals. After 1914, municipal support of all facets of housing reform increased as Social Democrats in key positions were able to push through their party's policies. The first alderman of housing was F. M. Wibaut, a leading member of the Social Democratic Workers' Party (Sociaal-Democratische Arbeiderspartij, SDAP); the head of the Housing Authority was Arie Keppler, a Social Democrat who had worked on housing issues in the city since the passage of the Housing Act.[16] In 1915, with the appointment as mayor of the Progressive Liberal Tellegen, former head of the Building and Housing Inspection Office, a powerful triumvirate in support of housing reform was in place. Material and labor shortages during the First World War caused the building industry to collapse, and the consequent housing shortages formed the chief justification for a massive investment of government funds. From 1914 to 1922, the dwellings constructed annually by the housing societies and the municipality outnumbered those produced by private construction, and as a result, the municipality substantially controlled housing production for the first time. Only after the war did the national government introduce subsidies to restimulate the private sector. By then, however, the institutions of social housing in Amsterdam had solidified and the public sector had established its regulatory powers.[17] Amsterdam had entered fully into a modern stage of housing reform, acknowledging public responsibility for housing quality and consolidating reform policies and procedures within the municipal bureaucracy.

By 1919, the Amsterdam City Council had approved nearly ninety housing projects comprising some 14,000 dwelling units to be built with funds under the Housing Act.[18] In neighborhoods throughout the city and its periphery, in the Indische, Transvaal, Spaarndammer districts and north of the river IJ, large housing projects sponsored by public monies were under construction. A public institutional framework to design, regulate, and construct housing had been established. During the next twenty years, that framework was employed in the city's southern extension plan. As the south expanded, Amsterdam's fame as a modern mecca of housing spread, helped in no small part by the remarkable architectural style being applied. Under municipal patronage, leading Dutch architects were commissioned, initially older designers like H. P. Berlage and K. P. C. de Bazel, later, more significantly, younger talents encouraged to work with the housing societies. In the designs of architects such as Michel de Klerk and Piet Kramer, a fresh wind pervaded Amsterdam's housing program, a spirit of progressiveness. Good housing had become a right, a public concern, an activity guided by experts, a vehicle for artistic expression. In the first decades of the century, the housing problem had been integrated into the public realm, municipal institutions were addressing the issues of social hygiene and visual order in the city, and the perspective of the modern urban reform movement permeated Amsterdam.

SOCIAL DEMOCRATIC MUNICIPAL POLICY

These accomplishments provided dramatic visual evidence of Amsterdam's success in tackling a problem shared with cities throughout Europe. Contemporary foreign observers admired the enlightened housing policy evinced at both the national and local level. The Dutch Housing Act was recognized as a model of comprehensive legislation, particularly in its linkage of urban planning and housing reform. The Amsterdam Housing Authority and the municipal council were lauded as progressive patrons of housing design by the international coterie that supported the values of the modern urban reform movement. Later historians have linked the ambitious housing programs of Amsterdam with those of Vienna, Berlin, and Frankfurt as examples of social democratic municipal policy.[19] In that comparison, Amsterdam stands out as the first city to achieve a comprehensive housing policy, the components of which were in place by the eve of the First World War.

Amsterdam's achievements were all the more remarkable given the lateness of Dutch industrialization and the late formation of a Dutch socialist movement. Several factors may have contributed to the early success of the Social Democrats in introducing a strong housing policy in Amsterdam. In the first place, foundations for such a policy were already in place by the time the Social Democrats became influential. The Housing Act itself, which created new scope for municipal action, was the product of radical liberal agitation for housing reform. The proponents of this national legislation were drawn from the same ranks as local proponents of increased government intervention and control of the urban infrastructure.[20] Between 1888 and 1895, a group of progressives on the city council had broken from Amsterdam's Liberal political club to form a radical splinter group that agitated successfully for municipal takeover of the gas, water, telephone, and tram concessions. The creation of a municipal land lease system at this time would later provide the basis for policies of municipal land management favorable to housing reform. The extensive powers granted municipalities under Dutch law facilitated local initiatives to extend the municipality's control. The Social Democrats were thus in a position to take advantage of an existing legal structure and an established policy of municipal autonomy.

Taking the lead from the radicals, who failed to create a significant party alternative to the liberals and socialists, some of Amsterdam's social democrats saw that they might use municipal reform to effect immediate improvements in the material well-being of the working class and pave the path to a socialist state. Willing to exploit existing political structures, the Social Democratic Workers' Party had in 1894 broken away from the Social Democratic Party over the issue of parliamentary participation.[21] Reformist in orientation, the Marxist SDAP welcomed into its ranks the former Radical and Fabian influenced P. L. Tak, who laid the foundations for its municipal program. In 1899, the party adopted a program of urban reform in support of municipally based provision of goods and services, including housing. The program called for municipal housing, slum clearance and renewal, stricter building ordinances and regulations, and the use of expropriation for municipal acquisition of land.[22] The SDAP's municipal policy was not intended to usher in socialist society at the municipal level, although the ultimate revolutionary goal of collective ownership of the means of production was not abandoned. As Tak formulated its goals, the party's municipal policy aimed first to raise workers' living standards to eliminate the poverty standing in the way of class consciousness, and second, wherever possible, to replace capitalism with collective management in order to demonstrate its usefulness and to gain experience for the later extension of collectivism.[23] The Social Democrats believed that immediate material results for the working class were propaganda for the socialist revolution and that on that basis collaboration with bourgeois government at the local level might be justified.

In Amsterdam, SDAP candidates began to win seats in the municipal council, one in 1902, three in 1905, and six in 1907. The party held adamantly to a policy of rejecting any ministerial seats in national government, and it would not consider filling the position of alderman at the local level unless it had a majority of votes in a city council. However, in the wake of winning 42 percent of the vote and fifteen of forty-five seats on the Amsterdam council in 1913, the party decided to accept a seat in the College of Aldermen on condition that the seat be given responsibility for housing, that is, in an area in which the party might anticipate tangible results. With this much debated decision, the SDAP took a step toward collaboration with bourgeois parties and away from its revolutionary focus. In 1907, the party had already been rent by the secession of a group of revolutionaries who formed the first Communist Party in Europe.

F. M. Wibaut, elected to the council in 1907 and through his membership on the Amsterdam Health Board (Gezondheidscommissie) already active in the municipality's housing affairs, was elected as the alderman charged with the new portfolio of housing in 1914.[24] Although he identified himself as Marxist, Wibaut's orientation to municipal reform had been strongly influenced by his reading of English Fabian socialism. Indeed, his chief biographer has identified his political affiliations as closer to that reform orientation than to revolutionary Marxism.[25] Wibaut could count on support for housing proposals from the small caucus of Progressive Liberals (the Vrijzinnig-Democratische Bond), the successors to the Radical Party, and a few left-leaning councilors from older liberal and conservative parties. Thus, even though the SDAP never attained a majority on the Amsterdam council, holding at its peak seventeen of the forty-five seats in the period between the wars, it was able to make common cause with reform-minded members of other parties.[26] Its municipal program had shifted its orientation to a less revolutionary position and had aligned the party more closely to radicals, left liberals, and others supportive of urban reform.

Indeed, after 1914, there was never a concerted opposition to the party's municipal program in Amsterdam. In response to the articulation of that program in 1899, other parties had developed their own municipal policies, although none matched the cohesiveness of the SDAP's.[27] It has been argued that the SDAP politicized the Amsterdam City Council, which until the 1880s was largely a club of local notables without a tradition of political caucus or debate.[28] The SDAP's growing presence in municipal government challenged complacency and stimulated a long postponed confrontation with issues of civic order. Commenting in 1918 after the end of the First World War on the shift of bourgeois parties to support of reforms they had rejected only a few years before, a Social Democratic councilor noted that in the previous five years the SDAP had seldom encountered organized opposition. The liberals were splintered and lacked leadership; representatives of the conservative religious parties, who had never organized to form a caucus, had for the most part "evolved" to more progressive views.[29] The absence of any concerted opposition allowed the Social Democrats to set a reform agenda to which, under electoral pressure, other parties could accommodate their views.

The broad base of support for urban reform was due to the breadth of Amsterdam's population affected by the problems of inadequate housing, urban congestion, and poor urban planning. The problems of the urban infrastructure were not solely those of the urban poor, but were also experienced by skilled workers and lower-middle-class residents, who by 1914 had the vote. This was the layer of society from which the SDAP largely drew its support. But the Social Democrats did not have a complete claim on their representation. These voters were also drawn to the religious parties, where their presence moved policy to a more reformist position. The early success of the Social Democrats' housing program was in part due to the rising political influence of these upper echelons of the working class. Even without a majority on the city council, the Social Democrats' housing proposals won support as the interests of this group swayed politicians toward reform, in some cases as a defense against socialism.

The Social Democrats played the leading role in bringing housing reform to the table in Amsterdam, but they never achieved the political strength to substitute government-controlled housing for the private market. Instead, they facilitated vigorous application of the provisions of the Housing Act and oversaw the development of a bureaucratic infrastructure to administer housing reform in the city. These less radical means for improving housing conditions for the working class represented a political compromise unacceptable to those further to the left. Indeed, with the introduction of universal suffrage in 1919, the SDAP lost votes to the more revolutionary parties, which shunned its reformist tactics as counterrevolutionary. By their willingness to work within the framework provided by the Housing Act, the Social Democrats stimulated formation of a municipal political consensus on housing reform, drawing support from the more progressive liberals and confessionals. Amsterdam took full advantage of the Housing Act between 1915 and 1922, spurred by the strength of the Social Democratic caucus in the municipal council, working with laws instigated by progressive groups, joined by a number of participating confessional organizations. The limited, but effective, program of housing reform achieved in Amsterdam was thus the result of politically pragmatic compromises on several sides. The Social Democrats accepted less than their long-term aim of restructuring the housing market, believing the gradual reform possible under the Housing Act would be a step toward that ideal. Liberals and confessionals eventually accepted municipal housing reform as a temporary measure to spur change within the private housing industry. It should also be noted that the disastrous material shortages of the First World War spelled the virtual cessation of private construction, and as in other economic sectors such as food and energy, conservatives supported limited wartime socialism as an emergency measure. Without the presence of a strong Social Democratic leadership in the municipal council, none of the neighborhoods built under government auspices that multiplied outside Amsterdam's nineteenth-century speculative ring would have been built. Their construction was enabled by the vision of municipal reform hammered out by Social Democrats at the turn of the century. But it is also important to recognize the constraints imposed on that vision by the limited participation of confessional and liberal groups in municipal reform. Amsterdam's housing reform entered into a public sphere defined by competing political interests. We turn now to the formation of that public sphere and its organizational implications for the city's housing reform.

Although the transformation of housing reform in Amsterdam from philanthropy to welfare followed a path roughly comparable to developments elsewhere, Amsterdam's housing achievements took shape within a social, political, and cultural context peculiar to the Netherlands. Welfare reform in the Netherlands must be seen in the context of a characteristic Dutch response to ideological diversity.[30] The limited support for the social legislation realized in the Netherlands by 1919 depended upon the creation of a zone of social control that each ideological persuasion could use to foster its own values. The housing achievements of the SDAP in Amsterdam were accordingly enabled by the institutionalization of a buffer zone between individual and state that could serve divergent ideologies. As we shall see, the creation of such a zone was critical to the development of the modern Dutch welfare state.

The Dutch state assumed its modern form through the assimilation of the Enlightenment tenets embodied in the French Revolution: the rational improvement of individual and society, the separation of church and state, the Rights of Man, and the concept of citizenship. First embraced during the 1795 Batavian Revolution, these liberal tenets were incorporated in the Constitution of 1848.[31] If the early politics of the new constitutional monarchy was characterized by the tensions between urban, secular bourgeois liberals and their conservative opponents, during the last third of the nineteenth century, social and political life in the Netherlands was dominated by the democratic integration into the state of those previously excluded from participation, notably the Catholic population and the working class. The rights of citizenship were granted to the Catholics when the state church was disestablished in 1848, and the slow spread of suffrage to all classes had been completed by 1919, facilitated by mass education and the gradual reduction and eventual elimination of financial tests for voters.[32]

Paradoxically, the agenda of secularization, education, and democracy constitutive of the liberal state had opened the door to the integration of social and political forces ideologically opposed to its tenets. On the right, religious groups such as the Catholics proclaimed the authority of the church and the family unit and challenged the secular model of the state. On the left, socialists pursued the revolutionary aim of overthrowing the liberal capitalist state to fulfill the utopian promises of the Enlightenment. The struggles to integrate the left and right as participants in the state produced the pluralistic society that characterized the Netherlands during the first half of the twentieth century. The threat to the state posed by the left- and right-wing critiques was defused by the integration of tempered versions of those critiques into the political process, an integration that was necessary if the state was to be preserved.

The catalyst for the formation of a pluralist social system was the Orthodox Protestant sect, which, unlike the mainstream Dutch Reformed Church (Hervormd), had refused to embrace the liberal constitution. In 1879, under the charismatic leadership of Abraham Kuyper, the Orthodox Protestants (Gereformeerd) founded the first mass political party in the Netherlands, the Anti-Revolutionary Party (Anti-Revolutionnaire Partij), so named to express its opposition to the values of the French Revolution. Their view of society was traditional, hierarchical, and organic, a rejection of liberal rationalism, secularism, and republicanism. The party's decision to participate in parliamentary politics meant abandonment of the aim of a theocratic state, realistically recognized as unattainable. But the largely lower-middle-class adherents of the party nonetheless found in it a bulwark against the liberal idea of religious belief as individual and private. Kuyper's genius was to recognize that modernism in the form of secular rationalism could only by fought with modern means; his political institution inaugurated modern party politics in the Netherlands.[33]

The political organization of the Orthodox Protestants was followed several years later by a proposal from the Catholic parliamentarian H. J. A. M. Schaepman to establish a Catholic political party, formed eventually in 1904. Political organization among the Catholic population was both emancipatory and reactionary, spawned by liberation from centuries of oppression and by fear of socialism.[34] Bound by a long history of exclusion, the Catholics formed a more unified block than the Orthodox Protestants, who were divided by many doctrinal and political splits, but both religious affiliations represented the persistence of old ideologies and defense of traditional, premodern social patterns.

Thus, ironically, the modern era of mass political participation was inaugurated in the Netherlands by the antimodernists. New institutions had been forged to preserve the conservative voice. The mass political party gave that voice power and protected the community of belief with an officially recognized minority status. For both the Catholic and Orthodox Protestant population, political party formation served the purposes of preserving group identity and providing a power base from which to wage the battle against secular values. Both groups rejected the atomistic model of society assumed by liberal political theory and were even more repulsed by the collectivism of the socialists. Against these credos, they offered an organic model of society based on Christianity, the family, and the Dutch monarchy. The battle against modernity was the explicitly articulated goal of their propaganda; Dutch politics was polarized between the traditional confessionals and the "modern" liberals and socialists.[35]

Parliamentary participation of the religious political parties, that is, the confessional parties, placed ideology and values squarely in the center of Dutch political life. As the liberal state moved to address the contemporary economic and social inequities of the "social question" recently identified by bourgeois reformers, opposition came not only from the conservative wing of the liberals, who espoused governmental minimalism, but also from the confessionals, who resisted interference by a secular authority whose values conflicted with their own. As government moved to regulate labor economics, workplace safety, education, and child labor, a new zone of politics, the politics of daily life, was opened in which the tendency to set collective norms was countered by confessional resistance.

Conflict was manifested most dramatically in the issue of government support of schools, an issue that dominated parliamentary politics for decades. The educational program at the very heart of the Enlightenment agenda for civilizing the masses was challenged by the confessional parties, which claimed the right to state subsidies for schools professing their own doctrines and values. Winning this struggle with the 1917 resolution dubbed the "Pacificatie," the confessionals employed modern political instruments in the service of conservative values and created a new semipublic institutional layer, supported by the state but given ideological autonomy.

Just as they had catalyzed the modernization of parliamentary politics through the formation of mass political parties, so too the confessionals responded to the modernist challenge of the nascent welfare state by establishing new social institutions to represent their views.[36] As myriad issues concerning daily life began to be addressed by the liberal state in order to redress social ills, an institutional buffer zone of social activities previously left to the influence of the individual, the church, or the marketplace emerged. Fearing that the state would impose progressive values through its regulation of daily life, the ideological segments within Dutch society created institutions of their own through which they might protect and promulgate their values. State subsidies were channeled through private religious and political affiliations so that ideological segmentation found expression in a sublayer of social and cultural activity that arose between the individual and the government. Social institutions subject to government regulation or eligible for government subsidy—schools, labor unions, hospitals, charities, and housing societies—were established according to religious and political color. Indeed, a rich local and national organizational life developed in which most areas of social activity, from recreational to commercial, from cultural to political, were segmented according to political and religious affiliation. Recreational organizations such as sports clubs, holiday camps, and choral societies formed on this basis. Even commercial life divided along these lines, identifying bakers, butchers, and department stores.

During the first decades of the century, an array of parallel institutions identified with particular segments were established, the confessional Catholics and Orthodox Protestants on the one hand, the socialists on the other. Affiliated organizations formed a self-enclosed society, a state within the state, within which it was possible to lead one's life. The Dutch term for such an affiliation was *zuil*, a pillar. The disadvantage of this terminology is the suggestion of a certain equivalence. In reality, the various segments did not enjoy separate but equal status in society. The blocks were not equivalent social organizations; the history and significance of each differed. Each segment had its own aims and issues, its own strengths and weaknesses, its own social structure, constituency, and internal dynamics. The groups were uneven in size, power, unity, and organization, although each gave rise to analogous institutions in journalism, broadcasting, labor organization, and housing.

The formation of the pillars thus coincided with and responded to the advent of the Dutch welfare state. As government intervention in many aspects of daily life increased, in particular subsequent to the accomplishments of the left liberal cabinet of 1901 that was also responsible for the Housing Act, the peculiar system of pillarized organization developed to preserve the control and autonomy of the confessional subgroups. Pillarization reached its height during the interbellum period, disintegrating for the most part only with the next social revolution, the shock waves of 1968.[37]

Pillarization represented rejection of a forced general normalization of society as a whole. Resistance to governmental imposition of norms was made possible by the existence of separate institutional vehicles for the expression of values. The segmented social institutions, organizations, clubs, and societies developed in reaction to the growing function of the state in all those areas of the "public interest" where it was acknowledged that government must be active, but where groups did not want to concede a standardized definition of the common good. Pillarization created pockets of institutional resistance, both conservative and progressive, to the centralized normalization of values.

Social segmentation along religious and political lines was a characteristic Dutch response to one aspect of modernization, namely, society's move to control and regulate its systems for the public good. Preserving sovereignty within one's own circle was the confessional response to state expansion. The creation of institutions to represent values other than state secularism accommodated pluralism without undermining the liberal state. The confessional resistance to modernity was thus the catalyst of modern Dutch society, first with its innovative organization of large numbers of newly enfranchised voters, and second as the proving ground of the segmented pluralism that came to constitute that society. Having lost the battle to rechristianize the Dutch state, the confessionals retreated into their protected sectors where they could benefit from welfare programs on their own terms, all the while participating in local and parliamentary government.

In this system of isolated social segments, the socialists occupied a special position. In many ways the generation of a socialist political party, socialist unions, newspapers, choral societies, cooperative, stores and housing societies signaled the creation of a socialist pillar analogous to those of the Orthodox Protestants and the Catholics. It is therefore possible to speak of an autonomous socialist culture, within which people grew up, lived, and to a certain extent shared a faith. The Social Democratic Workers' Party, which grew out of the Dutch labor and socialist movements of the nineteenth century, became associated with a growing number of cultural, educational, recreational, and economic organizations. Linked by a shared interpretation of working-class interests rather than a religious affiliation, lacking any strong hierarchy, and torn by many sectarian divisions, the Social Democrats may not have been as internally unified as the Catholics, but like the Dutch Catholics their solidarity was the product of an emancipatory mission.[38] However, the distinct cultural identity of the socialists was due as much to the fear and avoidance of their institutions by others as to their positive identification with a set of values. Pillarization was by no means a socialist strategy or goal. Indeed, such societal organization negated and undermined the class-based politics of the socialists because the religious groups demanded an allegiance that removed workers from the reach of class consciousness and endorsed a social imagery based on acceptance of the social hierarchy.

The segmentation of society into pillars and their peaceful integration into social and political life preserved the Dutch state, which even as it intruded into daily life came to be viewed as neutral, above sectarian differences. The ideologically opposed segments each acknowledged the right of the others to preserve and express their values without interference. In exchange for this acknowledgment, the confessionals sacrificed their ambitions for a church state, while the socialists tempered their revolutionary goals. With the agreement to disagree came the agreement to maintain the state above all differences. All came to have a stake in a shared, neutral polity in which their equal legitimacy as participants was recognized. As a result, open conflict was in general avoided. This peaceful compromise has been interpreted by some historians as the reason that class-based politics was prevented from occupying center stage in Dutch society. In this way, despite their rejection of the values of liberal capitalism, both the confessional and socialist pillars strengthened the foundations of the modern Dutch state.

The regulation of civic life that gave rise to institutionalized pluralism in the Netherlands depended on notions like "public interest" and "common good" to justify government intervention. Social legislation proposed to regulate areas of daily life for the benefit of the "common good." But pillarization made such concepts problematic, because the system of institutionalized segments constantly reinforced differences. Built into the segmented society was a continuous awareness of ideological affiliation; every activity of daily life was politicized, colored. The tension between collective and segmental identities and interests in the public sphere opened by reform legislation became constitutive of Dutch society, a particularly transparent version of the tensions in any democratic society between the imposition of collective, normative values and the resistance of plural voices.

As it became advantageous for those not aligned with the Enlightenment amelior-ism of the reform movement to endorse the ideology of government neutrality for the freedom it afforded their own emancipatory projects, most of society could be brought into the mainstream of support for social reform. The result was a defusion of antireformism, both of far left socialism, which rejected reform in favor of revolution, and of far right liberalism, which clung to laissez-faire economics. Segmentation of society, by virtue of its institutionalized protection of pluralism, deflected radical political conflict. Thus although the urban reform movement was instigated and shaped by those who espoused the modern attempt to ameliorate society through government intervention, the viability of that movement, its institutionalization, was made possible by its acceptance on the part of the antimodernists. Indeed, its characteristic methods, rules, and forms were shaped by the need to respond to the plural demands of the antimodernists. In the end, its strength, like that of the welfare state in general, sprang from the complex negotiation between the normalizing impulses of reform and the concession of autonomy to dissenters.

The pluralist agreement to share in the construction of the welfare state and address the politics of daily life can be seen in the way the word "social" was assimilated into the discourse of all groups participating in political life. "Social" lost its radical connotation as the confessionals and old liberals, under increasing pressure from the rise of working-class political organizations, moved toward acknowledgment of collective social responsibility. The liberals formed their Committee for Discussion of the Social Question in 1870, the Anti-Revolutionaries held their first Social Congress in 1891, and the Catholics, the last to organize for social reform, followed with a Social Week in 1908. The detachment of social reform from exclusive association with the socialists became an important tactic for liberals and confessionals to defuse the attraction of the social democratic movement. Right-wing parties continued to deny the existence of class struggle and opposed militant tactics such as the strike, but they developed their own unions and created their own organizations for social reform.[39] The word "social," bereft of its threatening associations with the overthrow of the existing political and economic order, came to represent instead the regulation of civic order and the improvement of material living standards. The "social" had come to indicate the management of daily life in the public interest, its broad definition a convenient obfuscation of the tensions between the ideological positions of those participating in the public sphere and of conflicts over how the public interest might be determined.

Two major political shifts marked the inauguration of the Dutch welfare state at the start of the twentieth century: the extension of full political participation to those who had previously been excluded and the introduction of greater regulatory powers to the government in areas where it had previously followed laissez-faire policies. The first was an emancipatory movement, the second normative. As a public dialogue was constructed about social issues such as housing, participants reacting against the faults of capitalist liberalism from both the left and the right, representing pro- and antimodernist positions, built modern institutional forms to define and represent their own social values so that both the emancipatory and normative impulse could be accommodated without overt conflict. This arrangement took on peculiarly Dutch forms, but was a response to a problem central to all welfare state formation: the reconciliation of individual freedom and collective control.

HOUSING REFORM AND IDEOLOGY

In the late nineteenth century, during an era overshadowed by the school issue, housing had not received much notice in Parliament, although there was a general consensus that the speculative nature of most housing production was inadequately serving the population. From 1874 to 1899, the housing issue was raised by only one representative, the Socialist Domela Nieuwenhuis during the 1888–89 session. In the following decades, all of the major political parties included some mention of the housing issue in their platforms. The housing question appeared to have become one aspect of social life capable of straddling political and religious divisions.[40]

By 1920, the ramifications of the Housing Act had been felt throughout the Netherlands, and an initial period of organizational adjustment had taken place, leaving in its wake new societies, professions, and bureaucracies. In Amsterdam, more than twenty housing societies had been approved to receive funds under the provisions of the act. For the most part, each was associated with one of the pillars of Dutch society.[41] A contemporary observer remarked that "in typical Dutch fashion, people set to work in groups according to sect or trade."[42] In 1910, the workers in one Amsterdam gasworks established a housing society that became socialist, while workers at the gasworks in another part of the city started a Catholic one.[43] Diamond workers, predominantly Jewish, joined three housing societies marked by three ideological orientations, one liberal, one socialist, and one religious.[44] By 1916, the head of the Amsterdam Housing Authority, Arie Keppler, was complaining about the profusion of societies. The situation was intensified at the end of World War I, when anticipation of expanded housing production, especially in Amsterdam South, led to the further proliferation of housing societies.[45] Keppler even complained that it had become hard to estimate the number of stores necessary when planning a neighborhood because the various religious and political factions each wanted their own bakeries, butchers, and grocers.[46]

The wide representation in the housing societies reflected general support for them as a vehicle of housing reform and their flexibility in serving a diversity of ideologies, even those in principle opposed to government intervention to improve housing. Like other organizational aspects of modernization, this institutional form was exploited by antimodernists for their own ends. Their willingness to make use of it contributed to its legitimacy, or perhaps more accurately, removed right-wing opposition to its exploitation by others. Housing reform was an issue so rooted in daily life that a wide political spectrum felt compelled to play some kind of role in defending it. The position of the housing society between the private and the public realm allowed it to accommodate diverse and conflicting strategies for urban reform. The housing society was able to project separate social and cultural agendas, to express varying interpretations of the home.

Workers had taken an active interest in housing improvement from the mid nineteenth century. From the 1870s, when labor first began to organize, the liberal league of unions, the ANWV (Algemeen Nederlandsch Werklieden-verbond), had called for housing reform. At its Easter meeting in 1890, the ANWV asked the government to give municipalities the power to condemn slums and build replacement housing.[47] But for the most part, the nascent labor movement concentrated on its primary economic and political goals, which were perceived as essential to the achievement of improved material conditions for the working class. During most housing controversies in the Amsterdam City Council, critics pointed to the failure of wages to keep up with rents, associating poor housing with low wages. Organized workers were often more interested in action to better their economic and political situation than in housing reform. In contrast, bourgeois reformers saw the housing issue as remediable without major social, economic, or political concessions. As a municipal union member put it soon after passage of the Housing Act, "now the housing question is somewhat peculiarly situated within the social question. In contrast to other aspects of the social question, such as wages, working hours and suffrage, those who have a stake in it do not care as much about the housing question as might reasonably be expected. On the other hand, there are those among the upper classes who don't care about wages and the like, but who feel strongly about the housing question."[48]

Housing offered the option of reform without structural social or economic changes and was therefore attractive to the radicals and progressives active in the bourgeois reform movement. This group, primarily responsible for passage of the Housing Act, engaged actively in housing reform in Amsterdam. A number of housing societies formed under the Housing Act had their origins in this bourgeois social movement, continuing the work of earlier philanthropic societies or worker self-help organizations. The first housing society in Amsterdam to seek recognition under the act was Oud-Amsterdam, which had previously built philanthropic housing in the Jordaan under the benevolent auspices of the monied class. The Amsterdamsch Bouwfonds was organized by reformers closely associated with a progressive circle of housing reformers who had also experimented with philanthropic housing in the decade before passage of the Housing Act. Other housing societies grew out of the liberal strategy of worker self-help. The Bouwmaatschappij tot Verkrijging van Eigen Woningen had started in 1868 with the aim of home ownership for workers (fig. 1.5). It eventually turned to subsidies under the Housing Act. The Handwerkers Vrien-

FIGURE 1.5 Members of the Bouwmaatschappij tot Verkrijging van Eigen Woningen, 1918. Photo courtesy of De Key Woningstichting.

denkring, a liberal mutual aid society primarily serving skilled diamond workers, generated its own housing society to build for members forced by slum clearance and condemnation to leave their homes in the Jewish district of Amsterdam.[49]

The strongest political proponents of housing reform were the Fabian-influenced Social Democrats, whose program of municipal socialism included government provision of housing. Housing reform also received support from the socialist labor movement. Louis M. Hermans, the socialist journalist, and H. H. Wollring, representative of the Amsterdam section of the Union of Dutch Carpenters, attended the meetings of the Public Health Convention (Nederlandsch Congres voor Openbare Gezondheidsregeling), which adopted their motion for a strong Housing Act in 1898. The Amsterdam Labor League (Amsterdamsche Bestuurdersbond) commissioned the 1901 survey of slum conditions, established a housing bureau, sent out circulars on housing conditions, and petitioned the Amsterdam City Council on housing issues.[50] The largest number of housing societies in Amsterdam were socialist in orientation, many of which were associated with labor unions or the cooperative movement. Membership in the Algemeene Woningbouw Vereeniging was dominated by diamond workers, models of the "modern" workers who formed the backbone of the Social Democrats' programs and who, for the most part, also belonged to the socialist labor union the ANDB.[51] Its initiators and trustees included Keppler and Wibaut. The housing society De Dageraad grew out of the social democratic cooperative movement. Other housing societies with a socialist tint were associated with labor unions. The ACOB represented schoolteachers active in the largely social democratic union of Amsterdam teachers. Amsterdam-Zuid and Zomers Buiten drew largely on municipal workers, particularly firemen, tram workers, and police. Worker-run housing societies were viewed as "a means for the organizational and administrative education of the working class and for the increase and strengthening of its feeling of responsibility."[52] Leaders of the Social Democratic Workers' Party participated as organizers and trustees in many of the societies in vigorous support of the party's program of municipal reform. Professional reformers with strong links to the SDAP also took steps to establish housing societies; De Arbeiderswoning, which provided rent-subsidized housing for the financially weak, was established by the Social Technical Society of Democratic Engineers and Architects (Sociaal-Technische Vereeniging van Democratische Ingenieurs en Architecten), many of whose members were SDAP members or sympathizers.

In contrast to the avid and vocal support of government action for housing improvement by the Social Democrats, when the First Christian Social Congress, sponsored by the workers' organization "Patrimonium," opened discussion of the social question in Orthodox Protestant circles in 1891, housing only received notice in passing. Patrimonium was established in Amsterdam in 1876 to represent the interests of Christian workers. The organization rejected strike action as a strategy and analyzed labor relations as a moral issue: steam power had turned the workman into a machine made of flesh; greed and selfishness had led the higher ranks of society to forget their duties and responsibilities. Patrimonium saw as its task cultural uplift and moral education. In lieu of labor action, one of the few activities it undertook was the founding of housing societies, beginning in 1886 in Kampen.[53] At the First Christian Social Congress, the potential role of parish philanthropy in the provision of housing for the poor was discussed and a lecture on "the household and labor" praised the benefits of home ownership for family life. In 1894, Patrimonium laid out its social program, which, having acknowledged the medical and moral dangers of bad housing, tepidly supported housing reform through tax relief and condemnation. The program also supported application of municipal land lease to facilitate home ownership. The 1897 election platform of the society supported expansion of expropriation as a means to improve housing. In 1913, the labor organization drafted a municipal program that supported municipal intervention in housing provision. In many respects, Patrimonium followed the line of the Anti-Revolutionary Party, which favored a patriarchal family, opposed the working mother, and emphasized the sovereignty of the nuclear family. But Patrimonium's position on municipal reform was more progressive than the party's, and working-class councilors representing the party sometimes voted with the Social Democrats on social issues.[54] The Anti-Revolutionary Party looked upon government expansion with distrust, preferred private responses to social welfare issues, and acted to protect property rights. The Anti-Revolutionaries never took up the cudgels for state-sponsored housing reform. Their most vocal spokesman on issues of planning and housing, Professor D. P. D. Fabius, representative on the Amsterdam City Council and member of the Amsterdam Housing Council, favored individual home ownership and the Amsterdam land lease system. In *Livingroom and Kitchen*, he praised the traditional image of home and hearth, citing the living room as the room where a mother's influence dominates, from which emanates the warmth that ties the family together.[55] These domestic images could, however, be served by housing societies. As early as 1910 the leaders of Patrimonium's Amsterdam branch decided to found a housing society. Overcoming their reservations about the Housing Act, they noted that "through the Housing Act is offered an organizational opportunity to build very reasonable workers' housing."[56] The prime mover in the founding and running of the housing society was secretary of the Amsterdam branch of Patrimonium, aided by a committee of leading members of the society, including an Anti-Revolutionary municipal council member.[57] Organization was hierarchical rather than grassroots: the statutes of the new society called for the appointment of officers and trustees by the parent organization. Establishment of the housing society was announced to the general membership in the pages of Patrimonium's newspaper in 1911, and recruitment of housing society members occurred only after housing plans were already formulated.[58] The founding of the housing society thus reflected the hierarchical character of the Orthodox Protestant pillar, but also, by its very existence, reflected the mixed-class composition of that pillar. Some segments of the Protestant labor movement even welcomed Wibaut's election to alderman of housing in 1914, noting that housing was an ideal they supported and that under the Housing Act workers could now pay as little as f2.50 (2.50 guilders) for "a home previously unimaginable," particularly those now available from Patrimonium.[59]

In Catholic circles, the moral influence of good housing was argued by political leader Dr. H. J. A. M. Schaepman and other important Catholic spokesmen. In 1902, a leading social Catholic claimed, "the way to heaven is easier to find in a roomy clean home than in a slum."[60] The Catholic legislative political program of 1896 noted the issue of housing, and Dr. Schaepman served as one of the organizers of the Dutch Public Health Convention. The housing question was one of the first agenda items of the Central Bureau for Catholic Social Action organized in 1905, with the national Catholic politician P. J. M. Aalberse (1871–1948) as its general secretary. Aalberse immediately organized a housing course for heads of diocesan committees to diffuse ideas locally. Attention was extended to the housing of the lower middle class, whose problems, it was felt, had been previously overlooked and who formed an important constituency in the Catholic political movement. Like the Anti-Revolutionaries, the Catholics did not pursue housing reform vigorously in the political arena, although Dr. Schaepman identified the improvement of workers' housing as an important facet of social reform in 1896 upon the five-year anniversary of the papal encyclical "Rerum

Novarum." At the first Catholic Social Week held in Utrecht in 1906, housing did not form a point of discussion, although at the 1908 Social Week, which took as its theme "The Municipality and the Social Question," J. M. A. Zoetmulder, leading Catholic housing spokesman and state inspector of housing, spoke on planning, building ordinances, and housing.[61] In addition to the usual blame placed on poor housing for alcoholism, immorality, contagion, and broken family life, the Catholic Social Action accused poor housing of being "socialism's most powerful propaganda."[62] The improvement of housing conditions would dispel socialist appeals to Catholic workers. Housing was viewed as a weapon in the papal war against liberal secularism, feminism, and modernism in culture and science: "Often more is achieved for Christian morals by building good housing than by decorating a church," it was argued.[63] Accordingly, although they formulated no cohesive municipal program, the Catholics too took advantage of the subsidies provided by the Housing Act. In Amsterdam, two Catholic housing societies were successfully established: Dr. Schaepman and Het Oosten.[64] Het Oosten was initiated in 1911 by a committee working in association with Catholic Social Action and J. M. A. Zoetmulder. Trustees included a Catholic Amsterdam architect and a Catholic municipal councilor.[65] The society was a product of the newly vocal segment of Catholics sympathetic to moderate social reform, whose fears that government involvement in housing would lead to socialism were allayed by the housing society's relative autonomy.

The first housing societies to form in Amsterdam after the Housing Act were the products of the liberal bourgeois reform movement. Once workers' housing societies began actual construction in 1909, a wave of new societies followed, including those of the confessional pillars. By 1919, 49 percent of the dwelling units approved by the municipal council under the Housing Act had been built by or were planned by housing societies with social democratic associations, and 18.4 percent by confessional housing societies. That year, in the elections for municipal council, the SDAP received 29.1 percent of the vote and the confessional parties received 27.9 percent. The disproportionate representation of the Social Democrats in housing society dwellings was a reflection not only of their more active engagement in housing reform, but also of their relatively homogeneous working-class following, in contrast to the mixed-class support of the confessional parties.[66]

Despite their resistance to government intrusion in the housing market and their vision of housing for the poor as a task for Christian charity, the confessional segments in Amsterdam began to take advantage of the opportunities opened by the Housing Act. Their participation can be read simply as a reflection of their presence in the Amsterdam population. It can also be interpreted as a defensive reaction against the menace of socialism, vitiating any monopoly the socialists might have on social reform and preserving the sanctity of the closed confessional community. Although the housing societies working with government loans built only rental units rather than the owner-occupied housing that might cultivate conservative values, their relative independence offered the confessionals the facility to shape urban housing in ways that would satisfy their vision of the family.

The housing societies represented a middle ground between individual home ownership and state-owned housing; they were not run by the government, they need not be run by their inhabitants, and they could be controlled by the party hierarchy. For the right wing, they were a moderate reform measure that might reduce worker discontent and the attractions of socialism. For the Social Democrats, on the other hand, the housing societies provided ammunition for the socialist critique, undercutting the capitalist definition of real estate as commodity. They were a natural extension of the widely supported cooperative movement in which workers reclaimed commodities from the inequities of the free market. They created an opportunity for socialist control that could encourage the gradual shift of society toward socialism.

The ambiguous position of housing reform as both a force toward socialism and a defense against it contributed to the organizational success of the housing societies. Each group was able to harness the institution of the housing society to promulgate its own norms of urban behavior, its own ideas of civic order. Only at the extremes of the political spectrum was there resistance to this kind of urban reform. The far left rejected the housing society as a drain on working-class energies that would be better invested in changing the structure of society. The far right rejected the intrusion of the housing society in the natural workings of the market. For the confessionals, liberals, and socialists, the housing society provided a serviceable vehicle for urban reform that required sacrifice of doctrinal insistence on charity, the market, and the revolution, respectively, as the true motors of social justice. Through their willingness to compromise, these ideologically opposed groups were able to harness a new institutional form for their own, diverse, purposes.

HOUSING REFORM AND SOCIAL ENGINEERING

By 1919, housing societies throughout the Netherlands had formed separate socialist, Catholic, and Orthodox Protestant federations that paralleled the national labor federations similarly affiliated with separate pillars.[67] Segmentation made political sense in that the internal organization and decisions of the housing societies reflected the values of their respective pillars: values about family life, the roles of the sexes, hierarchical or democratic concepts of social structure; individual or collective definitions of the social bond; ideological, religious, and cultural preferences. As the housing societies began to develop plans for housing projects, their values would have an impact on design decisions. The strength of segmentation in the Netherlands made it inevitable that sectarian divisions permeated and influenced housing policy and design. Despite the clear dominance of social democratic municipal reform in Amsterdam, the SDAP was forced by political conditions to accommodate other parties. Perhaps more important, the pillarized social context underscored the emancipatory nature of the housing societies as vehicles for the expression of group values.

This splintering was resisted by the nascent housing and planning professions, for whom design decisions were to be governed by the tenets of the new human sciences. The socialist reform expert Dirk Hudig argued against "segmentation" in housing societies, suggesting that talent would be spread thin, that the unnecessary multiplication of efforts would create administrative difficulties, and that political favoritism would influence council votes. Housing expertise is essentially apolitical, he claimed: "There is no party line on the preferable type of housing or rental policy, any more than there is on the design of a gasworks or the layout of parks."[68] Hudig himself had been one of the chief initiators in 1913 of a neutral national league of housing societies, the National Housing Council (Nationale Woningraad).[69] For Hudig and others dedicated to the development of the planning and housing professions, a rational model of social problem-solving precluded acknowledgment of pillar-based perspectives. They countered the politicization of the zone of daily life opened by new welfare legislation with the prospect of a politically neutral, impartial science of society. To generate legitimacy and power for their new expertise, they assumed an aura of political impartiality, following in the footsteps of earlier proponents of social reform who posited a science or technology of society based on rationality and impartial expertise.

The concept of a professional corps trained to apply social sciences to mend societal ills was espoused by both progressive liberals and socialists. The socialist theoretician Frank van der Goes claimed that "someday we will talk about the defects of society as impartially as we now do about the diseases of the body."[70] In the meantime, Van der Goes continued, the variety of opinions on the nature of society, its ills, and their reform could be compared with the superstitions that once held back scientific understanding. "There is no Catholic chemistry, no conservative mechanics, no Anti-Revolutionary botany," he noted. "But there is an Anti-Revolutionary politics, a conservative theory of society, and a Catholic solution to the social question. . . . It is as foolish to have an original opinion about politics as about electricity or surgery. It is certain that we will eventually manipulate the gears and levers of society with the same confidence as the doctor and the naturalist now manipulate their tools. We will cease to distinguish between liberal and conservative policies, just as we have stopped speaking of a sacred and profane physics."[71]

Arguments like Van der Goes's exerted a profound influence on the developing professions of social reform. If physics, chemistry, or medicine could be approached with a scientific objectivity free from politics, so too could social issues like housing and planning. Social problems could be "solved" by experts who modeled their professional identities on engineers; social ills could be "cured" by experts who modeled themselves on doctors. According to either metaphor, the authority of the expert is maintained by a claim to neutrality. Expert knowledge appears to be scientifically neutral and politically impartial; it is disassociated from the political divisions that make up society; and it comes to be identified with the public good. "A good law must be good for everyone in exactly the same way that a true proposition is true for all," wrote Condorcet in the late eighteenth century, when the optimism of the Enlightenment held out hope that universal laws might regulate social systems as they do the natural world.

Against the tendency of social organizations to follow the divisions between the pillars, the planning professions established an institutional bulwark of professional autonomy and neutrality. The organization of housing and planning expertise in the Netherlands was stimulated by the activities of the Central Bureau for Social Advice (CBSA), founded in 1898 in Amsterdam by the liberal industrialist J. C. van Marken (1845–1906) on the principle that the social question should be tackled by the application of the sciences to society.[72] The advent of reform legislation created a demand for appropriate professionals trained to execute the new laws. Recognizing that a new field of expertise lay open for development, Van Marken wrote a series of articles outlining the education and duties of the social engineer in the 1890s.[73] If a mechanical engineer was needed to oversee a factory's equipment, a social engineer was needed to oversee its social programs, he wrote, and those programs had to be as carefully designed as machinery. Van Marken's model for the new profession was the engineer, valued for his "competence, objectivity, and honesty."[74] The social engineer would demonstrate an indispensable, specialized problem-solving ability analogous to the mechanical engineer's, applying his expertise objectively. "Both the rights and duties of both boss and worker find in him an equally impartial defender," Van Marken contended in a statement remarkable for its naive faith in an Archimedean point of peaceful resolution between conflicting interests.[75]

The Central Bureau for Social Advice, modeled on American, French, and German precursors, embodied Van Marken's view of the new expertise of social reform, the human sciences that posited a neutral position vis-à-vis the social space opened by welfare legislation. Its stated aim was to "provide advice as requested to aid the foundation, organization, management, and administration of institutions whose aim is supporting the working class in its attempt to improve its economic position in any way."[76] This aim accorded with the progressive liberal strategy of social adjustments to preserve the status quo and the reform socialist aim of increasing standards of living through worker organization. The bureau provided advice to workers' organizations on a variety of social measures: health insurance, labor contracts, cooperatives, pension plans, unionization, and housing. While Van Marken himself represented the well-intentioned paternalism of the industrialist serving workers' interests as he defined them, the organization he founded was less conservative. It became an umbrella for reformers of all political persuasions, for workers' organizations as well as those of capitalists and confessionals, proffering as a solution for social ills a social technology that would mediate between their disparate interests.

From the first, the CBSA placed a high priority on maintaining its claim to both scientific and political neutrality. By associating scientific objectivity with fair political representation, the organization addressed the issue of normalization in a pluralistic society. The prominent Social Democrat P. L. Tak, reporting on the bureau's founding meeting, noted that "during the discussions, it appeared desirable that the matter be given a purely scientific, neutral character."[77] Attendance at that meeting was predominantly Progressive Liberal, but key representatives from other ideological segments were also present: W. C. J. Passtoors and A. S. Talma from the Anti-Revolutionaries; Dr. Schaepman of the Roman Catholics; Vliegen, De Vooys, and Wibaut of the Social Democrats.[78] The board of officers included representatives of the Anti-Revolutionaries, the Catholics, the Social Democrats, and the Liberals.[79] Political balance proved more difficult in the selection of the director and his assistant, since most of the solicitants were either Social Democrats or sympathizers. Although some suggested selection on the basis of competence and ability rather than political persuasion, given the organization's desire to underplay doctrinal differences, political considerations dictated that the appointment communicate the moderate character of the organization; it was felt that a director with pronounced socialist leanings might create opposition. The Progressive Liberal Treub was appointed director, with the Social Democrat Hudig his assistant.[80]

Throughout its twenty-two years of existence, maintaining a public image of nonpartisanship remained a constant preoccupation of the CBSA.[81] The first annual report noted with relief that requests for information came from a range of political persuasions, and that the bureau had achieved a reputation for its neutrality.[82] Because of the potential threat to that neutrality, the CBSA decided not to publish Hudig's dissertation on the Dutch labor movement, but this did not prevent it from appointing him successor to Treub as director in 1905.[83] Tak, at first skeptical of the nonpartisanship of the bureau, became convinced after its first year of operation that it could indeed function objectively.[84]

The CBSA thus sought to depoliticize social reform. Its ideology of neutrality negated social analyses based on class conflict or theology, conflating the objectivity of science and technology with the impartiality of fair representation. This model was instrumental in the development of welfare state institutions, promoting reform governed by expertise while accommodating the segmental character of Dutch society.

Social Democrats like Tak supported the CBSA and other organizations of the liberal reform movement because of a belief in the effectiveness of the human sciences shared with more conservative subscribers to the Enlightenment legacy. Tak defended his support for the School of Social Work, which was run by many of the same radicals and progressive liberals associated with the CBSA, by pointing out that his "honorable opponents" provided expertise for social reform that workers themselves could not: "The movement which we promise needs talents which the workers themselves cannot yet provide; thus they will fully appreciate it if young men and women wish to take advantage of this institution to render them services."[85]

> The fog of anarchy is clearing away with the daybreak of socialism. All kinds of institutions are beginning to appear and when they reach full growth they will take the place of anarchy in the future system. To achieve this a work force is necessary, but we can't supply the laborers, at least, not many, for we are too busy with the main business: the planting of social democracy in the hearts and minds of the workers. But it is pleasing to see now that the immediate care for many of the destitute has been assumed by trained members of the most well-intentioned bourgeoisie.[86]

Tak's assessment that expertise had a validity detached from politics permitted his support of institutions of professional reform grounded in the liberalism of his political opponents. "Trained experts" from the CBSA could serve the welfare of the working class whatever their political affiliation. This faith in the efficacy of social technology was not shared by the syndicalists or the orthodox Marxists, who split from the ranks of the Social Democrats in 1907.

Support for institutions like the CBSA on the part of the confessional parties came from the more progressive wings of the Orthodox Protestants and Catholics, who wished to harness the means of modernization for their own agendas but lacked expertise in their own circles. Particularly among the Catholic leadership, the lack of a professional-technical cadre was lamented, echoing the Social Democrats' arguments. The CBSA's authority as an umbrella organization for reform expertise was thus unassailed.

Housing was one of the first aspects of the social question the CBSA addressed. It began in 1898 by taking over a nonsectarian housing committee that had been founded by the Society for Public Welfare (Maatschappij tot Nut van 't Algemeen), a liberal reform organization whose eighteenth-century origins were reflected in its name. Participating on the committee were representatives of the Social Democrats, the Orthodox Protestant society Patrimonium, the Catholic Party, and the liberal labor organization ANWV, as well as delegates from two organizations representing housing expertise, the Society for the Advancement of Architecture (Maatschappij tot Bevordering der Bouwkunst) and the Public Health Convention.[87] This committee, reconstituted within the CBSA, advised organizations on the practical aspects of housing improvement, that is, on legal, financial, and technical issues, including the siting of housing in relation to workplace and transportation, street plans, the size and arrangement of housing.[88] It became the leading authority on setting up new housing societies, not only offering advice about legal, administrative, and financial issues, but also recommending architects.[89]

In 1901, the CBSA decided to establish a central office on housing for Amsterdam, to advise individuals and government on the possibilities for housing improvement offered by the proposed Housing Act. In October 1901, it invited housing reformers "belonging to the most disparate political orientations" to a meeting chaired by Liberal Arnold Kerdijk, which led to the founding of the Amsterdam Housing Council (Amsterdamsche Woningraad) that December.[90] After trying unsuccessfully to draw up plans in the new districts for a housing society for workers earning less than f12.00 per week, the council petitioned the city to reform its system of setting land lease rates. It carried out and published a series of studies on Amsterdam's parks, the condition of the old city, municipal housing, and a retrospective report on housing improvement in Amsterdam put out for the 1913 International Housing Congress.[91] The Housing Council grew into an important lobby for urban reform, whose influential members included a number of city councilors. Like the CBSA, it was officially a neutral organization and its work was actively supported by the confessional parties as well as the Social Democrats and Liberals, but again like the CBSA, its most active participants were Progressive Liberal and Social Democratic professionals.

Its success inspired Dirk Hudig, then director of the CBSA as well as an active member of the council, to suggest in 1914 the formation of a national organization for planning and housing. Hudig wanted to create an institute of research, consultation, publicity, and archives to centralize the activities of organizations already active in the field.[92] Although there was sufficient support among housing reformers, the First World War interrupted the proceedings, so that it was not until 1918 that the Dutch Housing Institute (Nederlandsch Instituut voor Volkshuisvesting) was founded. The board of officers consisted of representatives from organizations active in housing reform.[93] The institute became the central Dutch clearinghouse for information about housing and planning and the preeminent national authority on housing issues. It sponsored research, published the chief professional journal in the field (*Tijdschrift voor Volkshuisvesting*) from 1920, and joined forces with the international housing community. The Dutch Housing Institute thus represented the successful institutionalization of Van Marken's ideals. A relatively small coterie of reformers had established a national institution embodying the principle of nonpartisan expertise in the fields of housing and planning.[94]

The professionalization of planning and housing expertise took place within a series of organizations founded on the premise that the social engineer would provide solutions to society's ills, a concept that played a seminal role in defining the reform disciplines. Congruent with Van Marken's original formulation of the social engineer's impartiality, these organizations were characterized by a belief that political neutrality in the pursuit of social reform could be achieved by means of scientifically based social expertise and the fair representation of conflicting ideologies. The appearance of neutrality was essential for the legitimization of the new reform professions, first of all as a warrant for their scientific authority. But their neutrality also played a pivotal role in legitimizing a welfare state in which diverse ideological segments were integrated. To protect their own zones of autonomy, all social segments, conservative and progressive, had a stake in the creation and maintenance of a neutral public entity above partisan differences. Conflicting political segments joined in accepting the ideal of a neutral, nonpartisan polis, ruled by a code of fair representation, its impartiality supported by the objectivity of expert opinion. Professional expertise thus gained authority and privilege by legitimizing the ideal of governmental neutrality and at the same time was itself legitimized by its role in preserving neutrality. As the professional component of the modern reform movement assumed a key role in the maintenance of the state edifice, it helped sustain reform itself. Thus the assumption of neutrality within the reform professions served both the profession and the state. Nonetheless, the tension between normative statements by housing and planning professionals and the plural expression of values by individual, class, or ideological segment remained intrinsic to the public sphere of housing reform.

EMANCIPATION AND NORMALIZATION

The formation of the modern welfare state in the Netherlands was accompanied by the creation of new institutional forms such as mass political parties, labor unions, and housing societies. These were established by all the segments participating in parliamentary politics. Whether conservative or progressive, modernist or antimodernist, the ideological groups that composed Dutch society worked for their own interests through the new institutions of the welfare state. In the arena of housing reform, this meant the foundation of local housing societies defined by sectarian interests. Countering this institutionalized partisanship was the nonpartisan claim of the new reform specialists in housing and urban planning. The fact that the foremost representatives of expertise in social reform were themselves Progressive Liberals or Social Democrats, and thus professed modernists, did not prevent them from asserting the neutral character of their professional organizations. They established credibility not only through their claims to scientific neutrality, but also by cultivating a strategy of fair representation of the various pillars.

Experts and pillarized institutions formed a precarious partnership that maintained the authority and autonomy of each within the welfare state. The professionals were permitted to regulate themselves and to develop their disciplines without political interference, a freedom necessary for expertise to mature. The various subcultures of Dutch society were granted autonomy within the pillars of their parallel institutions. Together the premises of neutral expertise and segmental sovereignty allowed the Dutch welfare state to be launched with relative stability. Social regulation for the public good thus reflected both the emancipatory social movements that had given Catholics and workers a voice in the public realm and the reforming impulse that had prompted government intervention and defined its normalizing role.

Economic resurgence in Amsterdam had created a challenge to urban order. The issues were transportation, education, public safety, sewage, housing, and the provision of other public services. When housing reform was introduced into the public realm, particularly when the state assumed responsibility through the Housing Act, the segmentation of society generated competing visions of the future shape of urban life in Amsterdam. New organizations offered their objective expertise to override differences and provide justification for the imposition of norms in the name of the public good, while housing societies became the institutional means for expressing segmental values.

This formulation was, however, precarious and contradictory. It was based on the questionable assumptions that social expertise was objective and that segmental representation guaranteed political fairness. Within the new arena for action created by the power of professional knowledge and the power of political organization, each of which was being used to legitimize the new welfare state and its campaign for housing reform, lay inherent tensions: the conflict over the degree and nature of government responsibility, the scope and power of professional autonomy relative to the government and to the individual, the tension between the liberative aims implied by increasing living standards and the control required to implement them. In the middle zone between individual and state created in response to the Housing Act, these tensions continuously affected housing design. Although emancipation of groups previously excluded from the public realm meant that broader interests would be addressed, as issues such as housing improvement were introduced into the public realm, daily life became increasingly subject to normalization in a public dialogue shaped unevenly by political ideology, expertise, and those whose interests were at stake. The politics of daily life inaugurated with the welfare state was defined by the difficult coincidence of two processes, emancipation and normalization.

SOCIAL HYGIENE AND AESTHETICS

At the turn of the century, the Dutch industrialist J. C. van Marken recognized that the government's increased intervention in the politics of daily life would require the training of new experts in the fields opened by social legislation. Van Marken was not alone. As social legislation was adopted, a number of organizations acknowledged the need for new social technologies. These included professional societies, such as the Society of Delft Engineers, which reported in 1895 on the need for the development of a planning curriculum, and the Society for the Advancement of Architecture, which in 1892 sponsored a colloquium on the social question. Other societies that sponsored activities intended to encourage the development of housing expertise originated from the circle of bourgeois liberal and socialist reformers. The Society for Public Welfare and the League against Alcohol Abuse (Volksbond tegen Drankmisbruik), both bastions of liberal reform, sponsored scientific investigations into the housing question. Organizations like the Public Health Convention attracted professionals engaged in social reform.

Volunteers for the new role of social engineer were more likely to be found among the students at the Polytechnic School in Delft than among those training for the traditional professions at the universities.[1] In 1904, a group of Delft students established the Social Technical Society of Democratic Engineers and Architects, which endorsed a modern social agenda with an emphasis on urban planning and housing reform.[2] They petitioned Parliament in 1905 to create a new academic degree for the "social-technical engineer" at Delft, echoing an earlier suggestion by Van Marken for an interdisciplinary curriculum in social engineering, although the students were politically to

Van Marken's left. The society argued that new legislation such as the Health and Housing Acts required the services of specialists who understood not only the laws' legal and social implications, but also their technical significance. Civil servants administering housing, labor, and health laws were inadequately prepared because their training emphasized one discipline at the expense of the other. Since their education was so specialized, doctors, lawyers, architects, and engineers assuming administrative positions could not be expected to carry out the laws effectively. As the students argued: "An architect may design lovely facades, but what guarantee do they give that he knows the requirements of hygiene, social laws, or housing conditions?"[3]

Although a conservative Parliament did not approve the students' proposal, the assumptions that underlay it were pervasive among progressive engineers and architects: the belief in the efficacious application of expertise to social ills; the need for a new, synthetic curriculum based on the disciplines of social reform; the conviction that social reform should not be left to the amateur philanthropist or narrow specialist, but rather entrusted to the care of a professional corps newly trained in the emerging technologies of social reform. The Delft students' proposal was a spirited if naive attempt to define the interdisciplinary scope and methodological character of the new fields of the human sciences, a problematic that would prove to be a subject of contention between competing disciplines over the coming decades. In one respect, however, the students fully anticipated the tenor of those later debates: at the heart of their proposal lay a confidence in the authority and efficacy of expertise in the regulation of social order. This was to provide a broad ideological consensus for the development of the fields of knowledge that would operate in the space between the individual and the state created by new social legislation.[4]

As state and local government moved housing and planning further into the public arena after passage of the Housing Act in 1902, participation in the putative corps of social engineers was contested. What constituted housing expertise? Who was the planner? What models would provide the discipline and organization for the new professions of social engineering? Such questions were posed primarily by those contending for the positions opened by the government as it began carrying out the Housing and Health Acts, positions whose regulatory and executive power would be legitimized on the basis of expert knowledge. Battle lines were drawn over the definition of knowledge appropriate to the new social space created by reform legislation and over the nature of authority, and thus power, in that space. The fields of expertise called into existence by the ideology of social reform were accordingly constructed through a process in which the social and the political mediated the creation of knowledge.

The definition of new social reform expertise posed challenges to the existing professions.[5] Ancient disciplines, such as medicine and architecture, and modern professions, such as engineering, made competing claims for competence, but as the Delft students had anticipated, the multifaceted nature of the housing problem defied handling by any single field. New professions such as social work and urban planning also emerged to compete with the older professions. As doctors, engineers, and architects tackled the housing problem, struggles for authority between professions and conflicts over competency within disciplines erupted. These turf fights directly influenced the way authority over housing reform came to be organized in Amsterdam. Through these battles, the construction of a conceptual map of the housing problem emerged, albeit one in which the boundaries of analysis kept shifting as specific competencies and competing visions of the housing problem established spheres of influence. As a result, the bureaucratic structures erected to deal with housing reflected the spheres of influence emerging from the disciplinary battlefield. Knowledge was constitutively linked with power as the tensions between intellectual discourses and the corresponding creation of reform institutions delineated the fields within which housing design would be shaped, setting the limits and extent of control, defining the taxonomy of norms and the process whereby they would be established.

THE WANING OF THE MEDICAL DOMINATION OF HOUSING EXPERTISE

From the late eighteenth century, in the Netherlands as elsewhere, housing was perceived first as an issue of public health, and doctors, who played an essential role in identifying the health hazards of poor housing and in specifying remedies, assumed the lead as housing experts. Doctors, whose work took them to the warrens and alleys hidden to most of the bourgeoisie, were the first to report on the squalor of slum dwellings. Dr. S. S. Colonel's mid-nineteenth-century reports, read throughout the Netherlands, revealed the conditions of working-class neighborhoods to the educated classes.[6] His point that the deleterious environment of those neighborhoods had to be improved to control disease won support from leading liberals.[7] The sanitation movement led by Chadwick in England and the health reform movement of Dr. Virchow in Germany were both influential in the Netherlands, where the Dutch Society for the Advancement of Medicine took a lively interest in issues of water, sewage, and housing hygiene. Hygiene, a subject encompassing workplace conditions, public sanitation, the long workday and occupational hazards, as well as poor schools and housing, was designated a university subject in the Netherlands as early as 1865. In 1867, Dr. A. H. Israels started to teach it in Amsterdam. Doctors made the case for the relationship between poor living conditions and disease, becoming the leading proponents of improved housing and city planning. This medical analysis of the housing problem persisted into the twentieth century. Even after public sanitation was improved with municipal waste disposal, garbage collection, and water distribution, the eighteenth-century call for air and light continued to dominate housing solutions, an approach that permitted the technical specification of apparently objective norms.

Housing was perceived as a branch of the emerging discipline of social medicine, variously called public health and social hygiene.[8] Although members of established professions like law and architecture, as well as such new professional figures as the social worker and the urban planner, made contributions to housing, social hygiene remained under the aegis of the medical profession. At the first annual Public Health Convention in 1896, doctors were the ones who wrote out the requirements for a healthy home, and who led the discussion of proper city layout.[9] The medical perception of the housing problem contributed significantly to the polemics in favor of a national housing act, which was drafted in tandem with a national health act. During the first and second Public Health Conventions of 1896 and 1897, where the majority of participants were doctors, features eventually covered in the Housing Act of 1902 were discussed: building ordinances, planning requirements, housing standards, condemnation, and public housing. Engineers, architects, lawyers, labor representatives, and other professionals also participated, but the medical perspective dominated discussions.

Once legislation was in place, and public intervention in the regulation and production of housing was established, the focus of work in housing reform shifted to legal and technical means to solve the housing problem, drawing contributions from economists, engineers, and legal experts. Nonetheless, doctors tried to maintain their position of primacy and control, claiming to be the only experts whose understanding of the health implications of poor housing would permit the design of regulations, the administration of laws, and the planning of neighborhoods and housing to benefit public health. It followed that doctors should take the lead in setting standards for materials and design, while engineers would simply provide the technical assistance to carry out the medical specifications. The Delft engineers had hoped to avoid precisely this subordinate relationship between policy makers and engineers when they proposed the curriculum for a social-technical engineer whose range of expertise would allow him to operate effectively and independently in the social application of technology.[10]

The conflict between doctors and engineers for control of this new field came to a head on several occasions, including the execution of the Health Act of 1902. Previously, governmental health regulation had been minimal, primarily the licensing of legitimate practitioners and the limited policing of building practices. Regional health boards introduced in 1865 were advisory only and had negligible power or impact on living conditions. The proposed Health Act was intended to remedy this situation by providing a hierarchical organization for government health intervention in which a central health board would report directly to the Ministry of the Interior. At the regional level, chief health inspectors were to supervise health inspectors specialized in housing, medicine, and workplace safety. At the local level, a state appointed municipal health board composed of experts would pass judgment on local planning and housing proposals as well as other tasks related to maintaining public health.

The broad mandate of the Health Act, which defined public health to include issues of planning and housing as well as the control of epidemics and other health measures, reflected a shift to the more comprehensive social concerns of the ministry of Goeman Borgesius.[11] The government acknowledged this shift in emphasis by renaming "medical" inspection "public health" inspection, and by explicitly specifying that the state public health inspection need not be, and might not be, exclusively medical.[12] This acknowledgment and welcome of the contributions to public health from the nonmedical professions met with approval in the Society of Civil Engineers, whose committee to study the proposed Health Act reported favorably on the decision to rename the state inspection agency.[13] Doctors, on the other hand, were highly critical of the proposed changes. Objections came from both the Society for the Advancement of Medicine as well as the Public Health Convention. One bystander reported, "Most commentary from that circle presumes that they, the doctors, should be granted ultimate authority. This is understandable from their viewpoint since 'chaque curé prêche pour sa paroisse,' but we seriously doubt if it is the correct viewpoint."[14]

Most controversial was the question of who should head the central health board, a doctor, engineer, or legal expert. The doctors did not deny the necessity for assistance from other disciplines, especially in the housing field, but insisted on the primary authority of the medical profession, and on the supervisory role its leadership would provide. The Amsterdam Health Board, for instance, argued that the leadership in health must be given to the hygienists, that is, doctors of medicine, since health (*gezondheidsleer*) is a specialization of medicine (*geneeskunde*).[15]

Arie Keppler, the Delft engineer later to head Amsterdam's Housing Authority, disputed the doctors' claim to the title of hygienist, particularly social hygienist. The doctors claimed to be "the" hygienists, he noted, but he doubted their social commitment. One doctor who had studied the problem of tuberculosis and the home had suggested that the best measure to take against the disease was to advertise the benefits of light, air, cleanliness, and good nutrition. His remark, "You can provide the first three benefits in the back slums for nothing!" caused Keppler to reply scathingly,

> This is a doctor serving the poor, but can he ever have looked around at their housing? Has he ever been in one of the 2,000 or so cellar dwellings of Amsterdam, or in the alleys that scarcely get any light or air? Hasn't the doctor ever considered that cleanliness, not to mention the elimination of vermin, is almost impossible in an overcrowded one-room flat, where people wash, cook, and sleep? Or that when mother also has to go out and work, that there's no time or energy left to keep everything clean? But there he goes: "You can provide the first three benefits in the back slums for nothing." Wasn't he just destined to become a hygienist?[16]

The doctors had developed a scientific understanding of hygiene, Keppler argued, but they had not looked into its social implications until pressure from outside the medical profession forced them to do so. His comments underscored the failure of the medical profession to recognize the powerlessness of the individual in such dire conditions and the responsibility of society to set norms to protect the individual. Keppler identified engineers as more appropriate experts of social hygiene:

> Social hygiene will appear increasingly in the forefront, and I am convinced that there is bound to be a conflict of interests between the doctors on the one hand, and the engineers and the architects on the other.
>
> First the engineers had to battle against the lawyers over business management and administrative matters. Now, with the rise of the practice of hygiene and particularly applied hygiene, the medical and the technical experts will be crossing swords.[17]

The swords were crossed openly in Delft where Keppler and others had campaigned for the provision of adequate training in technical hygiene. They argued that the positions opened by the new social laws should be filled by properly trained appointees, claiming that the continuing failure to provide specialized instruction in technical hygiene at either the universities or Delft had contributed to the failure to find qualified hygienists to fill the positions created by the Health Act.[18] Under the auspices of the Social Technical Society of Democratic Engineers and Architects, Louis Heijermans, a doctor specializing in social hygiene and workplace conditions, gave classes in Delft from 1906 to 1909. The overwhelmingly favorable response to his lecture series led to further discussion of the need for instruction in hygiene, who should teach it, and what should be taught. Heijermans and others supported instruction by both medical and technical experts, but the government appointment in Delft eventually went to a doctor alone. His emphasis on the containment of contagious disease prompted students to demand the additional appointment of a technical specialist in housing and planning.[19]

The split between the medical and technical aspects of hygiene was also apparent in the changing organizational structure of Amsterdam's civil service. The reorganization of the bureaucracy illustrates vividly the eclipse of the medical profession in matters of housing and planning. A health board was originally installed in Amsterdam in 1864 as an advisory committee to the municipal council. It was composed of three council members, three doctors, a lawyer, chemist, architect, and veterinarian. From the first, this committee actively promoted thoughtful city expansion, studying the problem of workers' dwellings, the requirements of sewage and water, the relationship between mortality and population density, and other topics reflecting contemporary approaches to sanitation and hygiene. In the 1870s, the board carried out an important study of cellar dwellings, but it was not until the 1880s that it pressed for the creation of a permanent sanitary inspection agency for the city.[20] A municipal health service was established in 1893, under the direction of Dr. R. H. Saltet. Only a few years later, the Amsterdam Health Board recommended that a special bureau to study housing conditions be added to the health service, and this was accomplished in 1896.

Attention also focused on the inadequacies of contemporary building inspection, and on the scanty building code that provided its authority.[21] Although inspection procedures had been reorganized as recently as 1895, the collapse of several houses in 1899 led to renewed calls for overhaul of the inspection ordinance and office.[22] Since it was anticipated that the proposed Housing and Health Acts might precipitate further changes, the Amsterdam City Council decided to combine both building and housing inspection in one municipal agency. This notion had previously been rejected because it had seemed unlikely that a director would be found who could combine competence in both areas. The position of director of the Building and Housing Inspection Office was created and mandated to carry out a major revision of the building ordinance and to carry on the sanitary inspection of the city's housing stock. The Health Board, however, objected strenuously to the removal of housing inspection from the domain of the health service instead of maintaining separate inspections for building safety and for hygiene as in the past.[23] The medical lobby was even more incensed by the appointment of an engineer instead of a doctor as head of the new Building and Housing Inspection Office. In fact, the appointment was a particularly fortuitous one: J. W. C. Tellegen, a civil engineer, had distinguished himself nationally through his urban renewal work in Arnhem, the model of a well-informed, competent administrator. The doctors' objections to his appointment were countered by discussions of the nature of housing expertise. Although housing certainly should be the work of a hygienist, it was argued, a hygienist was not necessarily a doctor, for the meaning of the word had expanded to include the technician: "The housing question is that aspect of medicine that can be administered just as well, if not better, by a technical hygienist as by a hygienic physician," said one participant in the debate.[24]

Social hygiene as the discipline that would address the material dimensions of the social problem did not survive the battles for supremacy between the engineers and the medical profession. The term came to designate a more limited field, that of social medicine, which was to apply the techniques of medical and social research to the control of epidemics, the monitoring of consumer goods, and the provision of health care. A purely medical definition of the housing question was eventually superseded by a broader approach, although the perception of the problem as a public health issue persisted.[25] The Dutch *Journal of Social Hygiene* continued to publish articles on housing and planning throughout the first two decades of the twentieth century, and the health remedies of light and air continued to permeate discussion of proper housing design. However, the doctors yielded to others the leadership of the housing reform movement. One observer noted, "The difficulty of the housing question lies not in the formulation of hygienic requirements, but in the technical . . . side."[26] As government intervention broadened the field of endeavor, those working in housing reform discovered that the mere specification of sanitary requirements posed a lesser challenge than their translation into particular proposals for urban planning and housing design, that is, the conversion from minimal norms to positive forms. As the requirements for expertise grew, the locus of conflict about professional authority over housing and urban planning shifted to the engineers and architects.

URBAN PLANNING AS TECHNICAL AND AESTHETIC EXPERTISE

In the nineteenth century, urban planning in the Netherlands was viewed primarily as a technical problem of transportation and sanitation. Civil engineers were employed to locate and design transportation networks and public facilities such as bridges, harbors, railroad terminals, markets, and sewers. Amsterdam's most extensive nineteenth-century urban plans were prepared by engineers from the Public Works Department. The city engineer J. G. van Niftrik oversaw the design of the harbor extensions and the North Sea Canal, the filling in of canals to create streets in the city, and the extension of the sewage system, in short, all the technical infrastructure required by the city's growth.[27] In contrast, the scope of the city architect's position was generally limited; he merely had to oversee the design of public buildings. Since civil engineers working in public works departments were the supervisors of the Dutch urban extensions in the nineteenth century, it comes as no surprise that architects contributed little to the discussion of urban planning at the Public Health Conventions, or that engineers like Tellegen, with experience as director of public works in Arnhem, were the ones who cooperated with the doctors to draw up proposals for building ordinances and urban renewal policy. Nonetheless, in the field of city planning, civil engineers began to lose commissions to architects around the turn of the century.

Although civil engineering was long considered to be the appropriate training for urban planning, urban planning was not a profession per se. Before the end of the century, the problems of modern urban expansion were too new and their ramifications too unexplored to have produced either a corps of experienced urban planners or an established planning curriculum. Urban planning was not acknowledged as a specialized department of the Amsterdam municipal bureaucracy until 1924, with the founding of the city planning office in the Public Works Department. The Social Technical Society of Democratic Engineers and Architects proposed a chair of urban planning at Delft in 1904, but the failure of the public to recognize its legitimacy as a field of expertise is illustrated by Prime Minister Abraham Kuyper's remark during the parliamentary debate: "In earlier times in this country we knew how to lay out cities which still excite the admiration of Europe without any technical institute, without any lectures on planning, but at a time when people had energy and artistic sense."[28] Delft did not inaugurate a chair and department of city planning until 1926.

However, the failure of recent city extensions in Amsterdam and other cities to measure up to popular assessment of the aesthetic standards set by previous centuries inevitably led to a reexamination of planning expertise. Objections to the lifeless grids and the gray developments that had sprung up in Amsterdam in the 1880s and 1890s were expressed freely and frequently in the pages of journals and the deliberations of the municipal council. The Pijp, a triangular neighborhood of long narrow streets designed by Van Niftrik, was described as "the ultimate expression of *la vie grise*, the negation of all except empty boredom, a monument to laissez-faire and private enterprise, and also to the taste of the politicians."[29] Civil engineers began to lose credibility as urban planners.

The most influential Dutch voice in favor of more aesthetic planning was the architect H. P. Berlage. In 1892, Berlage summarized Camillo Sitte's new book on the aesthetic principles of city planning for Dutch architects.[30] Following Sitte closely, Berlage argued from historic examples that urban design and architecture had previously been unified in a manner lost in the nineteenth-century quest for individual expression. Urban planning would revive as an art form only with the artistic renewal of architecture, that is, with the emergence of a new general style that could objectively express the tenor of the times, as had all great styles of the past. Although Berlage claimed that the past was a source of artistic principles, not a copybook, the attention Sitte brought to bear on given historical forms led to a rediscovery of certain aesthetic effects: the enclosed square, curved street, irregular crossing, and the asymmetrical placement of focal buildings that creates a visual order conducive to the unified expression of place. Berlage, like Sitte, made the case that aesthetic as well as technical expertise was necessary for contemporary urban design and that architects alone had mastery over the appropriate skills. His own appointment in 1900 to design Amsterdam's southern expansion after the municipal council had rejected the plan of the city engineer ushered in a new era in urban design, with architects receiving commissions on the basis of their aesthetic expertise. There was plenty of work to be had, particularly in view of the requirement under the 1902 Housing Act that communities with a population of 10,000 or more draw up extension plans.

As architects in Amsterdam and elsewhere in the Netherlands began to receive planning commissions in the first decade of the twentieth century, their replacement of engineers did not go unchallenged. In 1914, the head of public works in Tilburg, J. H. E. Rückert, set off a spirited debate when he objected to the challenge architects were posing to a field traditionally led by engineers. While he acknowledged the previous failure of engineers to pay sufficient attention to the aesthetic dimension of planning, he suggested that the time of such ignorance was past, and that engineers were now in a position to guide all aspects of planning: economic, technical, social, legal, hygienic, and aesthetic. To give architects the lead and bring in engineers only to advise on technical matters such as bridges, paving, and sewage was an overreaction to past mistakes.[31]

A series of responses to Rückert's article quickly appeared in the engineers' and architects' professional journals. Each side freely acknowledged that planning demanded both technical and aesthetic expertise. The struggle between the two professions for leadership thus translated into a struggle over the legitimacy of their claims to that expertise. Each argued that it held a monopoly of expertise in its own discipline, while claiming mastery of the other. Thus the architect J. H. W. Leliman could say, on the one hand, "that designing an extension plan as such is neither the work of the architect nor the work of the engineer. Planning is . . . the work of a planner," but then go on to claim that the architect is the natural choice to be trained in the new discipline.[32] "At any rate, only an architect has the ability to shape space and mass as [planning] requires," wrote Berlage. Each side clearly had an eye out for its own interests, while the ever critical Keppler watched from the sidelines, chastising all parties for their lack of preparation for the task of planning. "There's a new job, gentlemen: who's going to bid the most for it?" he asked cynically.[33]

By basing their arguments on the question of appropriate expertise, and positing a dichotomy between aesthetic and technical criteria, the architects and engineers participating in this debate obscured the real issue at stake: the values that were being assimilated into their professional missions. This process can be seen in the controversy over the filling of old Amsterdam canals.[34] In 1902 the Public Works Department, still dominated by the civil engineering approach to planning, proposed filling in the Reguliersgracht in order to relieve local traffic congestion. The proposal was only the most recent in a pattern of construction that had created more streets in the center of the city to serve the interests of small business there. In reaction, speaking at the Antiquarian Association (Koninklijk Oudheidkundig Genootschap) in Amsterdam, artist Jan Veth gave the stirring lecture "Urban Desecration and the Reguliersgracht Question," in which he made an impassioned plea for recognition of the beauty of the old canal, "not the proudest, the grandest, or the most distinguished, but certainly the loveliest, the most intimate."[35] Veth's position defined a public interest in resisting planning decisions motivated solely by profit. The rising popular sentiment for the beauty of the old city was pitted directly against the practical, commercial interests favoring improved transportation; two interpretations of public interest, with far-reaching social and political implications, were put at loggerheads. The aesthetic objection to the plan drew from both conservative and progressive critiques of capitalist real estate. The conservative attack dwelled on the sanctity of the city's historical heritage, its symbolic representation of tradition, and the role of such symbolism in sustaining social order. The progressive attack viewed urban aesthetics as an essentially democratic good, benefiting all citizens equally, in contrast to the narrow economic interests of shopkeepers and businessmen. Those financial interests were defended by the engineers of the Public Works Department, who pursued a liberal policy toward land management that saw planning as an instrument to maximize profitable returns both for the city as landholder and for private concerns. The controversy on planning expertise between architects and civil engineers reflected the implicit incorporation of these competing definitions of public interest by the professions.

Repeated proposals made between 1902 and 1907 to fill the Reguliersgracht were defeated in the Amsterdam City Council in every instance, and eventually a solution to the transportation problem was found in the widening of a parallel street, the Vijzelstraat.[36] Meanwhile interest groups on both sides of the issue became increasingly organized. On the one hand, merchants and shopkeepers lobbied in favor of customer and delivery access, on the other hand, middle-class art and nature lovers organized to protect Amsterdam's civic heritage. In conservative organizations such as Genootschap Amstelodamum or Bond Heemschut, prominent citizens canvassed for the preservation of Amsterdam's beauty from disfigurement.[37] But protests against ugly planning had also become part of the cultural critique of capitalism, and the pages of P. L. Tak's progressive journal *De Kroniek*, a mouthpiece of the social reform movement, were also filled with criticism of the city's development.[38]

It was apparent to many concerned with Amsterdam's future that the efficacy of amateur lobbies was limited and that the services of experts in positions of authority were required to defend aesthetic values. The necessity for amateur lobbyists would be eliminated, reasoned Berlage, with the development of the science of planning, and as the values expressed in Jan Veth's encomium were incorporated by the planning professions. By 1914, Berlage's conception of planning had evolved since his initial encounter with Sitte's ideas, but he still adhered to the central precept that urban design is an artistic tool.[39] Economic, statistical, and hygienic analyses are thus the scientific foundations for city extension that the artist then organizes and manipulates into a great composition according to the aesthetic insights of his time. While Berlage struggled to categorize the city as the result of "artistic science" (*kunstvolle wetenschap*) or "scientific art" (*wetenschappelijke kunst*), he also held that only the architect had the creative expertise necessary to the task. Lest his acceptance of the scientific application of the art of planning be misconstrued, Berlage acknowledged that his insistence on architectural leadership was primarily a question of values. Some fear the scientific handling of the planning art, he commented.

> Municipal governments will have the tendency even more than now to consider the design of city plans as an issue only of science and not of art and therefore to commission plans from scientific men and not from artists. The recent controversy whether an engineer or an architect should design the extension plan of a city proves that this is not unthinkable. As for myself, I believe there is no doubt how to answer this question since it is simply governed by what one ultimately desires for the city as a whole. If one wishes that the plan satisfy all practical requirements with mathematical accuracy, then an engineer should make the plan; if, on the other hand, one wishes that the plan be a work of art, that is, that all parts be composed into a whole not only scientifically but also aesthetically and practically, then an architect should do it.[40]

In 1900, Berlage had himself been called upon by the Amsterdam City Council to replace the city engineer C. L. M. Lambrechtsen van Ritthem in the planning of Amsterdam's southern extension after Lambrechtsen's plan had been rejected by the council on aesthetic grounds.[41] Berlage's first project for the plan in 1904 was praised by the council as an aesthetic accomplishment, and a number of councilors expressed their satisfaction that a renowned architect had been given the commission (fig. 2.1).[42] Some accepted the premise that Berlage's role was primarily that of aesthetic form-giver, though they were nonetheless skeptical about the likely cost to the municipality. "Now I would be the last to blame the architect for that," said one council member. "He has simply fulfilled the commission as presented to him, according to his sensitive artistic nature. Nor is it the task of the architect to ask, if no limits have been set, if the patron can afford to start up such expensive undertakings."[43] Other councilors sharply criticized the one-sidedness of Berlage's planning considerations. P. L. Tak questioned the lack of economic study, charging that nowhere in the explanation of the plan, including Public Works' description of the improvements and estimates of their costs, could he find an analysis of the housing market in terms of income levels, rent, and demand for housing types from which to calculate the requirements for workers' and other housing. Tak suggested a planning process that would begin with the compilation of statistics in order to arrive at a sound housing policy on which, finally, both technicians and aestheticians might base their solutions: "Even the most brilliant drafting pen can't solve economic problems."[44]

Berlage's purely aesthetic interpretation was, however, compatible with article 28 of the Housing Act, which simply defined an extension plan as the layout of streets, canals, and squares, a definition reflective of the nineteenth century's limited conception of urban planning as physical planning. His plan was thus merely a drawing of proposed streets and a guide to the construction to be placed on them; it was a tool for giving shape to the city. Such a tool, however, carried untold cultural significance for Berlage, since he associated the development of the city with that of human civilization and the future development of architecture with that of the city.

> The city! What concept could possibly be as important as this one? It encapsulates the results, and to some extent the ends and the means, of human social life, the events of humanity's collective aspirations. The history of urban design is the very history of humanity; the development of the city is the development of human civilization. Accordingly, it should be kept in mind that to the extent that we can predict it, the architecture of the future shall be an art of the city, its fate must coincide with the development of the city, and it must be civic and democratic.[45]

Under the continuing influence of Sitte, Berlage viewed the opportunity to shape the city as an artistic challenge. If the city was a work of art, and the architect the artist, the intended viewers were the city's inhabitants, so that the art of the city was of necessity both civic and democratic. For Berlage, the highest role that the artist might ful-

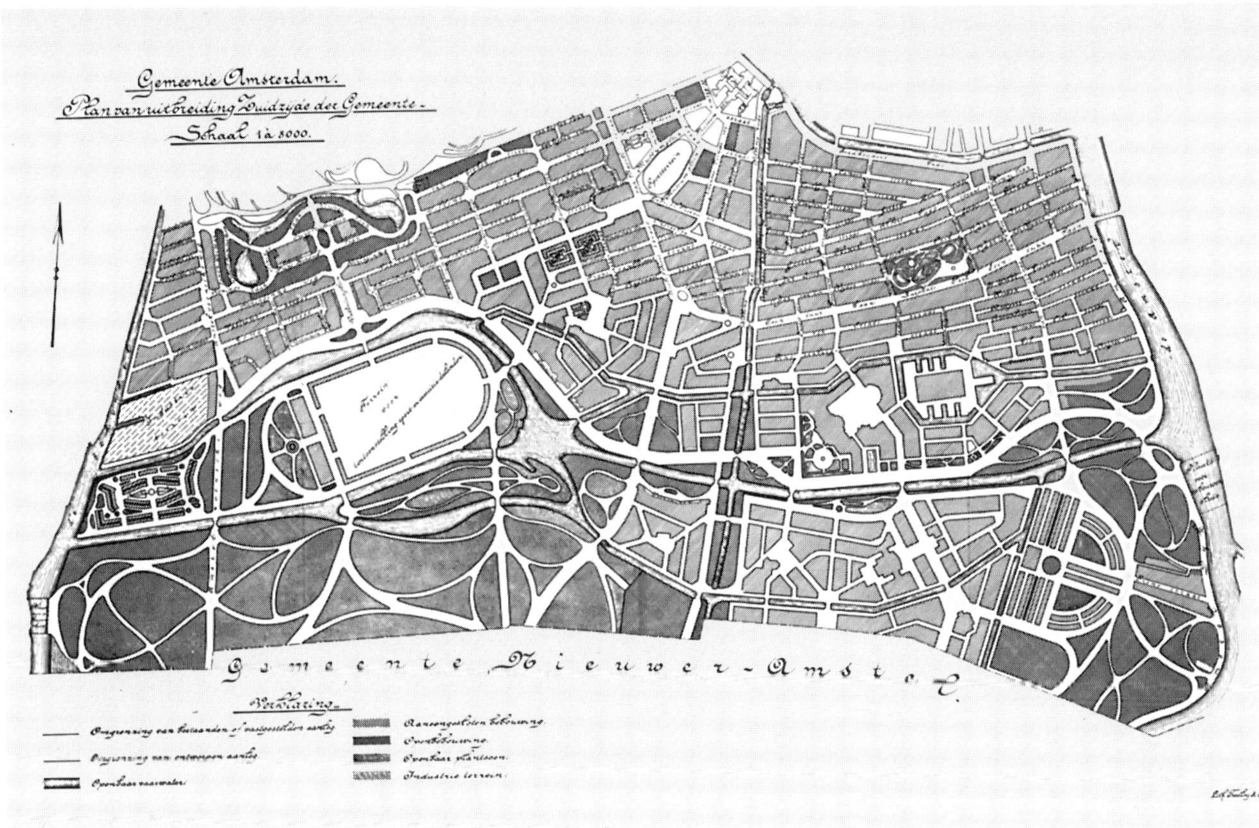

FIGURE 2.1 H. P. Berlage, plan for Amsterdam South, 1904. Gemeentearchief Amsterdam, negative E1640.

fill was that of interpreter of society to itself. In his capacity as artist, the architect was to interpret social and economic factors via his media of space and form. Urban design thus constituted the representation of the material conditions of the community, providing a visual manifestation of its lived realities.

This representational task could be satisfied only by the artist. The architect would bring visual order to the city through his interpretive creativity, something no mere technical approach could provide. Since urban design was a representational act, it must remain within the purview of the architectural profession alone. Berlage's approach admitted no authority to the engineers in this arena. Indeed, the restoration of meaning to the urban environment through visual means reflected Sitte's reaction against the fragmentation introduced by the engineer's practical but inexpressive pen and ruler. Essentially a romantic and democratic approach, Sitte's theory of urban design privileged the people's daily perceptions of the city, rather than the perspective of any prince or class. By emphasizing the experiential quality of the visual, the aesthetic itself became an avenue for the expression of political power in the city, a legitimization of the individual's orientation and of the collective civic identity expressed through the

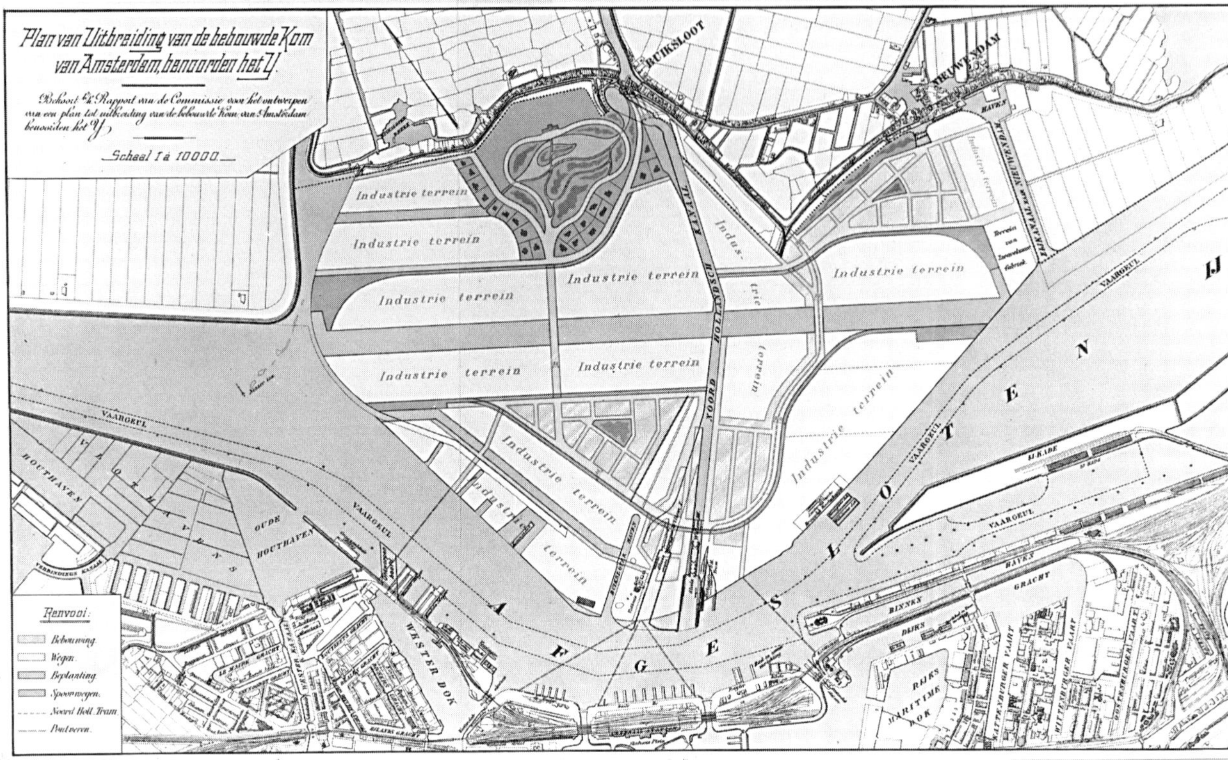

FIGURE 2.2 Plan for Amsterdam North, 1903. Gemeentearchief Amsterdam, negative E4493.

visual order created by the architect. The architect's representational conception, while expressive of political values and the product of political circumstance permitting the introduction of aesthetics into the public realm, removed urban design to an aesthetic plane distinct from the political and economic deliberations of urban policy-making. Berlage had recognized the ideological implications of city-shaping and had staked a claim for the architectural profession in the exploitation of urban design's potential for cultural expression.

Although the introduction of aesthetic values threatened the claim of civil engineers to professional hegemony over planning, it had no effect on the actual political and economic processes that animated planning decisions. Indeed, the contrast between the planning of Amsterdam North and Amsterdam South illustrates the relative marginality and isolation of aesthetic values in the political arena. Encouraged by the municipal council's evident concern to rectify the aesthetic lapses of the past, the architect H. J. M. Walenkamp had made a plea in 1901 for an aesthetically sensitive extension to Amsterdam North.[46] Walenkamp's vision of an all-embracing master plan for the north remained an architect's naive dream. In 1901, not long after it had given the commission for the Amsterdam South plan to Berlage, the city council appointed a committee to prepare a plan for the extension of the city north of the river

IJ. Unlike the extension to the south, where the allocation of land primarily to residential use had aroused little dispute, northern development raised long-standing questions about land use in relation to the expanding harbor and the possible location of heavy industry. In a deliberate move to take the matter out of the exclusive control of the municipal civil servants, the council created a committee headed by the mayor and made up of interested parties, such as the navy, the railroads, and the Chamber of Commerce, in addition to civil servants from Public Works, Building and Housing Inspection, and Commerce.[47] The inclusion of an architect was considered, but promptly dismissed, since the role of the architect was considered to be strictly limited to the aesthetic design of street plans, which could occur at a late stage of planning. The final report of the committee appeared in 1903 and made recommendations about land use. Lack of architectural participation had not prevented the committee from including rough layouts of residential districts (fig. 2.2). As the plan was executed over the next two decades, it was filled piecemeal with neighborhood plans prepared by a series of different architects.[48] This failure to provide a unified aesthetic overview was repeatedly decried both inside and outside the Amsterdam City Council. It was symptomatic of official relegation of aesthetic concerns to a subordinate consideration.

The definition of architecture's role as purely aesthetic marginalized its position in urban planning; the architect would be introduced to the planning process only after the policy decisions had been taken by the economic and political powers. However, the architect's claim to aesthetic expertise broke the engineer's stranglehold on urban design. Furthermore, and more important, architects' assertion of the aesthetic nature of urban planning was to exert significant influence on the architectural approach to housing design.

ARCHITECTURE AND THE HOUSING PROBLEM

During the second half of the nineteenth century, Dutch architects, accepting the public health orientation of housing reformers, had construed their contribution to the housing problem as technical; housing was viewed as a problem in hygienic construction. In the first two decades following the Housing Act, architects redefined not only their aesthetic treatment of housing, but also the criteria of architectural competence. The opportunities opened to architects by the Housing Act resulted in far-reaching changes both in the field's professional organization and its disciplinary focus. Housing was the activity through which the Dutch architectural profession modernized.

Architects had been encouraged to contribute to mass housing design from the late nineteenth century. In an 1892 study, a distinction was made between rural cottages, which could be built by journeymen, and urban housing blocks, which required the services of a trained architect.[49] Architect H. J. M. Walenkamp told Amsterdam architects in 1901 that they could contribute to urban beautification if they became involved in housing design.[50] In 1906, a national housing inspector warned architects in Amsterdam that housing design should not be left to the speculative builders, while J. W. C. Tellegen, the director of Amsterdam's building inspection, encouraged architects to become more involved with mass housing.[51] An Amsterdam housing inspector claimed in 1913 that the only way to assure hygienic design in housing was to hire good architects.[52]

When the Housing Act was passed in 1902, few architects considered housing to be an architectural problem. Addressing architects that same year, Tellegen urged them to view the act as opening a new field of expertise.

> It has been remarkable, but deplorable, that most housing has been built by people with little understanding of sound construction and that too little housing has been built by capable architects. If this can be changed, better housing conditions will result. The more architects move to accomplish something in this direction, and the more incompetent builders fade from the scene, the better conditions will be.[53]

There was little enthusiasm among architects for housing, and ten years later Arie Keppler, by then head of Amsterdam's housing section, took the profession to task for its lackluster response to the opportunities opened by the Housing Act.[54] Only the dramatic increase in the number of loans to housing societies, especially after the private building industry collapsed during World War I, pushed many architects into housing design.

When architects first became involved with housing in the nineteenth century, they dealt with the hygienic aspects of the problem already defined by doctors and reformers. The most pressing question was how to build healthful and cheap dwellings. As a consequence, the first architects to design workers' housing in Amsterdam, largely for philanthropic housing societies, did not view their task in aesthetic terms. Although well-known architects designed these projects, and sometimes explicitly expressed their intention to produce a pleasant effect, housing design was by no stretch of the imagination an outlet for architectural innovation.[55] Architects sought an appropriate level of sobriety: neither so plain that the building lost the expression of domesticity altogether, nor so decorated that it ceased to look like "workers' housing." Urban blocks of housing were treated either as large, single units, divided into central and end pavilions, or as imitations of row houses, with multiple repetitious gables (fig. 2.3).

The hygienic aspect of building dominated early discussions of housing among architects. When the major architectural society raised the housing issue in 1895 and again in 1898, it inquired which measures had been taken locally to respond to the hygienic requirements of housing, and then asked about the best ways to ventilate and

FIGURE 2.3 J. W. Zoutseling, Bouwmaatschappij tot Verkrijging van Eigen Woningen, 3e Hugo de Grootstraat and Van Houweningenstraat, 1888. Gemeentearchief Amsterdam, negative VH2340.

heat housing.[56] The intermittent housing articles appearing in the most widely read architectural journal, *Bouwkundig Weekblad,* focused on ventilation, heating, sewage, and the proper arrangement of the floor plan. During the preparations for the Housing Act, architectural journals turned to the legal side of housing, planning, and building ordinances; and during the first decade of the twentieth century, many of the articles on housing were written by civil servants, the municipal or state inspectors who contributed regularly on the technical, social, legal, and economic side of the issue.[57]

The first calls on architects to lend their expertise to the housing problem in Amsterdam drew on their knowledge of sound construction. Architects ran a study of Amsterdam slums initiated by the local temperance society in 1890.[58] In 1898, the main architectural society, along with the Public Health Convention, was invited to participate in the housing committee organized by the Society for Public Welfare. In the Amsterdam Housing Council, architects H. P. Berlage and J. E. van der Pek studied housing in relation to fire hazards, provision of parks, and the layout of extension plans.[59] In 1905, the Amsterdam Health Board, which already had two architects, decided to strengthen its architectural representation for a survey of slum housing to designate condemned dwellings.[60]

The hygienic aspect of housing was also the first to be incorporated into the architectural curriculum at Delft, after decades of lobbying for its inclusion. As early as 1892, arguments had been levied in favor of instruction in hygiene at the Polytechnic School.[61] A study of the curriculum in 1895 reached the same conclusion, suggesting that Delft add planning and art history as well as hygiene to the prescribed course of studies.[62] In 1905, as we have seen, the progressive society of architects and engineers, the Social Technical Society of Democratic Engineers and Architects, called for instruction in housing hygiene and planning at Delft, and their call was seconded by the students themselves.[63] Students advised the addition of courses on hygiene and planning because they felt architects should be competent to design workers' rental housing and city extensions. They asked for instruction in housing types, city blocks, street profiles, street plans, parks and squares, and monumental buildings.[64] The 1906 course on hygiene by Louis Heijermans included topics relevant to housing, but Arie Keppler, among others, deplored the fact that there was no specific instruction in workers' housing or planning.[65] In due course, instruction on the Housing and Health Acts, building ordinances, and other legal and sociological aspects of urban planning were taught by C. A. Verrijn Stuart from 1907 and J. H. Valckenier Kips from 1909.[66]

At the turn of the century, architectural expertise applied to housing was thus largely defined in terms of construction and hygiene, functional topics highly appropriate to the orientation of the Delft Polytechnic. But the low number of architects participating in the Dutch Public Health Convention indicates the limited interest most took in even those aspects of the problem. Nonetheless, those trying to encourage architectural participation continued to cast housing design as a hygienic rather than aesthetic problem. A writer in a 1901 issue of the *Bouwkundig Weekblad* tried to demonstrate that the floor plan was worthy of the greatest architectural consideration:

> It is noteworthy that in foreign countries the study of the floor plan is currently much the focus of attention, as is apparent from many books and journals. Professors at universities do not consider it beneath their consideration to take up that area. Indeed, in our opinion, to study that issue is more practical than delving into the aesthetic side of planning, or for that matter elaborate courses on religious or other monumental building types. Greater attention should also be paid in this country to that important problem, one might almost say *the* most important of all building problems, namely, the economic construction of "mass housing" in the broadest sense.[67]

In 1901, when the Society for the Advancement of Architecture sponsored a competition for a block of eight workers' dwellings, there were only 9 entries.[68] It sponsored a more successful competition for single family rural housing in 1908, with the express purpose of interesting architects in the housing problem. The 230 entries were exhibited in both the Hague and Amsterdam, and the best designs were later published in a book accompanied by the jury's report.[69] Here the fact that the jury was composed largely of municipal directors of public works and state health inspectors led inevitably to an emphasis on the social and hygienic aspects of housing. Simultaneously, the Amsterdam chapter of the society, with the assistance of the builders' organization Amstels Bouwvereeniging, sponsored a competition for a plot with eight workers' dwellings, the typical Amsterdam arrangement. However, none of the 9 entries was premiated.[70] Two years later, architects boycotted a competition for housing design sponsored by a housing society because of the basis on which the architect's fee was to be calculated.[71]

The narrow perception of the problem and the limited number of commissions before the Housing Act was fully put into effect combined to diminish architectural involvement in mass housing design. For architects, the traditional sources of prestige were important commissions and public recognition of their aesthetic accomplishments, neither of which were offered by mass housing. Architects did not yet view housing design as the translation of hygienic requirements into the language of space and form. Until housing design could be viewed as an appropriate social task, professionally recompensed, and until the housing problem could be perceived as an aesthetic challenge, architects would not be drawn into participation.

The recognition of housing as an aesthetic issue developed out of the architectural treatment of urban design. Although Berlage had introduced the new discipline of urban design, or *stedebouw*, in his 1892 summary of Camillo Sitte's work, the topic did not immediately become part of the architectural curriculum. In 1908, Berlage began teaching urban design to students of the newly established architecture academy in Amsterdam.[72] In 1912, the Society for the Advancement of Architecture petitioned the minister of the interior to establish a chair in planning and city extension at Delft. The society's proposal was seconded both by students and instructors in the Delft architecture department, who argued that while instruction in the technical, hygienic, economic, and legal aspects of planning was adequate, instruction in the aesthetic side was lacking altogether.[73] Later in the same year, the architectural society Architectura et Amicitia petitioned the minister to establish a chair in planning and city extension at the Academy of Fine Arts in Amsterdam.[74] When no immediate response was forth coming, the Delft student organization Practische Studie invited Berlage to give four lectures in Delft on "the aesthetic aspect of city planning."[75] In the following year, J. A. G. van der Steurs was appointed professor of architecture at Delft, introducing a course on the aesthetic principles of city extension and, incidentally, consolidating the architectural curriculum at Delft rather than at the academy.[76] By 1914, then, both the students at the aesthetically oriented architecture academy in Amsterdam and those at the technically oriented university in Delft were exposed to the teachings of Berlage on urban design.

In his 1914 lectures, following the planning theory of A. E. Brinckmann and Walter Curt Behrendt, Berlage held that harmonious urban development could only be achieved through the aesthetic unification of the housing block.[77] The blocks of residential development became the raw materials for shaping the city, and housing became pure architectural form. The street facade could be perceived as an aesthetic entity to be manipulated as a whole. Berlage thus introduced into Dutch architectural discourse a new conception of housing design, placing the subject directly into the mainstream of architectural debate. Once housing could be viewed as part of the aesthetic problem of urban design, it could become subject to the contemporary debate over the proper architectural forms for the times and the community. Housing, no less and perhaps more than any other building type, could become a vehicle for exploring the creation of a collective style. The emphasis of the architect's task in housing design would then shift from its previous focus on hygienic requirements to the translation of the collective experience of society. Housing might become a channel for communicating architectural ideas, in addition to being an economic, political, and social phenomenon in the province of politicians, doctors, and social workers. In short, housing design, like urban design, could become a representational act.

The disputes between and within professional disciplines to define the nature of housing expertise generated categorical distinctions that influenced the regulation of housing design. Foremost among these was the distinction between hygienic and aesthetic criteria. The persistence of the medical analysis of the housing problem and the rise of an aesthetic approach to housing and urban design had implications for the organization of housing expertise at the municipal level.

HOUSING EXPERTISE IN AMSTERDAM'S MUNICIPAL GOVERNMENT

Housing reform in Amsterdam was carried out by a relatively small coterie of specialists who exerted influence nationally. As they moved from positions within the charity organizations, from within the labor movement, or from the Delft Polytechnic, onto government advisory boards, into institutions of social reform and the municipal bureaucracy, the housing experts defined a shift of power from philanthropists wielding moral authority to professionals claiming authority on the basis of specialized knowledge. Philanthropic figures like Willem Spakler and C. W. Janssen, known for their financial support of private housing societies and social work organizations, faded in importance as trained associates like Johanna ter Meulen and Louise van der Pek-Went grew in stature and authority. Delft engineers such as Keppler and Tellegen took up important positions in the civil service, while architects like J. E. van der Pek and Berlage participated in a variety of reform organizations and committees in addition to designing housing projects. Many of these housing reform experts encountered each other time and again on committees and in organizations. The participants in the Amsterdam Housing Council, the CBSA, the School for Social Work, the settlement house Ons Huis, the League against Alcohol Abuse, and the Amsterdam Health and Welfare Boards overlapped considerably. With the introduction of municipal housing in 1914, the committee to advise its management was drawn from the same housing clique as were the trustees for the many housing societies formed to carry out the provisions of the Housing Act. This professionalized coterie, who represented the new reform expertise, introduced new perspectives on housing and urban planning that could not easily be accommodated by the existing bureaucratic structure. The struggles between the professions, the doctors, engineers, and architects, to define and lay claim to expertise influenced the way Amsterdam's government, bureaucracy, and advisory boards were organized to deal with the housing issue. New municipal committees and offices that would provide an institutional niche for the social values of the new disciplines had to be created; competing specializations sought to find advocates in the municipal government and positions inside and outside the bureaucracy from which to voice their point of view.[78]

The dichotomy between the technical and aesthetic approaches to urban design and housing was clearly reflected in the viewpoints of the various disciplines engaged in housing reform.[79] In 1896, a group composed of architects, lawyers, and hygienists had suggested that Dutch municipalities step in with both aesthetic and hygienic experts to oppose the incompetent design of speculative housing: "When granting building permits, municipal governments could place designs in the hands of competent judges to make suggestions for changes and improvements in form and color. For the general good, in any case, plans should also be judged . . . by a practical hygienist for dwelling hygiene."[80] This conceptual division of tasks was an outcome of the historical emergence of the "housing problem," first as an issue of practical hygienics, requiring technical skills, and only later as an issue requiring aesthetic skills. The logic of this division was reinforced by the physical structure of Amsterdam, where, as in most Dutch cities, the continuous fronts of row houses created a street facade visually detached from the repeated plans of the dwellings they contained, resulting in two distinct spatial components amenable to specialized treatment. Thus the city itself, through the traditional urban structure of city block and row house, fostered a separation between the hygienic treatment of the plan and the aesthetic treatment of the facade. The dichotomy between hygiene and aesthetics was not simply a matter of two equal, but competing definitions of the content of housing design. Each represented a specific discourse and problematic with its own particular history, its own values and methods, conceptions of the public good, and professional interests.

In Amsterdam, the impact of this conceptual splitting into the problem of the facade and the problem of the plan can be seen in the organization of the municipal review of proposals for housing projects to be built under the auspices of the Housing Act. The proposals were reviewed by expert advisory committees divided into two general areas of concerns, housing hygiene and architectural beauty. The Health Board, whose constitution was prescribed by the Housing Act, reflected the heterogeneous nature of the hygienic approach to housing. It reviewed proposed loans to housing societies, commenting primarily on the sanitary and lifestyle implications of the siting, orientation, and layout. It also tried to influence general city planning and neighborhood layout in an effort to foster better planning practices. When the committee reviewed new neighborhood plans for working-class residential areas, it actively encouraged a north-south street orientation for better sun exposure in the morning and afternoon. It also promoted the platting of parcels with wide street frontage and shallow depths, which would improve exposure to sun and air by increasing fenestration and allowing better ventilation.[81] The Health Board also criticized the floor plans of proposed housing projects and encouraged the development of new plan types. In 1918, Louise van der Pek-Went wrote that the board must continue to strive for better and larger dwellings: "Recently a great deal of consideration and cost has been bestowed on the exterior of workers' housing, but improvement of the dwelling place has not kept up at the same pace. If we wish to help housing along, we should concern ourselves first of all with the interior, and take care that it is not too cramped."[82]

Her concern about a disproportionate amount of attention paid to the facade of the dwelling was due to the effectiveness of architects addressing the aesthetic aspects of the housing problem. Architects were brought into the Public Works Department, traditional bulwark of civil engineering, to design neighborhood plans that met newly popular standards of aesthetics. A special committee composed exclusively of architects was established to advise the municipality on the aesthetic quality of proposed buildings. This so-called Committee of Aesthetics (Schoonheidscommissie) reviewed facades only, with the purpose of improving the appearance of the cityscape.[83] Although its jurisdiction was limited to designs proposed for municipally owned land, in effect the committee passed judgment on all new housing projects built under the provisions of the Housing Act, since housing societies built almost solely on municipally owned land. Accordingly, the design of housing facades became subject to the prevailing controversies within architectural circles.

Compelling social, economic, and political changes had led to the broad support for social legislation regulating aspects of daily life. The opening by that legislation of a new social space in which collective norms were to be regulated in the name of the public good marked the end of the individualistic moral authority of philanthropy and the emergence of a social discourse that drew its authority from the objectivity of expertise. But as separate areas of social expertise developed, their individual disciplines in turn shaped the new social space in which they operated, establishing the terms of analysis and setting the criteria of judgment. In other words, patterns of interaction within that social space of regulation, norm setting, and control were affected by the various perspectives and technologies of social expertise as well as by the sociopolitical structure of the space itself. Here both the aesthetic and the hygienic discourses on housing operated in tandem, each creating autonomous arenas for social interaction that were nevertheless subject to the tensions created by the objective conditions of the public sphere.

The hygienic definition of housing expertise was rooted in the early era of the bourgeois housing reform movement and persisted in the modern institutions of housing administration established under the Housing Act. On the Health Board, experts in medicine, architecture, and social work continued an analysis of the housing problem that emphasized the relationship between housing conditions and health. The deliberations of the Health Board considered designs for housing projects in this light; they viewed the floor plan as an instrument for the modernization of urban life. In requiring housing design to meet rising standards of hygiene, they entered perforce into political issues governing the degree of government intervention, they touched on issues affecting the lifestyles of those who were to benefit from their improvements, and they encountered the problem of establishing a standard plan type in a heterogeneous society characterized by segmental division.

Aesthetics, on the other hand, came late to housing reform, having played little role in the earlier bourgeois reform tradition, where, indeed, it had been met by both liberal resistance and confessional indifference. The product of an autonomous movement within architecture, the campaign for public aesthetic control gained widespread popular support. In particular, the demand for aesthetic housing design received support from the Social Democrats. The deliberations of the Committee of Aesthetics followed closely the contemporary debates within architectural circles about style and architectural competence. Under its aegis, housing design became a tool for the modernization of both the architectural profession and style. As a result, the committee became embroiled in conflicts that paralleled those of the hygienists: the proper extent of government intervention, the experts' influence on the tastes of those who were to benefit from their influence, and the problem of regulating urban visual order in a heterogeneous and segmented society.

In the following chapters, these two arenas of social interaction, the hygienic and the aesthetic, are explored: first in the translation of hygienic requirements into housing design, in particular in relation to the dwelling plan; second in the search for aesthetic quality in the design of housing facades. In both cases, the physical attributes of housing were intended as instruments of urban reform, as the tools of the social engineer. Reformers believed that design could serve social change and were prepared to use the institutions of the municipal bureaucracy to shape an urban environment, although their definition of what would improve the lives of its inhabitants often differed. Their efforts were served by the assimilation of the new disciplines of social reform into the municipal government and by the official recognition accorded the authority of hygienic and aesthetic expertise. The professional corps of social expertise envisioned by Van Marken had been formed; despite continuing dissention over the nature of that expertise and the political divisiveness of its application, it exercised a profound influence on the design of housing in Amsterdam.

PART TWO

SETTING HOUSING STANDARDS

At the turn of the century, in Amsterdam as in many other cities, the primary motivation for setting higher housing standards was hygienic. The connection between public health and housing conditions was uncontested. The deleterious effects of overcrowding, poor ventilation, inadequate water supply, and faulty sewage had become evident in the course of the nineteenth century. Contagious diseases knew no class boundaries, and the prospect of an inadequately housed urban population not only raised the specter of reduced economic productivity, but also threatened the lives of the urban elite. Setting housing standards to protect public health thus became a task of the public realm about which there was little or no dispute. In the Netherlands, the Housing Act of 1902 located responsibility for most housing standards at the level of the municipality, for example, identifying aspects of construction that a municipal building ordinance might regulate but leaving the actual setting of those requirements to the local authorities. Here the municipalities were aided by the housing and planning professionals who studied housing conditions and participated in the international discourse on housing issues. These hygienists, architects, civil engineers, doctors, and lawyers brought a wealth of knowledge and expertise to bear on municipal decision making.

It would be logical to expect that housing norms would rise in direct relation to improving economic conditions, that is, that public demands on housing standards would increase as a matter of course with the rise in living conditions generally. One might also expect that changing insights into the requirements of urban sanitation and housing hygiene would drive up housing standards. However, public housing standards were also mediated through highly politicized analyses of the housing problem, which depended on perceptions of the social structure, interpretations of class, assessments of who the housing was for, and opinions about the appropriate role of the government in providing it. Official housing standards were the result of negotiations between bureaucrats and politicians, as well as hygienic experts.

As we have seen in the preceding chapters, there was considerable division in Amsterdam over the interpretation of the public good and therefore over the government's role in serving it. Setting norms to serve the public good was accordingly polemical. Norms were a social construct, the product of interactions between experts, bureaucrats, and politicians in which each used their authority to influence the values expressed in housing standards. In this chapter, we examine several kinds of municipal decision making that affected housing design: the way members of the Amsterdam City Council and experts on the Health Board assessed proposals for housing projects, the way bureaucrats of the Public Works Department, Building and Housing Inspection Office, and Housing Authority carried out municipal land management, and the way politicians revised the building ordinance. These were some of the chief avenues by which participants in municipal government developed the local standards of housing to promote healthful living conditions.

RISING STANDARDS OF HOUSING

In 1909, the Amsterdam Housing Council predicted that the remarkable rise in workers' housing standards over the previous thirty years would continue: "Naturally we cannot be certain what the standard dwelling of a worker will be like in seventy-five years. But the indications are that it will be different, given the trendsetting changes already under discussion, though only occasionally carried out at present. The Housing Council is thinking, for example, of central heating, collective laundries, incinerators, baths, roof gardens, and community gardens."[1] That the council could imagine the latest modern conveniences in workers' housing when these were as yet uncommon in middle-class homes reveals their assumption that workers deserved the highest housing standards. Public discussion about workers' housing took place on the basis of such assumptions.[2] Setting standards for mass housing was tantamount to posing the question, "What design specifications are appropriate to workers and their families?" and in answering this question, housing experts, politicians, and the workers themselves drew on values that reflected their cultural and political leanings.

Much of the debate over housing policy and housing design in Amsterdam at the start of this century can be understood as the dispute between those who wished to extend government responsibility only to the regulation and maintenance of minimum standards and those who wished to harness the state's powers to create ideal, even utopian, norms. Over time, both camps shifted their standards higher; as the minimum conditions that society would tolerate in housing improved, the vision of ideal conditions grew correspondingly more ambitious. Improvement of economic conditions and the development of better technologies contributed to such shifts, but perceptions of class and status were equally relevant.

In 1855, the Royal Institute of Engineers (Koninklijk Instituut van Ingenieurs) reported that for the "least civilized of the lower classes" only publicly shared toilets were appropriate.[3] The Amsterdam Health Board took issue with that position in 1873, but their standards had not risen to the point of requiring a private toilet in each home. "Lack of a toilet does not constitute a basis for condemning housing," they stated.[4] Only in 1905 did the building ordinance in Amsterdam require a toilet in every dwelling.[5] Over the course of fifty years, hygienic standards had altered dramatically, aided by the advance of medical knowledge linking the spread of disease to inadequate sewage disposal. The sometimes ludicrous spectacle of overturned slops and chamber pots in the narrow stairwells of slum dwellings was slated to become obsolete. The role of medical insight in this shifting standard should not, however, obscure the equally important role played by the perception of what was appropriate to the lower classes. After fifty years, not only was the chamber pot to become a sign of the past, but the communal toilet was doomed to extinction.

The class boundaries marked by material culture were being redrawn. At the turn of the century, a private bath was not yet standard in middle-class homes. A 1901 book on housing hygiene directed at the middle class noted that "many still appear to consider a bathroom and baths luxurious items."[6] Nonetheless, Dr. Ben H. Sajet argued in 1915 that a bath in every home was a minimum hygienic standard, which should be included even in subsidized municipal housing.[7] Despite this medical conclusion, five years later the architect J. C. van Epen, a champion of higher standards for workers' housing, found that any workers' housing he designed that was equipped with bathing facilities was automatically labeled middle class.[8] Hygienic expertise had been insufficient to shift perceptions, and workers were still expected to use public baths. It was a matter of several more decades before this norm was as obsolete as the communal toilet.

The class dimension was pervasive in assessments of design features. Although back-to-back housing was universally condemned by hygienists and reformers, it was on occasion tolerated for the indigent. Many of Amsterdam's nineteenth-century philanthropic projects for the poor had used the back-to-back solution for the same space-saving reasons that led speculative builders to use it as a guarantee of profit in areas of high land prices (fig. 3.1A). By eliminating the typical enclosed alcove as bedchamber in their improved version of the back-to-back, reformers at the turn of the century hoped to eliminate some of the worst aspects of poor air circulation in that housing type. In 1896, J. E. van der Pek designed a variation on the back-to-back for a philan-

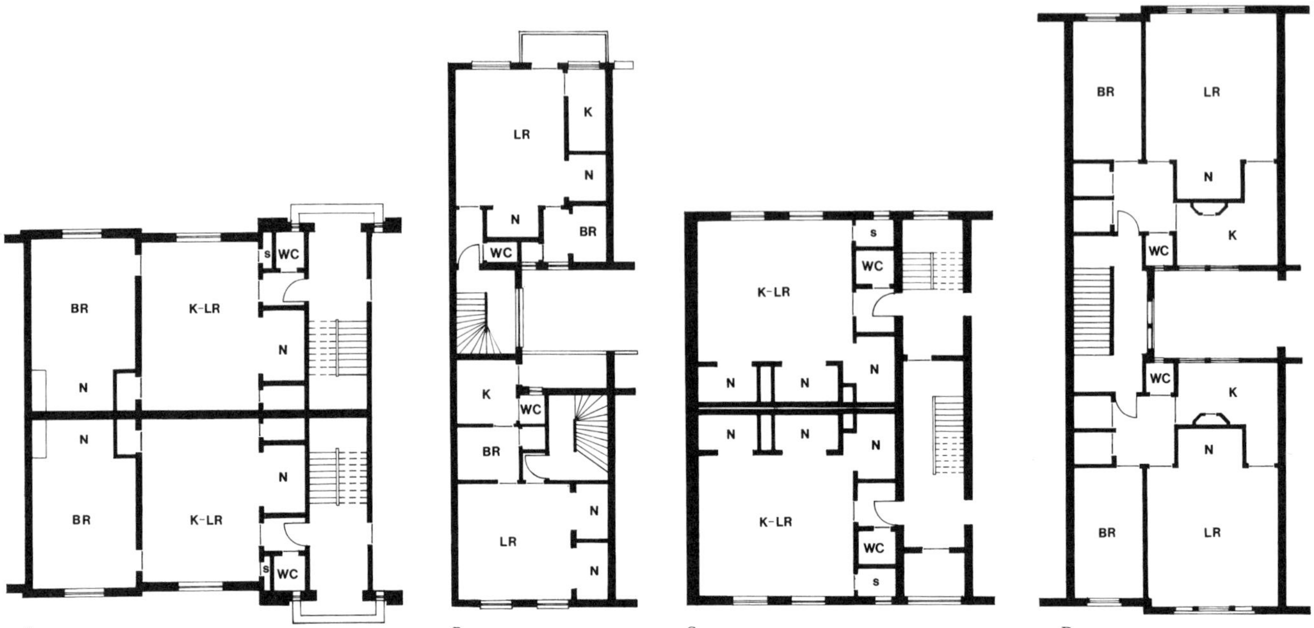

A B C D

FIGURE 3.1 Back-to-back dwelling plans: (A) P. J. Hamer, Vereeniging ten Behoeve der Arbeidende-klasse, Planciusstraat, 1854–56; (B) J. E. van der Pek, Bouwonderneming Jordaan, Lindengracht, 1896; (C) J. E. van der Pek, Polanenstraat, 1902; (D) H. J. M. Walenkamp, Het Westen, Roggeveenstraat, 1912.

thropic housing society, introducing small courts onto which faced kitchens and balconies (fig. 3.1B). Working with the same housing reformers in 1902, Van der Pek designed one-room back-to-back dwellings that tested the cheapest cost at which dwellings meeting minimum standards could be built and still yield 3 percent interest on the capital invested. Intended only for smaller families, for example, elderly couples or widows with daughters, this variation of the single-room dwelling was typical of Van der Pek's ingenuity. Party walls were constructed with cavities for soundproofing. Air ducts were introduced to the built-in beds, and the windows could be opened above and below for ventilation(fig. 3.1C).[9] The same reformers, working in the Amsterdam Housing Council, later developed a plan for back-to-backs intended for those "belonging to a very broad stratum of simple, mostly casual laborers."[10]

Reformers in Amsterdam continued to accept back-to-back housing for the poorest segment of the population into the second decade of the twentieth century. In 1911, the housing society Het Westen, building in the Amsterdam harbor district for casual laborers, proposed a plan similar to Van der Pek's on a particularly wide block whose dimensions had made development of low-cost housing difficult without recourse to the back-to-back solution. Here, as in Van der Pek's designs, an airshaft was introduced and the interior plan was arranged so that it served only kitchen, stairs, and toilets (fig. 3.1D). Nonetheless, the plan raised eyebrows in the Health Board, which pointed out that the constant daily use of the kitchen by mother and children made adequate ventilation and lighting in that room paramount.[11] In a closed session of the Health Board, the Social Democratic municipal councilor F. M. Wibaut and social worker Louise van der Pek-Went, both members of the Amsterdam Housing Council, objected to the plan. That such housing was considered good enough for refugees from condemned housing annoyed Wibaut. Van der Pek-Went admitted that her own housing society had built back-to-back dwellings years before, but stated that she would not build them now.[12] Het Westen's plan proved to be the last back-to-back to win council approval. In 1914, the back-to-back was definitively rejected in a proposal for subsidized municipal housing.[13] Henceforth, the back-to-back, no matter how ingeniously designed, was identified as below standard in Amsterdam. The housing norm for the most indigent had been raised to a level previously reserved for higher ranks.

The discussions about the back-to-back typified arguments about standards for low-cost housing design, reflecting assumptions about what was fitting for the working class and what was therefore appropriate as upper and lower limits of amenity. Was the private bath really middle class? Should back-to-back housing be eliminated even for subsidized housing? What conditions were so intolerable that even the lowest echelon of society could not be expected to submit to them? What conditions were so extravagant that the state could not justify applying taxpayers' funds to support them for workers' housing?

Each upward shift in norms indicated a change in the perception of acceptable minimum standards, that is, the minimum level of tolerability.[14] But the determination of that minimum level was not simply a translation of technological and material progress. Implicit in the setting of standards were assumptions about the structure of society. What one considered appropriate and adequate as housing standards depended on one's model of the social hierarchy.

THE SOCIAL STRUCTURE OF AMSTERDAM

When the Amsterdam City Council began to review proposals by housing societies for housing projects, one of the first issues to emerge was the question of what constituted workers' housing. The very framing of this question placed it historically. In the nineteenth century, the housing problem was viewed as the problem of housing the poor, that is, the charitable task of ensuring that even the indigent had adequate shelter. This identified dwellers as the recipients of philanthropy who through their position at the lowest level of society deserved compassion from the more privileged. The terminology "housing of the poor" conveyed an entire analysis of the housing problem. With the advent of the social welfare system represented by the Housing Act, the terminology shifted first to "workers' housing" (*arbeiderswoningen*), a word that identified the beneficiaries of social policy with a particular class, but one that could be interpreted to include a broad or narrow swath of the social hierarchy depending on one's political persuasion. Later, the more general and democratizing term "people's housing" (*volkshuisvesting*) came into use, suggesting the applicability of the law to the masses of society. This was followed by the current usage "social housing" (*sociale woningbouw*), emphasizing the social-legislative construct responsible for government-assisted housing in contrast to the free market sector. Each change in terminology has indicated a different phase of public intervention in the provision of housing.

In the period under discussion, the term "workers' housing" was used in distinction from "middle-class housing" (*middenstandswoningen*), so that a model of social hierarchy was implicit in the very use of the words. How one identified the worker determined how one interpreted "workers' housing." However, there were conflicting ways to interpret recent changes in Amsterdam's social structure.

Around 1850, Amsterdam's working population had consisted primarily of shopkeepers, craftsmen, skilled and unskilled workmen. Above them was a small group of nobility, patricians, and large-scale entrepreneurs, while below was another small group of the structurally poor. As Theo van Tijn has pointed out, Amsterdam at mid-century manifested the strata of a capitalist society, but one in which industrialization had but recently been imposed and with little real impact on its preindustrial social organization. The gap between the top layer of society and the rest, between *heren* and *volk*, gentlemen and people, was virtually unbridgeable.[15]

As the economy of Amsterdam grew during the last decades of the nineteenth century, the city's social composition and organization changed. As industry modernized, it was the newer, more concentrated, and technically advanced sectors such as heavy machinery and the chemical and electrical industries that expanded most quickly, while the artisanal, craft, and labor-intensive sectors declined in relative importance. As a result, an industrial working class emerged for the first time in Amsterdam, while traditional skilled labor and craftsmen underwent proletarianization. At the same time, with the rise of banking and insurance, and the expansion of the municipal government, there was a growth of white-collar jobs, for example, for clerks, bookkeepers, and bureaucrats.[16] The economic changes wrought during the last decades of the century did not affect all segments of the population equally. Many did profit directly and indirectly from the increase in per capita production made possible by new economic arrangements; but the impact of the new prosperity was uneven, and for many workers' families, life was precarious.

Around 1900, the working population in Amsterdam was divided by many nuances of social and economic position, which produced correspondingly diverse cultural positions. Distinctions occurred within the working class between those within the craft tradition and those without, those with pretensions to a middle-class lifestyle and those embedded in traditional workers' districts with their own local patois and social mores, the respectable and the rough, the unionized and the unorganized. The hierarchy of status was elaborate and unambiguous. The major divisions were the crafts, skilled labor, unskilled labor, casual labor, and the indigent. Within each division, the various industries could be ranked, and within each industry there was a keen awareness of the status accorded each of the different work positions. In the diamond industry, for instance, the cleavers far outranked the rose polishers on the social ladder. One author, writing in 1902 in a union newspaper, sketched the particulars of the working-class ranks. He placed the craftsmen at the peak of the hierarchy, especially the tailors, type compositors, and goldsmiths. Following the craftsmen were the trades: shoemakers, carpenters, joiners, plumbers, and tinsmiths. These, in turn, looked down on bell-ringers, lantern lighters, and nightwatchmen. At a second level were the factory workers, but among those the cotton factory workers were better than the bottle workers, the weavers better than the spinners. At a third level were found the workers who lived by the strength of their muscles. But even here there were internal divisions: the carriage driver was not at home to the hired hack. Below all three levels was the mass of the criminal and poverty stricken, "always fighting yet staying together, living from God knows what, finding employment in the dirtiest affairs and fame in the worst, and when missing usually gone to fill a slot in jail."[17] The hierarchy, then, consisted of fine gradations of status based on a variety of factors contributing to prestige: income, skill, job security, relative independence from the employer, and potential social mobility.

At the bottom of the social ladder, the mass of structural poor, which included the chronically unemployed and disabled, the widows and orphans for whom the prospect of financial stability remained obscure, had declined as a percentage of the population by the end of the nineteenth century. Their numbers had been reduced by the increased availability of work in the transport sector or in the harbor, where the change from sail to steam had made jobs available for unskilled workers from all walks of life, whether fresh from the country or unemployed from other trades.[18] However, lack of social security and unemployment insurance, the irregularity of work, and its often seasonal nature combined to create an underclass of underemployed, composed primarily of the families of casual laborers, sweated labor, and others with precarious sources of income, such as street hawkers. For many families, home industry was an activity in which all members participated, including the head of the family, who might also be working another form of casual labor. The struggle for subsistence in this segment of society was characterized not only by job insecurity and frequent shifts, but by simultaneous jobs.

While there was a wide gap between these casual laborers and the established working man with a stable position, much of the working class faced the vagaries of work opportunity. The precariousness of their economic position caused by living so close to subsistence and the lack of insurance to protect them against slack times meant that many of the less fortunate workers would fall temporarily or permanently into casual labor. Despite the high status attached to their income, job security, and education, as employer-dependent wage-earners, white-collar workers shared some of the perspectives of blue-collar workers.

Awareness of the political advantage of solidarity between all segments of the working class grew with the rise of the labor movement and socialist politics. Although perceptions of rank and status among workers continued to be sharp, among the socially progressive workers identification with a unified movement became increasingly feasible. Appeals to raise the working-class consciousness of craft and skilled workers emphasized the economic dependency they shared with those of lower status. The author who carefully delineated the status layers of the working class did so with the purpose of pointing out their common cause. Addressing the craftsmen, he asked: "Are you treated any better by the government and in society than they? Do you already have the vote, do you enjoy the full value of your labor, are your sons relieved of military service, are your daughters free of prostitution, is your retirement ensured, are you free at work, free to think, speak, and gather as you wish? No! And the poorest of the poor are oppressed in just the same way, so you should understand that their business, their struggle is your business and your struggle."[19] This attitude was the product of many decades of union and political organization.

The Dutch labor movement began in the mid nineteenth century with the organization of skilled craft unions. The typographers, for instance, were among the first workers to organize for material gain rather than merely for entertainment, education, or mutual aid, and they saw themselves as the leaders of the working class, as a labor aristocracy that would guide those lower in status.[20] This dual position, in solidarity against the capitalists but aware of the status differences within the working class, was particularly evident among the old crafts, with their proud exclusionary guild tradition. In contrast, the organization of casual, unskilled, and factory workers was slow to develop, although unskilled workers did participate in spontaneous and unorganized strike action during the second half of the nineteenth century to a degree the crafts did not.[21] Short-lived and loosely organized associations appeared often during or after such activity, but rarely developed into full-fledged permanent unions. Many of these unions individually, and later together as a federation, joined the Nationaal Arbeids Secretariaat (NAS), the umbrella organization of unions established in 1893 in close cooperation with the Socialist Democratic Party of Domela Nieuwenhuis. The NAS intended to act as a neutral labor board, but invitations to the liberal and confessional union federations were refused, leaving a strong bias toward socialist policy. The NAS, with its emphasis on spontaneity and its syndicalist aversion to central control, was more sympathetic to the unions of the unskilled workers, such as they were; and at the beginning of the twentieth century, it found its greatest support in the Amsterdam unions of the building trades, the harbor workers, and certain segments of municipal workers.

The situation of the diamond workers merits closer attention because of the special role this group played in the workers' union and political movement. From some 1,400 workers in 1865, the diamond workers grew to approximately 10,000 by 1890, thus forming the largest body of workers employed in a single industry in Amsterdam.[22] In 1894, the diamond workers joined together to form a federation of unions, the Algemeene Nederlandsche Diamantbewerkers Bond (ANDB). The new union contained many contradictory interests. Bosses and assistants both belonged, and all layers of the status hierarchy of workers, although the aristocracy of diamond workers, the diamond cutters, refrained for a number of years from joining. The socialists who organized the ANDB were part of a social democratic reaction against the anarchist leanings of the NAS. Through the work of the chairman, Henri Polak, the ANDB became the foremost representative of the so-called modern union movement that had grown up in England and Germany.[23] Polak and the rest of the union leadership worked to create a strong centralized organization, with high dues, strong strike support, disciplined strike action, and solid insurance covering sickness, injury, birth, and death. During the first decade of its existence, the ANDB used more than half its funds to support strike action. It repeatedly won strikes, winning concessions from the jewelers and factory owners, so that by 1904 the diamond workers enjoyed conditions surpassing those of any workers in Europe. The diamond workers were the first to achieve the nine-hour workday. The union established a standard wage scale, and settled wage disputes that arose between, for instance, the hourly and pieceworkers, the factory and home workers. It introduced a lunch break and eliminated exploitative practices like required purchases. It arranged a limit on the number of apprentices per year and worked to enforce it. The union was often supported in its struggles by members of the municipal government, by the liberal newspaper the *Algemeen Handelsblad*, and even by some of the more progressive jewelers. By 1904, the ANDB had become the model of the modern union in the Netherlands. Under the conditions of proletarianization that dominated the diamond industry in the 1890s, the highest- and lowest-ranked workers both perceived the need for collective action and considered themselves capable of such action.

The strategy of the diamond workers' union, unlike that of the syndicalist unions, was to aim for immediate improvement in material conditions. Whereas the syndicalists saw every strike action as a small step toward the civil disorder that would eventually usher in the revolution, the ANDB operated strictly on the basis of short-term practical goals. The ANDB was able to attract even those hesitant about joining union activity because of its attractive package of benefits, including maternity compensation. It grew quickly to include most diamond workers, 9,576 in 1911.

The ANDB refused to join the NAS, and it quickly perceived the necessity of establishing another central labor organization of unions sharing its viewpoint. By the turn of the century, a schism had developed within the leadership of the NAS that divided the parliamentary social democrats who in 1894 formed the Social Democratic Workers' Party (the SDAP) from the antiparliamentarian syndicalists associated with the Social Democratic Party.[24] In 1899, the ANDB took a leading role with the SDAP in founding a local board of "modern" unions, the Amsterdam Labor League, but it was not until 1906 that a national organization was founded, the Nederlandsch Verbond van Vakvereenigingen (NVV).[25] The NVV represented the moderate reformist position pioneered by the ANDB. It supported strong centralized unions with strong strike treasuries and salaried union employees. It was closely tied to the SDAP, but the differences between the economic and the political arms of the workers' movement were strong enough that these two bodies did not always see eye to eye.[26]

The SDAP, whose leadership included both former bourgeois left liberals and workers, ranged in support from the mildly reformist to Marxist revolutionary. It called for a wide-ranging package of social reform laws, universal suffrage, and Fabian-influenced municipal socialism.[27] Support for the SDAP came for the most part from the ranks of skilled workers and craftsmen. But it also represented the interests of the new lower middle class, who had come to experience the need for collective action and to perceive their powerlessness vis-à-vis their employers, a position they shared with other workers, whether wage earners or semi-independent, high or low status. Within the circles of the diamond workers, nearly 90 percent of the ANDB members voted SDAP, although only 10 percent were actual members of the party. Some 30 percent of the SDAP membership in Amsterdam, where the party was strongest, were diamond workers. In 1908, approximately 10 percent of the Amsterdam members of the Union of Dutch Teachers (Bond van Nederlandsche Onderwijzers) were members of the SDAP, a slightly higher percentage than that of the ANDB.[28]

In the mid nineteenth century, the gap between the privileged classes and the lower classes was wide, with few gradations of status between. By 1900, this structure had altered dramatically. A broad segment of society occupied the position of wage laborers, including the new industrial workers, a large group of white-collar workers, and the proletarianized craft and skilled workers, all of whom shared a precarious economic existence. Their shared plight was emphasized by the labor and political policies of the SDAP and NVV intended to propagate the idea of the modern "worker" exemplified by the diamond workers: a wide mix of workers of varying status and independence, disciplined, inspired by solidarity, and reform-minded rather than revolutionary. The word "worker" in the name of the Social Democratic Workers' Party encompassed a broad range of wage earners, from those who approached the middle class, like teachers, higher-paid diamond workers, and municipal bureaucrats, to industrial workers.

Who, then, were the workers intended by the term "workers' housing"? The Social Democratic definition was broad, although it emphasized the union-organized worker and deemphasized casual labor and the indigent. The Liberal definition, however, rested on a narrow vision of the social structure still anchored in mid-nineteenth-century perceptions. The targets of their housing policy were precisely the less-organized poor and casual labor; their conception of "worker" was status oriented, not class based. Thus skilled diamond workers, teachers, and civil servants who acted the role of exemplary workers for the Social Democrats might be considered middle class by Liberals. This difference in approach influenced the way housing design was interpreted and consequently how Amsterdam executed the Housing Act.

THRESHOLDS OF TOLERABILITY AND LUXURY

When the first housing projects proposed under the Housing Act came up for review in the municipal council, there was still resistance among right-wing members to the policy of state intervention in the housing market, though firm application of the condemnation powers of the Housing Act pressured all councilors to acknowledge the shortage of housing available for the lowest income levels. Even right-wing members voiced a willingness to support housing projects directed at poverty-stricken slum dwellers evicted from their homes by the municipality's condemnation measures.[29] The first projects of the housing societies, however, proposed designs clearly intended for a very different population, the organized workers with a steady income. State support for improving housing of the well-off worker was justified by progressives on the basis of the presumed "filtering" mechanism, whereby provision of new housing at upper levels would free up housing at lower levels so that all ranks would improve their housing options in a simultaneous shift upward.[30] But some right-wing councilors argued against supporting housing projects for financially stable workers, which directly competed with the private construction industry. They claimed that the intent of the Housing Act was only to aid construction for the direct benefit of those evicted from condemned housing.[31] It was clear that the first housing societies making use of the provisions of the Housing Act in Amsterdam were not proposing such minimal replacement dwellings.

When the housing society Eigen Haard proposed two-story housing in 1911, the first time that a low-rise project had been planned for an urban site in Amsterdam, a Liberal councilor objected to the plans as luxurious.[32] Another councilor reviewing housing plans in 1912 questioned whether they were "workers'" dwellings at all.[33] When the housing society Dr. Schaepman proposed plans in 1913 that included both living room and parlor, the question was raised again whether state support could be expected for housing beyond the simplest type.[34] The politicians of the right were applying a strict notion of minimal amenity to define workers' housing as housing aimed only at those on the lower rungs of the social ladder. Their definition did not include the higher-level, skilled workers.

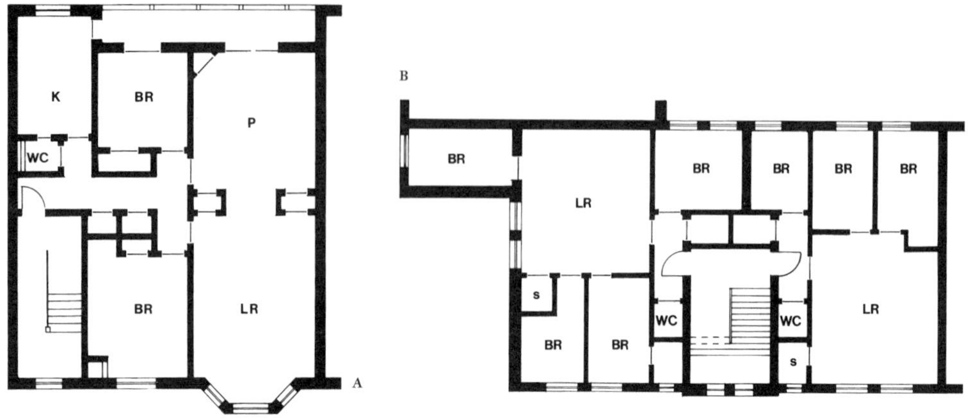

FIGURE 3.2 Dwelling plans approved under the Housing Act of 1902: (A) J. C. van Epen, ACOB, 1e Helmerstraat, 1909; (B) H. P. Berlage, De Arbeiderswoning, Javastraat, 1913.

As we have seen, workers themselves were keenly aware of their own status gradations and cultural differences. Such social distinctions had material counterparts. Workers' perceptions of housing were minutely attentive to the status conferred by the floor on which one lived, location in front or back of a block, or the presence of a parlor, and the dwellings of the housing societies could easily be assessed by these criteria. It was logical, then, that the dwellings being proposed and built by the housing societies should provide a range of housing types serving a variety of family patterns and reflecting differences in status as well as lifestyle. At one end of the spectrum, the teacher's housing society ACOB built four-story rows of apartments consisting of living room, parlor, two bedrooms, and kitchen (fig. 3.2A). The average dimension of more than ninety square meters far exceeded the typical teachers' home in commercial housing, and features like an electric lift for deliveries, wide stairs, bay windows, and well-insulated, soundproof walls further differentiated these flats from the ordinary speculative housing most of the ACOB members had been renting.[35] Approaching middle-class housing standards, these dwellings provided amenities for the teachers that reflected more accurately than their pay their status in the upper echelons of wage earners. In contrast, the subsidized housing for large families by De Arbeiderswoning, the socialist society that built replacement housing for displaced workers, for the most part casual laborers, provided only a living room, three small bedrooms, and a pantry with running water (fig. 3.2B). This too was a marked improvement over what these families had been renting, the single-room flats or cellar dwellings that provided the cheapest rental units for the indigent, but its lack of amenity reflected the lower standards considered adequate for the financially weakest.

If the top range of housing society projects was considered by some in municipal government to exceed the norms of workers' housing, even the low end was sometimes viewed as excessive. De Arbeiderswoning's simple arrangement was attacked on the council floor for providing more than the bare necessities. In 1913, a right-wing councilor claimed that by supporting the proposal of De Arbeiderswoning "we will be building housing in a certain sense more beautiful than many people need, or would rent if they could find it. So we are actually placing people in better homes than they would have chosen themselves and yet it is precisely these that the municipality plans to subsidize."[36] The alderman of public works countered, "This is not a case of helping a family to get a home that is better than its financial circumstances would warrant. Rather, it is a case of providing for a pressing need: to give poor people who have large families a humane dwelling."[37] That is, the government had the responsibility to determine the minimum housing standards to which every inhabitant of Amsterdam had a right, whatever their financial condition and whatever their own preference. Conflicting attitudes among politicians and reformers toward the nature of housing reform made what constituted a "humane dwelling" a matter of dispute. If, as followed from Liberal policy, the government's task was to provide housing for the poorest segments of the population, then standards were to be set on the basis of what was minimally tolerable for the poor, implying that what they received at the government's hands was a continuation of nineteenth-century patterns of charity. If, on the other hand, as followed from Social Democratic policy, the government's task was to provide housing for the broad segment of society that constituted the working class, then housing standards had to encompass a different notion of what were appropriate norms, implying that what workers were receiving from the government was a natural right to decent living conditions. Liberal and Social Democratic attitudes toward housing design reflected different assumptions about what amenities, if any, were appropriate for workers' housing.

The outward expression of class differences was almost unquestioningly accepted up to and through World War I. These differences were expressed culturally through language, clothes, and even the varying amenities of railroad waiting rooms. The notion that there was an appropriate level of display proper to each level of society was widespread, both among the bourgeoisie and among workers themselves. Thus, when the new municipal tram introduced cheaper commuter rates for workers, it was suggested that those riders be required to use special, less well-appointed cars. It was a sign of a new democratic spirit that Henri Polak, first Social Democrat on the municipal council, raised objections to the suggestion.[38] The idea of distinguishing working-class environs was, however, deeply rooted and cropped up repeatedly in municipal discussion.

In addition to the usual anticollectivist objections to municipal spending, middle-class attitudes toward working-class behavior had to be overcome before the city was willing to invest in trees, grassy squares, and playgrounds in working-class neighborhoods, even when these were justified on a hygienic basis. In a frank discussion of the

1911 budget, councilors on the Public Works Committee considered a proposal for a square with fountain in the Ferdinand Bolstraat to improve the monotonous character of the surrounding workers' district. Objections were raised: there was no reason for a square in that district; the district was unsuitable; it would be a waste of money.[39] At the same time, reservations were voiced about a proposal to introduce front yards along fifty meters of a street in the plan for a new workers' district north of the IJ. The gardens would be misused, with peas and potatoes grown next to flowers, and the results would be most unattractive.[40] Similarly, the idea of setting a limit on the height of the dwellings to be constructed north of the IJ was disputed. A councilor, who had been assuming that the intention was to create a *cité ouvrière* north of the IJ withdrew his objections to low-story developments with gardens only when informed that the inhabitants were not to be ordinary factory workers, but lower civil servants and factory foremen, who might be expected to make proper use of their gardens.[41]

Such arguments waned as Progressive Liberal and Social Democratic influence on the municipal council grew. Plans for new working-class districts began to include small green squares. The 1910 plans for Nieuwendammerham included a public square surrounded on all sides by houses. Berlage's 1910 plans for a large development of workers' housing in the Transvaalbuurt included a planted square. Nonetheless, workers' districts were still eyed with suspicion. In the Public Works Committee, opinion ran against creating "workers' ghettos," but there was also concern that workers' housing, if integrated with more expensive housing, would bring real estate values down.[42] The distrust of workers' districts is illustrated by municipal reaction when the Algemeene housing society began its negotiations for land in the Transvaalbuurt to carry out Berlage's plans. The city rejected the preliminary proposal, claiming "the execution of these plans would create back slums, which would lead to pollution and make extra lighting and surveillance necessary."[43] The Algemeene's officers took issue with this characterization of the plan, which had called for a pair of freestanding groups of two-story dwellings on a small block. As they put it to the mayor and aldermen, "with the epithet 'back slums' one is usually referring to something completely different than what we meant to build."[44] The Algemeene planned rents corresponding to the income of its members, largely diamond workers earning wages above the average worker's, hardly hardened slum dwellers.[45]

The Algemeene had in fact been forced by the municipality's conservative land policy to develop its plans in an out-of-the-way district. Although fear of creating separate workers' districts had been expressed by council members, the economically motivated pricing policy for leases on municipal land led to the creation of working-class enclaves in less desirable sections of Amsterdam. A Liberal council member defended the idea of replacing the existing cheap housing in the centrally located Jordaan district with high rental units, while designating a squalid and isolated section of the Spaarndammerbuurt for the construction of replacement workers' housing.[46]

With others, the Algemeene lent its support to the 1911 petition of the Amsterdam Housing Council, which complained to the municipality that the city's land policy was forcing workers to move to the least attractive districts, distant from the center, cut off by rail lines or near unattractive facilities such as prisons or abattoirs, and far from their traditional neighborhoods and workplaces.[47]

Until the revision of the plan for Amsterdam South and the resulting increase of available land in the 1920s, these were the districts open to workers' housing developments. But even when land in the new expansion plan for Amsterdam South began to be developed, workers' housing had to compete with middle-class housing for choice sites. Defenders of housing reform such as Tellegen and Keppler had to fight repeatedly to retain good sites for workers' housing societies in the new south plan.[48] Their interest in securing the best locations for workers' housing contrasted with the more prevalent opinion in the municipal council, which viewed the cheapest locations as adequate.

Liberal and socialist politicians and reformers split over housing reform, the former seeking minimum standards, the latter seeking excellence. The liberals justified government intervention on the basis of the need for replacement housing following state condemnations of unsafe dwellings. Slum clearance was the aim, and their first concern was to provide housing for the needy casual laborers and the destitute. This position defined housing reform as an extension of charity and poor relief, which justified an emphasis on sobriety and modesty in housing design. Reporting on the housing plight of the poor in 1903, Johanna ter Meulen expressed the minimalist attitude of liberal reformers when she wrote, "Let us build solidly, but with thrift and strict simplicity, only considering the threefold requirements of light, air, and privacy."[49]

For the socialists, housing was one aspect of a package of reforms intended to raise workers' material and spiritual level. Their primary aim was to serve the interests of workers, not the indigent. Ter Meulen admired individual reformers like Wibaut and Keppler, "whose dedication to the housing issue, free of any party interests, [was] unassailable," but she resigned from the housing society they founded for low-income families in disgust with socialist attitudes: "They spoke in an amazingly insensitive way about the very poorest, and in just as amazingly an oversensitive way about the workers."[50] Workers organized in the modern union movement, not casual labor or the poor, represented to the socialists the backbone of a modern utopia in which the highest standards of housing and planning would be applied. Their definition of the modern worker and his family, their needs and expectations, shaped the Social Democrats vision of housing norms.

The Social Democrats' aspirations for the working class overlapped considerably with those of left-leaning liberals. Both believed the material and spiritual development of workers could be encouraged through education and self-help, rational budgets, self-discipline, and good hygiene. Social Democrats cultivated reading, cultural activities such as choir singing, club membership, the avoidance of hard liquor, and other signs of civility also supported by liberal reformers. But their motivations were at odds. Liberal reform was essentially paternalistic, and its aims were to be achieved by maintaining the relative positions of the classes in the social hierarchy. The Social Democrats were actively cultivating a vanguard of responsible class leadership in their effort to win social justice and the radical reorganization of society. In their attempts to redistribute political power, they identified workers' deprivations as not only economic but also cultural, so that raising standards of residential amenity became a central part of their urban program. Government-sponsored housing was a right. But it was also preferable to the private real estate market because it could provide high standards undiluted by concerns for profit. Workers should chose to live in housing built under the Housing Act because it was the model of what housing should be, and not because they were forced into it by economic necessity.

The Social Democratic campaign to rectify the cultural deficit, however, was marked by anomalies. Although Social Democratic policy promoted the development of a working-class culture and considered bourgeois culture anathema, one means of ending workers' deprivation was to expose them to a high culture inextricably linked to the class enemy. This inherent duality of bourgeois and proletarian cultural models characterized housing reform, where the collectivist aims of socialist housing coexisted with cultural goals not unlike those of bourgeois reformers campaigning to civilize the working class. The Social Democrats' model of the modern worker was the diamond worker, who belonged to a union, the ANDB, whose membership was a bulwark of support for the SDAP. The ANDB's leader, Henri Polak, instructed workers in civility and taste in the pages of the union newspaper. The union headquarters were housed in a building designed in a modern style by H. P. Berlage and decorated with allegorical paintings by R. N. Roland Holst depicting working-class ideals. The ANDB embodied the synthesis of economic, political, social, and cultural renewal that the Social Democrats espoused and through which a distinctive working class-culture was to emerge. For these workers, the Social Democrats demanded the highest housing standards, although the definition of those standards lay ambiguously between those of middle-class housing and those being defined for the modern working class.[51]

Many workers themselves looked to middle-class behavior, possessions, and housing practices as models for respectable living, but found their views caught between the visions of working-class life projected by others. Although workers' hopes for self-improvement were considered laudable by liberal and socialist reformers alike, both groups were also interested in guiding those hopes toward the improved behavior they themselves considered appropriate for the urban working class. Liberals encouraged domestic virtues that fostered social order, maintenance of status differentiations, and sanitation. They discouraged imitation of the status symbols of bourgeois life. Social Democrats encouraged values useful to the class struggle, but disapproved the aping of bourgeois taste. From the perspective of workers, these messages may have been difficult to differentiate, particularly for those who identified most strongly with local neighborhood traditions that fit neither the liberal philanthropists' nor the Social Democrats' image of working-class life.[52]

Public debate on housing standards was affected by the conflicting approaches of reformers to the working class. The differences between reformers associated with the bourgeois urban reform movement and those associated with the Social Democrats led one group to define housing design as the task of fulfilling the minimum requirements of healthy living conditions and the other to view it as the task of providing the best housing possible. Both liberals and socialists acknowledged that there were differences between the problem of housing the poor and the problem of housing workers. Like the liberals, the socialists agreed that subsidized housing intended for the poor should meet lower standards than the housing built by independent workers' housing societies, but their demands for subsidized housing standards were higher than those of the liberals. They wished to raise the minimum that defined the "humane dwelling." The liberals, on the other hand, called for a similar differentiation between subsidized and society housing, but set lower standards for housing society dwellings than the socialists. For the latter, those housing projects were the first outposts of the socialist urban utopia where the modern working class could be nurtured, and they had to meet standards of excellence.

These attitudes, generated from different political values, permeated municipal debates on the proposals of housing societies and on housing to be built by the municipality itself. The much disputed proposal for municipal housing passed on the eve of the First World War was accompanied by a report recommending "a housing type as simple as possible."[53] The 1914 Health Board report suggested that there be a clear difference in amenity between the municipal housing, which was subsidized, and the housing society projects, which covered their own costs. When the first designs for municipal housing were up for review, the board wrote:

> The design of these plans poses a difficult task for the architect and the Housing Authority. On the one hand, he must never forget that these houses must be arranged so that there is a constant incentive for the dwellers to move to more expensive housing as soon as they can afford it, and he must build so that envy is not aroused in those who live in housing without municipal subsidy. On the other hand, the houses must still satisfy all the requirements of hygiene, and the decrease in attractiveness must not be achieved by means of a decrease in habitability.[54]

How were these requirements to be translated into design? The board had previously suggested such means as the absence of a separate kitchen (providing instead a pantry with running water off the living room), or lessening of privacy by increasing the number of dwellings given access from one street entrance, taking three earlier projects by De Arbeiderswoning as examples.[55] Discussion about the differentiation revealed conflicting positions on the Health Board. On the one hand were those who emphasized that the greatest simplicity should be sought, in the words of one committee member, that "as far as possible all the housing should be provided with what is useful and good, but not with what could be categorized as decoration."[56] Others redefined the minimum amenity. Dr. Ben Sajet argued that the more attractive a home, the easier it was to keep the dwellers out of the pub and that accordingly decoration was a necessity. The Social Democratic housing expert and council member H. H. Wollring suggested that rather than making the municipal houses less attractive, housing society projects should be made even more attractive.[57] This controversy serves as an illustration of the conflicting basis on which liberal and socialist reformers set housing norms. The interaction between these reformers established the upper and lower limits of the zone in which housing was subject to regulation. The lower threshold of tolerability established what was and was not acceptable in workers' housing, the upper threshold of luxury what was or was not appropriate. In determining what was a necessity and what a luxury, the experts became perforce involved in a discussion reflecting class perceptions that were closely determined by political position, whatever the issue of design.

STANDARDS OF LAND MANAGEMENT AND URBAN PLANNING

Conflicting definitions of housing norms also affected the management of municipal land holdings, which became a hotly contested political issue in the first decades of the century, particularly with the application of the Housing Act. There was considerable debate inside and outside the municipal council on what use to make of the municipality's essentially monopolistic control of land development, whether to pursue a conservative fiscal policy or a policy of land management for housing improvement.

The Public Works Department had long controlled all aspects of planning city extensions, constructing infrastructure, building municipal buildings, and administering the city's landholdings. It developed its procedures and working methods during the period of laissez-faire municipal policy. Under the former military engineer A. W. Bos (director of public works from 1907 to 1926), the department followed a liberal policy of land management whose primary aim was turning municipal holdings to a profit. In 1896, Amsterdam had rejected the practice of selling off its considerable landholdings, electing instead to lease its land in the hope of exerting direct influence on the city's future growth. In this way, land speculation, which was widely deplored and blamed for the failure to provide adequate low-cost housing, might be controlled.[58] Although the lease system was largely drafted by Progressive Liberals like Treub who had also led the drive to municipalize the utilities, conservative members of the council also supported municipal land leasing because they hoped to reform real estate practice through the elimination of small developers.[59] Housing reformers saw the system as one that could be harnessed to aid the improvement of housing by reducing the cost of land, which had been shown to be one of the root causes of high rents. They argued that housing societies should be charged a lower-than-market rate on land leased from the city, a position attacked by the right and just as fervently defended by the left.[60]

The municipal council was slow to introduce a committee that would represent the interests of housing improvement. In 1901, the mayor and aldermen rejected a proposal to set up a special council committee to handle questions arising from the new Housing Act, but during budget debates in 1908, the issue of a separate committee was raised again. One right-wing member questioned why the existing committee on public works, which had traditionally considered issues relating to the city's growth, could not handle housing. He was assured by the Social Democratic council member F. M. Wibaut that a housing committee needed members with other qualifications than those of the Public Works Committee.[61] In 1909, the alderman of public works suggested the need for a housing committee that would attend to the social arena rather than the technical emphasis of public works. The implicit political component of these comments was clear. A right-wing member noted that the Public Works Committee was considered to lack competence for social issues only because its members were politically conservative: "Since its seats haven't yet been filled by Social Democrats, the committee is declared unfit to fulfill a so-called social role. This and nothing else is the issue and the chairman will be the last to deny it."[62] In 1911, the accusation that the political composition of the Public Works Committee motivated the proposal for a housing committee was repeated.[63] When the Housing Committee was finally formed in 1912, its political composition was an immediate subject for discussion at the first meeting. There were no representatives from the right side of the council.[64] Thus the two committees concerned with urban expansion came to represent different political orientations pitting economic against social concerns.

The split was reflected in the organization and administration of housing matters in the municipal civil service. The Public Works Department continued its traditional task by construing urban planning as the physical planning of infrastructure and pursuing a conservative policy of land management. But two new agencies challenged that definition in their interpretation of the Housing Act: first, the Building and Housing Inspection Office, second, the Housing Authority, each of which was led by Delft engineers who espoused social planning values. In contrast to the Public Works Department, Building and Housing Inspection had been established as an instrument of hygienic reform. Under Tellegen, who became director in 1901, this office interpreted its mandate as the protection of housing quality. Building and Housing Inspection saw in the municipality's landholdings a means to control development. It argued on behalf of both private developers and workers' housing societies for the lowest possible lease rate in order to cut the high land costs that had long obstructed the building of decent low-cost housing. As the agency began to administer the Housing Act for the municipality, it tried to exert influence on the setting of rates. But Tellegen's attempts were perceived by Public Works as an infringement on its bureaucratic jurisdiction.[65] The two agencies remained at odds. When the Housing Authority was established in 1914 with the introduction of municipal housing, it took over many of the functions related to the Housing Act previously administered by Building and Housing Inspection and, under the guidance of Arie Keppler, similarly promoted a perception of urban planning that placed housing interests first.[66]

The differences in orientation between these agencies charged with managing the physical development of the city introduced a continuing tension within the Amsterdam bureaucracy. It surfaced repeatedly, as when the agencies disputed authority over the execution of Berlage's revised plan for Amsterdam South in 1915 (fig. 3.3). Advocates of housing reform, such as the Health Board and the Housing Committee, feared that Public Works would not represent the interests of housing adequately.[67] The Housing Authority and the Building and Housing Inspection Office each argued that they should share responsibility for the execution of the plan with Public Works "to do justice equally to the interests of all the agencies and those involved."[68] The director of the Building and Housing Inspection Office pointed out that the traditional technical responsibilities of the Public Works Department (the preparation of building sites, streets, canals, planting, and public buildings) had not prepared it for the new problems arising from administration of the Housing Act: applying the building ordinance, allocating land use, coordinating housing society activities.[69] The director of the Housing Authority wanted to control the assignment of land use, the setting of lease rates, and the layout of residential districts in the south plan. Since housing and planning are inseparable, he claimed "the agency that is specifically responsible for the interests of housing should participate in the creation of the urban plan in proportion to the weight of those interests."[70] Keppler had previously reproached the Public Works Department for its land pricing policy: "Others may consider their duty discharged by having set the land prices and assumed the period of amortization so that income will cover costs. We, on the other hand, ask for a feasible plan that will best accommodate the requirements for good, cheap housing."[71] The director of public works claimed that these agencies had not explained "why it is necessary to clarify or confuse land management by introducing elements that do not belong there."[72] These agencies lacked the information necessary for the correct assessment of land prices, he noted, and they were not responsible for achieving a balanced budget.[73]

The disagreement about planning methods and responsibilities between the Housing Authority and Public Works was not resolved at the time and came to a head on a number of occasions, typifying the planning milieu of Amsterdam into the 1920s. In

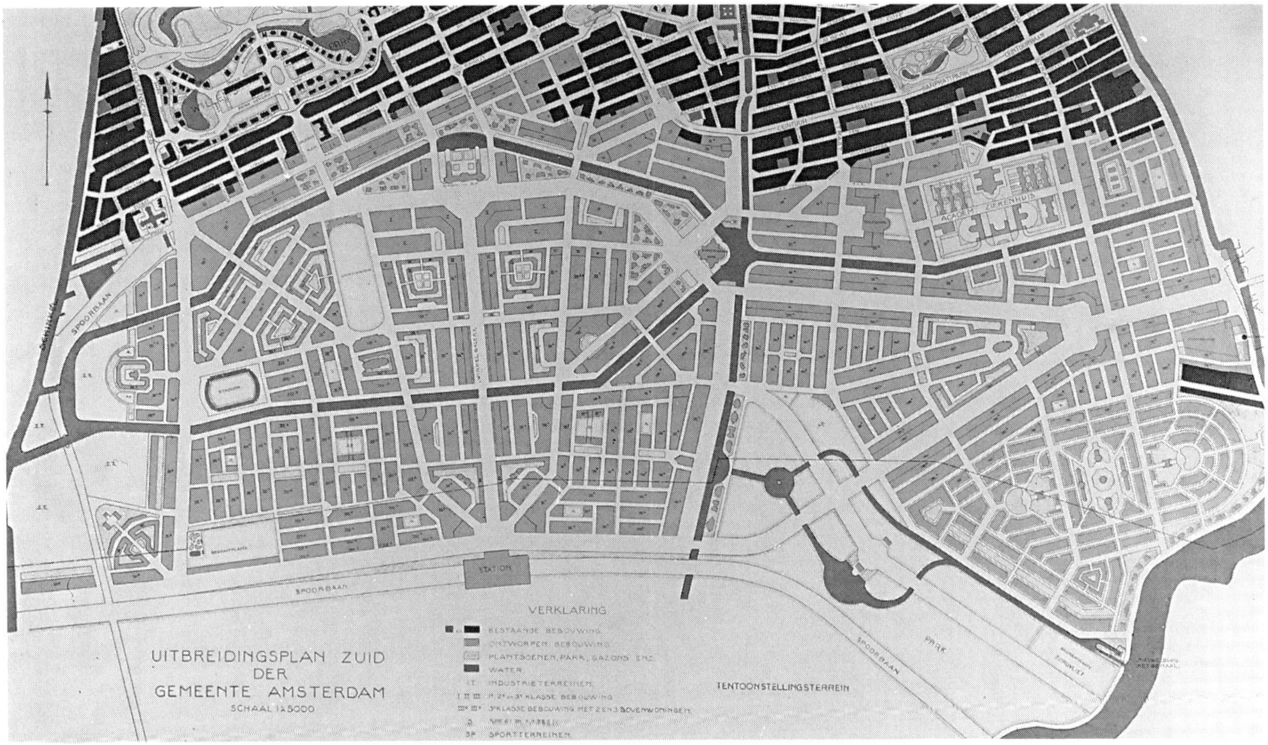

FIGURE 3.3 H. P. Berlage, plan for Amsterdam South, 1915. Gemeentearchief Amsterdam, negative F3798.

1918, their conflicts over the division of responsibility for municipal housing became a matter of public debate, as once again the Housing Authority argued for authority on the basis of its housing expertise, while Public Works banked on its seniority as municipal builder.[74] Clashes over authority in planning continued as the two agencies struggled to gain control of a separate municipal planning department.[75]

Although presented in terms of competence and expertise, the conflict between the municipal agencies was really about politics and planning methods. Public Works represented a continuation of nineteenth-century planning traditions in Amsterdam: advocacy for private development and two-dimensional, piecemeal planning in service to economic interests. Building and Housing Inspection and the Housing Authority advocated recent ideas of zoning, land use planning, and large-scale planning using municipal land in the service of social reform. Public Works defended its position as leader of Amsterdam's urban expansion because of its entrenched experience as well as its access to information about land values. Building and Housing Inspection and the Housing Authority claimed their access to building and housing statistics gave them authority. Only occasionally would the political underpinnings of the conflict surface publicly, as when F. M. Wibaut argued in the council that the entire municipal land management should be removed from Public Works to the Housing Authority. Wibaut claimed he always had the impression "that the Public Works Department treats land management as if it were a real estate business. That must come to an end. Land management must not be commerce in land, but rather the best possible management of the land in the service of housing provision, and nothing else."[76] This analysis, reflective of the Social Democratic municipal program, coincided exactly with the approach promoted by Wibaut's fellow party member Arie Keppler of the Housing Authority.

The Housing Authority and Building and Housing Inspection Office had assimilated into Amsterdam's bureaucracy the values of social reform through the introduction of new housing and planning expertise. The two Delft engineers, Tellegen and Keppler, promoted vigorous policies of urban reform through the application of the kind of social and technical expertise advocated by Progressive Liberals and Social Democrats like Van Marken and Tak. Their agencies became the chief voices within the municipal bureaucracy for using all possible means to raise workers' housing standards.

LEGISLATION TO IMPROVE HOUSING STANDARDS

The 1902 Dutch Housing Act addressed hygiene both negatively and positively: negatively through the condemnation of unfit dwellings and slum clearance to remove unfit dwellings, and positively through the requirement of a local building ordinance to ensure future construction of adequate housing. After some deliberation, the legislators had decided not to introduce national minimum standards, but to allow each municipality to respond to local requirements and traditions. Local autonomy placed responsibility on each community to establish its own criteria for acceptable construction. As a result, each community had to engage in a public debate to set those standards.[77]

In Amsterdam, the local response to this challenge was eased by the fact that the city had already begun the process of modernizing its building inspection department. The reorganization of the department well before passage of the Housing Act had been widely perceived as both progressive and innovative, while the choice of Tellegen to head the new service represented an enlightened shift to appointing technical experts to bureaucratic positions. It had placed a professional proponent of the urban reform movement in a key position of influence.

Tellegen's proposed building ordinance of 1905 set new standards of hygiene for all housing, both publicly and privately financed.[78] Its highly detailed specifications replaced an obsolete and incomplete ordinance. To increase light, it regulated the relation between building height and street width as well as the ratio of wall to window area, and it outlawed dwellings in alley courtyards. To increase ventilation, it required outlets from the toilet, a minimum ceiling height of 2.7 meters, and it abolished the cellar dwelling. It also prohibited construction of housing over five stories. Later, on the recommendation of the Health Board, the height of building north of the IJ was restricted to three stories.[79]

Tellegen's building ordinance was a milestone in Dutch housing legislation and the culmination of more than fifty years of discourse on housing reform. When it was put before the municipal council, it was resisted on the right as the dictate of an individual expert, though in fact the antecedents of the ordinance were clear.[80] It rested on discussions carried out at the Public Health Conventions, in reform journals, and at international conferences.[81] It reflected the hygienic approach to housing reform, its standards the product of a debate framed by concerns about healthful living conditions. But when the building ordinance was subjected to public debate in the council, it soon became apparent that setting housing standards involved far more than the scientific process recommended by Dr. Jenny Weijerman in his dissertation on building inspection.[82] The social and economic implications of minimum housing standards became a political issue. The principle of municipal regulation of building practice to ensure healthful housing construction was not disputed, but the setting of standards polarized the municipal council.

It had been generally recognized that raising building standards would raise construction costs, and that the general populace could not bear higher rents. Higher standards almost inevitably implied that the private building trades could not continue as they were organized. Confessional councilors, who represented real estate and builders' interests, predicted that the too-high standards and complicated requirements of the building ordinance would lead to increased rents, decreased building, and unemployment.[83] Social Democrats greeted the potential demise of the commercial builders as an opportunity for nonprofit housing societies and the municipality to step in. Tak used the occasion to argue against housing and real estate as business enterprises, claiming that the "profit-making side of housing and real-estate produces homes that many a good farmer would not accept for his cattle."[84] Accordingly, the socialists introduced amendments to increase the stringency of the standards, while the confessionals introduced amendments to decrease their requirements.[85] But aside from the policy implications for private or public housing, there was a discrepancy between the standards council members were willing to accept as appropriate. The socialists assumed that standards would continue to shift higher. Tak thought that even the most stringent standards introduced by the building ordinance would not last more than forty years.[86] In fact, by abolishing the alcove and built-in bed, an amendment proposed by the Social Democrats, the Amsterdam council preceded Rotterdam by more than fifteen years. But it did so over the objections of a Catholic council member, who asked whether the alcove was so bad for health that it had to be eliminated, given the financial consequences its disappearance would cause.[87]

The building ordinance did raise living standards in Amsterdam. Wider communal stairs, well-lit halls, better ventilation in new housing were immediate results.

Nonetheless, its influence was limited in a number of ways. Builders found ways to circumvent the letter of the law. Alcoves, for instance, were surreptitiously built after the building had passed inspection by adding partitions prior to occupancy.[88] And even when the building ordinance did perform as expected, it operated as a preventive rather than a prescriptive instrument. It could eliminate poor building practices, but it could neither guarantee that housing design would improve nor ensure how the housing would be used. A conservative councilor had argued against passage of the ordinance by blaming the inhabitants for producing bad housing conditions in the first place.[89] This attitude echoed that of nineteenth-century reformers, who claimed that workers had to be taught how to live in their homes, that a moral education was a necessary component of housing reform, and that instruction in the use of the home was the duty of the more "civilized" classes.[90] This moral dimension of housing reform continued to exert influence through the reformers who traced their origins to the philanthropic tradition.

Tellegen also admitted that a strong building ordinance was insufficient to produce better housing design, and he called for the derivation of better housing types. Research into the arrangement of rooms, the layout of housing blocks, and the organization of city neighborhoods would arrive at type solutions that would provide standards of design the housing societies might be encouraged to follow. This position represented the social engineer's strategy for housing improvement through a technology of design. It instrumentalized the floor plan of the dwelling, making it a tool of social improvement. It also implied that housing reform was like an engineering problem, with a "best" solution that might be imposed by virtue of its rationality.

Each of these responses, the moral call for teaching the working class how to use the home and the technical call for improved housing types, was addressed in the years following the introduction of the building ordinance. The following two chapters discuss these extensions of norm setting into the areas of behavior and design.

With the introduction of the Housing Act, the setting of public housing standards had become a part of the political life of the city. Although hygienic concerns remained the chief justification and hygienic experts occupied influential roles in advisory committees and in the municipal bureaucracy, the setting of standards was nonetheless as much a political discussion as it was a matter of expert opinion. Liberals, socialists, and confessionals brought cultural and political values to bear on the decisions they made regarding housing construction. As they reviewed proposals for projects, set rates for land leases, passed building ordinances, and deliberated on other planning decisions that would affect Amsterdam's housing conditions, the municipal council participated in a public dialogue charged with competing assumptions about the definition of community standards for the public good.

CIVILIZING THE WORKING CLASS

In 1919, a visitor to a block of subsidized workers' housing in Amsterdam was dismayed to find ducks in one home and birds whirling around a rabbit hutch in another. In various dwellings, she observed a cigarmaker at work, a shoemaker, as well as stacks of fruits and vegetables stored for sale. The visitor, a municipal social worker, was appalled by these irregularities in dwelling use. As for the paltry housekeeping, she commented, "Rooms are not cleaned regularly; floors are covered with tattered bits of rug and carpet. The stairs are unattended, the wash left too long, the beds not stripped in the morning, and the clothes poorly maintained."[1]

The urban poor had developed a number of strategies for surviving economic deprivation in the city. Many used their homes as workplaces for sweated labor such as wrapping cigars, labeling bottles, preparing and selling food. Boarders were taken into already crowded conditions to help pay the rent. Recent arrivals from the countryside kept livestock. The wash was left hanging to dry in the living room for fear of theft if it were left to hang in the attic, which was accessible to anyone in the building. One woman, warned by a doctor that drying damp clothes in the living room was a threat to her sick husband, asked sarcastically if she could dry them in his attic.[2] Lack of storage space led street hawkers to keep their wares, whether cabbages, potatoes, or carrots, under the bed. Families without sufficient beds or bed linen shared built-in bed-closets, rigged hammocks, or slept on the floor.[3]

Such behavior was viewed by reformers as irregular, neither conforming to their standards of civility nor fitting their notion of urban order. Reformers employed these two somewhat vague benchmarks in setting norms of behavior. Norms of civilized living and norms of urban order were for the most part defined negatively, that is, by identifying what did not conform, such as lifestyles that reproduced rural conditions in the city, or uncontrolled behavior that introduced noise, filth, or vandalism. More difficult was the definition of positive models of civilized behavior or urban order. Consequently, the methods developed to encourage or enforce adherence to reformers' norms often emphasized the repression of nonconformity. In short, although there was broad consensus among reformers about the definition of asocial behavior, there was little agreement on what constituted ideal social behavior. As G. K. Chesterton pointed out in 1910, "The social case is exactly the opposite of the medical case. We do not disagree, like doctors, about the precise nature of the illness, while agreeing about the nature of health."[4] In the case of social regulation, the ills were widely acknowledged, but what might constitute the state of health was in dispute. Reformers from a range of political persuasions with contradictory models of the ideal society all saw the usefulness of normalization in the achievement of their social and political goals, although their goals were rarely the same.

By defining a threshold of acceptable behavior, reformers also defined the behaviors that stood in resistance to their reform program and that might, from a different perspective, be viewed as not only reasonable, but advantageous and preferable. There was an important difference between the viewpoints of those who actively shaped norms and those who were to be passively shaped by them. For the first, norms represented social tools designed to cure social ills; for the second, they represented values that might be resisted or assimilated.

The selection of issues subject to normalization reflected the attitude and values of the norm setters. They reflected an analysis of what was wrong with housing conditions and what would constitute improvement. In the nineteenth century, what was wrong was for the most part identified as hygienic, while what might improve was primarily identified with changes in behavior. The housing problem was conceptualized as a set of specific concerns, each of which was viewed as posing hygienic challenges whose solution invoked behavioral change. A typical participant in the Dutch reform movement identified the chief housing issues as boarders, animals in the home, overcrowding, and the home used as a shop or workplace, that is, as a list of infringements by dwellers rather than conditions imposed on dwellers.[5] From the reformers' perspective, these inappropriate uses of the home threatened health and could be corrected by changing the behavior of the inhabitants. Even those reformers interested in combating the structural causes of poverty engaged in the battle against these symptoms. In their eyes, dwellers' ways of coping were backward and ill-informed, indications of laziness and ignorance. Focus was thus removed from any need for economic or social change to the moral character or rationality of the inhabitants themselves.

From the perspective of the urban poor, however, their behavior was a pragmatic response to economic conditions. Emotionally attached to accustomed means of self-preservation and maintaining self-esteem, workers perceived reformers' attempts to change their practices as unwarranted interference with familiar routines. Given the wherewithal, many workers would gladly have readjusted their habits, but without economic security they clung to habitual patterns of adaption. Many of their coping mechanisms, prevalent in the slums of old Amsterdam and its nineteenth-century districts, continued when the slums were abandoned for the new social housing of the twentieth century.

For many in the working class, the demands of daily life and work precluded the reproduction of bourgeois home and family life. Not only could they not afford the space and equipment necessary to maintain the bourgeois lifestyle, but their social circumstances constrained their choices. To counter the financial and medical burdens of old age, the elderly were put in institutions. The necessity to be close to work prevented poor residents from moving to less dense neighborhoods. Long hours at the workplace meant that some members of the family rarely encountered each other, and working at home destroyed the function of the home as a haven. The model of the nuclear family, a beloved image of Dutch culture, could not survive the conditions under which much of the working class lived.

For many, the nuclear family ceased to exist as a unit sharing a living space. In a large family, where children might be sent out to work as soon as they reached school-leaving age, some might be placed in domestic service, where they would live in the family of their employers. Sons went into the military service, where they lived in barracks. Sailors were absent from home for long periods of time. Some jobs, such as those in bakeries, encouraged the hired help to live on the premises because of the nonstandard hours of work. In a small concern, the help might live with the owner's family next to or on the work premises. In the case of medium-sized firms or factories, a dormitory system might be maintained. In such cases, it was not unusual for four or five workers to share a small bedroom or for a worker to find someone from a previous shift occupying his bed. Similar live-in working conditions existed for a variety of other jobs. Other alternatives for unmarried workers were renting rooms in boarding houses associated with pubs and boarding with a family. In either case it was likely that sleeping space would be shared. For the elderly, destitute, orphans, and the mentally ill, charitable institutes provided housing, typically in the form of a *hofje:* a courtyard behind the main street surrounded by individual rooms for each dweller, and often provided with a large meeting chamber for the regents of the institution.[6] A variety of factors thus contributed to the constitution of family life in a working-class home, a life markedly different from that of the middle class.

The nineteenth-century identification of the housing problem deemphasized the economic origins of urban dysfunctions and shifted the problem to one of character.[7] For nineteenth-century philanthropists tackling housing and other issues of the social question, morality was the obvious and unquestioned framework of analysis. Poverty was viewed as the result of character flaws; the lower classes were spendthrifts, lazy, crude, emotional, and immoral. Changes in personal behavior would improve their conditions. If the virtues of thrift, cleanliness, and regular habits could be inculcated, slum conditions could be eliminated. Housing reform, in this view, did not require changes in society's institutions but only the dedication of "civilizing" volunteers from the bourgeoisie, who would instruct the working classes on the proper use of the home. A corollary to this position was the proposition that housing of improved design would reform behavior.[8]

The nineteenth-century reform agenda linked cleanliness, home life, and moral character. That assumption of the reciprocity of hygiene and morality persisted into the twentieth century. In the era of professional reformers, it was still axiomatic that better housing would foster better behavior, while virtuous behavior would improve living conditions. In 1913, a respected Dutch reformer lectured that bad housing causes bad temper, household quarrels, philandering, alcoholism, waste of money, neglect of children, that it is the enemy of household virtues and leads to uncleanliness, disorder, and immorality.[9] In 1914, a doctor observed in a popular health magazine that "air, light, and sunshine enter the new dwelling, and with them tidiness, thrift, and domesticity."[10] Few attempts were made to demonstrate the relationship between housing and behavior statistically; and although research into other connections between health and housing was carried out, perceptions about housing and morality remained part of a common unquestioned lore.[11] The relationship between poor housing and alcoholism, which reformers had cited for half a century, continued to carry weight into the twentieth century, moving from the pages of reform tracts to journals of the reform professionals. In an 1898 novel written to enlighten working-class girls about the household virtues, a young visitor to the heroine's model home laments, "Oh, if only it were half as nice at home as it is here, then father would not go to the pub."[12] The same sentiments were echoed in the authoritative *Journal of Social Hygiene* in 1917: "The more unpleasant the home, the more likely the man of the house will seek refuge in the pub."[13] These ideas were introduced into municipal deliberations about housing in Amsterdam by reformers sitting on the health and housing committees.[14]

The moral perspective on housing hygiene, developed in the philanthropic institutions of the nineteenth century, persisted in various forms into the twentieth century to influence the way that government intervention might be applied to the housing problem. Liberal agitation for government intervention in housing had drawn strength from such assumptions. A memorandum to the proposed Housing Act incorporated much of the contemporary wisdom:

> A good healthy house is conducive to domesticity and cleanliness; a bad house, on the other hand, is conducive to disorder and wastefulness. It may be true that many women, no matter

> where they are, will always remain impractical and slovenly. But many others, even with the best of will, have given up the struggle because they have to live in a slum, nearly without light and air, where the stink is unbearable and where, even with the greatest care, the steadily increasing family can not be housed any more decently. Ten to one, these women would be better housewives and mothers if they were put into a better environment. And another factor should be considered. There are, unfortunately, many fathers who fritter away a large part of their wages outside the home. It would be unreasonable to contend that this would no longer occur if better housing were provided, but it would be just as unreasonable to maintain that the want of a cozy household hearth never sent a man off to the pub.[15]

Better housing was viewed as a means to reform working-class behavior.[16] Workers would be guided toward a new, orderly conduct in conformity with reformers' notions of modern urban civility.

Housing reform was but one component of a larger campaign to promote civic order that had arisen in the nineteenth century in the face of the overwhelming administrative and practical problems posed by rapid urban growth.[17] That campaign included the introduction of orderly infrastructure such as sewage, water, and public transportation and the regulation of social life. Police patrolled the streets; Amsterdam's yearly carnival was abolished in midcentury; and public holidays such as Hartjesdag, which had traditionally been occasions for high spirits and vandalism, were curtailed.[18] Housing reform was intended to contribute to this civilizing offensive, to the creation of a modern pattern of urban behavior that would foster social order and perhaps even reduce urban unrest.[19]

In the solidly working-class neighborhoods of Amsterdam, such as the northern part of the Jordaan, the Jewish Quarter, the old city center, and in the East and West Islands, community ties could be very strong. The bonds of language and kinship reinforced highly developed insular traditions and encouraged spontaneous resistance to strictures imposed from outside.[20] When workers moved out of these neighborhoods into new residential areas at the rim of the city, and when rural inhabitants took up residence in the city for the first time, familiar patterns of contact were lost, the workplace was separated from home, and housing form was changed. As workers' families were forced to adapt to new circumstances, housing reform afforded experts an opportunity to influence their behavior, to bring it into conformity with a modern vision of urban life.

Bourgeois reformers perceived housing as one of several means to shape working-class lifestyles in conformity with reformers' notions of civilized behavior. The word "civilized"—in Dutch *beschaafd*—was used by reformers to refer to themselves and also to the behavior they hoped to elicit from the working-class and poor. "Civilized" representatives from the bourgeoisie would, through personal contact and persuasion, attempt to alter the behavior of their charges. "Civilized" habits of living were the intended outcome of their interventions. The application of the word to both the reformers and those to be reformed communicated subtle differences. The word conferred moral authority to the reformers; applied to the beneficiaries of that authority it merely conveyed that a minimum standard of socially acceptable behavior had been met. Civility in the second case became a code word for conformity to social standards; it was a delicate linguistic construct suggesting a common ideal social order while implying social distinctions. When used to describe the middle classes, it became a bourgeois possession to which the lower classes could never aspire: one might speak naturally of "civilized ladies," but rarely of "civilized workers," who were more likely to be dubbed patronizingly *nette arbeiders*, "respectable workers." The word could, however, be applied to the behavior of workers, as in "civilized living." The use of "civilized" to demarcate a standard of behavior implied an assimilation of values by the lower classes, but one that would nonetheless maintain the social hierarchy.

The process by which the lower classes were to be civilized bears some comparison to what the sociologist Norbert Elias has identified as "the civilizing process," a general movement by society toward increasing self-control of emotions and self-discipline of behavior. Elias observes the tendency for those lower on the social hierarchy to adopt the behavior of those higher in the hierarchy, who have already moved further along through the civilizing process.[21] Indeed, under the influence of increasing material well-being and education, such changes could be seen among the working population of Amsterdam, as evidenced by aspirations for better education, better food and clothing, and finer furnishings. But the civilizing offensive of reformers must be distinguished from this independent sociological process; it was, rather, a conscious political project with specific aims. The urban working class was to be encouraged through a variety of means, including housing design, to conform to a set of behavioral norms designated as civilized by the dominant class. The civilizing process described by Elias occurred as workers confronted increased standards of living and changing urban conditions with their own values, which might or might not reflect the values of the bourgeoisie. Simultaneously, urban reformers instigated a parallel process of behavioral normalization intended to instill civilized behavior in the lower classes.

The civilizing project of middle-class reformers underwent a modern transformation with the shift from the philanthropic activities of the nineteenth century to the professionalism of the twentieth century. The amateur and personal basis of the former gave way to the expert and social-technical approach of the latter. When social technology replaced personal persuasion as the means of inducing civilized behavior, rationality displaced morality as the argument for change. We will examine some of the implications of that transformation, particularly the distinction between liberal and social democratic versions of the civilizing project and the effect of the working class's increasing role in its own civilizing process.

In bourgeois neighborhoods, rules of common decency, in some cases elevated to the status of law, dictated behavior in the semipublic areas of the house: carpets were to be cleaned only at given hours; the wash was never to be hung where it could be publicly observed. The cleaning of the stoop and the sidewalk in front of the house were the responsibility of its dwellers. Bourgeois sensibility dictated that the public nature of the street be acknowledged with strategies to enhance decorum and privacy.

This attitude of self-regulation and discipline could be instilled in the working class, reformers believed. The housing experts working with Amsterdam's municipal government sought to change working-class domestic behavior by a number of means: through education, through rules and legislation, and through housing design. These were continuations of reform techniques developed by philanthropic reformers of the nineteenth century: training through personal contact, brochures, and classes; rental regulations and other techniques for managing housing projects; the physical environment itself, either through the general civilizing benefit of improved, hygienic housing, or through the manipulation of housing design as reward or constraint. Regardless of whether or not these means actually changed working-class behavior, reformers believed in their efficacy and worked to make them part of the housing reform carried out by the government.[22]

Legislation was used to regulate housing usage. A "living" ordinance was proposed at the third Public Health Convention in 1898.[23] It influenced drafting of the articles of the Housing Act that permitted a building ordinance to limit the nature and use of the dwelling, the extermination of vermin, sleeping arrangements, the maximum number of dwellings in a building, and the relation between the number of inhabitants and the volume of space.[24] Although such limitations were set by the Amsterdam building code of 1905, the enforcement of those provisions remained impractical, and in any case they did not address many of the issues of appropriate use that reformers repeatedly raised: subletting, boarders, the use of the home as workplace, the keeping of animals, cleaning and laundry habits.[25] By and large, those issues were addressed by means of lease restrictions, which were first applied by the philanthropic housing societies of the nineteenth century. A rental agreement from 1885 forbade lodgers, doves, chickens, and four-footed animals in the house. The use of the home for any trade or manufacture without the permission of the housing inspector was forbidden, as were the sale and misuse of alcohol. Laundry was to be dried only in the attic. Most of these restrictions were adopted in the rental agreements of the new housing societies established under the Housing Act.[26]

Legal restrictions prohibited certain behavior, but most reformers also insisted that inhabitants, especially slum dwellers, needed to be taught how to use their new homes, blaming workers' behavior for their poor housing conditions.[27] If workers were made aware of the necessity of good housing, it was argued, they would leave their slums; that is, they would be willing to pay a higher proportion of their salary for better housing rather than squandering money on unnecessary luxuries. They would postpone marriage until they could afford decent housing and, once installed in improved housing, would exercise the virtues of thrift to maintain it properly.[28]

Experts were to provide proper guidance in the use of the home. The middle-class volunteers who had offered moral guidance were now to be supplanted by experts trained in the technologies of reform. Professional reformers communicated rational norms of social behavior, hiding the banner of moral authority under the cloak of expertise.[29] Instead of moral character flaws, ignorance and lack of education were blamed for poor behavior. The 1913 exhibition "De Vrouw" (The Woman), organized by middle-class feminists, displayed two contrasting workers' homes inhabited by the families of a model and a misguided worker. Although the families were equivalent in size and income, and the homes were both one-room dwellings at the same rent, the model worker had made wise use of his funds, arranging the house in a proper and hygienic manner. He had "also profited from all the social agencies which are a real benefit to the worker." The other worker "out of habit and obstinacy, enjoyed few of these advantages."[30] The blame had shifted: the worker was no longer lazy or immoral, but resistant to rational argument and the benefits of expertise. The economically weak had been cast in the role of cultural conservatives resisting modernization.

The *Journal for Social Hygiene* suggested that housewives should receive instruction in household care.[31] They could take advantage of Martine Wittop Koning's expertise on nutrition, and of the vocational school of the Society for the Improvement of Women's Clothing (Vakschool der Vereeniging voor Verbetering van Vrouwenkleeding).[32] Such expertise was made more accessible to working-class women through inexpensive evening courses in housing and hygiene. It was "better and more systematic" to learn scrubbing, washing, and polishing from a teacher than at home from mother, and "in particular, necessary hygienic ideas were better learned in school." A suggested curriculum on housing would discuss siting of the house vis-à-vis width of the street, wind, cleanliness of the surrounding area, neighbors, proximity of play areas, schools, and work. Instruction would cover dampness, window and room arrangement for light, air, water, and waste disposal, and the general ordering of the house to make as practical and hygienic use as possible of the rooms. A model budget and inventory of a worker's home would also be provided.[33]

Middle-class reformers of the late nineteenth century looked to Octavia Hill's work in England as a model for the education of the lower classes in household skills.[34] Indeed, social work developed into an established profession for Dutch middle-class women after Johanna ter Meulen and Louise Went trained with Octavia Hill in the 1890s and Hélène Mercier initiated settlement work in the Netherlands. These women transformed charity work; they trained experts in social reform and organized themselves professionally. At the School for Social Work, future social workers, including those being trained as housing managers, were taught economics and sociology, hygiene, and housing inspection by leading experts of the reform movement. They learned about housing surveys, housing types, housing law, and the private and public sectors of housing reform.[35] The Amsterdam Housing Council supported the work of these social workers, noting that it led to better use of the dwelling and taught the housewife about settlement work, child care, and hygiene.[36] When the municipality began construction of housing in 1915, it hired the school's newly trained social workers as housing inspectors.

As Johanna ter Meulen described the position, the housing inspector for a housing society or municipality participated in the selection of tenants, introduced the new family to the house, instructed them on its use, collected the rent in person, and was responsible for physical maintenance and keeping peace among the residents. Her weekly visits to the family to collect the rent should be businesslike, Ter Meulen explained, but after she had won the trust of the family, she might make suggestions about the housekeeping and housing arrangements.[37] In the journal she kept during the 1890s when she was housing inspector for her own philanthropic housing project, Ter Meulen noted the composition of the families in her charge, their income and employment, illnesses, marriages, and births. She lauded self-sufficiency and thrift, decried poor housekeeping, and threatened the argumentative with expulsion, praising one family with the words, "They pay faithfully and do what I say."[38] Her attitudes had changed little by 1913, when she advised a fellow worker who was taking up housing inspection for the municipality: "You will be just and kind to them. They will find you warm, supportive, and understanding. Your heart will go out to them, even when their deeds provoke criticism."[39] The idea of reform based on civility imparted by personal contact persisted alongside the promotion of education and technical training.

The most active advocates of social work were liberal and socialist reformers. Although social workers were generally drawn from liberal circles, their efforts to raise working-class living standards and educational levels were appreciated by the Social Democrats. P. L. Tak supported the School for Social Work and considered it as a means to further the spiritual development of the working class.[40] The Social Democratic housing alderman F. M. Wibaut claimed that he learned through his experiences on the Health Board that "the starting point for raising the civility of the working class is improvement of housing," an explicit endorsement of the civilizing project.[41] Wibaut was also an active supporter of the settlement houses operated by Ons Huis, a product of the bourgeois reform movement. But the socialist perspective differed considerably from that of bourgeois reformers. Tak and Wibaut would hardly have supported Ter Meulen's depiction of social work's goal as the rapprochement of the classes, the mutual acknowledgment of duties and responsibilities of one class to the other.[42] Her approach aimed at producing behavior socially acceptable to the existing social order. The Social Democrats, by contrast, were interested in encouraging the development of an organized and disciplined modern workforce whose rights were acknowledged, whose material well-being was improved, who participated in their own government, and whose civility was raised not in conformity with bourgeois models, but according to a new proletarian culture.

The Social Democrats would join forces with Progressive Liberal reformers to combat alcoholism and to promote hygiene and good nutrition, but they rejected any suggestion of bourgeois paternalism. Hudig commented on the socialist aversion to even well-intentioned and modest intrusion from the bourgeoisie into workers' lives.[43] While Ter Meulen herself carefully distinguished what she did from any form of interfering patronage, she did associate her work with the nurturing qualities of a mother. Remarking that Keppler had told her that he did not want a mother for those dwelling in municipal housing, she countered that "if he could say that, he did not know what a mother can be, for motherhood is the incarnation of unselfish love, and it fosters independence."[44] Ter Meulen's roots in philanthropy precluded any real understanding of the political program implied by the socialists' goal of uplifting the proletariat and left unquestioned the assumptions inherent in a model of social work that compared the social worker and her charge to parent and child.

The socialists agreed with liberals about the positive role of experts. The improvement of working-class life through the application of expertise was acceptable to the socialists in a way that middle-class moralism was not. The professionalization of reform shifted the locus of reformers' authority from morality to rationally applied expertise. This was consistent with the Social Democrats' embrace of social technology as a solution for society's ills. Moral analysis had placed the blame for social problems on personal failings; the Social Democrats claimed the worker's problems arose from his class position. With appropriate education, the worker could be encouraged to reach a new consciousness of that class position and to alter his behavior accordingly. The professional trained in the disciplines of social technology could help the worker achieve improved behavior through rational argument, without the paternalism that characterized middle-class reformers.

In practice, however, there were many similarities between the approach of the recently professionalized liberal reformers and that of socialist reformers. In neither case had the scent of nineteenth-century moralism completely disappeared. Values analogous to traditional middle-class norms can be detected in the socialist reform program, and the encouragement of such values was in itself similar to the bourgeois reform project based on the cultivation of character. The workers' material and spiritual deprivation would be countered not only by raising their consciousness of class position, but by self-improvement, cooperation, and collective effort. Some of these traits, under different names, were coincident with the virtues of responsibility, dedication, and hard work promoted by liberal reformers. Nor was the socialist goal of a modern working class dissimilar to the liberal desire to create a stable workforce. Both visions demanded discipline of workers, and in both cases workers resisting the message could be accused of resisting modernization. For the Social Democrats, the failure of an individual to politicize was tantamount to a failure of moral insight.

The Social Democrats believed that their vision of the appropriate organization of daily life could be inculcated by the same means used to spread liberal ideas of socially acceptable behavior. Through the Federation of Social Democratic Women's Clubs and its newspaper, *De Proletarische Vrouw*, the Social Democrats tried to arouse interest among women in bettering their housing.[45] They proposed crèches, public baths, collective laundries and kitchens. Housing could be modernized by the use of collectively owned machines, which would eliminate drudgery, and therefore, argued Mathilde Wibaut-Berdenis van Berlekom, the working-class housewife needed to be educated to appreciate communal provisions. In the case of the crèche, she noted that mothers were reluctant to accept the superiority of experts' techniques over their own. But, she argued, "we do not believe that motherhood in and of itself comprises pedagogical insight and talent. Children will be brought up best by those who have the best pedagogical aptitude. Meanwhile, if, for the moment, we do assume that the mother can provide the best upbringing and that she has been carefully prepared for the task of child rearing, then even so, that mother will be unable to apply the training principles that are necessary for the collective society without help from community institutions."[46]

The chief targets of socialist and liberal civilizing efforts were recent rural immigrants to the city and the entrenched urban underclass, the poverty stricken who had inhabited the slums of the city and were moving into new housing provided under the Housing Act. The former were encouraged to adjust their rural living habits to urban standards, and the latter were expected to adapt to the modern conveniences of their new living environment, primarily subsidized housing. Housing with subsidized rents drew the indigent, street hawkers, and casual labor rather than the skilled, unionized laborers, municipal workers, and lower civil servants, who could afford full housing society rents. But reform efforts were not limited to those forced to leave condemned housing in the slums. The image of modern urban home life promulgated by reformers was also meant to influence the better-off workers moving into the projects of the housing societies; they too were expected to take advantage of institutions offering intellectual and moral uplift.

The distinction between the ignorant poor and the model worker was made by both socialists and liberals.[47] Indeed, reformers made a series of distinctions between families already "civilized," families on whom housing might have a "civilizing" effect, families who brought standards down, and families that were designated "asocial."[48] The continued influence of the nineteenth-century civilizing offensive is apparent in these various categories. The philanthropic societies of the late 1800s, eager for respectable and well-behaved families, had screened prospective tenants for cleanliness, alcoholism, and steady employment before renting to them.[49] Under the Housing Act, the assessment of family background continued in housing societies, particularly when they were run by reformers rather than by the workers themselves.

In subsidized housing such as that provided by the socialist housing society De Arbeiderswoning and in municipal housing, social workers played a role in the screening and classification of families.[50] Unsatisfactory results when De Arbeiderswoning indiscriminately mixed families from rougher and better neighborhoods fueled arguments to separate the residents of municipal housing according to lifestyle and degree of civility.[51] The so-called respectable workers themselves did not wish to mix in what they called "a wooden shoe warehouse," a reference to the rural origins of the less "civilized" families. This was not always an issue of separating families by income; Keppler pointed out that income had little to do with how a family lived, meaning that cultural values derived from social background. The lifestyle of the harbor worker, his family life, education, and values, differed markedly from those of the tram conductor or diamond worker. When it came to assigning families to the municipal housing north of the IJ, which unlike most city-run units were low-rise, the city felt preference should be given to settled workers in municipal service rather than those emerging from the worst slums.[52] In contrast, the socially "unacceptable" or "asocial" families, "those who through their lifestyle appeared to be unfit to live in the same building with other families," were first to be assigned to supervised housing projects, where they could be suitably trained for eventual admittance to ordinary municipal housing.[53] In 1916, it was recommended that such families be placed in a separate housing complex with a central entrance and guard.[54] The municipality eventually built several projects designed to instruct troubled families and encourage them to move as soon as their living habits had improved.[55] The Social Democrats took the leading role in developing the system of educating "unacceptable" families, a policy reflective of the traditional Marxist disdain for the *lumpenproletariat*.[56]

Training the working class could serve different political ends. Liberals and socialists each addressed the issue of modernizing the masses, influencing their adjustment to the challenges of modern urban life, according to their respective convictions. For both socialists and liberals, the social worker and the controlled environment of housing sponsored by the municipality provided the expertise, institutional framework, and environment for inculcating the values of civility. Although their political goals were divergent, both groups admonished workers' families to join urban life by eliminating rural habits and developing disciplined behavior. For the liberals improved behavior might serve to preserve the status quo and avoid civil disturbance, while for the socialists it might help develop the disciplined cadres necessary for social change. The virtues to be imparted were on one side deference and obedience, and on the other solidarity and collectivity, but in each case the power and legitimacy of housing experts was acknowledged. It is difficult to specify to what extent the civilizing campaign actually influenced changes in working-class behavior; the campaign itself, however, was an indicator of reformers' attitudes and goals.

THE ORGANIZATION OF WORKERS' HOUSING SOCIETIES

The liberal reformers who drafted the Housing Act of 1902 expected that the new housing societies to be established under its auspices would follow the example of the nineteenth-century philanthropic societies founded by well-to-do citizens for the benefit of the less fortunate. In Amsterdam, several of those societies were the first to ask for official status under the new act. "Oud-Amsterdam," founded by Johanna ter Meulen with family money and the support of industrialist William Spakler, reorganized under the act in 1904. The Amsterdamsch Bouwfonds was established in 1906 by reformers previously involved in the Bouwonderneming Jordaan. Founded by leading housing experts, these societies stuck to the traditional reform model of demonstrating the financial feasibility of improved housing types to private developers. At their first meetings, the organizers of the Amsterdamsch Bouwfonds discussed building new housing types for teachers and other well-paid workers, whose steady incomes could guarantee the venture financially.[57] This was the form of organization recommended by A. van Gijn, secretary of the National Advisory Committee for the Housing Act. Housing societies were to take advantage of the organizational, financial, and administrative skills of the privileged classes to provide improved, noncharitable housing on a sound financial basis.[58] Conversely, Van Gijn's liberal political economy led him to oppose cooperative societies organized by workers themselves, since under the Housing Act, housing societies were charged exclusively with the improvement of housing, not with the material advancement of their members. Housing society construction was not intended by liberal reformers to compete with the real estate market but to guide it.

Other objections had been levied against worker-run housing societies in the reform literature. George A. M. Kallenbach argued in 1892 that workers were too inexperienced with the financing required for large-scale construction to manage a housing society themselves. If workers were to organize their own housing societies, he added, only the most intelligent and best positioned would gain any advantage from it. Since most workers prefer their poor but cheap housing, failing to see the advantage of a good home, he argued, it was preferable for reformers from the privileged classes to organize housing for them.[59] In their influential 1890 report on housing, Van Hasselt and Verschoor also gave consideration to the form of housing societies, weighing the advantages and disadvantages of worker-organized societies. Writing more than a decade before passage of the Housing Act, their chief objection to workers' societies was financial instability due to lack of capital and inexperience, but they also acknowledged the advantage of workers' insights into their own housing needs. Nonetheless, they doubted that worker-organized societies would produce better results, since "gentlemen may not be well enough informed about workers' needs, but generally workers are not well enough informed about business."[60]

By the time of the Housing Act, workers wanted higher standards than the housing philanthropic societies had to offer. One housing inspector at an older housing society in Amsterdam observed that the time was past when "many applicants considered it a great privilege to be allowed to secure one of the society's dwellings."[61] Workers who already had experience in organizations, such as mutual aid societies, unions, and cooperatives, were increasingly prepared to take housing reform into their own hands. Their growing empowerment challenged the pattern of housing reform inherited from the nineteenth century. The relations between philanthropist and grateful recipient had already been replaced by the relations between social reform expert and client. The latter relationship resembled the former in its hierarchy of power, but introduced power legitimized by expertise rather than by claims to moral superiority. Worker control of the institutions generated by the reform movement, such as housing societies, opened the possibility of another shift in roles. Workers might become the patrons of the professional experts hired to assist their endeavors, such as the architects commissioned to design housing for a worker-run housing society. In that case, there might for the first time be an opportunity for workers to dictate the reform agenda.

In 1905, the legality of cooperative housing societies organized by prospective dwellers became a parliamentary issue.[62] At the Public Health Convention, Tellegen challenged Van Gijn and defended cooperative housing societies as ethically preferable since those directly benefiting from the housing would tend to it themselves.[63] Keppler contributed to the controversy in a polemic in *De Kroniek* in which he looked askance at the societies founded with bourgeois capital: "In part they seem to me to be dictating from above, in part they remind me of *hofjes* [Dutch charitable housing institutions]."[64]

The national government ruled that cooperative housing societies were admissible under the Housing Act as long as their statutes included the clause that the housing would be rented at market levels, that is, that the society would be run exclusively for the betterment of housing, as the act required, and not for the financial benefit of the society's membership. Even with government approval of this form of organization, the establishment of cooperative societies was hampered. Only the better-educated workers, primarily those in the organized labor movement, had the experience, inclination, and resources for organizing housing societies. The likelihood of worker-initiated housing societies among unskilled and casual laborers was minimal. With fewer resources and high unemployment, these families had little experience of organization for self-help, so that traditional housing societies continued to have a mission. And even when cooperative housing societies were established and run by workers, official expertise tended to usurp whatever control workers might exert on the reform agenda. Keppler, who supported cooperative housing societies, urged workers to turn to the experts: "You workers struggle for better and cheaper homes. Let those who sympathize with you and have the ability exercise their talents to inform you about building plans, financial arrangements and the rest. Then we'll be on the right path."[65]

A number of factors contributed to the workers' deference to housing society experts. As in any client-professional relationship, those in the lay position deferred to the authority of expert knowledge. The workers' relative class position further defined the relationship, precluding the sort of power a middle-class patron has over professional help. The political beliefs of Social Democratic professionals might allow them to work on behalf of the workers' class interests, but their middle-class backgrounds and expertise cloaked them in an unassailable authority.

Faced with the experts' overwhelming experience, their well-developed perspective, and their advantageous social positions, it often proved difficult for workers to find ways to develop and express their own perspectives on the housing question, and thus fully assume the role of patron. At the second Public Health Convention, the labor activist H. H. Wollring argued that the unions could and should play an important role in housing reform. As the bodies whose business it is to lift up their members materially and socially, they are the natural gathering places of the workers' wishes and desires. The doctors and engineers may be ready to work for good housing, but the unions should not be passed over silently as participants.[66] But when Henri Polak tried to interest the ANDB in organizing a cooperative housing society in 1905, he received only 45 positive responses from a membership of more than 8,000. It seemed useless to proceed with the enterprise on the basis of so little interest.[67] Attendance at meetings on the topic of housing improvement was often scant, and the membership in housing societies remained low until there were signs that the venture was viable.[68] Workers either completely ceded the initiative in housing reform to the experts or relied heavily on expert advice in housing societies they themselves initiated.

In 1905, the first housing society in Amsterdam was officially recognized under the Housing Act. By 1907, three of the four recognized Housing Act societies had been set up by reformers, but in the years following, most were founded by workers on a cooperative basis, with workers as members and officers. These were largely based on existing organizations, unions in particular. The ACOB grew out of the Amsterdam section of the Union of Dutch Teachers. Rochdale emerged from a union of Amsterdam municipal workers. Eigen Haard was begun by workers in rail and tram manufacture associated with the cooperative store movement.[69] Many of these housing societies were organized by workers in government service: the teachers, transportation workers, and gas utility workers who had already generated a strong union movement. Most of the housing societies were affiliated with one of the religious/political pillars of Dutch society. Indeed, many were founded at the instigation of a central organization associated with that *zuil.*

Whatever their political or religious orientation, most of the societies turned to the experts for help. The CBSA Housing Committee helped nascent housing societies draft their statutes and maneuver through the red tape of the Housing Act to attain official status. The CBSA also provided them with contacts for trustees from among the corps of housing reformers and directed them to private sources of capital. It helped locate architectural assistance and gave advice on establishing a relationship with the architect. The CBSA's handbook on housing societies became the standard work on the subject and was often reprinted.[70] Although the CBSA answered housing inquiries from all over the country, its most frequent requests were from Amsterdam.[71] The Amsterdam Housing Council, which actively tried to stimulate the formation of housing societies in Amsterdam, offered similar services.[72]

Municipal bureaucrats also helped organize and guide the workers' housing societies. As director of the Building and Housing Inspection Office, Tellegen was closely involved with the housing societies. Keppler administered the Housing Act in Amsterdam within the inspection office, and from 1915 as director of Amsterdam's new Housing Authority. Both Tellegen and Keppler advised housing societies on procedure and worked with them on land acquisition and housing types. Tellegen was instrumental in setting up the building society of the Handwerkers Vriendenkring; Keppler helped found Rochdale, De Arbeiderswoning, the Algemeene, Eigen Haard, and others. The housing societies depended absolutely on the cooperation of these municipal representatives. Without their assistance and approval, the societies had little chance of putting through their requests for municipal financial assistance. Keppler and Tellegen thus wielded considerable influence on housing society decisions.

Another source of advice and guidance was the board of trustees each society appointed. Many of the housing societies, but particularly the liberal and socialist societies, included on their board of trustees at least one representative of the housing reform establishment. The confessional societies drew primarily from their own ranks.

The challenge of initiating large-scale housing projects, even when workers had organizational experience, should not be underestimated. It required administrative and financial skills, fluency with bureaucratic red tape, and the ability to reach decisions about all aspects of the housing project, architectural, technical, financial, and political. The challenge was met with widely varying degrees of sophistication, particularly in the pioneer years when all were inexperienced in the new procedures. It was not easy to find good administrators among housing society members, a difficulty not surprising when it is remembered that during the first years the work was taken on without salary by men already working long hours.[73] The letters to the CBSA requesting assistance display a range of proficiency, from awkward embarrassment and total unfamiliarity with the business world to smooth fluency in the special Dutch language of bureaucracy. As a result, not all the attempts to found societies succeeded, and of those that did, not all managed to achieve their goal of housing construction.[74] It often took years between the conception of a plan and its execution. Trying to whip up interest among the diamond workers, Henri Polak wrote optimistically but naively in 1905 that once established a society could expect to complete its first project in a year and a half. At the same time, Tellegen was warning the Amsterdamsch Bouwfonds, run by experienced reformers, that it could expect to wait several years for any municipal action on its request for aid.[75] Eventually, as the municipal council grew more progressive and as the private building industry declined during the First World War, the procedures for approving housing society projects became more efficient. But material shortages and rising construction costs often delayed projects, so that housing societies had to master the art of perseverance.

The bureaucratic difficulties besetting the new worker-run housing societies made expert guidance a necessity. The experiences of one cooperative housing society, a pioneer in Amsterdam, illustrates the forging of relationships between worker organizers, civil servants, housing experts, and the architect.

ROCHDALE COOPERATIVE HOUSING SOCIETY

The founding of Rochdale, the first workers' housing society in Amsterdam, illustrates the problems facing those trying to organize a cooperative housing venture. In April 1902, as the Housing Act was becoming law, an Amsterdam tram conductor suggested that municipal workers take advantage of its provisions.[76] The union, with approximately 1,700 members, followed a neutral political line, and was composed of Protestant and Catholic, as well as socialist and syndicalist members. Throughout the summer of 1902, a housing society was promoted in the pages of the union newspaper *De Gemeente-Werkman*.[77] In August a committee to study the proposal was formed, with representatives from the municipal departments of sanitation, telephone, waterworks, carpentry, and fire. But between the actual founding of the new society in 1903 and the actual building of the first project in 1909, the society faced a number of obstacles.

As the committee progressed in its discussions with the director and the alderman of public works, the idea of a cooperative housing society was attacked by union syndicalists whose revolutionary politics excluded the cooperative movement. At a January meeting of the municipal union, no less a figure than Domela Nieuwenhuis, leader of the syndicalist movement in the Netherlands, argued that cooperation served the interests of the capitalists and reactionaries, and siphoned workers' energies from the more important work of revolutionary struggle. One of the union members complained that the cooperative movement "absorbs the best talents in the union and once they have been made into businessmen not much more can be expected of them."[78]

The defenders of cooperation pointed out the immediate practical value of housing improvement, and argued that "cooperation is the nursery school that educates workers to be more powerful, self-conscious combatants for the place in society they deserve."[79] The membership as a whole was also divided on the issue. When the organizing committee sent out a questionnaire to survey interest in a housing society, some 800 of the 1,700 members responded, and of those, 400 appeared to be interested in supporting the venture.

By early 1903, the committee's report on the feasibility and advisability of establishing a society had received the approval of Tellegen, but with the outbreak of the 1903 Railroad Strike, all organization came to a halt. The Railroad Strike rent the shaky neutrality of the union. A strike by the union of municipal workers was narrowly avoided,[80] and radical disagreements over strategy within the workers' movement led to the withdrawal of Protestant and Catholic workers. Just as the housing society Rochdale was formally established in May 1903, the editorial board of *De Gemeente-Werkman*, which had supported the housing society throughout the controversies, split along sectarian lines. By 1904, there were two major unions of municipal workers in Amsterdam, one so-called neutral or independent, but primarily syndicalist, and one that espoused working-class electoral politics and the "modern" union movement of the Social Democrats, as well as two additional confessional unions. The socialist offshoot provided continued support for Rochdale, but in the course of these upheavals, the original leader of the housing society was deposed because of his affiliation with Anti-Revolutionary politics.[81]

Despite these political setbacks, at the time of its founding in May 1903 Rochdale had high hopes of building in four different districts within the year.[82] This naive optimism failed to take into account a long opening bout with the bureaucracy. It took until April 1904 to make the statutes of the new society public and to initiate application procedures for Housing Act status. Then Rochdale had to wait while the legality of cooperative housing societies was debated in Parliament. Finally in May 1906, having inserted the required clause in its statutes, Rochdale was admitted as a Housing Act society eligible for government loans. It was three more years, however, before Rochdale maneuvered through the local Amsterdam municipal system and built its first project, in fact, the first Housing Act project in Amsterdam.

The Rochdale organizers were placed in the difficult position of negotiating between bourgeois opponents on the right, who saw the workers' building cooperative as a threat to private property rights, and revolutionary socialists on the left, for whom their efforts represented cooptation. Their chief support came from progressive reformers. Any independent, worker-organized drive for the improvement of material conditions was dependent on these housing experts. The organizers of Rochdale accepted without question that the experts' served the workers' interests and paid little heed to warnings that reliance on them might undermine their own interests or contribute to their economic or political vulnerability. They responded to extreme left-wing skepticism with astonishment. The organizing committee answered one round of left-wing attacks by asking, "What can the committee expect now? That with the valued help of high-placed men striving for a working-class cause, it will have to defend that cause from the workers themselves?"[83] The need for this defense locates the society in the political niche of reform politics occupied by the Radicals, Progressive Liberals, and Social Democrats in which the educated worked for the benefit of the workers.

The Rochdale organizers' relationship with the experts was defined in part by their own lack of self-confidence and in part by the reality of their relative power. The housing reformers within the municipal government had access to political power as well as the power of technical and financial skills. The housing reformers in private organizations such as the CBSA were closely connected to the government and belonged to the same professional class. In their first article in *De Gemeente-Werkman*, the Rochdale workers modestly described their aim as getting the union's support to approach the CBSA with the question of how to proceed.[84] The organizers worked closely with Treub at the CBSA, Tellegen and Keppler at Building and Housing Inspection.[85] When grassroots support for the housing project was slow to develop, the director of the municipal tram service, J. H. Nieszen, was called in to give the effort a new impetus. The Rochdale organizers interpreted a lack of worker response to their efforts as hesitation in the absence of assurances from on high:

> For we understand exceedingly well what happened with our article. The business is too overwhelming for us. We have no knowledge of such matters and don't know how to proceed. The business appeals to us, but we don't dare to tackle it. And the end result is that nothing comes of it. We don't blame anyone and we admit freely we have often felt the same way.
>
> The author, who did not enjoy the privilege of finishing elementary school, personally feels all too keenly the disadvantage of a poor education to come down too hard on others when, for that reason, they shrink from a job which is probably far from child's play.
>
> But fear is a poor teacher!
>
> Let's overcome that fear. And since we now know that we can count on the support of a man like Mr. Nieszen and since, moreover, we can get advice from the CBSA, let's put our best foot forward.[86]

During the early period of Rochdale's organization, the organizers' dependence on the knowledge of outside authority was repeatedly acknowledged.[87] Upon reviewing the statutes drawn up for them by the CBSA, the members objected to the article calling for members of the society to serve on the board of trustees, since they "could hardly be more than puppets."[88] Similarly, relief was expressed at the idea that nonmembers could serve as officers of the society, since "the management of such a quickly developing cooperative is not so easy, and might well go beyond the members' intellectual powers."[89] In fact, the Rochdale organizers used the expertise and authority of their advisers to defend their venture against the doubts of skeptics, and to reassure potential members that their monetary investment in the form of membership fees was safe because the society would not take a step without the advice of Treub and Tellegen.[90] Exactly this reliance on help from the "big shots" made the venture suspect to the syndicalists.[91] But the Rochdale workers defended their usefulness: "Even though these gentlemen are not 'workers,' no one will want to deny that they have a right to participate in a business like this, and that their advice is valuable."[92]

THE PARLOR QUESTION

In the typical middle-class flat in Amsterdam, front and back rooms en suite, extending from the street to the garden side of the building, constituted the formal reception room and living room. This was a custom imitated by working-class families, albeit under less advantageous conditions. In homes of the most varied size and rental level, it was not uncommon to find a room set aside for only occasional use on Sundays, for company, or for important family events such as the celebration of an engagement. Here might be placed the best furniture, in almost pristine condition, along with cherished objects such as family photographs or prized china. A diamond worker's parlor in the Pijp during the first decade of the twentieth century was described by a member of the family: "The furniture in the parlor, which was only to be used for receiving visitors, was mahogany. It consisted of an oval table with a thick leg in the middle, a sofa, six chairs, and a cabinet (for family memorabilia). The upholstery was red plush protected from fading by antimacassars. Above the mantle, a gilt mirror (flaunting a crest), and a gilt clock under a glass dome (which I greatly admired), and a pair of vases."[93]

By the late nineteenth century, the parlor and its contents had been singled out for criticism by Amsterdam reformers as wasteful and extravagant. Hélène Mercier noted that in the two-room dwellings of one philanthropic society, the smaller room was usually set aside for use as a salon. She preferred the designs of another society, which were planned in such a way that both rooms had to be used daily, one as kitchen, the other as bedroom.[94]

Middle-class reformers campaigned against the parlor.[95] At a national conference on women and work in 1898, the feature was attacked, and there was a proposal to make it illegal or prohibited in leases.[96] A guide to hygienic housekeeping from 1901 condemned the parlor as a misuse of space: "It is not a habit that can be reconciled with the requirements of health to sleep in a small room or alcove while setting up one of the large rooms of the home as a salon or reception room."[97] The parlor was condemned as a health hazard: "Even when the dwelling is too small to begin with, there nonetheless has to be a parlor, usually hermetically closed off. Invariably that diminishes the space for sleeping—naturally to the detriment of health. Entire families close themselves up in an alcove at night like a tin of sardines."[98]

At the 1913 exhibition "De Vrouw," the model worker's family spent its days in the well-lit and well-ventilated space by the windows of its one-room flat. In the contrasting home, the room was divided into two parts, and the family sat between the stove and bed, while the area near the windows was left unused and set up for show.[99] To the argument that the parlor was morally objectionable because it encouraged improper pride and inappropriate expenditure were added objections based on hygiene and functionality.

The socialists, too, joined this campaign. Louis Heijerman's book on hygiene warned workers against the salon.[100] P. L. Tak described the parlor as an unfortunate space serving no purpose and pushed through an amendment to the Amsterdam building ordinance that prohibited division of flats with a volume of less than forty cubic meters into two rooms, one of which would be wasted as a parlor.[101] A propaganda brochure published by the Federation of Social Democratic Women's Clubs railed against the parlor. The brochure tells the story of a young couple who have just rented a home from one of the housing societies. The wife wants to dine in the kitchen and keep the front room as a parlor. Her husband offers advanced advice: keep the kitchen for washing and cleaning only, use the front room for dining.[102]

Despite reformers' admonitions, the parlor continued to enjoy popularity among a number of working-class families. Impractical as its use of space may have been for those whose small budgets commanded only limited floor area, the parlor was an outlet for a pleasure in display and decoration found in all layers of working-class society, no less than in the middle class. Workers wanted a home with salon, living room, and bedroom. The salon could serve not only as a decorated area to welcome guests, but also as sick room or study. One of the working-class representatives on the Amsterdam City Council spoke out for the necessity of increased wages so that workers could afford housing that met these preferences.[103]

Early in the planning stages, when Rochdale turned to the CBSA for help in managing the legalities of the Housing Act, it also turned to experts for advice on the design of its housing type. During a meeting with Tellegen, a member of the workers' committee preparing the groundwork for the society was taken aback when asked what housing type the organizers wanted. It was easier for him to identify what workers found undesirable: so-called barracks of repetitive housing blocks, insufficient sleeping locations, cramped space, too little storage. Dark halls, poor ventilation, and inadequate soundproofing were also common complaints. "But we hadn't formed a sufficiently clear idea of how it should be, how we actually want the dwellings to be arranged."[104] Tellegen pointed out that the Amsterdam Housing Council was searching for the preferred workers' housing type, and he sent Rochdale's committee to meet with architect J. E. van der Pek to discuss housing design. One of the first aspects of housing design Van der Pek discussed with the committee was the wastefulness of the salon.[105]

After a number of consultations, several housing types were agreed upon for Rochdale. Interestingly, in their report on the proceedings, the committee placed the strongest emphasis on the parlor. The committee had added it to the list of undesirable features and committed itself to gradually accustoming the members of the society to this reform. Lacking a vision of their own, they adopted the vision provided by the experts.[106] Rochdale went on to sponsor an architectural competition in 1908 that specified that the housing be so designed that no parlor could be set aside. In the nine Rochdale projects proposed by 1919, 98 percent of the dwellings had narrow kitchens and one living room, eliminating the possibility of creating a parlor (fig. 4.1). The society had assimilated the urban reform agenda in its housing design.

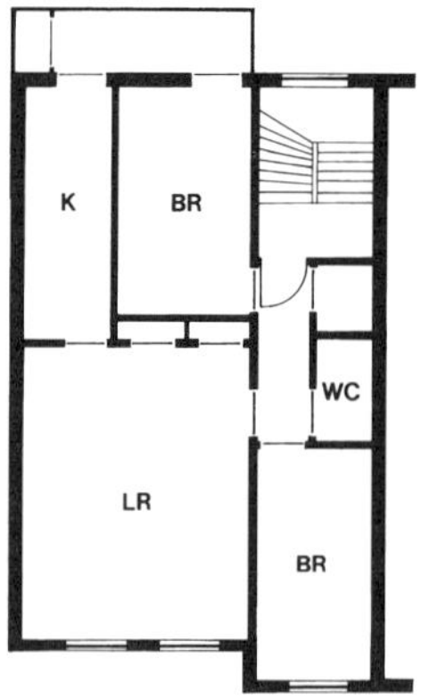

FIGURE 4.1
J. E. van der Pek, Coöperatieve Bouwvereeniging Rochdale, Van Beuningenstraat, 1908.

THE WORKING CLASS AND THE REFORM AGENDA

Most of the housing societies, including those organized by workers, took up as part of their mission the kind of moral and spiritual uplift encouraged by the experts. Housing societies adopted parts of the experts' reform agenda. Statutes were written to include screening of potential members and expulsion of misbehaving members.[107] Rochdale's job description for housing inspector included collection of rents, inspection of living conditions, and management of repairs, just as outlined by Johanna ter Meulen. However, Rochdale gave the job to a labor movement worker, H. H. Wollring, instead of to a "civilized and educated" middle-class lady, thus altering its cultural meaning from surveillance to self-management.[108] Other societies organized committees composed of the residents themselves to ensure good behavior, to settle disputes between neighbors, and organize social activities.[109] Workers also appeared alongside "gentlemen" on the boards of trustees: in the housing society Amsterdam-Zuid, the board of trustees was composed of two employees of the south gasworks, the director of the works, and two housing reformers, Hudig and Wibaut.[110] There was a clear distinction between the management of the subsidized housing projects, built by the municipality or by housing societies, in which surveillance was provided by professional social workers, and the cooperative housing societies organized by workers who provided their own management, voluntarily imposing behavioral restrictions taken directly from the reform agenda.

Despite the embrace of urban reform values by some workers, other more radical workers vociferously denounced what they perceived as the top-down control of housing design. In 1917, the socialist municipal workers' housing society Zomers Buiten remarked on the failure of nineteenth-century reform dwellings:

> Often we hear surprise expressed in architectural circles that the construction of workers' housing by housing societies elicits so little enthusiasm among the workers, even though it means that a piece of land and a number of houses have been removed from the predatory system of private ownership. This lack of enthusiasm does not seem so strange to us. Housing design has been shaped all too often by the opinions of well-meaning ladies and gentlemen or by architects who know little or nothing of the characteristics of the working-class family. They believed it incumbent upon themselves to give the workers homes they consider appropriate for workers, but which in fact did not satisfy the workers themselves.[111]

Many reformers were in fact well aware of the "characteristics of the working-class family" and responsive to their needs. Reformers recognized the need for variety in workers' housing, and some also encouraged the workers' participation in its planning. Hélène Mercier, writing in 1905, rejected uniformity of house plan, indicating the necessity of fit between the home and workers' needs: their financial level, the size of the family, and their kind of work. Even differences in level of education might affect needs, she noted, pointing to the increase in club and society life among some workers, which led to the need for a study in which to keep files and papers.[112] Some housing society projects were earmarked for families with specific needs. The Amsterdamsch Bouwfonds built dwellings for large families and a project for unmarried male workers. Its small housing units on Polanenstraat were reserved for young couples, the elderly, or widows with daughters. There were also reformers whose interest in raising standards led them to embrace the housing preferences of the workers themselves. In 1919, Dirk Hudig, the director of the CBSA, noted that housing standards would rise at an increasing tempo. He encouraged design of housing "too good" for the present, meeting the standards of the future. Unless building for the very simplest purposes, that is, for subsidized housing, Hudig wrote, a second living room, a parlor, should be included. Hudig argued in favor of the parlor as a space to keep the good furniture, to serve as study for husband and children, to use as a sick room, a reception room, a hallowed place in the home.[113] Reformers like Jan Kruseman, A. van de Wijk Groot, or G. Feenstra recognized the necessity of acknowledging workers' own definitions of their needs.[114]

Workers themselves had few opportunities to express their preferences, and when they did, their complaints were about the cramped quarters and poor construction of slum and speculative housing, not moral issues.[115] Sometimes a housing society established a members' building committee to review proposed housing types. Such committees often served to communicate the architect's ideas to the membership at large, through newsletters and meetings. Only occasionally did workers actually make suggestions. The building committees of the housing societies Het Oosten and the Bouwmaatschappij tot Verkrijging van Eigen Woningen were responsible for instructing their architects to include combined kitchen–living rooms. When the Handwerkers Vriendenkring presented architect J. H. W. Leliman's plans, its members suggested storage sheds for the carts and goods of the many street vendors among them.[116] For the most part, however, worker participation in the design process remained limited. At the instigation of Hudig and Keppler, Amsterdam housing societies established a federation in 1917, which most local housing societies joined. The federation provided a joint lobby for the interests of housing societies and was particularly effective in representing their views on rent hikes and other administrative issues when conflict arose with the municipal council. By and large, however, the federation did not become actively involved in the problem of housing design per se.

With the end of World War I, interest in responding sensitively to workers' needs led more reformers to call openly for working-class consultation in the design of housing. The Social Democratic council member and architect Zeeger Gulden, who designed for two socialist housing societies, called for input from working-class wives in a propaganda leaflet for the SDAP, appealing for their practical advice.[117] Hudig projected a role for housing society members in developing social programs and leisure activities to enhance the social development of housing complexes with sports and recreation facilities.[118] Where previously philanthropy, reformers, and the municipality had provided the impetus for creation of bathhouses, libraries, and playgrounds, Hudig saw workers taking more active roles in such programs. G. Feenstra, in his 1920 work on garden cities and housing, predicted a larger role for workers in setting standards for housing design. While emphasizing the role of expert leadership, Feenstra discouraged decisions on housing types without the participation of the workers themselves. He recalled reformers' castigation of the parlor as ostentatious and of eating in the kitchen as unhealthy, describing them as the reactions of people who decided about the interests of workers without asking for their input. Noting the success of modern workers' organizations and unions, he predicted that the workers would soon be determining their own house plans.[119]

The attitude of workers toward experts was paradoxically characterized both by deference and by a growing sense of their own power. Housing societies turned to experts in acknowledgment of their greater experience working with the housing problem. However, Ali de Regt has noted the loss of professional power by housing inspectors as workers' political power grew and they began to reject control from above.[120] The organizational arrangement of cooperative housing societies gave workers potential independence. By 1919, some left-wing organizers recognized that this potential was still largely untapped.

> If for once you objectively examine the power and influence of your building society, you will come to the conclusion that it has almost none, and that it is actually little more than a servant to all. It has to accept whatever the higher authorities decide is right. Everything is organized and decided on high. That's the real situation. Must it stay that way?
>
> We believe that the time has come that the working class itself become more involved with housing than it has in the past. For too long the design of workers' housing has been ordained

by outsiders. Certainly, we value the support and guidance given by reformers from other social milieus. We do not underestimate what has been accomplished by officials and interested individuals. But we believe that from now on, those who have a stake in it themselves must get involved and act more independently. The working class must be made to look at the housing question with its own eyes and find for it a fitting solution.[121]

Although this quote exaggerates the distance between working-class and middle-class perceptions of the housing problem, it indicates the problematic nature of power relations between reformers and the working class. However much workers were beneficiaries of housing improvement carried out on their behalf, the workers' positions as laymen and working class were subordinate to reformers' corresponding positions as experts and middle class. As the urban reform movement shifted from philanthropy to expertise, reformers and workers shifted their respective roles from that of benefactor and recipient to expert and client. Nonetheless, the hierarchical order of their relationship remained the same. It was a hierarchy that formed in relation to any expert whose origins were from another social milieu, even those who adhered to Social Democratic party politics.[122]

However, to view the housing society members as victims of a conspiracy to alter workers' behavior in conformity with a middle-class vision of social order is to oversimplify the situation. The ambitions of many workers, particularly those subscribing to the municipal reform principles of the Social Democrats, were consistent with that vision. When the Rochdale organizers were taken to task for accepting the reformers' proscription of the parlor, and the reformers were accused of paternalism, the housing society countered with the rational, technical arguments of professional housing reformers. They challenged anyone to design a housing type with a salon that also met the requirements of the Amsterdam building ordinance at affordable rents.[123] A worker who was active in the housing societies was by definition someone who had subscribed to some extent to the values of the housing reform movement and was already distinguishable from those who resisted the civilizing campaign. If the housing reform movement was a conspiracy of social control, many workers were willing collaborators. It is as inaccurate to depict the civilizing project crudely as something dictated to the working class as it is to claim that the worker-organized housing societies succeeded in accruing the power to act independently on behalf of the workers' interests.

The conception of housing as a moral influence on the working-class family was developed in the nineteenth century by liberal and confessional philanthropists. It became part of a connected set of efforts to "civilize" the urban workers, which included the campaign against alcoholism, the drive for compulsory education, and the elimination of unruly behavior. For the liberals, the betterment of working-class living standards, including housing, held out the promise of a more productive, less politically threatening, healthier working class, which would benefit society as a whole. For the extreme Protestant and the Catholic reformers, improved housing would foster the values of home and hearth as well as combat the dangers of socialism. The socialist reformers viewed housing as part of a comprehensive attempt to improve the lot of the working class, creating a well-educated, intellectually and politically prepared vanguard for a revolutionary dawn. All of these groups shared the idea that workers should be trained in correct behaviors and values; all had accepted the legitimacy of normalization, that is, of imposing norms of behavior. Housing was to be a means of civilizing the working class, although the vision of modern urban life varied from the capitalist state of the liberals embracing urban commercialism, to the socialist utopia proclaiming an era of emancipation, to the traditional values of the confessional parties defending the family against the dual threat of commercialism and revolution. The urban reform movement had witnessed a shift from a paternalistic extension of charity work in which personal persuasion used moral authority to influence behavior to the professional claim of rational expertise. But rational expertise did not eliminate the ideological subtext still evident in each strand of the movement. The reform movement had modernized its techniques, and each political group employed those techniques to shape a modern society that fit their values.

The shift of the urban reform movement from philanthropic paternalism to enlightened expertise did not completely alter the relations between the reformers and workers. Under government intervention, old patterns of deference persisted among the beneficiaries of housing expertise. But the politics of social change did color the complexion of those relations. The Social Democrats may have continued the campaign to influence working-class behavior, but their aim was the creation of a new proletarian culture with its own institutions. The powers of a political party, unions, and housing societies were activated in service to that end. Nonetheless, just as in the world of liberal middle-class reformers, the workers were the objects of a civilizing offensive, and the distinction between the aims and means of socialists and liberals was by no means always clear. As a result, the workers' relationship to representatives of the reform professions, such as the architects commissioned to design for the housing societies, was twofold. Workers were both patrons, with their own voice and authority, and clients, the recipients of well-intentioned reform. Indeed, within the context of the worker-organized housing societies, the identity of the actual architectural patron was unclear. Was it the administering civil servants in municipal agencies, the politicians authorizing funds and reviewing the projects, the housing reformers who determined standards, or the workers themselves? For the people living in the housing society projects, any role they might play as patron was compromised by their role as subject of the civilizing project.

It should be recognized, however, that the civilizing project was far from unified. Some members of the working class, taking advantage of new material and educational resources and of the greater financial security made possible by social laws and union organization, used their increased standard of living to fulfill dreams of respectability, imitating middle-class patterns of consumption and display, albeit in ways that were representative of their own economic and class status. There was also a behavioral counterpart to this material assimilation of cultural values. This civilizing process, driven by workers' own aspirations, must be distinguished from the campaign on the part of bourgeois reformers to bring middle-class values to the working classes. Here, the inculcation of such values as discipline, responsibility, and deference was motivated by bourgeois self-interest and was not intended to dismantle distinctions of status. Rather, it was a defensive move to maintain the social hierarchy by training a well-behaved underclass and improving its living conditions. The motivation was to foster urban order and thereby sustain the status quo. We can locate a liberal bourgeois reformer like Johanna ter Meulen in this position.

Progressive reformers working for the material and spiritual benefit of a modern working class in many ways pursued a civilizing campaign resembling that of their liberal counterparts, in that their values were also those of bourgeois culture. But in this case, the inculcation of values was accompanied by a democratizing mission intended to make available to workers the benefits of a culture they had previously been denied. Radicals and Progressive Liberals like Treub and Tellegen, Social Democrats like Hudig, Polak, and Wibaut belong to that group of reformers who interpreted the civilizing campaign as one that would bring about greater social justice and equality and improve workers' quality of life. In other words, they saw it as part of their larger emancipatory project.

Finally, we can identify a left-wing version of the civilizing project, which called for the creation of a new working-class culture based on the values of collectivism and solidarity, promising new forms of social and political organization. This campaign to bring new values to the working class launched a parallel campaign against bourgeois culture. Indeed, since most of these adherents of cultural modernism were themselves products of bourgeois culture, their campaign might better be described as reform from within. Their antibourgeois cultural campaign aligned them with the interests of the working class, but the role they assumed as determiners of values re-created the hierarchical relationship between those establishing social and cultural norms and those meant to conform to them that characterized all streams of the civilizing campaign.

Chapter Five

THE STANDARD PLAN

Dutch housing reformers, like their counterparts elsewhere, hoped to foster housing improvement by devising better dwelling types to replace the standard, and inadequate, plans of speculative housing. Unlike other methods of the housing reform campaign, for example, the setting of higher construction standards and instruction in "civilized" behavior, altering the standard dwelling plan required the development of new knowledge; it opened a new direction for the development of social technology. As soon as social workers, social hygienists, and architects began to view the plan as a social tool, the design of dwelling types became the location of an instrumental rationalism. The dwelling plan became the solution to a set of problems analyzed logically, an idealized, abstract space manipulated to conform with norms of urban order.

The active development and promotion of new housing types was meant to complement municipal regulation of construction practices. Tellegen had noted that a building ordinance worked only preventively, since it could limit poor construction and unhygienic practices, but could not force builders to invent and apply new models.[1] Housing societies constructing under the provisions of the Housing Act, however, might become vehicles for the introduction of improved plans devised by social hygienists, housing experts, and architects. Through the government's active participation in the development and approval of the housing societies' projects, it could encourage adoption of plan types it endorsed. Although the philanthropic societies of the nineteenth century had failed either to develop better plan types or to influence private developers, the new housing societies were expected to do both. Even those who did not support large-scale government sponsorship of housing argued that private builders, who lacked the time and money to search for good models themselves, would be forced by market demands to conform to the higher standards of the housing societies.[2] At the same time, the drive to find better housing types was also integral to the projects of those who saw in the creation of a substitute housing market the first step toward government-supplied housing that would eventually supplant the private market altogether.

The Amsterdam reformers defined their research into new models narrowly. In general, the traditional features of urban construction in Amsterdam were accepted: the customary four-story perimeter block remained the norm, and the floor plan maintained the front stair, side entrance, front-and-back orientation common to Amsterdam's urban housing.[3] Rather than a thoroughgoing reinvention of housing forms, the development of new plan types was a response to specific aspects of existing housing types. It was a reactive rather than an innovative response to the faults reformers identified in current dwelling types. Reformers pragmatically accepted the economic reality that mass provision of urban housing required large-scale construction and saw no problem in the fact that such an approach also required the local standardization of housing types.[4] Their objection was to the poor solutions offered by the private sector, and they viewed government involvement in housing provision as an opportunity to supply better models.

The search for improvement meant developing alternatives to what were perceived as the chief disadvantages of the single- and two-room dwellings found in the older slums and in the standard plans of speculative housing in new districts: lack of privacy, unsanitary sleeping alcoves, inappropriate and wasteful use of space, lack of light and air.[5] The reformers' solution was the rational reorganization of dwelling space within the confines of the existing urban pattern of construction.

The cultural value of the plan lay in its conceptual strength as a translation of reformers' analyses of the housing problem. Its transformation into lived space then subjected the plan to other criteria, namely, the response of families to its constraints and opportunities.

CIVILIZED LIVING

Liberal reformers and labor leaders alike reviled the single-room dwelling in which the family carried on all its daily activities of washing, drying, cooking, eating, sitting, living, working, playing, and sleeping, sometimes with members of the extended family or boarders, all in the same small space.[6] Its disadvantages were obvious: lack of privacy, inconvenience, and conflicting uses.

As you enter through the low door of a street-level house, then you find yourself immediately in the single room that constitutes the dwelling, which is about the size of what is called a reception room in a middle-class house. You can imagine how dark it is here if you consider that a high wall is less than a yard away, and that what little daylight falls through the single window has been absorbed by three black walls and an attic. In front of the window is a table with three chairs, a smokepipe nearby with a stove for heating and cooking underneath, a protruding bedstead with a dark curtain, two feet from the wall a table with cooking utensils on and around it. There you have the house and its inventory. No trace of plumbing, drain, toilet, coal bin, cabinet, or second bed, just signs of dampness in abundance.[7]

Of course, such arrangements were dictated by necessity rather than choice. The housing shortage, low wages, and high rents made it impossible for many workers to afford the larger dwellings they would have preferred. Although the skilled workman with a solid position might be able to manage the rent on an apartment with more than two rooms, for nearly half of Amsterdam in 1900 one or two rooms had to suffice. In 1899, 44.8 percent of all homes had only one or two rooms, the kitchen being counted as one. A full 37.4 percent of the homes occupied by more than two people were single-room dwellings.[8] Such overcrowded living conditions could be found in multiroom dwellings as well.

Separation of functions in the home became the main rationale behind the development of new dwelling types. The reformers identified specialization in the use of space as a measure of civility. In refined, upper-class homes, the separation of functions was highly developed: cooking, eating, sitting, sleeping, studying, receiving guests, entering the house, and so forth were all carried out in spaces designated for a particular use. Separation of function was taken to an extreme as houses were amply provided with specialized rooms, such as the office (*spreekkamer*), the pantry (*provisiekamer*), the drying attic with clothes rack and basket, the kitchen with a built-in counter (*aanrecht*), and so on.[9] The problem for reformers was to define for more modest dwellings the minimum number of necessary functions that would meet their requirements for civility, neither encouraging miniature versions of the middle-class home, which would include features that took up floor area unnecessarily, nor reducing the division of space to the extent that rooms had to fulfill conflicting functions. The problem was thus posed in terms of maximizing utility without creating overlapping uses of space considered detrimental to hygiene or morality.

Amsterdam's reformers insisted on three minimal conditions: the total separation of workplace from dwelling, the separation of washing and cooking from sitting and eating, and the separation of sleeping from any other function. The dwelling was accordingly to be the self-contained center of family life, where domestic activities could be carried out with privacy and order. Louise van der Pek-Went put it succinctly in her classes at the School for Social Work: "We call civilized living the habitation

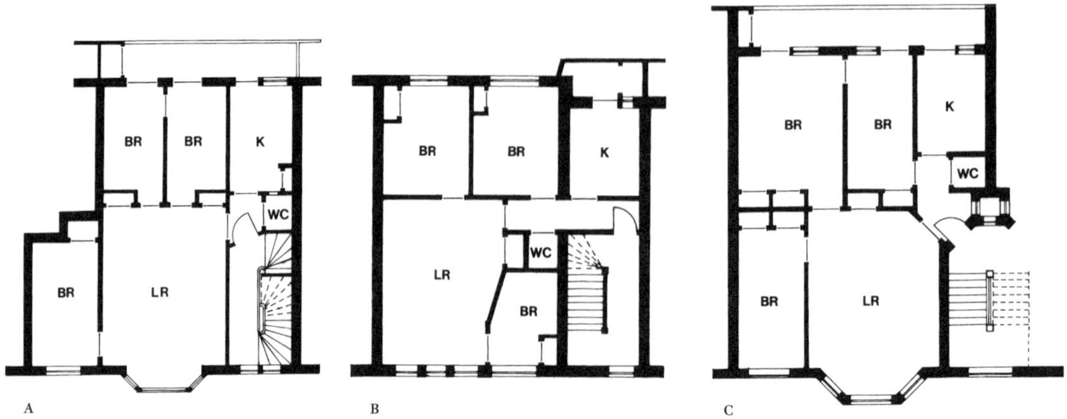

FIGURE 5.1 Examples of the preferred dwelling type: (A) H. P. Berlage, Algemeene Woningbouw Vereeniging, Tolstraat, 1912; (B) Michel de Klerk, Eigen Haard, Zaanstraat, 1918; (C) J. C. van Epen, Algemeene Woningbouw Vereeniging, 1915.

of the home such that living room, bedroom, kitchen, and so forth are separated as much as possible from each other. The less the civility, the greater the tendency to do everything in the same room. This tendency must be opposed as much as possible."[10]

In Amsterdam, discussion of the dwelling plan took place among the housing reformers within government, at the Building and Housing Inspection Office and the Housing Authority, and among those in advisory positions such as the members of the Health Board. These were the social workers, architects, and health officials who constituted expertise in social hygiene. Many of the same reformers were active in the Amsterdam Housing Council, which made a study of "the most advisable type for the worker's dwelling." Out of their deliberations emerged a consensus on a preferred plan type similar to that of Rochdale's first housing project. It consisted of a narrow kitchen, used exclusively for cooking and washing; a living room used exclusively for dining, sitting, and entertaining; and three separate small bedrooms used exclusively for sleeping (fig. 5.1). Ideally, the stair leading to the landing gave access to only one dwelling per floor, and the single entrance to the dwelling separated the hallway shared by other residents of the building from the dwelling itself. Behind the apartment door, the family would live in a discrete, private space of its own.

This set of specifications formed a general model that could be manipulated in response to the needs of a particular site to produce an actual floor plan. With the model they championed, reformers hoped to counteract behavioral tendencies working against their definition of civility by eliminating the necessity for conflicting uses in the home. Their model was both carrot and stick, intended to raise living standards while shaping them. Three bedrooms were an unheard of luxury to most low-income families; by encouraging housing societies to find ways to build them within workers' budgets, the reformers were contributing to higher standards of living. Aspects of their plan also aimed at preventing behavior of which they disapproved and at shaping the way a family lived in the home.

Housing reformers inside and outside government worked to make their preferred model the norm in Amsterdam. Officials in the Housing Authority exercised complete control over the plans of municipal and subsidized housing, although their relationship with the housing societies was purely advisory. Their influence was not negligible, but as long as housing societies conformed to the building ordinance they were free to build their projects as they wished. Reading the variations of plan types approved for Housing Act projects between 1909 and 1919 reveals the degree of acceptance and resistance met by the reformers' model plan. Despite some opposition, the attempt to normalize urban living through the introduction of a standard set of design criteria was largely successful. Equally significant, however, was the range of variation that the housing societies generated, reflecting alternative visions of urban lifestyle to the reformers' rational solution. This chapter traces the derivation of the reformers' model and then investigates the ability of the housing societies to express their vision of the ideal urban home within the confines of those imposed norms.

DERIVATION OF THE STANDARD PLAN

The changes reformers proposed constituted a reaction against nineteenth-century speculative housing conditions and workers' accommodations to them, rather than a radical break with traditional urban building patterns. Early-twentieth-century Dutch housing expertise translated the concerns of nineteenth-century reformers directly into housing requirements. Certain issues were repeatedly identified as critical to the design of dwelling type. A 1905 inquiry into the housing problem by Catholic Social Action emphasized the parlor question, lodgers, and the separation of sleeping places.[11] A questionnaire developed by the CBSA in 1908 for housing societies focused its attention on the parlor, the kitchen–living room, communal stairs, and the separation of sleeping spaces.[12] These lists of issues reflected the reformers' perception of the housing problem as one of hygiene and morality. Accordingly, in their search for an appropriate plan type for mass urban housing, reformers took positions on the moral and hygienic implications of each of these design problems.

Reformers contested the combination kitchen–living room. This was a room in which meals were prepared and eaten, the washing was done, the family gathered, and in which one or more members of the family might sleep if the number of bedrooms was insufficient.[13] Living conditions were thus only slightly better than in the one-room dwellings of speculative housing. The Amsterdam Health Board acknowledged only one advantage of the kitchen–living room over the narrow kitchen, separate from the living room. That was the ease with which mothers could mind their children while carrying out daily chores.

> The woman of the house in workers' families does not have help at her disposal for most of her work, especially in families who can only afford housing with low rent. She is thus forced during the preparation of meals, laundering, and other such activities for which the kitchen is intended to keep the children by her side in order to keep an eye on them. She is also forced by the nature of her activities to spend most of the day with her children in that kitchen, and thus to employ the kitchen as a living room.[14]

Nonetheless, the board favored housing types in which the kitchen could be used only for washing and cooking. It suggested that mothers could keep an eye on children through a connecting door between the kitchen and living room.

Several housing societies, however, incorporated kitchen–living rooms in their plans. From its first project, the Catholic housing society Het Oosten preferred a floor plan in which the kitchen was enlarged to a size permitting the family to dine in it, while a second, separate living room was used as a sitting room or parlor (fig. 5.2).[15] In this case, the presence of the parlor might relieve to some degree the burden of multiple uses to which reformers objected. The officers of Het Oosten decided to use this plan after consulting with their members, who had expressed dissatisfaction with existing housing types. In particular, the standard type built by speculative builders, consisting of front and back room with alcoves and small kitchen (fig. 1.4), elicited the complaint that the front room "is practically never used, and yet time must be spent dusting it every week."[16] This was a condemnation of the parlor from the point of view of workers' wives. On the other hand, Het Oosten's officers remained skeptical about the Rochdale type with the narrow kitchen praised by reformers, noting "that this praise was not fully endorsed by those who had moved into the dwellings."[17] They sought a solution that would separate dining and living rooms but still allow sufficient space for bedrooms. While the reformers favored separation of cooking from dining and sitting, Het Oosten opted for separating cooking and dining from sitting: "So that it was decided to make a fine square front room with as large a kitchen as possible, which, if so wished, could be used for serving meals. That eliminated the need for everything to take place in the living room because space was lacking in the kitchen. And the living room could become the cozy room so often described in books, but which all too frequently is lacking in workers' homes, since high rents cause them to make do with as little space as possible" (fig. 5.2).[18] This plan type was adopted by several other housing societies as well.[19]

Het Oosten's membership may have spoken out against the wasted space of a "front room" used as a parlor, but reformers feared that the second living room in their solution would result precisely in such use.[20] Louise van der Pek-Went objected to a similar plan proposed in 1918, noting that "the gentlemen specifically designate the front

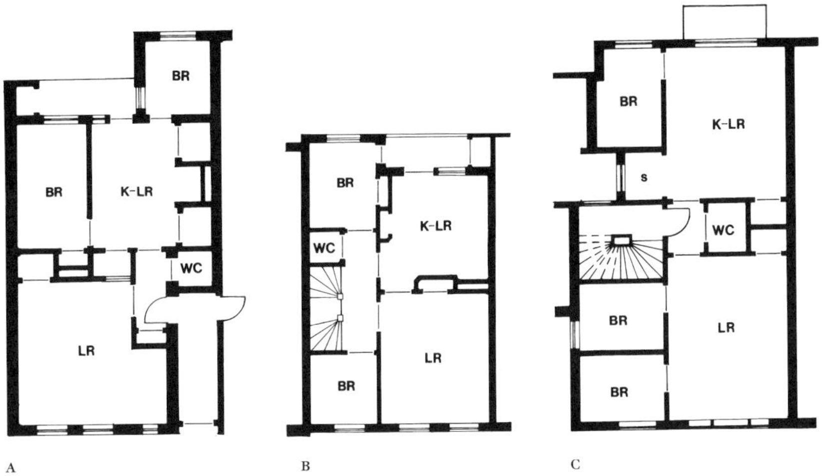

FIGURE 5.2 Dwelling plans with kitchen–living rooms: (A) J. J. L. Moolenschot, Het Oosten, Balistraat, 1913; (B) J. J. L. Moolenschot, Het Oosten, Nachtegaalstraat, 1914; (C) W. Greve, Jr., HIJSM, Madurastraat, 1912.

room as a salon. The actual dwelling thus takes place in the living room and bedroom. Of the forty-eight square meters of living area, twenty-eight are then used for living and twenty for salon. This is not a permissible ratio."[21] The kitchen–living room issue was thus linked to the question of the parlor. Here two kinds of arguments were used by reformers, a moral argument inherited from the nineteenth-century reform tradition that held that the parlor encouraged profligacy, extravagance, and false pride, and the functional argument that the limited space workers' families could command should be used as effectively as possible. That meant all space should be used continuously and that the light and air a front room provided should not be closed off because the room was reserved for special social occasions. There was also concern that in such a plan the two living rooms consumed floor area at the expense of the bedrooms, which became very small.

Reformers did approve one version of the kitchen–living room, but then only for subsidized housing. In fact, this deliberately inferior solution was intended to encourage its inhabitants to move to full-market housing. These flats were built by the municipality or by societies such as De Arbeiderswoning and the Handwerkers Vriendenkring to serve families moving out of condemned housing in Amsterdam's slums.[22] The floor plan was designed to provide minimal amenity as a reflection of the fact that these dwellings were rented below market value. In these units, a large living room with attached pantry was used for cooking, eating, and sitting (fig. 3.2B). The separate location of the sink in the pantry and the presence of separate bedrooms alleviated the hygienic objections of reformers to the kitchen–living room. Nonetheless, families

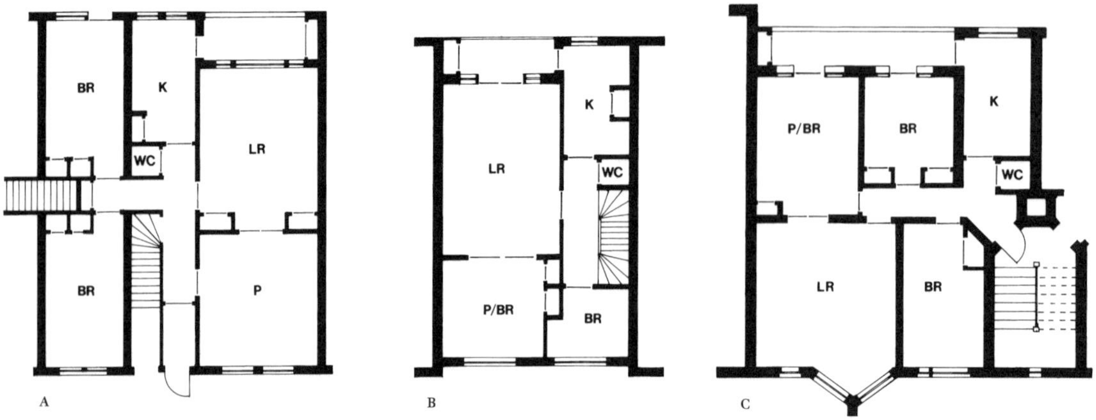

FIGURE 5.3 Dwelling plans with parlors: (A) H. P. Berlage and J. C. van Epen, Algemeene Woningbouw Vereeniging, Spreeuwpark, 1913; (B) T. Kuipers and A. U. Ingwersen, Patrimonium, Zwanenplein, 1917; (C) T. Kuipers and A. U. Ingwersen, Patrimonium, Polanenstraat, 1919; (D) J. C. van Epen, Algemeene Woningbouw Vereeniging, Josef Israëlskade, 1919.

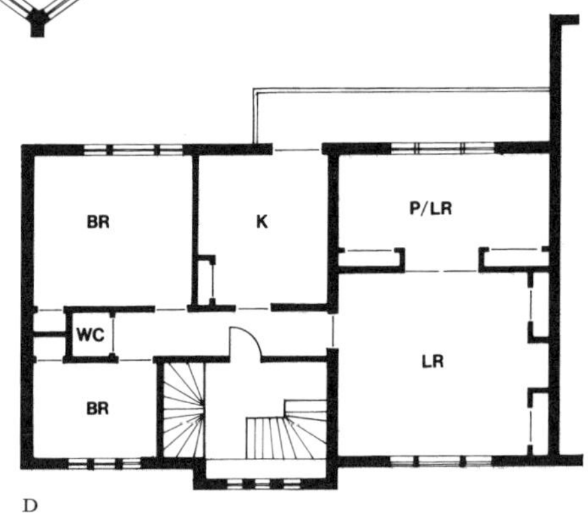

experienced some inconvenience in such housing units, notably the messiness caused by cooking, working, and living all in the same space.[23]

Like the Rochdale model, the subsidized type used a technique recommended by nineteenth-century reformers to prevent any room in the dwelling being set aside for use as a parlor, arranging the plan so that the living room had to serve daily as the dining room. A number of the housing societies did, however, construct housing types that provided a parlor, in contradiction to the reformers' model. In some cases, the plan imitated the middle-class pattern of two rooms, front and back, en suite (fig. 5.3). In other cases, as we have seen, the kitchen was enlarged to become a kitchen–living room, and the living room proper could then be put aside as salon (fig. 5.2). And some plans were intentionally ambiguous; a room designated for sleeping, usually located next to the living room, was arranged in such a way that it could easily serve the purpose of salon (fig. 5.3B–D).

Another issue that concerned reformers was how to provide a sufficient number of separate sleeping places. The campaign for three separate sleeping spaces in the home addressed middle-class fears of incest and immorality in working-class homes, first voiced in the nineteenth century. Ideally reformers wished to provide sleeping areas to accommodate parents and children of each sex. Neither the free market sector nor philanthropic housing had alleviated the problem of insufficient bedrooms. A 1909 survey of Amsterdam teachers gathered information about the sleeping arrangements of its members living in free market housing. The average family size was 3.34, while the average number of bedrooms was only 1.6 per dwelling. Altogether, more than a third of all sleeping spaces were not designated bedrooms, but rather attics, living rooms, alcoves, bedsteads, or other rooms.[24]

Within tight quarters, families created sleeping space wherever possible: closets, attics, and sometimes porches were pressed into service. Sometimes built-in "bunk beds" of two or more layers would be constructed by the dwellers to accommodate all members of the family. Children slept two, three, or more to a bed.[25] The rural custom of built-in beds (closets with a door or curtains to close off the bed during the day) was applied regularly in the city. As late as 1930, more than a third of the dwellings in the Western Islands and southern half of the Jordaan had built-in beds (*bedsteden*); in the Eastern Islands and northern half of the Jordaan, the proportion was well over half.[26] Whether philanthropic or private sector, the typical nineteenth-century Amsterdam dwelling offered a built-in bed or two in a room used as kitchen–living room, and another in the salon (figs. 3.1A and 5.4).[27] Of 2,356 housing society dwellings surveyed in 1899, all provided a bed built into the living room and most had only two rooms, so that many family members were forced to sleep in the same space.[28] In response to this situation, the reformers encouraged a plan that permitted sleeping only in designated bedrooms, preferably three separate spaces.

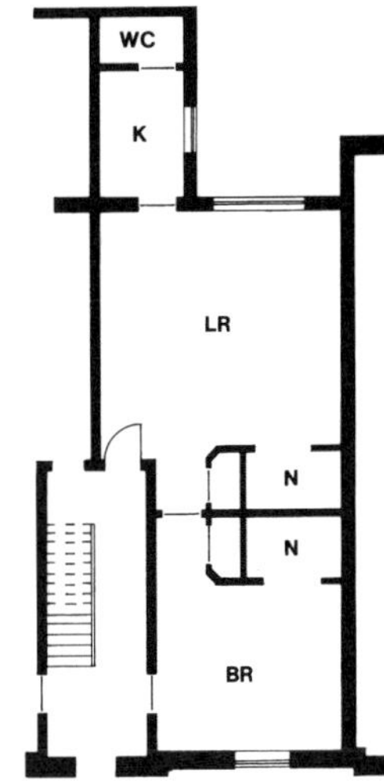

FIGURE 5.4
Dwelling plan with build-in bedstead: W. and P. J. Hamer, Vereeniging ten Behoeve der Arbeidersklasse, Jan van der Heijdenstraat, 1888.

In order to create spaces for sleeping, families often resorted to options considered unsatisfactory by reformers, such as attic bedrooms and built-in beds of various forms. The original built-in bed, a rural tradition, was a wooden closet with doors enclosing a space usually large enough for two people to sleep in. With its doors closed, the closet freed up the rest of the room for other uses. Working housewives with no time to make up the bed, those who felt a bed in the middle of the living room looked inappropriate, or those without separate beds and linens preferred this option, which allowed them to keep the sleeping arrangements out of sight.

The speculative builders' insertion of closed-off alcoves for sleeping was a widespread variation on the system. As a working-class councilor pointed out during the municipal debate on the 1905 building ordinance, workers would be happy to do without alcoves if they had the wages to afford dwellings with a bedroom in addition to a parlor and living room.[29] Their preference for alcoves and built-in beds made sense in the small one- and two-room dwellings they could afford. It was simply a remedy for lack of space.

This solution was rejected by those who, like Tak, considered that a "wrongheaded feeling for neatness interfered with hygienic practice."[30] As he argued successfully for the abolition of the built-in bed or bed closet in 1905, Tak noted, "above all we must get rid of some old-fashioned notions of respectability, which shall probably cause some commotion." In place of the built-in bedstead, Tak proposed the sleeping niche, a space the size of a two-person bed enclosed on three sides by walls. Here a free-standing bed and mattress could be placed, and if a light curtain were hung across the niche, the bed could disappear from view during the day but be ventilated at night.[31]

Before the war, nearly a third of the housing projects approved by the municipality included sleeping niches in the living room. Slightly less than half of those units also included a kitchen–living room, so that the second living room became a combination parlor and bedroom.[32] The rest consisted only of a living room with sleeping niche and a kitchen too small to eat in, so that the living room was the only space in which it was possible to dine, and also the only sleeping option.[33] Louise van der Pek-Went joined other reformers in condemning this practice. The living room should be used daily, but not for sleeping: "In my opinion, we must continue to disapprove of sleeping in living rooms. Either the living room is not used for living in and then there is too much space being sacrificed, or it is indeed used for daily living and eating, and then sleeping in that atmosphere is unhygienic."[34]

The continued dual use of the living room was inevitable considering the small size of the dwellings built by the housing societies and the naturally increasing size of families. The desire for more places to sleep, or for the separation of sleeping places, led people to use whatever available space they could find. Het Oosten purposely designed the living rooms of its first project so that one corner included two removable closets, providing a place for a two-person bed should the family increase or as children grew older (fig. 5.2A).[35] The Amsterdam Health Board tolerated some irregular sleeping arrangements in housing society plans because of its policy of encouraging at least three separate sleeping places in the home. At first this led the municipality to approve designs for bed niches in living rooms. But by 1914, this solution had fallen into disrepute among reformers.[36] After the abolition of the alcove and built-in bed in 1905, the municipality was also alert to the possibility that closets and other locations (such as the space under staircases) might be used for sleeping, and it moved to prevent such practices.[37]

In ordinary speculative housing, the attic provided space for an additional sleeping area if the residents converted their assigned storage partition into a bedroom. In the housing society projects, this practice continued. The attic was often divided by laths into storage or drying areas, but often those enclosures were finished off by the inhabitants for use as bedrooms. By including attic rooms as part of the building plan, housing societies hoped to provide a higher quality construction than the workers' makeshift efforts (fig. 5.5). However, reformers raised moral objections to this solution. Attic bedrooms were reached by the main stairwell, which gave access to all the flats in the building, and reformers objected to the potential for contacts between young people of the opposite sex without parental supervision. In 1905, as the Penal

Regulation Board reviewed the proposed building ordinance, it approved a proposal to require small locked entry halls in front of each attic room because "such intermixing of bedrooms for people from different families raises grave moral considerations."[38] In 1915, the Health Board took up the moral issue of attic bedrooms by asking eight Amsterdam housing societies if the rooms had led to undesirable consequences.[39] After reviewing the responses, the housing subcommittee concluded that the advantage of increased numbers of separate bedrooms offered by attic rooms was outweighed by the impropriety of bedrooms without sufficient guarantee of privacy. They approved only those attic bedrooms directly connected by private stairs to the corresponding flat below, and recommended that the conversion of attic storage areas be discouraged by limiting direct lighting, lowering ceilings, and using wire partitions.[40] Creation of a wholly private, self-contained dwelling unit was the aim. Keppler even argued that Rochdale's solution of a single bedroom permitted per attic, rather than several rooms for different families, was insufficient guarantee of privacy since there was no way to predict when residents of the other flats might choose to visit their storage area and the shared stair access would not prevent undesirable encounters.[41] Soon the housing societies no longer had any choice: the Health Board required them to provide internal stairs to the attic bedroom.[42] The Health Board had modified and legitimized the old working-class solution of finishing off the attic storage area to add another bedroom. The extra expense of the stairs and the elimination of rooms accessed only communally was justified by the civilizing effect of increased privacy. In the case of both alcoves and attic rooms, workers' strategies to achieve decency and privacy within the limits of their housing options were obviated by the provision of designated bedrooms in the reformers' model plan.

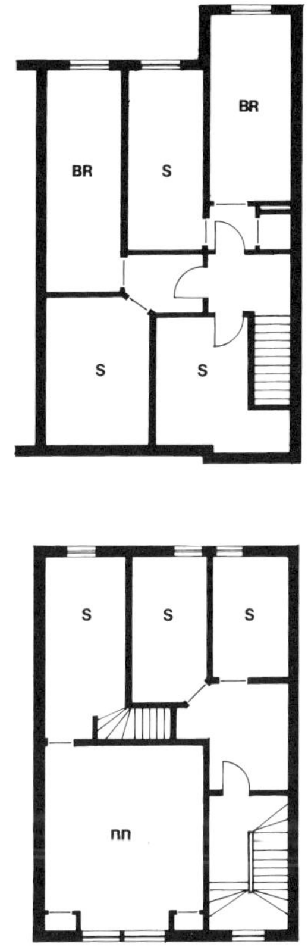

FIGURE 5.5 Attic bedrooms: (A) J. C. van Epen, Algemeene Woningbouw Vereeniging, Van Hallstraat, 1915; (B) J. C. van Epen, Algemeene Woningbouw Vereeniging, Amstelveenscheweg, 1918.

The reformers responded to the ills they perceived in speculative housing by developing a housing type that separated functions according to bourgeois norms. They identified their cultural position as rational, progressive, and modern, thus implying that any resistance to it was irrational, conservative, and traditional. The general scheme for the dwelling plan, with its acceptance of the existing urban fabric, its provision of three bedrooms, its small kitchen and separate living room, was represented as the only logical outcome of rational analysis. The exclusivity of this view, reducing space to an ideal, universalizing abstraction, prevented reformers from recognizing other, simultaneous meanings that might attach to the dwelling plan. Their mode of analysis automatically placed them in a position other than that of the inhabitants.[43]

The significance of the kitchen–living room differed in the eyes of workers and housing reformers. Workers reacted favorably to the advantages of carrying out childcare and kitchen chores in the same space, while finding no special disadvantage to dining in the kitchen. The reformers reacted unfavorably to the potential for abuse offered by the division of space into two living rooms. In their view, the disadvantages of the tiny kitchen they proposed were outweighed by the elimination of possible misappropriation of a living room as either bedroom or parlor. Workers' perceptions of the parlor also differed markedly from those of the reformers. A housewife, explaining her attachment to the parlor in reaction to reformers' designs that omitted it, asked "Why then deprive a woman of her illusions, when she in most cases enjoys so few of the pleasures of life any way, especially when she is bound to her home by needy children?"[44] The single living room, with no option for a separate parlor, eliminated a nicety many workers considered an important part of their living environment, a symbol of respectability and an object of pride. The small separate bedrooms answered a heartfelt need, but sometimes proved unserviceable for those without sufficient beds or linens. The reformers' priority was hygiene and efficiency, at the expense of workers' strategies to simulate middle-class amenities. Although the inadequacy of workers' solutions was largely a function of economic limitations, not backwardness, a tone of accusation and condemnation, rather than persuasion, often characterized the restrictions imposed by reformers. Paradoxically, workers' pursuit of the outward signs of respectability often resulted in solutions that brought them into conflict with those they imitated.

The reaction of reformers to those resisting their model for the dwelling plan can be observed in the municipal review of housing projects proposed by the Bouwmaatschappij tot Verkrijging van Eigen Woningen, a liberal workers' society established in the nineteenth century. After passage of the Housing Act, the society resisted turning to the government for financial support because it did not want to tie itself to the requirements of government reformers.[45] When it did finally seek Housing Act assistance, it was forced to leave the sleeping niche and kitchen–living room behind.

Many of the society's units combined a kitchen–living room with a living room that included a sleeping niche.[46] More than half of their units with kitchen–living room offered this dual use of the living room so disdained by reformers. The Bouwmaatschappij developed a housing type for small families that consisted simply of a kitchen–living room, living room with sleeping niche, and one bedroom (fig. 5.6). Between 1909 and 1914, these small units made up nearly a quarter of the dwellings built by the society.[47] In 1918, when the society proposed this type in three locations, including a new neighborhood in Amsterdam South, the Health Board objected.[48] In a letter to the board, the society ardently defended its use of the type. It pointed out the need to respond to families of different size and economic strength. It claimed that the sleeping niche was used by some small families primarily in case of illness or childbirth. Of all its dwelling types, this one received the most applications; it was preferred by many of the current members.[49] Despite these arguments on the basis of popularity, the Health Board ruled to eliminate both the kitchen–living room and the sleeping niche.[50]

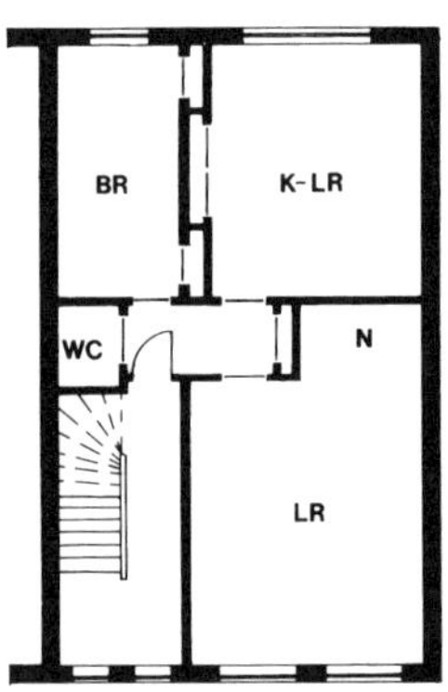

FIGURE 5.6 A. W. Weissman, Bouwmaatschappij tot Verkrijging van Eigen Woningen, 1e Hugo de Grootstraat, 1908.

Housing reformers in Amsterdam succeeded in enforcing their norms. More than two-thirds of the housing units approved for loans by the municipal council between

1909 and 1919 complied with the reformers' preferred model floor plan. The campaign to increase the number of bedrooms was particularly successful. In the housing society projects approved by the municipal council between 1909 and 1919, the percentage of dwelling units with at least three bedrooms increased markedly, while the percentage of dwellings with only one or two bedrooms dropped from almost one-half to one-third.[51]

Workers greeted the reformers' model housing types with varied responses. Of the 390 families still living in Uilenburg as it underwent urban renewal in 1912, 160 wanted to stay on rather than move to newly constructed replacement housing designed according to reform models.[52] Members of the municipal workers' union visited Rochdale's new housing soon after it was built in 1909. They described it favorably but felt obliged to explain the design and particularly the small kitchen to workers.[53] Others, as we have already seen in the case of Het Oosten, rejected that model.

There was a pattern to the resistance. For those who identified closely with confessional and liberal attitudes, the desire to imitate middle-class housing styles was stronger. The parlor and the kitchen–living room were more prevalent in both the confessional and the old liberal housing societies, whose members embraced a vision of society based not on class solidarity, but on a social hierarchy calibrated by symbols of status. Aside from its special application in subsidized housing as an incentive to move to better, unsubsidized housing, the kitchen–living room appeared only in projects built by conservative societies.[54] The confessional housing societies included parlors to a greater extent than any of the societies of different ideological persuasion; more than 40 percent of their units included a parlor, ten times more than progressive housing societies.[55] This tenfold difference reflected the degree to which the different groups subscribed to the housing reform agenda. The confessional societies used the provisions of the Housing Act advantageously for their members, but their aim was to help them to housing that was both affordable and approximated middle-class lifestyle. The accoutrements of respectability were a higher priority than the signs of modernity evident in the more functional plans of the reform movement. The architects of the confessional societies were not participants in that movement. They were not part of the circle of Progressive Liberals and Social Democrats who dominated the Health Board and the Amsterdam Housing Council. To the contrary, their municipal representatives were the most vocal opponents of municipal housing and stringent building standards. And their membership, composed mostly of highly paid workers, artisans, and petit bourgeoisie, was conservative in taste.

The modern union members, better educated and organized, accepted the reform agenda more readily. The socialist societies included the fewest parlors: only 4 percent included a specifically designated parlor; none used the kitchen–living room. It is not surprising that the reformers' model was adopted more freely by socialist housing societies. The socialist societies were run by workers and experts committed to the reform agenda. Some of their members may have resisted the message of modernization embraced by their leaders, but the roster of the trustees and officers of the societies came straight from the institutions of housing reform in Amsterdam. As we saw in chapter 4, liberal reformers rejected the parlor as an unnecessary loss of valuable space due to the vain desire to ape the manners of the middle class. Such arguments for minimalism became all the more acceptable to progressives and socialists when couched in terms of the rational allocation of space and the rejection of bourgeois habits in the name of a new proletarian culture.

Nonetheless, all the flats put up by the relatively well-off teachers belonging to the housing society ACOB included a designated "reception" room, although the teachers of this society were predominantly socialist (fig. 3.2A). For those who could afford the higher rents commanded by dwellings with two living rooms as well as bedrooms and kitchen, the parlor remained a goal no matter what their political persuasion.

High rent alone, however, did not fully account for the incidence of parlors. Although in general before the war there was some correlation between higher average rent in a project and the percentage of its units that could accommodate a parlor, several projects with low or average rents also included a significant percentage of possible parlors, and during and just after the war there was little relationship between rent and the availability of a parlor. Even those on a limited budget could find housing societies that made it possible to set aside a salon, resisting the reformers' ideal.[56] In fact, by 1919, altogether more than a quarter of the dwelling units approved for government loans by the municipal council permitted the creation of a parlor.[57]

Effective as the rationalism of the reformers' approach was in deriving a new model for the floor plan that would answer the failings of previous dwelling types, there was more at stake in the design of the dwelling than could be solved by logical analysis. Deeper still lay the problem of the image of the home, with its multiple cultural associations. Through the responses to the reformers' model, two conflicting images of the home emerged: first, the worker's home as a miniature imitation of the bourgeois house; and second, the creation of a new *wooncultuur*, a new culture of housing to represent the new emancipated social role of the working class. Each of these images carried social, political, and cultural connotations supported and contested by the participants in the creation of social housing. As we shall see, the generality of the reformers' model permitted the expression of these varied meanings within its norms.

SOVEREIGNTY AND COLLECTIVITY AS HOUSING IDEALS

The reformers' model dwelling plan represented little more than the amelioration of egregious faults in the existing types. Reformers protested against the results of laissez-faire real estate, which worked effectively to maximize profits but not livability.

Their own agenda endorsed the aim of improving housing conditions rather than increasing profits. Indeed, just as speculative developers applied the instruments of rationalism to extract the maximum profit from available space, the reformers employed their plan type rationally to maximize utility in the available space. The reformers' plan type was neutral, the product of applied geometrical logic, and it proposed no vision of the home aside from the assumption that it would house the nuclear family. The plan did not impose a specific social reading of the space, except, perhaps, for an unintentional indication of social position expressed by the subjection of the dwelling to minimum standards. Instead, a practical functionalism that suited both liberal and socialist perspectives dominated discussions of plan type.

Only in regard to questions of urban design, at the level of neighborhood planning, do we find reformers engaging in discussion of the phenomenological experience of "home" or the collective spirit of "community" as applied to the home. For instance, the garden city movement, which originated in England and exerted considerable influence in the Netherlands, including Amsterdam, raised the issue of appropriate domestic imagery, urban, rural, or suburban.[58]

For many, however, the bourgeois home provided a persistent model for mass housing, a myth of respectability held dear by some and interpreted in varying ways. It motivated the resistance of the Bouwmaatschappij to the reform model, the so-called middle-class appointments of the first ACOB projects, and occasional, more expensive units in confessional and socialist housing projects. The myth of the middle-class villa, an independent, autonomous dwelling, was defined in large part by the desire for a private, off-street entrance, a coveted expression of sovereignty over interior space. Such concern for privacy was already reflected in the reformers' plan, with its insistence on a single door giving access to all the rooms of the dwelling, and was shared equally by the Health Board and by workers themselves.

When nineteenth-century reformers introduced a central entrance giving access to eight units or more, workers objected and dubbed the housing "barracks." In 1896, the housing inspector for such a block explained the distaste many workers felt for the shared entryway: "When sixteen families live in one building and thus all gain entry to their homes through the same street door, the cream of the working class is not attracted."[59] Hélène Mercier, referring to the philanthropic housing societies that predated the Housing Act, also remarked on this objection: "The communal stair that one finds in all the Amsterdam housing societies is a nuisance for the dwellers and nondwellers alike. Every Dutch worker appears to have a deep-rooted dislike for anything that even remotely resembles a Parisian *cité ouvrière*, and a stairway that belongs to so many families can't help but suggest just that. We consider it a right to live in a home that is not part of a building whose front door is locked only at night and serves eight other families."[60]

Reformers were well aware of the unpopularity of the "barracks" and added their own set of objections to the type. G. A. M. Kallenbach's 1892 dissertation on philanthropic housing described in detail its disadvantages. He believed the communal use of hall, stairs, and attic led to uncontrolled conflicts between neighbors since the lower classes expressed their feelings and moods in a "livelier, less inhibited way."[61] Order and cleanliness were difficult to maintain in the common entry, halls, and stairs. Constant close contact with others might also pose a moral threat to family life. Kallenbach wished to distinguish between the friendly exchanges between neighbors overseen by the head of the family and the continuing, unavoidable contact between those living in the same building that led to theft, backbiting, illicit passion, and quarrels.[62]

One of the most documented problems of the communal hall and stairs was the issue of maintenance. Customarily, each family was responsible for cleaning the hall and stairs in their portion of the building, much as Dutch row house owners were responsible for the stoop and sidewalk outside their doors, and resentment against shirkers occasionally exploded.[63] Of the nineteenth-century housing societies, only the one run by workers rejected the barracks entry, choosing to give its ground-floor flats a separate entrance and placing a maximum of three flats off a common stair.[64]

The dislike for shared urban quarters continued into the twentieth century. Housing experts took note of the continuing prejudice of Dutch families against housing that required shared spaces.

> The ordinary Dutchman craves a home that comprises a separate building, an entire house, in which he does not have to encounter strangers either on the stairs or in the hallway. If he is not able to live in a detached house, then he wishes in any case a first-floor or second-floor dwelling to himself, that is, half of a house, that again comprises a separate entry. If that is not possible either, and he must be satisfied with a flat, then the small *portiek* apartment is introduced—a smaller portion of a building, but still with a separate entrance. This Dutch tendency can thus be typified as follows: the Dutchman wants to be in command of everything behind the street door. If necessary, he will not object to meeting a neighbor on a stair, but only one that leads to the street from outside his own street door. The entry and stairs inside his front street door must be his own turf, which no one can dispute with him.[65]

In four-story buildings, various attempts were made to achieve the goal of maximizing the number of families with their own street entrance, reducing the number of families sharing halls or stairs. The first proposals of the Amsterdam housing societies generally rejected the barracks solution of the nineteenth century, although permitted by the 1905 building ordinance to build a street entrance leading to a maximum of nine dwellings and a stair serving a maximum of six dwellings.[66]

Since the housing societies were motivated by the desire to increase the number of self-contained units and decrease the need to share access, they were willing to allocate more space to halls and stairs. Most three- and four-story buildings provided a street entrance for the ground-floor flats separate from the entry leading to the upper flats. A central stair leading to landings shared by two families was used much less frequently than a stair whose landings gave access to only one flat, although the double loading of the first solution saved space.[67] After the war, the double-loaded stair appeared in half of the projects with three or more stories, but it never became popular among the inhabitants of the buildings. Municipal authorities were not altogether satisfied with the communal stairs that were applied widely in municipal housing.[68] Some workers and housing societies were outspoken in their resistance to communal stairs.[69]

The strongest tendency to secure sovereignty in the home was to be found in the projects of the confessional housing societies. The high priority placed on creating self-contained dwelling units reflected the confessional societies' orientation to home and family. The Anti-Revolutionary leader Prof. D. P. D. Fabius defended the proposition that "every father should possess his own home."[70] Operating under the same financial constraints as the other Amsterdam societies, Patrimonium could not provide each father with his own detached house, but its first project did "strive to attain sovereignty of the individual home" by arranging as many independent entrances as possible.

The three main confessional housing societies rejected the barracks model of eight families entering through one street door, never applying it.[71] They were more active than any other group in experimenting with complex access systems designed to maximize private entrances (fig. 5.7). In several of Patrimonium's Amsterdam projects, an open porch gave access to eight families in a double parcel. Two doors inside the porch led directly to the two ground-floor apartments. A stairwell open to the street led to a landing with five doors. Two of these led directly to two second-floor flats. Two doors opened on two separate stairs each leading directly to a third-floor flat. The last door opened on stairs that climbed two floors to the fourth-floor entrances of the two top-floor flats. In this system, the significant break came at the first landing, where the locked doors divided the public from the private way. Of the eight families in the double plot, only the two on the top floor had to share a stair behind a locked door, but this arrangement required the construction of three separate and parallel stairways running from the first-floor landing.[72] Other projects by Patrimonium, Dr. Schaepman, and Het Oosten used similarly complex systems of access to achieve greater self-sufficiency.[73] Although only a few of the projects sacrificed valuable floor space to this degree, the confessional societies were consistent in applying as many techniques as needed to maximize the sovereignty of the dwelling.

The preference for separation of turf is also evident in the way the open space within perimeter blocks was allocated. That space could be shared communally or divided among the ground-floor occupants. Two-thirds of the projects approved between 1909 and 1919 elected to split all the open space for the benefit of the ground-floor flats; most of the projects erected by the confessional housing societies selected this option, which allowed families living on the ground floor the enjoyment of a private garden.

FIGURE 5.7
T. Kuipers and A. U. Ingwersen, Patrimonium, Vaartstraat, 1911: (A) ground floor, (B) first floor, (C) second floor, (D) third floor, (E) attic.

Nineteenth-century bourgeois reformers in the Netherlands had viewed collective facilities such as shared water pumps, dining rooms, or laundries as potential threats to morality and good conduct. Self-sufficiency of the dwelling was lauded as a means to minimize contact between neighbors and thus foster peaceful relationships free of bad influences.[74] Many reformers continued to concur with workers' preference for privacy, as long as it could be achieved economically. Too much expense devoted to this end was viewed as a wrongheaded pursuit of middle-class amenities. The Health Board's housing subcommittee looked into the allocation of considerable space to a stair system calculated to maximize the number of families with private access to their front door and found it an inappropriate attempt to make workers' dwellings into miniature gentleman's houses.[75]

In direct contrast with the confessionals' strong inclination toward sovereignty of the dwelling, the socialists promoted a utopian vision of collective facilities. They made a direct attack on the traditional definition of the sanctity of the home by proposing to move activities usually considered private, such as cooking, bathing, child rearing, and laundry, into collective facilities. Here the tradition of utopian social experiments such as the Fourier *familistère* formed a counterpoint to the reform tradition that emphasized the separation and autonomy of family life.

The socialists perceived collective facilities as a means to improve both the spiritual and the material well-being of workers. Mathilde Wibaut-Berdenis van Berlekom argued for the advantages of collective housekeeping, following the arguments of American feminists such as Charlotte Perkins Gilman. Public laundries, crèches, and collective dining facilities all might free the housewife of housework, yet maintain intimate family life. She praised the one-kitchen apartment house in which every fam-

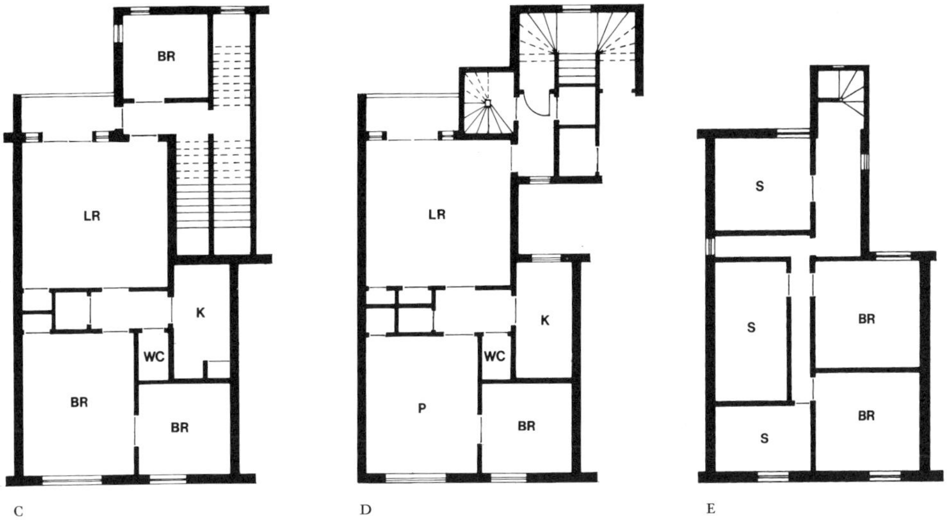

ily has separate quarters but shares space for dining, recreation, reading, play, and garden.[76]

The cooperative movement, heavily supported by the socialists, originated in consumer and producer cooperatives, but also gave rise to societies like De Dageraad, Amsterdamsche Coöperatieve Keuken, and Samenwerking, which had an impact on the housing movement.[77] The SDAP municipal program of 1899 drafted by P. L. Tak called for municipal baths, laundries, and housing. Such programs were carried out as the municipal council gathered more socialist votes, so that by 1920 the city ran municipal baths, laundries, and kitchens as well as its housing program.[78] The city also expanded its services to other areas formerly controlled within the private household: crèches, school lunches, public libraries, and vacation clubs.

Several of the socialist housing societies proposed extensive provision of collective facilities. Amsterdam-Zuid's original plans for a garden village included shared gardens, laundry, bathhouse, library, and a recreation hall.[79] The housing society Zomers Buiten made similar plans.[80] The preference of socialist societies for collective facilities extended to the gardens within the perimeter housing blocks. The open space was left undivided for collective use, or small gardens for the ground-floor occupants were combined with a large central, shared garden. Collective gardens were distributed unevenly among the housing societies. Twice as many socialist projects as confessional included collective gardens.[81]

Although the socialists carried out a continuous campaign in favor of collective facilities, there appears to have been a consistent resistance from some workers to services that took activities out of the home and into shared public space. Reformers had long protested the hygienic disadvantages of hanging the washing out to dry in the home, and workers themselves knew from experience the unsatisfactory and unhomelike atmosphere caused by the clothesline rigged in the living room. But municipal laundries were not greeted enthusiastically. Even in the largely socialist housing society Algemeene, dominated by diamond workers who were well acquainted with collective action, a 1915 survey on municipal laundries elicited only fourteen responses out of a thousand forms.[82] Housewives hesitated to use the municipal laundry for a number of reasons, all related to economic concerns. Some found the timing of the service inconvenient, since a family with few or no changes of clothing and linen could ill afford the week-long wait for the return of the laundry. Some feared mishandling of the belongings by the laundry staff. Others reacted to the invasion of privacy and disliked having strangers see their limited and ragged supplies. A number claimed it was less expensive to do the laundry at home.[83] Social Democratic propaganda in favor of the laundries suggested that workers' resistance could be overcome by education.

In a society where doing the laundry at home was a deep-rooted tradition, resistance was not surprising even in the face of persuasive practical arguments.[84] In 1920, Keppler asked various housing societies to find out whether their members preferred to have the laundry in or out of the house. All but Eigen Haard responded in favor of the laundry out of the house. The municipal laundry was reaching its maximum capacity and was slated to expand. But De Miranda, the Social Democratic alderman, wrote with concern that too many workers' wives were not taking advantage of the facilities, either because of shame, the expense, or the misguided belief in the impropriety of sending the wash out. People wanted the wash out of the house, but the collective system did not answer everyone's needs. It was not until 1925 that the municipality built the first laundromat that allowed the housewife to do her own wash, a solution that protected privacy, reduced expense, and eliminated turnaround. This semiprivate solution, like the public baths, took out of the home an activity inadequately served by contemporary dwelling standards.

Socialist convictions about the practicality of collective solutions hid an ideological commitment to such solutions. Workers dealing with their daily life problems were happy to embrace collective solutions when they were both practical and met their lifestyle requirements, but this was not always the case. Socialist disappointment in the failure of some workers to embrace collective solutions is apparent in the initial reactions to the proposal by Henri Polak to establish a housing society for the diamond workers' union. Polak began his campaign for a cooperative housing society in the pages of the ANDB's *Weekblad* in 1905. He described the beautiful, healthful, well-built, and well-organized houses the society could build to replace the cheap speculative housing in which most diamond workers resided. He suggested a plan for eighty families that might include, not only a collective garden, but collective laundry and bath. In calling for eighty participants, he was soliciting response from 1 percent of the ANDB's membership.[85] Only forty-one replied, most with some hesitation. Many expressed the desire to participate only if guaranteed a home independent of neighbors; others rejected the collective garden in favor of separate individual plots; still others refused to share stairs with other families. Polak criticized the respondents for their lack of community feeling and for their "narrow-minded individualism."[86]

Socialist leaders encountered resistance to their progressive ideas not unlike the resistance of workers to some of the changes in habit and design proposed by liberal housing reformers. The emancipatory project of the socialists could be fulfilled by two contradictory means, the attainment for workers of what had previously remained inaccessible across a class boundary or the manifestation of a new proletarian culture and rejection of bourgeois mores. The first represented *embourgeoisement;* the second suggested the possibility of redefining norms on new, utopian terms. It should, however, be emphasized that the domestic collectivism proposed by the Social Democrats was hardly radical. It was relatively conservative compared, for instance, to the more far-reaching proposals by their counterparts in the new Soviet Union. The Dutch Social Democrats accepted the nuclear family as the basic unit of housing design. Their proposals for shared facilities never implied a change in family structure. Nonetheless, many workers' families, even in the socialist ranks, aspired to middle-class domestic amenities rather than collective provisions.

For both socialists and confessionals, for those attracted to both modern and traditional images of the home, the small-scale low-rise alternative to the standard four-story urban perimeter block could express either the values of sovereignty or collectivity. Here the liberal reformers' functional plan could be lodged in a form that allayed fears of the evils of tenement dwelling held by reformers and workers alike. The low-rise satisfied the hankering for health, light, air, and greenery with the luxury of one's own street entrance creating the illusion of one's own detached villa. Workers and reformers both preferred the garden-apartment solution: each dwelling with its own front door, at most two families in one house, and no shared hall or stairs. Late-nineteenth-century reformers considered this the ideal and continued to work for this preference during the early twentieth century.[87]

Low-rise housing provided one way to increase the number of dwellings with street doors by discarding the urban housing pattern of a four-story perimeter block in favor of alternatives that would allow families to live "under their own roof," following the pattern prevalent in rural settings. Several housing societies of different political persuasions organized under the Housing Act with the specific intention of building this housing type. Zomers Buiten, founded in 1914 by socialist municipal workers, planned originally to build vacation resorts and later a garden city.[88] Ons Belang had its origins in the 1912 plans of a group of construction workers for a garden village.[89] Reformers like Tellegen, Keppler, and Hudig also played instrumental roles in encouraging housing societies to plan for low-rise projects. When Tellegen first met with the organizers of Amsterdam-Zuid in 1911, he presented them with the idea of building a garden village with recreational facilities, cooperative stores, and other features.[90] This plan had to be abandoned, but the Amsterdam housing reformers continued to push the idea. Eigen Haard began its construction with low-rise dwellings designed by Leliman in the Indischebuurt. The Algemeene's invitation to its founding meeting in March 1910 expressed the hope of building independent low-rise houses, and its first project, designed by Berlage in the Transvaalbuurt, included a row of low-rise units (fig. 5.8).[91] Hudig encouraged Patrimonium to follow the example of Eigen Haard and build low-rise housing types.[92] His writings on housing design extolled the virtues of the small-scale housing development.[93] Henri Polak promoted the garden village idea to the diamond workers, describing it as "broad curving lanes with large trees, individual houses surrounded by large gardens: here's a marvelous glimpse of Utopia."[94]

The municipality supported the attempt to bring low-rise housing to workers, although for the most part land near the center of the city could not be priced to allow it. The purchase of districts north of the IJ was seized as an opportunity to provide low-priced land suitable for small-scale development. In 1912, the council voted to restrict heights of buildings north of the IJ.[95] Eventually a series of low-rise projects appeared at the edge of Amsterdam's development: municipal projects in Watergraafsmeer, Buiksloterham, Nieuwendammerham, Nieuwendam, and Oostzaan put into

FIGURE 5.8 H. P. Berlage, Algemeene Woningbouw Vereeniging, Transvaalplein, 1913. Gemeentearchief Amsterdam, negative VH3454.

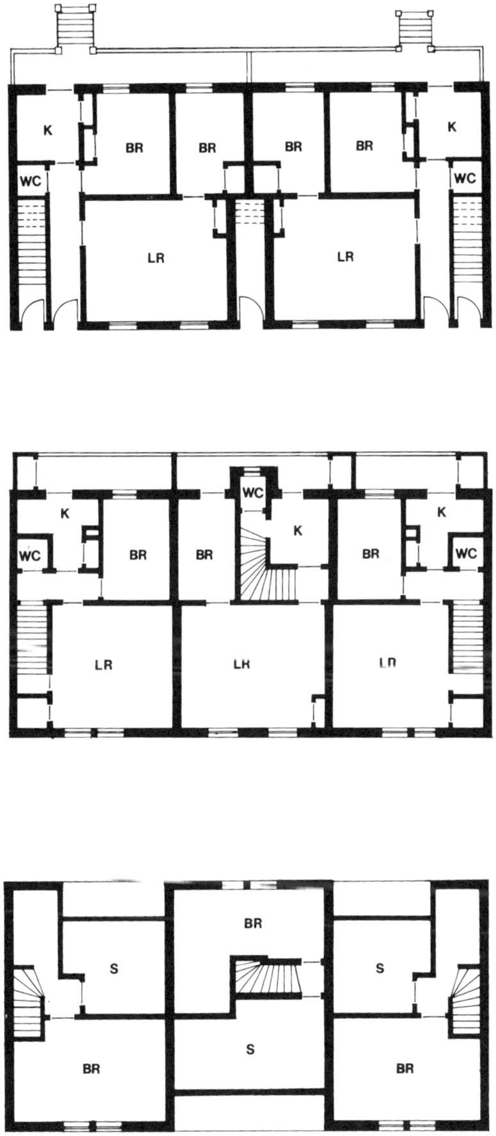

FIGURE 5.9 J. H. W. Leliman, Eigen Haard, Zeeburgerdijk, 1911: (A) ground floor, (B) first floor, (C) attic.

place by Keppler.[96] In the attempt to make low-rise housing affordable, a number of new housing types were invented that cleverly manipulated space. For instance, in Leliman's first project for Eigen Haard in the Indischebuurt, a standard five-dwelling unit was developed with two two-bedroom dwellings on the ground floor, and three three-bedroom dwellings occupying the second floor and attic. All five dwellings had direct, private access from the street (fig. 5.9).

The proportion of low-rise housing projects by the housing societies increased significantly during and after the war. More than a quarter of all the housing society dwellings approved between 1909 and 1919 were low-rise.[97] Both sides of the political spectrum supported it: the socialist-affiliated societies Eigen Haard and Algemeene particularly favored low-rise housing in their projects, and all four projects of the Catholic society Dr. Schaepman were two or three stories.[98]

On more expensive land, designs were applied with mixed housing of two, three, and four stories. Early projects by Leliman and Berlage for Eigen Haard and the Algemeene in the Indische and Transvaal districts introduced dwellings of varying heights adjacent to each other. Later, under Keppler's direction, an experiment was carried out in the Spaarndammerbuurt with an enclosed court design influenced by German and Dutch precedent, in which low-rise housing was surrounded by higher construction.[99] This planning idea was later applied to municipal housing in the Transvaalbuurt and Spaarndammerbuurt and was widely propagated in the execution of Berlage's plan for Amsterdam South.[100] The system created two kinds of public area. One, usually a street adjacent to standard four-story construction, demarcated the exterior of the block and might be pierced with bridged openings leading to the interior court. The second consisted of the interior of the block, which might or might not include a narrower, secondary road system, but usually provided collective open space dedicated either to a garden, playground, or schoolyard. With its perimeter of low-rise construction, protected by the wall of four-story construction on the outside, the interior courtyard became a symbolic village in the heart of the city. At Walenkamp's Zaanhof in the Spaarndammerbuurt, this rural connotation was underscored by the steeply roofed row houses that encircled a grass-filled common. At the same time, the courtyard could serve a myth of urban collectivity, as it did in the adjacent Polanenhof, a municipal project designed by De Bazel, where the interior wall of housing was built to the same four-story height as the exterior wall. This effect emphasized solidarity, particularly as the court itself was filled with the hard surface of a schoolyard rather than the green carpet of a garden as in the Zaanhof. The courtyard block was applied in many variations in Amsterdam, supplying imagery that served conservative evocations of quiet village life as well as collective urban fortifications aestheticizing proletarian solidarity.

It would be a mistake to conclude from the foregoing that the twin poles of the urban apartment and the suburban low-rise dwelling can be simply mapped on a political continuum from left to right. The small independent house in the garden village outside the dense city represented a rise in the standard of living supported enthusiastically by Social Democrats like Polak and Keppler as well as conservative confessionals. Several low-rise neighborhoods, notably Betondorp in Watergraafsmeer, became identified as Red neighborhoods,[101] while others, like Nieuwendammerham, were built up by a mixture of housing societies representing the full spectrum of Amsterdam's politics.

If the ethos of the small-scale neighborhood lent itself to various political interpretations, the large-scale housing block could also represent different images of urban living. The socialists, who saw it as an expression of collective experience, treated the entire block as a single aesthetic entity. Liberal reformers, who recognized the economic efficiency of large-scale housing projects but feared the moral disadvantages of barracks construction, encouraged the breakdown of the block into discrete units suggesting individual dwellings. Confessional housing societies such as Het Oosten or Patrimonium took advantage of large housing blocks to express group identity while providing as many front doors to individual dwellings as possible.

Although the large urban block remained the standard building practice in Amsterdam, there was a tendency toward an increase in the construction of low-rise projects after passage of the Housing Act. The number of projects of purely four-story housing declined markedly in the housing proposals from 1909 to 1919.[102] Three-story housing, particularly in Amsterdam South, grew in importance.[103] As a result of these developments, a greater number of dwellings were designed so that residents could enter their flats without contact with other inhabitants of the building. However, because of high land prices in Amsterdam, low-rise housing never replaced three- and four-story housing.

A range of ideologies was accommodated by the housing built in Amsterdam during the first decade of construction and planning under the Housing Act. The home as the province of the father-led family, the enlightened working-class family, the respectable family assuming the values of the middle-class reform effort were all encompassed within the normalized space of the rationalized reformers' model. Its neutrality vis-à-vis the image of the home permitted the subgroups within society to express their preferences without contradicting its essential aims. The flexibility of the reform model undoubtedly contributed to its resilience.

NORMALIZATION AND STANDARDIZATION

The reformers' specifications for the dwelling increasingly dominated the design and construction of housing projects sponsored under the Housing Act between 1909 and 1919. Of the projects that did not conform in one way or another, many did comply with reformers' requirements for separation of room functions. Only one-fourth of the units were constructed to permit a parlor.[104] After the war ended, no projects with either the kitchen–living room or the sleeping niche were approved.[105] Reformers had accepted the economic limitations that forced large working-class families into small flats and had tried to develop ways in which the family could lead what reformers considered a civilized existence within those confines. Since even the dwellings constructed under the Housing Act were limited in floor area, this meant that the reformers' goals were attained by sacrificing some of the ways workers had found to contend with their cramped space. A successful battle had been waged against both the travesties of the speculative builders' plans and workers' solutions to them.

The reformers' norms improved living conditions. By 1919, the housing societies that built under the auspices of the Housing Act had succeeded in raising housing standards beyond those of the nineteenth-century philanthropic societies. Inside the house there were more bedrooms, and the size of the units was larger.[106] The dwelling was hooked up to gas, electricity, running water, and had its own water closet.

Within the constraints of the reformers' model, there was ample room for variety in size, shape, and internal organization. The plan type was a form of normalization rather than standardization; that is, it called for compliance to a set of norms, not to a predetermined floor plan. Even with conformity to the requirements of the reformers, there was an increased variation in size and in floor plans in the housing projects. Not only was there a proliferation of floor plans reflecting the varying preferences and needs of the different housing societies, but within individual housing projects there was an increase in the variety of floor plans offered. Corner units and dwellings over openings into courtyards required further variations in floor plan. In some cases, such as the tendency of given societies to provide fewer or more bedrooms, we find variations compatible with reformers' requirements, merely reflecting different assessments of members' family size. In other cases, differentiations of plan type indicate ideological splits between the housing societies, whether emphasizing collectivity or self-containment. Some societies, such as the socialist societies Algemeene, Eigen Haard, or Rochdale, tended to embrace reformers' ideals like the new small kitchen. Others, such as the more conservative Bouwmaatschappij, Het Oosten, the railroad housing society HIJSM, and Patrimonium, preferred separate stair, separate door, a salon, and kitchen-living room.

This degree of variety, however, posed a problem in the postwar period when material shortages and a depressed economy led the national government to stress the need to cut costs, leading to a national discussion of standardization in housing construction. In Amsterdam, Keppler pursued an animated policy of experimentation with reorganization of the building trades, including construction of housing in concrete, which permitted hiring unskilled labor. Some reformers wished to push standardization as far as possible to decrease costs and increase productivity. In 1917, citing German and English opinion, Keppler wrote to Wibaut, "I will try as much as possible to apply standard housing types so that preparations can take place as quickly as possible."[107] In fact, only in the municipal housing projects of Amsterdam was much uniformity of housing type achieved. Between 1909 and 1919, the average number of different housing types in a single project increased, differentiated by number of bedrooms as well as by internal composition and arrangement of rooms. The reformers' model had been imposed, but within its confines a greater variety of response to families' needs had been introduced in Amsterdam than had been offered under the standardized repetitive plans of speculative housing or the housing of philanthropic societies.

The greatest pressure for standardization came from the national government. At a time of acute housing shortages in the aftermath of the First World War, the national government began encouraging private industry to reassert its dominance over housing production. In 1920, the achievements of publicly sponsored housing, particularly in Amsterdam, came under ministerial attack as excessively expensive and luxurious. In a meeting of the Health Board in April 1920, building inspector director H. van der Kaa accused the housing societies of building more expensively than private developers. Amsterdam had to defend the housing it had been so carefully nurturing against accusations that the private sector could build just as well and more cheaply.

Two reports from 1920 attested favorably to the standards achieved by housing societies in comparison to private developers. Explaining the higher cost per square meter of housing society dwellings, Keppler pointed out the many ways in which private builders failed to meet the demands for quality placed on housing societies, noting that private builders had only to meet the requirements of the 1905 building ordinance, while housing societies had to meet requirements set by the Health Board, Housing Authority, and the state housing inspector. Keppler pointed to the various corners cut by the private builder: using the cheapest bricks, poor carpentry, low or no attic, minimal balconies. Against this, the Health Board required that housing societies build living rooms at least four meters wide and connect attic bedrooms with the third floor by a separate stair. The Housing Authority also required materials and workmanship of high quality.[108] In a separate report, the Health Board made arguments similar to Keppler's. In many details, the housing societies adhered to higher construction standards: more and deeper closets, more painted doors, more gardens, higher and stronger roofs, sturdier balconies, better interior doors, and higher-quality finish to windowsills.[109]

Reactions both in defense of the housing societies and in support of Van der Kaa's accusations appeared in major newspapers and journals. At the national level, ministerial steps began to cut into the relative municipal independence that had characterized the first ten years of housing society construction. A series of ministerial circulars attempted to rein in costs by imposing rigid standards for Housing Act loans. At the same time, the government proposed subsidies to the private construction industry.[110]

One by one, the circulars began to designate new national norms for workers' housing. The circular of 30 July 1920 attempted to regulate the relationship between the spatial area of dwellings and the percentage costs to be covered by rent, with a maximum allowable volume of 300 cubic meters. The circular also underscored the necessity for the greatest sobriety possible in housing types. The minister of labor announced plans to present municipalities with a collection of standard housing types as a basis for further construction.[111]

Although reaction against the circulars was widespread, both among the reformers in the National Housing Council and in Catholic, Protestant, and socialist workers' circles, the objections focused on the lowering of the housing standard, not on the imposition of norms from above. In 1919, Dirk Hudig himself had proposed that a general minimum housing standard be set nationally, as in England.[112] But attempts to execute such an idea stirred up controversy. In 1918, at the yearly convention of the National Housing Council, Jan van der Waerden proposed the standardization of housing plans, provoking dramatic resistance from architects, housing society officials, and workers, many of whom protested that nationally imposed standards would not accommodate local and regional customs and building traditions.[113] In 1921, when the government published an album of fifty housing types, consisting of sketch plans for countryside, village, town, and city, the press and professionals again reacted strenuously against it.[114] The degree of normalization that had been imposed at the local level in Amsterdam had permitted flexibility and change. Widespread reaction against standardization only emerged when it threatened to be introduced at the national level; architects were particularly concerned that the publication of standard plans, which the government claimed were intended to assist rural communities without adequate professional resources, would act counterproductively to discourage communities from seeking architectural assistance.

The concept of standardization arose out of an awareness of the power of the machine; it promised the benefits of mass production. The technical problem of applying methods of mass production to the building industry to foster cheaper, faster construction of housing must, however, be clearly distinguished from the essentially social problem of normalization applied to housing design. Normalization entailed regularizing design according to norms resulting from the kinds of complex interactions described in chapter 3. Housing produced under the Housing Act was subject to normalization by virtue of its location in the public arena; through public debate, officials and experts generated specifications of the normal dwelling. Normalization was a solution to the problem of defining societal values. Standardization, on the other hand, offered the advantages of efficiency to housing production; it was a technical solution to the problem of limited resources.

Between 1909 and 1919, Amsterdam worked out its own system of housing norms. Housing reformers in positions of authority in civil service and on government advisory boards took the lead in establishing local norms and in setting limits on the permissible degree of deviation. The setting of norms by reformers occurred primarily in reaction to the slum conditions of the old city and the speculative housing of the new districts, but it also reflected the discrepancies between the reformers' vision of appropriate worker adjustment to modern urban life and the workers' own accommodations to modernity. The emergent norms were the result of complex political and cultural interaction at the local level, although couched in the official language of the expert.

When national housing policy shifted, there was an inevitable clash between national requirements and the local standards that had emerged during a period of negotiation between the interested parties.

In Amsterdam, reformers had set out to replace the inadequate housing produced by the free market. As they applied their expertise in the development of improved housing types, another battle line was drawn between the coping methods developed by workers to make a decent life for themselves in reduced circumstances and the new vision of appropriate urban housing pushed by the reformers, a battle viewed by reformers as a conflict between the forces of conservatism and those of progress and modernity. Raising living standards by setting higher norms for housing design undoubtedly contributed to the emancipation of the Dutch working class, along with the other hard-won guarantees of greater financial security provided by new social legislation. Such norms, although draped in the ideology of rationalism and neutrality, represented the values of urban order, civility, and modernity held by the experts, bureaucrats, and politicians who contributed to their construction. To the extent that these values did not reflect those of the inhabitants, to the extent that those inhabitants did not participate in the deliberations that produced housing norms, normalization imposed control as well as fostering emancipation.

Able to influence the design process through the institutions of housing expertise both within and outside the municipal government, the social engineers had effectively waged the battle for their modern model of civilized urban housing against the evils of speculative housing and the misjudgments of workers. However, their influence stopped short of imposing standardized plan types, so that within the constraints of the normalized plan there was room for plural views of the house. The floor plan of the dwelling could be harnessed by the housing societies to express their own values in addition to those of the reform movement. In this way, the housing societies gained an influence over the living environment that previously had never been exercised for residents of mass housing. Whereas the control of the speculative builder over housing decisions had been complete, leaving dwellers whose market power was minimal without any choice or input in the design of housing, the control exercised by housing reformers and the municipal government allowed for some interpretation of the hopes and desires of various groups in society.

Nevertheless, the housing societies proved to be more effective as vehicles for the urban reform agenda and sectarian interests than as instruments of lay participation. Housing societies reflected the ideals of home and community current among their members or organizers, articulating both class and traditional resistance to the anonymity of the rationalist model. Anticapitalist reaction from the left and from the right found room under the umbrella of liberalism's own correctives against the excesses of laissez-faire development. The substitute housing market through which the normalizing efforts of the progressive reform movement were carried out provided a vehicle for the expression of both sovereignty and collectivism in housing. But these ideals never gained the general force of social norms. The Social Democrats of Amsterdam, for instance, were never able to impose a citywide culture of collective domesticity as occurred in Frankfurt and Vienna in the 1920s. The only successful normalization was the use of the plan as a tool against the commodification of the dwelling, the counterpoint of social rationality against the rationalized space of real estate. The reform model shared with real estate the instrumentality of the plan, now functionalized in the campaign to improve living standards. This application of the dry logic of social hygiene provided a viewpoint distinct from the exploration of the image, vision, or myth of the home. That problematic was tackled in another discourse: the normalization of aesthetics.

PART THREE

CONTROLLING URBAN AESTHETICS

The liberal position on the relationship of government to the arts was established in the Netherlands in the 1860s by the framer of the Dutch constitution, J. R. Thorbecke, who insisted that art was not the business of government, that government should not act as judge or authority vis-à-vis art.[1] His position should not be misinterpreted as one of cultural indifference; he specified a number of ways government could foster development of the arts. But the economic laissez-faire model of the liberals, when applied to the arts, translated into the belief that the best way to foster artistic achievement was to leave the autonomous development of art to free competition among artists. Official art was to be avoided at all costs.

As Amsterdam's urban growth accelerated in the last decades of the nineteenth century, few of its politicians viewed urban aesthetics in the same light as hygiene, that is, as an aspect of the public realm to be regulated according to public standards. Unlike their counterparts in cities like Vienna or Paris, Amsterdam's bourgeoisie had failed to develop a strong monumental art that lent identity to the city and defined their social aspirations. In the absence of an urban iconography dedicated to the social ascendancy of the Amsterdam liberals, their mark on the city was associated with the monotonous and tasteless construction of the city's residential and commercial expansion. The liberal supporters of unobstructed real estate development, who dominated the city council, valued the midcentury doctrine of governmental abstention from aesthetic judgment, which unintentionally ordained their relative indifference toward urban aesthetics. As late as 1890, an Amsterdam council member who was arguing against approval of a developer's plan emphasized that his objections were not aesthetic. True, he considered the whole plan to be ugly, but the plan's aesthetics were the developer's business and the municipality had no right to demand beauty.[2] His logic reflected the liberal commitment to the inviolability of individual property rights, rights that might be infringed upon only if public safety were threatened.

But the definition of public safety was expanding in the period of progressive corrections to laissez-faire policy, supplanted by a concept of public welfare that incorporated many areas previously left to private discretion. Among those, the design of the urban environment was increasingly considered to deserve public scrutiny. It followed that public interest could justify government measures to protect urban aesthetics and amenities. While the public had no right to insist that all construction be beautiful, ran the new argument, the municipality could at least prevent ugliness. Reflecting the changing winds, in 1891 another Amsterdam councilor objecting to a developer's proposals reasoned that "the public way serves not only those living along it, but the entire city, and the municipality must not give permission to something that is in conflict with the universal laws of beauty."[3] Once the city's aesthetics were acknowledged as part of the public interest, the rights and freedoms of the individual could occasionally be curtailed in order to protect the common good, as they might be when public standards of sanitation and health were applied.[4]

Far from radical, the cause of civic art, that is, the promotion of urban aesthetics by means of planning and preservation, won broad political consensus.[5] As the century ended, awareness of Amsterdam's seventeenth-century architectural and planning heritage grew keener, its beauties observed all the more clearly in contrast with the recent eyesores resulting from rapid urban growth. Two problems emerged: the protection of the city's architectural heritage from demolition, alteration, or blight and the fostering of suitable new construction. The era when all proposals for development could be approved without questioning their impact on the visual character of the city had ended. But just as the government's increased intervention to maintain hygienic standards was accompanied by controversy over the setting of those norms, so too the degree and nature of aesthetic intervention became a matter of debate.

To maintain the liberal tenet of government impartiality, any limitations to be imposed on property owners could be justified only by assuming the existence of a public consensus about the standards of urban beauty. Liberal aesthetic policy adhered to several principles. First, it was assumed that beauty could be defined by "universal laws" as unassailable as natural laws. Next, both the fairness and objectivity of aesthetic judgments endorsed by government in the public interest were to be guaranteed by eliciting the advice of acknowledged experts acting without self-interest. Favoritism toward particular designers or authorization of a particular style would undermine impartiality and was to be avoided.

These tenets encompassed the two Dutch strategies for contending with potential conflict, whether doctrinal, political, or aesthetic: first, the legitimacy of authorized expertise; second, the fair representation of all parties. The conception of fairness in aesthetic judgment assumed that a line could be drawn by any aesthetic expert between what was and was not competent, without reference to taste or the contemporary context of artistic debate. Like the assumption that society might be cured of its ills by social hygienists or that a science of society could be objectively plied by social engineers, the liberal requirement of impartiality in matters of public aesthetic debate reveals the assumption that rationality is a sufficient basis for the arbitration of issues in the public realm. It reveals a willful blindness to the social connotations and political loading inherent in the exercise of public aesthetic judgments.

What made this position tenable was widespread agreement about what was ugly in Amsterdam's new construction and a growing appreciation for the beauty of its urban heritage. There was general consensus that the monotonous straight rows of housing filling the Kalff plan of 1877 were dreary and lifeless, and that the intervention of public authority was essential to prevent the continuation of similar urban desecration. The meetings of the municipal council during the first decade of the twentieth century record a steady stream of objections to unaesthetic urban planning emanating from all segments of the political continuum. Social Democrats and Anti-Revolutionaries took up the cudgels in defense of Amsterdam's urban beauty as often as the old Liberals. For the first time, council members attacked plans that proposed to fill in picturesque canals in order to create broad streets that would alleviate traffic congestion, a measure previously adopted with little objection. They objected to construction of massive buildings out of proportion with a building scale more characteristic of Amsterdam's past, and they called for better neighborhood design, for parks and greenery, and for the preservation of historic buildings.

The grounds for this consensus on civic beauty lay in a rejection of the late-nineteenth-century developments and a call to equal the aesthetic achievements of Amsterdam's heyday in the seventeenth century. However, there was little agreement among politicians about contemporary architects' responses to that call. Architects had divided into warring camps, espousing the historicist re-creation of the past on the one hand, the search for modern expression on the other. Although both political conservatives and progressives shared a distaste for the gray districts of the Pijp, the Dapperbuurt, the Kinkerbuurt, and the Staatsliedenbuurt, they were not direct participants in contemporary architectural debate. The heated polemics of aesthetic modernists and historicists were carried out within the societies and journals of the architectural profession. The evocation of the past by re-creating the styles of the Dutch Renaissance had been challenged by a generation of architects seeking to express modernity through a variety of new forms. Architects like H. P. Berlage, Willem Kromhout, K. P. C. de Bazel, and J. L. M. Lauweriks were pursuing fresh lines of exploration at the turn of the century, and their varied work, along with the parallel explorations of modernism in other countries, created an atmosphere of fierce partisan dissention among architects.

The general desire to correct the infelicities of Amsterdam's late-nineteenth-century growth provided the motivation to include urban aesthetics in the package of reforms embraced at the turn of the century. Urban reform came to encompass the visual order of the city as well as its social and sanitary order. The correction of the aesthetic disorder introduced by rampant development joined the other causes taken up by reformers in the general movement to correct the ills resulting from capitalist expansion. Urban aesthetics, like hygiene, became subject to the campaign to regulate aspects of everyday life according to public standards. Unlike hygiene, however, the control of urban aesthetics raised no issues of public safety and was never considered as an extension of police powers. It was, however, subject to a clearly delineated area of expertise, one in which the professional authority of the architect was unchallenged.

Yet despite that clear-cut authority, norms were no more easy to define in the case of urban aesthetics than hygiene. The subjective character of taste as it might be freely exercised by any individual made the authority of the expert even more questionable than in the case of social hygiene and made the relationship between expert and layperson more problematic. Furthermore, the partisan character of architectural criticism, all the more obvious in an era of stylistic conflicts, undermined the credibility of the experts' judgments. If the experts could not come to any agreement among themselves, what right did they have to impose any decisions on the community?

Still more important for the future control of public aesthetics in Amsterdam was its function as ideological expression, a function obscured by the liberal interpretation of urban aesthetics as an aspect of the public good amenable to objective, politically fair, and neutral treatment. Unlike hygiene, which might appear to be a technical problem despite its actual involvement in constructing the image of the home, the public regulation of urban aesthetics openly and unavoidably posed the problem of constructing the image of the city. Urban aesthetics was constitutively engaged in the problematics of representation. It was impossible to avoid the issue of who should determine the urban image. Control of urban aesthetics thus raised questions regarding the architect's role in public service and the nature of architectural patronage in a democracy.

The failure of the liberal policy of impartiality to acknowledge that the construction of meaning was at stake in the control of urban aesthetics meant that these issues were at first obscured. But as we shall see in this and the following two chapters, the advent of the public surveillance of urban aesthetics opened a realm in which professional, political, and class interests contested the right to define the representation of the city. Like hygienic reform, aesthetic reform could be embraced by those who wished to preserve the current social system as well as by those interested in dismantling it. The visual provided another means through which to define urban order and thus also opened another arena in which a struggle for control of that definition might take place.

In 1902, responding to a debate on the kind of aesthetic expertise most appropriate to the city of Amsterdam, P. L. Tak replied, "The only question worth addressing is how we can get the best for Amsterdam."[6] Not everyone agreed that getting the best was a mission of the government, and even among those who did, there was little agreement on what constituted the best. The seemingly rational goal of achieving the best for Amsterdam presumed an agreement on the criteria for aesthetic judgment that was to prove elusive in a period of stylistic strife and within a community torn by ideological divisions.

DESIGN IN THE PUBLIC SECTOR

During the nineteenth century, major public buildings in Amsterdam were designed by the city architect and major urban plans by engineers of the Public Works Department. These police stations, schools, hospitals, and other civic structures were generally characterized by an eclectic and uninspired historicism that favored the Dutch Renaissance. In 1895, the municipal museum was completed by A. W. Weissman, the city architect. Although praised for its functional arrangement of exhibition rooms, and particularly for its lighting, the traditional brick and sandstone exterior was heavily criticized in progressive cultural circles.[7] The museum proved to be Weissman's last major work as city architect and with his departure, Amsterdam abolished the time-honored office of municipal architect and placed the city's building department under the director of public works, a civil engineer, against the protests of the local architectural society.[8] Public discussion about the merits and demerits of appointing a new city architect ensued. While some imagined that a contemporary city architect might attain the architectural heights achieved by Hendrick de Keyser in Amsterdam's golden age,[9] the mayor and aldermen took another view. Arguing that appointment of an individual as city architect would necessarily lead to charges of favoritism, since architects can never agree among themselves on matters of taste, they rejected all proposals for reinstating the office. In so doing, they also avoided making an appointment that would have forced them to take an official position for or against tradition or modernity.[10]

Unofficially, many considered H. P. Berlage to be assuming the role of a contemporary Hendrick de Keyser. In 1896, after a long and controversial series of events, Berlage was appointed by the city to be designer of the new stock exchange building. In 1900, he was selected to replace C. L. M. Lambrechtsen van Ritthem, then director of public works, as the designer of the major southern extension of Amsterdam. Thus

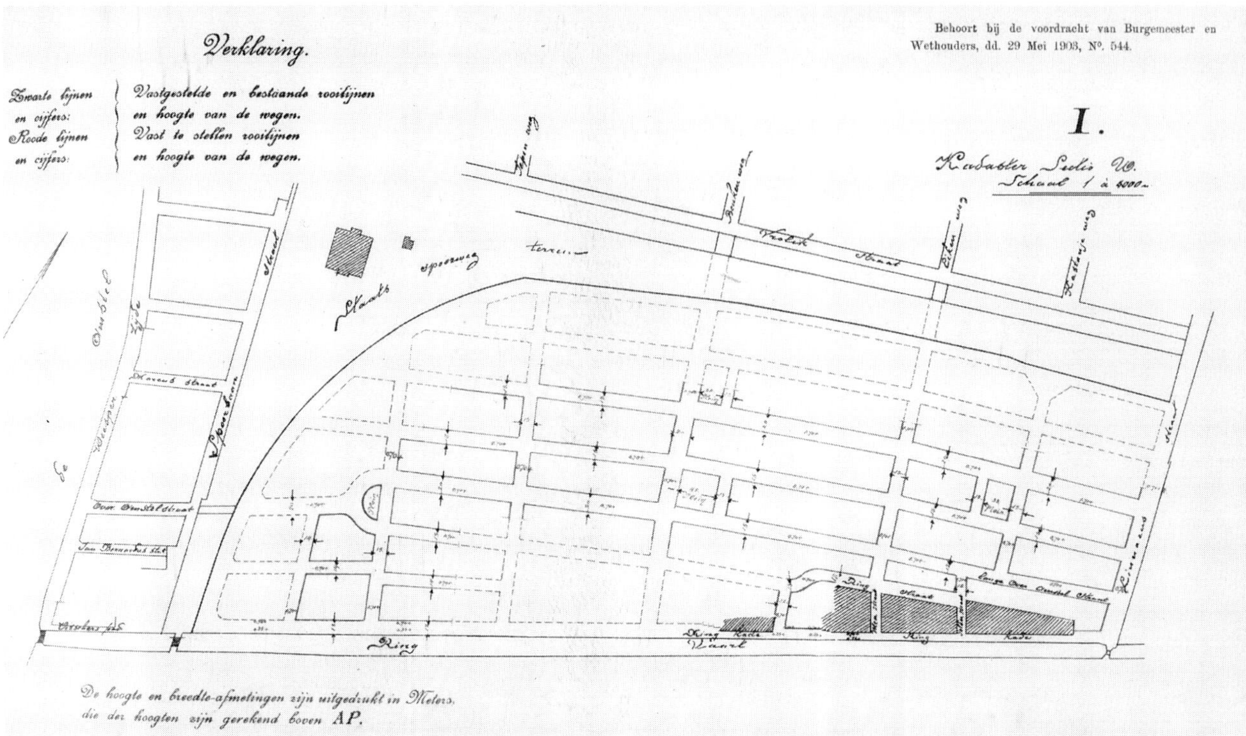

FIGURE 6.1
Plan for Transvaalbuurt, 1903. Gemeentearchief Amsterdam *Gemeenteblad* (1903), 1e Afd., proposal 544, 453–53

the two most important public design commissions in Amsterdam at the turn of the century, one for building, the other for planning, were placed in the hands of one of the most progressive figures of Dutch architecture.[11]

Berlage's appointment to design the southern extension of the city came after the plan proposed by Lambrechtsen had been rejected by the council on aesthetic grounds. Lambrechtsen had proposed to continue extension of the city in concentric rings cut by straight radial streets. This was castigated in the council as a repetition of the poor urban design of the nineteenth century, as an engineer's plan, as the product of ruler and drafting board.[12] These criticisms had become common parlance in part through Berlage's own role in popularizing Sitte's objections to the cold rationalism of the visual order created by real estate development and its erasure of any sense of place.

The rejection came amid accusations that the civil engineers of the Public Works Department were aesthetically incompetent. During the years in which execution of Berlage's southern extension plan was repeatedly delayed, a number of smaller neighborhoods were designed at the edges of the city. Time after time, the experience with the Lambrechtsen plan was repeated. The council rejected plans on aesthetic grounds, and Berlage was called in several times as an outside expert. In the first instance, a small corner of land by the Cellular Jail was redesigned by Berlage, after complaints that Public Works had mishandled the design. Another time he was called in at the

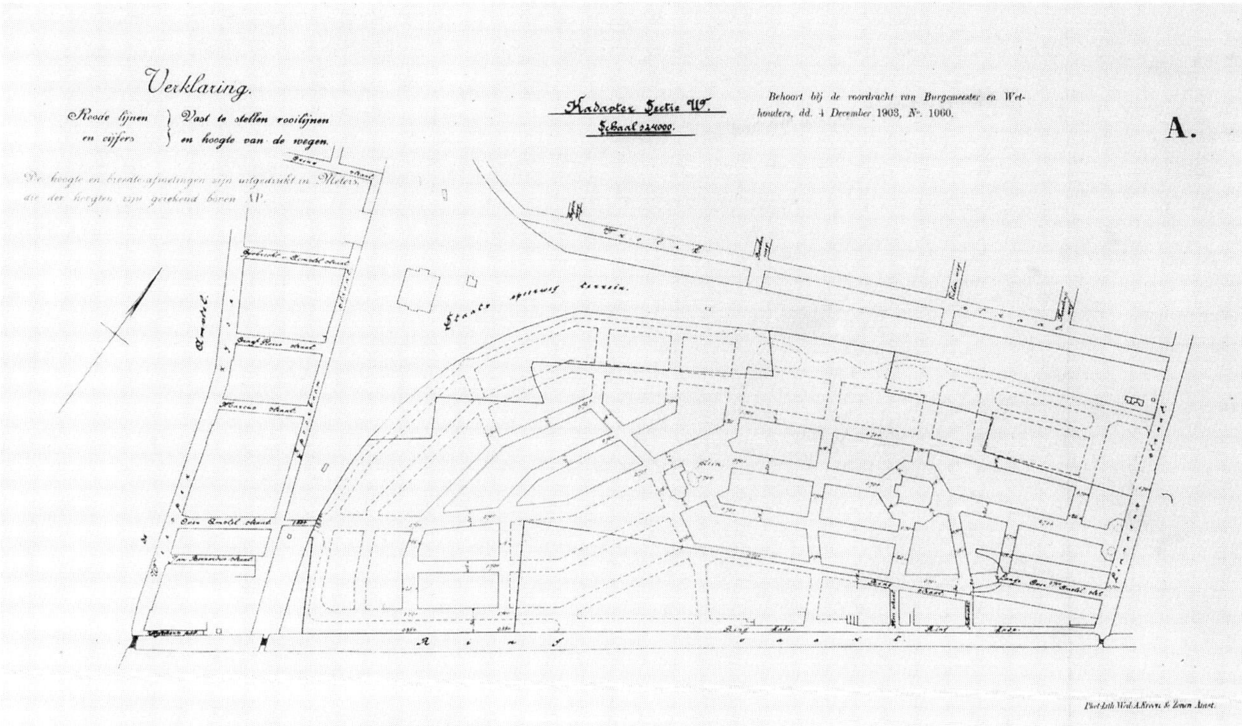

behest of right- and left-wing councilors to redesign a developer's plan for an entire neighborhood, the Transvaalbuurt. This neighborhood was laid out in an east-west grid without distinguishing features or differentiation between the streets. The Health Board claimed such monotony would have an adverse psychological impact on the inhabitants (fig. 6.1).[13] In the municipal council, Social Democrat Henri Polak decried the long narrow straight streets already so common in the new districts.[14] The tirade of an Anti-Revolutionary member typifies the attitude of the dissatisfied council:

FIGURE 6.2 H. P. Berlage, plan for Transvaalbuurt, 1903. Netherlands Architecture Institute, Berlage archive, negative 713.

> There can be no question of approving this plan in its current form. Not a moment's consideration should be given to building in this way. What is this plan? A few lines drawn horizontally and a few drawn vertically; that's the linear system. There can never be any question of allowing such a plan here, because we have far too much of the like already. Much of the new city has been spoiled and blighted by building in this way; no one disputes that construction has been carried out in a terribly ugly way.[15]

Berlage, brought in when the plan was rejected, designed a Sittesque plan with a wide main street bisecting the district, twisting angularly through the center of the neighborhood, and opening at two points onto squares designated for public buildings (fig. 6.2).[16]

Other outcries in the Amsterdam City Council against unaesthetic grid planning followed.[17] The last legacy of nineteenth-century planning was the 1911 design for completion of the Spaarndammer district, a harborside neighborhood in northwest Amsterdam. The original layout of this workers' district had been established in 1885 as long concentric curving blocks (fig. 6.3).[18] In 1911, the Public Works Department prepared a revised plan for the as yet unbuilt portion of the neighborhood (fig. 6.4).[19] Although it was a marked improvement over the first plan, including both a green square and a playground, the revision fell prey to the same complaints left- and right-wing politicians had been levying against the products of the Public Works drafting tables, "from that bureaucratic type who can draw straight lines so well."[20] Social Democrat F. M. Wibaut complained that the plan could have been designed by a mediocre draftsman with a ruler, whereas it should have been designed by someone expert in the field of city planning.[21] Interestingly, the Amsterdam Health Board also objected to the Public Works plan, but on the grounds that it did not meet hygienic norms. A subcommittee consisting of H. P. Berlage, Louise van der Pek-Went and J. T. J. Cuypers presented a sketch plan to indicate the nature of the Health Board's objections to the orientation and width of the housing blocks (fig. 6.5). They wanted the blocks to have a north-south orientation so that dwellings on both sides of the street would receive adequate sunshine; they suggested shallower blocks of thirty-three meters to encourage low-rise building and narrower streets for a domestic scale. The result, intended merely as an indication of the hygienic requirements and not as an aesthetic solution, was as much a grid as the most castigated "ruler-and-pen" plans.[22]

The controversy over the competence of Public Works designers was fueled by the claim of the alderman of public works that the Spaarndammer plan had indeed been designed in consultation with an expert in the field of city planning, J. M. van der Mey.[23] In 1910, the Public Works Department had hired Van der Mey, a brilliant young architect who had already won two major prizes, the Prix de Rome and the competition for the redesign of Dam Square in Amsterdam. Van der Mey's title at Public Works was aesthetic adviser; he worked part time in the department from 1911 to 1919, designing a bridge, a number of municipal building facades, and several neighborhood plans.[24] His appointment drew a mixed response of skepticism and applause. A right-wing architect and city councilor objected to Van der Mey's youth and lack of experience, though Van der Mey's adherence to a distinctly modern aesthetic style undoubtedly influenced his opinion.[25] Van der Mey proved to be the first of a series of gifted architects to join Public Works in a bid by the department to overcome its poor design reputation. His appointment signaled the department's response to criticism, its first break with the engineer's planning of the nineteenth century, and its first engagement of a designer involved in contemporary architectural discourse.

In 1913, Van der Mey prepared a plan directly at odds with the so-called engineer's approach. Developers had submitted a plan in 1912 for the southern half of the Indische district, where the long curving street in the older, northern half had already been

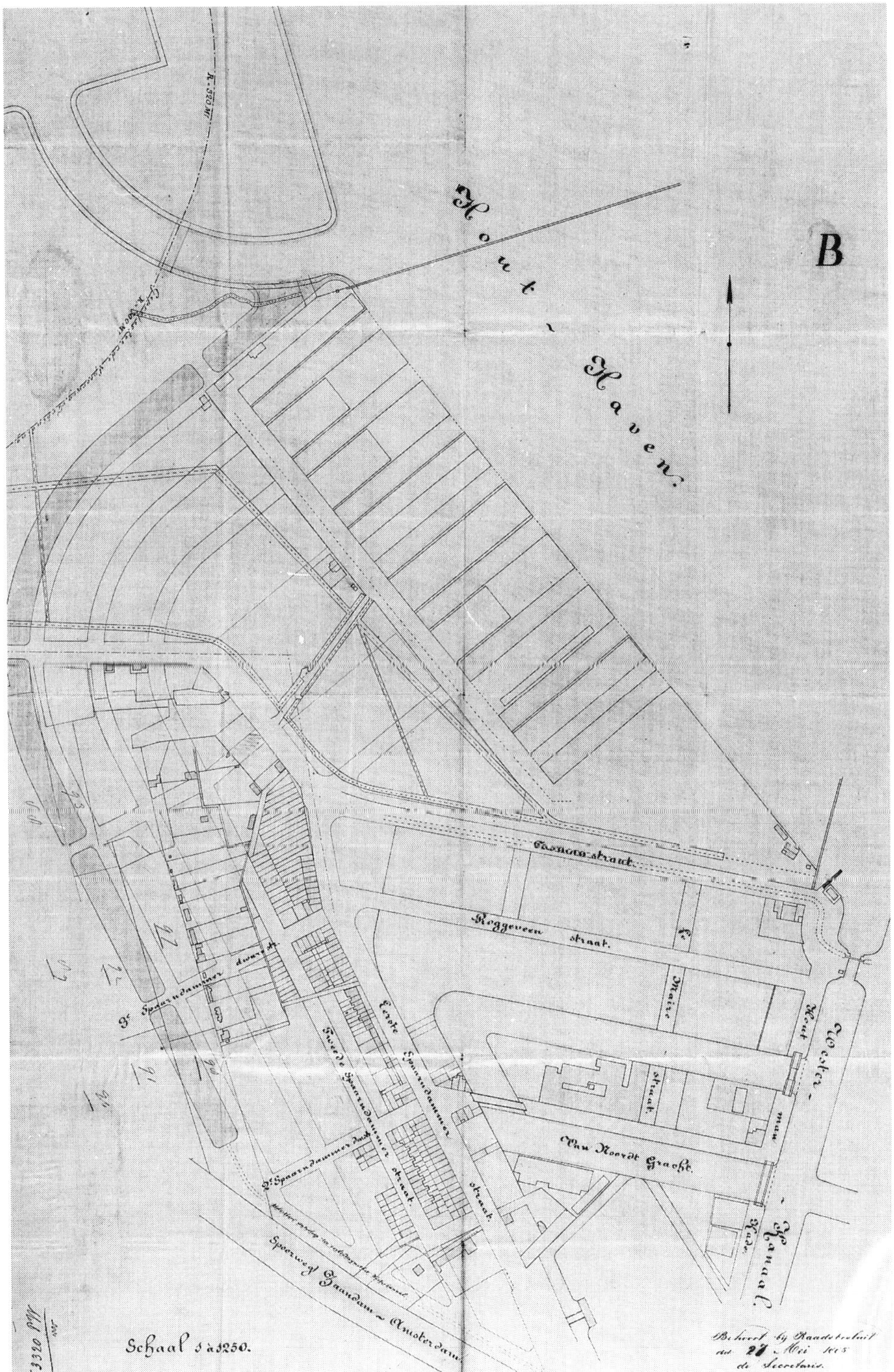

FIGURE 6.3 Plan for Spaarndammerbuurt, 1885. Gemeentearchief Amsterdam, archive 5180, 3320 PW 1885.

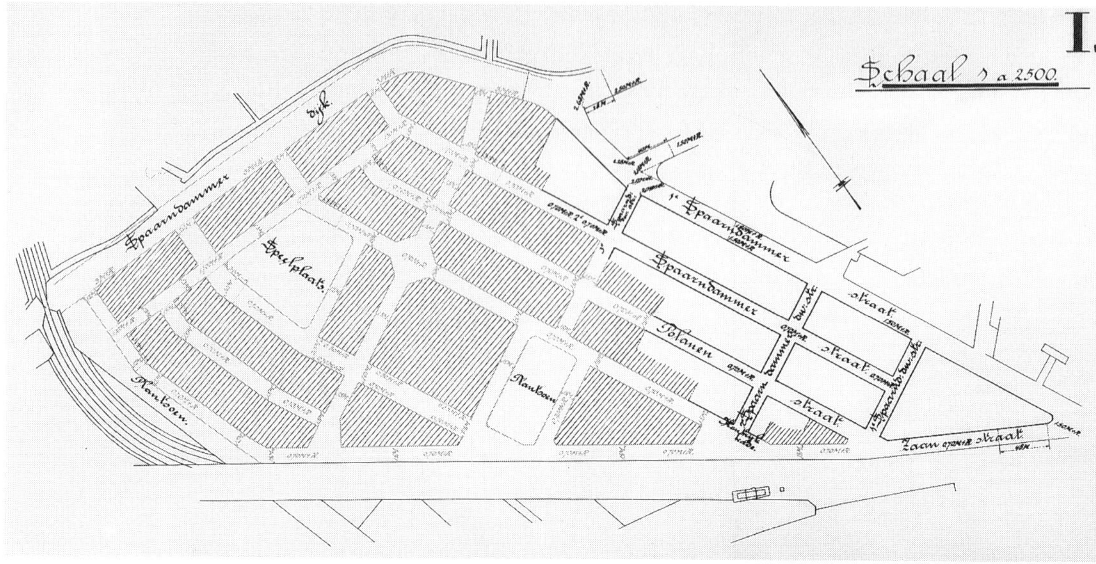

FIGURE 6.4 Public Works plan for Spaarndammerbuurt, 1911. Gemeentearchief Amsterdam, archive 5180, 8794 PW1912.

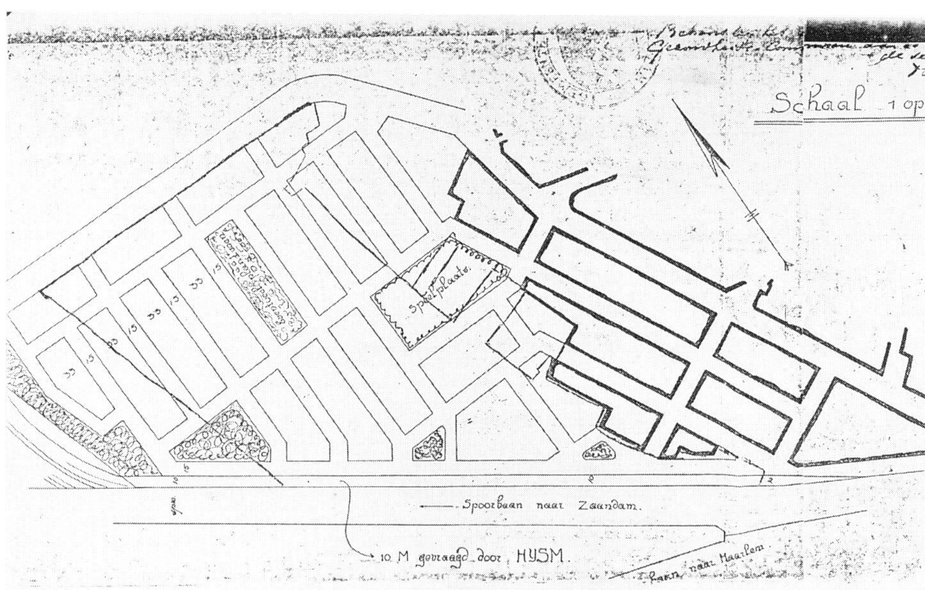

FIGURE 6.5 J. T. J. Cuypers (Health Board), plan for Spaarndammerbuurt, 25 November 1912. Gemeente-archief Amsterdam, 450 GC 1912.

the subject of council criticism (fig. 6.6).[26] The proposed plan repeated the monotonous narrow blocks of the northern half, and in accordance with the municipal council's newfound aversion to such arrangements, the developers were encouraged to find a more competent designer. They turned to the engineer J. G. van Niftrik, but his design raised objections from the Health Board, which insisted on a north-south orientation for the housing blocks.[27] Even after Van Niftrik revised his plan (fig. 6.7), the city took it upon itself to provide the developer with a plan designed by an "urban design expert," that is, a designer of the new stamp. There were several competing proposals for selecting an expert. Wibaut suggested a design competition, the Public Works alderman nominated Berlage, and the Building and Housing Inspection Office submitted its own design. This controversy over the selection of a designer for the Indischebuurt indicates the persistent confusion about what constituted the appropriate guarantee of aesthetic competency for public design. In the end, Public Works' in-house aesthetic adviser Van der Mey was appointed to redesign the area in 1913.[28]

Van der Mey's solution divided the area into two sections, organized symmetrically along a north-south axis in the western half and an east-west axis in the eastern half (fig. 6.8). The axiality suggested classical symmetry more than Sittesque irregularity. The plan not only satisfied the hygienic requirements for preferred orientation of the housing, but also created a main avenue, separate residential streets, and neighborhood focal points. It was a distinct improvement over the plans proposed by the developers.[29]

Van der Mey, however, was pessimistic about the execution of his plan, anticipating the likelihood that the blocks would be filled with incompetently designed housing. As "oases in the mostly dreary blocks," Van der Mey proposed well-designed public buildings such as schools, police stations, and fire stations. He explained that he had tried to "design an arrangement of blocks that would guarantee as reasonable a complex as possible, given that plans exert little influence when building commissions are in the hands of the aesthetically inept."[30] Here he was referring to the poor quality of the housing blocks erected by developers and the disappointing design of public buildings.

With its hiring of Berlage and Van der Mey, the city of Amsterdam endorsed the contemporary critique of the gridiron plan and threw off the nineteenth-century legacy of unaesthetic planning. But it soon discovered that this was not enough to secure an attractive cityscape. To achieve beauty in its urban expansions and complete the aesthetic reform program against laissez-faire planning, it would have to contend with the design of the buildings as well as the plans. Here there were few guidelines for aesthetic public policy. If a city architect was not to fulfill public commissions, who should? What methods offered the greatest likelihood of yielding good and fair results: design competitions, the appointment of an architect? And what kind of public control was appropriate over buildings erected in the private sector? These questions were discussed repeatedly in the first decades of the twentieth century.

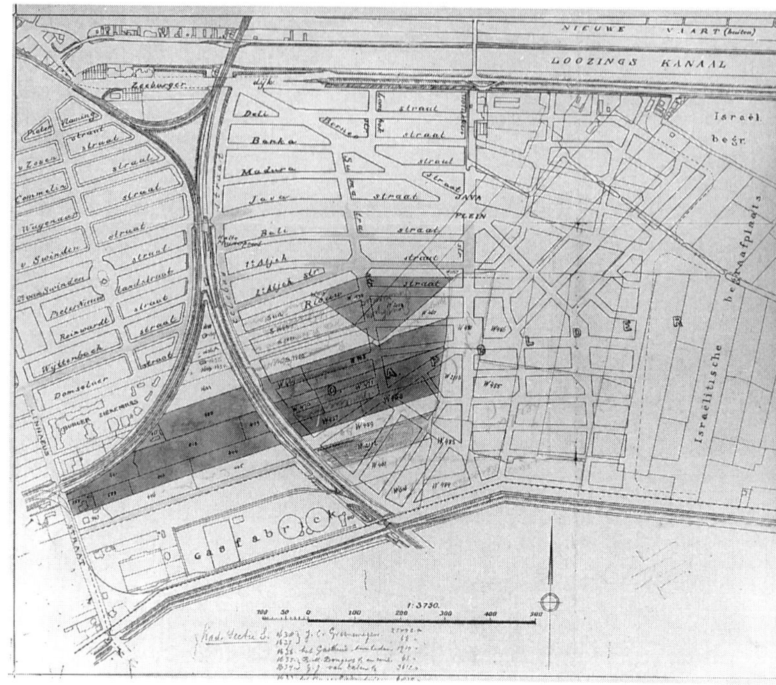

FIGURE 6.6 Maatschappij voor Grondbezit en Grondcrediet et al., plan for Indischebuurt, 1912. Gemeentearchief Amsterdam, archive 5180–2197, 1504 PW 1912.

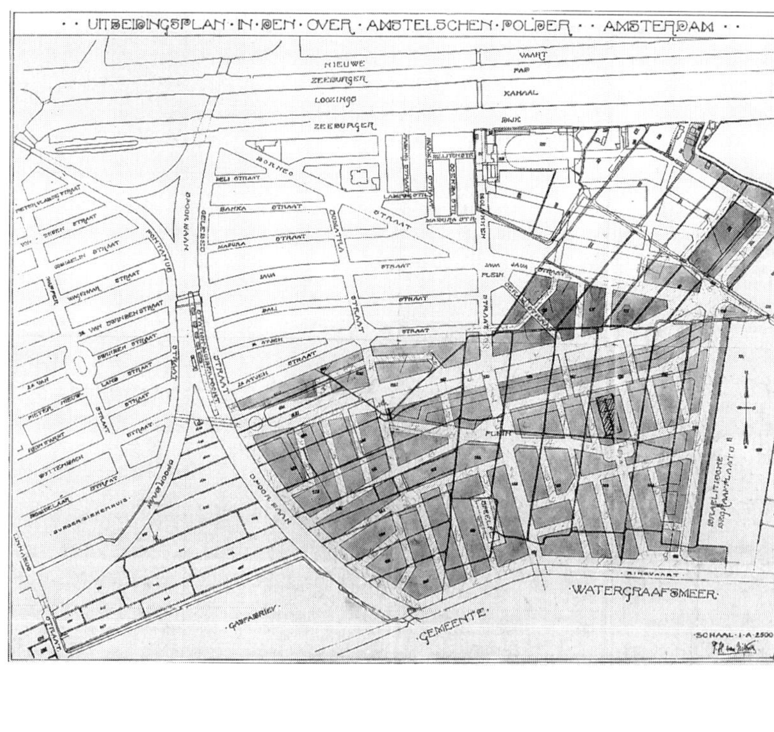

FIGURE 6.7 J. G. van Niftrik, plan for Indischebuurt, 1912. Gemeentearchief Amsterdam, archive 5213–501, Dienst PW 2456/1916, drawing 7.

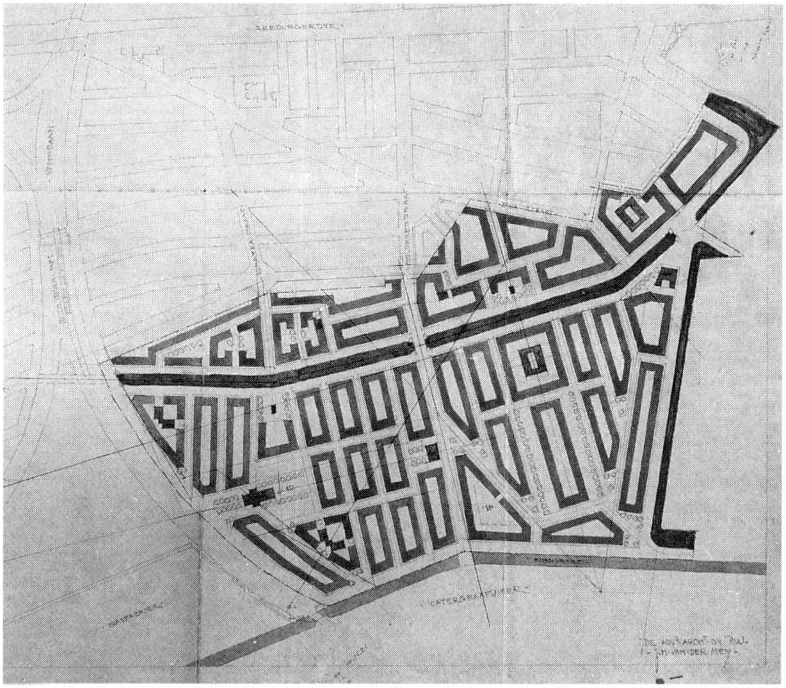

FIGURE 6.8 J. M. van der May, plan for Indischebuurt, 1913. Gemeentearchief Amsterdam, archive 5213-501, Dienst PW 2456/1916, drawing 22.

THE COMMITTEE OF AESTHETICS

The concerns Van der Mey expressed about the Indischebuurt echoed those of the municipal council itself. The council had repeatedly complained about the tasteless construction that spoiled the aesthetic potential of even the best plans. To remedy the situation, the government had searched for ways to encourage tasteful design, for instance, competitions for the best facade on a newly constructed street, a method introduced from Germany that had not proved fruitful.[31] In the 1890s, architects began to discuss the feasibility of architectural review boards. At a meeting of the Genootschap Architectura et Amicitia in April 1896, the establishment of an advisory committee of architectural experts was proposed. In 1897, the proposal was endorsed by both of the local architectural societies in petitions to the municipality. By May, the municipality had agreed to the formation of a committee to review designs proposed for the luxury district behind the Rijksmuseum. The committee was composed of six members, five of whom were appointed by the architectural societies, one by the mayor and aldermen.

From the start this committee, informally called the Committee of Aesthetics, limited its comments to facade design and left the monitoring of construction to the Building and Housing Inspection Office. Its purview was thus strictly aesthetic, and limited to that aspect of the design affecting the public way. Over the years, the committee's geographical jurisdiction and its powers gradually increased, but its advice remained limited to the design of facades. New neighborhoods, with less cachet than the prestigious Museumplein district, came under the committee's scrutiny. For instance, Berlage's 1903 plan for the Transvaal district, a neighborhood of low-income housing, carried the requirement that all facades constructed there be approved by the committee. The municipality could also request advice from the committee on buildings to be erected on any municipal land, although it exercised that option infrequently.[32]

The Committee of Aesthetics concentrated its first years on bringing more private building commissions into the hands of architects, insisting that minimal standards of aesthetic competence be set. This did not constitute a radical attack on developers, but was rather a broadening of the interpretation of government regulatory powers, a minor reform to bring aesthetic expertise to bear on urban development. P. L. Tak, commenting in 1904 on the newly published plans by Berlage for Amsterdam's southern extension, pointedly asked, "Who shall build the new city? Will it be bunglers or architects who expand Amsterdam?"[33] The committee answered by rejecting inept designs of conventional character and little architectural merit, often designed by inexperienced draftsmen or the developers themselves, and by encouraging developers to hire architects instead.

Although the committee might occasionally make suggestions for improvement of facade designs, it usually refrained from giving design advice. Builders whose facades were repeatedly rejected usually received the advice to find a "competent" designer. Their hopes of learning which architects would satisfy the commission's requirements were, however, frustrated, as the Building and Housing Inspection Office refused to make any recommendation of particular architects, which might be construed as preferential.[34] In 1911, holding to the principle of impartiality, J. W. C. Tellegen and the Committee of Aesthetics publicly invited architects willing to work for developers to register so that builders could chose freely from a list of posted names.[35] Meanwhile, Tellegen solicited names of Amsterdam architects willing to design facades from the city's main architectural societies.[36] Professional status as defined by membership in the architectural societies was the only requirement for placement on the Building and Housing Inspection list. However, the two societies had developed very different criteria for membership, representing two contrasting responses of the architectural profession to the challenges of modern urban society. The architects' reform and reconstruction of their own social roles had profound implications for the way the debate over public aesthetic control in Amsterdam developed.

THE CRITERIA OF ARCHITECTURAL EXPERTISE

The Dutch language uses three words to refer to architectural expertise: *architectuur* (architecture), *bouwkunst* (building art), and *bouwkunde* (building technique). Aside from foreign degrees and titles, only the initials b.i. (*bouwkundig ingenieur*, loosely translated as construction engineer) indicate formal university training in architecture. At the time under discussion, that training meant a degree from Delft and implied expertise in construction techniques. *Architect*, a title that anyone could claim in the absence of a system of registration, emphasized design and aesthetic expertise. *Bouwkundige* was a general term used for those involved with the construction of buildings, from the contractor to the architect.

Education alone could not provide a convenient benchmark for measuring architectural competence. Dutch architectural education had been neglected in the nineteenth century. Although architects had petitioned the government in 1841 to remedy the decline of Dutch architecture by establishing an academy for architectural instruction, it was not until 1861 that architecture courses were introduced at the Royal Academy in Delft, which had primary responsibility for training civil engineers. When the Royal Academy became the Polytechnic School in 1864, it introduced a degree in architecture, but this differed only slightly from the civil engineering curriculum. By 1895, the program had graduated only thirty-eight students, and new enrollments were negligible. A clamor for reform arose. Even after 1901, when the law regulating instruction at the Polytechnic allowed architecture to become independent of the civil engineering curriculum, training at Delft was largely academic and technical, rather than aesthetic and practical.[37] During the nineteenth century, there had been repeated suggestions that architecture might better be taught at the Academy of Fine Arts in Amsterdam, where instruction in architecture had ceased in 1870.[38] In the absence of such instruction, many had instead received their training in architectural offices, following drafting courses at night, or sometimes traveling abroad for higher education. Eventually, daytime work in studios could be supplemented by a more complete curriculum of evening course work at the academy of architecture set up in 1908 under the auspices of Genootschap Architectura et Amicitia. Here pedagogy followed a combination of practical and academic training, with an emphasis on aesthetic instruction.[39] Since there were many educational tracks, no single academic title could be used to designate architectural competence in the Netherlands.

With the rise in demand for architectural expertise in urban planning and housing, the need to distinguish competent architects became increasingly apparent to the Dutch architectural societies. Two competing definitions of architectural competence emerged, represented by each of the two main societies.[40]

The Society for the Advancement of Architecture, founded in 1842, published architectural periodicals; sponsored competitions, lectures, and exhibitions; and administered examinations for architectural surveyors and draftsmen. Given its role as leading organization for those interested in architecture, its membership was open and included architects, surveyors, draftsmen, building contractors, real estate developers, carpenters, and amateurs.[41] Only in 1888, when it introduced a table of fees for architectural services, did the society take on some of the character of a professional organization.

The other major architectural society in Amsterdam, Genootschap Architectura et Amicitia, was founded in 1855 by a group of young architects rejecting the older establishment. It too published periodicals, sponsored competitions, and opened its membership to a mixed array. But the specific mandate of Genootschap Architectura et Amicitia was to serve the interests of rising architectural talent.[42] Through the nineteenth century, the two societies differed in orientation: the first more involved with the protection of the profession, the second with advancing the discipline. The primary goal of the Society for the Advancement of Architecture was the representation of the architect's professional interests; Genootschap Architectura et Amicitia stated its primary goal as advancing architecture as an art form.[43]

With the extension of Dutch urban centers at the end of the nineteenth century, the interests of architects and builders separated, precipitating a change in the membership structure of these societies. As we have seen, the reaction against the aesthetic misdeeds of speculative building led to a clamor for competent architectural involvement in urban expansion. Architects began to understand that they must strengthen their professional lobby if they wished to influence urban design. As one architect put it, "Architects have too little professional consciousness because there are still too few actual architects among them."[44] As a result, the architectural societies began to close their ranks.

In the 1890s, the two societies began to discuss a merger to form a single architectural association to further their common intellectual and financial interests.[45] These were the first rumblings of a campaign to form a society for architects alone, which would primarily represent the social and economic interests of the profession. The path to the establishment of such a society was difficult and took a number of years to negotiate. The union of the two major societies failed to materialize, but both societies achieved internal reforms of their membership lists.

In 1908, a crisis over the direction of Genootschap Architectura et Amicitia and ongoing discussions about reorganization within the Society for the Advancement of Architecture led to the creation of a separate organization, the League of Dutch Architects (Bond van Nederlandsche Architekten, BNA). The BNA was founded by a group of prominent architects including K. P. C. de Bazel and H. P. Berlage. It explicitly took as its goal the furthering of the interests of the architectural profession. Membership was limited to professional architects, defined as those "practitioners of architecture who represent their patron with the works under their direction, who further the patron's interests, and who do not act as competing contractors, tradesmen, or agents, either independently, as a member of a firm, or as a managing partner."[46] The BNA established an honor code, which specified that architects could not realize any financial gain from their work apart from the officially recognized fee schedule. It also proscribed advertisement, plagiarism, and conflict of interest.[47] Although after much debate the BNA included the study of artistic issues as one of its aims, the organization was primarily established to regulate professional standards. It ensured the public that architects would act honorably, and it ensured architects that their economic rights would be protected.

After establishment of the BNA, the Society for the Advancement of Architecture began to consider a series of changes in membership qualifications intended to move it gradually toward operating as a professional society.[48] As the oldest and largest Dutch architectural society, it considered itself the leader; but from the turn of the century, it had been forced to recognize its own moribund state.[49] With particular anguish, it noted a loss of membership among younger architects against the gains of Genootschap Architectura et Amicitia.[50] Its threatened status as chief architectural society was made all too apparent after the embarrassing episode in Parliament in December 1907 when Victor de Stuers declared it incompetent on architectural matters because its membership included "brickmakers and perhaps even pastry chefs."[51] In 1911, the society changed its statutes to differentiate between architect members, extraordinary members (aspiring architects, engineers, draftsmen, surveyors), and subscribers. Only architects had voting rights. Architects were defined as those holding a diploma as construction engineer or architect, or those who could show sufficient evidence of practical work.[52] These distinctions attempted to establish a recognized cadre of professional architects on the basis of academic attainment and practical experience.

Clearly, the professional aims of the BNA and the reorganized Society for the Advancement of Architecture coincided. From 1911, a committee worked on the fusion of the two societies, and after considerable struggle they merged in 1919. One of the chief obstacles to overcome was the attachment of the older society to its traditional function as an umbrella organization representing all the building trades, and thus the general interests of construction. While the BNA had preferred to eliminate membership of architects working in the civil service, since as salaried workers their social and economic status was perceived as different from the independent architects, the Society for the Advancement of Architecture had long been their stronghold. They were finally permitted membership in the new organization, but not the right to become officers. Developers and others with commercial interests had already been excluded from membership; now salaried employees such as draftsmen and surveyors were also excluded, with the exception of those working toward the rank of architect. *Bouwkundig Weekblad*, the journal of the older society, continued as the newsletter of the profession. In the end, the combined societies formed the primary professional organization of Dutch architects.

The reorganization of Genootschap Architectura et Amicitia took a somewhat different route. The characteristic stance of the society pitted progressive young talent against a conservative architectural establishment. During the disputes of 1907 that led to the formation of the BNA, progressive architect Willem Kromhout and others had reconfirmed the society's aversion to professionalization and had insisted on the status of architecture as art.[53] Genootschap Architectura et Amicitia saw the necessity of separating out the builders and developers from the architectural experts among its members, but it sought to do so according to aesthetic criteria rather than architectural training or social and economic position. Aesthetic talent alone was the criterion for full membership. This idea had first been proposed in 1893 by Kromhout, who had suggested the formation of a society composed solely of outstanding architects that would serve aesthetic interests in much the way the Chamber of Commerce served commercial interests. In 1917, a group of young architects and artists, led by Jan Gratama and H. T. Wijdeveld among others, challenged the existing structure of the society and suggested a new organization that would grant voting membership solely on the basis of aesthetic criteria.[54] This proposal was adopted in modified form. Although there remained a large number of members without aesthetic pretensions, mostly from the building world, they had no voting rights. Only the delegated members, whose work had been approved by the society's admissions committee and who showed sufficient evidence of aesthetic talent, could vote and take positions on the editorial boards, in the society's governance, or on committees.

Since the society's aim was furthering the art of building, it had to guarantee that its members were accomplished artistically. By avoiding any requirements related to academic training or practitioner's status, the society left open to membership the ranks of salaried draftsmen and surveyors as well as artists in fields related to architecture. The society proclaimed its dedication to art with the publication in 1918 of *Wendingen*, a lavish magazine run by progressive architects, artists, and craftsmen. The contrast between *Wendingen*'s striking layout and the dry official pages of *Bouwkundig Weekblad* vividly illustrated the difference between the two main architectural societies.

Both societies sought to establish a cadre of architectural experts distinguished from the developers blamed for the incompetent urban extensions of the past fifty years, and both developed criteria to establish legitimacy and closed ranks. On the one hand, architectural expertise was defined on the basis of professional status associated with academic qualifications and independent practice, criteria that could guarantee a minimum standard of professional competence and allow the group to safeguard its economic well-being.[55] On the other hand, architectural expertise was defined without regard to rank, training, or independence, solely on the basis of aesthetic talent, as the foundation for further development of architecture as an autonomous discipline. The two orientations reflected the twofold character of architecture as profession and discipline, as trade and as art.

These differences directly affected discussion of the public review of architecture, raising the question of how such review might guarantee the competence of designers, that is, how it should go about hiring qualified architects. Should competence be assessed on the basis of professional status or on the basis of aesthetic qualifications? The Society for the Advancement of Architecture supported the first position, Genootschap Architectura et Amicitia the second. These differences also implied conflicting social orientations, the first invoking the profession, which through free competition within a closed market, protects its members; the second calling on the discipline, which by developing excellence through self-regulation, serves society. These competing definitions of legitimate expertise were also related to competing interpretations of the means and ends of aesthetic urban reform. On the one hand, the professionalization of design to correct the bungling of incompetents might prevent ugliness in the city. On the other hand, public selection of designers on the basis of aesthetic criteria might encourage the appropriate representation of the modern city, that is, the active stimulation of an urban image. Genootschap Architectura et Amicitia's spearheading of architectural renewal identified it more clearly with the latter position.

THE DEBATES ON PUBLIC AESTHETIC CONTROL

The fact that the city of Amsterdam owned most of the land on which development would take place gave the municipality wide scope within which to exercise design control. In its first phase, the Committee of Aesthetics operated to protect the public interest from the sorry results of incompetence by setting a higher standard of professionalism. Developers were repeatedly encouraged to hire competent architectural assistance to avoid denial of their building proposals. The committee, through the Building and Housing Inspection Office, was prepared to provide developers with a list of architects willing to design facades, all of whom by virtue of their membership in one of the architectural societies were assumed to be of sufficient competence. Although the committee would not recommend particular architects or guarantee that projects designed by those on the list would gain the committee's approval, in general it accepted designs by recognized architects. This approach supported the definition of architecture as a profession that was espoused by the Society for the Advancement of Architecture, and it served the interests of that society by promoting a closed market for architectural expertise. However, public oversight of the housing societies, which together with the municipality were to build the largest residential projects, gave the city a further avenue of influence. When Amsterdam began to apply the Housing Act more assiduously, the Committee of Aesthetics began to review architects' designs for housing society projects. In so doing, it expanded its task beyond influencing developers to hire competent designers to reviewing designs by architects.

Eventually, the review of fellow colleagues became the committee's most controversial activity.

As the committee began to review the work of architects themselves, a new set of criteria for judging architectural competence came into effect. The committee began to work as a design jury, applying an aesthetic standard, as did the Genootschap Architectura et Amicitia. Once the Committee of Aesthetics established itself as an aesthetic arbiter in the public realm, it opened itself up to criticisms of partisanship both from the government and by architects, who feared that official stylistic norms could threaten free competition.

Many architects viewed committees of aesthetics as necessary evils, required only because it was impossible to introduce a local ordinance requiring that all construction be designed by a registered architect, given the absence of national registration. Short of that, a committee could at least secure commissions for competent architects by insisting on a minimal degree of design competence. Others felt that the authority invested in the committees by architectural societies (on behalf of architecture) and the municipal government (on behalf of the community) should be wielded to encourage the positive development of architecture. Thus, in advancing the discipline, a committee of aesthetics might best serve the community. But if a committee took a position on taste and style, it would contradict the impartiality required by the government, the free competition between professionals, the free practice of the profession, and the free development of the discipline. The problem lay, then, in the question of whether the community was better served by the preservation of freedom or by aesthetic commitment.

The debate on the proper role of the committees of aesthetics centered on several principle issues. Should such a committee merely prevent ugliness, or should it actively advance architectural beauty? Would it be effective if it simply insisted that only architects receive design commissions, or must it influence the selection of those architects? Would the discipline of architecture be better served by a committee fostering a particular taste or style or by architecture being permitted to develop freely?

These issues arose repeatedly during the extensive discussions that took place among architects when the Amsterdam Committee of Aesthetics began to question the value the municipal government placed on its advice. The mayor and aldermen were under no legal obligation to follow the advice of the committee, whose status was merely that of an advisory board. In any case, the jurisdiction of the committee was sharply limited. But by 1910, the committee felt that even its limited mandate was being compromised, and it requested that it be reconstituted with greater powers. When the government dragged its feet, the committee responded in early 1911 with the complaint that it had been reduced to a position of "secondary significance."[56] Contributing to the committee's dissatisfaction was the apparent threat to its authority posed by another advisory board set up at the behest of the architectural societies.

The Committee of Urban Beauty (Commissie voor de Stadsschoon), established in 1911, was intended to protect the architectural heritage of the inner city.[57] Unlike the Committee of Aesthetics, it reviewed proposals for alterations to buildings and made specific design recommendations. Its working methods resembled to some degree the *Bauberatungstelle*, the system of design review developed in Germany in which review of construction included extensive design intervention on the part of municipally appointed experts.

By 1913, given the national interest shown in the problem and given a draft proposal for the reorganization of the Amsterdam Committee of Aesthetics, the Society for the Advancement of Architecture officially raised the issue of public design review among its membership. As might be expected given the society's raison d'être, after a year-long debate it came out in support of the exercise of professional freedom. Noting that the Committee of Aesthetics was an institution required only as long as the architectural profession remained unprotected by a registration act, it insisted that architects and nonarchitects should be distinguished, that is, handled by separate procedures, leaving the professionals largely free of review.[58] The society supported the creation of a closed professional environment in which architects might compete freely both with their ideas and for their profit.

One of the most vocal defenders of artistic freedom was the modernist disciple of H. P. Berlage, J. E. van der Pek. In 1912, he argued against expanding the powers of the Committee of Aesthetics. He objected to the way the committee had already moved from trying to improve the designs of builders to judging the work of other architects. It would harm architecture, Van der Pek warned, if members of the commission were asked to judge works by colleagues at the same or higher level of ability. Van der Pek feared that a reconstituted Committee of Aesthetics, even if composed to represent a variety of architectural opinion, could never judge new ideas objectively. The fresh expression of Berlage's Exchange Building would never have been realized, he claimed, had it been subjected to the judgment of a committee of architects. Throughout history, he argued, the avant-garde acts as a harbinger of the future, and it should never be stifled. Van der Pek feared a conservative Committee of Aesthetics might become a "spiritual tourniquet," and he too suggested that the committee continue to guide speculative builders, but leave the architects free. To great applause, he argued that certain architects, judged outstanding aesthetic leaders, should be altogether exempt from committee review.[59]

Van der Pek saw the committee's control as a potential danger for the free development of architectural ideas. Socialist and modernist as he was, he found a supporter in the aesthetically and politically conservative architect and politician C. B. Posthumus Meyjes, who pleaded, "May the responsibility for the advancement of architecture never be shifted from architects to some committee. That would deaden art rather than advance it."[60] Both progressives and conservatives had reason to fear the potential for the misuse of the committee's power. In 1913, cultural progressives, noting the close relationship between the Amsterdam Committee of Aesthetics and institutions dedicated to the preservation of historic architecture, such as the Committee of Urban Beauty and Bond Heemschut, feared the committee might obstruct modernist construction. Conservatives, on the other hand, had noted with concern the modernist position already assumed by the committee on several occasions, and feared it might continue to use its influence in the service of modernism. Given the heightened tension between the modernists and traditionalists, it was natural that conservatives and progressives were equally apprehensive that the other might assume control and impose a stylistic policy. Representatives of both sides dreaded the installation of an official art and wished to underline that neither the government nor the architects should use the Committee of Aesthetics to impose or create a style.[61]

Proponents of the Committee of Aesthetics took great pains to point out the potential for objective judgment from its members. They admitted the difficulty of putting aside personal preference and taste, but insisted that this was a matter of sensitivity and ethics: "Herein lies precisely the subtle, ethical side of the institution: personal taste may not count. No preference for any school may turn the scale. The greatest possible respect for the outlook of one's colleague should be asserted, even if it runs diametrically opposed to one's own opinion."[62]

The inherent relativism of this argument was anathema to some critics of the system of public aesthetic review, who felt it would cause greater harm than good. The level of architecture would not be raised and the development of architecture would not be furthered by impartial, nonpartisan committees, argued progressive artist R. N. Roland Holst in 1914: "A jury composed according to political, aesthetic considerations, in which for every man on the right a corresponding man on the left is selected, inevitably places the deciding balance in the hands of a pallid middle-of-the-roader, lacking in conviction. His taste in art turns toward the tame and insipid, toward art you can't hate, but that you can't love either, because it leaves you fairly indifferent."[63] For Roland Holst, and many others, the idea of impartial objectivity in aesthetic matters negated the commitment necessary for aesthetic advancement. An impartial committee on the government's model would prove incapable of promoting architectural improvement in Amsterdam. That could only be achieved by a committee willing to take a stand on the architectural issues of the day.

Many of those interested in P. L. Tak's challenge to get the best for Amsterdam believed they had to find means to circumvent the liberal legacy of public impartiality on aesthetic matters. But when the advisory committee openly engaged in stylistic politics, it met with stiff governmental resistance. Over the years, a number of disputes arose with the municipal government when the Committee of Aesthetics chose to champion a particular aesthetic position rather than following strict official impartiality. On several critical occasions, the mayor and aldermen unequivocally rejected attempts by the committee to dictate or proscribe building style. When in 1914 the Committee of Aesthetics tried to prevent acceptance of a museum design because of its conservative historicism, the mayor and aldermen disregarded its opinion. The committee members resigned in protest but later resumed their duties.[64] Tensions only heightened when in 1916 mayor and aldermen once again overturned a committee decision, this time against plans for an office building by a historicist architect.[65] In the letter explaining their rejection of the committee's advice, the mayor and aldermen made their position on government impartiality explicit: "The municipality can prohibit the freedom to erect buildings that disfigure the city; but in our opinion a municipal government or other governmental body does not have the authority to force the choice of a particular architectural style."[66]

The government was unwilling to take an official stand on what it perceived as an internal matter of the architectural discipline. This principled position made direct architectural advocacy in the public forum impossible. Posthumus Meyjes argued that committees of aesthetics must serve the public with impartial expertise:

> Does a committee of aesthetics have the right to try to lead architecture along the paths it believes to be the only true and beautiful ones? Committees of aesthetics were most certainly not instituted for that purpose, and these committees are surely not authorized to do so. They are only supposed to judge the submitted designs objectively and decide if a design is or is not in conflict with the general and fundamental requirements of aesthetics. They must abstain from prescribing a particular style with which the designer must comply.[67]

Yet from 1915 on, after its reorganization under a stronger mandate from the municipal council and as its membership shifted away from proponents of historicism, the committee increasingly viewed its mission as the active development of Amsterdam's architecture, a mission it interpreted as tantamount to promoting modernism.

Indeed, during its conflicts with the municipal government, the Committee of Aesthetics argued that the imitation of historical style was inappropriate in modern times. According to one member, the talented and progressive architect J. F. Staal, the question of whether one should build in an old style was as senseless as asking whether one should speak Celtic in Holland.[68] If the committee interpreted its task as promoting the beauty of Amsterdam, he argued, it had to take upon itself the responsibility to promote the development of architecture itself. The committee could not approve any building that "was a specimen of outlandish style imitation, like that perpetrated thirty or forty years ago, and a total negation of the development of architecture since that time." Staal aggressively proposed historical determinism, that is, the spirit of the age, as the foundation for aesthetic judgment.

> The individual's wishes must yield to the general interest in matters of building construction as it does in other social areas. This principle is presumably acceptable for any technical require-

> ments, but surprisingly when it comes to aesthetic requirements anarchy reigns. As a result, a great many building patrons believe that just because they foot the bills, they have the right to force the results of their taste[lessness] on the rest of the world and so dominate the environment where thousands must lead their lives years after they are gone, instead of subordinating their personal ideas to the general artistic insights and desires of their age.[69]

Staal saw the Committee of Aesthetics as the panel of experts that would protect the environment from works that ran counter to the spirit of the community and the times. The zeitgeist determined the one objectively correct style, the modern. Individual taste would have to defer to the aesthetic conventions of the collective community.

Without such sacrifice of individualism, no great era of culture could be achieved. This argument followed from the eclectic Hegelian historiography that equated high culture with style emanating from the processes of history, an interpretation made current by, among others, Berlage. Objectivity in aesthetics did not rest on timeless, universal principles, but on the suppression of the subjective (such as the nineteenth-century imitation of past styles) for the sake of an irresistible, historically determined formal trend. In this view, aesthetic objectivity derived ultimately from shared conventions. Berlage wrote: "Not only is every religion and every philosophy founded on dogma, but also art. For what is the art form of a particular style other than a dogma, the artistic dogma that all the artists of the same period accept as a collective notion? And it is precisely through the acceptance of such a dogma that the artists are capable of manifesting the highest aesthetic thought."[70]

How was the concept of art as dogma to be reconciled with the free practice of a profession? The public control of urban aesthetics touched on a tension between two phenomena of modern culture. The newly won freedom of the artist to pursue his discipline as pure art without the constraints of court or church patronage was challenged by the modern historiographical view that the artist was bound by the laws of history to serve society.[71]

When Berlage explicated the relationship between architecture and society in a 1919 publication, he repeatedly underlined the role of architecture as the social art. "Architecture is 'the social art,' the art that discloses the aesthetic idea of the community." "Like man, a building is a physio-psychological being, through which the spirit of society speaks." "[Architecture] is the artistic revelation of the soul of humanity itself. This profound psychological characteristic of architecture exacts extraordinary duties from the architect as artist. For every architectural activity is, as a social activity, therefore an act on behalf of the community, and the erection of every building is, as a social deed, therefore an act on behalf of the community."[72] The architect's role was thus to align himself with the community's soul, its aesthetic expression, the spirit of the people; his individualism must bow to the communal force that justifies architectural creativity and endows buildings with their highest purpose.

The endless discussions about the individual and society in Dutch artistic circles during the first decades of the century attest to the centrality of this issue. It was often framed as a choice between the subjective, but true development of individual talent and the true, objective development of style as an expression of community. The tension between these two missions suggested the uneasy relationship between the artist's identification with his profession and with his role in society. Berlage's formulation appeared to resolve the tension by making the advance of the discipline dependent on social engagement: by serving society the artist was serving art. But the irony of Berlage's conceptualization of a social art was that the stylistic "dogma" or convention that the artist was to obey in the name of the community required him to assume the role of interpreter of the community, that is, the provider of its style. Thus, in the very act of making the community the artist's patron, in itself intended as a liberative act, Berlage and those who followed his arguments withdrew the power of patronage from the public that was to be served and placed that power in the hands of the artist himself.

A complex set of interrelated issues was unlocked by holding urban aesthetics to public standards. The nature of the government's involvement depended on whether architecture was to be defined as a profession or as an art. The first required setting a norm of professionalism, the second a stylistic norm. Norms of professionalism could introduce standards of competence, which would eliminate those who did not meet the minimum requirements of professional status. Applied to all construction, this norm set a lowest common denominator, defining a limit to what was to be tolerated in any neighborhood in the city, no matter what the income level. This kind of control was hardly controversial, serving as it did the interests of the architectural profession and the interests of a society no longer ready to accept the poor quality of unregulated design. Norms of style, on the other hand, required the municipality to take a stand on aesthetic issues, acting positively to promote design excellence by patronizing architects judged to be at the leading edge and then forcing other architects to follow their lead. In this way, a committee of appointed architects, acting on behalf of the municipality, that is, on behalf of the community, could establish a position on the way architecture should develop in the city, in essence selecting and shaping the image of the city.

The choice between these two norms, professional and stylistic, was largely political. As in the case of social hygiene, it was the liberals and conservatives who favored a norm that set a lowest common denominator and the progressives and socialists who favored a norm that promoted excellence. In effect this meant that the Liberal council members favored establishing minimum standards of professionalism in the design of housing so that design competence could be guaranteed, whereas Social Democrats favored active promotion of the best possible design. But the difference in approach cannot simply be described as a difference between lower and higher standards. It also constituted different social visions of the nature of architecture. The choice between professional and aesthetic norms related to the difference between liberal defense of open competition and socialist defense of collective control. That these positions also coincided roughly with liberal defense of traditional styles and socialist espousal of modernism is not coincidental, given the association between traditional Dutch style and a national identity rooted in the seventeenth century on the one hand and the association between new architectural forms and a new social order on the other. But political position did not simply translate into aesthetic policy. Many liberals and cultural conservatives supported public engagement in urban aesthetics; some socialists and modernists were aware of the dangers of aesthetic dictation and official art. The public determination of the urban visual order was a troubled arena, governed by contradictory principles and conflicting criteria. It invoked conflicting positions on the nature of architecture as profession and art, the role of architectural service to society, the historical development of architecture, and ultimately notions of public interest and community. Expanding public power to regulate urban visual order required stretching the concept of public interest endorsed by liberal reformers. Their concept of public interest was embedded in the legalistic bonds of *Gesellschaft*, which assumed a society composed of individuals whose rights required protection. By contrast, the concept of community, or *Gemeinschaft*, emphasized the bonds of identity; it evoked a collectivity that could be expressed through aesthetic representation. The competing norms of professionalism and style thus also reflected a further distinction between the protection of the public interest and the aestheticization of community.

By the first decades of the twentieth century, there was general agreement in Amsterdam that the public interest would be served by imposing restrictions on laissez-faire development, but there was little agreement that the community would be served by government control of its expression. Any official stand on the urban image was riddled with unresolved tensions. The legitimacy of such authority was questioned; there were competing claims to control and competing definitions of the urban visual order. These tensions are explored in the next two chapters.

REFORMING WORKERS' TASTE

By the time the Dutch Housing Act went into effect in 1902, politicians and bureaucrats across the political spectrum agreed that workers' housing merited the attention of architects. Architectural expertise was viewed as indispensable for tackling the large-scale construction and complex functional requirements of mass housing. It was felt that builders of speculative housing had proved incompetent to solve these problems.

The very fact that architects were expected to take up the design of workers' housing indicated a shift on the part of authorities in the definition of a humane dwelling. What had previously been considered acceptable had ceased to be tolerated. The nature of the attention that architects should bring to the problem was, however, still a matter of dispute.

At midcentury, architects shared with housing reformers the opinion that their primary contribution to housing should be solid and sanitary construction. When the liberal architect J. H. Leliman and hygienist Dr. S. S. Colonel called for a varied treatment of facades in the Dutch philanthropic housing of the nineteenth century, they assumed that simple means would be used to achieve an architectural effect.[1] Aesthetic considerations were to be introduced to workers' housing only as a secondary amenity; beauty and decoration were to be sacrificed in favor of functionality and hygiene.[2] When the highly respected architect and city councilor P. J. H. Cuypers stated that "the worker has the right to live in a home that meets all the requirements of architecture that the housing of the more affluent does," the implication was that those requirements could be satisfied through modest means appropriate to the workers' social standing.[3] In liberal circles, where government intervention in the housing problem was still viewed as a charitable enterprise even after passage of the Housing Act, the nineteenth-century attitude toward "decoration" as an unnecessary luxury proved persistent. Workers' housing, it was felt, should somehow look like workers' housing, and one way to distinguish it was by restraining decoration.

Nineteenth-century reform literature was filled with admonitions to modesty, knowing one's place, behaving appropriately to class position. A reform tract thinly veiled as a novel presented the heroine as a model factory worker. Grietje Klien's apron had no lace; her hat was plainly colored and sported no "garden" of flowers for decoration. Her modest behavior elicited the following praise from a prospective employer: "You dress according to your place and your income. That is better than all the finery that some wear to look like a lady."[4] Just as young women were warned not to ape their betters, workers' dwellings were not to imitate upper-class villas. In the interests of thrift as well as maintenance of the status quo, the facade of a worker's home should display modest but tasteful domesticity without undue or expensive embellishment.[5]

Aside from any economic rationale, the injunction against unnecessary luxury was animated by the middle class's deep distrust of working-class judgment. Repeatedly workers were accused of misusing wages on drink, on improper diet, and on extravagant and frivolous expenditures. These objections appear in the writings of the leading social workers active in housing reform. Johanna ter Meulen complained of one housewife that she was well behaved but "enamored of finery and buying pretty things."[6] Hélène Mercier deplored what she perceived as the working-class woman's preference for proud display over daily duties: "She pays less attention to the preparation of the midday meal than to the polishing of her copper, but doesn't seem to realize that furnishings were placed in this world for people, not people for furnishings. As a result, instead of quiet and cozy togetherness her husband and children get treated to scrubbing and polishing when they come home."[7]

Working-class efforts to decorate the interior of the house were viewed with suspicion. Mercier was shocked at finding imitations of expensive furniture and knickknacks in the homes of the indigent slum dwellers of Amsterdam. Rather than viewing such possessions as a sign that the impulse for aesthetic expression survives under the most dire circumstances, reformers saw them as uneconomical and dysfunctional, an inappropriate extravagance: "To my surprise, I have found well-maintained bureaus and cabinets, shining copper, wall prints, large colored glass balls, porcelain dolls, and the like in dwellings as high as the fourth floor in the side alleys off 'Hol' and 'Hemelrijk.' And it is remarkable that nearly everywhere, even in the homes of [philanthropic] housing societies, the less cultivated the dwellers, the more so-called finery filled the room."[8] Mercier's comments date from 1887, but as late as 1916 De Bazel's plans for De Arbeiderswoning were praised because their design prevented the living room from becoming "a domestic museum of all sorts of junk."[9]

The reformers' distaste for what they felt was excessive luxury extended beyond housing for the casual laborers emerging from the slums, where it derived in part from arguments against wastefulness. Well-schooled, skilled laborers were also subjected to informal sumptuary laws. In 1906, Hudig recommended an architectural firm to a pair of typographers who had came to the CBSA looking for help in developing low-rise dwellings in the "open air" outside Amsterdam. Two years later, with designs in hand and a housing society recognized under the Housing Act, the typographers solicited capital from a list of well-known liberal philanthropists and reformers provided by the CBSA, but their quest was unsuccessful. Hudig reported to Keppler that the reformers "found the houses too beautiful, not workers' housing."[10]

Although socialists such as Hudig and Keppler could not agree with liberal reformers that workers' housing could be too beautiful, they were as likely as progressive liberals to condemn ostentatious taste, bourgeois or working class. Most socialist reformers would have agreed with Mercier's remark that "many a one-room dwelling bears a strong resemblance to the modern salon of the nouveau riche when it comes to the furnishings, both of them stockpiles of bric-a-brac."[11] The poor taste and gaudy display of the diamond workers who earned quick fortunes in the 1880s were often ridiculed. Socialist union organizer Henri Polak described their furnishings with disdain:

> The money had to be spent, and it went for the most tasteless, insipid things. . . . Right away new furniture was acquired . . . mahogany abominations, chairs, and sofas (called loveseats) covered with red velveteen, . . . silver chests (called *bonheur du jour*, Heaven knows why) decorated with ridiculous carvings, linen chests "of massive oak" for the family linen, and the damask tablecloths that, with their woven landscapes, hunt scenes, and arabesques, constituted the pride of the diamond workers' wives. The colors of the flowered carpets were blinding; the gilt clocks with candelabra, the gilt frames around the lithos "in the style of Koekoek," and the gas chandeliers shone with a glaring glitter.[12]

Polak's sharply critical description reveals as much about his own taste as it does about the workers' preferences. He and other socialist reformers tried to influence workers to abandon their impulse to acquire showy adornments. The morality tale published by the Federation of Social Democratic Women's Clubs in a brochure against the parlor also proffered suggestions for interior decoration. In place of fancy lamps and flowered carpets, overdecorated chairs and gilded picture frames, the heavy curtains that kept out the sun and other dust collectors that the wife in the story wants, the husband suggests plain and practical woven mats for the floor, simple caned chairs with cushions, and light, short curtains that can be left open to let in the sun during the day. The wife wants to keep her copper pieces, but echoing Mercier, her socialist husband suggests she consider decorations that will not require constant polishing, like a ginger pot or an old milk can filled with flowers. In response to his wife's objections that visitors will find the room he proposes strange and barren, the husband describes the typical parlor as a musty room cluttered with albums, knickknacks, and portraits.[13] The working class was expected to learn to prefer plain colors over printed wallpapers and carpets, simple furniture rather than false mahogany and imitation Louis XIV. The practical, undecorated, and logical was to replace the fussy, overelaborate, and awkward.[14]

The arguments socialist politicians brought to bear against the excesses of bourgeois culture, especially when imitated by the working class, drew directly from the arguments advanced by architects in support of progressive aesthetic reform. These arguments were pressed as strenuously on the middle class as on workers, but the movement for aesthetic reform had particular implications for workers. H. P. Berlage endorsed aesthetic reform in calling for the creation of a new, simpler aesthetic for the worker in contrast to the pretensions of sumptuous bourgeois construction. In his 1896 review of J. E. van der Pek's Goudbloemstraat housing, with its simple but decorative brickwork and glazed tiles, he praised the design not only for its solution to social and hygienic requirements, but for its aesthetic achievement, which he felt confirmed the possibility of a meaningful architecture in a workers' district.

> What is gratifying about this possibility is that the worker will now slowly begin to realize that art can also be for him. And if, as I hope, what we usually call "showy" architecture begins to discard its parvenu trappings of false beauty (which the worker, with a taste that could not conceivably be otherwise in these times, mistakes for real beauty since it appears rich and pretty), and if instead architecture becomes simple, then there will be an artistic and democratic confluence that will bring a beneficial unity to architecture, without the necessity that we must make workers' housing into showy architecture, or make showy architecture into workers' housing.[15]

Here Berlage sets out his agenda for the aesthetic reform of architectural design, influenced by the English Arts and Crafts literature of William Morris and Walter Crane.[16] The modernist critique of inauthenticity and dishonesty frequently levied at this time against architectural historicism is linked to the need to create an art for the worker. Architecture will only achieve a new "beneficial unity" when the false beauty of applied historical ornament is overthrown for simplicity, and when the revolution in taste is carried out for the sake of the worker. The struggle internal to architectural debate on the merits and demerits of historicism merges here with the political argument for throwing off old forms of social organization. The new aesthetic is to be a convergence of artistic and democratic ideals. Berlage followed Morris in claiming that architecture is for and of the people, for and of the community. However, the worker himself had to be educated to recognize his mistaken taste for false beauty and to recognize that a new art was emerging for him.

Aesthetic reformers, no less than housing reformers, believed that the public at large needed to be educated, in this case to understand art and to develop good taste.

Schools had failed to teach the lay public how to look at art, it was argued, so the public was now unable to appreciate the modern crafts movement.[17] The products of industrial processes, the argument continued, had debased the quality of everyday articles so that the consuming public were victims of the manufacturers. Members of the working class who had not previously been exposed to high culture would be uplifted intellectually and morally by art and architecture. Once workers were trained to understand examples of good taste, they could begin the intellectual and spiritual development for which they themselves yearned.[18] The crafts produced for the upper classes were unattainable to the proletariat, but a *gemeenschapskunst*, an art for the community in the form of objects for daily living, would educate and develop the worker.[19] If workers could be taught to adjust their lifestyles to the modern city, why not their tastes?

Both socialists and liberals used similar means to shape working-class attitudes: newspaper and magazine articles, lectures, exhibitions, and competitions. In October 1903, Amsterdam Social Democrats founded the society Art for the People (Kunst aan het Volk), its goal "the advancement and enjoyment of art by the working class."[20] In 1905, it sponsored an exhibition contrasting inexpensive but artistic living room interiors with tasteless examples.[21] In 1908, Berlage arranged and introduced an exhibition of good and bad wall decorations for the society.[22] He also lectured and wrote an essay for their widely reviewed 1910 exhibition displaying good and bad examples of everyday objects.[23] In 1912, the liberal settlement house society Ons Huis sponsored a competition for the complete furnishing of workers' dwellings, and exhibited the two winning entries alongside a counterexample.[24] Art for the People held a competition for the design of furniture for a worker's living room in 1916. The prizewinning furniture was displayed in a flat in De Bazel's housing for De Arbeiderswoning on Van Beuningenplein (fig. 7.1).[25]

The housing societies were also used for instruction in taste and furnishings. The teachers' housing society ACOB invited Henri Polak and architect J. C. van Epen to give their thoughts on how to build and arrange a good home, and Van Epen subsequently furnished a model room of the housing he designed for the Algemeene in 1910.[26] The housing society Amsterdam-Zuid had the department store De Bijenkorf furnish a flat in its first housing project.[27]

The message of these many examples and counterexamples was in general the same. Influenced by the Arts and Crafts movement, architects and artists preached the modern gospel of simplicity and truthfulness. They encouraged the unity of style, harmony and clarity of shape and color, and the reduction of elements. Logical forms reflecting function, convenience, and usefulness were encouraged. Materials were to be used according to their nature. Simplicity of design, reduction of ornamentation, and purity of form would create a clean, true decoration. At the 1910 exhibition organized by Art for the People, "crimes" against good taste were displayed and labeled:

FIGURE 7.1 H. van Dorp, prize-winning furniture, 1916. From *Bouwkundig Weekblad* 37, no. 6 (10 June 1916), facing 65.

chocolate busts of royalty, animal-shaped pen boxes, a series of prints on the Zeppelin flight, and hand towels emblazoned with patriotic sentiments.[28] The exhibition contrasted tawdry prints with tasteful lithographs, and hard-to-clean, overdecorated furniture with simple, easy-to-maintain pieces. Workers were warned against poor materials, old materials, falsification of materials, poor construction, inefficient construction, false representation of technique, plagiarism, overdecoration, historical styles, and loud, clashing colors. While these aesthetic admonitions were aimed against the mass culture that workers consumed, they carried the same message to the wealthy bourgeoisie, who could afford the goods offered at outlets of modern design such as Berlage's Binnenhuis or Liberty's Amsterdam affiliate Focke en Metzer.

Deeply influenced by Ruskin and Morris, the socialist Berlage argued the necessity of weaning the worker from middle-class tastes as strenuously as the liberal Mercier, though his aim could hardly have been more different. Rather than using material culture as a means to express the fixed place of workers in the social hierarchy, Berlage wanted architecture to represent a new democratic social order, to be the aesthetic embodiment of the worker's historic place. His position accorded well with the Social Democratic theorists who saw a bridge between aesthetics and politics. Modern aesthetic reform is a reaction against capitalism, explained P. L. Tak, whose weekly magazine *De Kroniek* gave Berlage and other progressive reformers, both aesthetic and political, a polemical platform. "Among . . . architects and decorative artists there is a growing demand for simplicity and truthfulness that is a clear reaction against the requirements of capitalism, so often in conflict with both."[29]

The middle-class reformer objected to the parlor on the grounds that it was a luxury the worker could ill afford and called the imitation of middle-class villas in working-class homes inappropriate. The socialists argued for similar ends by different means. In 1901, architect J. B. van Loghem suggested that the way to make modern design available to the proletariat was through large-scale reduction of decoration and the return to purer primitive forms.[30] He later warned against trying to transfer features of the villa into the worker's dwelling. His argument for simplicity was not that the worker should avoid display beyond his status, but that the diminutive re-creation of the specialized rooms of a middle-class house was false and useless rather than simple and true.[31] The modern aesthetic of sobriety might resemble the liberal rejection of decoration in workers' housing, but its intention was different. It was necessary to find an aesthetically worthy solution specific to the housing of workers, not because they did not deserve the quality of middle-class design, but because they deserved better.

Berlage's designs for workers' housing in Amsterdam displayed restraint and dignity (figs. 5.8 and 7.2).[32] The socialist housing society Algemeene described the modest aims of his 1910 housing designs: they would improve the quality and appearance of workers' housing; they would be better than anything that could be expected from a private builder; and they would be built without unnecessary trappings.[33] "Trappings" were presumably unnecessary because they were false and tasteless, not because workers should be denied any signs of wealth.

The simplicity of design found in the projects of the first modern architects to build in Amsterdam under the Housing Act contrasts sharply with the minimalism of both speculative and nineteenth-century philanthropic housing. Speculative housing was characterized by the cold grimness of its monotonous brick facades, whether unrelieved by decoration or plastered with shoddy applied ornament. The nineteenth-century housing projects frequently made reference to historic styles, either with the multiple gables of the Dutch Renaissance or with eighteenth-century decoration. They also frankly acknowledged their status as charitable enterprises, composing a block as if it were a single whole, emphasizing center and end bays in the visual hierarchy associated with institutional construction. In contrast, the modern projects by Van der Pek, Berlage, and De Bazel achieved a quiet dignity with modest means.[34] Berlage in particular used construction details like corbels to bring a sculptural varia-

FIGURE 7.2 H. P. Berlage, Algemeene Woningbouw Vereeniging, Tolstraat, 1922. Gemeentearchief Amsterdam, negative VH2536.

tion to his facades. De Bazel and Van der Pek both used multicolored glazed and unglazed brick to enliven the facade with geometric designs. Although their approach to design was as functional and economical as their speculative and philanthropic predecessors, the proponents of modern design sought to turn those limitations into virtues. The freshness of their forms surprised the eye with a simplicity that expressed distinction rather than impoverishment.

Despite the efforts made on their behalf, however, workers did not quickly accept the reformers' advice on taste. The sober, clean lines of De Bazel's subsidized housing at Van Beuningenplein earned it the sobriquet the "Lutheran Old Age Home."[35] The local populace dubbed Berlage's light-bricked and corbeled housing on the Javaplein "the beehive." Workers found that their furnishing and decorations fit poorly in the plain interiors. In his designs, De Bazel specified walls painted in flat colors and floors of tinted concrete for easy maintenance, but these proved unpopular with workers accustomed to do-it-yourself improvements such as colorfully patterned wallpaper and carpets.[36] A favorable review of Van der Pek's first housing for Rochdale emphasized the very simplicity that disturbed prospective inhabitants: "The immediate impression you get at the entrance is very friendly. Erected in clear red brick, with doors painted green and beautiful big windowpanes, the housing strikes one as most pleasant."[37]

At a number of the educational exhibitions, commentators noted that the visitors appeared to appreciate the examples of poor design more than the model rooms. Many workers rejected the unfamiliar forms of modern design, or as one reviewer commented critically, "the workers still place too much value on ostentatious forms and illogical display."[38] A socialist wrote impatiently: "It will be hard work to convince workers that they cannot get really good furniture for the money they have to spend, and that instead of filling their homes with poor, imitation furniture, they would do better to limit themselves to the most essential household effects."[39]

It was difficult for the aesthetic reformers to empathize with the preference for imitating "hopelessly" middle-class taste. A reporter at a 1920 exhibition of workers' rooms furnished by Van Epen jibed: "If the less well off cannot bring themselves to want to live in an interior characterized with as much liveliness, intimacy, and inventiveness as the inexpensive creation of this architect, then they deserve to sit pretty among their tea tables and chests for all eternity."[40]

Working-class steadfastness in the face of attitudes that, to the minds of reformers, were more logical, more economic, and more tasteful led some to disparage attempts to "educate" the working class.[41] They argued that the workers did not want to change, and that the reformers unjustifiably assumed a monopoly of knowledge. One critic argued against the campaign to bring art to the people, ridiculing "the pretention of setting oneself up as a sort of intellectual and aesthetic guardian over the people as if they were minors."[42] In a review of the 1921 exhibition of home interiors, another criticized the implicit paternalism of architects trying to alter working-class taste: "The attempts to raise the worker's dwelling to a satisfactory practical and aesthetic level will fail to achieve results as long as the workers themselves do not participate more in the attempts than they have up until now. It is simply a fact that everyone prefers, when decisions are being made that concern him, that some consideration be taken of what he himself wishes and feels."[43]

In the nineteenth century, architects had accepted the reasoning of bourgeois reformers by treating the aesthetic component of housing design as a luxury, to be applied minimally. The result was housing that visually projected its low social status. This representation of the social hierarchy was viewed as appropriate by conservative reformers; workers were meant to accept it just as they were intended to accept distinctions in clothing, language, and transport. The architect was thus an assistant in the social construction of reality as dictated by middle-class morality. Under the Housing Act, liberal politicians in Amsterdam fully expected the design of housing supported by the government to reflect its status in similar fashion. However, modernist values dictated that mass housing, no less than any other design for daily living, should embody new perceptions of form and space. As an outlet for autonomous advances within the architectural discipline, housing thus became a democratic art form applying modern aesthetics equally to the worker's flat and the bourgeois villa. Rather than a luxury, the aesthetic treatment of mass housing became central to its design. Nonetheless, the old power relations between housing designer and inhabitant were still played out. Although no longer armed with moralistic arguments in service to the existing social hierarchy, the doctrine of modernity required the architect to play the role of educator. Workers' taste was to be reformed, now in the name of their own liberation, although with little of their input.

"APPROPRIATE CONTEMPORARY MEANS TO AESTHETIC EXPRESSION"

At the 1918 National Housing Council Convention, Jan van der Waerden, then head of the Amsterdam Building and Housing Inspection Office, proposed nationwide standardization as a radical solution to the critical postwar housing shortage.[44] Van der Waerden's proposals were technical in nature, pointing out the efficacy of standardized manufacture of parts and the speed with which standardized plans could be constructed. Nonetheless, much of the criticism of his proposals was aesthetic.

Architects and workers alike protested the proposal, one of the few occasions workers spoke publicly on the issue of housing aesthetics. Representatives of labor unions and housing societies objected to the prospect of a nation of similar houses, without regional variation, and without room for individual expression. The solution of standardization suggested a return to the monotonous nineteenth-century townscape, which it had been hoped new housing would avoid.[45] Architects feared that standardization would deprive them of creative freedom.

Van der Waerden found a surprising defender in Berlage. Berlage responded not so much to defend the particular strategy put forward by Van der Waerden as to answer the aesthetic objections to standardization. He reminded the architects of the historic precedent for repetition in housing forms, citing aesthetically successful examples from the Rue de Rivoli and Place Vendôme in Paris to Regent Street in London. He chided the workers' representatives for seeking an individualism of form that was the very expression of the workers' class enemy. The fact that individualism is bourgeois should be sufficient to lead the workers to embrace the collective townscape with enthusiasm, he claimed. Berlage said that he had least expected objections to standardization from the side of the workers. "But it must be," he reasoned, "that the workers lack the insight and knowledge of building history that would teach them that the uniform row house has always existed and that it is the appropriate contemporary means to aesthetic expression."[46]

Berlage's study of urban planning, as we have already seen, had convinced him that mass housing was fundamental to the modern cityscape. The era of the individual house had ended, and the unified housing block provided the only form appropriate to contemporary urban conditions. Large-scale and standardized housing was an economic necessity that also catalyzed cultural expression. Its repetitious forms represented shared conventions that would serve not only workers' needs, and thus society's, but also the interests of architecture. For the worker, shared conventions meant that an aesthetic would emerge to represent the democratic community that included the worker and made him central to its culture. For architecture, shared conventions would make possible the emergence of a great culture to equal those of the past. Social democracy, for all its apparent materialism, embodies the moral idea that all men are created equal, argued Berlage. This idea would be the cornerstone of a new spiritual foundation to contemporary culture, just as religion had anchored ancient Greek and medieval culture, the two historical periods when art had fulfilled its potential as an expression of the community. The idea of democracy would provide the collective ideal from which a shared definition of beauty would be generated, an objective and unified style, rather than the subjective individualism at the heart of laissez-faire capitalism. For workers or architects to resist this development would be as futile as to resist the force of history.[47] According to Berlage's historical determinism, the architect would have to sacrifice his individualism to serve the collective impulse, and the dweller would have to give up his claim to be represented by an individual dwelling. The individual dwelling unit would disappear into the communal housing block as housing became a unified entity, the product of shared conventions, creating a collective rhythm along the street.

In this argument, architecture's rejection of old stylistic forms was associated with the rejection of old forms of social organization. Modernity's break with historic styles would also signify the proletariat's break from the falsity of bourgeois art and taste. The architect's task would be enlarged from simply designing in a modern way to leading workers to understand the historical imperative driving modern changes in society and daily life. In the words of J. F. Staal, socialist and architect, workers who had not understood the necessity of breaking with the aesthetics of the past had not understood their own interests: "Unthinking, the worker naturally holds up the bourgeois dwelling as the ideal for the worker's dwelling. The worker can only speak up on the issue of his own housing with the language of the bourgeoisie since he has not yet arrived at either an insight into his own interests or a translation of them."[48] Artist R. N. Roland Holst noted the distinction between the bourgeois philanthropists, who wished to share with the workers their own high culture, and the Social Democrats, who predicted that the future would bring forth for the people a new proletarian culture. The new culture would break with bourgeois individualism and generate a period of art animated by the concept of community. He announced the "beginning of a new nonindividualistic culture for Holland, the collective spirit that is now striving for new expression, and is moving toward a new beauty."[49] Bourgeois art was associated with the past, with the historical forms that evoked the era of Dutch mercantile glory. A new art, appropriate to the coming age of the proletariat, would have to generate new forms to express class consciousness. Thus the significance of aesthetic reform was not simply that it included the working class as part of the public requiring instruction in good taste, but that the working class was central to the nature of that reform. Social, political, and aesthetic changes appeared to be inexorably linked through the mechanism of historical determination.

Berlage's syncretic urban theory had laid the groundwork for a new conception of public urban aesthetics. It provided a political and historiographical interpretation of housing design that defined its representational function in the new urban order of the democratic *Grosstadt.* Sitte had defined city planning as "the monumental expression of civic spirit."[50] For Berlage, housing was the medium of city planning, the material through which the architect expressed the civic spirit. Workers' housing deserved aesthetic treatment not only because workers deserved humane dwellings, but because mass housing itself constituted the building blocks of the city. The architect's role was to express the spirit of the community in his designs. His treatment of housing would serve to enlighten the working class, bringing them in contact with a beauty previously reserved for the wealthy. This was a worthy goal supported by socially minded architects and reformers. But beyond the benefit to workers, Berlage's conception of mass housing held out a promise to architecture's own development: only with the design of mass housing would architects be able to express the new age. Aesthetics rather than hygiene would drive architects' approach to the housing problem, no longer an added luxury, but a concern integral to its solution. Conversely, mass housing would become integral to the development of architecture, the agent of its formal transformation. The implications of these insights were to be worked out, however, not by Berlage's own generation of pioneering modernists, but by newer, rising talents.

THE ASCENDANCY OF THE AMSTERDAM SCHOOL

In 1916, the Committee of Aesthetics reviewed H. J. M. Walenkamp's design for the Zaanhof. It found that the design "in no way displays the character of workers' housing with its luxurious intentions, particularly the towers and the numerous gables, which will greatly increase the cost of construction and maintenance."[51] The emphasis on restraint and the call for the avoidance of extravagance typified the liberal attitude. A year later, the committee argued along quite different lines, criticizing the dull monotony of a project designed to house people forced to move from condemned slum housing. Its reproach to the architect was that architectural quality should be considered essential to even the most modest housing. The architect's defense that the subsidized character of the building required a subdued treatment carried little weight with a committee that now viewed all housing design as an aesthetic challenge.[52] Influence had shifted from traditionalists and modernists of the rationalist stamp to younger talents, who were challenging rationalism with a new emphasis on the imaginative and expressive character of architecture.

This fresh approach is discernable in the jury report of the 1917 competition for housing facades sponsored by Genootschap Architectura et Amicitia. The judges defined aesthetic criteria for workers' housing in terms of its emotive qualities: "The architecture must be powerful and simple, the incarnation of the coming class consciousness of the worker. Yet the architecture must not be too harsh and the exterior must reveal the 'friendly' living room, where the worker, after his hard day's labor, can rest amid his family. The overall color must display a liveliness since the people need it and will always continue to need it."[53] The simplicity demanded here was not meant to produce a bleak sobriety, but to take into consideration the responses of the dwellers. The jury expected the architect to design with the preferences and the needs of the worker in mind. The Social Democratic bureaucrat Arie Keppler, in urging architects to contribute to the aesthetic solution of workers' housing, had encouraged them to "understand what the working class needs and what it considers attractive."[54] When Art for the People was first set up, Social Democrat W. H. Vliegen had commented: "Whoever wishes to bring art to the people must fit that art to the people's capacity for understanding."[55]

These sentiments reflected a common set of attitudes toward the working class. Workers were cast as recipients of art served by artists and architects, whose job it was to cater to their needs. The role consigned to workers was not that of artistic patron, that is, a wielder of power, but that of a patient in the hands of an aesthetic caretaker. That the needs, wishes, and imagination of the worker were to be taken into consideration at all marked an important recognition of working-class aesthetic response. By acknowledging the legitimacy of that response, Social Democrats furthered their mission of working-class spiritual and cultural uplift. But the attempt to cultivate workers' taste by taking their preferences into account was based more on architects' assumptions about those tastes than on any actual study of them. The modern architect, who rejected the ostentation of bourgeois styles and the falsity of historicism, had been challenged to find an aesthetic language both pleasing to the people and reflective of modernity. But in this process of interpretation, it would be his own assumptions

FIGURE 7.3 Jan Gratama and G. Versteeg, municipal housing, Transvaalbuurt, 1917. Netherlands Architecture Institute.

about working-class aesthetic preferences that he translated into forms compatible with the modern architectural agenda. In his capacity as aesthetic expert, he would then take the lead in showing members of the working class what they should like.

Jan Gratama presented his design for municipal housing in the Transvaal district, which sported red tile roofs, multicolored woodwork, glazed brick and stone, as a response to the worker's psyche (fig. 7.3): "We feel that our primary duty is to make cheerful workers' dwellings. There is no type of dwelling more offensive to the worker than institutional housing, with its endless, monotonous rows of cells. Moreover, the drab pessimism, which comes from a lack of enthusiasm for life among the intellectual bourgeoisie, in no way forms an important element in the psyche of the modern worker. He has the right to enjoy life and he yearns to do so. Cheerful houses! Colorful and lively!"[56] The emancipatory luster of this statement, which with all goodwill values the worker's "right to enjoy life," is somewhat tarnished by the architect's presumption that he can ascribe to the worker the terms of that enjoyment.

One architect in particular met the challenge of using modern means to design architecture intended to please the working class. Michel de Klerk brought a vigorous animation to the treatment of mass housing that galvanized the conception of what such housing could be. He appeared not only to have answered the call for a powerful new expression of mass housing, but to have firmly negated the "endless, monotonous rows of cells."

De Klerk was one of several young architects who had come under the influence of Ed Cuypers, a student of the English Arts and Crafts movement. With Van der Mey and Kramer, De Klerk had in 1911 helped design an office building facing the harbor of Amsterdam that exploded with textural brick complexities and an intricate sculptural iconography. This potent combination of material and meaning found a following among the younger generation of architects who gathered in the architectural society Architectura et Amicitia. The emerging style developed suburban and urban faces, the first drawing on vernacular sources to produce cottages and villas of fantastic form; the second, in the design of housing, offices, and bridges, schools, and street furniture, coining a new set of expressive conventions saluting the city.[57]

De Klerk first tackled the problem of urban housing in several projects for developers, first a middle-class housing block in the Museum district, then workers' housing in the Spaarndammerbuurt (1913–15). Under the Housing Act, he initially worked for the housing society Eigen Haard, designing two more housing projects in the Spaarndammerbuurt near the first (1914–18 and 1917–21) (figs. 7.4 and 7.5). Later he collaborated with Piet Kramer in Amsterdam South on a large project for the society De Dageraad (1920–23) (figs. 7.6 and 7.7). He continued his housing work with designs for developers in Amsterdam South (1921–23), his career cut short by his untimely death at age thirty-eight in 1923.[58]

With these works, De Klerk transformed what modernism had to offer mass housing design. Applying the lessons of the English Arts and Crafts style to the local traditions of bricklaying, he put his considerable graphic imagination to work on the street facade, turning it into an expressive organism in which doors, window frames, rooflines, and stairwells became sculptural events on the swelling surface of the street wall. Other young talents of the new generation of Dutch modernists joined what by 1916 was dubbed the Amsterdam School and followed De Klerk's lead in developing a new architecture of daily urban life.[59]

These architects reinforced urban identity by focusing intently on the nature of their material, brick, the traditional material of Dutch city-building, exploring its sculptural potential to the fullest extent. Coining idiosyncratic forms whose curves suggested organic sources, they introduced new shapes to Dutch architecture that implied a variety of associated meanings. Although they rejected direct quotation from the symbols of Amsterdam's architectural heritage, the step gable, the inventive decorations of mannerist classicism, and the stately orders of Palladianism, their buildings seemed to provide an answer to the seventeenth-century core of the city, a response that found in the large-scale housing project features that might be transformed into contemporary symbols of urban identity.

The Arts and Crafts critique of industrial production pointed to a decline in the quality of design brought about by the false use of materials, the replacement of the artisan by the machine, and the loss of aesthetic authenticity due to industrial standardization. These accusations were used to justify a preindustrial aesthetic in which the rural vernacular served as chief model. The Amsterdam School accepted the arguments against the failings of industrial culture, but did not reject urban culture. These

FIGURE 7.4
Michel de Klerk, Eigen Haard, Spaarndammerplein, 1918. Gemeentearchief Amsterdam, negative VH2372.

architects took the techniques Arts and Crafts employed against the dull banality of industrial production and used them to transform the city. Rather than despairing of the urban condition, they accepted the realities of large-scale construction and multiple dwellings and denied the assumption that these necessarily implied monotony and uniformity. The very piles of bricks that elicited such negative reactions when formed into the endless straight rows of tenements in the Pijp were now animated to create a contrasting image. This was not the city of fragmentation, discontinuity, and alienation, but a city composed of a continuous fabric, harmoniously woven, flowing along the streets in waves of motion, designating the tempos of contemporary life.

As De Klerk's designs for workers' housing were realized, they met with opposition

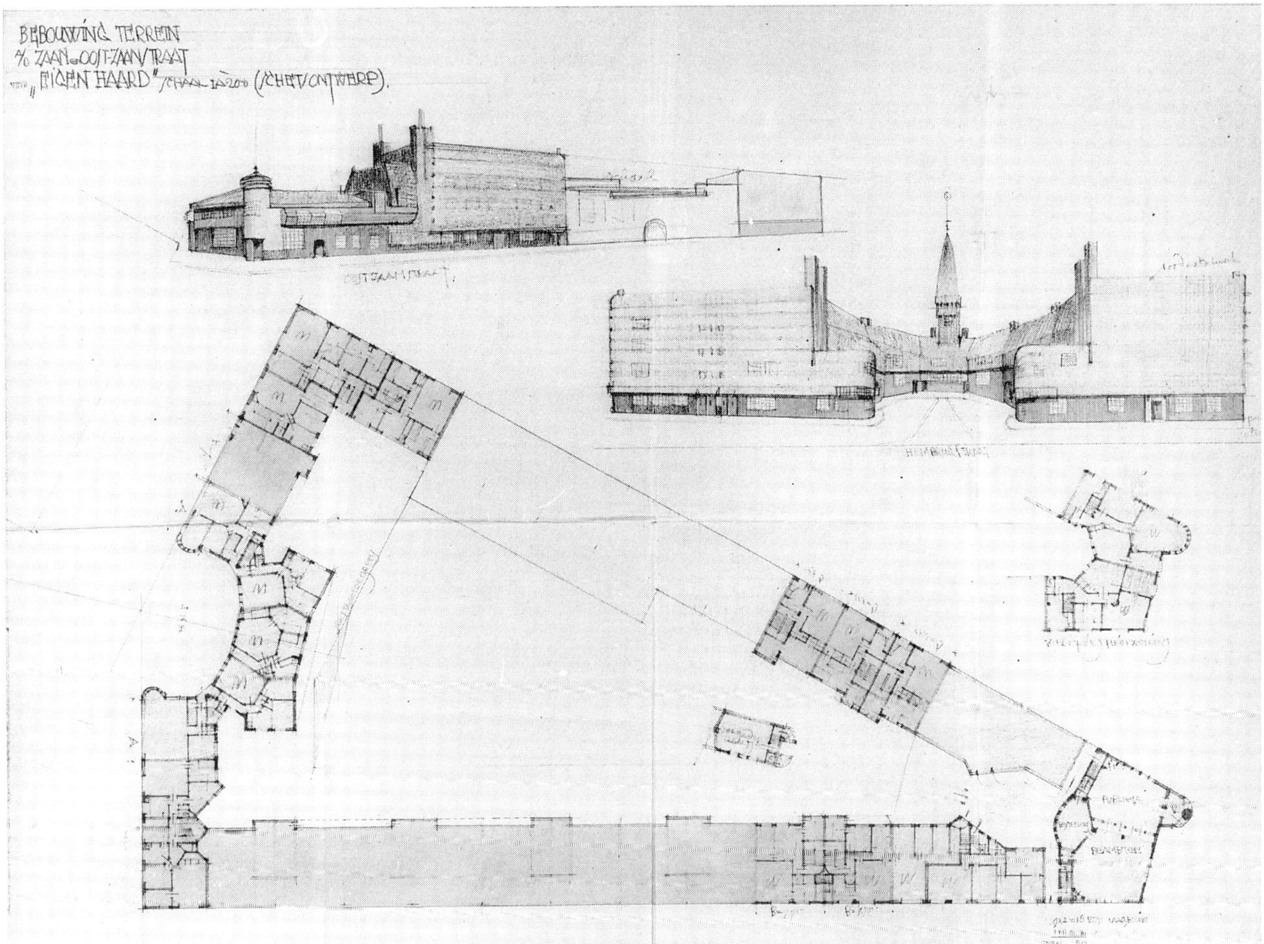

FIGURE 7.5 Michel de Klerk, Eigen Haard, Oostzaanstraat, Hembrugstraat, and Zaanstraat, 1917. Gemeentearchief Amsterdam, archive 5187, 2533 VH 1917.

from several sides. De Klerk's formal vocabulary made use of brick to create textures and sculptural forms that could not be justified by function and that often disregarded the expression of construction. They were accordingly anathema to the older generation of Dutch modernists, who adhered to the rational precepts of Viollet-le-Duc.[60] For the followers of Cuypers and Berlage, architectural beauty reposed in constructive truth and functional reality. In contrast to the architecture of simplicity and necessity with which they had spearheaded the renewal of design in the battle against historical imitation, the exhibitionist vitality of De Klerk's designs invoked a threatening irrationality. When De Klerk's first housing projects were shown at Genootschap Architectura et Amicitia's 1915 exhibition, the then Berlagian Jan Gratama reacted with mixed admiration and suspicion. De Klerk's designs won Gratama's praise for their sharp contrast with "the dull housing blocks with their endless rows of similar windows, their dull doorways, the pitiful roofs, their total lack of rhythm," compared to

FIGURE 7.6 Michel de Klerk, De Dageraad, gardens behind Henriette Ronnerplein, 1923. Gemeente-archief Amsterdam, negative 2432.

which the exhibited facades were full of fantasy, imagination, and strange shapes. He noted the "piquant" contradiction between the monumentality of De Klerk's housing blocks and their playful details. But he feared as well that De Klerk's work bordered on decadence, and that through it architecture might become merely a game.[61]

The work of De Klerk and his followers also lay open to accusations of frivolity, overdecoration, and willfulness from those Liberals and Anti-Revolutionaries clinging to Calvinistic notions of what was appropriate to workers' housing. The municipal advisory committee on housing considered De Klerk and Kramer's Dageraad housing in the Coöperatie district too whimsical, with its waving facades of brick that reach a climax of curves at the corners (fig. 7.7).[62] Members of that committee also objected to the costs incurred by De Klerk's last housing block in the Spaarndammer district for Eigen Haard, with its dramatic, but merely symbolic, tower and its elaborate masonry twisted into a profusion of textures (fig. 7.5).[63] Such objections echoed nineteenth-century arguments against the inclusion of anything but the functionally necessary in low-income housing.

While many Social Democratic housing reformers concurred with the functional approach to plan design, they also valued the aesthetic treatment of mass housing. Among the reasons liberal reformer Johanna ter Meulen broke off her association

FIGURE 7.7 P. L. Kramer, De Dageraad, Burgemeester Tellegenstraat, 1923. Gemeentearchief Amsterdam, negative 2431.

with the socialist housing society De Arbeiderswoning was that "no one except Keppler thought about frugality during construction. They were only content if it were beautiful, a lovely facade, something to show off."[64] The Social Democrats' belief in design as a moral tool of spiritual uplift and political consciousness made it clear to them that workers deserved the best architects. Socialists in the Amsterdam bureaucracy and city council promoted excellence in workers' housing design. Keppler argued repeatedly for the aesthetic side of housing as a legitimate and prominent part of the housing problem. F. M. Wibaut also encouraged aesthetic exploration and repudiated bad design. Perhaps already under the influence of De Klerk's new housing projects, he complained in 1915 that designs for the housing society Het Oosten showed no new thought, implying that workers' housing should display stylistic innovation.[65]

Social Democratic support of aesthetic uplift for the working class made some members of the party incline toward the innovative forms of De Klerk and other young talented architects. Unhampered by the rational principles that made some architects hesitate in their appreciation of the Amsterdam School, many leading Social Democrats were impressed by the new style. Indeed, it was a more effective carrier of their utopian message than the sober modernism of Berlage. Berlage's work, with its call for collective conventions to displace the clashes of individualistic self-expression, could be interpreted as a reaction against capitalism. But his architectural rationalism, applied for the sake of the community, represented the redirection of capitalist norms. Instead of profiting the few, the powers of industrialization would be harnessed to benefit the many, and socialist rationalism would supplant the rationalism of the market. For Berlage, architectural beauty resided in an aesthetic objectivity that was the product of a rational struggle with the requirements of material, construction, and function. The Amsterdam School, by contrast, countered capitalist rationalism by challenging the principle of rationality itself. Through its exploitation of the power of imagery to animate material, it provided a new aesthetics of place, community, and modernity.

The faceless, utilitarian, and commercialized urbanism of industrial capitalism constituted a modern space in which traditional bonds of community were fragmented and traditional spatial markers rendered meaningless. The notion that through aesthetic, that is, representational, means the perceived loss of place and community might be healed gave birth to both progressive and regressive mythologies of social and visual cohesiveness. The restoration of meaning as an antidote to the experiential chaos produced by the capitalist version of modernity became a tactic of political aestheticization adopted by both left- and right-wing ideologies. Resistance to utilitarian and universalized urban space was sought in what David Harvey has called the "particularism of the local."[66] In the Netherlands, the forms of the preindustrial rural vernacular and of the Dutch Renaissance became symbols of traditional visual coherence for the right wing, evoking a past of imagined social solidarity and stability. The lush forms of the Amsterdam School provided the left-wing with an alternative representation of social solidarity and stability, conjuring a utopian future.

The political ideology of the Dutch Social Democrats rested on the concept of a working class that derived from Marxist analysis of the economic conditions linking the interests of all workers, from the casual dockworker to the skilled typographer. Propaganda for class consciousness, the dawning awareness of shared interests that would spur political action, exploited nostalgia for a "rooted community" by idealizing class solidarity. With songs, banners, and posters, the SDAP articulated its notion of a working-class community defined by the virtues of solidarity, steadfastness, and righteousness. The aesthetics of community also motivated architects like those judging the Architectura et Amicitia competition, who required housing design to be "the incarnation of the coming class consciousness of the worker." When liberals claimed that government-supported housing should look like workers' housing, their intent was to mark the distinctions between the social ranks. The socialist support for a proletarian style equally intended an aesthetic differentiation from bourgeois styles, but in this case the purpose was to indicate solidarity, to express class consciousness. The representational arsenal of symbolism and iconography exploited by conservatives to defend the status quo would now be used in the struggle to communicate the myth of class, thus laying the foundation for a restored sense of community. The architects of the Amsterdam School developed a rich array of symbols for the collective nature of mass housing: the blanketing roof, the balcony extending along several dwellings, the rhythmic composition that suggested a harmonious movement along the street.

The richness of the Amsterdam School's forms also aestheticized place, providing a location of resistance to the monotonies of laissez-faire development. The architects' response to the industrial imagery of repetition and standardization was to create the illusion of the craftsman's specificity of design. Repeated doors and windows were given idiosyncratic forms and were placed in a larger frame of reference, the city block, with its own strong repeated imagery. The result was a strong sense of place despite the repetition necessary to mass housing construction. Indeed, repetition was exploited to create rhythmic streetscapes composed of pulsing elements.

The Amsterdam School provided an imagery for the modern city based not on fragmentation but on continuity. The style employed the traditional unit of city building, the perimeter block, and the traditional building material of the city, brick. Out of these was formed a seamless urban fabric in which visual metaphors of urban identity were incorporated. The speed and motion of modern urban life found expression in the flowing patterns of brick, the waving surfaces of the facades, and the compositional effects that stressed the street's directionality. Other factors also reinforced the creation of local identity. The peculiar organic shapes of ornamentation coined an urban vernacular specific to Amsterdam. The shaping of the housing block with sculptural corners, roofs, entrances, and the occasional tower established urban landmarks that distinguished neighborhoods one from the other.

Finally, the Amsterdam School celebrated modernity, although it occupied an unusual position among the strands of architectural modernity competing in the first decades of the century. It employed many of the visual means associated with the historical styles against which modernism rebelled: perspective, monumentality, iconography, ornament. It accepted masonry, the closed perimeter block, and the continuous urban landscape. Nonetheless, it rejected the imitation of historical style, invented a new visual language of forms, gave preference to collective over individual expression, and embraced the large scale, repetition, regulation, and speed of the city. The Amsterdam School occupied the part of modernity that still privileged individual experience. Its humanist modernism honored the subject, acknowledged the subject's point of view, and granted the validity of the sensual experience of architecture. In short, it rejected historicism but not the tactic of visual metaphor. What particularly distinguished the Amsterdam School from functionalism, aside from its focus on community and place rather than the aestheticization of hygiene and the machine, was its embrace of the experiential and its delight in representation. The style indulged the pleasure of making sense out of forms. For the bourgeoisie, the Amsterdam School built suburban villas that evoked the rural milieu through an interpretation of its forms and materials. For the working class, it built mass housing that celebrated the city, the collective, and the new. Through housing design, the modern city was to be transformed into a powerful expression of collective energy. The liberative implications of this urban mythology were evident to Social Democrats, who eventually identified the Amsterdam School as a symbol of their program of municipal reform.

The sobriety of the housing designed by older modernists like Berlage and Van der Pek contrasted sharply with the dreamlike flights of fantasy that characterized De Klerk's housing. The staid dignity of the older modernists' work resembled too closely the puritan moralism of liberal philanthropy. To create a new architecture of democracy, Berlage asked on numerous occasions that the architect and client sacrifice individuality for the sake of collective conventions. Such a sacrifice became more palatable when the collective repetition of mass housing was enlivened by the playfulness of the Amsterdam School.

ARCHITECTURAL PATRONAGE AND HOUSING DESIGN

In 1918, as Amsterdam prepared for the expansion of Amsterdam South, Arie Keppler expressed his doubts about the quality of the future development. His reservations were based on his experience working with housing societies over the previous decade. Only where he had insisted that De Klerk be appointed to build did Keppler feel he had achieved a good result.[67] He placed the blame for unsatisfactory results elsewhere squarely on the choice of "second-class" architects, referring in particular to those selected by the housing societies.[68]

Although the Housing Act did not make it a requirement, housing reformers encouraged the housing societies to hire competent architects. Dirk Hudig and H. C. A. Henny stressed in their handbook for housing societies that an architect would not merely help with the appearance of the housing, but, in their view more important, would improve the layout, hygiene, and solidity of construction.[69] In their positions in the Building and Housing Inspection Office and as trustees to a number of societies, Keppler and Tellegen exerted some influence on the choice of architect by Amsterdam housing societies. Typically, they presented the officers of the society with names and helped them chose from the list.[70] Reform organizations such as the CBSA and the Amsterdam Housing Council offered similar advice. One group of workers wrote plaintively to the CBSA, "Can your agency possibly recommend to our society a competent, and more to the point, a sincere and honest architect?"[71] Stylistic preference was not one of their criteria.

By and large religious or political affiliation, not style or taste, was the deciding factor in a housing society's choice of architect. A shared affiliation offered a guarantee of trustworthiness and a likelihood that the ideological preferences of the group would be understood. Kuipers and Ingwersen, known for their design of Orthodox Protestant churches, were a natural choice as architects for the Orthodox Protestant housing society Patrimonium. Similarly, Amsterdam-Zuid, the housing society initiated by socialist municipal workers, turned to the Social Democratic architects Gulden and Geldmaker. As one architect complained: "In our little country with its hundred or so shades of politics and religion, there are just so many cliques, with the result that Catholic housing societies chose Catholic architects, Protestant housing societies chose Protestant architects, and Social Democratic housing societies chose Social Democratic architects, each according to their own party."[72] The requirement of affiliation at times led to choices among lesser-known and less-talented architects, and once a housing society associated with one architect, it was unusual for it to commission another for subsequent projects.[73] As a result, Keppler's doubts about the architectural quality of housing society's projects were in some cases justified.

Ideological factors also influenced the quality of the architectural choices made by the housing societies. The *zuilen* exhibited divergent attitudes toward the patronage of art and aesthetics. The Anti-Revolutionary Party concurred with the Liberals on the principle of governmental impartiality toward the arts, although their justification for this policy, in contrast to the Liberals', stemmed from the religious character of their political theory. Abraham Kuyper articulated the Orthodox Protestant position on the arts, stating the belief that art and religion occupy distinct spheres. It followed that the Orthodox Protestant attitude was one of complete indifference to artistic achievement and that they felt no obligation to encourage government involvement in the arts. Architecture in particular was looked upon as inappropriate to Calvinist expression, since their orthodoxy claimed no need of palaces or cathedrals.[74]

For the Catholics and Social Democrats, the arts represented a somewhat different opportunity. Each viewed the arts, and especially architecture, as an integral part of their respective emancipatory projects. As soon as Catholics were granted rights in the early nineteenth century to practice their religion, church building and restoration brought Catholic architectural patronage to the fore. It was no coincidence that the initiators of the Dutch historic preservation movement were Catholic, as were the leading neo-Gothic architects whose association with the theories of Viollet-le-Duc placed them in the forefront of late-nineteenth-century architectural reform. For the long-oppressed Catholic community, architectural and artistic activity offered a means to reassert identity.

The socialist position on the arts displayed some similarities to the Catholic. Among Social Democrats, as we have seen, the cultural betterment of the working class was viewed as apt preparation for political work as well as a logical extension of the campaign to improve material conditions.[75] Leading Dutch Social Democrats absorbed the lessons of William Morris and supported contemporary artists seeking new, modern modes of expression that might represent through form and image their utopian aspirations for society.

One might expect these attitudes to be directly reflected in the architectural patronage of the affiliated housing societies. However, it is difficult to ascertain how much importance the individual housing societies attached to architectural quality, since they did not openly express much interest in defining the architectural style they preferred. All hoped for an improvement over the dull monotony of the speculative builders' vocabulary, but the newsletters, annual reports, and journals of the societies give little indication of stylistic preference. Het Oosten expressed the desire for a standard facade that would identify the society's projects throughout the city, whereas Patrimonium was pleased that its architects had avoided uniformity and monotony in the facades designed for the society.[76] The socialist housing society Algemeene reported that its membership lists expanded when it was announced that Berlage would design their first housing project.[77] To the many diamond workers who joined the Algemeene, Berlage was familiar as the designer of their union headquarters. Familiarity may have played as much a role as aesthetic preference in the evident enthusiasm for his commission. As architectural patrons, the housing societies rarely hired their architects on the basis of aesthetic preference and provided their architects with few or no aesthetic guidelines.

In the climate of aesthetic reform, both liberal and socialist advocates of public aesthetic review agreed that the expert alone could provide workers with the appropriate environment through the interior and exterior design of housing. As in the case of the housing plan, both liberals and socialists subscribed to a benevolent paternalism. Both wished to see workers move from their imitation of bourgeois taste to accept designs by experts who could interpret the workers' needs and desires. When the Committee of Aesthetics began its work, the housing societies were thus put in somewhat the same position as speculative builders had been: free choice of designer by the building patron was to be limited by experts in aesthetics acting to secure competent design. The housing society's role as patron of architecture was to be curtailed, its control and power diminished.

The means by which design control was to be wrested from the housing society was a matter of some discussion. The Committee of Aesthetics had been limited in the influence it could exercise over developers' choice of architect. A. W. Weissman, a former city architect as well as a member of the committee, complained in 1912 about the little control the committee had, noting that even if it repeatedly rejected a design, it could not insist that the commission then be given to a good architect, "which would be the only guarantee for a decent design."[78] Weissman's statement implied that the architects themselves, represented by the Committee of Aesthetics, were the only appropriate judges of architectural competence and that nonexperts could not make sound decisions, a position endorsed by the architectural societies themselves.[79]

In 1916, J. F. Staal suggested that the committee simply appoint an architect when proposals indicated total aesthetic incompetence.[80] The builders, he argued, could not be expected to make good choices on their own: "For such a choice it is necessary to have a broad interest in the architectural world, something that can be expected from the Committee of Aesthetics itself, but not from some builder whose interest is more or less only to his own advantage. A developer chooses a designer for his building sites preferably from among cheap, second-rate, or underaged workers, brick dealers' sons, assessors or mortgage bank agents, their relatives, and the like."[81] The Liberal Weissman and the Social Democrat Staal were in agreement that the committee had a central role to play in assuring that commissions be made to qualified architects, although their criteria for architectural qualification were at odds. However, attempts to put into practice any concept of control by expert authority unlocked strong resistance in favor of the builder's freedom of choice.[82]

The case of the housing societies was somewhat different than that of the builders because they had generally already engaged the services of a recognized architect before their housing plans reached the scrutiny of the Committee of Aesthetics. Nonetheless, the experts doubted the ability of the housing societies to make good selections. As a housing inspector put it, "It can hardly be left to the members of a housing society to decide what is beautiful and what is ugly in architecture."[83]

That conviction was hardened in the summer of 1919, when the mayor and aldermen asked the municipal council to approve plans for two housing projects proposed by the Bouwmaatschappij tot Verkrijging van Eigen Woningen, one in Amsterdam South, the other north of the IJ.[84] Both projects were designed by A. W. Weissman.

The Bouwmaatschappij began its work in 1868 as the first worker-organized housing society in Amsterdam and had built 940 housing units by the time the Housing Act was passed in 1902. Design and construction were supervised by an in-house drafting office. In 1908 the society, which prided itself on independence, leased land from the municipality for the first time and had to submit its project to the Committee of Aesthetics for approval.

The design was by L. van Buuren, chairman of the society's Building Committee, and it differed little from the standard designs the society had been erecting: drab, repetitious blocks with Dutch Renaissance gables. The Committee of Aesthetics rejected the design at once and, in accordance with its position of encouraging professional design, instructed the society to find a more competent designer for the facade. Weissman, by then the chairman of Bond Heemschut as well as member of the Committee of Aesthetics, took on the job of directing changes in the facades to meet the requirements of the committee. He was also consulted for the Bouwmaatschappij's next project and hired to design the facades for the society's subsequent housing.[85]

In 1918, the society proudly presented Weissman's designs for two projects to his colleagues on the Committee of Aesthetics. The projects seemed grim and dull, espe-

FIGURE 7.8
A. W. Weissman, Bouwmaatschappij tot Verkrijging van Eigen Woningen, Josef Israëlskade, 1924. Gemeente-archief Amsterdam, negative VH2455.

cially in comparison to recent brilliant facades by De Klerk and others. Weissman had made no attempt to treat the housing block as a plastic mass. Repeated elements, such as gables, bays, and windows, appeared irregularly, without rhythmic emphasis. The surface of the facade was unadorned. In both his low- and high-rise projects, Weissman had made little advance over the stark, utilitarian facades of nineteenth-century philanthropic housing (figs. 7.8 and 7.9).

When the Committee of Aesthetics reviewed Weissman's plans for Amsterdam South in May 1919, it commented on their "exceedingly barren character."[86] After its first rejection of the design, Weissman indicated his willingness to add a few gables and bays. But the committee denied the possibility of corrective measures and rejected the plans definitively. In a scathing letter to the mayor and aldermen, it explained the basis of its rejection. Even against the standards of massive simplicity to which Weissman apparently adhered, the design lacked any qualities of logical or aesthetic power. The low-rise housing planned north of the IJ took little advantage of the open setting, transposing the very same door, window, and roof details applied to the

FIGURE 7.9
A. W. Weissman, Bouwmaatschappij tot Verkrijging van Eigen Woningen, Meeuwplein, 1921–23. Gemeente-archief Amsterdam, negative VH3023.

large four-story blocks in Amsterdam South. The committee claimed that the designs showed no evidence of aesthetic capability and recommended that the designer be required to get aesthetic assistance.[87] Not a little of the animosity expressed in the rejection letter must have been due to the enmity between Weissman and supporters of the Amsterdam School, who by then made up the majority of the committee's members.[88]

Keppler concurred with the committee's recommendation and was prepared to assign the building site to another society if the Bouwmaatschappij refused to cooperate.[89] "I would deeply regret approval of these plans," he wrote. "Amsterdam has achieved a reputation at home and abroad for its attention to new workers' districts. The execution of the plans by architect Weissman would harm that reputation severely."[90]

Weissman defended his design by citing the constraints imposed on art by practicality, economics, and the building ordinance, the standard defense of liberal housing reformers for inattention to the aesthetic side of housing design.[91] More interesting was the housing society's defense of its architect. Dismissing the report as "nice generalities and principles," the society petitioned the mayor to override the committee's advice. It explicitly acknowledged its inability to judge the architecture, but it justified its choice of Weissman, pointing out that he was not only a publicly recognized architect who had carried out responsible commissions for the city, but a long-time member of the Committee of Aesthetics itself, an expert on the history of architecture.[92] From the society's point of view, it had hired a competent architect of good repute, someone who had originally been brought in to respond to the committee's requirements. It would deeply regret postponement of its plans merely because of "a difference of opinion about architecture between the Committee of Aesthetics and the architect Weissman." For these workers, professional standing was sufficient guarantee of architectural competence, and the aesthetic debates among architects were of no relevance.

Mayor and aldermen quickly moved to approve the designs, citing the extraordinary postwar housing shortage as a reason to avoid any construction delays.[93] But in the aftermath of this decision, Keppler and the Committee of Aesthetics began to insist that the collective control of urban aesthetics in Amsterdam had to be strengthened and that the choice of architect could no longer be left to the housing societies.

Several factors contributed to their conviction: belief in the public interest in an aesthetic environment, commitment to the aesthetic side of the housing problem, a desire for Amsterdam to take a lead in architecture, and the perception that no amount of review by the Committee of Aesthetics or any aesthetic adviser could compensate if the designs to be coordinated were inferior. Finally, distrust of lay judgment of architectural competence sealed the notion that both the community and architecture would be better served if architectural choice were placed in the hands of experts.

In general, the relationship between architect and patron involves an exchange of cultural and economic power. The architect brings a cultural capital that endows him with authority, and the patron's economic capital gives him the power to hire and dismiss the architect. However, in periods of aesthetic reform, such as the rise of modernism, the architect has more leverage in that exchange, for his role expands to that of instructor, guiding the patron's taste. In Amsterdam, the architect's cultural power was even further strengthened as working-class housing societies began to commission projects. The architect's social position vis-à-vis his working-class employers was entirely the reverse of where he stood in relation to bourgeois patrons. He was no longer subordinate, or at best equal to, those who paid for his designs, but their social superior. As a result, the housing societies were not able to assume the full power usually attributed to the patron. To a certain extent, they might better be viewed as recipients of advice extended in their own interest. Their position was thus less that of the progressive bourgeois sponsor seeking up-to-date recommendations than of the client receiving guidance from a social worker.

In 1919, appalled by the results of the Bouwmaatschappij incident and looking ahead to the large-scale development of Amsterdam South, Keppler initiated a discussion with the Committee of Aesthetics about measures that might be taken to improve future development in Amsterdam.[94] The committee shared Keppler's concerns. The Bouwmaatschappij affair had reconfirmed the members' belief that the officers of the housing societies were not competent to judge the aesthetic qualifications of their architects.[95] In many instances, they noted, the chosen designers were unable to handle the large housing commissions. The poor massing, lack of rhythm, and other failings of recent projects were proof that many architects lacked the fundamental ability and talent necessary for the design of mass housing.[96]

Keppler sent a memorandum to Mayor Tellegen describing the city as the "caretaker of an aesthetic urban design" and suggesting that housing must be designed by "the best architects of our land." The only way to accomplish this, he maintained, was the forced assignment of good architects to the housing societies. As a radical solution, he proposed that architects be assigned when building sites were allocated to housing societies. "The construction must be designed by the best architects of this country, while the execution can be assigned to other architects. This will mean that not every housing society will be able to appoint a designing architect. The architects who do the designing will have to be designated by the government, which is the caretaker of an aesthetic urban design."[97]

In response to Keppler's proposal that housing be designed by "the best architects," Tellegen raised the pertinent question, "Who are they?"[98] By giving the government the job of assigning architectural commissions, Keppler implied that the government not only had the authority to answer that question, but was better equipped to answer it than the housing societies. Keppler's commitment to providing workers with the best architecture led him to propose a form of collective architectural patronage that excluded the workers' direct participation. The role of the architect, the expert, was to fulfill the workers' aesthetic needs, providing architecture appropriate and pleasing to the working class, but not eliciting the workers' own opinion.

Keppler wished to give the municipality total control over urban aesthetics. He felt his goals would be best served by centralizing architectural patronage in the civil service, which would guarantee selection of excellent architects. In the heated context of postwar politics, following the successful socialist revolution in Russia and the aborted one in Germany, many shared his conviction that government bolstered by expertise could serve the common good by centralizing decision-making. "A new time has come," he wrote to the mayor, "old forms of organization will now no longer suffice."[99]

His interest in centralized control of style was shared by some of the architects most committed to modernism, although they viewed themselves, not the civil servants, as the logical authorities. By 1920, caught up in the postwar fervor for a new society, J. F. Staal envisaged a new role for the architectural societies that would counter once and for all the inadequate aesthetic choices of lay patrons, both builders and housing societies. Staal contended that the architectural societies should appoint architects to all building commissions. Bourgeois sentiment for freedom of competition had to be overcome, he claimed; and as for the freedom of the patron to chose his architect, Staal's experience on the Committee of Aesthetics had convinced him that such choices only hindered the development of architecture: "The architectural societies will only be able to exercise their right to assign the architects for all architectural commissions if the democratic view that the community is best served when each of its members serves his own interest gives way to the communist view that personal interests are served when the interests of the community are well served."[100] According to Staal, workers no less than the bourgeoisie must sacrifice individual taste for the benefit of the collective. Like Keppler, Staal sought means to provide the community with the best architecture through the centralization of aesthetic control and removal of choice from the people themselves. Architecture was to be left in the hands of the architects because only they could guarantee its advancement, and the advancement of architecture would serve the community.

In this climate, it is no surprise that a proponent of free professional competition raised his voice in protest. Theo Rueter argued vociferously in favor of a centralized bureau that would ensure that all qualified architects had equal opportunities to acquire lucrative housing commissions. His perspective reflected the liberal orientation toward aesthetic reform, which held that the public interest would be best served by requiring the involvement of competent, that is, professionally qualified, architects.[101]

This dispute continued the debate on the opposing definitions of architectural competence identified with the two architectural societies and played out in the Committee of Aesthetics. One side contended that the public interest would be served by setting a minimal standard of design professionalism, the other that the community would be served by collective, expert guidance of urban aesthetics. The former position adhered to a free market model of competing architectural ideas; the latter insisted that the market could not be trusted to benefit community interests, which should be protected by public aesthetic norms.

Staal and others argued that because architectural style is historically determined only a self-selected architectural corps could objectively identify the style of the age and thus provide the community with appropriate architectural expression. Since it required a particular expertise, the search for an expression of the community necessarily excluded participation of its lay members. The ideal architecture for the community was thus representational, rather than representative. That is, it would interpret the community rather than reflect popular taste. In short, as Reinink has written of the early Dutch modernists, they "were committed to furthering a future 'community art' in service to the people, but still without the voice of the people. At the same time, we find that this intellectual superstratum, precisely through the furthering of a future 'community art,' paradoxically elevated itself to an elite."[102]

Staal proposed that only those architects who had passed the aesthetic test of Genootschap Architectura et Amicitia's jury would be granted commissions. Far more than a simple guarantee of architectural competence and expert control, this solution was in fact calculated to create conditions wherein the young, progressive architects of the Amsterdam School would determine the new face of the city. Like most of the public arguments about urban aesthetics in Amsterdam, this struggle between proponents of modern and traditional styles was carried out under the guise of principled discussions about the proper exercise of public patronage. Keppler and Staal's arguments for centralized control appeared to be about the appropriate locus for public aesthetic authority, the Housing Authority legitimized by its public function on the one hand or the professional societies legitimized by their expertise on the other. But their arguments were in fact framed with full awareness that the authority each wished to empower would exercise that power to patronize modern architecture. Similarly, conservatives were well aware that their arguments for architectural patronage based on freedom of expression and professional status would enable traditionalists to build. The struggles to determine the legitimacy of authority in matters of public patronage were therefore integral to the struggles between conservatives and progressives in politics and aesthetics.

Both liberals and socialists agreed that workers' housing should be designed by architects. Liberals were satisfied that architectural standards would be upheld if housing were in the hands of competent professionals. They acknowledged the ugliness of unlimited development and accepted the Berlagian formulation of the urban plan as a large-scale, harmonious, orderly development. While abstaining from expressing stylistic preference, they shared the Calvinistic attitude that aesthetic considerations were a luxury in low-cost housing, an economic if not a moral extravagance. Restrained aesthetic expression reflected their economic and moral ideology. For the Social Democrats and their sympathizers, aesthetic treatment was a tool of spiritual uplift, a basic right, and the aesthetics of housing a positive opportunity for expression of ideology. The socialists demanded that housing be placed in the hands of the best aesthetic talents. The best talents should be tapped to serve the worker, and the best architecture should not be interpreted as too good for the worker because, in the socialist view, the worker deserved nothing less as reward for his toil.[103] Liberals justified public control of urban aesthetics with the Enlightenment ideal of rationality in which universal laws of beauty operated. This position was countered by the Social Democrats' insistence on the proletariat's right to excellence in design and the assimilation of the value placed by leading architects on the collective expression of the community.

The question of aesthetic control in Amsterdam was succinctly and ironically restated by one councilor in 1917: "Who will determine how the city will look? The individual builder? mayor and aldermen? or Public Works?"[104] As the city began to fill

Berlage's plan for the southern extension with housing projects, this issue became more pressing. Amsterdam was confronting the problem of identifying the legitimate arbiter of taste in a democracy. In the first flush of applying the Housing Act, it had become apparent that acceptance of urban aesthetics into the public realm had opened a new dimension in which power could be exercised. What had previously been a matter of private decision making had been claimed for the public. The problem then became twofold: What constituted the public realm, and who had the authority to speak on its behalf? Did that authority lie with the individual citizens, their elected representatives, or the bureaucracy? Or did it perhaps lie with the aesthetic experts, the architects? Each of these participants could argue for their legitimacy as arbiters of public design: the individuals on the basis of free choice, the politicians because of their status as public representatives, the bureaucracy and architects on the basis of their expertise.

The problem of public aesthetic control took on a particular coloration when it came to the design of housing. Given the semipublic nature of housing provision under the Housing Act, the identity of the architectural patron for housing projects was already uncertain. Many had a stake in housing design: the housing societies, the politicians, the bureaucrats, housing reformers, and the architects themselves. Each of these players was well placed to influence architectural decisions for the city. The housing societies hired their architect. The politicians approved the housing proposals. The civil servants guided the planning process for housing projects. The architects exercised design control through the Committee of Aesthetics. Only one thing was certain: that the workers who occupied the housing would not themselves play the role of architectural patron. No one trusted the workers on aesthetic matters. Liberals accused them of extravagance. Socialists accused them of ignorance. Rational modernists accused them of illogic. The modernists of the Amsterdam School accused them of bad taste. Everyone assumed that in matters of taste, the workers were misguided and required education. They were more clients than patrons, their role established as recipients of well-intentioned decisions made on their behalf. Nevertheless, this was a distinct advance over the days before government intervention, when speculative builders were free to pursue profit rather than respond to market demands. Working-class residents had not been able to exert any power as consumers in the tight housing market; in the welfare state there was then no reason to perceive their passive role as a loss of power.

The right of workers' families to housing that met public standards of architectural design had been established in Amsterdam; the construction of those standards and the specific visual choices were not, however, to be in the hands of the inhabitants themselves. Instead, competing claims were made for the control of urban aesthetics. As we shall see in the next chapter, this debate revolved around competing models of the public realm.

NORMALIZATION OF THE FACADE

During the first decades of the twentieth century, those responsible for overseeing urban development in Amsterdam contributed to a lively discussion about the appropriate means to institutionalize public standards of urban aesthetics. That there should be a visual order to the development of the city, an order to be enjoyed equally by all of its inhabitants, was a goal widely accepted by the time that the Amsterdam Committee of Aesthetics was established in 1898. The exact nature of that visual order, its extent, its character, and the means to bring it about were, however, still subject to debate. The creation of public norms for urban aesthetics raised a set of difficult issues: What means of deriving and establishing such norms would be consistent with a democratic society? Whose values were to define such norms and what vision of the city, if any, should be expressed through them? In innovative, if often problematic ways, Amsterdam's architects, politicians, and civil servants answered these questions through a series of experiments and negotiations within and between the municipal institutions in charge of design and urban planning.

Architects and politicians blamed the laissez-faire policy of the nineteenth-century municipal government for the unsatisfactory results of the city's development. H. P. Berlage, for one, believed a solution to this lack of control could be found through government-imposed norms similar to the eighteenth-century ordinances that had created regular, orderly urban ensembles in France and elsewhere. But he recognized that the politics of twentieth-century Amsterdam would not permit the high-handed, centralized control possible under autocratic rule. In place of the absolute political authority vested in earlier design ordinances, the authority behind any contemporary aesthetic norms would have to be democratic.

Democracy in the Dutch liberal state was served by the assumption that a public realm existed within which rational, critical discourse on matters of public concern could take place.[1] The institutions of the public realm wielded authority only to the extent that they appeared to be acting on the public's behalf, for the public good. In Amsterdam, the norms of urban aesthetics were to be determined and administered by the municipal councilors and the Committee of Aesthetics. This combination of political representation and expert discourse was meant to guarantee that the public good would be served fairly. But as we have already seen in the deliberations of the Committee of Aesthetics, the definition of the public good was itself a matter of some dispute.

When the participants in the public realm consisted only of liberal, educated, propertied voters, the assumption of a homogeneous public good had been uncontested because the values of one interest group were universalized. By the end of the century, new issues and new participants had entered the public realm, and its institutions were pressured to acknowledge the conflicting values and norms of the many interest groups that composed society. With the admittance of previously excluded groups into the public realm, the question of who the public was became subject to conflicting interpretations. The liberal answer continued the eighteenth-century notion of a society made up of equal and independent citizens with individual rights and common interests. This was challenged by confessional and socialist notions of community, inspired by separatist and utopian impulses, respectively. Each of these conceptions of the public had its own history of meaning; each served its own ideological ends. The shifting development, jurisdiction, and practice of the Committee of Aesthetics can be viewed as an account of its maneuverings to satisfy the proponents of these varied conceptions.

The notion of "public interest" rooted in Dutch liberalism was based on the assumption that the public, into which all citizens had been equally assimilated, had common concerns that could be addressed through rational discourse. Government was permitted to repress individual liberties for the sake of the greater good, but the concept had to be judiciously applied to avoid undermining individual rights. Achieving a balance between private and public interests accordingly required a legalistic, not simply a rational disciplinary, discourse. The official discussions and documents that record the work of the Amsterdam Committee of Aesthetics are couched in this language. They convey a sensitivity to both individual rights and public responsibilities, weighed against each other impartially.

Such a balance could be maintained easily as long as the committee's work was the enforcement of universal laws of beauty, equally applicable to all, and impartially applied for the benefit of all. Natural laws of beauty could be explicated by experts; the idea of natural laws assumed the existence of a rational discourse on the nature of beauty. That assumption permitted the committee to operate smoothly within the limits permitted by liberalism. As long as the Committee of Aesthetics operated under these conditions, conflict between aesthetic experts and government could be minimized.

However, another notion of the public realm raised more complex issues for the administration of public aesthetics. The notion of "community" arose in reaction against the atomizing effects of liberal economics. Instead of the homogeneous, abstract, and universalized citizen depicted by liberalism, this notion emphasized a collective identity. It served new participants in the public realm, groups whose interests did not coincide with that of the liberal bourgeoisie. On the right, "community" rested in the imagery of the organic society melded together by the institutions of monarchy and church. On the left, working-class solidarity and class consciousness provided a new basis for community. By emphasizing identity, community invoked self-representation. Unlike the public interest, it was a concept that favored image, privileging a narrative or representational discourse over a legalistic one.

When the notion of community was introduced into the discourse on aesthetic urban control, it disturbed the procedures that had been established to balance individual and public interests. "Community" implied the representation of collective identity through the production of an urban image. This posed a whole new set of dilemmas for the administration of an urban aesthetics. First, the positive specification of a collective urban image required government to assume the position of originator and promulgator of that image, a role with obvious historical precedent in autocratic regimes, but with a troubled history in democracies. More important, both left- and right-wing versions of community assumed a social consistency that was as questionable as liberal interpretations of public interest. Given the marked divisions of class and religion in Dutch society, the location of a shared polity was unclear, making both "public interest" and "community" problematic notions. Neither concept addressed conflict within society; each term assumed the existence of shared values. Both were constructed to appear natural, although they were equally ideological.

Public patronage of the arts, like any other matter of public policy, brought the internal conflicts within society to the fore. In a monarchy, for example, visual forms that would express the ruler's power and ideology could be imposed without impediment. In other words, not only was political power centralized, but that power easily found unified expression. But what of aesthetic patronage in a democratic society, with its inevitable conflicts of interest? If the polity was not unified, how could its aesthetic expression be? How might a complex and divided society begin to determine universally applicable aesthetic norms or seek to express itself as a whole through collective imagery?

Reacting to the perceived lack of unity in the nineteenth-century city, public consensus in Amsterdam supported some kind of restitution of visual order, whether through the application of universal laws of beauty, a sense of harmony, the expression of the genius loci, the representation of community, or some other means. Such aims could be served by government acting in the name of the people. But whose vision of urban beauty should prevail? Who in a democracy should determine architectural quality? Was the government to serve as the public arbiter of taste? How far should government power extend in order to secure a beautiful city? In this chapter, we will examine how far Amsterdam's municipal government went in the direction of imposing aesthetic norms on urban development and describe the range of government intervention as it was delimited by competing notions of the public realm. Urban aesthetics, no less than hygiene, became a means for defining urban order and thus an avenue for the expression of power. In a democracy no less than a monarchy, architectural style was not simply a matter of taste, but a political tool. The introduction of urban aesthetics into the public realm had opened up a new arena where its power could be contested.

REGULATION OF THE STREETSCAPE

By 1911, the Amsterdam Committee of Aesthetics was lobbying the municipality to increase its powers and regularize its legal standing, having grown frustrated with the passive role it was forced to play in the city's development.[2] In 1915, the committee was reorganized after long negotiations with the municipal government. No longer simply an advisory committee to mayor and aldermen, the committee was now appointed by the municipal council and enjoyed a new, extended mandate to judge facades proposed on all land leased or owned by the city.[3] It could also initiate comment on any matter it considered of import to the city's appearance.

Despite this extension of its jurisdiction, however, the Committee of Aesthetics still exerted only limited influence on the quality of architectural design in the city. It was now authorized to review construction on all municipal land and therefore, in effect, on all housing construction, but as before its actions were restricted to suggesting revisions for proposed facades. The impact of this system on the emerging cityscape was disappointing to many council members and architects, who pointed to the committee's failure to foster good design even where there were competent street plans.[4] De Lairessestraat, lined with facades approved by the committee, was a favorite butt of council criticism. The fear that the measures devised for aesthetic control might still allow new districts to arise as dull as the much despised Pijp led some council members to suggest that the designer of a street plan should also have some role in the determination of what was to built upon it. To some it was becoming apparent that to secure better architectural design for the city, the government would have to do more than merely enforce standards of professional competence. It would have to introduce aesthetic criteria of its own.

The Committee of Aesthetics had always reviewed isolated facades. Extension plans merely established street patterns and gave no indication of the third dimension, no standards for the street profile or planting, and no consideration of the aesthetic relationship between facades. Under such a system, the Committee of Aesthetics could do nothing to promote harmonious, coordinated construction on plans, so that even where architectural talent was employed, the results might be discordant.

Harmonious coordination of street facades had, however, become a goal articulated by architects and others. The value placed on stylistic harmony is apparent in the criticism levied by the architect G. Versteeg against recent construction in the Museum district, where facades had been carefully monitored by the committee: "One is struck with the surfeit of contradictions here. You have buildings by the most prominent and pace-setting architects, and when they are put together they create a completely absurd overall effect. This ensemble distresses me more than any incoherent collection of speculative building could." The Committee of Aesthetics, he insisted, would have to be more restrictive: "Not only will it have to watch that what is built meets aesthetic requirements, but further, until we once again possess a general artistic expression emanating from the spirit of the time and culture, it must see that the overall image of the street and square displays an aesthetic unity or a harmonious interplay of form and color."[5] According to Versteeg, government should actively step in and participate in art, not simply to protect urban beauty, but to provide, through legal enforcement, a created unity in the absence of a natural collective expression. Versteeg suggested that government can "act to regulate and assure that different blocks are treated with architectural unity."

Berlage argued much the same thing in a series of lectures at Delft in 1913. Under the influence of the urban theorists Brinckmann and Behrendt, Berlage maintained that a unified streetscape provided the key to a harmonious and monumental cityscape.[6] In his lectures, he identified the beauty of a city as an organic unity between its buildings and the spaces between them, that is, the streets and squares. A beautiful city is not composed of separate entities, but is itself a single entity that becomes a total work of art only when both the plan and the buildings on it have been designed as one.[7] The street becomes the passageway between squares, which are, so to speak, the rooms where great public buildings may be placed. Along the streets, housing flows without distinction between the individual units. The facades cover the houses behind them, emphatically unifying the space along the street. The city becomes a single organism, moved by a general impulse and filled with a great spirit.[8] Berlage had embraced Brinckmann's credo that city planning is the shaping of space with housing.[9]

Berlage noted that coordination between the urban plan and its third dimension was characteristic of eras that achieved a style representative of their cultures. That general style animated all artists in a given society, each interpreting it according to his individual ability. But, Berlage argued, this coordination had proved impossible in

Amsterdam at the turn of the century. Architectural unity could only be achieved by overcoming the destructive subjectivism of the times. With nine-tenths of all building in the hands of speculative developers, that is, incompetent designers, it was not surprising that well-designed street plans were spoiled. During a period of chaotic stylistic conflict, the desire for harmony could only be satisfied by imposing aesthetic unity. In the absence of a collective culture, society could take measures to achieve harmony by enforcing a certain regularization of form. It was only natural, then, to reexamine earlier building restrictions that had achieved unity between street plan and construction.[10]

Berlage looked to the eighteenth century for models. He pointed to examples where separate facades were combined into unified blocks by standard cornice heights, roof profiles, and fenestration, and he drew attention to the princely regulations that established standard facade types in France and Germany.[11] Berlage defended the imposition of unity with such artificial means by quoting the eighteenth-century theoretician Abbé Laugier: "If one wishes a city to be well built, then one must not leave the facades to the discretion of individuals. Everything along the street must be stipulated and subjected to the judgment of the public authorities in agreement with what has been established. Not only must the location where one is allowed to build be fixed, but also the way in which one is required to build." Berlage admitted, "This sounds to us rather despotic, to some extent intolerable, yet at that time the art of building and particularly of urban design, achieved a high level."[12]

Berlage concluded that the individual architect must bow to norms imposed by the community. The need to control the individual for the sake of the collective stood behind the inception of such institutions as committees of aesthetics, he argued. The chaotic results of personal taste when unrestrained by tradition made public controls necessary. The only way to produce a unified cityscape under the current stylistic conditions was to have one person design an entire street or have several architects cooperate.[13] There must be an overall coordination between the city blocks, and between the plan and what is built on it. The designer of the plan must therefore indicate the nature of the building to be placed on his plan.

With this vision of a city constructed of unified blocks, Berlage outlined the program for future attempts to achieve architectural quality in Amsterdam's new districts. His translation of the planning theories of Brinckmann and others provided the impetus for increased municipal involvement in shaping the city. The implications of his position, worked out through the municipal institutions of planning and housing design in the following ten years, eventually led to the public imposition of stylistic harmony, in essence, a system that encouraged the normalization of the facade in a manner that paralleled that of the dwelling plan.

In the memorandum to his revised plan for Amsterdam South of 1915, Berlage restated the main points of his 1913 lectures, now providing practical guidelines for the harmonious development of the city: Large-scale development of housing should be encouraged; building permits should be granted only for entire streets or squares; and when several builders construct on the same site, they should cooperate to create a unified whole. Such large-scale construction could, of course, only be undertaken by major developers or by housing societies with adequate resources and talent.[14]

Berlage found a sympathetic audience among some members of the Amsterdam municipality. The newly reorganized Committee of Aesthetics was receptive to the idea of design coordination; the new head of the Housing Authority supported the position; and within Public Works, the architect J. M. van der Mey made similar proposals. In 1915, Van der Mey argued that he should oversee the construction of his own plan for the Indische district, stressing the importance of unity between plan and architecture. The approval of facades by the Committee of Aesthetics did not guarantee unity of construction, he argued, so it was necessary for an aesthetic adviser to take control.[15] This would ensure that proposed construction, as the product of a single architectural mind and taste, would create a sense of consistency and harmony within new neighborhoods.

Van der Mey's ideas met with resistance from the right. His proposal to supervise construction in the Indische district was rejected by the Public Works Committee. Its members did not want to impose restrictions on private developers, who they felt would be anxious to proceed with construction quickly and unimpeded.[16] For liberals and confessionals, the developer's financial interests outweighed any public aesthetic concerns and were not to be made subject to what was viewed as excessive government control.

Compared with the private housing developers, the semipublic housing societies working with public monies under public supervision provided less controversial opportunities for the exercise of aesthetic control by those municipal authorities who favored it. Even before he headed the separate Housing Authority created in 1915, Arie Keppler had been working to coordinate the building efforts of housing societies. As supervisor at the Building and Housing Inspection Office, he began a series of experiments in 1913 to improve the design of workers' residential districts.

Keppler started in the Spaarndammer district, where the original plan proposed by Public Works had been criticized for its old-fashioned gridiron pattern. As housing societies began to apply to the city to lease land there, Keppler began to consider ways of bringing contemporary concepts of urban design into the neighborhood.[17] He was impressed by the successful application in Arnhem and Leipzig of the *hof*, that is, a large perimeter block pierced with openings leading to housing lining an interior

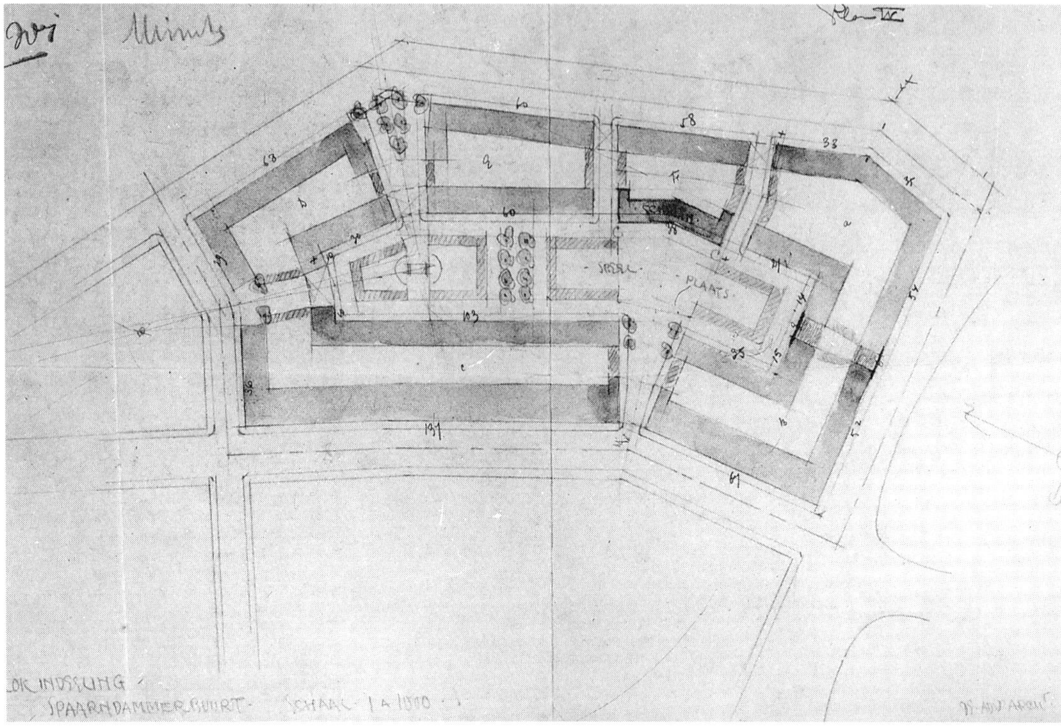

FIGURE 8.1 J. M. van der Mey, plan for the Zaanhof, 1913. Gemeentearchief Amsterdam, archive 5213–630, Dienst PW 1616/1921.

courtyard.[18] He roughly sketched such a block with low two-story houses and a school on the inside, surrounding an open playground, and higher three- and four-story houses on the exterior rim. He then engaged Van der Mey's help in developing the design.[19] The resulting complex, the Zaanhof (fig. 8.1), was the first application of a design concept that would be used repeatedly in the 1920s in Amsterdam South to bring light, air, and green space to mass housing. Although it bore some resemblance to the courtyards of *hofjes*, philanthropic housing established as early as the sixteenth century, the Zaanhof differed considerably in design. The *hofjes* usually formed a single rim of low housing opening directly on a small courtyard, whereas the Zaanhof formed a double ring of housing around a large courtyard surrounded by a narrow road.

Keppler arranged for the architects of the three participating housing societies to meet with him and Van der Mey to coordinate their designs on the plan. With the exception of the school design, the entire interior perimeter was assigned to one housing society and thus designed by one architect, in this case H. J. M. Walenkamp working for Het Westen. His gabled fronts reinforced the rural motif already suggested by the enclosed green (fig. 8.2). The exterior rim was executed primarily by Patrimonium's usual architects, Tjeerd Kuipers and A. U. Ingwersen, who designed four-story housing with the repeated turrets of a medieval fortress protectively encircling the lower housing (fig. 8.3). Their design was interrupted along one side by a rather sober continuation of the four-story wall by W. Greve designing for the housing society HIJSM. Although the three designs shared neither materials, color, nor style, the whole complex formed a unified entity by virtue of Van der Mey's design of a strong enclosure penetrated by passageways. As a result, the entire block succeeded in creating a visually coordinated neighborhood. Breaking with the district's grid pattern, it formed an enclave that exuded closeness and community, from within emulating the peacefulness of a village green, on the exterior suggesting cohesive solidarity. The Zaanhof was the first attempt by the municipal authorities in Amsterdam to coordinate urban design and control the shape of the city by means of housing built under the Housing Act. It received considerable praise.[20]

With the founding of the Housing Authority and the reorganization of the Committee of Aesthetics in 1915, the possibilities for design coordination based on cooperation between municipal institutions were soon realized. Soon after the Housing Authority was established with Keppler at its head, Jan Gratama, then editor of the *Bouwkundig Weekblad* and a member of the Committee of Aesthetics, suggested that a special committee be appointed to lead the architectural coordination of municipal housing projects.[21] Continuing his efforts to encourage aesthetic conformity in hous-

FIGURE 8.2 H. J. M. Walenkamp, Het Westen, Zaanhof, 1920. Gemeentearchief Amsterdam, negative D39061.

FIGURE 8.3 T. Kuipers and A. U. Ingwersen, Patrimonium, Spaarndammerdijk, 1919. Gemeentearchief Amsterdam, negative VH2388.

ing design, Keppler and the new Committee of Aesthetics went to work at once to create the kind of leadership Gratama had suggested. In this attempt to gain control of neighborhood planning, those seeking to improve the quality of architecture within a harmonious cityscape were often pitted against those defending fiscally motivated conceptions of land development.

Writing to the Committee of Aesthetics in November 1915 about several projects to be built along the Krommeniestraat in the Spaarndammer district, Keppler raised the issue of coordination between architects building within the same block. The projects were adjacent to an existing row of housing by De Klerk on the Spaarndammerplantsoen and only a few blocks from the Zaanhof. De Klerk's design, which had been carried out for the private developer Klaas Hille, was the first housing project to use the flamboyant brickwork already applied in Van der Mey, De Klerk, and Kramer's collaboration at the office building the Scheepvaarthuis. In an early sketch (fig. 8.4), De Klerk articulated the flow of material and the rhythmic accents of stairwell and windows that would characterize the final project. The sketch suggests the organic nature of the street facades Berlage called for, not least because in it De Klerk extended the stylistic treatment to hypothetical housing on the same and nearby blocks.[22] Keppler expressed an interest in achieving such stylistic coordination in reality.[23] But although Keppler, the Committee of Aesthetics, and the architects working for housing societies assigned to the adjacent blocks participated in lengthy debates about how

FIGURE 8.4 Michel de Klerk, sketch for housing block on the Spaarndammerplantsoen, 1913. Netherlands Architecture Institute, De Klerk archive, no. 29.

FIGURE 8.5 Michel de Klerk, drawing of housing project for Eigen Haard, Spaarndammerplantsoen, 1915. From *Bouwkundig Weekblad* 36, no. 28 (6 November 1915), facing 210.

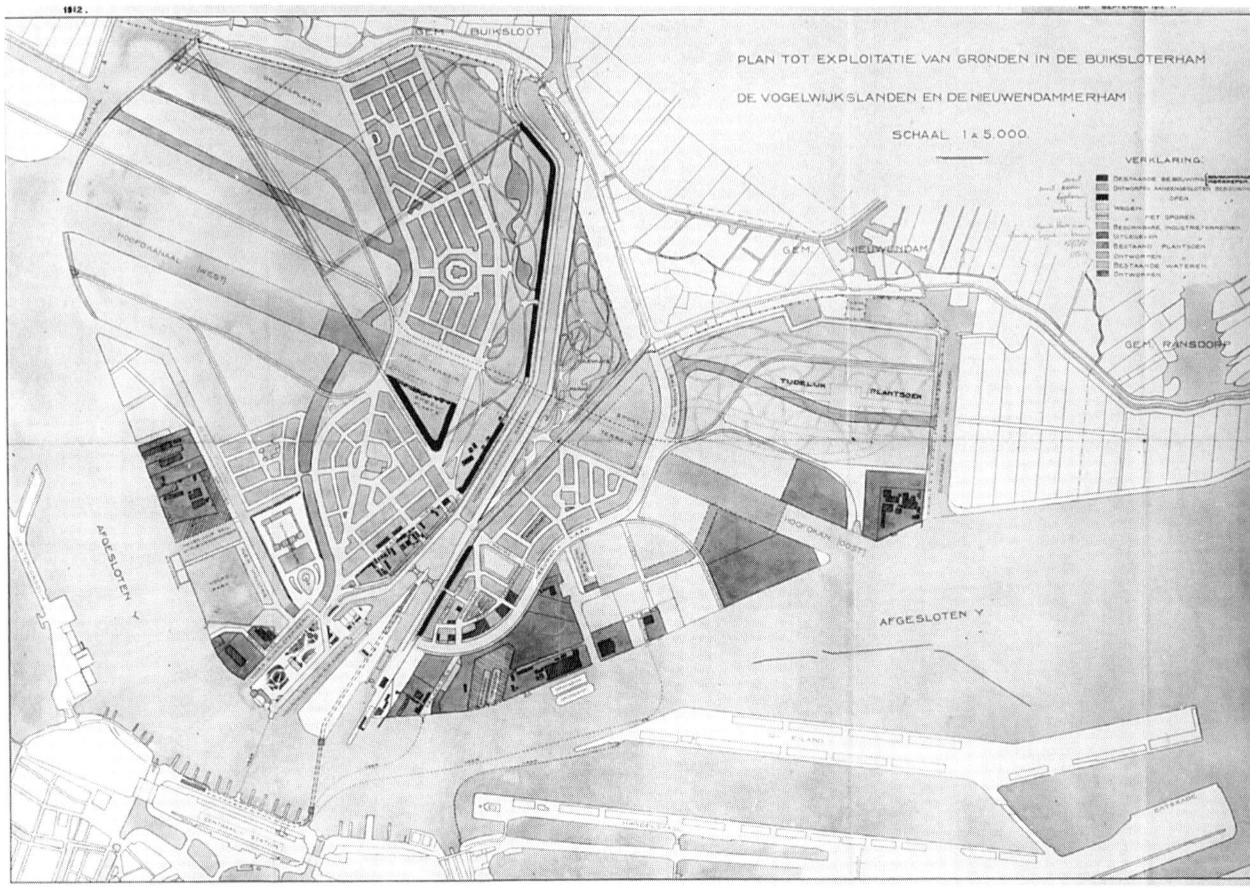

FIGURE 8.6 Public Works, plan for Amsterdam North, 1910. Gemeentearchief Amsterdam, archive 5180, 6587 PW 1912.

to combine the designs, their discussions only underlined the difficulty of combining what proved to be radically different styles in one block.[24]

De Klerk had also designed a block of housing for Hille parallel to the first block and across the Spaarndammerplantsoen. When inflation and shortages cut off the private building sector at the onset of World War I, Hille had been forced to abandon the project, but Keppler was able to convince the building society Eigen Haard to take it on, so that the unity of the square could be preserved. On the third side of the square, Gulden and Geldmaker made plans for the housing society Amsterdam-Zuid that De Klerk felt would not disturb his design. As a result, a stylistically unified square was created, not unlike the image De Klerk himself had envisaged in his drawing of the project (fig. 8.5).[25] This experience prompted the Committee of Aesthetics to propose to the mayor and aldermen that in the future entire blocks be assigned to a single housing project to facilitate coordination of architectural treatment.[26]

Keppler's successes in the Spaarndammer district were paralleled by other experiments in neighborhood planning. In 1910, Public Works had prepared a provisional

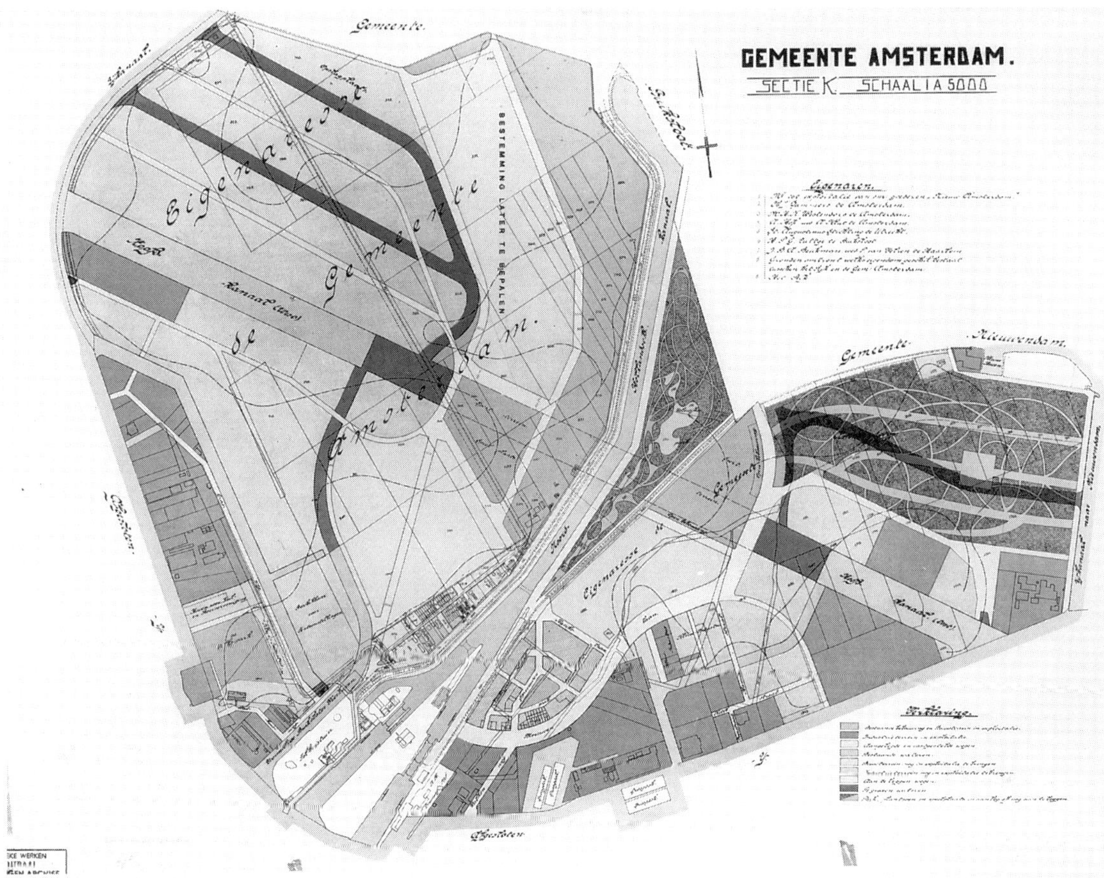

FIGURE 8.7 Public Works, plan for Amsterdam North, 1914. Gemeentearchief Amsterdam, negative 3349.

street plan for a new district north of the IJ, including the northern half of Nieuwendammerham (fig. 8.6), but approval of the plan was postponed until the general extension plan for North Amsterdam could be approved.[27] By the time the general plan neared completion in 1914 (fig. 8.7), housing societies had begun to request land there. The district was attractive not only because of its proximity to jobs in the harbor, but because the plan called for restriction of building heights to a maximum of three stories. Under new regulations, the housing societies applied to the Building and Housing Inspection Office for land, rather than to the Public Works Department, which had previously controlled all municipal land allocation, an acknowledgment of the increasing significance of housing interests. Keppler, as head of the housing division, now hoped to take over some of the plan-making functions of Public Works. Long critical of Public Works' approach to neighborhood design, he attempted to bring modern planning concepts to bear on the housing plans for which he was responsible.

At the beginning of 1914, Keppler asked Public Works if he could control the

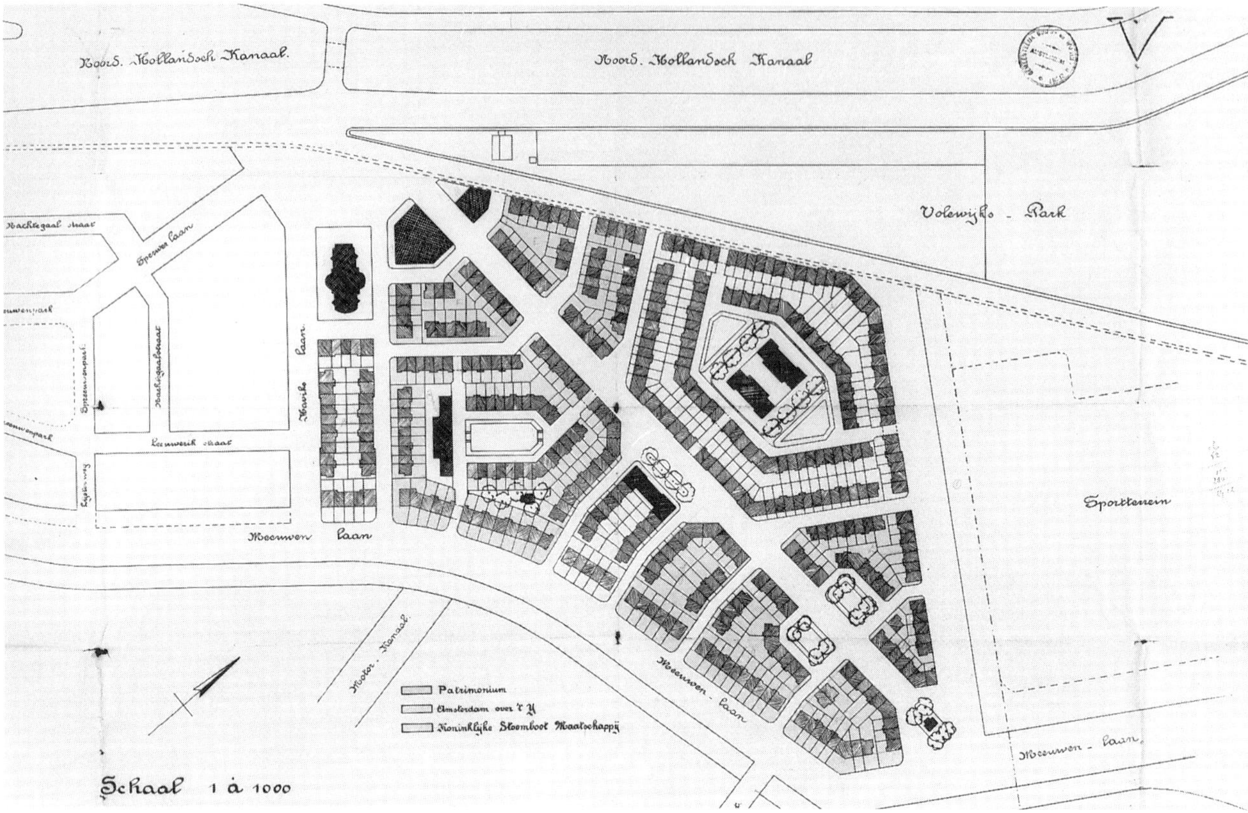

FIGURE 8.8 Municipal Housing Authority, unexecuted plan for Nieuwendammerham II, 1916. Gemeentearchief Amsterdam, archive 5180, 4955 PW 1914.

design for the new district. In collaboration with several architects working for housing societies that had requested land in the area, he drew up a street plan for the northern half of Nieuwendammerham.[28] The plan consisted of a diagonal traffic road separating two courtyard complexes designed like the Zaanhof, with a rim of housing on the exterior and a quiet courtyard lined with low housing on the inside (fig. 8.8). Schools placed in the courtyards and along the street formed focal points, a reaction against the prevailing custom of hiding schools within the space enclosed by perimeter blocks.[29] However, Keppler's bid to influence neighborhood planning was curbed by A. W. Bos, the director of public works, who was infuriated by Keppler's attempt to take over his department's planning functions. Bos called on his aesthetic adviser Van der Mey to redesign the plan.[30]

When Keppler and Tellegen saw that the new plans designed by Van der Mey sent to them in July 1914 did not make use of the *hof* concept they were so actively promoting, they protested to the alderman of housing.[31] Although Bos did not favor the procedure, Van der Mey, who had previously worked with Keppler in the design of the Zaanhof, once again began coordinating a joint plan between housing society architects. Keppler specifically asked that his plans facilitate the assignment of entire blocks to single architects in order to better the aesthetic treatment of the neighborhood.[32]

After numerous revisions, Van der Mey's plan finally met the approval of all parties (figs. 8.9 and 8.10). His plan established two main axes intersecting at an oblique angle, with a church at the pivot point. The side streets were narrow and short. Although Van der Mey did not use the *hof* concept, a similar intimacy was achieved by grouping the housing around open spaces to form quiet enclosures.[33] Here, as at the Zaanhof, the neighborhood street plan had been manipulated to create a sense of community and to facilitate architectural coordination between housing projects.

Keppler supervised the division of Van der Mey's plan among the six participating housing societies.[34] Then he began the second part of his experiment. He brought the architects of the six housing societies together to discuss the architecture of the neighborhood.[35] He requested the Committee of Aesthetics to consider the six projects simultaneously, rather than following the customary procedure of reviewing their facades individually. Working in coordination with one another, the architects pre-

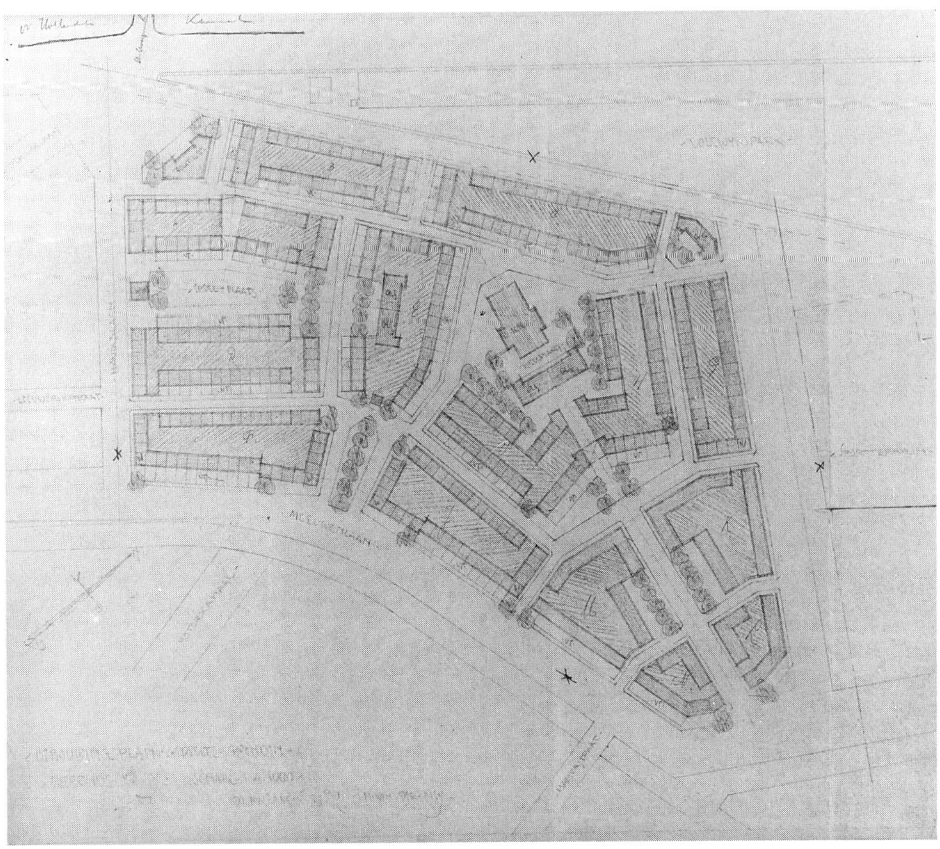

FIGURE 8.9 J. M. van der Mey, sketch plan for Nieuwendammerham II, 1916. Gemeentearchief Amsterdam, archive 5180, 4955 PW 1914.

pared perspective drawings and bird's-eye views (figs. 8.11 and 8.12). In their review, the Committee of Aesthetics made recommendations for the coordination of materials and rooflines.[36]

The neighborhood in Nieuwendammerham made a striking contrast to earlier housing developments in Amsterdam. When Berlage's plans for Amsterdam South came up for approval in the council in 1917, housing alderman Wibaut displayed sketches of Nieuwendammerham to stifle objections that designing by city block, as recommended by Berlage, necessarily meant dull monotony.[37] The following year, Keppler applied a similar system of architectural coordination to the Coöperatie district in Amsterdam South.[38] There, in contrast to the development north of the IJ, the process was applied to the dense urban fabric of three- and four-story housing. Work-

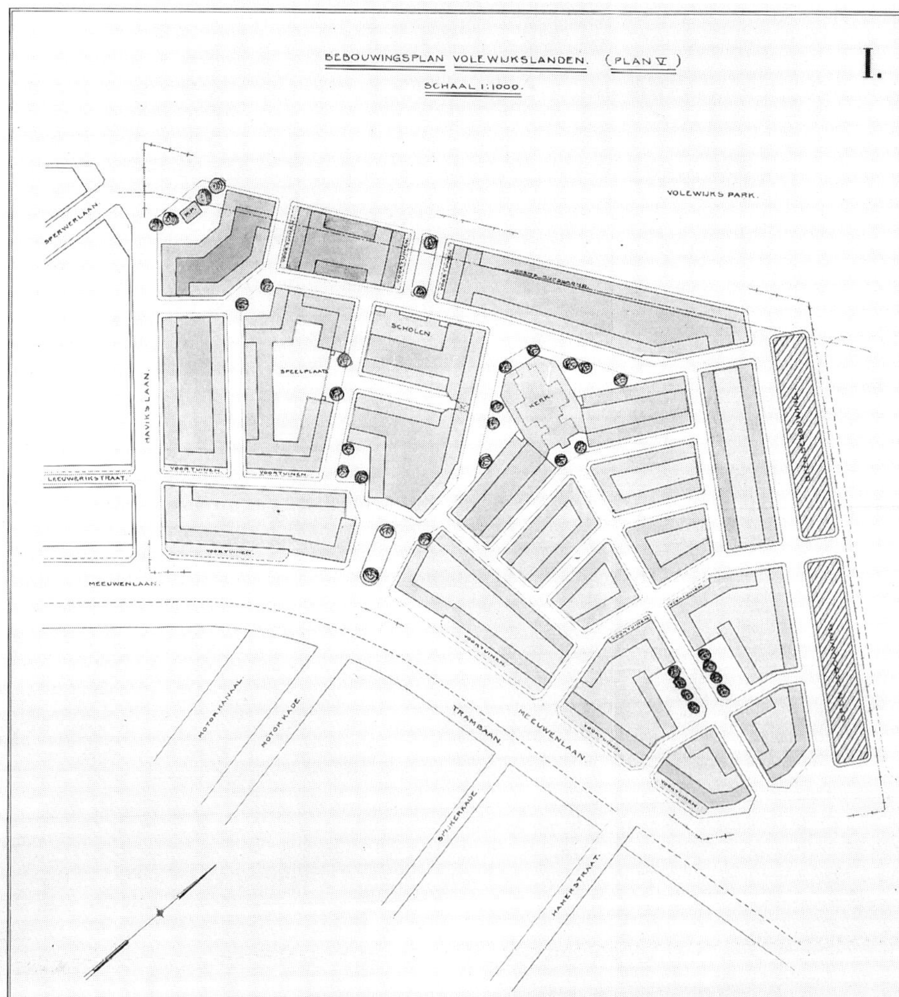

FIGURE 8.10 Public Works, plan for Nieuwendammerham II, 1916. Gemeentearchief Amsterdam, archive 5187, 1609 VH 1916.

FIGURE 8.11 Jan Gratama and G. Versteeg, Eigen Haard, bird's-eye perspective of Nieuwendammerham II, 1918. Netherlands Architecture Institute, Gratama archive, negative 90.

FIGURE 8.12 Jan Gratama and G. Versteeg, Eigen Haard, Nieuwendammerham II, 1918. Netherlands Architecture Institute, Gratama archive, no. B8.

ing for De Dageraad, Michel de Klerk and Piet Kramer designed a remarkable project in which the housing along a central street seemed to flow in waves, culminating at billowing corners, while the dwellings that edged two matching open spaces clustered under swelling rooflines (figs. 7.6 and 7.7).[39] To either side of this impressive complex, architects working for other housing societies designed less flamboyant but similarly positive evocations of the urban condition.

Although the housing societies provided a ready opportunity for design coordination, in the case of municipal housing, which the council authorized in 1915, Keppler was able to exert total control as director of the Housing Authority. Rather than turn to the architects of the Public Works Department, he selected private architects to design the first three housing projects. The choice fell on three architects with experience in urban housing design: J. E. van der Pek, K. P. C. de Bazel, and H. P. Berlage. In each case, Keppler was able to arrange the innovative coordination of plans and buildings. For De Bazel's project in the Spaarndammer district, Keppler took over the area of a playground, originally intended for housing societies (fig. 6.4). Once again engaging the services of Van der Mey, the neighborhood was redesigned to form

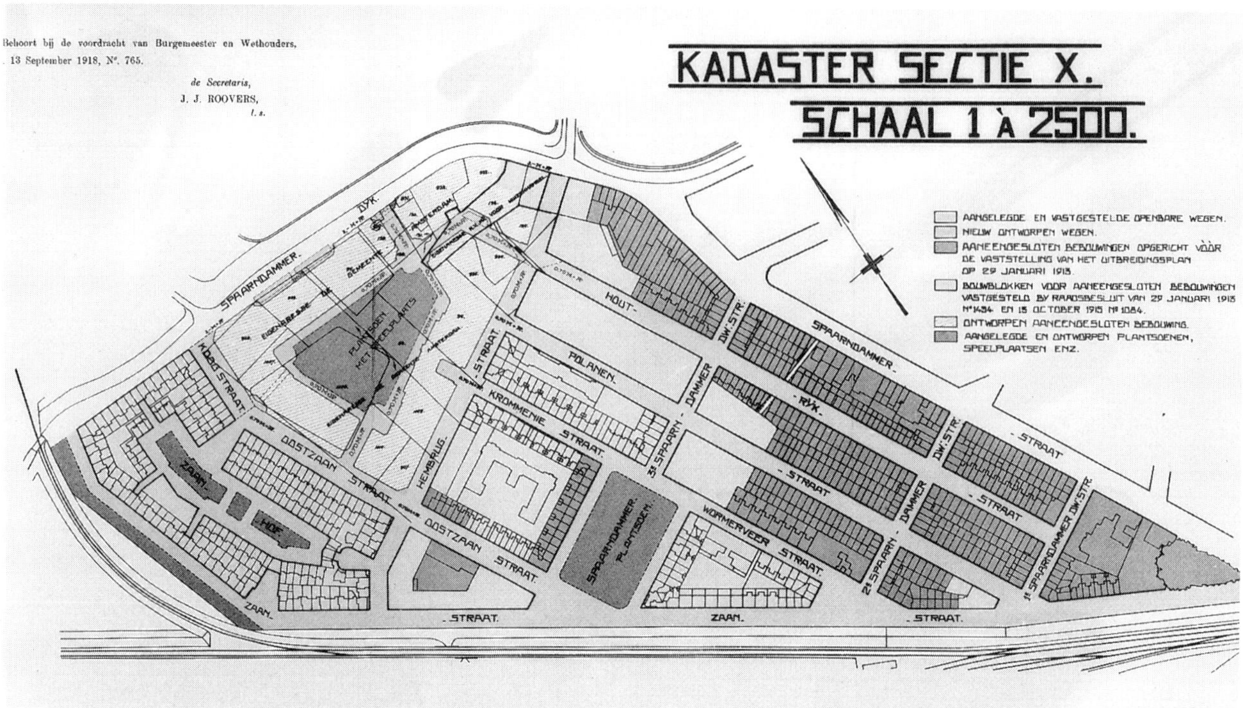

FIGURE 8.13 Public Works, revised plan of Spaarndammerbuurt including the Polanenhof, 1918. Gemeentearchief Amsterdam, archive 5187, 3079 VH 1918.

FIGURE 8.14
K. P. C. de Bazel, municipal housing, Polanenhof, 1923. Gemeentearchief Amsterdam, negative VH8215.

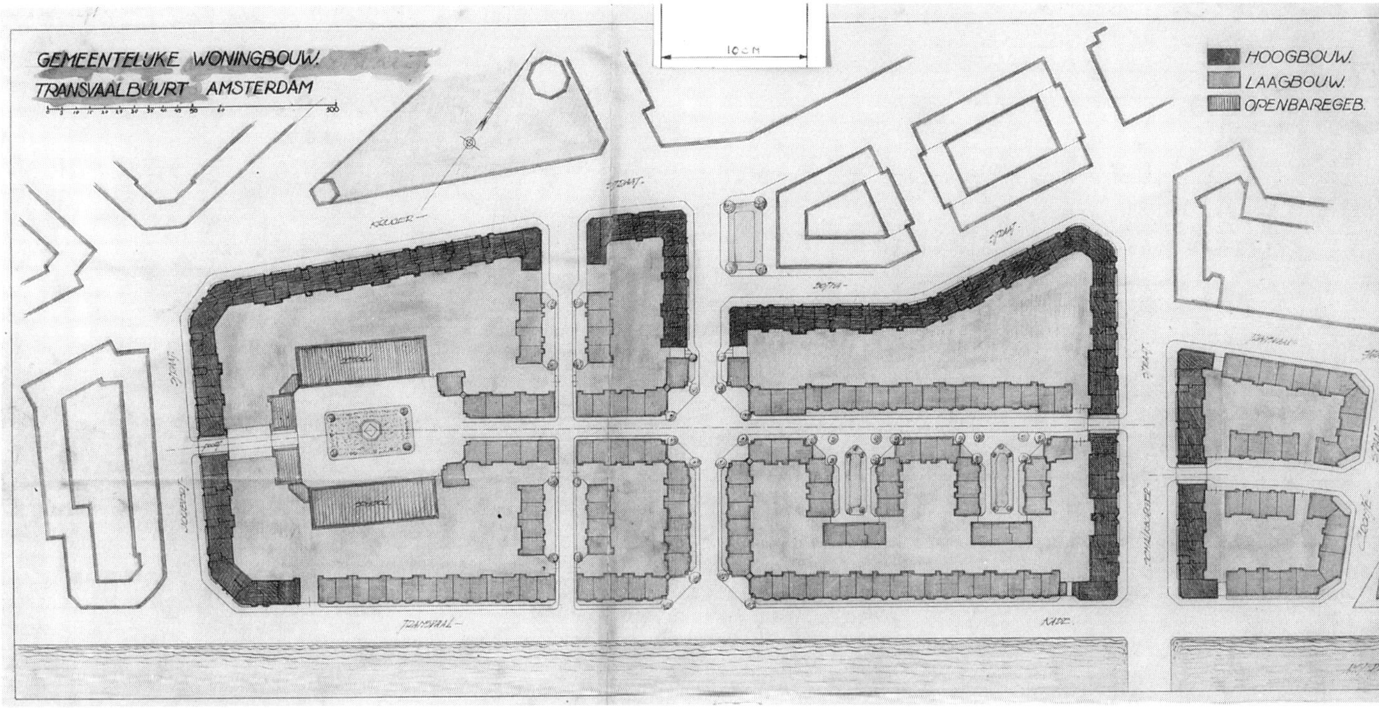

FIGURE 8.15 H. P. Berlage, Jan Gratama, and G. Versteeg, plan for municipal housing in the Transvaalbuurt, 1915. Netherlands Architecture Institute, Gratama archive, negative 3961.

FIGURE 8.16 H. P. Berlage, Jan Gratama, and G. Versteeg, municipal housing, Kraaipanstraat, 1923. Gemeentearchief Amsterdam, negative VH2574.

FIGURE 8.17 J. E. van der Pek, plan for Buiksloterham, 1916. Gemeentearchief Amsterdam, archive 5187, 670 VH 1917.

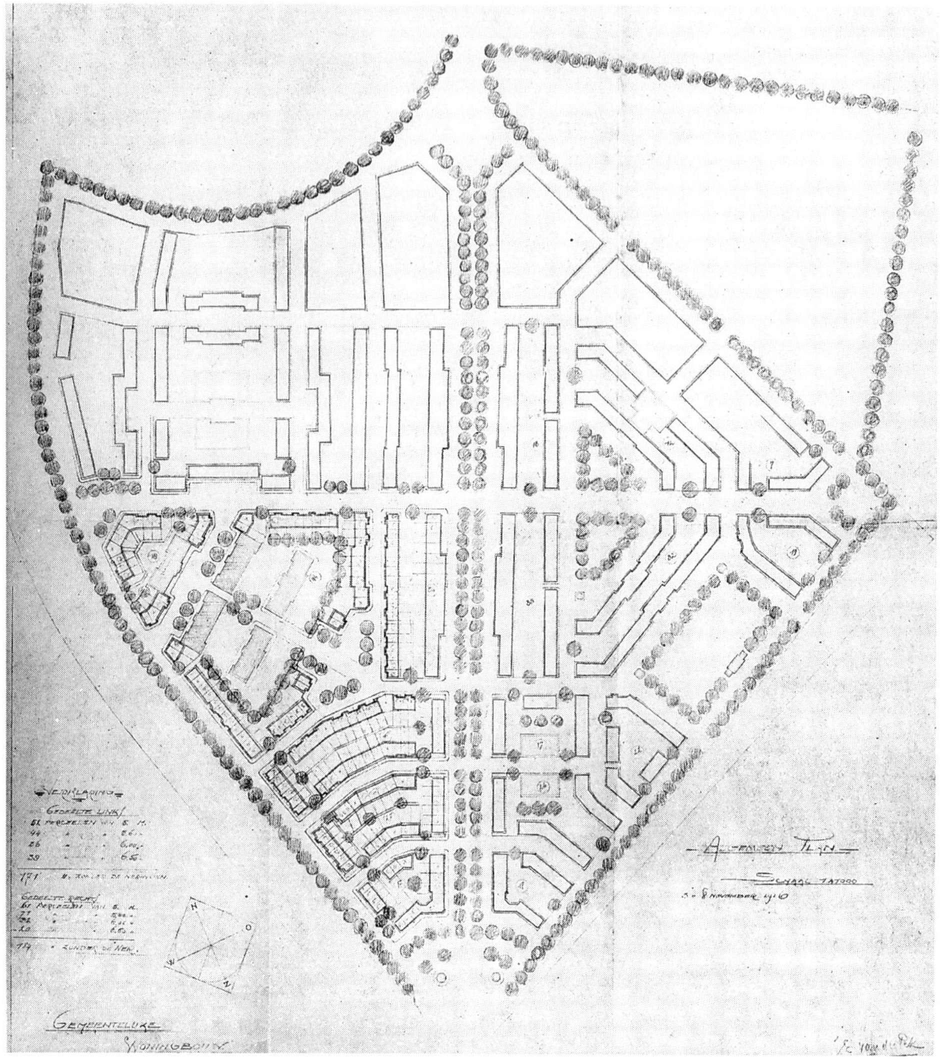

another *hof*, just east of the Zaanhof (fig. 8.13). Although De Bazel's severe facades, with their small, thinly spaced portals leading to collective entries for eight families, did not possess the intimacy of Walenkamp's design for the Zaanhof, the newly named Polanenhof did achieve a sense of neighborhood identity through its continuous protective bulwark, in striking contrast to the dismal rows of housing on the nearby streets of the 1885 plan (fig. 8.14).

Berlage engaged the assistance of Jan Gratama and G. Versteeg for the municipal housing in the Transvaal district. Here Berlage's street plan of 1903 was altered to form a series of U-shaped courts influenced by Unwin (figs. 8.15 and 8.16). The result was similar to the concept of the protective *hof*, with high four-story buildings encircling the low two-story housing facing the small courts. The lively colors of the brick facades were further enhanced with colored tiles and painted wood trim to form an intimate oasis within the city.

The third project for municipal housing was designed as a garden suburb by Van der Pek in Buiksloterham north of the IJ (figs. 8.17 and 8.18). Symmetrical patterns of short curved streets intertwined with ample green space. Solidly constructed, pleasantly grouped low-rise housing lined the street. Although the results of these municipal housing projects reflected a sober functionality and were certainly less innovative than later projects by De Klerk and his followers, they did permit the municipality to achieve a consistency of architectural treatment unparalleled by earlier philanthropic housing.

Keppler, the socialist civil servant trained at Delft, worked hard within the municipal bureaucracy to realize Berlage's vision of coordinated design for residential areas. Using the control given him as head of the Housing Authority, he pushed for better street plans and housing designs. Under this system, the government had become actively involved in controlling the aesthetic quality of neighborhood design: a leading architect, attached to the Public Works Department designed street plans and, in conjunction with the Committee of Aesthetics, acted as aesthetic adviser to their construction, while cooperating housing architects were supervised by Keppler himself.

FIGURE 8.18 J. E. van der Pek, municipal housing, Bremstraat, 1921. Gemeentearchief Amsterdam, negative VH3469.

Although Keppler's experiments took municipal aesthetic control far beyond the original mandate of the Committee of Aesthetics, they did so without threatening the professional autonomy many architects wished to preserve. Design coordination between architects selected by housing societies, or those selected by the municipality for its own housing, raised no alarms. Nonetheless, Keppler's efforts did stretch the principle of government intervention on behalf of the public good beyond the limited definition current in the 1890s when the municipal council first began to consider its role in the regulation of urban design. With adoption of the principle of harmony, a door had been opened to increasing government control of the urban visual environment.

CONTROLLING STYLE

At least one member of the Amsterdam municipal council argued that the logical consequence of Berlage's 1915 memorandum on the plan for Amsterdam South was government control over architectural style: "Must we leave the construction of this new city to the building owners, when the plans have been made by Berlage who has his own views of architecture? Or must the council set limits to the type of construction? I believe that we cannot refuse to regulate the construction so that it will be in the same style as Berlage has designed his city."[40]

Municipal regulation of style was a radical proposal. The Committee of Aesthetics took the official position that it could not reject design proposals merely on the basis of taste. At one of its first meetings after the 1915 reorganization, the members expressed that position explicitly. However, the point was also made that designs of all architects, even those with established reputations, would be subject to the committee's review and no architect might be excluded from scrutiny simply because of his qualifications.[41] As it became dominated by those sympathetic to the younger, more progressive architectural talents, the Committee of Aesthetics increasingly tapped these comprehensive powers of review to provide stylistic direction to Amsterdam's construction.

Under the guise of impartial criticism, the committee pressured housing societies to have their projects designed in the style of the Amsterdam School. Although design reviews were always couched in terms of architectural competence alone, the bias of the committee's judgments was nonetheless clear to observers and participants alike. In 1918, one of the councilors representing real estate interests bitterly complained: "Anyone who submits a building design and does not belong to one of the favored architectural societies is blacklisted. No design of his will be approved, while designs of those from certain groups, whether they are experienced or green, will pass the committee without any objections."[42]

Proposals by De Klerk and his contemporaries were almost invariably passed by the committee without comment.[43] But the vast majority of housing projects were sent back for revision, often repeatedly. In some cases, the design was rejected outright. As in the case of private developers, the committee then tried to convince the housing society to find another designer. But the close relationship between architect and housing society meant that architects were rarely dismissed. Instead, the society would acquire an aesthetic adviser. In 1917, for instance, the Catholic housing society Dr. Schaepman was forced by the committee to hire an assistant for its architect. The society turned to J. C. van Epen, one of Berlage's disciples, and the project was then approved.[44] In 1920, after designs for another project were rejected repeatedly over a period of six months, the housing society was again forced by the committee to hire an assistant who was considered compatible with the Amsterdam School architects building in the same neighborhood.[45]

In 1919, the committee reviewed plans submitted by Het Oosten's longtime architect J. J. L. Moolenschot.[46] The sketch plan convinced them that the architect needed the assistance of a designer "who could be expected" to produce an aesthetically reasonable solution for the facades.[47] Having just had its rejection of Weissman's designs overruled by the mayor and aldermen, the committee was in general wary of dismissing any design outright. The problem, as one member of the committee spelled out, was whether such a nondescript design, which was not bad, but certainly not good, might be accepted or whether, in the interests of furthering the city's beauty, the committee should take a stronger stand.[48] In the end, the committee rejected Moolenschot's design despite the possible disapproval of the mayor and aldermen.

While the stated justification for the committee's design review was maintenance of high design standards "in the interests of furthering the city's beauty," in reality its judgments often simply reflected the aesthetic preferences of its members. In 1919, Het Oosten was working with the architects M. J. E. Lippits and N. H. W. Scholte to design a housing project in Amsterdam South. Lippits had already established a solid reputation as a housing architect; nonetheless his plans for Het Oosten were rejected.[49] The Committee of Aesthetics judged them designs of such low quality that they could not be improved.[50] This rejection proved embarrassing when it came to be known that Lippits and Scholte had already submitted their designs to Berlage, who, as aesthetic adviser to the city for the south extension, had approved them.[51] Given their different architectural convictions, it is not surprising that Lippits's restrained style was more acceptable to Berlage than to the committee.

Followers of Berlage's rationalist style, were now regularly required by the Committee of Aesthetics to revise their schemes, the style no longer considered appropriate for workers' housing. The committee found scant value in the designs of J. H. W. Leliman, editor of the architectural journal *De Bouwwereld*, which was fiercely critical of the Amsterdam School. Leliman, whose father had been one of the first architects to take up the task of designing philanthropic housing projects, was also one of the few architects consistently committed to the housing issue.[52] Under the Housing Act, he had designed the first projects erected by the housing society Eigen Haard (fig. 5.9). In 1916, he also became the architect for the Handwerkers Vriendenkring. His first designs for that society (fig. 8.19), however, had to be submitted and resubmitted numerous times to the Committee of Aesthetics before final approval was granted. His next design for Eigen Haard, located in the Spaarndammer district adjacent to De Klerk's first Hille project, was definitively rejected by the Committee of Aesthetics in 1917, but the decision was overturned by the mayor and aldermen because of the housing shortage (fig. 8.20). In its memorandum justifying the rejection to the mayor and aldermen, the committee made it clear that it was using as its standard of judgment Berlage's concept of the unified housing block: "In the first place, in the opinion of the committee, the only correct aesthetic solution for such a complex (serving a single use and designed by one person) is a single block, and consequently an architectural composition such that the aforementioned unity of function is expressed externally."[53]

Leliman's design, consisting of a string of units, with varying heights, bays, and stairwells, lacked the unified block treatment required by the Committee of Aesthetics. After the committee's rejection of the design, Eigen Haard, which had worked with Leliman since its first project in 1910, turned to De Klerk, an appointment for which Keppler took credit.[54] The result was the flamboyant triangular block incorpo-

FIGURE 8.19 J. H. W. Leliman, Handwerkers Vriendenkring, Spitskopstraat, 1920–25. Gemeentearchief Amsterdam, negative VH2616.

FIGURE 8.20 J. H. W. Leliman, Eigen Haard, Hembrugstraat, 1918. Gemeentearchief Amsterdam, negative VH2351.

rating a post office, school, and tower located across from the Spaarndammerplantsoen, where De Klerk had already designed two parallel housing blocks (fig. 7.5).

The Committee of Aesthetics rejected designs by Weissman and Leliman, both outspoken critics of the Amsterdam School, only to see the mayor and aldermen override their decisions. Rejection was a radical step, which the committee applied only when it saw no possibility of a design's improvement. Since both Weissman and Leliman were widely acknowledged as competent architects, style alone must have been the basis for the judgment. Their simple and utilitarian versions of traditional Dutch architecture were the direct descendants of nineteenth-century philanthropic housing, reflective of the liberal values of restraint and thrift, and anathema to the committee's taste.

Even Berlage, who had uncontestably contributed to the aesthetics of housing design, was not exempt from the committee's criticism. When it reviewed his flat-roofed and somber Tolstraat housing for the Algemeene, the committee was "surprised to receive a design of such low quality."[55] Most telling was the committee's treatment of J. C. van Epen, one of the most gifted of the Amsterdam housing architects. His designs in Amsterdam South for the housing societies Algemeene, Rochdale, and ACOB provided the city with some of its most lyrical passages of housing architecture (figs. 8.21 and 8.22). The simple manipulation of alternating bays and battered buttresses created a rhythmic street facade both lively and humane. The facades were animated by orange and green woodwork. The fact that Van Epen used little more than the raw materials

FIGURE 8.21 J. C. van Epen, Rochdale and ACOB, Cornelis Krusemanstraat. From *Bouwkundig Weekblad* 39, no. 49 (7 December 1918): 285.

of construction to create his aesthetic effects separated him definitively from the playful, decorative craftsmanship of De Klerk favored by the committee. Although Van Epen's designs did not stimulate the imagination and fantasy to the degree of De Klerk's most fascinating work, his housing created citadels of security and hominess. But the flat roofs and uncompromising simplicity did not please the Committee of Aesthetics, which openly disagreed with his design. It grudgingly approved his project in Krusemanstraat with the comment that in the future it would not look favorably on such sober architecture.[56]

Van Epen, chafing from the ignominy of the committee's public rebukes, angrily accused it of destroying the artist's initiative because it forced him to sacrifice his individual search for art. Committees of aesthetics, he wrote, made art into fashion, stifling artistic development.[57]

After World War I, it became increasingly difficult for housing societies to build in Amsterdam unless their designs in some way reflected the aesthetic ideas of the Amsterdam School. Kuipers and Ingwersen, the architects of Patrimonium, were forced in their plans for both the Coöperatie and Stadion districts to revise their gabled facades for a more plastic and decorative treatment (fig. 8.23 and 8.24D). The committee's

FIGURE 8.22 J. C. van Epen, Rochdale and ACOB, Bertelmanplein, 1921–22. Netherlands Architecture Institute, Van Epen archive.

attitude persuaded housing societies to turn to the Amsterdam School for their architects. One by one the housing societies were encouraged to hire architects working in the new style.

The committee's strong endorsement of the style developed by Michel de Klerk and his followers is not difficult to understand. The style provided a convincing answer to the challenges set by Berlage's 1915 memorandum on the plan for the southern extension of the city. Adherents of the Amsterdam School carried out Berlage's suggestions with aplomb, in particular, the shaping of entire blocks with the fluid treatment of the street wall. Their plastic interpretation of brick, developed independently as an exercise in expressionism, could be applied successfully to mass housing. The aesthetic impulse that had originally motivated the initiators of the new style, that is, the interpretation of the vernacular building material in a fresh language of highly charged textural surfaces and symbolic forms, lent itself to further development at the scale of the street wall. Thus translated, an architectural technique earlier applied to villas, office buildings, and middle-class apartments demonstrated its appropriateness for mass housing, transforming the city block into a vibrant, pulsing whole with the rhythmic movement of imaginative forms.

FIGURE 8.23 T. Kuipers and A. U. Ingwersen, Patrimonium, Lutmastraat, 1919–1921. Gemeentearchief Amsterdam, archive 5187, 6449 VH 1920, BWT dossier 26782.

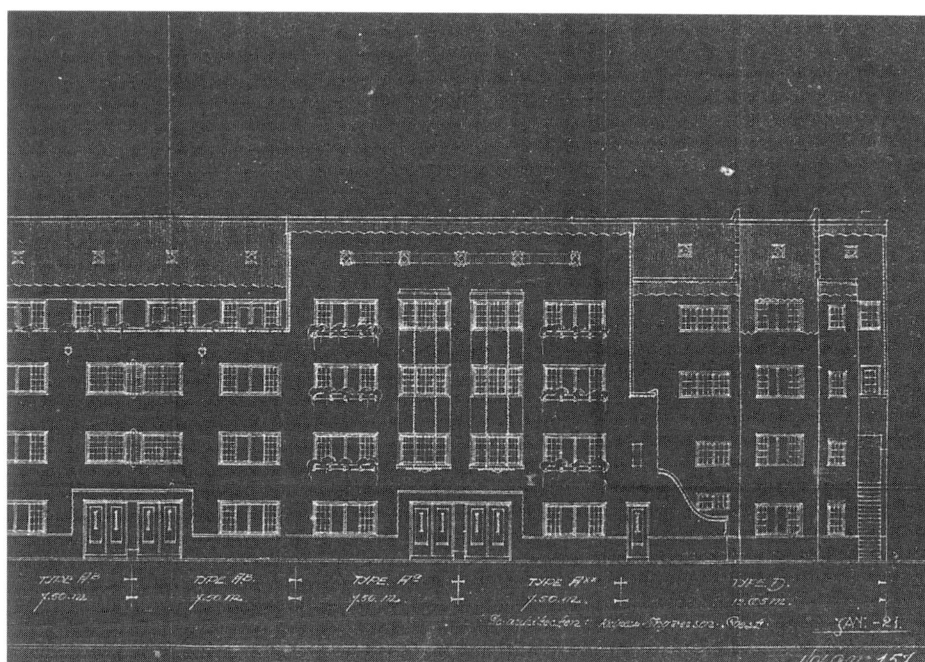

This focus on the external skin of the buildings was entirely consistent with the organizational environment in which housing design was carried out in Amsterdam. The split between facade and plan was a product of traditional row house construction; it was a preexisting condition to which the architects of the Amsterdam School conformed. The conceptual separation of plan from facade had been embodied in the regulation of housing design, which, as we have seen, confined the aesthetic judgments of the empowered committee strictly to the exterior of the building. This conceptual, constructive, and regulatory distinction between facade and dwelling plan identified the design of the facade as the "artistic" task. The architects of the Amsterdam School, closely affiliated with the architectural society Architectura et Amicitia, which defined architecture as art rather than construction or social hygiene, were also content to construe the "architectural" aspect of housing design, that is, the design of the facade, as the "artistic" component. Their modernity lay in the contemporaneity of their forms and their rejection of historicizing styles, not in any of the new insights into the relationship between interior and exterior space that characterized Russian and German modernism, or for that matter, the experiments of De Stijl. The Amsterdam School would frequently be subjected to accusations of superficiality, both by contemporary and later critics. Certainly the style's achievements in housing design lay in the intense focus on surface. But that focus should be understood in the light of the graphic originality of De Klerk, and the subsequent applicability of his imaginative forms to the street wall. These were apposite responses to the way the aesthetic problem of housing design had been posed. First, the professional and bureaucratic setting had split consideration of the plan from the facade, following the tradition of row house construction in Amsterdam. Second, Berlage's promotion of urban design as the shaping of the city with housing blocks implied a sculptural approach well suited to the plasticity of the Amsterdam School, but it also evoked the interface between street and block such that emphasis fell on the facade.

The message of the forms developed by the Amsterdam School architects also justified the support of the Committee of Aesthetics. The organic continuity of shapes along the street wall reinforced both urban identity and community solidarity. First it provided a contemporary answer to seventeenth-century patterns, a modern alternative to the historicist solution of re-creating past forms. The expressive forms of the Amsterdam School conveyed a sense of place by creating an extended visual chain of meaning through the city.[58] The utopian aspirations inherent in this program of urban expressionism were consistent with the official aims of the Committee of Aesthetics: to provide aesthetic guidance to construction in a city offended by the results of laissez-faire development in the late nineteenth century. That Amsterdam might achieve an urban aesthetic surpassing that of its past or at least worthy of that heritage was a widely shared desire. For a broad audience, the possibility of creating a new set of identifying imagery and forms through the city legitimized official encouragement of a consistent style. On the other hand, the expression of community solidarity, through what Helen Searing has described as a "proletarian iconography," satisfied the socialist program of bringing culture to the workers, a program espoused by a number of the committee members.[59] The accessible and legible forms of the facades gave additional impetus to a style born of individual genius, but assimilable as community expression.

While these may have been compelling reasons for the Committee of Aesthetics to favor architects espousing the style of the Amsterdam School, their practice of rejecting designs that did not conform to that style was naturally attacked. To the objections by such architects as Leliman that the Committee of Aesthetics was too one-sided, J. F. Staal answered, "the equivalence of many-sidedness with mediocrity is far too well known."[60] Leliman, often subject to the committee's rejections, had good reason to disapprove of its policies. Others, however, also argued in favor of architectural variety in the city. The Social Democratic councilor Loopuit, fearing monotonous results from Berlage's plan for *blokbouw* in Amsterdam South, argued on several occasions for a variety of architectural expression in Amsterdam: "We shall have to have various architects with various talents, various views, and various styles for the building of this city."[61] The defenders of aesthetic control claimed that such a pluralist position precluded excellence. Rather than explicitly arguing in favor of a specific style, the Committee of Aesthetics couched its recommendations in general terms of architectural excellence and architectural harmony, the vagueness of these concepts lending an appearance of objectivity.

Had the Committee of Aesthetics not exercised design review or exerted influence on the selection of architects for housing commissions, the success with which Amsterdam created harmonious residential districts during the 1920s would never have been achieved. But the committee itself did not give rise to the style it propagated. The formative years of the Amsterdam School occurred before the committee's intervention to spread the style, and the style's widening acceptance did not contribute to its further development. Indeed, one might argue the opposite and claim that the style weakened with increased application.[62] The committee did not create art; it eliminated what did not fit its norms. As one defender of the committee's work expressed it: "Even though the Committee of Aesthetics cannot create a work of art, it can certainly contribute to the pure understanding of art if it keeps on rejecting the barren results stemming from either antiquarianism or the stupid greed of patrons."[63] The rejection of historicism and incompetence and the encouragement of unity and harmony justified in its own eyes the committee's decisions in favor of the Amsterdam School. In the end, the Committee of Aesthetics operated less as a vehicle for architectural creativity and innovation and more as a public enforcer of stylistic uniformity. In this way, its activities seemed an answer to Berlage's call for a modern equivalent to eighteenth-century design ordinances. The Committee of Aesthetics normalized facade design to achieve the stylistic unity that was believed necessary as an expression of the times and of the community.

CREATING HARMONY

At a meeting of the Committee of Aesthetics in May 1919, Keppler warned the committee against limiting its judgment to separate facades. He noted that his previous attempts to achieve aesthetic harmony had ultimately proved unsatisfactory because he could not appoint the architects himself or effectively coordinate those selected by the housing societies. Keppler noted that satisfying results had been achieved only where he had succeeded in securing a commission for De Klerk.[64]

Keppler and the committee discussed a variety of methods that might be used to achieve architectural harmony in urban housing. Although they purposely rejected the possibility of outright appointment of architects to the housing societies, they did try to come up with other methods of control.[65] The committee might group architects with matching styles by district. If a housing society wished to build, it would have to go to the district where its architect was assigned. Alternatively, the lessee of the most prominent site for each district might select an architect with the approval of the Committee of Aesthetics. This lead architect would then give each of the other housing societies assigned to the neighborhood their choice between two architectural candidates. Public Works architect A. R. Hulshoff wished to see one of the members of the Committee of Aesthetics assigned as a district aesthetic adviser to direct the participating architects. Keppler suggested that Berlage draw up a list of the architects who would be allowed to design in a district in the southern extension plan. The common thread of all these proposals was the conviction that districts should be constructed by architects of similar stylistic inclinations. Berlage concurred, and commented that his southern extension plan should ideally be built so that each of the clusters of blocks composing it would be designed by one architect. Short of that, he approved of a list of related architects to be assigned to a cluster of blocks.[66] This was in fact the concept he had espoused in his 1914 lectures and in the memorandum to the plan.

Developments by both private developers and housing societies applied several of these methods over the following years. Eventually, the Committee of Aesthetics was able to institutionalize the coordination of style. Thus, the committee exerted its influence on style most effectively by promoting the harmonious development of neighborhoods under centralized aesthetic leadership. The seemingly neutral and indisputable goal of aesthetic harmony could be used as leverage to gain official sanction for adherence to the Amsterdam School. Although the number of housing projects that displayed extraordinary quality of design was limited, the construction of entire districts stylistically consistent with those projects magnified their impact.

As a result of the May 1919 meeting of the Committee of Aesthetics, Hulshoff, a proponent of the Amsterdam School, became the adviser for the development of the northern portion of Buiksloterham, north of the IJ.[67] Hulshoff was to consult with the designers of the various housing societies building in the district as they planned their projects. This was a marked increase in involvement over the committee's previous experiments in coordination, where it had simply judged a group of facades after the architects consulted among themselves. Yet it was still not considered a complete success by the committee's members, "since the combination of architects was too arbitrary, given that the selection was made by the housing societies without any consultation about the choice of architects among themselves."[68]

In the Stadion district in the south plan, public aesthetic control increased still further. Jan Gratama, architect for the Algemeene housing society, assumed aesthetic leadership of the district. Gratama provided guidance in the selection of architects and the assignment of blocks to the eight participating housing societies. The choice of architects largely represented the Amsterdam School, and some societies turned for the first time to new architects from among its adherents.[69] Control was incomplete: Het Oosten still worked with J. J. L. Moolenschot, whose designs had so frequently been rejected by the Committee of Aesthetics.

Together with the Housing Authority, Gratama revised the street plan for the district and provided the street sections, the silhouettes of street facades, the planting plan, the color of the brick and woodwork, and the flat roofline (fig. 8.24).[70] After the accusations of willful excess that attended De Klerk's work in the Spaarndammer district, Gratama was careful to justify his towers as storage area. The result of his endeavors was a stripped down, simplified brickwork that created a strongly unified appearance for the district. Nowhere did Gratama explicitly refer to a preferred style, but this system clearly gave the aesthetic coordinator control. In the publication describing the district, aesthetic control was justified by the failure to achieve harmonious development when the housing societies were left on their own.[71]

Harmonious construction of neighborhoods was also the result of changes within the Public Works Department. The Committee of Aesthetics had tried to expand its powers to review public as well as private construction in 1916. Its request to review all Public Works designs, industrial buildings, and extension plans was rejected by the Public Works Committee, which argued that the presence of Van der Mey was sufficient guarantee of aesthetic quality.[72] As an acknowledged professional, Van der Mey was presumably exempt from review. The continued hiring by Public Works of architects sympathetic to the Amsterdam School accomplished what the Committee of Aesthetics had been after: a forward-looking and up-to-date design department for the city.[73] Within the new districts of coordinated design, municipal buildings such as schools and post offices were designed in the style of the Amsterdam School by a staff of architects in the Public Works Department under the supervision of Hulshoff. As their designs for bridges and street furniture spread through the city in the 1920s, a chain of consistent visual imagery linked the new districts to the old. In 1916, a municipal councilor summarized the shift in Amsterdam's public patronage of architecture:

> Only a few years ago, architectural design by Public Works was the laughing stock of Amsterdam and the rest of the country. Public Works' output at that time was published in the architectural press to show how *not* to do things. Complaints about Public Works came into the council repeatedly. Happily, at this point Public Works has noticeably started off in a new direction. It is gratifying to be able to point out that Public Works is no longer a laughingstock as far as architecture is concerned, so that Amsterdam will now lead in architecture as it already does in other matters and as it should do.[74]

Finally, private developers were also led to promote cooperation among their architects. The Amstel's Bouwvereeniging, a confederation of approximately seventy local builders, confirmed Berlage's judgment that large-scale development companies could carry out the plan of Amsterdam South. The developer planned a district of two thousand middle-class housing units with government subsidy in 1921. It provided the housing plans but appointed Hulshoff to provide centralized aesthetic leadership for the design of the facades. With architects Jan Gratama, Jan de Meyer, and J. F. Staal, Hulshoff formed a committee appointed by the municipal council. The committee revised the site plan, set building heights, divided the site into architectural units, established the aesthetic standards, and selected seventeen architects to design the facades with the approval of the builders. The result was a remarkable example of stylistically unified housing and some of the most interesting of the Amsterdam School facades (fig. 8.25). Although in an account of his aesthetic leadership, Hulshoff made no mention of the stylistic preferences of the committee, the visual power of this neighborhood came from the architects' consistent application of the fresh insights of Amsterdam's new expressionism.[75]

A similar coordination of facade design under centralized guidance occurred in the private development of Amsterdam West. A committee was set up consisting of the developer, three architects, and several civil servants. The committee divided the privately owned site into architectural units and proposed architects for each. Here again the builder, Van der Schaar, provided the plans, while the architects designed only the facades. This arrangement proved awkward because the facades had to pass through two stages of approval, first the special committee and then the Committee of Aesthetics.[76]

Such duplication of work was avoided in the Indische district, where a special subcommittee of the Committee of Aesthetics was formed in 1922 to foster harmony and judge the facades of the eastern half of the district, a system eventually applied to the entire city.[77]

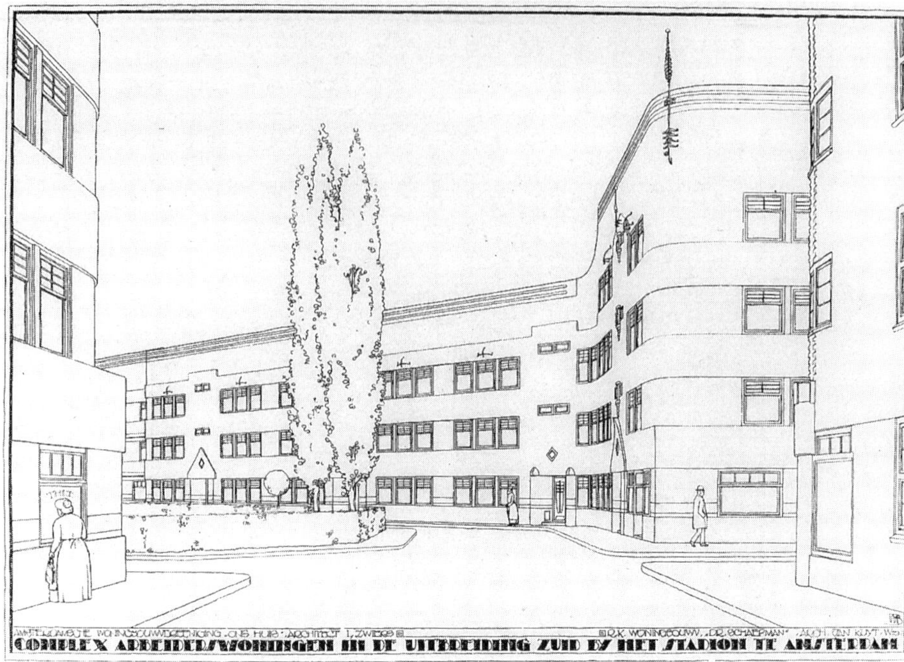
COMPLEX ARBEIDERSWONINGEN IN DE UITBREIDING ZUID BY HET STADION TE AMSTERDAM

A

B

COMPLEX ARBEIDERSWONINGEN IN DE UITBREIDING ZUID BY HET STADION TE AMSTERDAM

C

D

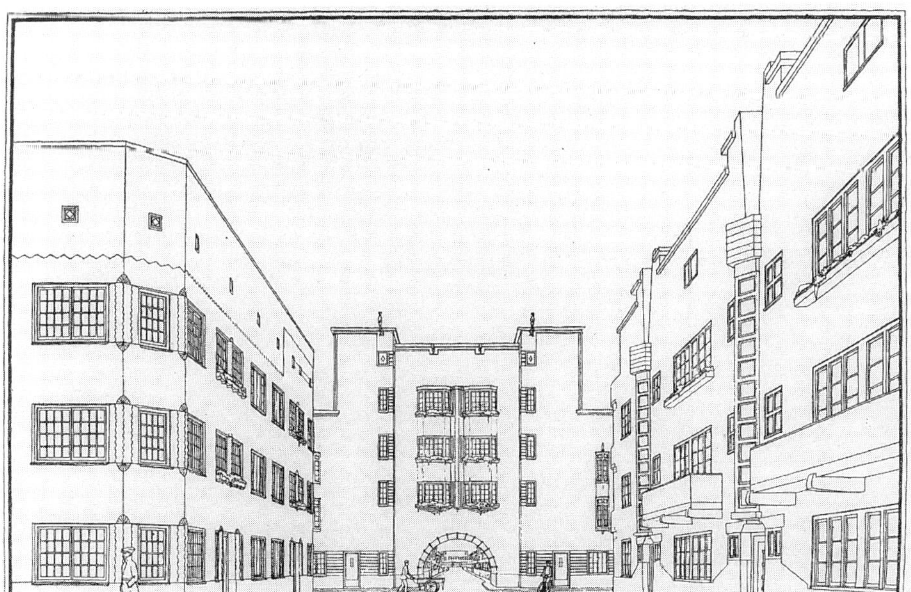

FIGURE 8.24 Stadion housing complex, Amsterdam South: (A) L. Zwiers (Ons Huis), Jan Kuyt (Dr. Schaepman); (B) J. J. L. Moolenschot (Het Oosten), Nicolaas Lansdorp (municipal housing); Willem Noorlander (Ons Belang); (C) Jan Gratama and G. Versteeg (Algemeene Woningbouw Vereeniging), Nicolaas Lansdorp (municipal housing); (D) T. Kuipers and A. U. Ingwersen and E. Roest (Patrimonium); Jan Gratama and G. Versteeg (Algemeene Woningbouw Vereeniging), C. J. Blaauw (Onze Woning). From *Bouwkundig Weekblad* 42, no. 47 (19 November 1921): 300–303.

FIGURE 8.25 Margaret Staal-Kropholler and Nicolaas Lansdorp, Holendrechtstraat, 1922. Gemeente-archief Amsterdam, negative 11203-34.

The new system evolved with the reorganization of the Committee of Aesthetics in 1924. The city had embarked on this second reorganization of the committee when the building ordinance was changed in 1922 to include a general regulation protecting Amsterdam's urban beauty.[78] The new regulation implied, among other things, an expansion of the committee's jurisdiction from buildings on municipal property to buildings on any land within the city. The 1924 reorganization enlarged the committee's bailiwick, as well as altering its composition and expanding its tasks, granting powers it had long sought.[79] The committee would advise mayor and aldermen not only on the design of extension plans, but on the nature of any construction in proposed extensions. It could also coordinate architectural specifications for the plans, establishing in sketch form the standards future building proposals would have to meet.[80]

After its reorganization, the Committee of Aesthetics set up a subcommittee for a district in Amsterdam South. The subcommittee worked with Berlage, Public Works, and the Building and Housing Inspection Office to coordinate the plan and its construction. It produced sketches and silhouettes of the blocks, indicating height, number of stories, roof type, and the locations for architectural emphasis.[81] The coordination of plan and construction that Van der Mey had called for as early as 1916 had at last been realized.

The proponents of aesthetic control now pressed the municipality to assume the power to appoint architects. In a meeting of the Public Works Committee in 1925, Zeeger Gulden proposed that the city appoint the architects to build on municipal land.[82] The architectural society Architectura et Amicitia petitioned the city in the same cause. But as it had on previous occasions, the municipality rejected such proposals and adhered to the principle of aesthetic impartiality. In 1926, the mayor and aldermen issued a statement about the policy of aesthetic control in Amsterdam. They admitted that the current system of setting aesthetic specifications could not prevent facades that "barely harmonize with each other as a result of the completely different ideas of the designers," and that appointment of architects might lead to the greatest possible harmony. Nonetheless, they rejected the infringements on freedom that municipal appointment of architects would entail.[83]

The executive branch would not endorse any governmental intervention beyond the setting of design specifications. Accepting the notion of unified street facades and the need to assign entire blocks to one architect, the municipality proposed to establish a standing subcommittee of the Committee of Aesthetics to designate specifications and to judge proposed facades. This subcommittee would also institute the proposal made years before that builders requesting land from the city should submit a sketch of the proposed building for approval before the lease could be granted. Like the subcommittee previously set up for a district of the south plan, this subcommittee was to be composed of both civil servants and architects.[84] The architects would carry out the business of the subcommittee: advising on the street and building plan, setting the widths of facades, making up street silhouettes, dividing the construction into architectural units, judging preliminary sketches for lease applications, and giving final approval to all proposed facades.[85]

The mayor and aldermen clearly felt that harmony should be the primary goal of their proposal to control aesthetic development of the city:

> The separate judgment of each facade cannot lead to a result in which the aim of beauty is achieved. A facade may possess worthwhile characteristics and still not correspond with what surrounds it, so that buildings put up according to separate plans may not form a coordinated whole. In spite of the care given to the external appearance of the separate facades, the whole area then produces an unsatisfactory impression. In our opinion, unity and harmony must be present between the various buildings in each city district, even when they are of varied architecture.[86]

This stance thus supported the idea of architectural unity but avoided official dictation of stylistic choice.

Within a year of the government's statement, aesthetic subcommittees of architects had been set up for Amsterdam South, North, East, and West. Thus by 1926, Berlage's vision of Amsterdam's extension had not only been brought to fruition in a number of districts, the municipality's acceptance of the precepts enunciated in his 1915 plan for Amsterdam South had led to the creation of legislation and institutions to guarantee their continued application. The 1926 proposal implemented many of the recommendations for aesthetic control that had been debated over the previous decade.

OFFICIAL HARMONY

With the reorganization of the Committee of Aesthetics and the designation of subcommittees for the various districts of the city, the municipality felt it had reached the limit of its possible intervention in urban aesthetics. Short of designating an official style, it had gone as far as it could to achieve architectural harmony.

> Now that developers remain free in their choice of architect, as long as that choice falls on a designer of sufficient competence, the establishment of some kind of "official architectural style," which might have resulted from the deadening influence of a system in which the municipality appointed architects, has been avoided. Indeed, we believe that the system we propose, aimed at achieving harmony in construction, will not limit anyone's efforts and will provide full scope for their talents. Land to be built will be divided into a relatively large number of units so that various architects will design the facades, each according to his own ideas. The committee of architects can make sure that incompetent architects are excluded, but, should the wish to do so arise, it may not suppress any expression of personal opinions.[87]

This position represented the official compromise between the principles of aesthetic harmony and freedom of expression.

There was, to be sure, a discrepancy between the official version of public aesthetic control and the actual operations of the Committee of Aesthetics. The municipal policy against "official architecture" was to a great degree countermanded by the fact that the Committee of Aesthetics had in effect already made the Amsterdam School the standard style of the city. While the stylistic consistency of Amsterdam's new districts drew praise internationally, at home it drew accusations of unfair prejudice against those outside the Amsterdam School. One architect wrote, "Our Committee of Aesthetics has lowered itself to pedantry, to acting as if it were an exam committee testing for a diploma in the architecture of the day."[88] This was exactly the sort of charge the committee had hoped to avoid through its efforts to achieve stylistic unity in Amsterdam by means that were, at least publicly, consistent with government impartiality. At all times, the committee's injunctions to design in a style that would coordinate with the Amsterdam School were couched in neutral language. The experiments in neighborhood design coordination never explicitly referred to architectural style, instead requiring the acceptably neutral goal of "harmony" achieved at the hands of an "aesthetic expert." Such subterfuge was necessary if public control of urban aesthetics was to be sustained, but its terms reveal the political tensions underlying public oversight.[89]

"Expertise" and "harmony" were thus critical notions in the project of public aesthetic control. Although undisputed as a requirement, "expertise," as we saw in chapter 6, gave rise to competing definitions of architectural competence, and the conflict between the professional and aesthetic definitions shaped the debate on urban aesthetics. "Harmony" was an even more complexly constructed norm. As an aesthetic criterion, "harmony" was a malleable concept that could take on different colorations depending on ideological orientation. When interpreted simply as the felicitous agreement between parts, it was given the status of a universally applicable principle of beauty. As such, it satisfied the liberal bourgeois requirement that a public criterion of urban aesthetics be rationally and impartially applicable. It was a concept that fit easily into the abstract and legalistic discourse required for administration of the public realm, providing a demonstrable test for designs.

But "harmony" could also refer more specifically to a quality often ascribed to preindustrial urban planning and architecture. In this sense, it became a goal for modern urban design. The original impetus for public control of urban aesthetics arose from the reaction against the chaotic and uncontrolled forms of speculative development, which were compared disadvantageously to the achievements of previous centuries. "Harmony" thus became part of a battery of criteria applied to urban aesthetics that evoked nostalgia for an apparently lost cultural heritage. It could be applied as a justification for the preservation of those parts of the city surviving intact from the past and as a measure of the success of new developments in living up to those standards. As a criterion of urban aesthetics, "harmony" suggested the importance of restoring lost order and maintaining local identity. In Amsterdam, the coordination of the three major canals and the houses built along them in the seventeenth century were viewed as exemplary of the city's visual character and therefore set the local standard of urban design.

"Harmony" also entered into the rhetoric of the collective utopian community envisioned by Berlage as the basis for architectural and artistic renewal. The democratic ideals of mass society would serve the spiritual role previously played by religion and thus provide the central idea animating modern civilization. Shared artistic conventions would emerge as a matter of course from these collective ideals, so that modern civilization could develop a characteristic artistic culture to rival those of past civilizations. The rampant individualism of the nineteenth century was to blame for the chaos of its visual culture; in its place would come the visual harmony that is the sign of a great civilization. Architecture, as the most social of all the arts, would express the great ideas of its times and thus achieve harmony and style again. Harmony in this case was interpreted as the very hallmark of civilization.

But harmony also carried connotations of solidarity and cooperation, virtues of the collective endeavor encouraged by socialism. It formed part of the rhetoric of class consciousness through which the people would form a harmonious front against the bourgeoisie. An aesthetic counterpart to this political conception envisioned the incarnation of working-class solidarity in harmonious urban form.

Thus, for a variety of reasons, the shaping of a visually harmonious city became acceptable to a broad spectrum of Amsterdam's residents. For the facade, as for the dwelling plan, normalization, in the sense here of the imposed conformity to an architectural style, could be put to use for different ideological purposes. Visions of civic order, of urban and community identity, could be fostered through the control of mass housing design. Keppler's experiments in the coordination of design, Berlage's vision of mass housing blocks, and the Committee of Aesthetics' efforts to bring harmonious stylistic treatment to new neighborhoods could be justified within the limits of both liberal and socialist rhetoric.

The representational capacity of the Amsterdam School was not incidental to the effort to achieve urban harmony. As a modern architectural style that had not abandoned representation and that aestheticized community and place rather than function or hygiene, the Amsterdam School occupied a position distinct from both the rationalism of Berlage and that of the Nieuwe Bouwen, the Dutch functionalist movement of the 1920s. We have examined the way that the textural and plastic richness of brick was exploited by the architects of the Amsterdam School, rejecting historicist mimicry yet maintaining links to the traditional craftsmanship and urban vernacular of Amsterdam's perimeter block. This permitted the simultaneous readings of urban identity and collectivity, readings that were also sustained by the aesthetic criterion of "harmony."

Berlage had called for a democratic architecture reflecting the economic and constructional realities of industrial urban life. A new style for the age would represent mass society through a *gemeenschapskunst*, an architecture of the community that would replace the false forms of commercialized mass culture. In his vision of the southern extension of Amsterdam, there was to be no outward sign of class distinction. Large-scale construction would give rise to standardization, a solution applicable to both middle- and working-class housing. All classes would be served equally by architects striving to express the character of the age objectively. Berlage saw mass housing as architecture's opportunity to articulate the truths of the modern urban condition. Rationally applied modern materials and standardized construction would shape and define the city and thus give expression to the community.

However, when Berlage's projection of a collective streetscape was fulfilled by the Amsterdam School, it introduced meanings of community he had not anticipated. The style was put to use to express class consciousness, rather than the democratic mass society Berlage envisioned. Berlage's notion of community, based on a spiritual rather than a Marxist socialism, did not altogether coincide with that of the Social Democrats. The Social Democratic director of the Housing Authority, Keppler, wanted the best for the working class and saw his job as service to a community defined by class. Under the direction of the SDAP, the shaping of urban image would foster working-class civilization and spearhead class consciousness. Architectural style would become a liberative tool of social change. Providing culture to the working class, in itself a compensatory project, defined a new political role that fell to socially engaged professionals. In bringing beauty to working-class neighborhoods and stimulating their dreams, architects would contribute to the creation of community identity and solidarity among workers. This task corresponded only in general with the service to community demanded by Berlage's modern historiography of architecture. Its aim was to serve a community defined by Marxist teleology rather than mass society.

The high point of the Amsterdam School as an architectural style was its application in a few extraordinary housing complexes, where, as Helen Searing has amply illustrated, class solidarity was brilliantly aestheticized. In the Spaarndammerbuurt at the Eigen Haard housing projects, De Klerk alone, and in the Coöperatiebuurt at the Dageraad project, De Klerk with Kramer demonstrated the capacity for architecture to express community politicized by class consciousness. These were, however, isolated incidents of architectural genius and political commitment. They took form within a larger urban framework that depended on a less politicized notion of community. They joined other projects that formed the greater urban fabric Amsterdam was weaving to mend itself after the ravages of late-nineteenth-century urban development. This larger tapestry represented the development of a local urban vernacular, translating modern conditions into a new collective expression of place. The Amsterdam School answered the call not only for an expression of community defined by class, but also for one defined by urban identity. The style served not just the notion of community, or "the people" as defined by the Social Democrats, but perhaps even more, the ideal community of Berlage's theory. In short, it provided an iconography of the of the modern city itself, expressing the utopian dream of harmony between classes, the peaceful transformation of the urban industrial world into a shared and just community.

As the Amsterdam School spread across the facades of entire neighborhoods, it fashioned a representation of the new welfare society: large scale, urban, pacified (fig. 8.26). In the large blocks that formed Amsterdam South, different classes were sheltered together. Under harmonious facades, housing societies of totally different ideological perspectives were united. The result was not revolutionary, politically or architecturally. The housing blocks were not embattled bastions of class resistance or cultural transgression. Rather, through the creation of place, they merely resisted the laissez-faire system of housing construction and urban development.

The new neighborhoods that arose under the enlightened public patronage of Amsterdam were founded on the notion of an invented sense of community that drew on harmony, peace, and solidarity, unimpeded by awareness of tensions within society.

FIGURE 8.26 Amstellaan, Amsterdam South. Postcard from collection of author.

Here, place could compete with class as the source of collective identity and as the location of resistance to capitalism. Creating a modern urban *Heimat*, the Amsterdam School occupied a peculiar position. The style's expressive capabilities resisted conservative historicism with its innovative modern forms. It participated in the international movement to renew architecture, the city, and society. At the same time, it resisted the internationalism of industrial rationality through its coinage of a local urban vernacular. David Harvey notes that the aesthetics of place is a part of modernity that provides both resistance to the universalizing impulse and an alternative to class loyalty.[90] In Amsterdam, the successful public campaign to wrest control of urban aesthetics from profit-making real estate interests resulted in a collective expression of community that celebrated urban identity. That strategy fostered both the radical construction of a class-based community and the more moderate representation of urban order.

The public patronage of urban aesthetics in Amsterdam can be analyzed on several levels. It can be reduced to an internal architectural debate between modernists and traditionalists, that is, between those throwing off the yoke of historical style and those embracing it. Those aesthetic struggles can also be interpreted in political terms, pitting the progressive aim of creating an architecture for the people against the conservative expression of bourgeois individualism and traditional vested interests. The struggles between modernists and traditionalists, or between progressives and conservatives, were framed inside yet another discourse, one about expertise, legitimacy, and authority. Once it was made a public issue, the aesthetics of the city became a contested area of control, with the public, the government, and the experts making competing claims as the appropriate sources of norms. The struggle to control urban aesthetics in Amsterdam not only released competing stylistic and professional interests, it also invoked competing models for legitimate decision making in the public arena.

Given the peculiar nature of Dutch segmented society and the means found to maintain social stability through the development of a pluralist political structure, the contradictions encountered in the public patronage of architecture are striking. They illustrate in a particularly transparent manner the general contradictions inherent to public aesthetic patronage within modern democracies. In the absence of autocratic forms of patronage, conflicts between competing claims of authority naturally arise. Amsterdam's early experience with public housing design cannot simply be reduced to a question of taste, to a conflict in which conservative housing societies espousing conservative styles resisted a modernism imposed by well-intentioned experts. It exemplifies the inherently political nature of taste making and the particular geography of aesthetic control in democratic societies.

Ideally, the public patronage of architecture would lead to the democratic creation of collective memory and shared culture. But the splits and tensions within society make such an ideal problematic. The democratic and liberative principle of self-expression contradicts the enforced expression of the collective. This was the issue at the heart of Berlage's own representation of the problem of attaining a modern expression. By associating the collective expression of the community with a deterministic zeitgeist, he manifested the contradiction between the liberative, democratic aims of his utopian vision and the normalization required by the administration of aesthetic harmony. This contradiction between emancipation and normalization lay at the very heart of the Enlightenment project of modernism; it was constitutive to the example of publicly sponsored housing design in Amsterdam.

BETWEEN THE CALCULUS OF NECESSITY AND THE RHETORIC OF IDENTITY

Identical straight streets and unvarying rooflines; monotonous colors of faded brown, red and dull gray; identical bricks, bricks, bricks, below, above, and on either side; millions of bricks stacked up into houses that line up into streets that form into endless enclosures around empty sites, where the wind raises clouds of dust day in and day out. And in all of the identical houses in all of these identical streets are identical rooms, and even the ennui is identical.—"Snarepijperij," *De Kroniek* (1897)

Through variations in color and form, the inhabitants recognize their own home, their own windows. Here they feel that they dwell, not that they have been stowed away. . . . Here's proof that it is possible to expand the city in a way that elevates us out of the uninspired.—E. Kuipers, "Arbeiderswoning complexen van M. de Klerk"

Modernism, seen as a whole, explored the dialectic of place versus space, of present versus past, in a variety of ways. While celebrating universality and the collapse of spatial barriers, it also explored new meanings for space and place in ways that tacitly reinforced local identity.—David Harvey, *The Condition of Postmodernity*

The late-nineteenth-century construction of speculative housing districts around the old core of Amsterdam was driven by the technical exigencies of mass production and its economic advantages. Repetition resulted in cheaper housing. It also created what one author called "the stultifying regularity of the office symbolized in streets."[1] By 1897, among those rejecting urban form created through the minimalist calculus of necessity, equating the monotonous urban grid with bureaucratic mentality had become a commonplace trope. Capitalism, unrestrained, had imposed a visual order on the cityscape, one that suggested the isolation of individuals and the fragmentation of society, where the rationalization of space and the collapse of time erased any representation of place and community. The Pijp is "a neighborhood where you can walk into someone else's house twenty-five times without even noticing, where all the houses are numbered cells for the prisoners of life; a neighborhood like a huge prison in which an infinite number are condemned to hard labor for life, with Necessity as guard and Death as release."[2] The prison imagery underscores the message that space has become undifferentiated; one cell is much like another. Time has collapsed into an endless routine, since the calculation of profit is indifferent to its passage. Space has extended endlessly into a Cartesian grid of measurement subject to those calculations. This vision of the late-nineteenth-century city captures the perception of the carceral society, its members imprisoned and controlled, subject to the analytical rationalities of capitalism's maximization of profit.

The analysis is visual: it transcribes a social critique onto an image so that the urban landscape is privileged as a symbol of modern society. In turn, the analysis suggests the way out of the prison: the restoration of differentiated time and place through new urban forms. Such aesthetic control might liberate the city from the suppression of identity and permit the expression of community. The rhetoric of identity was as old as Pugin's arguments for a return to the Gothic as a means to counteract what he perceived as modernity's dehumanizing application of the Classical. Social harmony required the restitution of shared mythology; the atomized and fragmented society could be reintegrated through the expression of identity. Those reacting against the nullifying order of the nineteenth century city might, then, place their faith in the reforming powers of visual forms.

Simultaneous with the critique of the urban grid's rational order was a condemnation of the chaos resulting from the capitalist marketplace. In an unregulated real estate market, the city expanded out of control. The result was the clutter and contrast of competing forms, irregular and undisciplined. This problematic also evoked a visual critique, stimulating calls for a homogeneous expression of place and community that would result in visual harmony. According to this analysis, an urban order maximizing human welfare, rather than profit, was required to ameliorate the dire conditions resulting from the unregulated real estate market. In the absence of public standards, buildings collapsed, proof of shoddy materials and poor workmanship. Disease was rampant, not only because of uncontrolled construction that permitted unhygienic arrangements, but because of the uncontrolled behavior of those occupying urban dwellings. The chaos of the *Grossstadt* had to be counteracted by the imposition of order and control. Liberation from the ravages of one system required the imposition of another.

I have attempted to illustrate modernity as a continuing dialectic of control and liberation. Under the laissez-faire policies of the late nineteenth century, the modern city had allowed the imposition of an order driven by the profit motive. The freedoms granted the individual entrepreneur had resulted in the carceral urban landscape, its repetitious monotony signifying the entrapment of the masses. The reaction against that particular configuration of liberation and control, order and disorder, took recourse in the power of normalization, applying the disciplines of hygiene and aesthetics to the urban landscape. One calculus of necessity was thus replaced by another, the public interest supplanting profit as a goal, identity now affirmed rather than denied. In Amsterdam, which entered this phase of modernity like many other European cities, a particular synthesis of the aesthetic and hygienic juggled and rebalanced contradictions between space and place, past and present, with an equipoise that hid the social tensions that produced it.

By 1920, the city of Amsterdam had reacted collectively against the order and disorder, the freedoms and controls, of the laissez-faire urban landscape. It had normalized the dwelling plan and style of housing built under municipal auspices. The plan included a living room, a separate small kitchen, and three bedrooms. The style consisted of the brick expressionist forms coined by De Klerk and his followers. These new standards represented a radical improvement over the plans and facades of the speculative housing that had arisen in the last decades of the nineteenth century. Not only were the plans more humanely functional, but the harmonious coordination of housing facades erected in the style of the Amsterdam School created neighborhoods of dignity and character.

These changes occurred within the context of a newly structured institutional environment. Architectural patronage had been reorganized. In place of speculative developers, the municipality and housing societies legally required to act exclusively in the interests of housing quality now commissioned designs. The Amsterdam Housing Authority had been established to oversee housing production and design. The government was assisted by a new advisory apparatus that included experts in housing hygiene and urban aesthetics. The Amsterdam Health Board and Committee of Aesthetics provided a filter of expertise through which housing proposals had to pass. Architects were now responsible for the design of housing and the plans of residential districts. Engineers, doctors, social workers, urban planners, and architects had recharted their professional turf in the effort to join the field of opportunity opened by the public review of housing design.

In the name of the public interest, unregulated construction of housing was curtailed; and through the regulation of the cityscape, a new urban order was instated, one that inverted the order of the laissez-faire city. The visual cacophony of individualism was replaced by the stylistic harmony of entire neighborhoods. The monotony of gray, spiritless streets produced by capitalist reckoning gave way to a rhythmic surge of pulsing facades suggestive of collective urban energy. Light and air infused housing constructed to meet legislated minimum standards. The inadequate, compacted floor plans of the typical speculative dwellings yielded to variations on the standard reform plan that answered previous failings of privacy, hygiene, and amenity. Here, as a commentator remarked about a project by De Klerk, the city's inhabitants might "feel that they dwell, not that they have been stowed away."[3]

Housing design had been appropriated into the protective custody of the public realm where government bureaucracy and professional expertise would guarantee its cultivation for the improvement of living standards and the reshaping of mass urban culture. Theodor Adorno has noted the potential for cultural stewardship that cooperation between bureaucracy and expertise offer: "The relation between administration and expert is not only a matter of necessity, but it is a virtue as well. It opens a perspective for the protection of cultural matters from the realm of control by the market, which today unhesitatingly mutilates culture." Culture might thrive under that protection from the marketplace, but Adorno also acknowledged "the twisted feeling of irreconcilability in the relation of culture and administration."[4] We have observed that patterns of tension inherent to the relation between culture and the administrative apparatus of welfare became apparent through the complex struggles for power and representation disclosed by public control of housing design in Amsterdam. The replacement of the market as generator of housing norms resulted in numerous negotiations between the newly organized actors in the newly constituted field of housing design, between the discordant perspectives of clients and experts, experts and bureaucrats, middle class and working class. Among experts, there were conflicts over professional turf and over the means of legitimizing authority. Within the architectural profession, there was a need to explore the potential conflicts and overlaps between its allegiance to the autonomous development of the discipline, its role in service to society, and its self-preservation as profession. Setting collective cultural norms in a society with democratic assumptions generated contradictions between the rule of discipline and the rule of law. These forces and the tensions between them constituted the social geography of housing design's cultural field.

We have examined these issues of power relations as they were played out in two discourses, social hygiene and aesthetics. In the course of engendering norms of healthy urban living and norms of urban beauty, each discourse became central to the reform of housing design, assimilated into a protected noncommercial zone, where each was harnessed to serve the campaign to enhance urban order. Each was changed through its participation in the new field of power.

The two discourses responded in parallel to the same social processes at work within that field, each developing its own institutions, bureaucracies, experts, and norms. In each case, we have observed the creation and definition of appropriate expertise, the establishment of new institutions, and their application to the civilizing project and reform of working-class behavior and taste. In both cases, we have examined disputes over the appropriate nature and degree of government intervention. Within each discourse, a professional class, legitimized by government, attempted to shape aspects of daily life formerly controlled by the market or individual. These experts set the norms of orderly behavior and established the norms of visual order. Accordingly, each generated resistance: working-class resistance to middle-class reform values, lay resistance to professional authority, conservative resistance to the extension of government control, and professional resistance to government interference. The relationships between the public, the expert, and the municipal government were altered as both the plan and the facade were instrumentalized for the improvement of workers' living conditions and the creation of a new urban order. Both became locations for power struggles; both acted as conduits of emancipatory and controlling intent.

But the plan and facade functioned separately because of the differing natures of their underlying discourses. The plan operated repressively; it was used to constrain the usage of the home to inhibit behavior identified by urban reformers as inappropriate. By contrast, the facade operated as a means for expression, a canvas for the representation of civic harmony. The plan became a device to fashion an urban lifestyle, the facade a means to create collective identity. Thus the plan addressed the family, private life, and interior space; the facade addressed the city as a whole, public and exterior space.

Hygiene and aesthetics were each mobilized by a different kind of discourse. Hygiene was subject to the scientism of objectivity; aesthetics was embedded in the historicity of the city and its image. Hygiene was applied as a technology of behavior modification intended to improve living conditions and increase civility. Aesthetics applied the representational function of architecture, long the political tool of the *ancien régime*, in the service of mass society, in the name of "the people." Two metaphors of urban reform, the city as an unhealthy organism and the city as a work of art, encapsulate their contrasting methods and imply their contrasting disciplinary bases. That dual frame for the normalization of the dwelling, housing as an entity both experienced and representational, was central to this phase of the modern urban project.

The resulting synthesis demonstrates the contention that physical urban form is analogous to social form and that regulation of urban form according to norms might shape society. Paul Rabinow's comments on such a synthesis, made in the context of French modernism, are apt:

> Urbanism's synthesis of historical and natural elements into an object—the planned city as a regulator of modern society—can be seen as one of the most complete examples of modernity. This synthesis was exemplary in its demonstration of man's ability to exploit, in a comprehensive functional form and in the name of the general welfare of the population, previously naturalized elements (geography, demography, and hygiene) as subjects of pragmatic knowledge; it was exemplary as well in its awareness of history (of monuments, styles, and cultures) as the ground on which society's future form could be legitimized.[5]

In Amsterdam's social housing, the natural and the historical were exploited in ways that rebalanced the tensions between restraint and liberation in a new configuration. The orders and disorders of the laissez-faire city were replaced with a regime of normalization in the name of public welfare that imposed its own patterns of control and emancipation.

The regulation of the plan took the values that had been espoused by the philanthropic housing movement of the nineteenth century and recast them in the rational terms of hygienic discourse. Moral admonitions against profligacy and wastefulness, extravagance and unnecessary luxury, were translated into neutral terms such as efficiency and functionality. The rational space of real estate, viewed as an undifferentiated, abstract entity, was now subjected to logical manipulation according to rationally derived hygienic norms. Such norms could be used to establish the minimum requirements for the home, requirements that were given the appearance of scientific validity by the authority granted the experts who generated them. Norms identified what was not tolerable, and what was minimally tolerable. Here we find a close correspondence between liberal and Calvinist restraint and social democratic scientism, each subscribing to a calculus of necessity whereby the impartial application of rationality to universalized space might result in an appropriate corrective to the problems created by the housing produced under laissez-faire policy. For liberals, the setting of norms was dependent upon assumptions about the social hierarchy and served the purpose of preserving the status quo, reproducing society; for the socialists, setting norms implied the first step toward the collective rationalization of daily life, an ultimately oppositional, revolutionary goal. Both replicative and oppositional political persuasions supported norm setting under the guise of neutrally applied expertise. For both, space became subject to an instrumental rationalism, distinguishable from the functionalism of the laissez-faire era because the public welfare had been introduced into the equation.

In contrast, regulation of the facade invoked values developed by the aesthetic disciplines in the last decades of the nineteenth century. German idealism had generated a modern historiography of art that considered the greatness of a culture to be manifested in its collective expression. Accordingly, the architect's proper role in society was to translate that society to itself. Modern Dutch architects, such as Berlage, who espoused this view saw architecture as the paramount art representing the community, a *gemeenschapskunst*, community art, construed as a democratic art acting in response to the needs of the people. This viewpoint furnished the justification for high art in a democratic era as well as a defense of artistic autonomy: the people deserve art, and the artist, in particular, the architect, must be left unhampered to reveal the objective style of the times in service to the people. In the interests of artistic advancement, architects thus shared with housing reformers the desire to wrest housing design from the marketplace. Both would benefit from the creation of an official public sphere protected from commercial interests and defined by a disinterestedness that would serve the city and discipline alike.

But liberal democracy reached an impasse when confronted by the determinism at the heart of this modernist historiography. The claim that the means of expression appropriate to the times, the place, and the community could be derived objectively was legitimated by expert opinion, but its derivation from that disciplinary logic put it on a collision course with official neutrality. The modernist imperative rooted in the rule of discipline contradicted liberal freedom rooted in the rule of law.

Nonetheless, the determinism central to modernist historiography offered a way to express collective order that answered liberal needs. In the case of the facade, as in the case of the plan, the liberal desire for urban order coincided to a certain degree with that of the socialists. The creation of visual harmony was viewed by both as a means to civilize the city; formal manipulations of the physical provided means for controlling the city. Public control of urban aesthetics became essential to the liberal espousal of measures to mitigate the results of laissez-faire development; it was also assimilated into the social democratic program of cultural uplift. As new, unified neighborhoods arose, the collective image did not represent restoration of some preindustrial myth of community, but rather a distinctly modern urban solidarity against commodification. The normalized facades formed a tribute to mass society. The visual harmony that was imposed through their stylistic coordination at the behest of architects and municipal authority demonstrated the inscription of the *res publica* on the city, identified as much with the bourgeoisie as the proletariat.

The control of housing design through the dual framework of plan and facade took advantage of the contrasting rationalities of hygiene and aesthetics: the functional and the historiographic, respectively. The norms applied to the plan were the product of a discourse in which space was viewed as a continuous abstraction to be handled with efficiency and objectivity. The plan type was an abstraction of the idealized home that satisfied certain objective hygienic needs. It rationalized space in a systematic response to the reformers' checklist of hygienic ills. In contrast, the norms applied to the facade were generated by a historical rationality: the objective manifestation of the true expression of the times. The facade thus applied a logic to time. It represented the present moment in all its specificity in contrast to the undifferentiated time of the late-nineteenth-century city. If regulation of the plan substituted the calculation of human welfare for the calculation of profit, regulation of the facade substituted for the mass production of cells the rhetoric of a collective urban identity. Rather than the atomization and fragmentation of urban society, the harmonized facades of Amsterdam's social housing reaffirmed differentiated space. The harmony of the facades became an analogue for the reconciliation of the community as a whole, and for the pacification of diverse ideological groups. The new neighborhoods represented the new urban order of mass society.

Civic identity is forged in competition with an unwieldy range of allegiances: to self, family, class, profession, religion, community. It depends ultimately on the construction of an alternative sense of collectivity, an acknowledgment of public interests despite class and sectarian divisions.[6] Such a sense of collectivity can be served by the aestheticization of place, a tactic tapped by both the right and the left to counteract the universalizing tendencies of modernity. This was exemplified in turn-of-the-century Amsterdam, where the normalization process engendered by the public review of housing design inspired a standard urban vernacular whose political message was ambiguous. It represented liberal adherence to the universal principal of aesthetic harmony, mobilized for the creation of a visual analogue to civic order. It also represented the social democratic achievement of a visual representation of the working masses. The social democratic municipal agenda, tempered by compromise with progressive liberalism, played into a conciliatory system that forged a society segmented by class and religious divisions into a single civic order. That civic order was represented by new forms of urban identity.

Form represses all trace of the social processes that produce it. Nonetheless the forms assumed by plan and facade in Amsterdam were the products of the new social processes that have been described in this study. Their apparently transparent translation of collective identity and collective values reflects the visual's treacherous ability to represent reconciliation. The wholeness and completeness of an image, its totalizing capacity, belies the realities of the tensions that gave rise to it. Normalization of the plan suggested the existence of a collective set of values as ephemeral as the collective society represented on the facade.

Amsterdam arrived at collective norms for plan and facade that suggested a reconciliation that never existed between ideologies. The much admired harmony of Amsterdam's new residential neighborhoods hid the conflicts and tensions that underlay their creation, a product of the system of neutrality and accommodation that permitted the city's ideological segments to coexist. Visual harmony represented a neutrality above sectarian interests; it suggested a shared civic identity and proclaimed a new era of mass society. The apparent consensus about the nature of the family dwelling expressed through the definition of a minimal plan type suggested the success of modern rationality in maximizing the use of space for the public good. Aesthetics and hygiene had each been manipulated to serve a collective social entity.

AMSTERDAM IS INTERESTING as an effort to reconcile, however tensely and precariously, the universalizing rationalism of the Enlightenment project with the expressive aesthetics of particularity.[7] In Amsterdam, the functionalist realism of mass production was embraced as the appropriate expression of the times at the same time that the critique of atomization demanded the expression of place. For a brief period, the calculus of necessity and rhetoric of identity were synthesized, but this fragile construct quickly broke down. In the 1920s, the rationalization of the plan overtook and colonized the facade. The abstract perception of space required for the discourse of the plan had anticipated the terms necessary for the functionalist approach of avant-garde architects. An antiaesthetic denial of place-making in favor of rational construction discredited the dichotomy of plan and facade that characterized the Amsterdam synthesis. However, this antiaesthetic introduced its own internal contradictions by espousing the representation of cleanliness and sanitation while denying the need for representation itself. Despite its own antiaesthetic disclaimer, progressive architectural discourse supplanted the aestheticization of place with the aestheticization of hygiene. These developments made the tension between regionalism and internationalism inherent to modernity more apparent. Whereas resistance to the universalizing and atomizing tendencies of capitalist rationality had generated a progressive move toward the regionalism of local expression, the internationalist opposition to the constraints of the parochial produced an emancipatory reaction in the other direction. The mythifying of place as a means to satisfy nostalgia for lost order and community was then monopolized by the conservative right. Not until the 1960s would the left rediscover the progressive myth of the local.

In Amsterdam during the first decades of the twentieth century, the embrace of aesthetics encouraged architectural engagement in mass housing design without radicalizing the terms of the architectural problem into domestic engineering for the working class, as occurred, for example, in Martin Wagner's Berlin and Ernst May's Frankfurt. Nor did Amsterdam achieve the radical socialist culture of Vienna or Frankfurt. Despite the introduction of public libraries, bathhouses, and collective gardens, the social democratic vision of a new urban lifestyle occurred only in isolated neighborhoods within Amsterdam. Collective housekeeping and proletarian iconography appeared only in limited pockets.[8] Instead, Amsterdam's housing reform straddled civic order and utopian vision. It reconciled the values of nineteenth-century middle-class aesthetic and hygienic reform with the vision of a social democratic utopia. In Amsterdam, socialist collectivism was always tempered by the progressive liberal ideal of the well-managed city, and the visual was used to manifest the reconciliation of societal splits. Amsterdam, in contrast with Vienna's utopian lifestyle, Frankfurt's aesthetics of hygiene, or London's rural nostalgia, represented civic harmony.

Nor did Amsterdam's housing reform create a bourgeois urbanism like Burnham's contemporary Chicago plan of 1909. Despite superficial similarities, the campaign for urban aesthetics in Amsterdam was distinct from the City Beautiful movement in the United States. Berlage's plan for Amsterdam South shared some of the grand visionary characteristics and baroque references of Burnham's plan for Chicago, but the motivations were entirely different. Burnham's plan recast the city as the imperial seat of capitalism, whereas Berlage's plan emphasized the collective dimension of the city. The aesthetic reforms of the City Beautiful movement did not address social issues. In

Chicago, tenement reform was considered a distraction from the central issue of giving shape to the city, whereas in Amsterdam aesthetic and housing interests were considered coincident.

Amsterdam's housing projects thus occupy a position somewhere between the Vienna of the Ringstrasse and of the Karl Marx Hof, assimilating the bourgeois project of order and harmony of the first while rejecting the exclusiveness of its audience, but never aspiring to the collectivist reconstructionism and militancy of the second.[9] The boundaries of its housing design were defined by resistance to laissez-faire policy on the one hand and the utopian reorganization of urban life on the other.

When this particular configuration broke down between the wars, it was due to a number of factors. As noted already, the ceding of the progressive edge to the Nieuwe Bouwen, the Dutch version of functionalism, rearranged the forces in the architectural field. The death in 1923 of De Klerk, the creative genius of the Amsterdam School, was also significant. In addition, the changing policy of the national government in favor of encouraging the private construction industry eventually eroded the municipality's hold on housing production and shifted power in the political field. Nonetheless, the institutionalization of housing design in the public realm achieved during the first decades of the century proved to be a lasting contribution. During the initial decades of public housing reform, an institutional environment had been created within which the norms of housing design could be discussed. In the following decades, housing design remained caught in a web of contradictions and tensions, even as its forces altered and rearranged themselves. The parlous role of the expert in relation to the government and the nominal client, the dweller, continued. The complexities of mass culture in relation to high culture remained. The tensions between social service and disciplinary allegiance persisted, although the particular tension between the role of the architect as social engineer and artist was never again as pronounced as during the pioneering decades of housing reform. Even as class structure was transformed and *verzuiling* dismantled, the public dialogue on housing quality maintained a space within which Dutch society established its norms and forms. In an extensive study of Dutch public housing, Noud de Vreeze has remarked that the changes in housing after 1901 did not simply increase the standard of living and alter the technologies of housing, but also fostered a continuous debate on social visions and priorities, inspirations and ambitions, that reflect a history of housing ideals.[10] Despite the inherent conflicts between the lived and the representational, between the emancipatory and controlling elements of its project, Amsterdam first earned its reputation as a mecca of housing by establishing a location within which this particular question of modernity could be pursued free of commercial interest, bringing order and identity to the city.

APPENDIX

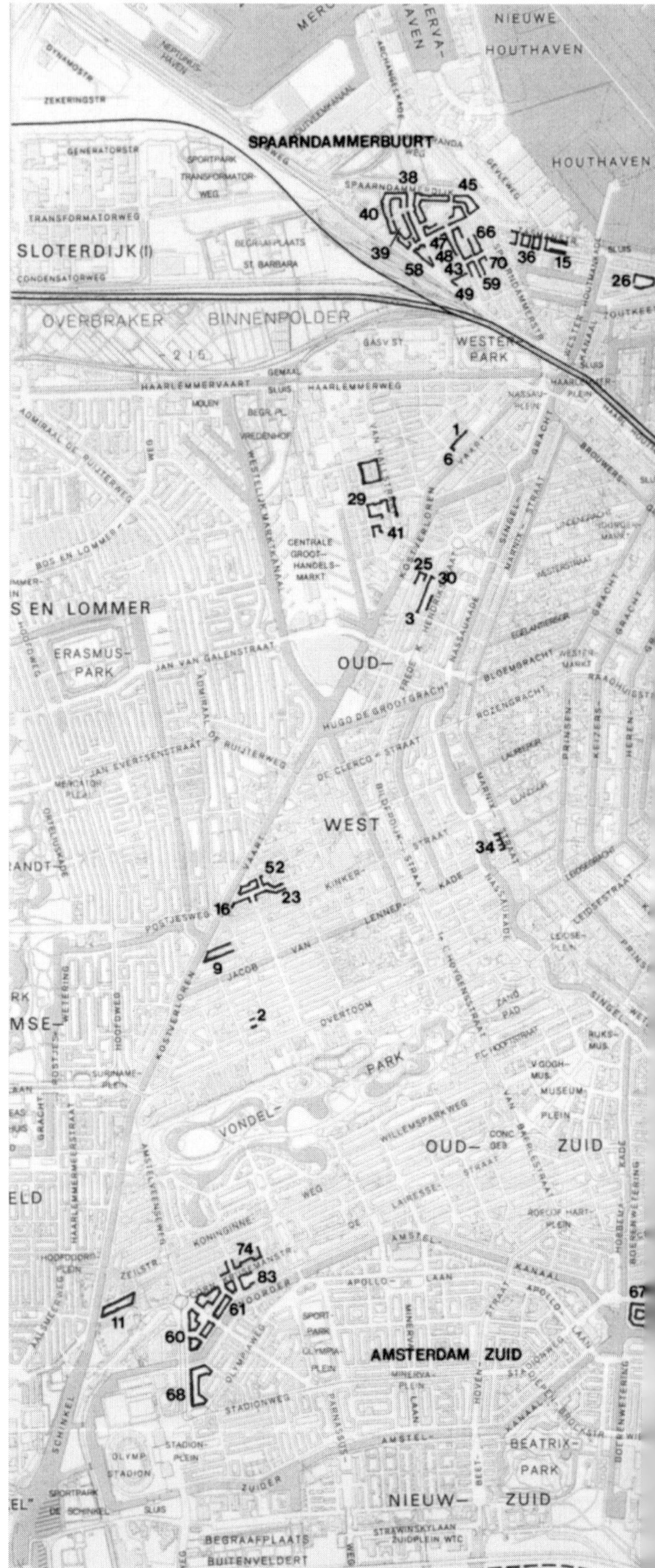

SITE MAP OF HOUSING PROJECTS

APPROVED BY THE MUNICIPAL COUNCIL

FROM 1908 TO 1919

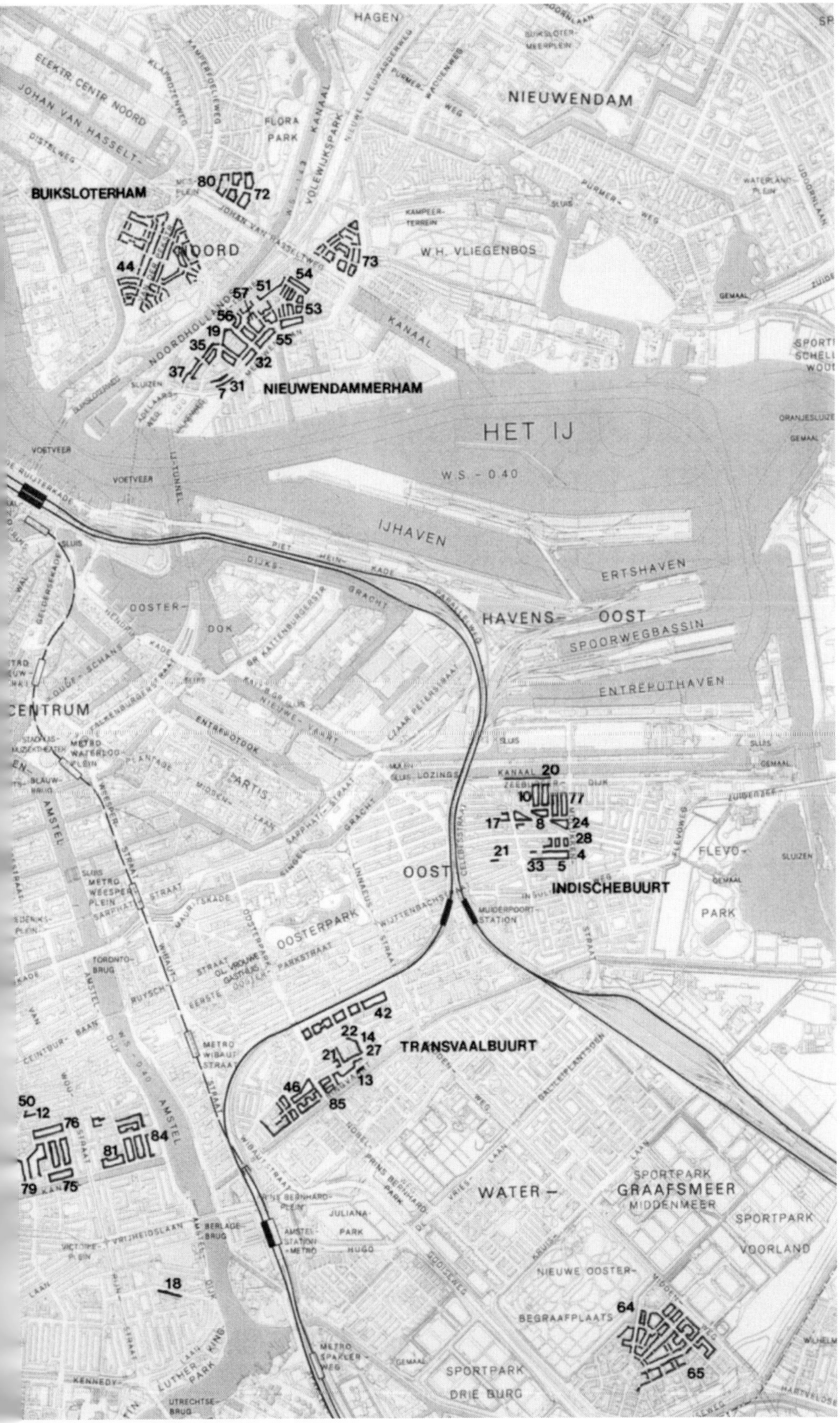

HAGEN
NIEUWENDAM
FLORA
PARK
KANAAL
BUIKSLOTERHAM
NOORD
W.H. VLIEGENBOS
KAMPEER-
TERREIN
NIEUWENDAMMERHAM
HET IJ
W.S. - 0.40
IJHAVEN
ERTSHAVEN
HAVENS- OOST
SPOORWEGBASSIN
ENTREPOTHAVEN
OOSTER-
DOK
CENTRUM
ARTIS
OOST
INDISCHEBUURT
FLEVO-
PARK
OOSTERPARK
TRANSVAALBUURT
WATER-
GRAAFSMEER
SPORTPARK
MIDDENMEER
SPORTPARK
VOORLAND
NIEUWE OOSTER-
BEGRAAFPLAATS
SPORTPARK
DRIE BURG
AMSTEL
JULIANA-
PARK
80
72
44
73
57
51
54
56
53
19
55
35
32
37
7
31
20
10
77
17
8
24
28
21
33
5
4
42
22
14
21
27
13
46
85
50
12
76
84
81
79
75
18
64
65

Housing Projects Approved by the Amsterdam Municipal Council from 1908 to 1919

(Project numbers refer to the site map)

No.	Approval	Construction	Housing Society	Location
1	1908	1912	Rochdale	Van Beuningenstraat
2	1908	1910	ACOB	1e Helmerstraat/2e Boerhaavestraat
3	1909	1911	Bouwmaatschappij tot Verkrijging van Eigen Woningen	1e Hugo de Grootstraat
4	1909	1911	Rochdale	Balistraat
5	1910	1912	Amsterdamsch Bouwfonds	Balistraat
6	1910	1910	Rochdale	Van Beuningenstraat
7	1910	1912	Dr. Schaepman	Meeuwlaan
8	1911	1912–15	Bouwmaatschappij tot Verkrijging van Eigen Woningen	Borneostraat
9	1911	1913	Rochdale	Jacob van Lennepstraat
10	1911	1913	Eigen Haard	Zeeburgerdijk
11	1911	1914	Patrimonium	Vaartstraat
12	1912	1913	Algemeene	Tolstraat
13	1912	1913	Algemeene	Transvaalstraat
14	1912	1913	ACOB	Pretoriusplein
15	1912	1914	Het Westen	Tasmanstraat
16	1912	1915	Rochdale	Hasebroekstraat
17	1912	1914	HIJSM	Madurastraat
18	1913	1915	Amsterdam-Zuid	Trompstraat (Trompenburgstraat)
19	1913	1915	Algemeene	Spreeuwpark
20	1913	1917	Eigen Haard	Zeeburgerdijk

Units	Architect	Archive Numbers
28	J. E. van der Pek	BWT 5717; 6654 PW 1908
48	J. C. Van Epen	BWT 15154; 3636 PW 1909
220	A. W. Weissman	BWT 2387, 16359, 16360, 16517; 8055 PW 1909
88	J. E. van der Pek	BWT 14794; 731 PW 1910
83	J. E. van der Pek	BWT 18455; 1232 PW 1911
20	J. E. van der Pak	BWT 2629; 8340 PW 1910
45	J. H. Rijnja	BWT 16604
472	A. W. Weissman	BWT 23422; 972 PW 1912
188	J. E. van der Pek	BWT 20626; 2350 PW 1912
160	J. H. W. Leliman	BWT 19909, 19910, 9132 PW 1912
220	T. Kuipers/A. Ingwersen	BWT 18794; 2614 PW 1912
48	H. P. Berlage	BWT 9678; 4228 PW 1912; 855 VH 1919
178	H. P. Berlage	BWT 18995, 22033, 5720; 5758 PW 1912
12	J. C. van Epen	BWT 907
340	H. J. M. Walenkamp	BWT 19284
322	W. Noorlander	BWT 11485, 7925; 3929 PW 1913
84	W. Greve Jr.	BWT 13215; 4797 PW 1913
88	Z. Gulden/M. Geldmaker	BWT 21918
179	H. P. Berlage/J. C. van Epen	BWT 23210, 233211; 280 VH 1914
94	J. H. W. Leliman	BWT 11811; 1542 VH 1915

No.	Approval	Construction	Housing Society	Location
21	1913	1915	Het Oosten	Balistraat/Smitstraat
22	1913	1915	ACOB	Pretoriusplein
23	1913	1915	Amsterdamsch Bouwfonds	Hasebroekstraat
24	1913	1915	Bouwmaatschappij tot Verkrijging van Eigen Woningen	Javaplein
25	1913	1915	Bouwmaatschappij tot Verkrijging van Eigen Woningen	Zaagmolenstraat
26	1913	1916	Amsterdamsche Vereeniging tot het Bouwen van Arbeiderswoningen	Barentszplein
27	1913	1915	Patrimonium	Laingsnekstraat
28	1913	1915	De Arbeiderswoning	Javastraat
29	1913	1916	De Arbeiderswoning	Van Hallstraat
30	1913	1916	De Arbeiderswoning	Zaagmolenstraat
31	1913	1915	Dr. Schaepman	Meeuwlaan
32	1913	1915	Eigen Haard	Meeuwlaan
33	1913	1915	Rochdale	1e Atjehstraat
34	1913	1915	Amsterdamsch Bouwfonds	Marnixstraat
35	1914	1916	Patrimonium	Nachtegaalstraat
36	1914	1914	Het Westen	Nova Zemblastraat
37	1914	1916	Het Oosten	Nachtegaalstraat
38	1915	1918	HIJSM	Oostzaanstraat
39	1915	1920	Het Westen	Oostzaanstraat
40	1915	1919	Patrimonium	Oostzaanstraat
41	1915	1919	Algemeene	Van Hallstraat
42	1916	1921–25	Handwerkers Vriendenkring	Retiefstraat
43	1916	1918	Amsterdam-Zuid	Spaarndammerplantsoen
44	1916	1921	Municipal Housing Authority	Buiksloterham

Units	Architect	Archive Numbers
123	J. J. L. Moolenschot/M. J. E. Lippits/ N. H. W. Scholte	BWT 21718, 21719, 21721; 35 VH 1914
12	J. C. van Epen	BWT 23150; 664 VH 1914
101	J. E. van der Pek	BWT 22803, 23608, 23609; 2038 VH 1914
132	A. W. Weissman	BWT 2761
40	A. W. Weissman	BWT 21919; 1132 VH 1914
237	J. Waal	BWT 3584, 26302
27	T. Kuipers/A. Ingwersen	BWT 21965; 5139 PW 1912
169	H. P. Berlage	BWT 18242; 2716 VH 1916
302	K. P. C. de Bazel	BWT 24179, 25288
70	H. P. Berlage	BWT 24010; 939 PW 1913; 2717 VH 1914
102	J. H. Rijnja	BWT 21926, 21687; 2255 PW 1913
65	J. H. W. Leliman	BWT 19561; 2166 VH 1914
43	Z. Gulden/M. Geldmaker	BWT 21818, 23612; 2167 VH 1914
330	J. E. van der Pek	
41	T. Kuipers/A. Ingwersen	BWT 24249; 828 VH 1915
283	H. J. M. Walenkamp	BWT 19283; 549 VH 1915
87	J. J. L. Moolenschot/M. J. E. Lippits/ N. H. W. Scholte	BWT 24062
104	W. Greve Jr.	BWT 24158; 1320 VH 1916; 545 VH 1915
118	H. J. M. Walenkamp	BWT 28300; 975 VH 1915; 2483 VH 1917
264	T. Kuipers/A. Ingwersen	BWT 24510; 1025 VH 1917
161	J. C. van Epen/H. P. Berlage	BWT 21977, 21978, 30363
332	J. H. W. Leliman	1840 VH 1919; 3398 VH 1918; 1250 VH 1915; 60 VH 1920; 1222 VH 1920
44	Z. Gulden/M. Geldmaker	BWT 24892; 85 VH 1916; 2678 VH 1916
560	J. E. van der Pek	656 VH 1916; 447 PW 1917

No.	Approval	Construction	Housing Society	Location
45	1916	1923	Municipal Housing Authority	Polanenhof
46	1916	1922–31	Municipal Housing Authority	Transvaalbuurt
47	1916	1918	Eigen Haard	Polanenstraat
48	1916	1918	Het Oosten	Krommeniestraat
49	1916	1918	Eigen Haard	Zaanstraat
50	1916	1918	Algemeene	Tolstraat
51	1917	1919	Patrimonium	Zwanenplein
52	1917	1919	Rochdale	Bellamystraat
53	1917	1919	Eigen Haard	Zwanenplein
54	1917	1919	Het Oosten	Fazantenstraat
55	1917	1921	Amsterdam over 't IJ	Meeuwlaan
56	1917	1920	Dr. Schaepman	Eksterstraat
57	1917	1920	Algemeene	Havikslaan
58	1918	1920	Eigen Haard	Zaanstraat
59	1918	1918	Amsterdam-Zuid	Polanenstraat
60	1918	1922	Algemeene	Pieter Lastmankade
61	1918	1921	Rochdale	Pieter Lastmankade
62	1919	CANCELED	Eigen Haard	Zeeburgerdijk
63	1919	CANCELED	Het Oosten	Molukkenstraat
64	1919	1925	Eigen Haard	Watergraafsmeer
65	1919	1925	Algemeene	Watergraafsmeer
66	1919	1921	Patrimonium	Polanenstraat
67	1919	1923	Het Oosten	Ruysdaelkade
68	1919	1923	Patrimonium	Amstelveenscheweg
69	1919	1923	Amsteldijk	Josef Israëlskade
70	1919	1920	Amsterdam-Zuid	Polanenstraat

Units	Architect	Archive Numbers
629	K. P. C. de Bazel	
650	H. P. Berlage/J. Gratama/G. Versteeg	BWT 32343, 36341, 35425
52	J. H. W. Leliman	BWT 26337
90	J. J. L. Moolenschot/M. J. E. Lippits/ N. H. W. Scholte	BWT 24893, 25303
60	M. de Klerk	2099 VH 1916; 1907 VH 1917
35	J. C. van Epen/H. P. Berlage	BWT 29835; 2377 VH 1917
150	T. Kuipers/A. Ingwersen	BWT 32941; 891 VH 1918
23	G. F. LaCroix	1232 VH 1918
224	J. Gratama/G. Versteeg	BWT 22102; 539 VH 1918
75	J. J. L. Moolenschot/M. J. E. Lippits/ N. H. W. Scholte	1231 VH 1918
165	H. J. M. Walenkamp	BWT 32803; 3201 VH 1917; 3996 VH 1918
86	J. H. Rijnja	3794 VH 1918
140	J. C. van Epen	BWT 22265; 2394 VH 1918
102	M. de Klerk	BWT 249231; 855 VH 1919
106	Z. Gulden/ M. Geldmaker	BWT 26014; 106 VH 1919
295	J. C. van Epen	BWT 34443, 35213, 35428
360	J. C. van Epen	BWT 34437, 35140, 36768
299	J. H. W. Leliman	
144	J. J. L. Moolenschot/M. J. E. Lippits/ N. H. W. Scholte	
562	J. Gratama/G. Versteeg	BWT 43235, 43959, 52174
532	J. Gratama/G. Versteeg	BWT 37656, 38022, 43558
87	T. Kuipers/A. Ingwersen	BWT 38018; 3392 VH 1919
318	M. J. Lippits/N. H. W. Scholte	BWT 22108
273	T. Kuipers/A. Ingwersen/E. Roest	BWT 26782; 649 VH 1920
318	J. Stuyt	BWT 35972; 1127 VH 1921
52	Z. Gulden/M. Geldmaker	BWT 35171; 3393 VH 1919

No.	Approval	Construction	Housing Society	Location
71	1919	1922	Amsterdam-Zuid	Josef Israëlskade
72	1919	1923	Ons Belang	Mosveld
73	1919	1923	Onze Woning (Bouwmaatschappij tot Verkrijging van Eigen Woningen)	Meeuwlaan
74	1919	1922	Ons Huis	Cornelius Krusemanstraat
75	1919	1923	Rochdale	Josef Israëlskade
76	1919	1923	Patrimonium	Lutmastraat
77	1919	1921	Onze Woning (Bouwmaatschappij tot Verkrijging van Eigen Woningen)	Molukkenstraat
78	1919	1924–25	Onze Woning (Bouwmaatschappij tot Verkrijging van Eigen Woningen)	Josef Israëlskade
79	1919	1922	De Dageraad	P. L. Takstraat
80	1919	1926	Protestantsche	Mosveld
81	1919	1925	Eigen Haard	Granaatstraat
82	1919	1922	Dr. Schaepman	Lutmastraat
83	1919	1921	ACOB	Pieter Lastmankade
84	1919	1921–26	Algemeene	Saffierstraat
85	1919	1922	Algemeene	Cronjestraat

Units	Architect	Archive Numbers
274	Z. Gulden/M. Geldmaker	BWT 35975
218	W. Noorlander	BWT 35424
352	A. W. Weissman	BWT 35139, 36711, 45699
		BWT 35204
120	F. A. Warners	BWT 35426; 199 VH 1920
378	Z. Gulden/M. Geldmaker	
180	T. Kuipers/A. Ingwersen	BWT 21966
80	A. W. Weissman	4634 BH 1919
		BWT 36789, 43338; 6176 VH 1922
423	A. W. Weissman	BWT 35979; 3359 VH 1921
292	P. L. Kramer/M. de Klerk	BWT 44184; 6185 VH 1924
68	A. H. Van Wamelen	
169	P. J. Hamer	BWT 38024
150	J. H. Rijnja/J. Kuyt	BWT 36084; 7238 VH 1920
86	J. C. van Epen	BWT 17794
489	J. C. van Epen	BWT 35423, 36331, 43663; 665 VH 1920
18	J. C. van Epen	BWT 36063; 4712 VH 1919

NOTES

ABBREVIATIONS

ACOB Amsterdamsche Coöperatieve Onderwijzers Bouwvereeniging

ANDB Algemeene Nederlandsche Diamantbewerkers Bond

ANWV Algemeen Nederlandsch Werklieden-verbond

AZ Algemeene Zaken

BNA Bond van Nederlandsche Architekten

BWT Bouw- en Woningtoezicht

CBSA Centraal Bureau voor Sociale Adviezen

GAA Gemeentearchief Amsterdam

GC Gezondheidscommissie

HIJSM Hollandsche IJzeren Spoorweg Maatschappij

IISG Internationaal Instituut voor Sociale Geschiedenis

NAS Nationaal Arbeids Secretariaat

NVV Nederlandsch Verbond van Vakvereenigingen

PW Publieke Werken

SC Schoonheidscommissie

SDAP Sociaal-Democratische Arbeiderspartij

STVDIA Sociaal-Technische Vereeniging van Democratische Ingenieurs en Architecten

VH Volkshuisvesting

VHBO Voortgezet en Hooger Bouwkunst-Onderricht

WD Woningdienst

1. Helen Searing, "Amsterdam South: Social Democracy's Elusive Housing Ideal," *VIA* 4 (1980): 59.

2. American, Italian, and Dutch scholarship opened the field, beginning with two American dissertations: Suzanne Frank, "Michel de Klerk, 1884–1923: An Architect of the Amsterdam School" (Ph.D. diss., Columbia University, 1969), reissued in her *Michel de Klerk, 1884–1923: An Architect of the Amsterdam School* (Ann Arbor: UMI Research Press, 1984), and Helen Searing, "Housing in Holland and the Amsterdam School" (Ph.D. diss., Yale University, 1971). Two exhibitions have yielded catalogs: Ellinoor Bergvelt et al., *Amsterdamse School, 1910–1930* (Amsterdam, 1975), exhibition catalog, Stedelijk Museum; Wim de Wit, ed., *The Amsterdam School: Dutch Expressionist Architecture, 1915–1930* (Cambridge: MIT Press, 1983), exhibition catalog, Cooper Hewitt Museum. See also Maristella Casciato, *La scuola di Amsterdam* (Bologna: Zanichelli Editore, 1987). A relevant exhibition catalog that was published too late to be consulted in the preparation of this book is Manfred Bock et al., *Michel de Klerk: Bouwmeester en tekenaar van de Amsterdamse School, 1884–1923* (Rotterdam: NAi, 1997).

3. In addition to the sources cited in note 2, see Suzanne Frank, "Michel de Klerk's Designs for Amsterdam's Spaarndammerbuurt, 1914–1920: A Contribution to Architectural Lyricism," *Nederlands Kunsthistorisch Jaarboek* 22 (1971): 175–213; Helen Searing, "Eigen Haard: Workers' Housing and the Amsterdam School," *Architectura*, no. 2 (1971): 148–75; Searing, "Amsterdam South"; and Searing, "With Red Flags Flying: Housing in Amsterdam, 1915–1923," in *Art and Architecture in the Service of Politics*, ed. Henry A. Millon and Linda Nochlin (Cambridge: MIT Press, 1978), 230–69.

4. Donald Preziosi gives a provocative account of art history's methodological quandaries in *Rethinking Art History: Meditations on a Coy Science* (New Haven: Yale University Press, 1989). For a recent interpretation of Alois Riegl, see Margaret Iversen, *Alois Riegl: Art History and Theory* (Cambridge: MIT Press, 1993).

5. Pierre Bourdieu, *The Field of Cultural Production: Essays on Art and Literature* (New York: Columbia University Press, 1993). "In defining the literary and artistic field as, inseparably, a field of positions and a field of position-takings we also escape from the usual dilemma on internal ('tautological') reading of the work (taken in isolation or within the system of works to which it belongs) and external (or 'allegorical') analysis, i.e. analysis of the social conditions of production of the producers and consumers which is based on the—generally tacit—hypothesis of the spontaneous correspondence of deliberate matching of production to demand or commissions. And by the same token we escape from the correlative dilemma of the charismatic image of artistic activity as pure, disinterested creation by an isolated artist, and the reductionist vision which claims to explain the act of production and its product in terms of their conscious or unconscious external functions, by referring them, for example, to the interests of the dominant class or, more subtlely, to the ethical or aesthetic values of one or another of its fractions, from which the patrons or audiences are drawn" (34).

6. Ibid., 30. For a succinct definition of his term "field," see also Pierre Bourdieu and Loic J. D. Wacquant, *An Invitation to Reflexive Sociology* (Chicago: University of Chicago Press, 1992), 96–115, where he specifies the relational quality of the concept and indicates the relative auton-

omy of fields: "In highly differentiated societies, the social cosmos is made up of a number of such relatively autonomous social microcosms, i.e., spaces of objective relations that are the site of a logic and a necessity that are *specific and irreducible* to those that regulate other fields" (97). Further explanation of the notion of field is to be found in Pierre Bourdieu, *In Other Words: Essays towards a Reflexive Sociology* (Stanford: Stanford University Press, 1990), 192–94.

7. Bourdieu has acknowledged that his use of the metaphor of theater is similar to its use by E. P. Thompson for describing the dynamic reciprocal relations through which classes define themselves. For extended use of the theater metaphor, see E. P. Thompson, *Customs in Common: Studies in Traditional Popular Culture* (New York: New Press, 1991), 9, 57, 74, 83. The prevalence of metaphors of "theater" and "spectacle" in cultural analysis is discussed in Stephen Daniels and Denis Cosgrove, "Spectacle and Text: Landscape Metaphors in Cultural Geography," in *Place/Culture/Representation*, ed. James Duncan and David Ley (London: Routledge, 1993), 57–59.

Bourdieu also makes use of "game" as an analogy for field: "In a field, agents and institutions constantly struggle, according to the regularities and the rule constitutive of this space of play (and, in given conjunctures, over those rules themselves), with various degrees of strength and therefore diverse probabilities of success, to appropriate the specific projects at stake in the game. Those who dominate in a given field are in a position to make it function to their advantage but they must always contend with the resistance, the claims, the contention, 'political' or otherwise, of the dominated" (Bourdieu and Wacquant, *Invitation to Reflexive Sociology*, 102). What is consistent among these metaphors, and embedded in the use of "field" itself, is the analysis of human interaction through a spatial metaphor. Daniels and Cosgrove discuss such geographical metaphors as boundaries, terrain, and site in "Spectacle and Text." Michel Foucault discusses the implications in his work of such spatial metaphors as field, region, and territory in *Power/Knowledge: Selected Interviews and Other Writings, 1972–1977*, ed. Colin Gordon (New York: Pantheon Books, 1980), 68–70. See also *The Foucault Reader*, ed. Paul Rabinow (New York: Pantheon Books, 1984), 254: "Once knowledge can be analyzed in terms of region, domain, implantation, displacement, transposition, one is able to capture the process by which knowledge functions as a form of power and disseminates the effects of power. There is an administration of knowledge, a politics of knowledge, relations of power which pass via knowledge and which, if one tries to transcribe them, lead one to consider forms of domination designated by such notions as field, region and territory."

8. Gilles Deleuze, "The Rise of the Social," in *The Policing of Families*, ed. Jacques Donzelot (New York: Random House, 1969), ix–xvii.

9. E. H. Gombrich, "In Search of Cultural History" and "Art History and the Social Sciences," in *Ideals and Idols: Essays on Values in History and in Art* (London: Phaidon, 1979), 24–59, 131–66.

10. Bourdieu, *Field of Cultural Production*, 13.

11. Ibid., 37.

12. Bourdieu, *In Other Words*, 140–42.

13. For studies of the urban reform movement in Germany, France, and the United States, see Brian Ladd, *Urban Planning and Civic Order in Germany, 1860–1914* (Cambridge: Harvard University Press, 1990); Paul Rabinow, *French Modern: Norms and Forms of the Social Environment* (Cambridge: MIT Press, 1989); and Paul Boyer, *Urban Masses and Moral Order in America*,

1820–1920 (Cambridge: Harvard University Press, 1978). Boyer's study encompasses several strands of the moral reform movement, among which he identifies the attempt to effect moral reform through environmental betterment, or "positive environmentalism" (179–87, 220–83).

14. The term "substitution market" is employed by Nicolas Bullock and James Read, *The Movement for Housing Reform in Germany and France, 1840–1914* (Cambridge: Cambridge University Press, 1985), 523–30.

15. Ibid., 534. Bullock and Read place this transformation in Germany and France in the period following World War I. In the Netherlands, the transformation began in the decade preceding World War I and was completed during the war, in which Holland was a noncombatant.

16. Max Weber, *The Protestant Ethic and the Spirit of Capitalism* (New York: Charles Scribner, 1958); Henri Lefebvre, *Everyday Life in the Modern World* (New York: Harper and Row, 1971); Jürgen Habermas, *The Theory of Communicative Action*, vol. 1, *Reason and the Rationalization of Society*, trans. Thomas McCarthy (Boston: Beacon Press, 1984).

17. Max Horkheimer and Theodor W. Adorno, *Dialectic of Enlightenment*, trans. John Cumming (New York: Continuum, 1982), ix. "The instrument by means of which the bourgeoisie came to power, the liberation of forces, universal freedom, self-determination—in short, the Enlightenment, itself turned against the bourgeoisie once, as a system of domination, it had recourse to suppression" (93).

18. Rabinow, *French Modern*, 171.

19. Michel Foucault, *The Order of Things: An Archaeology of the Human Sciences* (New York: Random House, 1971).

20. "I believe that the process which has really rendered the discourse of the human sciences possible is the juxtaposition, the encounter between two lines of approach, two mechanisms, two absolutely heterogeneous types of discourse: on the one hand there is the re-organization of right that invests sovereignty, and on the other, the mechanics of the coercive forces whose exercise takes a disciplinary form. And I believe that in our own times power is exercised simultaneously through this right and these techniques and that these techniques and these discourses, to which the disciplines give rise invade the area of right so that the procedures of normalization come to be ever more constantly engaged in the colonization of those of law. I believe that all this can explain the global functioning of what I would call a society of normalization" (Foucault, "Two Lectures," in Gordon, *Power/Knowledge*, 107). Foucault's most influential book to consider normalization is *Discipline and Punish: The Birth of the Prison*, trans. Alan Sheridan (New York: Vintage Books, 1979). A useful discussion of the issues raised by normalization is found in John Caputo and Mark Yount, "Institutions, Normalization, Power," in their *Foucault and the Critique of Institutions* (University Park: Pennsylvania State University Press, 1993), 3–19.

21. See, for example, Allan Megill, *Prophets of Extremity: Nietzsche, Heidegger, Foucault, Derrida* (Berkeley: University of California Press, 1985), 197; David Harvey, *The Condition of Postmodernity: An Enquiry into the Origins of Cultural Change* (Oxford: Basil Blackwell, 1989), 9; Jürgen Habermas, *The Philosophical Discourse of Modernity: Twelve Lectures* (Cambridge: MIT Press, 1987).

22. Charles Taylor, "Foucault on Freedom and Truth," in *Foucault: A Critical Reader*, ed. David Couzens Hoy (Oxford: Basil Blackwell, 1986), 81–82.

23. Karl Polanyi, *The Great Transformation: The Political and Economic Origins of Our Time* (Boston: Beacon Press, 1957).

24. Lefebvre has noted the contrast between the abstract conceived space of the architect and the lived space of the user. "It is in this space that the 'private' realm asserts itself, albeit more or less vigorously, and always in a conflictual way, against the public one" (Henri Lefebvre, *The Production of Space* [Oxford: Basil Blackwell, 1991], 362).

25. Harvey points to the multiple contradictions and ambiguities resulting from the modernist project to affect the aesthetics of daily life, given the modernist allegiance to the creative aura, which yields "a highly individualistic, aristocratic, disdainful (particularly of popular culture), and even arrogant perspective on the part of cultural producers" (*Condition of Postmodernity*, 22).

26. In *Marxism and Literature* (Oxford: Oxford University Press, 1977), Raymond Williams suggests that a sociology of culture will overcome and supplant the division between "art" and its institutions, instead "insisting on what is always a whole and connected social material process" (140); "the full possibilities of the concept of culture as a constitutive social process, creating specific and different 'ways of life'. . . were for a long timed missed" (19).

27. Lefebvre maps out distinctions between the spatial practices of an era, the spatial representations produced by architect and planner, and the spatial experience as lived, that is, the perceived, the conceived, and the lived (*Production of Space*, 33–39, and passim).

CHAPTER ONE

1. "Verslag van den Gemeentelijken Gezondheidsdienst over 1897," *Gemeenteverslag* (1897), app. 9, 62. A firsthand account of life in the Amsterdam slums of the early twentieth century can be found in C. J. Smitz, "Memorie van een 85-jarige Amsterdammer," 1977, MS, GAA.

2. On the economic revival of the Netherlands, see Joel Mokyr, *Industrialization in the Low Countries, 1795–1850* (New Haven: Yale University Press, 1976); J. A. de Jonge, *De industrialisatie in Nederland tussen 1850 en 1914* (Amsterdam: Scheltema en Holkema, 1968); and Theo van Tijn and W. M. Zappij, "De negentiende eeuw," in *De economische geschiedenis van Nederland*, ed. J. H. van Stuijvenberg (Groningen: Wolters-Nordhoff, 1977), 201–308. The urban implications of Amsterdam's economic revival are explored in Michiel Wagenaar, *Amsterdam, 1876–1914: Economisch herstel, ruimtelijke expansie en de veranderende ordening van het stedelijk grondgebruik* (Amsterdam: Historisch Seminarium van de Universiteit van Amsterdam, 1990).

3. Writing in 1905, Van Nierop viewed rural depression as the only cause for immigration to Amsterdam, as there was no great industry to attract workers, and the employment opportunities in the harbor, small shops, and sweated labor would not attract workers. L. van Nierop, *De bevolkingsbeweging der Nederlandsche stad* (Amsterdam, 1905).

4. The Kalff plan was filled with a series of discrete plans by developers. In the west and east harbor areas (the Redeker Bisdom concession of 23 March 1879), Barentszstraat was built in 1878, the Spaarndammerbuurt started in 1883, and Funen (Blankenstraat) in 1884–87. The greatest amount of construction took place in the Kinkerbuurt, the Pijp, and the Dapperbuurt, whose long, dull narrow streets contrasted sharply with the pleasantly curving streets of the Willempark villa district and the monumental plans for the Museumbuurt.

5. The classic study of the Jordaan is H. T. Dijkhuis, "De Jordaan: De ontwikkeling van een volkswijk in een grote stad," *Economisch-Historisch Jaarboek* 21 (1940): 1–90. Chapters 3 and 4

discuss the housing problem from 1813 to 1914. More recent histories of Amsterdam's planning and housing history in the nineteenth century include F. Galesloot, *De gemeente uitgelegd: Stadsuitbreidings- en woningbouwpolitiek in Amsterdam in de 2de helft van de 19e eeuw* (The Hague: NIROV, 1983); Arnold van der Valk, *Amsterdam in Aanleg: Planvorming en dagelijks handelen, 1850–1900* (Amsterdam: Planologisch en Demografisch Instituut van de Universiteit van Amsterdam, 1989); and Wagenaar, *Amsterdam.*

6. The annexation of Nieuwer Amstel in 1896 swelled the percentage of residents living outside the Buitensingel, but the growth of the new districts (Kinkerbuurt, Dapperbuurt, Pijp, Staatsliedenbuurt) made the greatest contribution to the increase (Amsterdamsche Woningraad, *De verbetering der volkshuisvesting te Amsterdam* [Amsterdam, 1913], 18).

PERCENTAGE OF AMSTERDAM'S POPULATION BY AREA

Year	1879	1889	1899	1909
Center	14.7	10.7	7.3	5.2
Old City	75.0	65.6	51.7	42.1
New City	10.2	23.7	41.0	52.7

7. The builder had little or no means of his own. Usually it was the land speculator who originated the entire process of development. With a construction mortgage, the builder was able to erect housing, but there was always the pressure to produce it as quickly and as cheaply as possible for immediate sale so that the mortgage would be paid off with minimum interest and maximum profit. For none of those involved in the financial transaction was the quality of the housing a criterion of success. Given the high demand for housing, even the eventual owners had little to gain from higher quality. As a result, foundations were faulty, the paint chalky, and the brick unsound. On a number of occasions, buildings collapsed while still under construction.

8. An excellent analysis of housing conditions and housing reform in Amsterdam from the mid-nineteenth century to 1913 can be found in Amsterdamsche Woningraad, *Volkshuisvesting te Amsterdam*. See also Louise van der Pek-Went, "Woningtoestanden voor de Woningwet," in *Beter wonen: Gedenkboek gewijd aan het werk der woningbouwverenigingen in Nederland* (Amsterdam: Arbeiderspers, 1938), 13–33; Frank van Wijk, "Volkshuisvesting te Amsterdam, tussen 1850 en 1914" (masters thesis, University of Amsterdam, 1974). The housing types constructed in the new developments of Amsterdam are analyzed by the Amsterdamsche Woningraad, *Rapport over de volkshuisvesting in de nieuwe stad te Amsterdam* (Amsterdam, n.d.). The report was prepared by Johanna ter Meulen, Dirk Hudig, Arie Keppler, J. E. van der Pek, and H. H. Wollring.

9. Good sources for the cost of housing in Amsterdam at the turn of the century are Louis M. Hermans, *Krotten en sloppen*, illustrations by Albert Hahn (Amsterdam: Van Gennep, 1975), and the pioneering work by Johanna ter Meulen, *Huisvesting van armen te Amsterdam* (Haarlem: H. D. Tjeenk Willink, 1903). A general source for Dutch housing statistics is Sociaal-Technische Vereeniging van Democratische Ingenieurs en Architecten, *Woningtoestanden in Nederland: Cijfers en grafische voorstellingen bewerkt naar de woningstatistiek van 31 December 1899* (Rotterdam, 1906), and *Arbeidersbudgets, jaarbudgets van zeventig arbeidersgezinnen in Nederland: Rapport*

eener enquete der Sociaal Democratische Studie Club te Amsterdam, no. 69 (Amsterdam, 1912), 20–24. The housing survey reported in the *Gemeenteverslag* (1897), app. 9, table 6, notes an average rent for one room, f2.14; two rooms, f2.02; three rooms, f1.82; four rooms, f1.79.

10. Hermans, *Krotten en sloppen*. A widow's fear of being sent to live in the charity home for old women is poignantly recorded in this account of Amsterdam slum life.

11. Journals that published on the housing issue included *De Economist, Sociaal Weekblad, Sociale Kroniek, De Gids, Staatkundig en Staathuishoudkundig Jaarboek*. See also H. L. Drucker, "Het woningvraagstuk," *De Gids* 62, part 1 (March 1898): 444–84; Hélène Mercier, *Over arbeiderswoningen* (Haarlem: H. D. Tjeenk Willink, 1887); *Verslag van het eerste Nederlandsch Congres voor Openbare Gezondheidsregeling* (The Hague: F. van Rossen, 1896), 38; C. W. Janssen et al., *Doel en werken der Bouwonderneming Jordaan* (Amsterdam, 1900); Antonie Roell, "Wetgeving op de huisvesting der arbeidende klasse" (Ph.D. diss., University of Leiden, 1892); Daniel Josephus Jitta, *Iets over de verbetering der volkshuisvesting te Amsterdam in verband met werkverschaffing* (Amsterdam, 1893); George A. M. Kallenbach, *Over de pogingen door particulieren in het werk gesteld tot verbetering der arbeiderswoningen* (Leiden: A. H. Adriani, 1892); J. van Hasselt and L. Verschoor, *De arbeiderswoningen in Nederland: Beoordelend overzicht samengesteld door de commissie van onderzoek naar hetgeen in verschillende gemeenten des lands gedaan is ter verkrijging van verbeterde arbeiderswoningen* (Amsterdam: Maatschappij tot Nut van 't Algemeen, 1890); and H. L. Drucker, H. B. Greven, and Jan Kruseman, *Het vraagstuk der volkshuisvesting* (Amsterdam, 1896). An excellent survey of the activities of the philanthropic housing societies in nineteenth-century Amsterdam is Carel Schade, *Woningbouw voor arbeiders in het negentiende-eeuwse Amsterdam* (Amsterdam: Van Gennep, 1981). Schade has also studied a specific project in "Honderd-vier woningen in het Plantsoen: Woningbouw voor arbeiders in Amsterdam, 1851–1856" (master's thesis, University of Amsterdam, 1973). See also Jan Kruseman, "Woningbouwvereenigingen voor de Woningwet," in *Beter wonen*, 35–45.

12. The 1896 study by Drucker, Greven, and Kruseman, *Vraagstuk der volkshuisvesting*, carried out under the auspices of the Society for Public Welfare, a politically neutral organization with roots in eighteenth-century secular idealism, argued forcefully and influentially for national housing legislation.

13. See, for example, the account of a philanthropic housing experiment by Janssen et al., *Bouwonderneming Jordaan*. The successes and failures of the experiment are discussed in Clara Brinkgreve, *De Bouwonderneming Jordaan: Een experiment in de volkshuisvesting aan het einde van de negentiende eeuw* (The Hague: Nederlands Instituut voor Ruimtelijk Ordening, 1985).

14. *Wet van 22 Juni 1901* (Staatsblad no. 158), *Houdende wettelijke bepalingen betreffende de Volkshuisvesting* (hereafter cited as *Woningwet*). The history of the Housing Act has been treated extensively: Nederlands Instituut voor Volkshuisvesting en Stedebouw, *De Woningwet, 1902–1929: Gedenkboek samengesteld ter gelegenheid van de tentoonstelling gehouden te Amsterdam, 18–27 October 1930* (Amsterdam, 1930); Jan Kruseman, *De volkshuisvesting onder de Woningwet: Geschiedkundig overzicht en herinneringen* (Haarlem: H. D. Tjeenk Willink, 1940); H. G. van Beusekom, *Getijden der volkshuisvesting: Notities eener geschiedenis van een halve eeuw* (Alphen aan den Rijn: Samson 1955); Jacques Nycolaas and Rein Geurtsen, "Zeventig jaar Woningwet, nog eens zeventig jaar woningnood," *Plan*, no. 9 (September 1972): 17–21; "De Woningwet van 1901 tot 1931," *Plan*, no. 10 (October 1972): 28–34; Niels Luning Prak, "Zeventig jaar Woningwet: Huizen,

plannen, voorschriften," *Plan*, no. 11 (November 1972): 29–44; Frank Smit, "Geboorte van de volkshuisvesting: Een moeizame bevalling," *Wonen TA/BK*, no. 13 (July 1973): 5–13; Frank Smit, "Gemeente als vliegwiel voor volkshuisvesting," *Wonen TA/BK*, no. 14 (July 1973): 18–26; Jacques Nycolaas, *Volkshuisvesting: Een bijdrage tot de geschiedenis van woningbouw en woningbeleid in Nederland, met name sedert 1945* (Nijmegen: SUN, 1974); H. F. J. M. van der Eerenbeemt, "Wat leidde tot de Woningwet," *Spiegel Historiael* 11, no. 10 (October 1976): 516–25, Peter de Ruijter, "Voor volkshuisvesting en stedebouw: Over woninghervormers en de beweging voor een goede stedebouw, 1890–1920" (Ph.D. diss., University of Amsterdam, 1986).

15. A comparable ambivalence in the support for a substitution market for housing has also been noted for Germany and France, Nicolas Bullock and James Read, *The Movement for Housing Reform in Germany and France, 1840–1914* (Cambridge: Cambridge University Press, 1985), 531.

16. On Wibaut's life and politics, see his autobiography, *Levensbouw: Memories* (Amsterdam: Querido's, 1936), and G. W. B. Borrie, *F. M. Wibaut: Mens en magistraat, ontstaan en ontwikkeling der socialistische gemeentepolitiek* (Amsterdam: De Arbeiderspers, 1968).

17. For a chronological account of twentieth-century housing policy in Amsterdam, see Egbert Ottens, *Ik moet naar een kleinere woning omzien, want mijn gezin wordt te groot: 125 jaar sociale woningbouw in Amsterdam* (Amsterdam: Gemeentelijke Dienst Volkshuisvesting, 1975), and the annual reports of the Building and Housing Inspection Office and the Housing Authority.

18. See the list of projects in the appendix. For a complete list of Amsterdam housing projects to 1991, see *Sociale woningbouw Amsterdam, Atlas* (Amsterdam: Federatie van Woningcorporaties, 1992).

19. See, for example, Manfredo Tafuri et al., *Architettura socialdemocrazia Olanda, 1900–1940* (Venice: Arsenale Cooperativa Editrice, 1979).

20. Peter de Ruijter has pointed out that many of the members of the progressive liberal association the Liberale Unie, which formed in 1885, played an important role nationally in housing reform: H. L. Drucker, Hendrik Goeman Borgesius, Arnold Kerdijk, P. L. Tak, J. W. C. Tellegen, and M. W. F. Treub (De Ruijter, *Volkshuisvesting*, 110). The last three were of particular importance in Amsterdam.

21. On the history of the SDAP in Amsterdam, see P. Hoogland, *Vijf en twintig jaren sociaaldemokratie in de hoofdstad* (Amsterdam: Ontwikkeling, 1928).

22. "Ontwerp-gemeenteprogram en toelichting hierop van J. H. A. Schaper," *Verslag SDAP Congres* (Amsterdam, 1899), 22–27. P. L. Tak first drafted a municipal program in 1899, which served as the outline for the program adopted by the SDAP later that year. This predated the municipal program adopted by the Socialist International in Paris in 1900. The three programs are reproduced in Borrie, *F. M. Wibaut*, 307–13.

23. Ibid., 84.

24. The question of whether the SDAP should or should not fill the alderman's position is discussed in ibid., 97–104. Wibaut received fifteen votes from the SDAP, five from the Progressive Liberals (VDB), and two from the Liberal Party.

25. Ibid., 224–25.

26. Representation in the Amsterdam City Council shifted as follows:

	1903	1911	1918	1919
ARP	7	5	4	3
R.-K. Staatspartij	6	4	3	7
CHU	4	3	1	2
Oud-Liberalin, Midden-stand	-	4	4	-
Liberals	20	16	13	6
VDB	7	5	5	4
SDAP	1	12	15	13
SDP, SP	-	6	-	-

27. The Progressive Liberal Party (Vrijzinnig-Democratische Bond, VDB) adopted a municipal program similar to the SDAP's in 1903; the ARP followed in 1908, and the Liberale Unie in 1915. For an analysis of the municipal programs of the various parties, see P. F. Maas, *Sociaal-Democratische gemeentepolitiek in Katholiek Nijmegen, 1894–1927* (Nijmegen: Janssen, 1974), 58–71.

28. Borrie, *F. M. Wibaut*, 81.

29. J. van der Tempel, "Verslag 1918," no. 283, Wibaut archive, IISG.

30. Lijphart's pathbreaking analysis of this phenomenon in 1968 has spawned a vast literature. The discussion that follows has benefited from a number of studies, primarily Siep Stuurman, *Verzuiling, kapitalisme, patriarchaat: Aspecten van de ontwikkeling van de moderne staat in Nederland* (Nijmegen: SUN, 1984). See also Arend Lijphart, *The Politics of Accommodation: Pluralism and Democracy in the Netherlands* (Berkeley: University of California Press, 1968); Hans Daalder, "Politicologen, sociologen, historici en de verzuiling," *Bijdragen en Mededelingen Betreffende de Geschiedenis der Nederlanden* 100, no. 1 (1985): 52–64; J. C. H. Blom, "Onderzoek naar verzuiling in Nederland: Status quaestionis en wenselijke ontwikkeling," in *Broeders sluit U aan: Aspecten van verzuiling in zeven Hollandse gemeenten*, ed. J. C. H. Blom and C. J. Misset (Amsterdam: De Bataafse Leeuw, 1985), 10–29; S. Stuurman, "De Nederlandse staat tussen verzuiling en moderniteit," in *Balans en perspectief: Visies op de geschiedwetenschap in Nederland*, ed. F. van Besouw et al. (Groningen: Wolters Noordhoff, 1987), 262–283; Erik Hans Bax, "Modernization and Cleavage in Dutch Society: A Study of Long Term Economic and Social Change" (Ph.D. diss., University of Groningen, 1988); Robert Henry Cox, *The Development of the Dutch Welfare State: From Workers' Insurance to Universal Entitlement* (Pittsburgh: University of Pittsburgh Press, 1993).

31. For the history of Dutch liberalism, see E. H. Kossman, *De Lage Landen, 1780–1940: Anderhalve eeuw Nederland en België* (Amsterdam: Elsevier, 1976), and Gerrit Taal, *Liberalen en Radicalen in Nederland, 1872–1901* (The Hague: Martinus-Nijhoff, 1980).

32. Suffrage before 1850 varied considerably from region to region. Starting in 1850, a series of laws gradually extended suffrage to men. Nationally in 1850, 11 percent of men age twenty-three or older had the right to vote; in Amsterdam, the percentage was less than 6 percent. Suffrage was granted to those who paid at least a minimum amount in taxes. In 1888 that was 26 percent nationally; in 1896, 49 percent; and in 1910, 63 percent of men age twenty-five or older. Universal male suffrage was introduced in 1917 for men at least twenty-three years old; two years later the same rights were granted to women. For a discussion of the extension of suffrage,

see Hans Daalder, "Politieke instellingen en politieke partijen," in *De Nederlandse samenleving sinds 1850: Wording en samenhang*, ed. F. L. van Holthoorn (Assen: Van Gorcum, 1985), 318–21.

33. The standard histories of the Protestant workers' organization are R. Hagoort's *Patrimonium: Gedenkboek bij het gouden jubileum* (Amsterdam: Het Nederlandsch Werkliedenverbond Patrimonium, 1927), and *Het beginsel behouden: Gedenkboek van het Nederlandsch Werkliedenbond Patrimonium over de jaren 1891–1927* (Amsterdam: Het Nederlandsch Werkliedenverbond Patrimonium, 1934). See also D. Th. Kuiper, *De Voormannen: Een sociaal-wetenschappelijke studie over ideologie, konflikt, en kerngroepvorming binnen de Gereformeerde wereld in Nederland tussen 1820 en 1930* (Meppel: Boom/Kok, 1972), and Jan de Bruijn, ed., *Een land nog niet in kaart gebracht: Aspecten van het protestants-christelijk leven in Nederland in de jaren 1880–1940* (Franeker: Wever, 1987). The Protestant labor movement is discussed in Erik Hansen and Peter Prosper, "Religion and the Development of the Dutch Trade Union Movement, 1872–1914," *Histoire Social* 9, no. 18 (November–December 1976): 357–83. The Orthodox Protestants, or Gereformeerd, represented a radical break from the Dutch Reformed Protestants, or Hervormd.

34. The Catholic movement is described in L. J. Rogiers and N. C. de Rooy, *In vrijheid herboren: Katholiek Nederland, 1857–1953* (The Hague: Pax, 1953); L. J. Rogier, *Katholieke herleving: Geschiedenis van katholiek Nederland sinds 1853* (The Hague: Pax, 1956); and J. M. G. Thurlings, *De wankele zuil: Nederlandse katholieken tussen assimilatie en pluralisme* (Deventer: Van Loghem Slaterus, 1978).

35. A helpful overview of the political segmentation of this time is to be found in Isaac Lipschits, *Politieke stromingen in Nederland: Inleiding tot de geschiedenis van de Nederlandse politieke partijen* (Deventer: Kluwer, 1977). The changing political platforms of the various parties and societies at the turn of the century are collected in Nicolaas Oosterbaan, *Politieke en sociale programma's*, 5 vols. (Utrecht, 1897–1909).

36. Typical for the degree of social organization along segmental lines was the division within the labor unions. Dominated by socialism in the nineteenth century, when the labor movement began to gain power in the first decade of the twentieth century, three federations of labor unions formed, the social democratic NVV (Nederlandsch Verbond van Vakvereenigingen) in 1906, the Protestant CNV (Christelijk Nationaal Vakverbond) in 1909, and the Catholic Roomsch Katholieke-Vakbureau in 1909.

37. A discussion of the causes for the post–World War II dismantling of pillarization can be found in Paul Pennings, *Verzuiling en ontzuiling: De lokale verschillen* (Kampen: J. H. Kok, 1991), 185–211.

38. On the history of socialism in the Netherlands, see Ger Harmsen and Bob Reinalda, *Voor de bevrijding van de arbeid* (Nijmegen: SUN, 1975); Pieter de Rooy, *Een revolutie die voorbijging: Domela Nieuwenhuis en het Palingoproer* (Bussum: Fibula-Van Dishoeck, 1971); Ger Harmsen, *Historisch overzicht van socialisme en arbeidersbeweging in Nederland: Van de begintijd tot het uitbreken van de eerste wereldoorlog* (Nijmegen: SUN, 1971). The early history of the SDAP is recounted in V. H. Vliegen, *Die onze kracht ontwaken deed: Geschiedenis der SDAP in Nederland gedurende de eerste 25 jaren van haar bestaan* (Amsterdam: De Arbeiderspers, 1938), while the first decades of the SDAP in Amsterdam is commemorated in Hoogland, *Vijf en twintig jaren sociaal-demokratie*. The history of the socialist labor movement is given in F. de Jong, *Om de plaats van de arbeid: Een geschiedkundig overzicht van ontstaan en ontwikkeling van het Nederlands Verbond van Vakverenigin-*

gen (Amsterdam: De Arbeiderspers, 1956), and J. M. Welcker, "Een ongemakkelijk bondgenootschap: De Sociaal-Democratische Arbeiderspartij en het Nederlandsch Verbond van Vakvereenigingen tussen 1906 en 1913," in *Heren en arbeiders in de vroege Nederlandse arbeidersbeweging, 1870–1914* (Amsterdam: Van Gennep, 1978).

39. The early days of the social movement are described in A. C. J. Vrankrijker, *Een groeiende gedachte: De ontwikkeling der meningen over de sociale kwestie in de negentiende eeuw in Nederland* (Assen, 1959).

40. See, for example, the comments of H. L. Drucker in "Het woningvraagstuk," *De Gids* 62, part 1 (March 1898): 444–54. In 1892, the Radical Party adopted a housing plank, followed by the Liberale Unie in 1897. The 1897 election platform of the Nederlandsch Werklieden Verbond Patrimonium supported expansion of expropriation as a means to improve housing. The SDAP introduced housing in its campaign material in 1897.

41. The following is a list of housing societies that had either built or were planning to build in Amsterdam in 1920: ACOB, Algemeene, Amsteldijk, Amsterdam over 't IJ, Amsterdam-Zuid, Amsterdamsch Bouwfonds, De Arbeiderswoning, De Dageraad, Dr. Schaepman, Eigen Haard, Handwerkers Vriendenkring, HIJSM, Ons Belang, Ons Huis, Onze Woning, Het Oosten, Patrimonium, Protestantsche, Rochdale, Het Westen, Zomers Buiten.

42. H. V[ries, Mzn.], "Onze bouwplannen in Amsterdam," *De Handwerksman* 22, no. 4 (August 1912).

43. The socialist society was Amsterdam-Zuid, the Catholic society Het Oosten, eventually the largest Catholic housing society in the country.

44. The socialist society was the Algemeene, the liberal society the Handwerkers Vriendenkring, and the orthodox Jewish society Oholei Jacob. The last two societies were specifically set up in 1912 for those living in the renewal district Uilenberg. The society Oholei Jacob was set up to build near the old neighborhood, but proved unsuccessful in its efforts (RA 941, no. 311, CBSA archive, IISG).

45. In order to reduce the bureaucratic tangle, Keppler insisted that only existing societies be designated building sites. As a result, some societies never succeeded in building. When Keppler received a request from the Amsterdam Musicians' Society to set up yet another housing society, he asked the mayor and aldermen to put an end to the proliferation (Arie Keppler to alderman of housing, 13 December 1916, 5156 WD 1916, in 3759 VH 1916, archive 5187, GAA). Mayor and aldermen agreed to Keppler's proposal on 2 March 1917. Keppler also suggested consolidation of existing societies (29 October 1917, 5605 WD 1917, in 3678 VH 1918, archive 5187, GAA). Rochdale, ACOB, Eigen Haard, and Algemeene did develop housing plans together in the Stadion district and in Watergraafsmeer.

46. Arie Keppler at Health Board meeting of 15 December 1917, Notulen van de besloten vergaderingen van de Gezondheidscommissie (1917), archive 5269, GAA. Neutrality was required, however, of societies requesting straight government subsidies. Attempts to establish the St. Nicolaasstichting, a housing society for poor Catholic families, foundered on the requirement for neutrality. The socialist society De Arbeiderswoning was only able to receive a subsidy because its housing was open to dwellers of all persuasions. The Handwerkers Vriendenkring was organized to provide new housing for dwellers from the primarily Jewish renewal district Uilenburg, but it formed a special case because of the demolition of houses and forced

evictions. The Amsterdamsche Vereeniging tot het Bouwen van Arbeiderswoningen also received a municipal subsidy. When reviewing the proposal for municipal housing in 1914, the Health Board considered as one of its advantages the provision of housing regardless of religious or political affiliation (Health Board, "Verslag van de bevindingen en handelingen der Gezondheidscommissie te Amsterdam in 1914," *Gemeenteverslag* [1914], app. 1, 23).

47. Barend Bymholt, *Geschiedenis der arbeidersbeweging in Nederland* (Amsterdam: Van Looy, 1894), 2:612. For more on worker involvement in the call for housing reform, see Schade, *Woningbouw voor arbeiders*, 44, 141–45. For the early history of the ANWV, see B. H. Heldt, *Algemeen Nederlandsch Werklieden-verbond, 1871–1896* (Leeuwaarden: Coöperatieve Handelsdrukkerij, 1896).

48. [Glimmerveen], "Werk aan de winkel," *De Gemeente-Werkman* 1, no. 1 (26 April 1902).

49. Handwerkers Vriendenkring, *Gedenkboekje ter gelegenheid van het 30-jarig bestaan: Bevattende een kort overzicht van de geschiedenis der vereeniging, 1869–1899* (Amsterdam, 1899), and *Gedenkschrift der Stichting Bouwfonds Handwerkers Vriendenkring* (Amsterdam, 1937).

50. L. M. Hermans's work appeared in "De tehuizen van de Amsterdamsche proletariërs," *De Jonge Gids* (1898–99). His book *Krotten en sloppen* was circulated by the union leadership among members of the diamond workers' union, the largest Amsterdam union (Hermans to ANDB, 21 May 1901, ANDB archive, IISG).

51. The society had 9,929 members as of 1 January 1915, of whom 223 were diamond workers, 384 were skilled labor in other areas, and 109 were municipal workers (Algemeene Woningbouw Vereeniging, *Jaarverslag* [1914]).

52. J. H. van Schlosser, "Neutraliteit in den woningbouw," *Volkshuisvesting* 1, no. 15 (24 April 1920): 1.

53. Bernard Kruithof, "Trouw aan het beginsel: De Christelijk-sociale beweging in Nederland van 1876 tot 1909," in *Tijdschrift voor Sociale Geschiedenis* 7 (December 1981): 351, 353.

54. Maas, *Sociaal-Democratische gemeentepolitiek*, 62–65.

55. D. P. D. Fabius, *Huiskamer en keuken: Een tweetal schetsen* (Leiden: Donner, 1897). For an example of the social thought of the Reformed pillar, see J. R. Slotemaker de Bruine, *Christelijke-sociale studiën* (Utrecht: G. J. A. Ruys, 1910), and Herman Bavinck, *Het Christelijk huisgezin* (Kampen: J. H. Kok, 1908).

56. *Patrimonium's Bode* 4, no. 4 (1 Oct 1912).

57. D. Schut, Prof. P. A. Diepenhorst, and Ds. J. C. Sikkel.

58. W. J. Bossenbroek had written to the CBSA for examples of statutes in July 1910; meetings and exchanges with the CBSA followed (W. J. Bossenbroek to CBSA, 6 July 1910, RA 861, CBSA archive, IISG). On 10 July 1910, a preparatory committee consisting of Patrimonium leaders set up the organization's Amsterdam housing society (*Patrimonium's Bode* 2, no. 6 [1 March 1911], and no. 12 [1 June 1911]).

59. *De Amsterdammer: Chr. Volksdagblad*, 31 March 1914.

60. Alfons Ariens, "Gemeenschappelijke of persoonlijke eigendom van arbeiderswoningen," *Katholiek Sociaal Weekblad* 1, no. 45 (8 November 1902): 483.

61. *Mededelingen Katholieke Sociale Actie, 1905–1908.*

62. *Vlugschrift*, no. 7, June 1906. For a representative view of Catholic social policy, see J. D. J. Aengenent, *Leerboek der sociologie* (Leiden: Futura, 1909).

63. Ariens, "Gemeenschappelijke," 483.

64. Plans for another Catholic society, the St. Nicolaasstichting, faltered. The society planned to build rent-subsidized housing for poor Catholic families with many children. Societies requesting such rent subsidies were required to be completely neutral (28 January 1913, 22265 BWT 1913, in 165 VH 1913, archive 5187, GAA).

65. Ad Bevers, *Oost-West thuis best: Gedenkschrift bij gelegenheid van het vijftigjarig bestaan der R.K. Wbv. "Het Oosten" te Amsterdam* [1962], 17–21. The inspector was J. M. A. Zoetmulder, the architect Joseph Cuypers, and the councilor J. N. Hendrix.

66. The fact that the highest percentage of dwellings built under the Housing Act in Amsterdam belonged to housing societies associated with the Social Democrats was discussed in the municipal council in 1920. The confessional councilor Douwes claimed that land was being unfairly allocated to what he called "revolutionary" housing societies. Wibaut countered this characterization of the housing societies, noting that revolution and housing rarely go together. Douwes provided the following accounting of current housing society dwellings: Social Democratic, 2,397; neutral, 1,362; Catholic, 522; Protestant, 706. Including projected construction, the figures were Social Democratic, 9,577; neutral, 2,322; Catholic, 1,840; Protestant, 1,321 (*Gemeenteblad* 2 [1920], meeting of 1 December 1920, 1804–5).

67. Social Democrats founded the Bond van Arbeiders-woningbouw-vereenigingen, based in Rotterdam, which published the journal *Volkshuisvesting* from 1920. The Bond van Protestants-Christelijke Woningbouwvereenigingen "Patrimonium" and the R.-K. Federatie van Diocesane Woningbouw-Centrales represented confessional housing societies. All three were overshadowed by the activities of the neutral National Housing Council, established in 1913, housed during its first years at the CBSA, and later closely allied to the Dutch Housing Institute. L. G. Gerrichhauzen argues that the confessional housing federations did not play an important role until after the Second World War (*Het Woning-corporatiebestel in Beweging* [Delft: Delftse Universitaire Pers, 1990], 105–9).

68. Dirk Hudig, "De woningbouwvereenigingen op politieke grondslag," *Gemeentebelangen* 15, no. 6 (15 November 1919): 83–85. See also his article "Adviesbureaus voor bouwvereenigingen," *Sociale Voorzorg* 1 (June 1919): 547–84 and H. J. Nieboer, "De financieele kant van het woningvraagstuk," *Socialistische Gids* 5, no. 1 (January 1920): 34.

69. On the history of the National Housing Council, see B. G. A. Kempen and N. van Velzen, *Werken aan wonen: 75 jaar Nationale Woningraad* (Almere: Nationale Woningraad, 1988), and De Ruijter, *Volkshuisvesting*, 238–39.

70. "One can state with a great degree of certainty what causes particular disturbances in bodily functions, and what will result from particular medications and diets, because the symptoms of disease and recovery have been carefully observed. But one cannot state the causes for the poor constitution of society, or what one should do to eliminate those causes. At least there is no authoritative theory, no collection of general observations that would more or less apply equally throughout the civilized world. There is no clearly formulated system of probable causes and effects that one could consult as a matter of course as cases arise. No, not unlike the practice of medicine in backward regions, everyone has to doctor society on his own. The possibility that there could actually be a general classification of the symptoms involved is held in doubt and even denied" (Frank van der Goes, "Sociaal onderwijs," *De Nieuwe Gids* 7, part 1 [1891–92]: 131–41).

71. Ibid. Van der Goes argued that all opinion on society should be based on the science of society. "De noodzakelijkheid dat men zijne meeningen over de samenleving, ontleene aan niets dan aan de wetenschap van de samenleving, wordt nog maar zeer zwak gevoelt."

72. Van Marken was director and chief shareholder of a factory in Delft, as well as a progressive bourgeois reformer. The factory was De Nederlandsche Gist- en Spiritusfabriek. Van Marken belonged to the circle that included Arnold Kerdijk, M. W. F. Treub, B. H. Pekelharing, Johanna ter Meulen, and others. He participated in the Committee for Discussion of the Social Question and published in progressive journals such as *Vragen des Tijds*, *Sociaal Weekblad*, and *De Kroniek* as well as his factory newspaper *De Fabrieksbode*. Van Marken, who considered himself more "social than the socialists," believed the private industrialist should bear responsibility for the welfare of his workers. F. M. Wibaut writes in his autobiography of a visit to the Van Markens' home around 1892. When Van Marken related that he had instructed the architect to build him a house somewhat larger and somewhat differently arranged from those of the workers, but in the same spirit, Wibaut responded with the comment that they must have been amazed when they saw the house (Wibaut, *Levensbouw*, 373). Van Marken introduced a number of innovative social experiments at his own factory, including profit sharing, pension funds, health insurance, savings plans, disability payments, life insurance, and a cooperative store. In the style of Cadbury, Lever, and Krupp, he hired an architect and landscape architect to design an industrial park where he and the workers could live in peaceful proximity to the plant. A detailed description of Van Marken's factory reforms is to be found in Jan Muntendam, *Loon naar werken: Enkele sociale aspecten van het werk van J. C. van Marken* (Deventer: Kluwer, 1971). On Agneta-Park, see J. C. van Marken, *Het Agneta-Park en de N.V. Gemeenschappelijk eigendom* (Delft, 1889).

73. J. C. van Marken, "Sociale ingenieurs," in *Uit het fabrieksleven: Herdruk van hoofdartikelen in de Fabrieksbode van J. C. van Marken* (Delft: Van Marken, 1906), 3:312–29. The series of four articles started appearing in 1893 and were reprinted as a whole in 1898. Van Marken envisaged the social engineer at work in three areas: in the factory to design and manage social programs; in government to administer social legislation; and in higher education to train industrialists in labor relations, health, welfare, and safety. The social engineer would be trained in economics, labor law, housing, hygiene, engineering, administration, and accounting. Van Marken's factory paternalism and theory of the social role of the engineer parallel closely the work of Émile Cheysson described by Paul Rabinow, *French Modern: Norms and Forms of the Social Environment* (Cambridge: MIT Press, 1989), 172–84.

74. Van Marken,"Sociale ingenieurs," 325.

75. Ibid., 329.

76. Statutes of the CBSA, 1899, CBSA archive, IISG. In the late 1890s, Van Marken corresponded with a member of the Association for Improving the Condition of the Poor in New York who invited him to become a foreign contributor to a proposed "Bureau of Social Information." An existing Bureau of Social Economics was already writing for the press and consulting on such topics as cooperatives, social laws, public health, and municipal policy, providing "an American view of the social engineer" (*Amsterdamsch Nieuwsblad*, 4 January 1899). The Musée Social financed in Paris by the industrialist Comte de Chambrun in 1895 and the German Centralstelle für Wohlfahrtseinrichtungen also inspired Van Marken and his adopted son

J. C. Eringaard to establish a Dutch office to consult on social measures. On the principles of the Musée Social, see Rabinow, *French Modern*, 182–84; on the early development of the CBSA, see Is. P. de Vooys, *Sociaal Weekblad*, no. 50 (1898). An article by J. C. Eringaard in *Sociaal Weekblad*, no. 47, 19 November 1898, suggested the usefulness of a Dutch social bureau. It received more than a hundred sympathetic responses, prompting a meeting in Utrecht on 27 December 1898 that resulted in the appointment of a temporary set of officers: J. C. Eringaard, J. C. van Marken, Alfons Ariens, W. H. Vliegen, Arnold Kerdijk, and M. W. F. Treub. Treub refused the nomination, but was later appointed director (CBSA, Notulen Bestuursvergaderingen, 1898–1921, CBSA archive, IISG). For the history of the CBSA, and particularly the role of Dirk Hudig in the organization, see De Ruijter, *Volkshuisvesting*, 230–36.

77. [P. L.] T[ak], "Bureel voor Sociale Adviezen," *De Kroniek* 5, no. 210 (1 January 1899): 2. The word "neutral" itself was not without its political overtones, which could vary with usage. During the school struggle, which overshadowed all Dutch politics during the second half of the nineteenth century, confessional parties had contested the liberal notion that the state support only "neutral" nondenominational schools. It was argued that a "neutral" curriculum in history omitting reference to divine intervention was as partisan to an Anti-Revolutionary parent as a fundamentalist reading of history would be to a liberal parent. Neutrality often served as a password for liberal, as in the designation of some liberal unions as "neutral." Institutions such as the Society for Public Welfare, which called themselves neutral, openly supported the liberal school position. Even where neutral meant silence on political issues, that silence could be interpreted as a political position. Thus the socialist Wibaut took the reform Toynbee organization Ons Huis to task for its neutrality on strikes, which he compared unfavorably with English settlement house behavior (F. M. Wibaut, "Toynbee-werk," *De Kroniek* 4, no. 188 [31 July 1898]: 247–48).

78. CBSA, *Jaarverslag* (1899–1900), 5.

79. CBSA meeting of 4 January 1899, Notulen Bestuursvergaderingen, CBSA archive, IISG. The first definitive board of officers was elected on 11 September 1899 and included representatives from all four pillars: Arnold Kerdijk, chairman; Louise Went, vice-chairman; J. C. Eringaard, treasurer; P. J. M. Aalberse; G. M. Boissevain; R. A. de Monchy; A. S. Talma; J. F. Vlekke; W. H. Vliegen (replaced by P. L. Tak in 1900).

80. CBSA meetings of 16 May and 30 May 1899, Notulen Bestuursvergaderingen, CBSA archive, IISG. The fear of being too closely associated with socialism was not ungrounded. In 1903, the CBSA was attacked for its socialism in the Delft City Council (CBSA, *Jaarverslag* [1905–6]). The School for Social Work, founded by Progressive Liberals closely associated with the Society for Public Welfare and the CBSA, was confronted with parents unwilling to allow their daughters to enter what they felt was a bastion of socialist subversion. M. G. Muller-Lulofs speculated that such fears led to the closing in 1903 of the original School for Social Work founded in September 1899 by Kerdijk. The school started up again in September 1904 (M. G. Muller-Lulofs, *De School voor Maatschappelijk Werk* [Amsterdam, n.d.]). On the founding of the school, see Arnold Kerdijk, "Een opleidingsinrichting in wording," *Sociaal Weekblad*, 22 April 1899. See also E. C. Knappert, *De School voor Maatschappelijk Werk, 1899–1924* (Amsterdam, 1925?).

81. Its labor committee was composed of four members, one representative each from the

liberal ANWV, the socialist ANDB, the Calvinist Patrimonium, and the Roman Catholic Volksbond.

82. CBSA, *Jaarverslag* (1899–1900), 3.

83. CBSA, *Jaarverslag* (1905–6).

84. T[ak], "Bureel voor Sociale Adviezen," 2; [P. L.] T[ak], "Sociale adviezen," *De Kroniek* 6, no. 270 (25 February 1900): 58.

85. [P. L.] T[ak], "Opleiding voor socialen arbeid," *De Kroniek* 5, no. 233 (11 June 1899): 186. Tak's socialist perspective is in striking contrast to the liberal proponents of social work. See A. van Gijn et al., *Persoonlijke bemoeiingen van meer ontwikkelden in 't belang van minder ontwikkelden (Toynbee-werk)* (Amsterdam: Maatschappij tot Nut van 't Algemeen, 1895).

86. [P. L.] T[ak], "Sociale arbeid," *De Kroniek* 10, no. 475 (30 January 1904): 34.

87. Maatschappij tot Nut van 't Algemeen, "Punten ter beschrijving van de Algemeene Vergadering," 1 June 1898, no. 265, archive 211, GAA. An invitation to a meeting on 5 November 1898 was refused by Th. Ligthart, secretary of the Nederlandsch Aannemersbond, who wrote that "het bevorderen van een bouw van goede arbeiderswoningen, tot op heden ligt buiten de werkkring van den Ned. Aannemersbond." The members of the Society for Public Welfare's preparatory committee (Commissie van Voorbereiding in zake de Centrale Commissie van het Woningvraagstuk) were H. L. Drucker (Public Health Convention), E. Fokker, M. W. F. Treub, D. W. Stork (Society for Public Welfare), B. H. Heldt (ANWV), Klaas Kater (Patrimonium), W. C. J. Passtoors (Ned. R.K. Volksbond), W. H. Vliegen (SDAP), G. F. V. L. van Zuilen (Society for the Advancement of Architecture).

88. "Adres van de Commissie van Voorbereiding in zake de Centrale Commissie van het Woningvraagstuk," 7 December 1898, no. 265, archive 211, GAA. On 16 January 1899, the preparatory committee met with representatives of more than thirty societies and appointed a permanent housing committee, but since the CBSA was concurrently being organized, the Society for Public Welfare's committee decided to wait in order to coordinate their housing endeavors. In October, the society's committee met with the board of the CBSA and decided to associate the housing committee with the CBSA. The CBSA was to select five from the current committee to form the new housing committee. These were appointed on 12 March 1900: Johanna ter Meulen, C. W. Janssen, A. H. Rakers, H. L. Drucker, J. W. C. Tellegen, and J. W. Weijerman, secretary (CBSA, *Jaarverslag* [1899–1900], 11–13; CBSA meetings of 19 September 1899 and 12 March 1900, Notulen Bestuursvergaderingen, CBSA archive, IISG).

89. See the many responses to queries in the CBSA archive, IISG, and Dirk Hudig and H. C. A. Henny, *Handleiding voor woningbouwverenigingen* (Zwolle, 1911).

90. The original board of officers were M. W. F. Treub, J. W. Jenny Weijerman, Louise Went, D. P. D. Fabius, and P. L. Tak ("Verslag van de werkzaamheden van den Amstrerdamsche Woningraad gedurende de vyf eerste jaren van zyn bestaan [januari 1902–augustus 1906]," typescript, Wibaut archive, IISG).

91. A number of these works were later republished by the Dutch Housing Institute.

92. CBSA meeting of 9 June 1914, Notulen Bestuursvergaderingen, CBSA archive, IISG. Hudig listed the existing housing organizations as the National Housing Council, Congress for Social Hygiene (Congres voor Sociale Hygiëne), Bond Heemschut, Association of Dutch Municipalities (Vereeniging van Ned. Gemeenten), Economic Society (Vereeniging voor

Staathuishoudkunde), the three engineers' societies, the four main architectural societies, and the National Housing Board (Rijkswoningcollege).

93. Peter de Ruijter, "De oprichting van het Nederlands Instituut voor Ruimtelijk Ordening en Volkshuisvesting," *Stedebouw en Volkshuisvesting* 59, no. 11 (November 1978): 541–52; CBSA, *Jaarverslag* (1917–18), 6–8. The organizations represented on the board were the Society for Public Welfare, Public Health Convention, League against Alcohol Abuse, Bond Heemschut, Society for the Advancement of Medicine, Society for the Advancement of Architecture, League of Dutch Architects, Architectura et Amicitia, Social Technical Society of Democratic Engineers and Architects, Royal Society of Engineers, CBSA, National Housing Council, Amsterdam Housing Council, National Housing Board, Association of Dutch Municipalities, Amsterdam, Rotterdam, and the Hague. The history of the institute is given in Peter de Ruijter, *Voor volkshuisvesting en stedebouw: Voorgeschiedenis, oprichting, en programma van het Nederlands Instituut voor Volkshuisvesting en Stedebouw, 1850–1940* (Utrecht: Stichting Matrijs, 1987).

94. Biographical accounts exist for many of the leading housing reformers: H. van der Weide, *Het werk van Mr. Dirk Hudig* (Alphen aan den Rijn: Samson, 1970); Jan Kruseman, *De volkshuisvesting onder de Woningwet: Geschiedkundig overzicht en herinneringen* (Haarlem: H. D. Tjeenk Willink, 1940); Wilhelmina C. Blomberg, *Aan de bakermat van de Amsterdamse Volkshuisvesting: Louise Went, 1865–1951* (Amsterdam: Gemeentelijke Dienst Volkshuisvesting, 1985); Cornelia L. de Lange, "Johanna Elisabeth ter Meulen 11 augustus 1867–11 februari 1937," *Amstelodamum* 57 (1965). With the successful establishment of the Dutch Housing Institute, the Amsterdam Housing Council soon came to the conclusion that it had fulfilled its mission and that it had been superseded (Jan Kruseman to F. M. Wibaut, 27 February 1920, no. 288, Wibaut archive, IISG). It dissolved in 1920, and was followed in 1923 by the CBSA, and in 1924 by the STVDIA. The CBSA and STVDIA, organizations that had stimulated work in many aspects of social reform, ceded to the independent professional organizations they had helped launch. To the extent that they had fostered the development of organized expertise, they had lost their own raison d'être.

CHAPTER TWO

1. On student life, see A. J. C. de Vrankrijker, *Vier eeuwen Nederlands studentenleven* (Voorburg: Boot, 1939). On the occasion of a speech given by socialist Jan van der Waerden just after his election as president of the student body, Tak wrote optimistically about the wave of social responsibility displayed by the Delft students at the turn of the century, an attitude he hoped would spread to the universities (P. L. Tak, "Een Delftsche toespraak," *De Kroniek* 5, no. 251 [15 October 1899]: 330–31). B. H. Pekelharing, a progressive professor of law and economics who taught at Delft from 1874 to 1908, observed that even the more conservative students at the Polytechnic were beginning to expand their social horizons (B. H. Pekelharing to F. M. Wibaut, 5 March 1897, no. 5, Wibaut archive, IISG).

2. These were forty of the students and former students of B. H. Pekelharing, who worked with the Committee for Discussion of the Social Question and joined Treub as an editor of *Sociaal Weekblad* from 1893 to the end of 1897. He was also involved with such organizations as the Society for Statistics. Many of the students inspired by Pekelharing's lectures on labor history

later became leading Social Democrats, such as the Van der Waerden brothers Theo and Jan, Hettinga Tromp, J. W. Albarda, and Israel P. de Vooys. For more on this circle, see Walter Thijs, *De Kroniek van P. L. Tak: Brandpunt van Nederlandse cultuur in de jaren negentig van de vorige eeuw* (Amsterdam: Wereld Bibliotheek, 1956), 70. The Delft society's aim was the furthering of the general welfare, the growth of a democratic state, and the promotion of the interests of engineers. The STVDIA archives and library are to be found at the International Institute of Social History. The group addressed a variety of social issues, including housing and planning. They published reports, organized a garden city competition, and petitioned the government for the revision of the Housing Act. At Delft, they sponsored lectures on social and economic subjects that emphasized the social function of the engineer. One student commented that the difference between the Society of Delft Engineers and the STVDIA could be read in their statutes, the older society defining its purpose purely in terms of the interests of the profession, the younger one making explicit a commitment to social improvement (Sr., "De ingenieur," *Technisch Studenten-Tijdschrift* 1, no. 9 [15 February 1911]: 217–18.

3. Pieter Bakker Schut, "Ambtenaren ter uitvoering der sociale wetgeving," *De Kroniek* 9, no. 461 (24 October 1903): 339. In the proposed curriculum, the social technical engineer would receive training in mathematics, physics, chemistry, mechanics, architecture, planning, drafting, hygiene, economics, statistics, social and administrative law. See "Adres der Sociaal-Technische Vereeniging van Democratische Ingenieurs en Architecten" (January 1905), which refers directly to Van Marken's articles as precedent. The address was signed by Pieter Bakker Schut, L. Doedes, F. G. Unger, G. Versteeg, and Jan van Hettinga Tromp and reprinted in *De Ingenieur* 20, no. 5 (4 February 1905): 66–69. A detailed description of the curriculum appears in Pieter Bakker Schut and L. Doedes, "Sociaal-technische ingenieurs," *De Ingenieur* 20, no. 6 (11 February 1905): 81–84. The amendment was supported by progressives such as Pekelharing and Tellegen outside Parliament and H. H. van Kol and Treub inside, but it was withdrawn and never put to a vote (discussion of proposal for a degree in social engineering, *Handelingen van de Tweede Kamer* [1903–4], 4 March 1904, 1467–69). The debate is summarized and the results described in *De Ingenieur* 20, no. 9 (4 March 1905): 127–28. In 1905, Van Kol again attempted to have the field approved for study and did succeed in getting Parliament to accept the possibility of the Technical Institute introducing new fields with the approval of its governing body and without the necessity of parliamentary approval (*Handelingen van de Tweede Kamer* [1904–5], 1085–91). On Van Marken, see chapter 1, note 72.

4. The members disbanded the STVDIA in 1924 when their crusade to establish the legitimacy of the new social technologies could claim victory: "Men is het er over eens dat de verlangens die bij de oprichting voorgezeten hebben, voor een groot deel door de gebeurtenissen achterhaald zijn, en dat dit op zich zelf een verblijdend verschijnsel mag heeten. Dat het militante karakter eenigzins verloren is gegaan, moet toch wel daar aan worden op toegeschreven, dat het juist de oprichters en de leidende figuren uit de vereeniging zijn die thans aan de oplossing van de maatschappelijke problemen medewerken, en daarbij zelfs de richting aangeven, zoodat de vereeniging van zelf hare werkzaamheid op een nieuw gebied moet overbrengen" (STVDIA meeting of 20 April 1921, Notulen Bestuurdersvergaderingen, STVDIA archive, IISG).

5. By midcentury, many of the professions had organized societies to represent their inter-

ests, for example, doctors in the Society for the Advancement of Medicine (Maatschappij tot Bevordering der Geneeskunst), engineers in the Royal Society of Engineers (Koninklijke Instituut van Ingenieurs) and the Society of Civil Engineers. The Society for the Advancement of Architecture (Maatschappij tot Bevordering der Bouwkunst) represented commercial as well as professional interests until it underwent reform in the first decade of the twentieth century, eventually merging with the newly formed League of Dutch Architects (BNA) (see chapter 6). Each of these organizations was instrumental in creating a new powerful professional class in the Netherlands, and each had a vested interest in maintaining its position of professional control. For a discussion of the way professional societies served the specialized class interests of their members under conditions of the free market economy, see Magali Sarfatti Larson, *The Rise of Professionalism: A Sociological Analysis* (Berkeley: University of California Press, 1977), 66–79, and Eliot Freidson, *Profession of Medicine: A Study in the Sociology of Applied Knowledge* (New York: Dodd, Mead, 1970), 335–82. For an excellent discussion of the derivation of professional autonomy from a mastery of knowledge and a commitment to a service ideal, see William J. Goode, "The Theoretical Limits of Professionalization," in *The Semi-Professions and Their Organization*, ed. Amitai Etzioni (New York: Free Press, 1969), 291–92.

6. S. S. Colonel, *Middelburg voorheen en thans: Bijdragen tot de kennis van den voormaaligen en tegenwoordigen toestand van het armwezen aldaar* (Middelburg, 1859). For six years city medical officer in Amsterdam and best known for his work in Middelburg, Colonel was an active propagandist for improved workers' housing. See, for example, S. S. Colonel, "Het bouwen van arbeiderswoningen," *De Economist* 24, part 1 (1875):257–80, 525–40.

7. J. A. Verdoorn, *Volksgezondheid en sociale ontwikkeling* (Utrecht: Het Spectrum, 1968), 176–79. The fact that the miasmic theory of the spread of disease continued to receive support in the Netherlands, even after the conclusive evidence that water is the carrier for cholera, explains their stress on garbage and sewage disposal. In Amsterdam, happily, the water supply was modernized at an early date, and from 1854 fresh water from the dunes was piped in and available to the city, the distribution being skewed, of course, in favor of the wealthier districts (44–47). See also H. F. J. M. van den Eerenbeemt, *Arts en sociaal besef in Nederland in historisch perspectief* (Tilburg: Gianotten, 1969), 33–34.

8. For a description of the origins and differences between these terms as used in the Netherlands, see Pieter Muntendam, *Plaatsbepaling van de sociale geneeskunde*, Handelingen van de Sociaal-Wetenschappelijke Raad, new series no. 2 (Leiden: Instituut voor Sociale Geneeskunde, 1966), 9–12. While arguing in the Lower House of Parliament for the introduction of instruction in social and technical hygiene at the Technical University at Delft, Van Kol defined social hygiene to include the cleaning of public water, sewage, hygiene of public ways, measures for traffic and the extension of cities, improvement of workers' housing, study of the housing problem, and the building of schools, factories, public baths, abattoirs (*Handelingen van de Tweede Kamer* [1903–4], 4 March 1904, 1467). In the *Journal of Social Hygiene*, which published the convention's proceedings and related articles, the editors distinguished between hygiene proper and social hygiene. Hygiene they considered to be a purely medical science, whereas social hygiene was construed as interdisciplinary, drawing on technical, legal, economic, and policy fields (*Tijdschrift voor Sociale Hygiëne en Openbare Gezondheidsregeling* 1 [1899]: 3). The comparable relationship of housing reform to public health and hygiene in Germany and

France is discussed in Nicolas Bullock and James Read, *The Movement for Housing Reform in Germany and France, 1840–1914* (Cambridge: Cambridge University Press, 1985), 86–109, 342–56.

9. See, for example, Dr. G. v[an] O[verbeek] de Meijer, "Woningshygiëne," and Dr. Wintgens, "De eischen eener gezonde woning," in *Verslag van het eerste Nederlandsch Congres voor Openbare Gezondheidsregeling* (The Hague: F. van Rossen, 1896), 19–22. Doctors also studied ventilation with a view to suggesting proper materials. See, for example, Benjamin Swaab, "De natuurlijke ventilatie van kleine woonvertrekken in Amsterdam" (Ph.D. diss., University of Amsterdam, 1901), and the more popular reporting of P. B. Middendorp, "Versche lucht en zonlicht in onze woning," *Het Groene en het Witte Kruis* 11 (1914–15): 59–71, 77–87. Among the active, nonmedical, participants in the annual public health congresses were L. M. Hermans and H. H. Wollring (both Social Democrats representing the Amsterdam labor organization the Amsterdam Labor League), Jan Kruseman, and J. W. C. Tellegen ("Het woningvraagstuk op het Gezondheidscongres," *Tijdschrift voor Sociale Hygiëne* 1, no. 5 [1899], 5–39).

10. R. A. van Sandick, "Sociaal-technische ingenieurs," *De Ingenieur* 20, no. 5 (4 February 1905): 70.

11. Dominicus Cannegieter, *Honderdvijftigjaar Gezondheidswet* (Assen: Van Gorcum, 1954), 106; Van der Eerenbeemt, *Arts en sociaal besef*. Some participants in the parliamentary review of the proposed health act suggested broadening it to include the application of all social laws, including the inspection of workplace safety, labor, nuisance, and workman's compensation (G. Oosterbaan, *De Gezondheidswet en de Woningwet* [Groningen:Wolters, 1901], 10). The Health Act is the *Wet van 21 Juni 1901 (Staatsblad No. 157) tot regeling van het Staatstoezicht op de Volksgezondheid* (hereafter cited as *Gezondheidswet*).

12. "Dat te veel uit het oog is verloren dat het Staatstoezicht tot behartiging der belangen van de volksgezondheid niet behoeft of mag zijn uitsluitend een *geneeskundig* Staatstoezicht" (*Het ontwerp van de Gezondheidswet, met memorie van toelichting* [Zwolle: De Erven J.J. Tijl, 1899], 27). See also the discussion of the relative role of doctors and other professionals in the *Handelingen van de Tweede Kamer* (1902), 1194–95, in which the authoritarian manner of doctors is taken to task.

13. The committee, composed of two doctors, two engineers, and a lawyer, also expressed the concern that the introduction of experts from various nonmedical specializations was not the equivalent of training specialists in social hygiene itself, that is, inspectors trained originally in one profession or another who had gathered the interdisciplinary training and experience necessary to an understanding of social hygiene (Vereeniging van Burgerlijke Ingenieurs, *Verslag der commissie in zake eene nieuwe regeling van het Staatstoezicht op de Volksgezondheid* [January 1900]).

14. [F.] v[an] E[rkel], *Bouwkundig Weekblad* 20, no. 7 (17 February 1900): 51.

15. The best discussion of this controversy is to be found in Cannegieter, *Honderdvijftigjaar Gezondheidswet*, 111–17. Objections to the Health Act appear in Amsterdam Health Board, *Rapport over het wetsontwerp tot regeling van het staatstoezicht op de volksgezondheid* (Amsterdam, 1900); J. Zeeman et al., "Rapport der Commissie van praeadvies over het ontwerp Gezondheidswet," *Medische Weekblad*, 2 December 1899, 37–44; *Rapport van de Commissie uit den Geneeskundigen Raad voor Noord-Holland aan den genoemden raad in zake het ontwerp van de Gezondheidswet* (Amsterdam, 1900); Amsterdam Health Board, "Verslag van de werkzaamheden van den Gezondheids-

commissie over het jaar 1900," *Gemeenteverslag* (1900), app. 8, 3. A dissenting voice was heard from Dr. J. W. Jenny Weijerman, who approved of cooperation with other professions and suggested that the doctor work with, not above, the others (J. W. Jenny Weijerman, "Het Ontwerp Gezondheidswet," *De Gids* 18, part 1 [1900]: 447–71). See also Peter de Ruijter, "Voor volkshuisvesting en stedebouw: Over woninghervormers en de beweging voor een goede stedebouw, 1890–1920" (Ph.D. diss., University of Amsterdam, 1986), 220–22.

16. Scrutator [Arie Keppler], "Hygiënisten," *De Kroniek* 12, no. 611 (8 September 1906): 282–83. Keppler questioned the qualifications of doctors as social hygienists in the article "Heren medici en de social hygiëne," *De Kroniek* 11, no. 570 (25 November 1905): 370–71. He also attacked two articles in which a doctor gave medical figures the credit for leading social hygiene, described as a new field of cooperation between medicine and sociology (Scrutator [Arie Keppler], "Sociale-hygiëne," undated MS, no. 35, Tak archive, IISG). The articles in question were Dr. D.B., "Sociale hygiëne," *De Kroniek* 12, no. 592 (28 April 1906): 133–34, and no. 593 (5 May 1906): 138–39.

17. Arie Keppler, "Medische en technische hygiënisten," *De Ingenieur* 23, no. 4 (25 January 1908): 60.

18. The positions at issue were chairman of the central health board or the chief inspectors (Scrutator [Arie Keppler], "Iets over het staatstoezicht op de volksgezondheid," *De Kroniek* 10, no. 520 [10 December 1904]: 395–97).

19. The Higher Education Act of 1904 permitted instruction in technical hygiene at Delft, but the option had not yet been exercised (STVDIA, *Het onderwijs in de hygiëne aan de Technische Hooge School te Delft* [Amsterdam, 1909]; Sr. [H. E. Suyve], "De hygiëne en haar toepassingen," *Technisch Studenten-Tijdschrift* 1, no. 6 [1 January 1911]: 143). Prof. Dr. J. G. Sleeswijk was inaugurated as professor of technical hygiene on 6 December 1910, with the lecture "De veelzijdigheid der hygiëne."

20. "Verslag over de bewoonde kelders in de Gemeente Amsterdam," *Gemeenteverslag* 1 (1874), app. A. The cellar study noted that of the 1,151 residents of Amsterdam who died in the 1886 cholera epidemic, 12.3 percent lived in cellars, while only 7.94 percent of the total population lived in cellars. The committee's advice on laying out streets in 1872 was not acceptable to the municipal council, however. When the committee requested a municipal ordinance requiring the raising of polder land before development, the municipality claimed this exceeded municipal authority. From the 1870s, the left-liberal press published increasingly on the social question, including the housing issue. Women influenced by Octavia Hill's work in England published their observations of the housing problem. See Hélène Mercier, *Over arbeiderswoningen* (Haarlem: H. D. Tjeenk Willink, 1887); Johanna ter Meulen, *Huisvesting van armen te Amsterdam* (Haarlem: H. D. Tjeenk Willink, 1903). The liberal penchant for collecting statistics before analyzing potential action contributed to the meager start of social science in the Netherlands and led to the founding of the Society for Statistics, after German example (*Gedenkboek uitgegeven ter gelegenheid van het 25-jarig bestaan der Centrale Commissie voor de Statistiek, 1892–1917* [The Hague, 1917]). Figures on housing density and rents were published in the society's monthly reports from time to time, but only with the establishment of the Central Bureau of Statistics, under the influence of liberal minister N. G. Pierson, did a housing survey at national level get carried out with the 1899 census.

21. Chapter 9 of the General Police Ordinance (Algemeene Politie-Verordening). The history of the Amsterdam Health Board and the Municipal Health Service can be found in Verdoorn, *Volksgezondheid*, 295–322.

22. See discussion in the Amsterdam City Council, *Gemeenteblad* 2 (1900), meeting of 22 March 1900, 314–43.

23. Amsterdam Health Board, "Verslag van de werkzaamheden van den Gezondheidscommissie over het jaar 1900," *Gemeenteverslag* (1900), app. 8, 4. The municipal decision to combine the building and housing inspection is found in *Gemeenteblad* 1 (1901), no. 276, 19 March 1901, 194–96. The existing housing inspection as organized in the health service was simply moved en masse to the new agency, with the same inspector (F. van Erkel) and the same staff.

24. D. Schut, *Gemeenteblad* 2 (1900), meeting of 21 December 1900, 1416. Discussion of reorganization and appointment in *Gemeenteblad* 2 (1900), meeting of 21 December 1900, 1409–26, and Notulen besloten vergaderingen Gemeenteraad (1899–1900), meeting of 12 December 1900, archive 5079/282, GAA, 704–5.

25. Hornstra, "Begrip sociale geneeskunde," 45; Cannegieter, *Honderdvijftigjaar Gezondheidswet,* 145; Arie Querido, *The Development of Socio-medical Care in the Netherlands* (London: Routledge and Kegan Paul, 1968), 50.

26. Jenny Weijerman, "Het Ontwerp Gezondheidswet," 450.

27. A manuscript of J. G. van Niftrik's autobiography "Leven en werken" is available at the Gemeentearchief Amsterdam.

28. *Handelingen van de Tweede Kamer* (1903–4), sixtieth meeting, 4 March 1904, 1470–71. The use of German terms in the original Dutch suggests that Kuyper considered planning an alien discipline. Victor de Stuers defended planners and castigated the government for ignoring the importance of planning.

29. "Snarepijperij," *De Kroniek* 3, no. 113 (7 March 1897): 78.

30. H. P. Berlage, "De kunst in stedenbouw," *Bouwkundig Weekblad* 12, no. 15 (9 April 1892): 87–90; no. 17 (23 April 1892): 101–2; no. 20 (14 May 1892): 121–24; no. 21 (21 May 1892): 126–27; Camillo Sitte, *Der Städtebau nach Seinen künstlerischen Grundsätsen* (Vienna, 1889).

31. The main articles contributing to this controversy are J. H. E. Rückert, "Stedenbouw: Een arbeidsveld van den ingenieur bedreigd," *De Ingenieur* 28, no. 48 (29 November 1913): 1034–36; G. P. Nijhoff, letter, *De Ingenieur* 28, no. 50 (13 December 1913): 1069; Jan Gratama, "Een arbeidsveld van den ingenieur bedreigd?" *Bouwkundig Weekblad* 34, no. 1 (3 January 1914): 46; W. F. C. Schaap, "Wie is de stedenbouwer?" *Bouwkundig Weekblad* 34, no. 2 (10 January 1914): 14–16, no. 3 (17 January 1914): 27–29; L. H. E. van Hylckama Vlieg, "Stedenbouwers," *Bouwkundig Weekblad* 34, no. 3 (17 January 1914): 31; K., "Een gevaar . . . doch waardoor?" *Bouwkundig Weekblad* 34, no. 5 (31 January 1914): 55–56; J. H. E. Rückert, "Stedenbouw," *De Ingenieur* 29, no. 10 (7 March 1914): 199–200; J[an] de M[eyer], "Stedenbouw," *Architectura* 22, no. 13 (28 March 1914): 107–8; W. F. C. Schaap, "Nogmaals 'Wie is de stedenbouwer?'" *Bouwkundig Weekblad* 34, no. 16 (18 April 1914): 189–90. The debate about urban planning expertise is also discussed in De Ruijter, "Volkshuisvesting en stedebouw," 292–96.

32. J. H. W. Leliman, "Stedenbouw: Een arbeidsveld van den architekt bedreigd," *De Bouwwereld* 11, no. 50 (10 December 1913): 377–80.

33. Arie Keppler, "Stedenbouw," *De Ingenieur* 28, no. 51 (20 December 1913): 1089.

34. With the increase in commerce and population in Amsterdam, and the abandonment of the canals for transportation of goods, pressure was building by the 1880s to fill canals to provide wider transportation routes. Of particular concern were the linkages between the old and the new parts of the city, and discussion began early in the new century about alterations to the radial routes, the Utrechtsestraat, Reguliersgracht, Vijzelstraat, and Spiegelstraat.

35. Jan Veth, "Stedenschennis," in *Bedreigde schoonheid* (Amsterdam: P. N. van Kampen, 1916), 13–42.

36. In 1907, options considered by the council included the following: widening Utrechtsestraat at f4,000,000, widening Spiegelstraat at f4,350,000, and filling Reguliersgracht at f530,000. The decision to fill the Vijzelgracht and widen it to twenty-five meters was budgeted at f3,350,000 in the proposal from the mayor and aldermen (*Gemeenteblad* 1 (1907), no. 367, 2 April 1907, 243). Discussion of the proposal is in *Gemeenteblad* 2 (1907), meeting of 15 May 1907, 622–47; Notulen besloten vergaderingen Gemeenteraad (1905–6), meeting of 19 September 1906, archive 5079/285; and Notulen besloten vergaderingen Gemeenteraad (1907–8), meeting of 2 January 1907, archive 5079/286, GAA.

37. Founded in 1909, Bond Heemschut was modeled after a similar German society as a watchdog organization composed of interested laymen, literary figures, artists, and architects. For a discussion of the origins and motivations of Bond Heemschut, see Egbert J. Hoogenberk, *Het idee van de Hollandse stad: Stedebouw in Nederland, 1900–1930, met de internationale voorgeschiedenis* (Delft: Delftse Universitaire Pers, 1980), 39–40 and De Ruijter, "Volkshuisvesting en stedebouw," 256–68.

38. A typical instance is Jan Stuyt, "Oud en nieuw in Amsterdam," *De Kroniek* 4, no. 207 (11 December 1898): 400.

39. For a study of the development of Berlage's planning theory, see Manfred Bock, "Stedebouw," in the exhibition catalog *H. P. Berlage: Bouwmeester, 1856–1934* (The Hague, 1975), 51–72, and *Anfänge einer neuen Architektur: Berlages Beitrag zur architektonischen Kultur der Niederlande in ausgehenden 19. Jahrhundert* (The Hague: Staatsuitgevrij, 1983), 81–120; and Vincent van Rossem, "Berlage and the Culture of City Planning," in *Hendrik Petrus Berlage: Complete Works*, ed. Sergio Polano (New York: Rizzoli, 1988), 66–90. Berlage's role in the development of the aesthetic side of urban planning is also discussed in De Ruijter, "Volkshuisvesting en stedebouw," 243–55.

40. H. P. Berlage, "Stedenbouw," *De Beweging*, 10, no. 6 (June 1914): 271.

41. Notulen besloten vergaderingen Gemeenteraad (1899–1900), meeting of 8 March 1900, archive 5079/282, 451–69; Public Works Committee meeting of 9 March 1900, Notulen van de Commissie van bijstand in zake Publieke Werken (1900), archive 5087, GAA, 20–21.

42. Berlage's "architectonic explanation" of the plan claimed only to be an aesthetic description and warned that financial considerations had not been the primary consideration. The explanation expressed exactly the limited nature of his concerns: to provide Amsterdam with a plan for expansion that might, in contrast to those of the recent past, be an embellishment (H. P. Berlage, "Architectonische toelichting tot het plan van uitbreiding der stad Amsterdam tusschen Amstel en Schinkel" [September 1900], in *Gemeenteblad* 1 [1904], no. 876, 7 October 1904, 1717–25).

43. Council member Van Dijk, *Gemeenteblad* 2 (1904), meeting of 21 December 1904, 1300.

44. P. L. Tak, *Gemeenteblad* 2 (1904), meeting of 21 December 1904, 1304–5; meeting of 11 January 1905, 46–47. Berlage's planning practice changed markedly, as evidenced by the planning report accompanying the 1915 revised plan for Amsterdam South, which explains the traffic considerations and housing plans worked out with the appropriate authorities (H. P. Berlage, "Memorie van toelichting behoorende bij het Ontwerp van het uitbreidingsplan der Gemeente Amsterdam" [March 1915], in *Gemeenteblad* 1 [1917], no. 851, app. A, 901–15).

45. H. P. Berlage, "Stedenbouw," *De Beweging* 10, no. 3 (March 1914): 226–27.

46. H. J. M. Walenkamp, *Amsterdam in de toekomst* ([Amsterdam], 1901). Walenkamp suggested that the northern extension mirror the concentric canals of the seventeenth-century half moon.

47. The appointment of a committee was opposed at first by mayor and aldermen. Long and trying discussions resulted in a number of revisions to the list before the final choice was ratified on 26 June 1901. See "Uitgebreide bebouwde kom der Gemeente benoorden het IJ," *Gemeenteblad* (1900), no. 385, 17 April 1900, 303–6; "Praeadvies op het voorstel-van Nierop tot het benoemen eener commissie voor de exploitatie der terreinen aan de overzijde van het IJ," *Gemeenteblad* (1900), no. 921, 23 October 1900, 1561-64; Notulen besloten vergaderingen Gemeenteraad (1901) meeting of 12 June 1901, archive 5079/283, 115–17; *Gemeenteblad* 2 (1901), meeting of 26 June 1901, 556-57; Notulen besloten vergaderingen Gemeenteraad (1901), meeting of 9 January 1901, archive 5079/283, 4-10. A new director of public works, Van Hasselt, replaced Lambrechtsen, who retired miffed by the rejection of his plan for the southern extension. Van Hasselt proposed a revision of a Van Niftrik plan for the area north of the IJ on 4 May 1900. The Chamber of Commerce petitioned for a committee to study the plan in September, suggesting experts in trade, harbor, industry, railroad, and housing to decide on land use in the north.

48. Public Works prepared a partial street plan in 1910 for one neighborhood where several housing societies were to build and followed with a complete plan for the remaining neighborhoods in 1912. An extension plan prepared in 1914 by Tellegen at the Building and Housing Inspection Office rejected the street plans prepared by Public Works and indicated only designated land use (*Gemeenteblad* 1 [1914], no. 902, 29 July 1914, 814–15). Nieuwendammerham was designed by an architect especially assigned to Public Works (J. M. van der Mey, 1916), Buiksloterham by a private architect working for the Housing Authority (J. E. van der Pek, 1917), Nieuwendammerham III by a housing society architect (A. W. Weissman, 1918), and the area north of the municipal housing in Buiksloterham by the city architect (A. R. Hulshoff, 1921).

49. George A. M. Kallenbach, *Over de pogingen door particulieren in het werk gesteld tot verbetering der arbeiderswoningen* (Leiden: A. H. Adriani, 1892), 18.

50. "Toch zoudt ge van Uw kant véél kunnen doen, heeren Architecten! bijv. door U bezig te houden met het Woningvraagstuk meer dat dit tot heden—zonderling genoeg!—is gescheid" (Walenkamp, *Amsterdam in de toekomst*, 19).

51. *Bouwkundig Weekblad* 26, no. 19 (1906): 252.

52. Mels Meijers, "Volkshuisvesting: De architecten en de woningbouw," *Bouwkundig Weekblad* 37, no. 28 (1916): 212.

53. Quoted in *Bouwkundig Weekblad* 22, no. 45 (8 November 1902): 425–26.

54. Arie Keppler, "De architect en het woningvraagstuk," *Architectura* 20, no. 47 (23 November 1912): 398–400, lecture at 1305th meeting of Architectura et Amicitia.

55. On the housing designs of J. H. Leliman, see Carel Schade, *Woningbouw voor arbeiders in het negentiende-eeuwse Amsterdam* (Amsterdam: Van Gennep, 1981), 191.

56. *Bouwkundig Weekblad* 15, no. 48 (30 November 1895): 306–7.

57. For instance, F. van Erkel, W. C. Schaad, D. E. Wentink, and J. L. B. Keurschot.

58. Volksbond tegen Drankmisbruik, *Verslag van een onderzoek naar den toestand der arbeiderswoningen te Amsterdam (oude stad)* (Amsterdam: De Bussy, 1893). According to Schade, half of the temperance organization in 1893 were architects (*Woningbouw voor arbeiders*, 175 n. 44).

59. See, for example, Amsterdamsche Woningraad, *Rapport over de Amsterdamsche parken en plantsoenen* (Amsterdam, 1909), reporters: H. P. Berlage, J. van Hasselt, Dirk Hudig, Jan Kruseman, and C. A. den Tex; *De volkshuisvesting in de nieuwe stad te Amsterdam* (Amsterdam, 1909), reporters: Johanna ter Meulen, Dirk Hudig, Arie Keppler, J. E. van der Pek, H. H. Wollring.

60. Amsterdam Health Board, "Verslag van de bevindingen en handelingen der Gezondheidscommissie," *Gemeenteverslag* (1905), app. 9, 1.

61. At the architectural convention held in celebration of the fiftieth anniversary of the Society for the Advancement of Architecture, D. E. C. Knuttel gave a lecture entitled "Het onderwijs in de hygiëne aan architecten." For an account of the lecture and the discussion following, see *Bouwkundig Weekblad* 12, no. 19 (7 May 1892): 114–15, and no. 23 (4 June 1892): 140.

62. The study compared the Delft program to other European Polytechnics: Zurich, Vienna, Stuttgart, Munich, Karlsruhe, Aachen, and Berlin (Vereeniging van Burgerlijke Ingenieurs, *Verslag der Commissie in zake het Technisch Onderwijs: Benoemd ingevolge het besluit van de Algemeene Vergadering der Vereeniging van Burgerlijke Ingenieurs op 18 Juli 1891* (The Hague, 1895).

63. *Rapport van de Centrale Commissie voor Studiebelangen* (Delft, 1906 and 1908). A number of student designs for housing appear in the student publication at Delft, the *Technisch Studenten Tijdschrift*, particularly in 1911 and 1912. The course suggested by the STVDIA included the influence of housing on health, lighting, heating, ventilation, siting, statistics, urban renewal, and building ordinances ("Memorie van toelichting bij het adres der STVDIA," *De Ingenieur* 20, no. 5 [4 February 1905]: 66).

64. N., "Verslag ledenvergadering 'Practische Studie,' 3 maart 1913," *Technisch Studenten-Tijdschrift* 3, no. 11 (15 April 1913): 336; "Jaarverslag Handelingen Centrale Commissie voor Studiebelangen 1913," *Technisch Studenten-Tijdschrift* 4, no. 9 (1 March 1914): 235–36.

65. STVDIA, *Het onderwijs in de hygiëne aan de Technische Hoogeschool te Delft* (Amsterdam, 1909). In 1911, Dr. Sleeswijk was brought in by Delft to teach technical hygiene. It was not a required course. The housing hygiene section covered ventilation, heating, lighting, and sewage. The 1913 course included housing conditions, workers' housing, the hygienic side of planning, and garden cities (*Programma der lessen* [Delft, 1911–13]).

66. See J. A. Veraart, "Recht en Economie," in *Technische Hogeschool te Delft, 1905-1955*, ed. A. F. Kamp (The Hague: Staatsdrukkerij, 1955), 168-73.

67. [F.] v[an] E[rkel], "Woningbouw," *Bouwkundig Weekblad* 21, no. 43 (26 October 1901): 401–2.

68. *Bouwkundig Weekblad* 21, no. 20 (18 May 1901): 184–85. Results described in 22, no. 17 (26 April 1902): 157–56.

69. See *Bouwkundig Weekblad* 28, no. 4 (1908): 53–54, for the description of the competition. The jury was W. van Boven, inspector of health in the Hague, L. Krook, director of public works in Zwolle, J. H. W. Leliman, architect, W. F. C. Schaap, director of public works in Arnhem, and D. E. Wentink, inspector of health in Utrecht. See *Eengezins-werkmanswoningen* (The Hague: Mouton, 1908).

70. The jury was J. H. W. Leliman, A. D. N. van Gendt, J. W. C. Tellegen, P. van Exter, C. H. Eldering. See *Bouwkundig Weekblad* 28, no. 11 (1908): 174–75; no. 31 (1908): 589–91.

71. Adjustments had to be made to the official fee tables for architects in order to provide for multiple construction of the same design as required by housing projects. Rochdale's 1910 competition was the first to move beyond the design of a housing prototype to the design for an actual site. The housing society hoped to build the winning design on the site already designated to it by the municipality. However, all the major architectural societies objected to the conditions of the competition. Both the prize money and the promised architectural fee were too low, they claimed. The problem was simply that the existing table of architectural fees was based on a direct percentage of the total building costs. There was no way to take into consideration the fact that the designer of a housing block would only design a limited number of housing types for repetition. A series of meetings did nothing to resolve the matter, and the jury insisted on retaining Rochdale's original conditions. There were few entries as a result; two entries were premiated, but no first prize was awarded. J. E. van der Pek eventually ended up designing the project. The jury consisted of architects H. P. Berlage, Jan Gratama, J. E. van der Pek, and housing inspector J. M. A. Zoetmulder, as well as officers of the society, including Arie Keppler. The following year the leading architectural society, the Society for the Advancement of Architecture, submitted a revised fee schedule for housing blocks that created a new category of work type and reduced the percentages to be applied to the construction costs. See *Bouwkundig Weekblad* 29, no. 50 (11 December 1909): 594, no. 52 (25 December 1909): 617–18; *Bouwkundig Weekblad* 30, no. 16 (16 April 1910): 190–92, no. 18 (30 April 1910): 215–16, no. 32 (6 August 1910): 278–79, 382; no. 41 (8 October 1910): 491–92; and *Bouwkundig Weekblad* 31, no. 26 (1 July 1911): 304. During the war, the enormous increases in building material costs caused the housing societies once again ask that the architectural fee be reduced, and the architectural societies agreed to use 25 percent above 1914 costs as a basis for figuring the architectural honorarium.

72. Alongside Berlage's lectures on the aesthetics of planning, Tellegen lectured on the Housing Act and Van der Pek taught design of workers' housing. See VHBO brochures, 1908–1909, 1909–1910. Technical Science was a required course and covered hygiene, ventilation, heating, sewage, the Housing Act, and building ordinances. City Extension and Planning was an elective. The VHBO had seventy students in 1912. The program was a three-year evening course; see chapter 6.

73. C. H. Schwagermann, "Het onderwijs in stedenbouw aan de T.H.S. te Delft," *Bouwkundig Weekblad* 32, no. 49 (7 December 1912): 593–94; and letter to the Society for the Advancement of Architecture from the Department of Architecture at Delft, "Leerschool in den stedenbouw aan de Technische Hoogeschool," *Bouwkundig Weekblad* 32, no. 50 (14 December 1912): 601–3.

74. *Architectura* 20, no. 46 (16 November 1912): 387–88. The minister of the interior refused on 22 January 1913 to decide the question of the chair until the question of the future of the Academy of Fine Arts was settled.

75. Some 120 students attended Berlage's lectures, an indication of the desire for the aesthetic approach to planning (*Bouwkundig Weekblad* 33, no. 51 [20 December 1913]: 20). For the complete set of lectures at Delft, see H. P. Berlage, "Stedenbouw," *De Beweging* 10, no. 3 (March 1914): 226–47; no. 4 (April 1914): 1–17; no. 5 (May 1914): 142–57; no. 6 (June 1914) 263–79, or the transcription by C. H. Schwagermmann, "Het aesthetisch gedeelte van stedebouw," *Bouwkundig Weekblad* 33, no. 51 (20 December 1913): 20; *Bouwkundig Weekblad* 34, no. 1 (3 January 1914): 6–8; no. 2 (10 January 1914): 17–20; no. 9 (28 February 1914): 98–100; no. 10 (7 March 1914): 116–18; no. 11 (14 March 1914): 126–28; no. 12 (21 March 1914): 138–40; no. 16 (18 April 1914): 186–89; no. 17 (25 April 1914): 198–202.

76. Van der Steur's inaugural speech of 1914, "Architecture Should Only Be Taught at the Technical Institute," hit another blow at the continuing dispute between supporters of the Royal Academy of Fine Arts and those of the Technical Institute. Van der Steur's point was that only Delft was equipped to do equal justice to both the technical and the aesthetic side of architecture. This was largely a sterile debate, echoing to some extent the contemporary debate between architects and civil engineers over planning.

77. Berlage, "Stedenbouw." As noted above, Berlage's lecture was recorded by C. H. Schwagermann in *Bouwkundig Weekblad*; it was later reworked by Berlage for *De Beweging*, influenced by a reading of Walter Curt Behrendt, *Die Einheitliche Blockfront als Raumelement im Stadtbau: Ein Beitrag zur Stadtbaukunst der Gegenwert* (Berlin: Bruno Cassirer Verlag, 1911), and A. E. Brinckmann, *Deutsche Stadtbaukunst in der Vergangenheit* (Frankfurt: H. Keller, 1911).

78. For a different perspective on the development of housing expertise, see De Ruijter, "Volkshuisvesting en stedebouw," 217–39.

79. Noud de Vreeze has also noted the significance during this period of the dual interpretation of urban planning from both a technical (*wetenschappelijk-programmatische*) and an aesthetic (*artistiek-architectonische*) point of view. See Noud de Vreeze, *Woningbouw, inspiratie en ambities: Kwalitatieve grondslagen van de sociale woningbouw in Nederland* (Almere: Nationale Woningraad, 1993), 200.

80. "Speculatie-bouw," *Bouwkundig Weekblad* 16, no. 24 (13 June 1896): 148–49, report of the Amsterdam chapter of the Vereeniging ter Bevordering van Fabrieks- en Handwerksnijverheid in Nederland: A. J. Cohen Stuart, Ed Cuypers, Jan Kruseman, E. de Lange, J. F. Staal, C. T. J. Louis Rieber.

81. The Health Board influenced the planning of the Indische district and presented a model plan for the Spaarndammerbuurt. J. T. Cuypers in the Health Board presented a sketch plan in response to a Public Works plan for the Spaarndammerbuurt (Health Board, 13 November 1918, 153 GC 1918, archive 5269, GAA). P. L. Tak had complained about standard planning practice during the building ordinance debate: "Wat niet in de verordening is bedwongen is het gebruik, dat de terreinspeculanten maken van hun grond. Een terreinspeculant doet mij altijd denken aan een vischboer met gerookten elft. Die snijdt zijn elft zoo dun mogelijk uit en evenzoo worden de bouwterreinen zoo dun mogelijk uitgesneden, aan de straat zoo smal mogelijk gemaakt" (*Gemeenteblad* 2 [1905], 21 June 1905, 826).

82. Louise van der Pek-Went to Health Board, 15 November 1918, 255 GC 1918, archive 5269, GAA.

83. The committee, originally established in 1898, was dubbed unofficially the "Schoonheids-

commissie," literally, "Beauty Commission." For its history and development, see Helen Searing, "Housing in Holland and the Amsterdam School" (Ph.D. diss., Yale University, 1971), 215–23; Marijke Beek, "Ambtenaren en architecten: Een schoonheidscommissie als kunstenaar," in *Berlage en Amsterdam Zuid,* ed. Karin Gaillard and Betsy Dokter (Rotterdam: Uitgeverij 010, 1992), 26–45; Marijke Beek, *Het aanzien waard? Geschiedenis van de welstandszorg in Nederland* (Deventer: Kluwer, 1985); and chapters 6, 7, and 8 below.

CHAPTER THREE

1. Housing Council petition to Amsterdam City Council, November 1909. In a footnote, the Housing Council modestly admitted that all these changes were probably not imminent.

2. At the exhibition "De Vrouw" in 1913, the architect Greta Derlinge designed a model dwelling for the middle class that was equipped with central heating, warm water, electric light, and a modern kitchen. A bath and washroom was provided by Henri Brugman (*Catalogus van de tentoonstelling "De Vrouw," 1813–1913* [Amsterdam, 1913], 235–37). One twenty-year-old male visitor to the exhibition commented that the maid's room was too luxurious with its washstand, bed, and cupboard. He claimed that a built-in bed in the attic was sufficient and that anything better would spoil her ("Het een en ander over Het Huis 1913," *De Vrouw,* no. 12 [30 August 1913]: 2).

3. "Verslag aan den Koning over de vereischten en inrigting van arbeiderswoningen door eene commissie uit het Koninklijk Instituut van Ingenieurs" (The Hague, 1855).

4. From the Health Board's report on the condition of cellar dwellings, by a committee formed 26 October 1872 (Health Board, "Rapport over de Amsterdamsche Kelderwoningen [Amsterdam, 1873]).

5. Dr. Wintgens, "De eischen eener gezonde woning," *Verslag van het eerste Nederlandsch Congres voor Openbare Gezondheidsregeling* (Amsterdam: F. van Rossen, 1896). Item 15 stated that every home should be equipped with a toilet with connection to the outside air, and that in multistoried housing there should be at least one toilet on each floor.

6. P. H. Schreuder and N. Cariot, *De huishouding in al haar onderdeelen volgens de laatste en hygiënische eischen* (Amsterdam, 1901), 55.

7. Committee on Municipal Housing meeting of 14 December 1915, Notulen van de Commissie van advies in het beheer der Gemeentewoningen (1915), archive 5103, GAA.

8. Letter in *Het Volk,* 16 June 1920. Van Epen actually introduced showers into his workers' housing by designing a one-square-meter closet to be converted by the worker. On Van Epen's career as a housing architect, see M. C. Kuipers, "Gezond en vrolijk wonen: Over het werk van J. C. van Epen, 1880–1960" (master's thesis, University of Leiden, 1976).

9. The reformers were Van der Pek's wife, Louise van der Pek-Went, Dr. P. W. Janssen, Hélène Mercier, and Wilhelmina C. van der Hoeven ("Dagloners woningen te Amsterdam," *Bouwkundig Weekblad* 23, no. 6 [7 February 1903]: 57–58). Rents ran f1.45–2.20.

10. Amsterdam Housing Council petition to minister of the interior, n.d., Wibaut archive, IISG. Their plan was for double parcels fifteen square meters, with a very small kitchen, two small bedrooms, two closets, toilet, and hall, renting for f2.00–2.50.

11. Health Board to alderman of public works, 22 December 1911, 391 GC 1911, in 9028 PW 1911, archive 5180, GAA. Het Westen's architect was H. J. M. Walenkamp.

12. Health Board meeting of 18 December 1911, Notulen van de besloten vergaderingen van de Gezondheidscommissie (1911), archive 5269, GAA. In fact, the following year, the Amsterdamsch Bouwfonds in which Van der Pek-Went actively participated did propose back-to-back housing with an internal courtyard on the Hasebroekstraat. This was again intended for cheap dwellings, this time subsidized (Amsterdamsch Bouwfonds, meetings of 26 April and 1 November 1912, Notulenboek ledenvergaderingen Amsterdamsch Bouwfonds, archives of the Algemene Woningbouw Vereniging). The Health Board rejected the plans and the Bouwfonds wrote to the board asking under which conditions it would approve back-to-backs (Amsterdamsch Bouwfonds to Health Board, 4 January 1913, archive 5269, GAA). Het Westen's project proved to be the last in Amsterdam to include back-to-back housing. On the proposal for Het Westen, see *Gemeenteblad* 1 (1919), no. 1175, 24 Oct 1911, 2825. See also *Gemeenteblad* 1 (1912), no. 257, 23 February 1912, 245; and discussion *Gemeenteblad* 2 (1912), meeting of 13 March 1912, 366–69. Early objections to Het Westen's plan as old-fashioned came from the Public Works Committee (meeting of 19 October 1911, Notulen van de Commissie van bijstand in zake Publieke Werken [1911], archive 5087, GAA, 263). Plans for the second block next to the first eliminated the back-to-back option and broke up the unwieldy block with cross streets. More than 1,035 families signed up to rent the 328 dwellings of the second block (A. Staalman, chairman of Woningbouwvereeniging Het Westen, to the director of the Building and Housing Inspection Office, 3 June 1914, 549 VH 1914, archive 5187, GAA).

13. J. W. C. Tellegen, "Rapport van den directeur van het Gemeentelijk Bouw- en Woningtoezicht over het voorstel tot woningbouw van de Raadsleden Wollring, c.s." (25 June 1914), *Gemeenteblad* 1 (1914), no. 1297, 2 October 1914, 2695–2729.

14. Lefebvre notes that as the idea of "housing" takes on definition, it is accompanied by its corollaries of minimal living-space, minimal facilities, and a programmed environment, which together define the lowest possible "threshold of tolerability" (Henri Lefebvre, *The Production of Space* [Oxford: Basil Blackwell, 1991], 316).

15. Theo van Tijn, "Voorlopige notities over het ontstaan van het moderne klassebewustzijn in Nederland," *Mededelingenblad: Nederlandsche Vereniging tot Beoefening van Sociale Geschiedenis*, no. 45 (May 1974): 37–39.

16. The overall shift in social structure appears most dramatically if we compare the relative weighted sizes of three groups. Around 1850, the old lower middle class, consisting of the shopkeeper, entrepreneur, and craftsman, was 28 percent of the working population; the new lower middle class, consisting of the semiprofessional and management, was 11.2 percent; workers constituted 60.8 percent (41.2% skilled, 19.6% unskilled). In 1920, these figures were, respectively, 12.8 percent, 22.9 percent, and 64.3 percent. The figures for 1920 refer to men only and have been derived from "Resultaten der volks- en beroepstelling 31 December 1920 van Amsterdam," *Statistische Mededeelingen*, no. 72 (Amsterdam, 1924), table 12. With women included the percentages are, respectively, 11.1, 23.2, and 65.6. The figures for 1850 are taken from Jacques Giele and Geert Jan van Oenen, "Theorie en praktijk van het onderzoek naar de sociale structuur," *Tijdschrift voor Sociale Geschiedenis*, no. 5 (May 1976): 183. Their methodology is described in the article "De sociale structuur van de Nederlandse samenleving rond 1850,"

Mededelingenblad: Nederlandsche Vereniging tot Beoefening van Sociale Geschiedenis, no. 45 (May 1974): 231. For another perspective, see I. J. Brugmans, "Standen en klassen in Nederland gedurende de negentiende eeuw," in his *Welvaart en historie: Tien studien* (The Hague: Martinus Nijhoff, 1970), 140–60.

17. *De Gemeente-Werkman* 1, no. 1 (15 February 1902). For the Netherlands, research on class identity and class consciousness includes Van Tijn, "Voorlopige notities," and Jacques Giele, "Arbeidersbestaan: Levenshouding en maatschappijbeeld van de arbeidende klasse in Nederland in het midden van de negentiende eeuw," *Jaarboek voor de Geschiedenis van Socialisme en Arbeidersbeweging* (1976), 21–91. Also relevant to these issues is the introduction to Giele's collection of workers' autobiographical statements in his *Arbeiderslevens in Nederland, 1850–1914* (Nijmegen: SUN, 1979). This is the first collection of Dutch workers' autobiographies since the socialist journalist J. F. Ankersmit published *Arbeiderslevens* (Amsterdam: Ontwikkeling, 1919).

18. A detailed study of unemployment, specifically the policies developed in Amsterdam, is to be found in Pieter de Rooy, *Werklozenzorg en werkloosheidsbestrijding, 1917–1940: Landelijk en Amsterdams beleid* (Amsterdam: Van Gennep, 1978).

19. *De Gemeente-Werkman* 1, no. 1 (15 February 1902).

20. On the history of the Dutch labor movement, see Ger Harmsen and Bob Reinalda, *Voor de bevijding van de arbeid* (Nijmegen: SUN, 1975). Also helpful is the bibliography on socialism and the workers' movement in the Netherlands by Ger Harmsen, *Idee en beweging: Bekommentarieerde bibliografie van de geschiedenis van socialisme en arbeidersbeweging in Nederland* (Nijmegen: SUN, 1972). For the early history of the ANWV, see B. H. Heldt, *Algemeen Nederlandsch Werklieden Verbond, 1871–1896* (Leeuwaarden, 1896).

21. Jacques Giele has noted that the unskilled and casual laborers were more prominent in this sort of action than is generally to be observed in other industrializing countries at the time (Giele, *Arbeidersbestaan*, 36–37).

22. The following discussion of the diamond workers is based on the classic work on the subject, Henri Heertje, *De Diamantbewerkers van Amsterdam* (Amsterdam: Centen's, 1936) and on Theo van Tijn, "De Algemene Nederlandsche Diamantbewerkersbond: Een succes en zijn verklaring," *Bijdragen en Mededelingen Betreffende de Geschiedenis der Nederlanden* 88 (1973): 404–5.

23. A scholarly biography of Henri Polak is provided in Salvador Bloemgarten, *Henri Polak: Sociaal democraat, 1868–1943* (The Hague: SDU Uitgeverij, 1993). Polak was particularly influenced by the British Fabian Socialists and translated several works on labor union history and theory by Sidney and Beatrice Webb.

24. The syndicalists influenced by the French movement favored decentralized unions without professional union leadership, low union dues (generally f.10 per week), and consequently a weak treasury for strike support. Its political program called for the general strike to be used as a tool leading to revolution.

25. For a general history of the NVV, see Frits de Jong Edz., *Om de plaats van de arbeid: Een geschiedkundig overzicht van ontstaan en ontwikkeling van het Nederlands Verbond van Vakverenigingen* (Amsterdam: De Arbeiderspers, 1956).

26. J. M. Welcker, "Een ongemakkelijk bondgenootschap: De Sociaal-Democratische Arbeiderspartij en het Nederlandsch Verbond van Vakvereenigingen tussen 1906 en 1913," in *Heren*

en arbeiders in de vroege Nederlandse arbeidersbeweging, 1870–1914 (Amsterdam: Van Gennep, 1978).

27. The early history of the SDAP is recounted in V. H. Vliegen, *Die onze kracht ontwaken deed: Geschiedenis der SDAP in Nederland gedurende de eerste 25 jaren van haar bestaan* (Amsterdam: De Arbeiderspers, 1938).

28. P. Hoogland, *Vijf en twintig jaren sociaal demokratie in de hoofdstad* (Amsterdam: Ontwikkeling, 1928).

29. Discussion about continuation of the Health Board's program of condemnation heightened in 1908 and 1911, as can be seen in the arguments put forth whenever massive condemnations were proposed in those years. These heated discussions paved the way for acceptance of municipal housing in 1914.

30. The "filtering" theory was much debated in the Netherlands and abroad. J. W. C. Tellegen demonstrated its failure in the report he wrote as director of the Building and Housing Inspection Office preparatory for the introduction of municipal housing ("Rapport," 2698–99).

31. Socialists rejected the filtering notion. They supported subsidized municipal construction for the poorest and self-supporting housing society construction for the better-off workers. A typical discussion on the topic is to be found in *Gemeenteblad* 2 (1908), meeting of 15 April 1908, 365; *Gemeenteblad* 2 (1909), meeting of 7 April 1909, 370–408; and *Gemeenteblad* 2 (1912), meeting of 19 March 1912, 484.

32. P. W. Sutorius, *Gemeenteblad* 2 (1911), meeting of 26 July 1911, 1004.

33. D. P. D. Fabius on the Rochdale proposal for Hasebroekstraat, *Gemeenteblad* 2 (1912), meeting of 20 November 1912, 2200.

34. Housing Committee meeting of 15 April 1913, Notulen van de Commissie van bijstand in het beheer der zaken van Volkshuisvesting (1913), archive 5102, GAA. In fact, in Amsterdam this issue of setting a limit resolved in favor of a standard that at times conflicted with national policy. In 1913, Minister Heemskerk rejected proposals for seven housing society projects in Amsterdam, stating that he would only approve the simplest of plans. With a change of ministry, the plans were approved by Cort van der Linden. Struggles over the definition of working and middle-class housing continued after the war. For instance, Z. D. J. W. Gulden objected to the 1920 housing proposal for Ons Huis in Watergraafsmeer because the housing had been designated as "middle class" to conform with national standards. Gulden objected that acceptance of such a designation would make it impossible to propose a similar housing type as workers' housing (Housing Committee meeting of 12 January 1920, Notulen van de Commissie van bijstand in het beheer der zaken van Volkshuisvesting [1920], archive 5102, GAA).

35. The dwellings on Boerhaavestraat by J. C. van Epen followed the same plans he used for the housing on Pretoriusstraat. The survey is in *De Volksschool* 8, no. 8 (3 March 1909).

36. D. P. D. Fabius on De Arbeiderswoning proposal, *Gemeenteblad* 2 (1913), meeting of 21 May 1913, 907.

37. Th. F. A. Delprat defending De Arbeiderswonging proposal, ibid., 908.

38. *Gemeenteblad* 1 (1903), no. 1053, 30 November 1903, 2093. Henri Polak stated, "Eindelijk zou hij wenschen, dat de 'verplichting om, zoo mogelijk, plaats te nemen in een bijwagen' niet worden geschapen. Er zit iets stuitends in dat voorschrift. De tram is een democratisch vervoermiddel, dat geen onderscheid van rang, stand of klasse kent, noch kennen moet. Het zal

goed zijn, geen enkelen maatregel te nemen, waardoor om zoo te zeggen, eene scheiding tusschen bokken en schapen wordt in het leven geroepen."

39. Public Works Committee meeting of 6 July 1910, Notulen van de Commissie van bijstand in zake Publieke Werken (1910), archive 5087, GAA, 231.

40. *Gemeenteblad* 2 (1910), meeting of 27 July 1910, 914–29. An unfavorable view of these gardens appeared in a later report of the director of public works (no. 2559, 6 March 1913), in which he expresses the expectation that they would not be well-maintained. Posthumus Meyjes in the Public Works Committee also expressed concern: "Bijna overal waar voortuintjes zijn aangelegd, is, in plaats van een tuintje, een rommel ontstaan, die het uiterlijk aanzien geducht schaadt" (meeting of 10 April 1913, Notulen van de Commissie van bijstand in zake Publieke Werken [1913], archive 5087, GAA, 231). On the issue of parks in Amsterdam, see H. P. Berlage, J. van Hasselt, Dirk Hudig and Jan Kruseman, *De Amsterdamsche parken en plantsoenen* (Amsterdam: J. A. de Bussy, 1909), report of a commission of the Amsterdam Housing Council, which argues for greater municipal intervention in the provision of urban green space and particularly for a large urban park. See also J. P. Thijsse, "De parken-kwestie," *Algemeen Handelsblad*, 5 January 1908. In 1911, the mayor and aldermen, acting on an earlier proposal by councilor Vliegen, proposed a woods north of the IJ (*Gemeenteblad* 1 [1911], no. 1257, 14 November 1911, 2925–27). For a history of urban parks in the Netherlands, see Maurits van Rooijen, *De groene stad: Een historische studie over de groenvoorziening in de Nederlandse stad* (The Hague: Vereniging van Nederlandse Gemeenten, 1984).

41. C. B. Posthumus Meyjes at Public Works Committee meeting of 17 March 1910, Notulen van de Commissie van bijstand in zake Publieke Werken (1910), archive 5087, GAA, 105.

42. See, for example, Public Works Committee meetings on Lepelstraat, 26 May 1906, 104–6; on Museumterrein, 25 May 1908, 83–84; and on the Overtoom, 3 February 1910, 62, in Notulen van de Commissie van bijstand in zake Publieke Werken (1910), archive 5087, GAA.

43. "Door de uitvoering van die plannen zouden toch z. g. achterbuurtjes ontstaan die tot verontreiniging aanleiding zouden geven en extra verlichting en bewaking noodig zouden maken" (Housing Committee to alderman of public works, 1 April 1911, 8691 PW 1910, archive 5180, GAA). The Algemeene's plans, by H. P. Berlage, had proposed a pair of freestanding groups of nine dwellings each on the area, which became a square facing directly on the public way.

44. Letter to mayor and aldermen, 5 July 1911, reprinted in Algemeene Woningbouw Vereeniging, *Jaarverslag* (1911). The final plans are in BWT dossiers 18995, 22033, 5720.

45. The annual reports of the Algemeene list membership by occupation. Rents were f2.50 to f5.50.

46. F. J. Perquin on housing locations, *Gemeenteblad* 2 (1909), meeting of 1 November 1909, 1422–23. The future of the Notweg area, site of caravan encampments, was the subject of considerable discussion.

47. Algemeene Woningbouw Vereeniging, *Jaarverslag* (1911), 25–26; Amsterdam Housing Council, petition to the Amsterdam City Council, January 1911, Wibaut archive, no. 295, IISG. Municipal land priced low enough to allow construction of workers' housing was located behind the Cellular Jail, on Tasmanstraat, in the Indische and Transvaal districts, which were

cut off by railroad lines, and in Spaarndammerbuurt, which was distant from the center. The council responded to the petition later that spring (*Gemeenteblad* 2 [1911], meeting of 18 May 1911, 593).

48. In 1918, a typical dispute erupted over the distribution of land to private developers and housing societies. The city had proposed that several riverside blocks within the new southern plan should be split so that private developers might build the side facing the Amstel River and the housing societies might build on the back. In the Public Works Committee, defenders of private real estate interests raised objections to joining the better and lesser class of housing in one block (J. N. Hendrix in Public Works Committee meeting of 18 June 1918, Notulen van de Commissie van bijstand in zake Publieke Werken [1918], archive 5087, GAA, 70). In response, Keppler proposed that the housing society Algemeene build the entire site, but with more expensive units under new state provisions. He had originally not pursued the plan "because Housing Act housing would be less appropriate to the character of the rest of the construction along the Amstel" (Arie Keppler to alderman of housing, September 1918, 3211 VH 1918, archive 5187, GAA). The Public Works Committee countered by suggesting the riverfront site be reserved entirely for first-class private construction, and that any workers' housing to be built should only be sited behind a transitional strip of middle-class housing, itself behind the riverfront site (meeting of 24 December 1918, Notulen van de Commissie van bijstand in zake Publieke Werken [1918], archive 5087, GAA, 359–60). Mayor and aldermen decided in 1919 to allow the Algemeene to carry out its plan (J. W. C. Tellegen to alderman of public works, 22 April 1919, 983 VH 1919, archive 5187, GAA). In defense of this decision, Tellegen, by then mayor of the city, argued that this area was in any event less likely to attract the high rents desired by private interests, given that the tram line linking it downtown already carried "a totally different clientele" than those found in first-class housing, referring to the working-class inhabitants of the adjacent district, the Pijp (Tellegen to alderman of public works, 7 March 1919, 313 VH 1919, archive 5187, GAA). The attractive site was preserved for workers because of its proximity to an existing workers' district. It was eventually built up with one of architect J. C. van Epen's most engaging projects. National policy following World War I favored support of private developers. For the continuing debate over the designation of land for private developers and housing societies, see Public Works Committee to mayor, 13 March 1919, 904 PW 1919, archive 5180, GAA. The letter of minister of labor P. J. M. Aalberse of 4 December 1920 makes clear the government intention to encourage private developers to start work again after the war (A.I. no. 27166 1920).

49. Johanna ter Meulen, *Huisvesting van armen te Amsterdam* (Haarlem: H. D. Tjeenk Willink, 1903), 68. She projected a minimum dwelling for f1.50 rent consisting of at least one large room with a stove and one or two side rooms.

50. Johanna ter Meulen to Johanna van Vlissingen, 20 December 1914, no. 29, archive 492, GAA. Wibaut was chairman, W. A. Bonger, the socialist criminologist, was treasurer, and the socialist bureaucrat Keppler had asked Ter Meulen to act as secretary.

51. For a discussion of working-class identities in Amsterdam and their social and political orientation, see Nancy Stieber, "The Professionalization of Housing in Amsterdam, 1900–1920" (Ph.D. diss., MIT, 1986), chap. 2.

52. The classic study of the civilizing process by Elias identifies two phases of the spreading

of conduct from one class to another, first an assimilation of conduct from the superior to the inferior class and second a repulsion as the inferior class gains in social power and self-confidence. See Norbert Elias, *Power and Civility: The Civilizing Process* (New York: Pantheon Books, 1982), 2:311–12.

53. Tellegen, "Rapport," 2720. The simplest possible housing meant four-story buildings with units consisting of living room, kitchen, and bedrooms. Tellegen rejected the back-to-back housing solution because it was inflexible and did not permit redesign as housing standards rose.

54. Health Board report to mayor and aldermen on municipal housing proposal, 128 GC 1916 (24 May 1916), in *Gemeenteblad* 1 (1916), no. 622, 26 May 1916, 539.

55. Health Board, "Verslag van de bevindingen en handelingen der Gezondheidscommissie," *Gemeenteverslag* (1914), app. 1, 23.

56. Health Board meeting of 15 May 1915, Notulen van de besloten vergaderingen van de Gezondheidscommissie (1915), archive 5269, GAA.

57. Committee on Municipal Housing meeting of 14 December 1915, Notulen van de Commissie van advies in het beheer der Gemeentewoningen (1915), archive 5103, GAA. The first municipal projects, designed by De Bazel, Van der Pek, and Berlage, Gratama, and Versteeg, excluded separate kitchens, eliminated internal hallways, and minimized entry halls.

58. For the nineteenth-century background to municipal land management, see L. Jansen, "De grondpolitiek van Amsterdam in de negentiende eeuw" (Dienst van Publieke Werken, Amsterdam, 1965, mimeograph), G. T. J. Delfgaauw, "De grondpolitiek van de gemeente Amsterdam" (Ph.D. diss., University of Amsterdam, 1934), and Arnold van der Valk, *Amsterdam in Aanleg: Planvorming en dagelijks handelen, 1850–1900* (Amsterdam: Planologisch en Demografisch Instituut van de Universiteit van Amsterdam, 1989).

59. Simon Zadoks, *Geschiedenis der Amsterdamsche concessies* (Amsterdam: Holkema en Warendorf, 1899); L. Jansen, "Het Amsterdamse Erfpachtstelsel van 1896–1909," (Dienst van Publieke Werken, Amsterdam, mimeograph), 6, 14–15.

60. "Memorie van beantwoording van het Algemeen Verslag der Afdeelingen van den Gemeenteraad van Amsterdam over de Gemeentebegrooting voor het jaar 1906," *Gemeenteblad* 1 (1905), no. 977, 11 October 1905, 2251. The mayor and aldermen rejected the suggestion from the council to shorten terms of leases and thereby charge a lower canon. They admitted the possibility of exceptions to the rule where it might provide important social benefits to the community. Jansen cites the case of the Volksbadhuis Sparta, which asked for a reduced canon in 1901, but was refused by the mayor and aldermen ("Erfpachtstelsel," 28–31). The mayor wanted to establish a clear distinction between decisions made by the municipality in its role as land developer and those it made to subsidize worthy social ventures.

61. *Gemeenteblad* 1 (1902), no. 1035, 15 October 1902, 2049–50; *Gemeenteblad* 2 (1902), meeting of 31 October 1908, 1180–84.

62. Zadok van den Bergh and C. B. Posthumus Meyjes at the Public Works Committee meeting of 19 May 1909, Notulen van de Commissie van bijstand in zake Publieke Werken (1909), archive 5087, GAA, 127–29. It was not until 1914 that the Public Works Committee got its first Social Democrats, Van den Tempel and Vliegen. Posthumus Meyjes belonged to the Christelijk-Historische Unie.

63. *Gemeenteblad* 2 (1911), meeting of 18 May 1911, 612.

64. Housing Committee meeting of 7 October 1912, Notulen van de Commissie van bijstand in het beheer der zaken van Volkshuisvesting (1912), archive 5102, GAA. The members of the first Housing Committee (Commissie van bijstand in het beheer der zaken van Volkshuisvesting, Raadsbesluit no. 954, 4 Sept 1912) were F. M. Wibaut, G. T. J. de Jongh, B. E. Asscher, H. H. Wollring, and Th. F. A. Delprat, chairman and alderman of public works.

65. Director of public works to J. W. C. Tellegen, 12 October 1906, 6738 BWT 1906, archive 5221, GAA; Public Works Committee meeting of 27 February 1908, Notulen van de Commissie van bijstand in zake Publieke Werken (1908), archive 5087, GAA, 38–40. It was especially important to lower land costs after passage of the 1905 building ordinance, which raised building standards and thus construction costs (Jansen, "Erpachtstelsel," 49–53).

66. Keppler, brother-in-law of the first housing alderman in Amsterdam, fellow Social Democrat F. M. Wibaut, objected to the way the new alderman's portfolio was organized and felt that the SDAP should not accept the portfolio under those conditions. In a letter to Wibaut, he noted that the alderman did not have authority over all the municipal agencies that would affect housing. Specifically, he noted that land management and extension planning remained under the jurisdiction of the alderman of public works. Keppler's comments anticipate the structural conflict that would characterize the municipal bureaucracy during his stint as head of the new Housing Authority (Arie Keppler to F. M. Wibaut, 16 January 1914, Wibaut archive, IISG).

67. Housing Committee meeting of 15 February 1916, Notulen van de Commissie van bijstand in het beheer der zaken van Volkshuisvesting (1916), archive 5102, GAA; Report of the Health Board subcommittee on extension plans, 12 March 1915, 56 GC 1915, archive 5269, GAA.

68. Director of the Housing Authority and director of the Building and Housing Inspection Office to alderman of housing, 16 March 1916, 685 VH 1916, archive 5187, GAA. Shared responsibility was advocated in March 1916 by the directors of the Building and Housing Inspection Office and the Housing Authority, who suggested that a permanent committee, including the director of public works, prepare street plans and set rates. The director of public work's reaction to this suggestion was negative.

69. The Building and Housing Inspection Office director's proposal to make his own agency central to planning grew from his perception of its neutrality and from a sense of competence about planning expertise: "An extension plan is more than the drawing of a ground plan with the boundaries of streets, squares parks, and canals. It must also be seen as a division of the city according to the type of building (perimeter block, villas, with or without front yard, etc.) and also as a division by districts into zones that either permit or prohibit the activities proscribed by the Nuisance Law. In short, a plan describes the use of the various building lots and their division according to the kind of building. It is a plan of renewal or demolition of the old city and a plan of evacuation to the new districts for the inhabitants. It is a plan of land management that must principally provide for adequate construction and decent housing, and that treats the creation of a good street network at minimum cost as secondary while placing the building plan foremost. If this describes a plan, then the preparation and execution of such a plan should occur at the agency that is established for the advancement of those interests, and that understands their special requirements, where all the matters related to the building and housing

problem can be judged and where all the relevant statistical materials should be gathered" (director of building and housing inspection to alderman of housing, 18 September 1916, 114[2] AZ 1916, in 2342 VH 1916, archive 5187, GAA).

70. Arie Keppler, "Nota betreffende voorbereiding stadsplannen," 20 September 1916, 2342 VH 1916, archive 5187, GAA. Keppler suggested that a committee of the three agencies be responsible for determining land use and prices, but that the Housing Authority bear sole responsibility for the plans of the districts where Housing Act housing was to be built, reserving for Public Works only the technical execution of the plans. Building and Housing Inspection would designate building zones, prepare street plans for private builders, and negotiate for municipal land leases. The Housing Authority would study housing needs, and prepare street plans for districts built by the housing societies and the municipality.

71. Arie Keppler, "Voorlopige nota, terzake financieele uitkomsten, te verwachten bij de exploitatie van het aaneengesloten Gemeentelijke grondbezit in 'Uitbreiding Zuid' bij de uitvoering van het gewijzigd uitbreidingsplan," 15 February 1916, 717 WD 1916.

72. Director of public works to alderman of public works, 12 April 1916, no. 2713/doss. 921 G.E., in 1674 PW 1916, archive 5180, GAA.

73. Keppler wrote to the housing alderman in August insisting on his need to influence the street plans and land costs in cooperation with the two other agencies. The number of demands he had received from the housing societies for land in the southern extension propelled Keppler to seek this involvement (Arie Keppler to alderman of housing, 5 August 1916, 3280 WD 1916, in 2342 VH 1916, archive 5187, GAA). As a result of this letter, Wibaut met with the Public Works alderman and set up a September meeting to discuss relations between the agencies. Wibaut asked each of the three to come up with firm proposals.

74. This conflict can be followed in the debates of the municipal council during 1918 and in numerous memoranda on cooperation between the two municipal agencies.

75. On the clash over the municipal planning department, see W. J. Bruyn, "Delegatie bij planvoorbereiding: Een kritische nabeschouwing over het algemeen uitbreidingsplan van Amsterdam, 1935" (Ph.D. diss., Katholieke Hogeschool, 1976), 26–39.

76. F. M. Wibaut, *Gemeenteblad* 2 (1919), meeting of 31 July 1919, 1730. Wibaut was speaking in defense of Keppler upon the motion by Zwart, Hendrix, Roell, Van Os, and Ter Haar to rebuke him (*Gemeenteblad* 1 [1919], no. 509, 30 May 1919, 983).

77. *Woningwet*, Staatsblad no. 158, 22 June 1901, arts. 2 and 3. The law required standards for the siting of buildings, the floor level and height of the building, the measurements of the living areas, stairs, and entries, toilets, availability of water, fire prevention, prevention of dampness, solidity, elimination of smoke, water, and sewage, adequate light and air.

78. "Ontwerp Bouwverordening," *Gemeenteblad* 1 (1905), no. 387, 3 April 1905, 397–571.

79. Health Board, "Verslag van de bevindingen en handelingen der Gezondheidscommissie te Amsterdam," *Gemeenteverslag* (1909), app. 1, 15.

80. J. N. Hendrix arguing against Tellegen's proposed building ordinance, *Gemeenteblad* 2 (1905), meeting of 21 June 1905, 820; echoed by P. W. Sutorius, *Gemeenteblad* 2 (1905), meeting of 23 June 1905, 1032. The ordinance was approved by a vote of 28 to 8.

81. For the discussion of building requirements, see the proceedings of the first and second Public Health Conventions: *Verslag van het eerste Nederlandsch Congres voor Openbare Gezondheids-*

regeling (Amsterdam: F. van Rossen, 1896) and *Verslag van het tweede Nederlandsch Congres voor Openbare Gezondheidsregeling* (Amsterdam: F. van Rossen, 1897). Also J. W. Jenny Weijerman, *Woningtoezicht* (Haarlem: H. D. Tjeenk Willink, 1899); H. L. Drucker, "Het woningvraagstuk," *De Gids* 62, part 1 (March 1898): 470–74; Dr. R. H. Saltet, "Verslag van den directeur van den Gemeentelijke Gezondheidsdienst betreffende zijne reis in Engeland tot onderzoek van het sanitair toezicht op woningen aldaar" (October 1895), in *Gemeenteblad* 1 (1896), no. 563, 11 August 1896, 565–78. For comparable developments in Germany, see Nicolas Bullock and James Read, *The Movement for Housing Reform in Germany and France, 1840–1914* (Cambridge: Cambridge University Press, 1985), 96–110.

82. Jenny Weijerman, *Woningtoezicht*, 26.

83. D. Schut, C. B. Posthumus Meyjes, J. N. Hendrix on proposed building ordinance, *Gemeenteblad* 2 (1905), meeting of 21 June 1905, 819–31.

84. *Gemeenteblad* 2 (1905), meeting of 21 June 1905, 822.

85. See *Gemeenteblad* 1 (1905), no. 590, 6 June 1905, 793–98; no. 591, 8 June 1905, 799–808; no. 622, 15 June 1905, 821–24; no. 625, 19 June 1905, 831–55.

86. *Gemeenteblad* 2 (1905), meeting of 21 June 1905, 823.

87. J. N. Hendrix on elimination of alcove, *Gemeenteblad* 2 (1905), meeting of 23 June 1905, 945.

88. Mels Meijers, "Volkshuisvesting: De architecten en de woningbouw," *Bouwkundig Weekblad* 37, no. 29 (1916): 216–19.

89. D. Schut on proposed building ordinance, *Gemeenteblad* 2 (1905), meeting of 21 June 1905, 829.

90. In both the 1890 study sponsored by the Society for Public Welfare and Jenny Weijerman's doctoral dissertation (published as *Woningtoezicht*), the position was maintained that paupers need to be given a moral education and taught how to use the home.

CHAPTER FOUR

1. A. v[an] d[e] Wijk-Groot, "Verslag over de arbeiderswoningen: Blok AW I and AW V," June–December 1919, 5730 VH 1919, archive 5187, GAA.

2. J. W. Smit on workers' accommodations to poor housing, *Gemeenteblad* 2 (1905), meeting of 23 June 1905, 943.

3. Families were occasionally given bedframes through charity or through the housing society itself. In 1920, Keppler told of a family found wandering in the streets who were brought into temporary municipal facilities at a school on Wittenburgerstraat. They were later transferred into housing for asocial families and finally given a subsidized home with kitchen and four bedrooms in the Handwerkers Vriendenkring project. However, the family did not use two of the bedrooms because they had no linens and had no money for them (Housing Committee meeting of 12 January 1920, Notulen van de Commissie van bijstand in het beheer der zaken van Volkshuisvesting [1920], archive 5102, GAA).

4. G. K. Chesterton, *What's Wrong with the World?* (London: Cassell, 1910), quoted in Georges Canguilhem, *The Normal and the Pathological* (New York: Zone Books, 1991), 258.

5. J. W. Jenny Weijerman, *Woningtoezicht* (Haarlem: H. D. Tjeenk Willink, 1899), 65.

6. In the *Staatsenquête* of 1890, the witnesses make many references to these housing conditions.

7. Not all middle-class reformers were persuaded by arguments blaming the victims for their social problems. In an impassioned disavowal of the middle-class interpretation of overcrowded housing conditions, Brooshooft points to the hypocritical use of the word "overpopulation" by reformers arguing that workers should postpone marriage. This places the responsibility on workers' moral restraint rather than on the low wages that create the difficulty of supporting children in the first place (Pieter Brooshooft, *Officieele en feitelijke waarheid: Bijdrage tot de kennis van onze arbeiderstoestanden* [The Hague: Haagsche Vereeniging voor Kindervoeding, 1897], 39).

8. The Dutch reformer's civilizing offensive in relation to charity work and housing is discussed in Ali de Regt, *Arbeidersgezinnen en beschavingsarbeid: Ontwikkeling in Nederland, 1870–1949, een historisch-sociologische studie* (Amsterdam: Boom Meppel, 1984), 143–98, and in Leon Deben, "Van onderkomen tot woning: Een studie over woonbeschaving in Nederland, 1850–1969" (Ph.D. diss., University of Utrecht, 1988).

9. Jhr. Mr. Rethaan Macare, quoted in *Tijdschrift voor Sociale Hygiëne* 15 (1913): 344.

10. P. B. Middendorp, "Versche lucht en zonlicht in onze woning," *Het Groene en het Witte Kruis* 11 (1914–15): 85.

11. In 1890, Van Hasselt and Verschoor, noting that no long-term observations had yet been made, hesitated to draw conclusions about the relationship between the improvement of housing and a decrease in alcohol consumption (J. van Hasselt and L. Verschoor, *De arbeiderswoningen in Nederland: Beoordelend overzicht samengesteld door de commissie van onderzoek naar hetgeen in verschillende gemeenten des lands gedaan is ter verkrijging van verbeterde arbeiderswoningen* [Amsterdam: Maatschappij tot Nut van 't Algemeen, 1890], 229–30). The League against Alcohol Abuse initiated the inquiry. Because of the assumed connection, the league had a continuing interest in housing reform. It had commissioned the 1893 Amsterdam study, later participated in the formation of the Society for Public Welfare housing committee, and set up its own housing committee. Public discussion of the relationship between poor housing and pub attendance dated from the mid nineteenth century (see W. de Sitter, "Een woord over de openbare gezondheidsregeling," *De Economist* 2 [1853]: 137), and in the early twentieth century the league was still investigating the connection.

12. Marie Sparnaaij, *Het leven en werken, het lijden en strijden door onze fabrieksarbeiders* (The Hague: Drukkerij "Vrede," 1898), 41. Sparnaaij's novel was a thinly veiled series of admonitions to factory workers to eat better, exercise, wash more often, and to cultivate virtues such as loyalty, sobriety, neatness, thrift.

13. V.d. B[reggen], "Woning en ziekte," *Tijdschrift voor Sociale Hygiëne* 19 (1917): 48.

14. In one of the first meetings of the council's advisory committee on municipal housing (Commissie van advies in het beheer der Gemeentewoningen) in 1915, alcoholism was declared by Dr. Ben H. Sajet to be one of the consequences of bad housing (meeting of 14 December 1915, Notulen van de Commissie van advies in het beheer der Gemeentewoningen [1915], archive 5103, GAA).

15. "Memorie van toelichting," *Woningwet*, Staatsblad no. 158, 22 June 1901, 2, 3.

16. The comparable American project to bring moral order to the urban masses through

housing reform is discussed in Paul Boyer, *Urban Masses and Moral Order in America, 1820–1920* (Cambridge: Harvard University Press, 1978), 179, and Gwendolyn Wright, *Moralism and the Model Home: Domestic Architecture and Cultural Conflict in Chicago, 1873–1913* (Chicago: University of Chicago Press, 1980).

17. The campaign for urban and civic order in Germany is treated in Brian Ladd, *Urban Planning and Civic Order in Germany, 1860–1914* (Cambridge: Harvard University Press, 1990), and in the United States in Boyer, *Urban Masses.* The Dutch problem of training recent rural immigrants to meet norms of urban behavior is comparable to the training of foreign immigrants to adjust to American urban life.

18. Yearly carnivals (*kermis*) had long provided an outlet for the pent-up frustrations of working-class life, and a tradition of riotous and sometimes violent behavior had grown up in various neighborhoods, for example, Hartjesdag in the Dapperbuurt. A move to reduce the carnival festivities from two weeks to one precipitated riots in working-class neighborhoods. The most dramatic outbursts occurred in 1886 in the Jordaan, after several years of extreme unemployment, especially in the building trades. One carnival activity, eel catching, was forbidden in Amsterdam. Participants sitting in boats would attempt to pull an eel from a rope strung taut over the canal, and bets would be laid on the possible winner. In 1886, a crowd gathered at the Lindengracht canal to wager on the outcome of an eel-catching contest. Violent protests, lasting several days, took place when the police and military put a stop to the event. Although the authorities claimed that the protest was socialist inspired and the popular press portrayed it as such, there was no evidence of any organized socialist participation. The Palingoproer ("Eel riot") was, rather, a spontaneous expression of the frustrations of long, cold winters with high unemployment (Piet de Rooy, *Een revolutie die voorbij ging: Domela Nieuwenhuis en het Palingoproer* (Bussum: Fibula–Van Dishoeck, 1971).

19. In the aftermath of the divisive Railroad Strike, Charles Boissevain's proposal to the Public Works Committee for the construction of a garden city north of the IJ was a rare instance in which housing was openly discussed as a means to keep workers happy with their lot: "Door de best mogelijke woningtoestanden te scheppen b.v. door aanleg van een tuinstad zou men wellicht langzamerhand een tevreden en gelukkige arbeidsbevolking kunnen krijgen en kon zich daar eene moderne industriestad vestigen, waar het verblijf in de fabrieken niet langer een last zou zijn en waar maatschappelijke misstanden als de tegenwoordige woningen ontbraken" (meeting of 12 October 1905, Notulen van de Commissie van bijstand in zake Publieke Werken [1905], archive 5087, GAA).

20. The Eastern Islands, a stronghold of the Amsterdam dockworkers, were famous for insularity, and residents were said to spend their entire lives on their island, considering a visit to central Amsterdam a major outing.

21. Norbert Elias, *Power and Civility: The Civilizing Process* (New York: Pantheon Books 1982), 2:310–11. The linearity of Elias's analysis, which suggests a single route of progress along the path of self-control and self-discipline, obscures the more interesting problem of what forms such self-control might take, forms that were by no means determined by a teleology of progress and were therefore open to social construction.

22. Ali de Regt makes a similar point and warns against crediting the reformer's civilizing offensive with too much effectiveness (*Arbeidersgezinnen*, 244).

23. "Het woningvraagstuk op het Gezondheidscongres," *Tijdschrift voor Sociale Hygiëne* 1, no. 5 (1899): 23–27.

24. *Woningwet*, art. 2.

25. "Bouwverordening," *Gemeenteblad* 1 (1905), no. 387, 3 April 1905, chap. 5, arts. 323–30, 478–80.

26. Vereeniging ten Behoeve der Arbeidersklasse, no. 49, archive 297, GAA. Dirk Hudig and H. C. A. Henny included a model rental agreement as an appendix to their *Handleiding voor woningbouwverenigingen* (Zwolle, 1911).

27. See, for example, Jenny Weijerman, *Woningtoezicht;* D. B. van der Meulen, *Uw huis en uwe woning* (Amsterdam: Maatschappij tot Nut van 't Algemeen, n.d.); or A. van Gijn, *Verslag van het tiende Nederlandsch Congres voor Openbare Gezondheidsregeling* (Amsterdam, 1905), 29. The primary impulse toward training the working-class had emanated from such liberal reform circles as the Society for Public Welfare, whose work encouraging thrift and education through its savings banks and libraries extended to brochures on nutrition, hygiene, housekeeping, and the proper way to arrange a home.

28. A. van Gijn, *Woningbouw en Woningwet: Modelstatuten voor vereenigingen als bedoeld in de Woningwet* (Haarlem: H. D. Tjeenk Willink, 1904), 45.

29. De Regt, *Arbeidersgezinnen*, 149.

30. Gedenkboek van de tentoonstelling "De Vrouw, 1913" (Amsterdam, 1913), 28.

31. V.d. Breggen, "Woning-ziekte," *Tijdschrift voor Sociale Hygiëne* 19 (1917): 50.

32. Catalogus van de tentoonstelling "De Vrouw, 1813–1913" (Amsterdam, 1913), 202–3.

33. *Het huishoudonderwijs aan de Herhalingsschool: Rapport van eene Commissie uit den Bond van Leeraressen bij het Huishoudonderwijs* (Amsterdam, 1905), 4, 45. The committee included M. D. Wittop Koning. One textbook on home economics estimated the cost of the tools needed for cleaning and housework at f36.61. M. Bosch and C. J. W. van der Ploeg-Deggeler, *Onderhoud van huis en huisraad* (Almelo, 1905), 1.

34. Van Hasselt and Verschoor, *De arbeiderswoningen*, 3. The philanthropic housing societies hired housing supervisors who collected rent, knew the tenants, and kept an eye on them, but Van Hasselt and Verschoor regretted the absence of such civilizing influence in the Netherlands as the lady rent collectors trained by Octavia Hill.

35. Treub taught economics, Jenny Weijerman hygiene, and Louise van der Pek-Went housing inspection. On the School for Social Work, see P. L. T[ak], "Opleiding voor socialen arbeid," *De Kroniek* 5, no. 233 (11 June 1899): 186, and "Sociale arbeid," *De Kroniek* 10, no. 475 (30 January 1904): 33–34; M. G. Muller-Lulofs, "Sociale opleiding," *De Gids* 21, part 4 (1903): 288–310; Clara Brinkgreve, *De Bouwonderneming Jordaan: Een experiment in de volkshuisvesting aan het einde van de negentiende eeuw* (The Hague: Nederlands Instituut voor Ruimtelijk Ordening, 1985), 46–47; Wilhelmina C. Blomberg, *Louise Went, 1865–1951: Aan de bakermat van de Amsterdamse Volkshuisvesting* (Amsterdam: Gemeentelijke Dienst Volkshuisvesting, 1985). Ali de Regt discusses the professionalization of social work in the Netherlands (*Arbeidersgezinnen*, 183–88).

36. Hudig and Henny, *Handleiding voor woningbouwvereenigingen*, 89–90.

37. Johanna ter Meulen, *De woningopzichteres* (Dordrecht, 1921).

38. Johanna ter Meulen, "Verslagboekje betreffende de bewoners der verhuurde perceelen," 1897, no. 39, archive 492, GAA.

39. Johanna ter Meulen to Johanna F. [Han] van Vlissingen, 13 November 1913, no. 29, archive 492, GAA.

40. P. L. Tak, "De Amsterdamsche Woningraad," *De Kroniek* 8, no. 371 (1 February 1902): 33–35.

41. F. M. Wibaut, *Levensbouw: Memories* (Amsterdam, 1936), 137.

42. Johanna ter Meulen, *De beschaafde vrouw als opzichteres over arbeiderswoningen* (Amsterdam, 1898).

43. Hudig and Henny, *Handleiding voor woningbouwvereenigingen*, 91.

44. Johanna ter Meulen to Johanna van Vlissingen, 18 June 1915, no. 29, archive 492, GAA.

45. After the introduction of women's suffrage, the SDAP used the housing issue to motivate women's interest in politics and, through its promise of housing improvement, to win their support. Fearing that confessional parties would win the women's vote, the socialists' increased their housing propaganda during the 1919 elections. See, for example, J. H. Sch[aper], *Hoe woont gij? Een woord aan de arbeiders en hunne vrouwen* (Amsterdam: SDAP, 1906); Z. D. J. W. Gulden, *De vrouw en haar huis* (Amsterdam: Bond van Sociaal-democratische Vrouwenclubs, [1923]); *De Proletarische Vrouw*, passim. The activities of the Federation of Social Democratic Women's Clubs are discussed at length in Cita Hartveld, *Moderne zakelijkheid: Efficiency in wonen en werken in Nederland, 1918–1940* (Amsterdam: Uitgeverij Het Spinhuis, 1994), 172–84.

46. Mathilde Wibaut-Berdenis van Berlekom, "De vrouw en het gezin," *De Socialistische Gids* 3 (November 1918): 816. The article reveals the influence of the American feminist Charlotte Perkins Gilman. The educated classes showed greater interest in the possibility of kitchenless houses, which would free the wife from housework, yet maintain intimate family life. The middle-class housing society Samenwerking was active in this area, see below, chapter 5, notes 76 and 77.

47. De Regt, *Arbeidersgezinnen*, 142, 243.

48. De Arbeiderswoning, *Jaarverslag* (1915–16), 10–12. The report suggests that the noise level and behavior of the inhabitants depended on their origins and the number of children. Berlage's housing in the Indischebuurt came to be called the "beehive" because of the noisy swarms of children living there.

49. Hélène Mercier discusses the standards of selection for the Vereeniging ten Behoeve der Arbeidersklasse in *Over arbeiderswoningen* (Haarlem: H. D. Tjeenk Willink, 1887), 139. Johanna ter Meulen, acting on behalf of the Vereeniging tot het Bouwen van Arbeiderswoningen, refused to allow the municipality to force her to take in unfit dwellers, but she did not wish to restrict selection to only the "easiest" inhabitants (Johanna ter Meulen to Johanna van Vlissingen, 4 June 1914, no. 29, archive 492, GAA).

50. Johanna ter Meulen discusses this aspect of the housing inspector's job in *De woningopzichteres*, 13–14. In its first meetings (9 November and 14 December 1915, 9 May 1916), the council committee for the management of municipal housing took up the issue of segregating certain families. In the 1920s, two special communities were established for asocial families.

51. Committee on Municipal Housing meetings of 9 November 1915 and 9 May 1916,

Notulen van de Commissie van advies in het beheer der Gemeentewoningen (1916), archive 5103, GAA.

52. Keppler argued that the housing north of the IJ was intended for the industrial workers employed there and for those still living on the Eilanden, Czaar Peterstraat, and the Indischebuurt, that is, those from poor housing. Because of wartime housing shortages, many municipal workers ended up in the municipal housing in Buiksloterham, and friction developed between them and the subsidized dwellers. Even with the sifting process, the housing shortage after World War I led to mismatches of neighborhoods and dwellers. A 1923 investigation of privately built housing in the Amstelkwartier reported dissatisfaction among the middle-class dwellers for whom that housing was intended because the living habits of many of their working-class neighbors were so different from their own. But the interlopers were dissatisfied as well, since the neighborhood lacked the typical appurtenances of the working-class neighborhood: market, pub, active street life, pawn shops, stores, and street festivals. A worker would rent a dwelling at f600–800 a year and sublet rooms in order to afford it. His tenants would include casual laborers such as streethawkers. The introduction of lower-paid workers to its middle-class housing created a set of problems for the Amstels Bouwvereeniging: for instance, the storage in rooms of fish (fresh, smoked, sour and salted!) fruit, and flowers. There was an interesting discrepancy between the work of the main renter and that of the lodgers: the former usually a white-collar office worker or salesman, the latter unskilled workers, hawkers, assistants, or harbor workers (Woningdienst, *Verslag van het onderzoek naar de woningtoestanden in het z.g. Amstellaankwartier* [Amsterdam, n.d.]).

53. "Woningbouw van Gemeentewege," *Gemeenteblad* 1 (1914), 2 October 1914, 2680.

54. The municipal housing committee as a whole reacted against further splitting these families (Committee on Municipal Housing meeting of 22 June 1916, Notulen van de Commissie van advies in het beheer der Gemeentewoningen [1916], archive 5103, GAA). Another issue was the class origins of housing inspectors: should they be well-bred, middle-class girls trained by the School for Social Work or lower-class girls? (meeting of 4 July 1916).

55. The families were placed first in a converted school, then in special housing constructed in Zeeburgerpad and Asterdorp. The designs were severe: one-story, one-family dwellings, consisting of living room, kitchen and two to four bedrooms, with flat roof, iron windows and doors, limited woodwork, brick pavement in place of gardens, and a single guarded entrance (*Gemeenteblad* 1 [1921], no. 14, 7 January 1921, 22–24). The Communist councilor Wijnkoop objected that the design looked like a prison (*Gemeenteblad* 2 [1921], meeting of 27 January 1921, 222–28). See also De Regt, *Arbeidersgezinnen*, and Adrianne Dercksen and Loes Verplanke, *Geschiedenis van de onmaatschappelijkheidsbestrijding in Nederland, 1914–1970* (Meppel: Boom, 1987).

56. De Regt, *Arbeidersgezinnen*, 212.

57. Amsterdamsch Bouwfonds meetings of 30 August 1905 and passism, Notulenboek ledenvergaderingen Amsterdamsch Bouwfonds, archives of the Algemene Woningbouw Vereniging.

58. Van Gijn, *Woningbouw en Woningwet.* Van Gijn favored encouraging private enterprise over the government-aided housing societies: "Bij de voorziening in de behoefte van arbeiderswoningen, zoolang onze maatschappij niet geheel volgens de droomen van het collectivisme gewijzigd is, de particuliere bouwnijverheid wel altijd de grootste rol zal vervullen" ("Hoe kan

van het standpunt der Woningwet de bouw van arbeiderswoningen worden bevorderd?" *Tijdschrift voor Sociale Hygiëne* 7 [1905]: 146). The role of the societies was to improve the housing type such that the entrepreneur was forced to improve his. This same argument had been made by Drucker earlier. Van Gijn and the drafters of the Housing Act assumed that government funds would be used for housing only when private enterprise failed, and that the housing societies would continue to operate on the same basis as the philanthropic societies of the nineteenth century. They were unprepared for the cooperative ventures proposed by workers themselves. In defending private enterprise by insisting that housing societies charge market rents, Van Gijn cut short the dreams of some workers.

59. George A. M. Kallenbach, *Over de pogingen door particulieren in het werk gesteld tot verbetering der arbeiderswoningen* (Leiden: A. H. Adriani, 1892), 2.

60. Van Hasselt and Verschoor, *De arbeiderswoningen*, 210–12.

61. J. van Altena to Jan Kruseman, 15 March 1896, no. 49, archive 297, GAA. The society was the Vereeniging ten Behoeve der Arbeidersklasse.

62. Tak, Treub, and Borgesius, socialist, progressive liberal, and old liberal respectively, supported acceptance of cooperative societies.

63. "Tiende Congres voor Openbare Gezondheidsregeling," *Tijdschrift voor Sociale Hygiëne* 8 (1905): 86–87.

64. Scrutator [Arie Keppler], "Coöperatieve Bouwvereenigingen," *De Kroniek* 11, no. 573 (16 December 1905): 396.

65. Ibid., 397.

66. *Verslag van het tweede Nederlandsch Congres voor Openbare Gezondheidsregeling* (Amsterdam: F. van Rossen, 1897), 78–79.

67. They may have been put off by his phrasing: "Het moeten menschen zijn, in staat en bereid een sommetje te storten in het aandeelen-kapitaal—eenige honderden guldens wellicht" (H[enri] P[olak], "Wonen," *Weekblad ANDB* 11, no. 45 [10 November 1905]).

68. Many of the yearly reports of the housing societies comment on the low attendance at meetings, especially in the first years of organization before construction of housing began.

69. The early histories of many of the housing societies are recorded in union newsletters, commemorative publications, or in the first annual report of the society. See, for example, Coöperatieve Woningbouwvereeniging Rochdale, *Jaarverslag* (1908); *Rochdale 50 jaar: Jubileumboek uitgegeven ter gelegenheid van het 50 jarig bestaan van de coöperatieve bouwvereeniging "Rochdale" te Amsterdam* (Amsterdam, 1953); G. C. J. Drijfhout, *De gouden mijlpaal 1909, 8 september 1959: Gedenkboek uitgegeven ter gelegenheid van het Gouden Jubileum van de woningbouwvereniging "Eigen Haard" te Amsterdam* (Amsterdam, 1959), 19; E. S. Ottens, *Woningbouwvereeniging "Eigen Haard," 1909–1984* (Amsterdam, 1984). For the genesis of the ACOB, see *De Volksschool* (1902–12)and *Woningbouwvereniging ACOB, 1905–1995: Een historische momentopname* (Amsterdam: Woningbouwvereniging ACOB, 1995).

70. The *Handliedingen voor woningbouwvereenigingen* by Hudig and Henny was first published in 1911.

71. These are collected in the archives of the CBSA in the International Institute of Social History. Between 1900 and 1922, the CBSA handled fifty-four requests for advice from Amsterdam societies.

72. After meeting with Henri Polak, leader of the diamond workers' union, Louise van der Pek-Went suggested that "you submit your well-formulated wishes to the housing council so that it can help you establish a society for the improvement of the housing conditions of the diamond workers. This will be the first step that the ANDB must take, whereupon a request for a subsidy from the city can follow" (Louise van der Pek-Went to Henri Polak, 10 November 1905, no. 3055/18, ANDB archive, IISG).

73. In a letter to Treub, then head of the CBSA, the socialist worker H. H. Wollring, who took an active role in housing reform, insisted on being paid for his time when a meeting was canceled. His family could not do without the pay, he wrote. Such direct glimpses into the financial difficulties of worker participants in the housing movement appear only occasionally (H. H. Wollring to M. W. F. Treub, 19 December 1901, no. 19, CBSA archive, IISG).

74. A group of teachers ran into misunderstandings with their architect, whose plans had overshot their budget but who demanded payment nonetheless. They wrote to the CBSA for guidance in finding an honest architect (correspondence between M. W. F. Treub and the Coöperatieve Bouwvereeniging "Eigen Haard," 1901, RA 152, no. 234, CBSA archive, IISG). One society, having looked elsewhere for advice, came to the CBSA contritely confessing that it would not stray again (H. Glimmerveen to M. W. F. Treub, 4 January 1904, letter 4273, RA 374, no. 248, CBSA archive, IISG). Hudig at the CBSA tried to help a group of typographers, whom he referred to as "these fellows" (*deze luitjes*), to build two-story row houses in Watergraafsmeer, but their plans foundered (Hudig letter, 18 November 1908, RA 637, no. 248, CBSA archive, IISG).

75. Polak, "Wonen." The society decided to build first with private capital.

76. H. Glimmerveen, "Werk aan de winkel," *De Gemeente-Werkman* 1, no. 1 (26 April 1902). The union was the Centrale Gemeentewerkliedenbond. H. Glimmerveen and P. Roeland were the primary organizers of Rochdale.

77. "Woning-coöperatie," *De Gemeente-Werkman* 1, no. 20 (28 June 1902); "De nieuwe Woningwet," no. 23 (19 July 1902); "Woning-coöperatie," no. 24 (26 July 1902); "Bouwcoöperatie," no. 29 (30 August 1902).

78. Domela Nieuwenhuis and C. B. de Best, quoted in "Verslag Openbare Cursusvergadering der Vereeniging van Stadsreinigers E.m.M., 14 December 1902," *De Gemeente-Werkman* 1, no. 47 (3 January 1902).

79. "Bouwcoöperatie," *De Gemeente-Werkman* 1, no. 46 (24 December 1902).

80. A. J. C. Rueter, *De Spoorwegstakingen van 1903* (Leiden: Brill, 1935), 297, 330, 323–26, 344.

81. *Rochdale 50 jaar*, 27; *De Gemeente-Werkman* (1902–3); *De Amsterdamsche Gemeentewerklieden* (1906–7). The neutral union was the Centrale Bond van Gemeentewerklieden and the socialist was the Bond van Amsterdamsche Gemeentewerklieden.

82. P. Roeland to M. W. F. Treub, 14 May 1903, letter 3337, RA 374, no. 248, CBSA archive, IISG.

83. *De Gemeente-Werkman* 1, no. 49 (17 January 1903).

84. "Werk aan de winkel," *De Gemeente-Werkman* 1, no. 1 (26 April 1902).

85. *Rochdale 50 jaar*, 31–2; RA 374, no. 248, CBSA archive, IISG. Roeland met regularly with Keppler.

86. *De Gemeente-Werkman* 1, no. 19 (21 June 1902).

87. For instance, one letter from a "faithful reader" noted the need for support from more educated people such as "bosses": "Zeer zeker is steun van meer ontwikkeld noodig, bv. van onze chefs" (Een abonné and getrouw lezer Z., *De Gemeente-Werkman* 1, no. 22 [12 July 1902]); Roeland made a similar comment in a letter to Treub: "Zal zoodanige poging kans van slagen hebben dan zullen wij de hulp moeten hebben van mannen die door hun maatschappelijk aanzien en kennis ons ter zijde willen staan" (P. Roeland to M. W. F. Treub, 14 May 1903, letter 3337, RA 374, no. 248, CBSA archive, IISG).

88. The membership preferred nonmember trustees (H. Glimmerveen to M. W. F. Treub, 13 September 1903, letter 3958, RA 374, no. 248, CBSA archive, IISG). In 1908, Rochdale did have a worker trustee, L. W. Tol, who served alongside J. H. Nieszen, director of the municipal tram service, and J. Menno Huizinga, a doctor. Officers of the society included Keppler and Henny alongside the workers C. Koster, P. Roeland, and C. Melon.

89. "Bouwcoöperatie," *De Gemeente-Werkman* 1, no. 27 (16 August 1902).

90. "Vakvereeniging en bouwcoöperatie," *De Gemeente-Werkman* 1, no. 25 (2 August 1902). "Wie nu weet dat de heer Tellegen . . . en als technicus naam heeft, en als hoofdambtenaar der Gemeente geacht mag worden met de stemming van het Prinsenhof bekend te zijn . . . die zal moeten toegeven dat waar de heer Tellegen dezen raad geeft, ze iets meer dan gewone beteekenis heeft" ("Bouwcoöperatie," *De Gemeente-Werkman* 1, no. 46 [24 December 1902]).

91. *De Gemeente-Werkman* 2, no. 57 (14 March 1903). The willing participation and encouragement of the high-placed (*hooge oomes*) was surely a "snake in the grass" according to C. J. de Best.

92. H. Glimmerveen, *De Gemeente-Werkman* 2, no. 58 (21 March 1903).

93. J. C. van Dam, *Sociaal logboek, 1900–1960: Spiegel van vooruitgang* (Amsterdam: De Brug–Djambatan 1960), 25.

94. Mercier, *Over arbeiderswoningen*, 137, 140–41. Mercier disapproved of the designs for the Vereeniging ten behoeve der Arbeidersklasse and approved of Salerno's because the first permitted use of a parlor while the second did not.

95. The parlor was variously called the salon, mooie kamer, pronkkamer, nette kamer, or kamer aan kant.

96. *Catalogus van de Nationale Tentoonstelling voor Vrouwenarbeid* (Amsterdam, 1899), 164.

97. P. H. Schreuder and N. Cariot, *De huishouding in al haar onderdeelen volgens de laatste en hygiënische eischen* (Amsterdam, 1901), 17.

98. *De Gemeente-Werkman* 1, no. 39 (8 November 1902).

99. Catalogus "De Vrouw 1813–1913," 202–3.

100. Louis Heijermans, *Gezondheidsleer voor arbeiders* (Rotterdam: W. L. and J. Brusse, 1905), 148.

101. *Gemeenteblad* 2 (1905), meeting of 21 June 1905, 946. When it reviewed the proposed building ordinance in 1903, the Amsterdam Health Board had considered altering the requirement for minimum dwelling volume to discourage parlors. The article in question provided that every dwelling consist of at least two rooms, together containing at least forty cubic meters: "A minority wished to reword this provision so that if there is a total space of forty cubic meters the dwelling may only consist of one room. They fear that if two rooms are allowed in that vol-

ume the larger would be used as a parlor, the smaller for a living room, according to the well known custom of our people" (*Gemeenteblad* 1 [1905], no. 590, 2 June 1905, 795).

Since the majority on the Health Board believed the disadvantages of the one-room dwelling outweighed those of the parlor, it did not support this amendment, but later the municipal council passed an equivalent amendment proposed by the Social Democrats Tak and Polak. They introduced an amendment to the building ordinance requiring one room of at least forty cubic meters or two rooms of at least fifty cubic meters, which was passed by the council 21 to 10 (*Gemeenteblad* 1 [1905], no. 622, 15 June 1905, 822; *Gemeenteblad* 2 [1905], meeting of 22 June 1905, 918–20).

102. A. Ogterop, *De gezellige woning* (Amsterdam: Bond van Sociaal-democratische Vrouwenclubs, n.d.).

103. *Gemeenteblad* 2 (1905), meeting of 21 June 1905, 942–43.

104. *De Gemeente-Werkman* 1, no. 31 (11 October 1902), and no. 39 (8 November 1902).

105. J. A. Snikkers letter, *De Gemeente-Werkman* 1, no. 50 (24 January 1903): 2.

106. Arie Keppler reviewed the completed Rochdale housing and reported favorably on the floor plan, which "forces dwellers to break with the system of a room put aside" ("Woningwet-woningen," *Bouwwereld* 8, no. 41 [13 October 1909]: 326–28). But the Arnhem housing inspector J. Keurschot attacked the design as evidence of paternalism in "Sociale hygiëne en techniek," *Bouwkundig Weekblad* 29, no. 47 (20 November 1909): 561–63. The officers of the Rochdale housing society took umbrage at this interpretation and challenged him to design a dwelling with a salon that also met the requirements of the Amsterdam building ordinance at affordable rents (P. Roeland and Ch. Koster, "Keurschot-Rochdale," *Bouwkundig Weekblad* 29, no. 49 [4 December 1909]: 590–91).

107. H. Glimmerveen to M. W. F. Treub, 15 September 1903, letter 3958, RA 374, no. 248, CBSA archive, IISG. Rochdale insisted on making a three-quarters vote necessary for expulsion from the society because the quarter vote suggested by the CBSA might lead to political misuse of the vote.

108. Rochdale, "Opzichters instructie," January–December 1914, RA 104, no. 324, CBSA archive, IISG.

109. For example, the committee for the society Algemeene organized musical events, outings for children, and use of the shared garden area.

110. H. Lucassen, *Vijftig jaar Woningbouwvereeniging 'Amsterdam Zuid,' 1911–1961* (Amsterdam, 1961).

111. Zomers Buiten, *Jaarverslag* (1917), 33.

112. Hélène Mercier, "De volkshuisvesting te Amsterdam," *De Gids* 69, part 1 (1905): 124. Johanna ter Meulen also discusses housing needs (*Huisvesting van armen te Amsterdam* [Haarlem: H. D. Tjeenk Willink, 1903], 68–70).

113. Dirk Hudig, "De bouwvereenigingen en de nieuwe tijd," *Woningbouw* 3, no. 1/2 (March 1919): 3.

114. The issue of storage arose repeatedly in reformers' discussion, and it was closely tied to the issue of work at home. Reformers wished to remedy the evils of the home as workplace, but their rejection of facilities at times worked against the workers' own needs. Kruseman suggested a few bicycle sheds at Amsterdamsch Bouwfonds' Indischebuurt housing (meeting of 7 July

1910, Notulenboek ledenvergaderingen Amsterdamsch Bouwfonds, archives of the Algemene Woningbouw Vereniging); in 1919, Van de Wijk-Groot suggested the need for workplaces and storage areas in De Arbeiderswoning houses; in 1921 the neighborhood renters' society "Over het Y" supported by the neighborhood renters' society "De Eilanden," asked the municipality for work and storage areas for workers who worked at home (*Gemeenteblad* 2 [1921], meeting of 20 April 1921, 887).

115. The wood partitions used to form the alcoves in speculative housing contributed little to privacy, and even the fire walls between parcels or the floors between stories were far from soundproof. Residents complained bitterly of the noise. One witness blatantly referred to the lack of conjugal privacy. Commenting on the quality of construction in the new districts, Van Veelen states, "Doch daar zijn zij door den bouw op winst bejag zoo luchtig, dat men, wanneer men het sexueele verricht, door den buurman kan worden gehoord" (testimony of Jacob Johannes van Veelen, age twenty-six, Amsterdam, 30 September 1891, *Enquête, gehouden door de Staatscommissie, benoemd krachtens de wet van 19 Januari 1890* [Stadsblad no. 1], *Verhooren*, 3:22). For an account of the complaints about public order made by Amsterdam inhabitants between 1865 and 1920, see Rineke van Daalen, "Nauwbehuisd en dichtbevolkt: Gemeentelijke voorzieningen en klachten uit de burgerij, Amsterdam, 1865–1920," *Sociologisch Tijdschrift* 12, no. 2 (October 1985): 274–307.

116. *De Handwerksman* 24, no. 1 (July 1914), and no. 2 (August 1914). This simple requirement was controversial among reformers who considered the separation of work and residence important. Only 5.3 percent of the members of the Handwerkers Vriendenkring worked in food, 82.9 percent were diamond workers. See S. R. de Miranda, *Gedenkschrift der Stichting "Bouwfonds Handwerkers Vriendenkring"* (Amsterdam, 1937).

117. Gulden, *De vrouw en haar huis*. Gulden, who worked for Amsterdam-Zuid and Zomers Buiten, noted in a council meeting that an English architectural journal had labeled Amsterdam the mecca of the working class (*Gemeenteblad* 2 [1922], meeting of 17 May 1922, 635).

118. "De bouwvereenigingen en de nieuwe tijd," 4. The idea of the housing societies as small villages, organizing cultural and social life through consumer cooperatives, playgrounds, vacations, savings and insurance, improvement of furniture and living standards, is expressed in a report on a lecture by C. van Doorn: J. H. v[an] S[luis], "De sociale taak der woningbouwcorporaties," *Volkshuisvesting* 2, no. 22 (August 1921): 395.

119. G. Feenstra, *Tuinsteden en volkshuisvesting in Nederland en buitenland* (Amsterdam: Van Mantgem en De Does, 1920), 37, 165.

120. De Regt, *Arbeidersgezinnen*, 188–98.

121. *Wat wil de Bond van Arbeiderswoningbouwvereenigingen in Nederland?* (Watergraafsmeer, 1919).

122. J. M. Welcker describes the irritations that arose between the largely working-class labor organizers of the NVV and the politicians of the SDAP, who were for the most part from educated, bourgeois backgrounds ("Een ongemakkelijk bondgenootschap: De Sociaal-Democratische Arbeiderspartij en het Nederlandsch Verbond van Vakvereenigingen tussen 1906 en 1913," in *Heren en arbeiders in de vroege Nederlandse arbeidersbeweging, 1870–1914* (Amsterdam: Van Gennep, 1978).

123. P. Roeland and Ch. Koster, "Keurschot-Rochdale," *Bouwkundig Weekblad* 29, no. 49 (4

December 1909): 590–91. A visitor from the municipal labor union from which Rochdale drew most of its members (Bond van Nederlandsche Gemeentewerklieden) reported on the society's first housing project once it was occupied. His article responded directly to complaints that the new dwellings were cramped, narrow, and impractical. True, he admitted, the kitchen was small, but a kitchen is not a living room (*De Gemeente-Werkman* 10, no. 10 [7 October 1911]).

CHAPTER FIVE

1. One method of promoting improved plans was publication of housing types that met reformers' criteria. At the first Dutch Public Health Convention in 1896, Dr. Menno Huizinga suggested publication of a "housing book," a compilation of small dwelling plans, and reformers in Amsterdam repeated his call after the housing act was in place (*Verslag van het eerste Nederlandsch Congres voor Openbare Gezondheidsregeling* [Amsterdam: F. van Rossen, 1896], 56). A few years later, Dr. J. W. Jenny Weijerman made the same point (*Woningtoezicht* [Haarlem: H. D. Tjeenk Willink, 1899], 65), and in 1902 P. L. Tak called for the collection of housing types designed by experts from other countries ("De Amsterdamsche Woningraad" *De Kroniek* 8, no. 371 [1 February 1902], 33–35).

2. A. van Gijn quoted in *Verslag van het tiende Nederlandsch Congres voor Openbare Gezondheidsregeling* (Amsterdam: F. van Rossen, 1905), 26.

3. One of the few original housing types cleverly placed three second-floor units above two ground-floor units, each with its own street entrance. See Leliman's Eigen Haard housing in the Indischebuurt (fig. 5.9).

4. For a contemporary analysis of the building industry, see Commissie van Onderzoek benoemd door de Gemeenteraad 30 januari 1897, *De toestand der werklieden in de bouwbedrijven te Amsterdam* (Amsterdam, 1898).

5. For sources on housing conditions and housing reform in Amsterdam from the mid nineteenth century to 1913, see above, chapter 1, note 8.

6. At the second Public Health Convention, Wollring spoke against the single-room dwelling, identifying living room, bedroom, kitchen, and attic as the minimum requirements of a dwelling (*Verslag van het tweede Nederlandsch Congres voor Openbare Gezondheidsregeling* [Amsterdam: F. Rossen, 1897], 102). The Amsterdam Labor League petitioned the municipality in 1905 to effectively prohibit the single-room dwelling.

7. Hélène Mercier, *Over arbeiderswoningen* (Haarlem: H. D. Tjeenk Willink, 1887), 118–19.

8. Of 971 houses investigated in the Jordaan by the Building and Housing Inspection Office in 1896, 64.8 percent of the inhabitants lived in one- or two-room homes, and 24.1 percent lived in a one-room dwelling with more than two occupants. The occupancy rate was highest for one-room dwellings, decreasing as dwelling size increased:

1 room	3.5 people per room
2 rooms	2.0 people per room
3 rooms	1.5 people per room
4 rooms	1.2 people per room

(figures derived from "Verslag van den Gemeentelijken Gezondheidsdienst over 1897," *Gemeente-*

everslag [1897], app. 9, table 4, 55). Subsequent investigations in the Jordaan (331 dwellings in 1898 and 335 dwellings in 1899) produced analogous results. In the Jodenbuurt in 1898, the investigators found occupancy rates of 3.9 people per one-room dwelling in the Jodenhouttuinen and 5.11 per one-room dwelling in the Valkenburgerstraat ("Verslag van de werkzaamheden van den Gemeentelijke Gezondheidsdienst over 1899," *Gemeenteverslag* [1899], app. 9, table 3, 81–83, and "Verslag van de werkzaamheden van den Gemeentelijke Gezondheidsdienst over 1900," *Gemeenteverslag* [1900], app. 9, table 3, 77–80).

9. An interesting contemporary description of a middle-class Amsterdam house is given in D. S. Meldrum, *Home Life in Holland* (New York: Macmillan, 1911), 10–47. On the evolution of the Amsterdam town house see, A. W. Weissman, *Het Amsterdamsche woonhuis van 1500–1800* (Amsterdam, 1885); H. J. Zantkuyl, *Bouwen in Amsterdam: Het woonhuis in de stad* (Amsterdam: Architectura et Natura, 1993); Rudolf Meischke, *Het Nederlandse woonhuis van 1300–1800* (Haarlem: H. D. Tjeenk Willink, 1969); C. J. A. C. Peeters, "Het negentiende-eeuwse woonhuis in Nederland," *Jaarverslag Vereniging Hendrick de Keyser* 53 (1971): 28–37; and Niels Luning Prak, *Het Nederlandse woonhuis van 1800 tot 1940* (Delft: Delftse Universitaire Pers, 1991).

10. Louise van der Pek-Went, quoted in Clara Brinkgreve, *De Bouwonderneming Jordaan: Een experiment in de volkshuisvesting aan het einde van de negentiende eeuw* (The Hague: Nederlands Instituut voor Ruimtelijk Ordening, 1985), 48.

11. *Mededeelingen van het Centraal Bureau van de Katholieke Actie*, no. 3 (December 1905).

12. The CBSA asked societies about innovations, by which it specifically meant any practical or hygiënic innovations such as "alcove ventilation, top opening windows, incinerators, separate places to sleep, furnaces, bath, collective gardens, roof gardens, dumbwaiters, drying attics." Its concern for the correct use of the dwelling is borne out in further questions about the role of the housing inspector as an influence on the family and its life style (Dirk Hudig, 24 December 1908, no. 194, CBSA archive, IISG).

13. On German and English reactions to the kitchen–living room see Nicolas Bullock and James Read, *The Movement for Housing Reform in Germany and France, 1840–1914* (Cambridge: Cambridge University Press, 1985), 151–52.

14. Health Board, 22 December 1911, 391 GC 1911, archive 5269, GAA.

15. The type was used in the two projects by HIJSM and the first three projects by Het Oosten; other societies using the type were the Amsterdamsche Vereeniging tot het Bouwen van Arbeiderswoningen, Bouwmaatschappij, Patrimonium, and in a single instance the Amsterdamsch Bouwfonds for large families. There were a total of 1,856 kitchen–living rooms, 1,148 with a second living room. The figures cited here and in the following analyses are based on a study of the dossiers in the Building and Housing Inspection Office for each of eighty-seven housing projects approved by the municipal council between 1908 and 1919.

16. Quoted in Ad Bevers, *Oost-West thuis best: Gedenkschrift bij gelegenheid van het vijftigjarig bestaan der R.K. Wbv. "Het Oosten" te Amsterdam* [1962], 28.

17. Ibid.

18. Ibid.

19. A number of societies chose the option of the living room in addition to the large kitchen–living room. The Bouwmaatschappij tot Verkrijging van Eigen Woningen used it in 42.4 percent of the dwelling units approved by the municipality by 1919, Het Oosten in 47.5

percent, Amsterdam Vereeniging tot het Bouwen van Arbeiderswoningen in 83.12 percent, and HIJSM in 97.9 percent. This option did not necessarily mean that the livingroom was put aside as parlor; it was often used as a bedroom or daily sitting room or both. But the possibility for its use as salon was there, and this lead to objections by the Health Board.

20. In 1,148 of the 1,856 kitchen–living rooms this would have been possible, that is, in 9 percent of the housing societies in this study.

21. The society was the Bouwmaatschappij tot Verkrijging van Eigen Woningen (Louise van der Pek-Went, 22 November 1918, 255 GC 1918, archive 5269, GAA).

22. The Handwerkers Vriendenkring distinguished its nonsubsidized units by including a full kitchen in them. Slightly more than half the units were subsidized.

23. Complaints were registered in the first annual report of De Arbeiderswoning. Enlargement of the pantry to include space for a gas range would allow it to be used for cooking in addition to washing and cleaning, and thus alleviate the problem (De Arbeiderswoning, *Jaarverslag* [1 October 1915 to 31 December 1916], 6). Seventy-four new houses by De Bazel for the society in Van Beuningenplein did get larger pantries. When similar plans were proposed for municipal housing in 1914, Tellegen defended them by pointing to the precedent for such rooms in a housing project in the Indischebuurt (fig. 5.2). Investigation of the latter by a subcommittee of the Health Board had resulted in a favorable report, but Tellegen had failed to mention that all the dwellings that included a kitchen–living room in that project also included another living room. The project in the Indischebuurt was by HIJSM (discussion of "Woningbouw van Gemeentewege," *Gemeenteblad* 2 [1915], meeting of 31 March 1915, 443).

24. According to reformers' standards, 35.6 percent of all sleeping arrangements were irregular. Alcoves were used for sleeping in more than half (52.3 percent) of the dwellings, attic rooms in 14.6 percent, living rooms and salons in 29 percent. The survey of the Bond van Nederlandsche Onderwijzers was published in *De Volksschool* 8, no. 8 (3 March 1909).

25. In 1903 in a class of forty-eight children, twenty-eight (58.3 percent) slept with two others or more in a bed or mattress on the floor (*De Volksschool* 2, no. 10 [27 May 1903]).

26. "De bevolking van Amsterdam," part 2, "De uitkomsten der tienjaarlijksche volkstellingen van 1830 tot 1930," *Statistische Mededelingen*, no. 100 (Amsterdam, 1934), table 39.

27. A typical example is the 1889 housing of the Bouwmaatschappij tot Verkrijging van Eigen Woningen in the Dapperbuurt.

28. J. W. Jenny Weijerman, *Overzicht van de door verschillende woningvereenigingen op aanvrage der [Arnhemsche] Tentoonstellingscommissie verstrekte statistische gegevens* (Amsterdam, 1899). The results showed housing society dwellings of the following sizes: one room, 319; one with alcove, 229; two rooms, 1,693; three rooms, 112.

29. J. W. Smit, *Gemeenteblad* 2 (1905), meeting of 23 June 1905, 942.

30. P. L. Tak, ibid., 946. Louis Heijermans also mentioned workers' liking of alcoves (*Gezondheidsleer voor arbeiders* [Rotterdam: W. L. and J. Brusse, 1905], 147). This intolerance for the bedstead was fairly recent. Van Hasselt and Verschoor had assumed the necessity of the bedstead because they accepted two conditions: the two-room dwelling and the worker's use of the rooms as living room and salon. At the same time, they wished to encourage use of both rooms for sleeping in order to encourage the separation of the sexes: "In een woning met één kamer kunnen daarom, naar onze meening, bedsteden niet worden gemist; maar ook in woningen van

twee vertrekken zal dit bezwaarlijk gaan. In de eerste plaats toch zal, waar de gelegenheid hiertoe bestaat het wenschelijk zijn, om de slaapplaatsen voor de verschillende sexen te scheiden, en moet dus de gelegenheid tot slapen zoo mogelijk in beide vertrekken bestaan; maar bovendien zal een arbeidersgezin, wanneer het over twee vertrekken kan beschikken, niet het ééne als woon- het andere als slaapkamer inrichten. Waar twee vertrekken zijn, wordt het eene steeds tot een soort pronkkamer bestemd, en nu moge dit verkeerd zijn, toch meenen wij, dat het onjuist zoude wezen, hiermede geen rekening te houden" (J. van Hasselt and L. Verschoor, *De arbeiderswoningen in Nederland: Beoordelend overzicht samengesteld door de commissie van onderzoek naar hetgeen in verschillende gemeenten des lands gedaan is ter verkrijging van verbeterde arbeiders-woningen* [Amsterdam: Maatschappij tot Nut van 't Algemeen, 1890], 144).

31. *Gemeenteblad* 2 (1905), meeting of 23 June 1905, 956. Tak noted the use of the storage space under the bed: "Een alcoof kan nog gelucht worden, maar in een bedstede kan nooit doorstrooming gemaakt worden. Men houdt daar een geur, dien het zeer lang vertoeven van een of meer menschen achterlaat, en die tenslotte in het houtwerk trekt. Die geur is niet te beschrijven, het is niet muf, het is . . . men kan er niets anders van zeggen dan dat daar hangt een speciale bedstedegeur. Dat is het effect van hat slapen van menschen in houten kasten, welke zoo spoedig mogelijk na het verlaten worden gesloten en gesloten gehouden."

32. Eleven of thirty-five housing projects included the sleeping niche before 1914, that is, 1,009 units, of which 450 also included the kitchen–living room.

33. This was a housing type applied by Het Westen, the Bouwmaatschappij, and to a lesser extent by Rochdale and Patrimonium.

34. Louise van der Pek-Went to Health Board, 22 November 1918, 255 GC 1918, archive 5269, GAA.

35. Bevers, *Oost-West*, 27.

36. Wollring in the Housing Committee meeting of 19 May 1914 objected strenuously to the use of bed niches by Het Westen and the Bouwmaatschappij (Notulen van de Commissie van bijstand in het beheer der zaken van Volkshuisvesting [1914], archive 5102, GAA).

37. See, for example, the discussion in *Gemeenteblad* 2 (1907), meeting of 23 January 1907, 131–46, and Housing Committee meeting of 25 February 1913, Notulen van de Commissie van bijstand in het beheer der zaken van Volkshuisvesting (1913), archive 5102, GAA. Builders designated areas as storage, but reformers were concerned that the space would be used for sitting or sleeping. Closets under stairs were particularly suspect. In 1920 the Communist councilor N. J. Collij complained that the Housing Authority forced a housing society to put up a partition to prevent use of the area under the stairs for sleeping (*Gemeenteblad* 2 [1920], meeting of 1 December 1920, 1814).

38. *Gemeenteblad* 1 (1905), no. 625, 16 June 1905, 8356. In response, D. Schut and J. N. Hendrix claimed that attic bedrooms are as safe as hotel rooms and thus do not require an entry hall (*Gemeenteblad* 1 [1905], no. 591, 8 June 1905, 803).

39. Eight societies answered the inquiry, but the results were inconclusive. The two societies that had built attic bedrooms (HIJSM and Algemeene) had not experienced any difficulties. Three societies (Het Westen, Bouwmaatschappij, Oud Amsterdam) were already convinced of the evils of attic bedrooms and did not construct them. Rochdale provided attic bedrooms only for the third-floor flat, rejecting a larger number specifically to avoid undesirable relations. Only

the Handwerkers Vriendenkring had applied a solution favored by the Health Board: attic bedrooms accessible from the third-floor flat via an internal stairway. Both the Handwerkers Vriendenkring and the Algemeene noted that areas designated as attic storage for each flat were likely to be arranged as bedrooms as soon as the family needed more room. Hence it was preferable to design attic spaces that would provide adequate light and air for eventual bedrooms. The Algemeene's architect, J. C. van Epen, pointed out that he did not know if the attic rooms had led to undesirable relationships between male and female members of different families, but even in the absence of such bedrooms, there was still no way to avoid the occurrence of such relations.

40. "Verslag van de Subcommissie voor de zaken betreffende Volkshuisvesting," February 1916, 1012 VH 1916, archive 5187, GAA. The Health Board immediately objected to further plans by the Algemeene to build attic bedrooms and asked it to replace the three attic rooms reached by the main stairs with a storage area and rooms with private stair connection. The Algemeene agreed to the experiment in some of its units, although it objected to the idea of placing the largest family on the third floor. Since the plans for the project called for collective stairs for six families, there was particular pressure for the Health Board to remedy the lack of privacy that could result from attic bedrooms for six different families (Health Board, 14 April 1915, 87 GC 1911; 12 June 1915, 150 GC 1915, archive 5269, GAA).

41. Arie Keppler in Housing Committee meeting of 28 July 1916, Notulen van de Commissie van bijstand in het beheer der zaken van Volkshuisvesting (1916), archive 5102, GAA, 76–79. In 1917 Keppler noted: "Many societies appeared to be of the opinion that the necessity of using a communal stair was a great drawback, and that a separate connection offered such great advantages that one simply had to bear the increased costs" (meeting of 17 April 1917, Notulen van de Commissie van bijstand in het beheer der zaken van Volkshuisvesting [1917], archive 5102, GAA, 29–30).

42. Objections from the fire department put an end to the practice a few years later.

43. David Harvey discusses at length the consequences of Enlightenment rationalism applied to space in *The Condition of Postmodernity: An Enquiry into the Origins of Cultural Change* (Oxford: Basil Blackwell, 1989), 252.

44. Letter of 15 January 1884 in response to Van Marken's plans for Agneta-park, published in J. C. van Marken, "Nog eens de woningplannen," *De Fabrieksbode*, 19 January 1884; reprinted in J. C. van Marken, *Uit het fabriekleven, 1869–1905: Hoofdartikelen uit de Fabrieksboden* (Delft: Van Marken, 1906), 1: 268–69. Van Marken answered, having calculated the weekly cost of adding the salon at f19.00 per year, that this "sacrifice for an object of luxury" was too large.

45. J. Mol, *Gedenkboek uitgegeven ter gelegenheid van het 50-jarig bestaan van de Vereeniging "Bouwmaatschappij tot Verkrijging van Eigen Woningen"* (Amsterdam, 1918). On the Bouwmaatschappij, see Mercier, *Over arbeiderswoningen*, 154. The society was established in 1868 to build low-rise housing for workers' families at a low rent that would contribute to eventual ownership. When this goal appeared unfeasible, the standards quickly shifted to rental housing for two families. The society was founded by workers, including Klaas Ris, a well-known member of the socialist movement, but its board of overseers was composed of such liberals as H. S. van Lennep, Gijsbert van Tienhoven, G. M. den Tex, Jan Kruseman, H. C. A. Henny, J. H. van Eeghen (*Volkshuisvesting* 1, no. 19 (12 June 1920): 272–74.

46. This type was also used by the Amsterdamsche Vereeniging and Het Oosten.

47. Twenty-four percent, or 212 units of 868 units.

48. The proposed locations were in the Indischebuurt, Amsterdam South, and Nieuwendammerham north of the IJ. "Sleeping in a living room continually raises dust and during a number of hours of the day it creates a disorderly appearance because of the stripped linens" (Health Board to Arie Keppler, 20 December 1918, 270 GC 1919, in 217 VH 1919, archive 5187, GAA). Cooking and washing in a room used for sitting were also criticized, and the committee suggested that with a direct connection between kitchen and living room, mothers could keep an eye on their children, thus eliminating the usual argument in favor of the kitchen–living room. Architect J. B. van Loghem pointed out that a direct connection between living room and kitchen was not considered stylish ("Algemeene wenken aan woningbouwvereenigingen," *Woningbouw* 2, no. 4 [October 1918]: 5–6). According to the Health Board, a subcommittee that interviewed two women living in the contested housing type expressed a preference for a living room without sleeping niche and for a small kitchen instead of the kitchen–living room (Health Board to Arie Keppler, 20 December 1918, 270 GC 1919, in 217 VH 1919, archive 5187, GAA). Wentink, state housing inspector, also objected to the continuation of the small version with sleeping niche as almost obsolete: "If this idea does not receive constant attention, I am afraid that the expansion of Amsterdam in the long run will begin to look like a patchwork and we will continue to huddle in barracks which, by their very nature, will set back the improvement of housing one hundred years" (23 October 1918, no. 663, 241 GC 1918, archive 5269, GAA).

49. Bouwmaatschappij tot Verkrijging van Eigen Woningen to Jan Kruseman, 20 November 1918, 241 GC 1918, archive 5187, GAA. This small type was not the cheapest unit; it rented for f3.70, while another unit with living room and two bedrooms rented for f3.60.

50. Housing Committee meeting of 18 March 1919, Notulen van de Commissie van bijstand in het beheer der zaken van Volkshuisvesting (1919), archive 5102, GAA. The Housing Committee decided to permit the society to complete an existing block with this plan, but new projects had to eliminate both the disputed kitchen–living room and the sleeping niche.

51. Comparison of housing society dwellings:

	1909–14	1915–18	1919	TOTAL
4 rms or fewer (1 or 2 br)	48.9%	40.3%	34.6%	41.3%
5 rms or fewer (3 or more br)	51.1%	59.7%	65.4%	58.7%

From 1911, the state housing inspector J. M. A. Zoetmulder began to insist that more units include three bedrooms. In 1919 this became state policy (H. C. A. Henny to F. M. Wibaut, 28 February 1911, no. 22, Wibaut archive, IISG).

52. One hundred of those cited proximity to work and familiarity as their reasons for wishing to stay. The replacement housing was that of the Handwerkers Vriendenkring in the Transvaalbuurt (H. de Vries, "Op Onderzoek op Uilenburg," part 2, *De Handwerksman* 22, no. 8 (December 1912).

53. *De Gemeente-Werkman* 10, no. 10 (7 October 1911).

54. The societies that chose the option of the living room in addition to the large kitchen–living room were the Bouwmaatschappij tot Verkrijging van Eigen Woningen, Het Oosten, Amsterdam Vereeniging tot het Bouwen van Arbeiderswoningen, and HIJSM.

55. Twenty-four percent of their units supplied specifically designated parlors; 42 percent included parlors if convertible living rooms and bedrooms are included. Other societies that included parlors in around 10 percent of their units were HIJSM (10.6%), Dr. Schaepman (11.5%), the Algemeene (12.6%), and Bouwmaatschappij (12.8%). Eigen Haard and the Algemeene had plans that allowed bedrooms to be used as parlor, and several societies built a second living room in addition to a large kitchen–living room.

56. The correlations between rent and the percentage of units with possible parlors were prewar .50, wartime 0.15, postwar 0.02. The projects that provided parlor space fit into two categories. Those with a designated parlor in a significant percentage of units were, with two exceptions, above average in rent. Those with below average rent and parlor space usually followed the pattern of living–room kitchen and separate living room.

57. True parlors were included in only 8.5 percent of the housing society units approved by 1919, but if the variations are also included in the count, slightly over one quarter of the units (26.2%) permitted the user to create a salon. During the war, there was a steep decline in the percentage of housing society dwellings with true parlors or rooms that could be used as parlors:

	1909–14	1915–18	1919
Units with potential parlors	34.7%	12.4%	26.4%
Units with parlors	11.4%	1.2%	10.3%

58. On the influence of Ebenezer Howard in the Netherlands in general and Amsterdam in particular, see Frank Smit et al., *De Droom van Howard: Het verleden en de toekomst van de tuindorpen* (Amsterdam: Gemeentelijk Woningbedrijf Amsterdam, 1991).

59. The block belonged to the Vereeniging ten Behoeve der Arbeiderklasse (housing inspector letter, 12 February 1896, no. 49, archive 297, GAA).

60. Mercier, *Over arbeiderswoningen.* See discussion in the Public Works Committee meeting of 14 December 1911 (Notulen van de Commissie van bijstand in zake Publieke Werken [1911], archive 5087, GAA, 333), where apartment houses are also disparaged by the middle and upper classes. Van Hasselt and Verschoor claim that "de wensch om heer en meester in zijn eigen woning te zijn, is aan ons volkskarakter in die mate eigen dat de inrichting van woningen, waarbij elke bewoner geheel onafhankelijk is van zijn buurman, zeker moet worden verkozen boven elke andere" (*De arbeiderswoningen,* 153).

61. George A. M. Kallenbach, *Over de pogingen door particulieren in het werk gesteld tot verbetering der arbeiderswoningen* (Leiden: A. H. Adriani, 1892), 12.

62. Ibid., 14–16. Kallenbach's arguments are borrowed from Dr. E. Sax, *Die Wohnungszustande der arbeitenden Classen und ihr Reform* (1896).

63. The municipal social worker, Van de Wijk-Groot, recorded the difficulty of getting housewives to comply regularly with this cleanup (A. v[an] d[e] Wijk-Groot, "Verslag over de arbeiderswoningen: Blok AW I and AW V," June–December 1919, 5730 VH 1919, archive 5187, GAA).

64. Hélène Mercier, "De volkshuisvesting te Amsterdam," *De Gids* 69, part 1 (1905): 119. The society was the Bouwmaatschappij tot Verkrijging van Eigen Woningen. Mercier attrib-

uted the decision against the double-loaded stairway to the expression of the workers' disdain for the barracks since the Bouwmaatschappij was the only worker-run society at the time.

65. Dr. Nederbracht, "Praeadvies," quoted in *Volkshuisvesting* 3, no. 11 (1 March 1922): 188. The *portiek* was an entry porch reached by stair from the street that usually gave direct access to two dwellings on the second floor, and further access to a stair leading to flats on upper floors. It was particularly prevalent in the Hague, but it was also used extensively by the confessional housing societies in Amsterdam.

66. The prohibition against a greater number of families gaining access from the same door originated from the need to control quarantines.

67. Of all projects with three or four floors, 70.7 percent included separate first-floor entries. Van Epen did some with street entry to all four families for ACOB and the Algemeene. Separate first-floor entries remained common, but double stairs increased in usage. Twenty-two of the fifty-eight projects with three and four stories (37.8%) included the double stair, in eight of thirty projects for 1909–14, in seven of fourteen projects for 1915–18, and in seven of fourteen projects in 1919; that is, half of the projects over two stories used double stairs.

68. "The system of housing in which a great number of families reach their homes through the same street door and along the same stairway does not appear to be satisfactory" (discussion of Van Beuningenplein housing, *Woningdienst Verslag* [1918], 57).

69. Workers themselves objected to the multifamily entry; see, for example, *Volkshuisvesting* 1, no. 14 (24 March 1920), and no. 17 (14 April 1920); Eigen Haard, *Jaarverslag* (1925). Eigen Haard wrote that workers wanted "good houses, not six families living off one stairway." State housing inspector Wentink also objected when the Algemeene proposed a plan in which eight families shared an entry. These stairs were wide, well lit, and bore no resemblance to either the steep slum stairs of the past or nineteenth-century philanthropic *kazernes*, but they remained unpopular and presented special problems of maintenance since two families per floor were responsible for cleaning.

70. "Het verdient aanbeveling te bevorderen, dat elke huisvader in het bezit gerake van een eigen woning" ("Patrimoniums woningstichting," *Patrimonium's Bode* 4, no. 5 [1 November 1912]).

71. The model was applied in three projects of De Arbeiderswoning, three of Bouwmaatschappij, two of the Algemeene, two of Rochdale, two of Eigen Haard, one each of Amsterdamsch Bouwfonds, De Dageraad, Amsteldijk, and Amsterdam-Zuid.

72. Although this system secured individual entries, it also introduced deeply recessed stairs open to the public way, which drew objections from the police, Keppler, and the Health Board (Public Works Committee meeting of 23 August 1916, Notulen van de Commissie van bijstand in zake Publieke Werken [1916], archive 5087, GAA, 68). Objections were to the deep open stairs at HIJSM's Oostzaanstraat project. A later report by the Housing Authority on *portiek* housing disapproved of projects by Patrimonium and Amsterdam-Zuid (Arie Keppler to mayor, 4 February 1919, 860 WD 1919, in 378 VH 1919, archive 5187, GAA). Plans with *portieks* by Gulden and Geldmaker for Rochdale and Amsterdam-Zuid were rejected by the Housing Committee at its meeting of 3 March 1919 (mayor to Keppler, 5 March 1919, 378 VH 1919, archive 5187, GAA). The *portiek* was accordingly rejected as an option when Rochdale and

Amsterdam-Zuid proposed them in 1918 for projects in Amsterdam South, but other alternatives were found.

73. Two projects by Patrimonium in Amsterdam South introduced three street doors for each set of four dwellings, so that both ground- and second-floor flats had their own street door, and only those living on the third and fourth floor had to share door and stairs. Dr. Schaepman also used a variation of this system in Amsterdam South. In a project by Het Oosten, the deeply recessed stairs of the *portiek* were replaced by external stairs leading to a second floor landing from which four doors opened, two directly to each of the two second-floor apartments, two to stairs leading to third- and fourth-floor flats.

74. Carel Schade, *Woningbouw voor arbeiders in het negentiende-eeuwse Amsterdam* (Amsterdam: Van Gennep, 1981), 70–71 and passim.

75. Health Board housing subcommittee, 23 January 1915, 22 GC 1915, archive 5269, GAA.

76. Mathilde Wibaut-Berdenis van Berlekom, "De vrouw en het gezin," *De Socialistische Gids* 3 (November 1918): 808–29. Her husband, the alderman of housing in Amsterdam, was also interested in the one-kitchen or central-kitchen house (Housing Committee meeting of 17 February 1914, Notulen van de Commissie van bijstand in het beheer der zaken van Volkshuisvesting [1914], archive 5102, GAA).

77. The most successful example of the application of cooperative principles to housing occurred not in workers' housing but in the middle-class housing complexes of the Amsterdamsche Coöperatieve Woningvereniging "Samenwerking," established in 1908. This society, which did not qualify for the government support offered to low-cost housing, was organized to improve the quality of housing for the middle class in Amsterdam and built units rented at over f400 per year. Born of the cooperative movement, its blocks came to include four consumer cooperatives (Centrale Coöperatie voor Woninginrichting, Centrale Coöperatie voor Aardappelen en Groenten, Centrale Coöperatie voor Zuivel, Amsterdamsche Coöperatieraad voor Brandstof en Aardappelen). In 1912, the society met with the Amsterdamsche Coöperatieve Keuken to discuss the idea of housing for singles and young families that would include a central kitchen. Discussion of a one-kitchen house continued through 1916, and the society eventually built the experimental Het Nieuwe Huis in the 1920s. Its first complexes were designed by the architect M. J. E. Lippits, but the largest and most impressive complex, constituting an entire neighborhood in Amsterdam South, was designed by J. C. van Epen. Here were also to be found cooperative stores for dairy products and groceries, household goods and furniture. By 1925, the society had built 774 dwellings, 10 stores, and 4 studios. A number of Amsterdam's housing reformers were closely associated with Samenwerking, including Tellegen. The National Housing Council was housed in Het Nieuwe Huis (*Twintigjarig overzicht 1908–1928 Amsterdamsche Coöperatieve Woningvereniging "Samenwerking"* [Amsterdam, 1929]; Samenwerking, *Jaarverslagen*).

78. At the second Public Health Convention in 1897, H. H. Wollring had called for municipal laundries. The municipal council approved municipal bath houses in 1908 (*Gemeenteblad* 1 [1908], no. 844, 24 July 1908, 719–21; discussion in *Gemeenteblad* 2 [1908], meeting of, 30 September 1908, 796).

79. Amsterdam-Zuid, *Jaarverslag* (1915), 3.

80. Zomers Buiten, *Jaarverslag* (1917).

81. Rochdale and the Algemeene had most (five and six of nine projects respectively). Enthusiasm for collective facilities appears to have been most widespread among the progressive segments of the middle class, rather than among workers, socialist or otherwise; see note 76 above.

82. Algemeene Woningbouw Vereeniging, *Jaarverslag* (1915), 12.

83. See Van de Wijk–Groot, "Verslag over de arbeiderswoningen." The nature of working-class reactions to the municipal laundries has been the subject of controversy. See Ali de Regt, "De vorming van een opvoedingstraditie: Arbeiderskinderen rond 1900," *Amsterdams Sociologisch Tijdschrift* 5, no. 1 (June 1978): 37–61; Ulla Janz., "Gemeentelijk koken en wassen in Amsterdam, 1915–1939," *Amsterdams Sociologisch Tijdschrift* 7, no. 4 (March 1981): 501–32.

84. Mercier wondered in 1887 if the age-old Dutch custom of washing underclothes and linens in the bedroom/living room would change even if a laundry were built nearby (*Over arbeiderswoningen*, 213). The socialist perspective of the Federation of Social Democratic Women's Clubs is presented in *De wasch uit de woning* (Amsterdam, n.d.); *Een wasscherij van de Gemeente* (Amsterdam, 1917); and S. R. de Miranda, *De vrouw, de woning, en de waschtobbe* (Amsterdam, 1924).

85. H[enri] P[olak], "Wonen," *Weekblad ANDB* 11, no. 45 (10 November 1905).

86. He gave up altogether when only four more letters came in ("Coöperatieve Woningbouw," *Weekblad ANDB* 12, no. 4 [26 January 1906], and no. 5 [2 February 1906]). There were two sorts of reactions toward cooperatives: a petit bourgeois desire for individualism and a far left anarchist reaction against bourgeois cooperation. During the organization of the housing society Rochdale, some municipal workers viewed the cooperative as taking energy from the real revolutionary struggle (*De Gemeente-Werkman* [1902–3], passim).

87. See, for example, G. E. V. L. Zuylen, *De volkshuisvesting: Voordracht gehouden voor de Haagsche afdeeling der Maatschappij tot Bevordering der Bouwkunst* (The Hague: Mouton, 1908), 7: "Het is immers onbetwijfelbaar dat eene kleine afzonderlijke woning voor ieder familie, liefst met tuintje of bleekveld er bij, het ideaal is."

88. Bourneville was their example (Zomers Buiten, *Jaarverslag* [1917]). The society established a housing society, Tuindorp, in 1916, which finally carried out plans in Nieuwer Amstel and Buiksloterham in 1924. See *Tuindorp: Maandblad van de woningbouwvereniging Tuindorp.*

89. They planned to build in Sloten, assisted by architect Willem Noorlander, but the plan fell through and the society built 218 small houses in Buiksloterham between 1919 and 1923 (*Ons Belang* 40, no. 1 [1965]).

90. H Lucassen, *Vijftig jaar Woningbouwvereeniging 'Amsterdam Zuid,' 1911–1961* (Amsterdam, 1961), meeting 1 January 1911.

91. Algemeene Woningbouw Vereeniging to ANDB, March 1910, no. 3078/22, IV, ANDB archive, IISG.

92. Dirk Hudig to W. J. Bossenbroek, 17 September 1910, RA 861, no. 302, CBSA archive, IISG.

93. Dirk Hudig and H. C. A. Henny, *Handleiding voor woningbouwverenigingen* (Zwolle, 1911), 12.

94. Henri Polak at a meeting of the Union of Dutch Teachers, 12 January 1906, reported in *De Volksschool* 5, no. 3 (7 February 1906). For contemporary views on the garden city, see Jan Bruinwold Riedel, *Tuinsteden* (Utrecht: Van Boekhoven, 1906); G. Feenstra, *Tuinsteden en volks-*

huisvesting in Nederland en buitenland (Amsterdam: Van Mantgem en De Does, 1920); S. J. Fockema Andreae, "The Garden City Idea in the Netherlands before 1930," *Stedebouw en Volkshuisvesting* 44 (1963): 95–107.

95. In the Public Works Committee, Charles Boissevain supported the idea of garden suburb development in the belief that such housing types produced happy and contented workers (meeting of 12 October 1905, Notulen van de Commissie van bijstand in zake Publieke Werken [1905], archive 5087, GAA, 126).

96. On Keppler's efforts to apply the garden city ideal to Amsterdam. See Frank Smit, "Van tuinstedebouw tot stedelijk uitwaaiering," *Wonen TA/BK*, no. 13 (1975): 5–17; Frank Smit, "Pleidooi voor een naïef realistische stedebouw," *Wonen TA/BK*, no. 13 (1976): 5–20; Wil Swart, *Van sinaasappelkistje tot kangoeroe-woning: Het Amsterdam-Noord van Arie Keppler* (Amsterdam: Wijkopbouworgaan Midden–Noord Amsterdam, 1992). The first prize plan in the STVDIA competition for a garden town was incorporated into Berlage's 1915 plan for Amsterdam South, but never executed.

97. Only 14 percent of the dwelling units approved between 1909 and 1914 were two stories, in contrast to more than a third (35.4%) of those approved in 1919.

98. For Eigen Haard six of its nine projects, for Algemeene six of its nine projects.

99. The *hof* concept was published in the 1910 planning competition for Gross-Berlin, but the more immediate influence was several projects in Arnhem. The application of the *hof* in Amsterdam is discussed further in chapter 8.

100. See Francis F. Fraenkel, *Het plan Amsterdam-Zuid van H. P. Berlage* (Alphen aan den Rijn: Caneletto, 1976).

101. A vivid description of Betondorp appears in Frits de Jong Edz., *Herinneringen van een rode jongen* (Amsterdam: Stichting beheer IISG, 1989).

102. The number dropped from 68.6 percent of the projects approved before the war to 20 percent of the projects approved in 1919 (1909–14: 24 projects, 68.6%; 1915–18: 12 projects, 57.1%; 1919: 4 projects, 20%).

103. Distribution of stories in housing society projects:

NO. OF DWELLINGS

Stories	1909–14	1915–18	1919	TOTAL
2	665	1110	1728	3505
3	261	6	1831	2098
4	3823	1880	1316	7019
TOTAL	4750	2996	4875	12620

PERCENTAGE OF DWELLINGS

Stories	1909–14	1915–18	1919	TOTAL
2	14.0	37.0	35.4	27.8
3	5.5	0.2	37.6	16.6
4	80.5	62.8	27.0	55.6

104. Housing societies that built almost exclusively designs that did not permit a parlor were Amsterdam-Zuid, Amsteldijk, Ons Belang, Handwerkers Vriendenkring, Rochdale, De Arbeiderswoning, Het Westen, De Dageraad, and the Protestantsche.

105. One postwar exception was the Bouwmaatschappij tot Verkrijging van Eigen Woningen, which was permitted after some discussion to complete a block previously begun in the Indischebuurt that included plans with both kitchen–living room and sleeping niche.

106. Between 1909 and 1919, the average number of rooms per dwelling increased, from 3.59 before the war, to 3.89 during the war, to 3.94 in 1919.

107. Arie Keppler to the alderman of housing, 13 November 1917, 4067 VH 1917, archive 5187, GAA.

108. Memo from the director of the Housing Authority, n.d., 2729 VH 1920, archive 5187, GAA. Housing society construction cost 33 percent more than private construction in 1913, 53 percent more in 1919.

109. These comparisons between private builders and housing societies were based on the study of some fifteen projects around 1913 and 1919. A comparison of the plans indicates the higher quality of the housing society designs (Health Board report, 20 December 1920, 7714 VH 1920, archive 5187, GAA). This issue was taken up in the newspapers and journals; see, for example, a rebuttal to H. van der Kaa by Z. D. J. W. Gulden, "Het particulier initiatief en de woningvoorziening," *Volkshuisvesting* 1, no. 19 (12 June 1920): 271–72.

110. Circulars of *Staatscourant*, 25 June 1919, 30 July 1920, 12/13 November 1920, 1 June 1921, 28 December 1921; subsidies approved by Koninklijkbesluit no. 29 of 8 November 1920 (*Staatscourant*, no. 238 [7 December 1920]).

111. Circular of 30 July 1920. Later circulars similarly suggested limitations to current Amsterdam practice. These norms were attacked by architects for suggesting standards that the city had already surpassed. See the response of the Club van Amsterdamsche Woningbouw-Architecten to the minister of labor, defending Amsterdam housing standards and particularly its aesthetic achievements against the minister's call for sobriety and functionality in design (*Bouwkundig Weekblad* 42, no. 2 [8 January 1921]. In particular, the ministerial circular of 1 November 1922 set the policy against five-room dwellings, which would allow creation of a second living room, a policy explicitly directed against the parlor in low-income housing.

112. Dirk Hudig, "De bouwvereenigingen en de nieuwe tijd," *Woningbouw* 3, no. 1/2 (March 1919): 4.

113. Jan van der Waerden, "Maatregelen waardoor de bouw in massa bevorderd wordt: Normalisatie in de uitvoering, in het bizonder wat betreft de te verwerken onderdeelen," in *Praeadviezen voor het Woningcongres, 11 en 12 februari 1918*, by M. J. A. Moltzer et al. (Amsterdam, 1918), 67–96. The immediate reaction to his lecture can be found in Nationale Woningraad, *Stenografisch verslag van het Woningcongres op 11 en 12 februari 1918* (Amsterdam, 1918), 107–62. Gwendolyn Wright discusses the conflicting responses to standardization of suburban house plans in the United States during the same period in *Moralism and the Model Home: Domestic Architecture and Cultural Conflict in Chicago, 1873–1913* (Chicago: University of Chicago Press, 1980), 246–53.

114. *Album bevattende een 50-tal woningtypen voor met Rijksvoorschot te bouwen woningen* (The Hague: Departement van Arbeid, 1921). The Dutch Housing Institute sent an address to the

minister of labor in protest of the album (*Volkshuisvesting* 2, no. 15 [21 April 1921]) after organizing a meeting to discuss the book (26 February 1921); a similar meeting was held by the BNA (*Bouwkunding Weekblad* 42, no. 7 [12 February 1921]: 45–49). The architects responded by publishing an album of recent examples of housing design: H. P. Berlage et al., *Arbeiderswoningen in Nederland* (Rotterdam: W. L. and J. Brusse, 1921).

CHAPTER SIX

1. The debate that gave rise to Thorbecke's famous statements on art is placed in historic context in Warna Oosterbaan Martinius, *Schoonheid, welzijn, kwaliteit, kunstbeleid en verantwoording na 1945* (The Hague: Gary Schwartz/SDU, 1990), 85–87. The best introduction to the relation of government to the arts in the Netherlands for the period before the Second World War is the 1939 study by Emanuel Boekman, Social Democratic alderman of the arts in Amsterdam, *Overheid en kunst in Nederland* (Amsterdam: Menno Hertzberger, 1939).

2. Daniel Josephus Jitta, *Gemeenteblad* 2 (1890), meeting of 27 February 1890, 77.

3. P. J. H. Cuypers, *Gemeenteblad* 2 (1891), meeting of 25 November 1891, 143.

4. The socialist council member Z. D. J. W. Gulden expressed this position in terms acceptable to even a diehard liberal: "The beauty of the city belongs to every inhabitant and pedestrian, and in order to protect it, the rights of the building owners must be slightly limited" (Public Works Committee meeting of 10 October 1918, Notulen van de Commissie van bijstand in zake Publieke Werken [1918], archive 5087, GAA, 295).

5. Amsterdam, following other European cities, participated in the movement for public art. Charles Buls of Brussels played a leading role in the movement, for example, through his book *L'Esthétique des villes* (Brussels: Bruylant-Christophe and Cie., 1898), and through the first International Congress on Public Art (Brussels, 1898).

6. [P. L.] T[ak], "Een gemeente-architect," *De Kroniek* 8, no. 396 (26 July 1902): 243.

7. J. E. van der Pek, the articulate follower of H. P. Berlage, accused Weissman of lacking any sense of composition, contour, lines, colors, details, or truth ("Het Gemeente-Museum te Amsterdam," *De Kroniek* 1, no. 41 [6 October 1895]: 322–24). He was answered by Weissman in *De Opmerker* of 12 October 1895 and responded in *De Kroniek* on 20 October. Weissman had been fired from his position as city architect in June 1894 after using an artificial sandstone on the museum against orders from the mayor and aldermen, although in fact discussion about his departure had predated that event. The history of the commission is given in Joost Braat, "De bouw van het Stedelijk Museum, 1892–1895," in *Amsterdam: Het beschouwen waard*, ed. Jan M. Baart et al. (Amsterdam: Stadsuitgeverij; Gemeentelijk Bureau Monumentenzorg, 1993).

8. Address to the Amsterdam City Council, *Bouwkundig Weekblad* 15, no. 4 (26 January 1895), 267.

9. Address to the Amsterdam City Council by Architectura et Amicitia, *Bouwkundig Weekblad* 22, no. 39 (27 September 1902): 247, and by the Society for the Advancement of Architecture, *Bouwkundig Weekblad* 22, no. 39 (27 September 1902), 248. See also Gerrit van Arkel's response (*Gemeenteblad* 1 [1902], no. 664, 24 June 1902, 839–40) to the mayor and aldermen's proposal (*Gemeenteblad* 1 [1902], no. 595, 7 June 1902, 775–79). Van Arkel raised the issue of the need for

a municipal architect in budget discussions of 1900 and 1901. In 1902 he proposed an aesthetic adviser (*Gemeenteblad* 1 [1902], no. 1018, 7 October 1902, 2023; discussion, *Gemeenteblad* 2 [1902], meeting of 22 October 1902, 1467).

10. *Gemeenteblad* 1 [1902], no. 902, 5 September 1902, 1899–1900.

11. Max Eisler compared Berlage to Hendrik de Keyser in *De Bouwmeester H. P. Berlage* (Vienna: Hoelzel, 1921), 17. On the history of the Beurs commission, see Guido Hougewoud, "De Amsterdamse Beursprijsvraag," *Nederlands Kunsthistorisch Jaarboek* 25 (1974): 277–365, and A. W. Reinink, *Amsterdam en de Beurs van Berlage: Reacties van tijdgenoten* (The Hague: Staatsuitgeverij, 1975). Berlage's commission for the Exchange Building was due to the efforts of M. W. F. Treub. Berlage's relationship to the city of Amsterdam is the subject of Manfred Bock et al., *H. P. Berlage en Amsterdam* (Amsterdam: Meulenhoff/Landshoff, 1987).

12. The municipal council, having preferred the practical efficacy of the Kalff plan to the extravagant Haussmanian proposals of Van Niftrik, reversed its unimaginative orientation with the rejection of Lambrechtsen's plan. During a first round in 1899, the plan was defeated by the council solely on the basis of political disagreement about the proposed system of expropriation. By 1900, agreement had been reached on the expropriation issue, but the resubmitted design still met with criticism from council members, this time on aesthetic grounds (Notulen besloten vergaderingen Gemeenteraad [1899–1900], meeting of 8 March 1900, archive 5079/282, 451–69; Public Works Committee meeting of 9 March 1900, Notulen van de Commissie van bijstand in zake Publieke Werken [1900], archive 5087, GAA, 20–21).

13. Health Board report, 29 April 1903, 166 GC 1903, archive 5269, GAA; *Gemeenteblad* 1 (1903), no. 544, 29 May 1903, 453. The plan was originally submitted in 1881 by the developers N. V. Bouwmaatschappij "Ringvaart" and "Over-Amstel" for a district subsequently annexed by Amsterdam and was resubmitted for approval by Amsterdam in 1903.

14. *Gemeenteblad* 2 (1903), meeting of 17 June 1903, 667.

15. D. P. D. Fabius, ibid., 669.

16. *Gemeenteblad* 1 (1903), no. 1060, 4 December 1903, 2123, approved 23 December 1903. The plans were ready by 23 July 1903.

17. In 1908, the F. M. Wibaut denounced proposals to carry out a plan dating from 1897 for part of the Indische district. The dominating feature of the plan was a series of slightly bowed streets, crossed at an acute angle by the main street. Wibaut objected to the dreary views that the long curving streets would produce, and noted that the council's ideas about urban design had progressed since the plan had first been proposed twelve years before. The northwest quadrant of the Indische district, which stretches from the railroad along the Zeeburgerdijk to the Nieuwe Diep, had already been laid out as a workers' district according to the 1897 plan (*Gemeenteblad* 1 [1897], no. 200, 24 March 1897, 137), but the southern half was revoked by council decision (*Gemeenteblad* 1 [1900], no. 114, 21 February 1900, 1555; Raadsbesluit no. 892, 2 October 1901). The northeast quadrant was probably designed by Berlage (*Gemeenteblad* 1 [1902], no. 1183, 21 November 1902, 2227). Wibaut's proposal to change the plan was rejected because it was out of turn (*Gemeenteblad* 1 [1908], no. 923, 9); the plan had already been accepted by the council and only its execution was being decided.

18. *Gemeenteblad* 1 (1885), no. 233, 11 May 1885, 228–39, approved 27 May 1885 for N. V. Hollandsche Hypotheekbank.

19. The city wished to clean up the neighboring caravan settlement in the Notweg (*Gemeenteblad* 1 [1912], no. 1434, 31 December 1912, 3279).

20. *Gemeenteblad* 2 (1903), no. 577, 17 June 1903, 670.

21. *Gemeenteblad* 2 (1913), 29 January 1913, 95–100. Wibaut compared the ugly oblique corners to those he had complained of in the Indische district. He also complained about the anticipated high density construction and claimed "Op het gebied van uitbreidingsplannen zijn we op het punt de Chinezen van Europa te worden." The plan was approved 22 to 14. For J. H. W. Leliman's objections, see "Amsterdam: Het uitbreidingsplan Spaarndammerbuurt en de volkshuisvesting," *Bouwwereld* 13, no. 12 (19 March 1913): 69–72.

22. The plan was drawn by the architect J. T. J. Cuypers (25 November 1912, 450 GC 1912, in 8794 PW 1912, archive 5180, GAA). After meeting with the chair of the Health Board, the mayor and aldermen overruled the board's objections (mayor and aldermen to Health Board, 14 December 1912, 8794 PW 1912, archive 5180, GAA). There is also a lost plan for this area by J. E. van der Pek: a plan for the Overbraken Binnenpolder in connection with plans by the Amsterdam Housing Council for a housing society. The plans never came to pass, but Van der Pek's drawing was sent to the director of public works in February 1911 (H. C. A. Henny to mayor and aldermen, February 1911, 1359 PW 1911, archive 5180, GAA).

23. Van der Mey's involvement in the Spaarndammer plan was strictly advisory, although he was accused by Keppler, among others, of gross incompetence in its design. Keppler wrote an open letter to Van der Mey (published in *Bouwkundig Weekblad* 33, no. 7 [15 February 1913]: 83), and Van der Mey responded in self-defense (*Bouwkundig Weekblad* 33, no. 9 [1 March 1913]: 108). Jan Gratama accused Public Works of hiding its own incompetence behind Van der Mey's name in "Kroniek III," *Bouwkundig Weekblad* 33, no. 10 (8 March 1913): 109–11. In the municipal council discussions of the 1914 budget in October 1913, Delprat admitted that others had designed the plan and Van der Mey only looked at it (*Gemeenteblad* 2 [1913], meeting of 29 October 1913, 1821). Van der Mey had in fact designed an alternative plan, rejected by Public Works because it reduced the amount of exploitable land. He had exerted little influence on the Public Works design, which displayed the chamfered corners and underlying grid typical of the department.

24. W. J. de Groot, "De aesthetische aansprakelijkheid voor de bouwwerken door den dienst der Publieke Werken Amsterdam in de laatste jaren uitgevoerd," *Bouwkundig Weekblad* 40, no. 25 (21 June 1919): 151–52. Van der Mey worked for Public Works until 1 May 1919, but most work after 1 May 1915 was by the architects under A. R. Hulshoff, with the exception of the bridges by Piet Kramer. On Van der Mey's career, see Helen Boterenbrood and Jurgen Prang, *Van der Mey en het Scheepvaarthuis* (The Hague: Staatsuitgeverij, 1989).

25. C. B. Posthumus Meyjes at Public Works Committee meeting of 29 December 1910, Notulen van de Commissie van bijstand in zake Publieke Werken (1910), archive 5087, GAA, 391–94.

26. Plan for Indischebuurt, 29 February 1912, 1504 PW 1912, archive 5180, GAA. The developers were N. V. Bouwmaatschappij "Insulinde," Maatschappij voor Grondbezit en Grondcrediet, and Maatschappij "Amsterdam" te Exploitatie van Bouwterrein.

27. The Health Board did like a revised plan by Van Niftrik, but wished the area to be designated for two- and three-story buildings (Health Board to director of public works, 23 May

1913, 164 GC 1913, in 4278 PW 1913, archive 5180, GAA). This proposal was rejected by A. W. Bos, the director of public works (Bos to alderman of public works, 3 June 1913, Dienst PW 6226 doss. 265, in 4278 PW 1913, archive 5180, GAA).

28. Wibaut suggested a competition for the plan, saying that if there could be a competition for the Dam, why not for a workers' area (*Gemeenteblad* 2 [1912], meeting of 17 April 1912, 529–30). Alderman Delprat defensively suggested that Berlage design the plan so as to avoid the accusation from the council that Public Works did not consult an expert. The Building and Housing Inspection Office sent its plan to Bos without result. The planning of the Indische district is also discussed in Boterenbrood and Prang, *Van der Mey*, and Paul Spijker, *De Indische buurt: Geschiedenis van een Amsterdamse wijk* (Amsterdam, 1986).

29. Revised plan for the Indischebuurt, 4278 PW 1913, archive 5180; doss. 2456/1916 Dienst PW, archive 5213, GAA. Van der Mey based his plan on Van Niftrik's, the Health Board's report, and the director of public work's comments. He intended to include a "walk" along the central boulevard, connecting to a *wandel allee* in the eastern half, a church playground, and a monumental complex in the west. Because of the necessity of waiting for a report on future railroad plans, approval of the plan was put off until 1918 (*Gemeenteblad* 1 [1918], no. 851, 27 September 1918, 2895–99, approved 9 October 1918). The Health Board was pleased with Van der Mey's plan aesthetically and hygienically, but still wished for lower building heights (Health Board to director of public works, 19 December 1913, 322 GC 1913, archive 5269, GAA).

30. J. M. van der Mey, "Memorie van toelichting bij schets-uitbreidingsplan in den Overamstelschen polder," 22 September 1913, in Dir. PW no. 12399, doss. 265, 1913, archive 5213, GAA.

31. For example, the council's decision of 15 February 1882 (Raadsbesluit no. 8550) to give an award of f10,000 to the most beautiful facade on the Ruyterskade was never applied.

32. In 1903, the Committee of Aesthetics passed judgment on 91 out of 1,909 new buildings; in 1912, 409 out of 1,072. From around 1911, it became the custom to have the Committee of Aesthetics review all buildings to be constructed on land leased from the city. In 1905, Social Democrats Henri Polak and P. L. Tak tried unsuccessfully to amend the proposed building ordinance so that inadequate aesthetic treatment might be grounds for refusing a building permit (*Gemeenteblad* 1 [1905], no. 622, 15 June 1905, 821; discussion and rejection *Gemeenteblad* 2 [1905], meeting of 21 June 1905, 872–76). For a general history of architectural review boards in the Netherlands, with some specific mention of Amsterdam, see Marijke Beek, *Het aanzien waard? Geschiedenis van de welstandszorg in Nederland* (Deventer: Kluwer, 1985).

33. [P. L.] T[ak], "De uitbreiding van Amsterdam," *De Kroniek* 11, no. 525 (14 January 1905): 410.

34. Public Works Committee meeting of 10 July 1913, Notulen van de Commissie van bijstand in zake Publieke Werken (1913), archive 5087, GAA.

35. In September 1911, the committee published an open letter to that effect in *Bouwkundig Weekblad*, *Architectura*, and the *Telegraaf* (*Bouwkundig Weekblad* 31, no. 37 [16 September 1911]: 447; *Architectura* 19 [1911]: 298). The working methods of the Committee of Aesthetics were described at a 1913 meeting of the architectural members of the Society for the Advancement of Architecture (*Bouwkundig Weekblad* 33, no. 44 [November 1913]: 536).

36. The Society for the Advancement of Architecture submitted a complete list of its Amsterdam members and asked Architectura et Amicitia to do the same ("Honorarium Gevelontwerpen," *Bouwkundig Weekblad* 31, no. 26 [1 July 1911]: 304).

37. From 1891 to 1900, seven new students enrolled at Delft for the degree program in architecture. From 1901 to 1910, seventy-seven enrolled. See *Gedenkschrift van de Koninklijk Academie en van de Polytechnisch School, 1842–1905: Samengesteld ter gelegenheid van de oprichting der Technische Hoogeschool* (Delft, 1906); A[drien] Huet, *De regeling van het hooger onderwijs en de vorming van ingenieurs en architecten* (Delft, 1873); A. Le Comte, *Het goede recht der kunst aan de Polytechnische School: Afschiedswoord aan zijne leerlingen* (Delft: J. Waltman, 1894); J[an] V[eth], "Bouwkunst aan de Rijksacademie te Amsterdam," *De Kroniek* 5, no. 225 (16 April 1899): 121–22; " *Rapport over het onderwijs tot opleiding van bouwkundig ingenieur aan de Polytechnische School te Delft ingediend aan de afdeeling 's Gravenhage van de Maatschappij tot Bevordering der Bouwkunst* (The Hague, 1895); F. Westendorp et al., eds., *De Technische Hoogeschool te Delft van 1905–1930* (Delft: J. Waltman, 1930).

38. This argument continued into the twentieth century. See the inaugural address of Prof. J. A. G. van der Steur, *De opleiding van den architect behoort uitsluitend te geschieden aan de Technische Hoogeschool* (Rotterdam: Nijgh en Van Ditmar, 1914). The address was attacked by the BNA and Architectura et Amicitia. It was written in reaction to a parliamentary speech by Victor de Stuers calling for full architectural training at the Rijksacademie der Beeldende Kunsten in Amsterdam.

39. "Verslag oprichtingsvergadering Voortgezet en Hoger Bouwkunst," *Architectura* (1908): 107. In 1908–9, fifty-six students were enrolled. The training was called "Advanced and Higher Architectural Instruction" (Voortgezet en Hooger Bouwkunst-Onderricht), which in 1915 was sponsored by Architectura et Amicitia, BNA, and the Society for the Advancement of Architecture. Instructors included leading architects such as Berlage, De Bazel, Walenkamp, and Kromhout.

40. The following account of the struggle to define the architectural profession in the Netherlands can be understood in the light of what Larson writes about the unification of a profession: "In this process, particular groups of people attempt to negotiate the boundaries of an area in the social division of labor and establish their own control over it. Persuasion tends to be typically directed to the outside—that is, to the relevant elites, the potential public or publics, and the political authorities. Conflict and struggle around who shall be included or excluded mark the process of internal unification of a profession" (Magali Sarfatti Larson, *The Rise of Professionalism: A Sociological Analysis* [Berkeley: University of California Press, 1977], xii).

41. Ordinary membership was extended to architects, surveyors, contractors, and materials suppliers. Extraordinary membership was extended up to age twenty-three. Amateur membership was granted to nonpractitioners. In 1908, the membership list was as follows: architects, 315; engineers, 61; Delft students, 19; teachers, 10; crafts artisans, 11; draftsmen and surveyors, 111; contractors, 45; manufacturers, 52; societies and institutes, 18; material suppliers, 22; building workers, 31; others, 78 (*Bouwkundig Weekblad* 28, no. 12 [21 March 1908], 186).

42. A chronological account of the society is to be found in Jeroen Schilt and Jouke van der Werf, *Genootschap Architectura et Amicitia* (Rotterdam: Uitgeverij 010, 1992).

43. Accounts of a comparable period of professionalization by architects in other countries

can be found in Martin S. Briggs, *The Architect in History* (Oxford: Clarendon Press, 1927); Barrington Kaye, *Development of the Architectural Profession in Britain: A Sociological Study* (London: Allen and Unwin, 1969); Frank Jenkins, *Architect and Patron* (New York: Oxford University Press, 1961); Raymonde Moulin et al., *Les architectes: Métamorphose d'une profession liberale* (Paris: Calmann-Levy, 1973); Spiro Kostof, ed., *The Architect: Chapters in the History of the Profession* (New York: Oxford University Press, 1977); Judith Blau, *Architects and Firms: A Sociological Perspective on Architectural Practice* (Cambridge, MIT Press, 1984). English resistance to professionalization of architecture is expressed in R. Norman Shaw et al., eds., *Architecture, a Profession or an Art? Thirteen Short Essays on the Qualifications and Training of Architects* (London: John Murray, 1892).

44. Jan de Meyer quoted in *Architectura* 20, no. 47 (23 November 1912): 400.

45. *Bouwkundig Weekblad* 18, no. 27 (2 July 1899): 209. Willem Kromhout had suggested a Dutch architectural league in 1893 and his lecture on the topic on 20 November 1895 before Architectura et Amicitia had evoked considerable discussion. Kromhout's original idea, however, was to create an elite group of gifted architects of proven talent, not the idea of a professional society to represent the profession's social and economic interests. Unsuccessful attempts were made at fusion in 1898 and 1904.

46. Members also had to be twenty-eight years old and have practiced for three consecutive years as an independent architect. For the BNA letter of invitation and description, see *Bouwkundig Weekblad* 28, no. 11 (14 March 1908): 163–65. The final statutes are in *Bouwkundig Weekblad* 28, no. 20 (16 May 1908): 363. For the history of the BNA, see M. P. van der Linden, "De oprichting van de Bond van Nederlandsche Architecten (1908) en zijn fusie met de Maatschappij tot Bevordering der Bouwkunst (1919)," *Bouwkundig Weekblad* 76, no. 20 (17 May 1958): 239–44.

47. The code was based on Julien Guadet's 1907 code for the Société Central des Architects Français.

48. The first such proposal, that only architects have the vote, came on 11 March 1908 (Van der Linden, "Oprichting van de Bond van Nederlandsche Architecten," 241).

49. At the eighty-third meeting of the society in May 1901, J. H. W. Leliman, Jr., castigated the officers for not acting on the fusion of 1898 and summarized the inactivity of the society: "Wat doet ge? Niets. Wanneer doet ge dat? Nooit. Waar doet ge dat? Nergens." *Bouwkundig Weekblad* 21, no. 35 (31 August 1901): 326.

50. In 1899, it had 494 ordinary, 12 extraordinary, and 73 amateur members. Amsterdam's branch had 74 ordinary members and 5 extraordinary members.

51. See "Een woord van protest," *Bouwkundig Weekblad* 27, no. 51 (1907): 803–4.

52. In addition, architect members had to be at least twenty-six years old and to have worked three consecutive years independently. In 1915, there were 2 honorary, 213 architect members, 14 aspirants, 25 assistants (*medewerkers*), and 441 subscribers. The statutes were again changed on 22 December 1914, introducing the requirement that architects refrain from commercial activity, removing nonarchitects from membership altogether and placing them in the category of assistant.

53. Kromhout and twelve other young architects had formed a committee for Architectura et Amicitia following Kromhout's 20 November 1907 lecture "Ons Genootschap zoals het was, is en kan zijn." The committee proposed, among other things, the creation of membership based

on aesthetic competence. See Linden, "Oprichting van de Bond van Nederlandsche Architecten," 240.

54. See *Architectura* 25, no. 14 (7 April 1917): 101–2, or no. 27 (7 July 1917), following 220. On Architectura et Amicitia, see Helen Searing, "Housing in Holland and the Amsterdam School" (Ph.D. diss., Yale University, 1971), 206–15.

55. The society stood parallel to other societies established to protect the economic interests of their members such as the Union of Contractors (Aannemers Bond), or the society for salaried employees, the ANOTB (Algemeene Nederlandsche Opzichters en Teekenaars Bond). The rights and privileges of this last group remained a hotly contested issue during the reorganization of the architectural societies, since many draftsmen, surveyors, and other salaried assistants aspired to full independent professional status after their period of service in another's studio. Were they to be treated as apprentices, as aspiring architects, or as workers? That is, did they share the architect's interests, or were their economic interests different? For those emphasizing the aesthetic nature of architecture, the economic distinctions were irrelevant. For a discussion of the architecture societies and education in relation to class position, see Rein Geurtsen, "De tol-grenzen van de architectenpractijk," *Wonen TA/BK*, no. 4 (April 1973): 11–20.

56. Letter from the Committee of Aesthetics to the mayor and aldermen, 25 January 1911, quoted in a letter from the Committee of Aesthetics to the mayor and mldermen, 1 April 1914, published in *Architectura*, 22, no. 14 (4 April 1914): 110–12. In 1910, the committee had seen its advice on the design of a police office and a department store ignored by the municipality.

57. The archives of the Commissie voor het Stadsschoon are in the Gemeentearchief, archive 458, nos. 1–8. The establishment of the committee was preceded by a study of the preservation movement by the Society for the Advancement of Architecture in 1910. The final report of the study was written by S. de Clercq, Jan Gratama, Herman van der Kloot Meijburg, and J. H. W. Leliman, "Heimatschutz en bouwkunst," *Bouwkundig Weekblad*, 30, no. 50 (10 December 1910): 592–95.

58. B. J. Ouendag, F. J. Kubatz, and P. G. Buskens report in *Bouwkundig Weekblad* 34, no. 21 (23 May 1914): 244–45. This report advised the installation of an architectural advisory office on the model of the German Bauberatung to which the rejected plans of nonarchitects could be sent for correction. Rejected plans by nonarchitects would either have to be redrawn by an architect or submitted for revision to a public architectural advisory bureau to be set up by the architectural societies. Although the advisory office could exert direct influence on the designs of nonarchitects, architects were to be guaranteed their artistic freedom and need not follow the notations of the Committee of Aesthetics. Several years later, another committee of the Society for the Advancement of Architecture studied the problem and concluded that advisory offices should not be allowed in large cities where developers could always afford to pay for professional architectural help. The report subscribed to the system of a list of local architects, that is, that the Committee of Aesthetics aid the hiring of architects. It defined architects as members of architectural societies that set sufficient requirements of competence for membership (*Bouwkundig Weekblad* 38, no. 25 [23 June 1917]: 145–46).

59. J. E. van der Pek, "Reorganisatie der Schoonheidscommissie," *Architectura* 20, no. 8 (24

February 1912): 62–63, and "De taak en bevoegheid der Schoonheidscommissiën," *Bouwkundig Weekblad* 33, no. 23 (7 June 1913): 273–5. The general debate on the topic was held by the Society for the Advancement of Architecture on 28 May 1913. See Jan Gratama, "Schoonheidcommissies en Openbaar Bouwkundig Adviesbureaux," *Bouwkundig Weekblad* 33, no. 32 (9 August 1913): 389–91.

60. C. B. Posthumus Meyjes, "Het typisch karakter onzer oude steden en de taak der Schoonheidcommissies," *Bouwkundig Weekblad* 37, no. 34 (23 December 1916): 250.

61. On the other hand, both sides could agree that the prevention of ugliness by eliminating the nonarchitect was legitimate. See Pieter Bakker Schut on the avoidance of official art in "Schoonheideischen en de Bouwverordening," *Gemeentebelangen* 12, no. 6 (1916): 103.

62. Jonas Ingenohl, "Schoonheidscommissiën," *Bouwkundig Weekblad* 33, no. 23 (7 June 1913): 272.

63. R. N. Roland Holst, "Kunst als regeeringszaak," *De Gids* 78, part 2 (1914): 531. This was part of an argument on the failure of state architecture and the juries for the Rotterdam City Hall and University of Groningen buildings.

64. The building was the Colonial Institute by the architect J. J. Nieukerken. Discussion of the incident occurred in the municipal council (*Gemeenteblad* 2 [1914], 25 March 1914, 623–32). See also Committee of Aesthetics to mayor and aldermen, 1 April 1914, published in *Architectura* 22, no. 14 (4 April 1914): 110–12. On the history of the Colonial Institute, see Jacobus Woudsma, *Een markant gebouw in Amsterdam-Oost: Het Koninklijk Instituut voor de Tropen* (Amsterdam: Koninklijk Instituut voor de Tropen, 1990).

65. The insurance company Koninklijke Hollandse Lloyd planned an office building by Evert Bremen in the harbor area. Since a small portion of the site fell on government-held land, the approval of the municipality was required. With approval of the Public Works Committee, the municipality went ahead and passed the proposal despite the Committee of Aesthetics' objections to the design (Committee of Aesthetics to mayor and aldermen, 23 September 1916, SC no. 42, archive 458/20, GAA).

66. Mayor and aldermen to Committee of Aesthetics, 25 November 1916, SC no. 46, archive 458/20, GAA.

67. Posthumus Meyjes, "Het typisch karakter onzer oude steden," 250. This statement was made in reaction to the committee's rejection of the design of an office building in historical style.

68. Committee of Aesthetics meeting of 4 January 1917, Notulen vergaderingen der stemgerechtigde leden der Schoonheidscommissie, archive 458/14, GAA. An entire issue of Architectura et Amicitia's journal was devoted to J. F. Staal: *Forum: Driemaandelijks Tijdschrift van het Genootschap Architectura et Amicitia* 36, no. 3–4 (August 1993).

69. J. F. Staal, 23 September 1916, SC no. 342, archive 458/20, GAA.

70. H. P. Berlage, "De bouwkunst als maatschappelijke kunst," in *Schoonheid in samenleving* (Rotterdam: W. L. and J. Brusse, 1919), 102.

71. This tension within modernity is discussed in David Harvey, *The Condition of Postmodernity: An Enquiry into the Origins of Cultural Change* (Oxford: Basil Blackwell, 1989), 29.

72. Berlage, "Bouwkunst als maatschappelijk kunst," 93, 103, 112.

1. Carel Schade, *Woningbouw voor arbeiders in het negentiende-eeuwse Amsterdam* (Amsterdam: Van Gennep, 1981), 196.

2. G. E. V. L. van Zuylen, "De toepassing der hygiëne bij den bouw van goedkope woonhuizen," *Bouwkundig Weekblad* 12 (4 June 1892): 114.

3. P. J. H. Cuypers, *Bouwkundig Weekblad* 12 (4 June 1892): 115.

4. Marie Sparnaaij, *Het leven en werken, het lijden en strijden door onze fabrieksarbeiders* (The Hague: Drukkerij "Vrede," 1898), 59, 164.

5. J. van Hasselt and L. Verschoor, *De arbeiderswoningen in Nederland: Beoordelend overzicht samengesteld door de commissie van onderzoek naar hetgeen in verschillende gemeenten des lands gedaan is ter verkrijging van verbeterde arbeiderswoningen* (Amsterdam: Maatschappij tot Nut van 't Algemeen, 1890), 141.

6. Johanna ter Meulen, "Verslagboekje betreffende de verhuurderspercelen," no. 39, archive 492, GAA, 68.

7. Hélène Mercier, *Over arbeiderswoningen* (Haarlem: H. D. Tjeenk Willink, 1887), 239.

8. Ibid., 238. Ali de Regt discusses the role of the social worker as adviser on the internal arrangement of the house (Ali de Regt, *Arbeidersgezinnen en beschavingsarbeid: Ontwikkeling in Nederland, 1870–1949, een historisch-sociologische studie* [Amsterdam: Boom Meppel, 1984], 163).

9. *Algemeen Handelsblad*, 23 May 1916.

10. Dirk Hudig for CBSA to Arie Keppler, 18 November 1908, no. 278, RA 6371, CBSA archive, IISG. Hudig sent the representatives of the typographers' society Ons Doel to the architects Vorkink and Wormser, then developing an extension plan for Watergraafsmeer, who designed plans for four two-story blocks of six dwellings each. The reformers solicited included Dr. C. W. Janssen, Willem Spakler, H. L. Drucker, and Johanna ter Meulen, all liberals readier to give assistance to slum housing reform than to improvement of the housing of ordinary workers, the cause promoted by the socialist reformers Hudig and Keppler.

11. Mercier, *Over arbeiderswoningen.*

12. Henri Polak, "De strijd der diamantbewerkers" (1896), 13–14, quoted in Henri Heertje, *De Diamant-bewerkers van Amsterdam* (Amsterdam: Centen's, 1936), 38.

13. A. Ogterop, *De gezellige woning* (Amsterdam: Bond van Sociaal-democratische Vrouwenclubs, n.d.)

14. See the description of the bad example of furnishings described in the Ons Huis exhibition, *Architectura* 20, no. 27 (6 August 1912), 226, or Henri Polak's many articles in the *Weekblad ANDB.*

15. H. P. Berlage, "De arbeiderswoningen aan de gedempte Lindengracht," *De Kroniek* 2, no. 98 (8 November 1896), 360–61.

16. Crane's 1892 *Claims of Decorative Art* was translated by Jan Veth, a frequent contributor to *De Kroniek*, as "Art and Society," *Kunst en samenleving* (Amsterdam: Scheltema en Holkema, 1894). The translation was reviewed by Frank van der Goes in "Socialisme en kunst," part 3, *De Kroniek* 1, no. 26 (1 September 1895): 282. Van der Goes himself translated William Morris's *New from Nowhere* in 1897. A series of essays on art by Morris was published in Dutch as *Kunst en maatschappij* (Amsterdam: Soep, 1903), with a biographical introduction by Henri Polak.

17. See, for example, L. H. E. van Hylkema Vlieg, "Bauberatung," part 4, *Bouwkundig Weekblad* 33, no. 47 (22 November 1913): 576–78.

18. See, for example, Frans Coenen, *Kunst aan het Volk* (Baarn: Hollandia-Drukkerij, 1909).

19. L., "Naar aanleiding van de Expositie van Architectura et Amicitia," *De Kroniek* 7, no. 334 (18 May 1901): 157–58.

20. [P. L.] T[ak], "Kunst aan 't Volk," *De Kroniek* 10, no. 516 (12 November 1904): 360–61. P. L. Tak, F. M. Wibaut, and H. P. Berlage supported the organization. In 1908, its membership was 2,000 (Vereeniging Kunst aan het Volk, "Daden der vereeniging, 1903–1907," Tak archive, IISG). For a scholarly discussion of taste reform in the Netherlands between 1900 and 1940, see Mark Adang, "Breng me in uw huis, laat me uw woonkamer zien, en ik zal u zeggen wie gij zijt! Het denken over kitsch en smaakopvoeding in Nederland," *Nederlands Kunsthistorisch Jaarboek* 28 (1977): 209–59, and his chapter, "'Tegen leelijkheid en smaakmisleiding' Twee tentoonstellingen (uit 1905 en 1910/11) in het Stedelijk Museum te Amsterdam," in *Wonen in het verleden, 17e–20e eeuw: Economie, politiek, volkshuivesting, cultuur, en bibliografie*, ed. P. M. M. Klep et al. (Amsterdam: NEHA, 1987), 129–40. On the history and activities of Art for the People, see his "'Eens zal de dag, opgaand, vinden arbeid en schoonheid vereend': Over socialisme en kunstopvoeding in Nederland aan het begin van de twintigste eeuw," in *Met den toverstaf van ware kunst: Cultuurverspreiding en cultuuroverdracht in historisch perspectief*, ed. M. G. Westen (Leiden: Martinum Nijhoff, 1990), 71–104.

21. W. P[enaat], *Kunst aan 't Volk: Catalogus met de beschrijving van de tentoonstelling gehouden in het Stedelijk Museum van Amsterdam* (Amsterdam, 1905).

22. In 1909 there was also an exhibition in the Hague by the similar society Art for All (Kunst aan Allen), with good and bad examples of workers' home interiors. See v. H., "Tentoonstelling van 'Kunst aan Allen,'" *Bouwkundig Weekblad* 29, no. 22 (29 May 1909): 264–65.

23. See Jan Gratama, "Tentoonstelling van Smaak- misleiding," *Bouwkundig Weekblad* 31, no. 2 (14 January 1911): 13– 15.

24. "Tentoonstelling van meubeleeringen voor arbeiderswoningen in 'Ons Huis' te Rotterdam, Juni, 1912," *Architectura* 20, no. 26 (29 July 1912): 220–21, no. 27 (6 August 1912): 226–27. The designs were for two workers' families, one set of furniture for 300 guilders, the other for 450.

25. Lambertus Zwiers, "Meubelen voor een arbeiderswoonkamer," *Bouwkundig Weekblad* 37, no. 6 (10 June 1916): 65.

26. Henri Polak and J. E. van Epen, *De Volksschool* 5, no. 3 (7 February 1906).

27. Amsterdam-Zuid, *Jaarverslag* (1915). Berlage and Van Epen also furnished a flat in the Transvaal district for the Algemeene. Other exhibitions included: "Het huis en zijn inrichting," 1 May to 7 June 1920, by the Nederlandsch Vereeniging van Huisvrouwen, for which Van Epen designed low-cost and expensive rooms; and "Tentoonstelling voor Woning-inrichting," 20 May to 1 July 1921 at the Stedelijk Museum, with work of Piet Kramer and others, organized by A. R. Hulshoff. Keppler and Wibaut established the Centrale Coöperatie voor Woninginrichting, which furnished model dwellings, brought designers and manufacturers together, and distributed modern furniture.

28. H. P. Berlage, *Korte Uiteenzetting van het doel der tentoonstelling van Smaakmisleiding* (Amsterdam: Kunst aan 't Volk, 1910). The exhibition systematically laid out the sources of bad taste,

categorizing them under the headings of material errors, construction errors, and decorative errors. This was according to a scheme originated in Germany by G. E. Pazaurek, who wrote *Geschmacksverirrungen im Kunstgewerbe: Führer für die neue Abteilung im Köningl. Landes Gewerbemuseum* (Stuttgart, 1909). See Adang, "Breng me in uw huis," note 1.

29. Tak, "Kunst aan 't Volk," 361.

30. [J. B. van] L[oghem], "Naar aanleiding van de Expositie van Architectura et Amicitia," *De Kroniek* 7, no. 334 (18 May 1901): 157–58.

31. J. B. van Loghem, "Algemeene wenken aan woningbouwvereenigingen," *Woningbouw* 2, no. 4 (December 1918): 5–6.

32. Helen Searing, "Berlage and Housing: 'The most significant modern building type,'" *Nederlands Kunsthistorisch Jaarboek* 24 (1975): 133–80. Berlage's design included work for De Arbeiderswoning, the Algemeene, and the municipality. For the latter, he contributed the urban design, while the architects Gratama and Versteeg designed the housing.

33. Algemeene Woningbouw Vereeniging, *Jaarverslag* (1911), 19.

34. J. E. van der Pek built projects for the Amsterdamsch Bouwfonds and Rochdale in the Indischebuurt and for the municipality in Buiksloterham north of the IJ. De Bazel built for De Arbeiderswoning and in the Spaarndammerbuurt for the municipality.

35. *Algemeen Handelsblad*, 23 May 1916: "Luthersche Besjeshuis."

36. K. [P. C.] de Bazel, "Woningbouw aan het van Beuningenplein, van Hallstraat, van Hogendorpstraat en de Kempenaerstraat, door de vereeniging 'De Arbeiderswoning' te Amsterdam," *Woningbouw* 1, no. 2 (April 1917): 9–15.

37. A.A.L., "Uit de Afdeelingen, Amsterdam," *De Gemeente-Werkman* 10, no. 10 (7 October 1911).

38. *Architectura* 20, no. 26 (29 July 1912): 220.

39. E. Kuipers, "Arbeiderswoning-complexen van M. de Klerk," *Woningbouw* 3, no. 4 (October 1919): 30–32. The review criticized workers who filled De Klerk's Eigen Haard complex on Wormerveerstraat with a poor imitation of "capitalist" furniture. This is clearly a socialist speaking, but the argument is exactly the same as a liberal's.

40. Joh. L. in the *Telegraaf* of 27 May 1920, on J. C. van Epen's design for a modest home in the exhibition organized by Nederlandsche Verereeniging van Huisvrouwen, "Het huis en zijn inrichting," 1 May 1920 to 7 June 1920.

41. For example, v.H., "Tentoonstelling van 'Kunst aan Allen,'" *Bouwkundig Weekblad* 29, no. 22 (29 May 1909): 264–65.

42. Cornelius Veth, "Kunst aan 't Volk," *Pro en Contra* 5, no. 6 (1909): 13. Veth argued that people wanted entertainment, not art, and that few people of any class had real interest in art. Art, he said, cannot be served up on a silver platter. Art appreciation must be learned, and rather than offer popularized art to adults, it would be better to start proper training at an early age.

43. J. P. M[ieras], "Amsterdamsche Tentoonstelling van Woning-inrichting in het Stedelijk Museum," *Bouwkundig Weekblad*, no. 25 (18 June 1921): 161. Mieras goes on to write scathingly of those whose designs prescribe hygiene and taste to workers.

44. Jan van der Waerden, "Maatregelen waardoor de bouw in massa bevorderd wordt: Normalisatie in de uitvoering, in het bizonder wat betreft de te verwerken onderdeelen," in *Praeadviezen voor het Woningcongres, 11 en 12 februari 1918*, by M. J. A. Moltzer et al. (Amsterdam,

1918), 67–96. He proposed government-organized and centralized housing production. The state would purchase and distribute materials for construction, and local authorities would erect the housing. To maximize efficiency and cost-effectiveness, housing plans would be standardized throughout the country. Van der Waerden figured that nine housing types would be needed, single-family dwellings in detached, row, and corner types; two-, three-, and four-family dwellings in row and corner type.

45. The discussion following Van der Waerden's presentation appears in Nationale Woningraad, *Stenografisch verslag van het Woningcongres op 11–12 februari 1918* (Amsterdam, 1918), 107–62. Van der Waerden's response to his audience follows on pages 165–74.

46. H. P. Berlage, *Normalisatie in woningbouw* (Rotterdam: W. L. and J. Brusse, 1918). This is a further elaboration of Berlage's comments at the convention. A negative appraisal of standardization appeared in *Normalisatie in den woningbouw* (Amsterdam: Nederlandsch Instituut van Volkshuisvesting, 1920), the results of the investigations of a committee consisting of H. C. A. Henny, Arie Keppler, W. Verschoor, Piet Vorkink, J. Versteeg, W. K. de Wijs.

47. This discussion of Berlage's historical perspective is based on his "Over architectuur," *De Kroniek* 1, no. 2 (6 January 1895): 9–10, no. 8 (17 February 1895): 58–59; "Over architectuur," *Tweemaandelijksch Tijdschrift* 2, part 3 (November 1895): 202–35 (includes J. E. van der Pek's article "Bouwen-in-Stijl" of March 1894); "Kunst en maatschappij," in *Studies over bouwkunst, stijl, en samenleving* (Rotterdam: W. L. and J. Brusse, 1910), 1–44; "Kunst en gemeenschap," *De Beweging* 7, part 4, no. 12 (December 1911): 225–38; "De bouwkunst als maatschappelijke kunst," in *Schoonheid in samenleving* (Rotterdam: W. L. and J. Brusse, 1919), 91–123.

48. J. F. Staal, "Af- en toe wendingen," *Wendingen* 1, no. 10 (October 1918): 16.

49. R. N. Roland Holst, "Kunst als regeeringszaak," *De Gids* 78 (1914): 518.

50. Camillo Sitte, "To Our Readers," *Der Städtebau* 1, no. 1 (1904), reproduced in George R. Collins and Christiane Crasemann Collins, *Camillo Sitte: The Birth of Modern City Planning* (New York: Rizzoli, 1986), 323.

51. Committee of Aesthetics meeting of 23 March 1916, Notulen van de werkvergaderingen der Schoonheidscommissie, archive 458/16, GAA. The committee also planned to tell Keppler that they objected from an aesthetic viewpoint to such designs. They also objected to the gateway by Kuipers for Patrimonium. There was some dissent on the issue, although later the point was clarified with the admission that more extravagance was permissible where the housing was not being subsidized by the state (meeting of 20 April 1916).

52. J. H. W. Leliman to Arie Keppler, 4894 WD 1917.

53. Jan de Meyer, H. T. Wijdeveld, and J. B. van Loghem, "Juryrapport Geval Prijsvraag Arbeiderswoningen," *Architectura* 25, no. 15 (14 April 1917): 114. See also *Architectura* 25, no. 4 (27 January 1917): 19–20. Searing discusses the significance of this competition in "Housing in Holland and the Amsterdam School" (Ph.D. diss., Yale University, 1971), 225–27, and "'Eigen Haard:' Worker's Housing and the Amsterdam School," *Architectura* no. 2 (1971): 172–74.

54. Arie Keppler, "De architecten en volkshuisvesting," *Architectura* 20, no. 47 (23 November 1912): 398–400.

55. W. H. V[liegen], "Leekgedachten over kunstbeoefening," *De Kroniek* 10, no.465 (1904): 370.

56. Jan Gratama, "Gemeentelijke woningbouw.: Transvaalbuurt, Amsterdam," *Bouwkundig*

Weekblad 41, no. 4 (24 January 1920): 19–23. See also a favorable review by J. G. Wattjes, "Woningbouw in de Transvaalwijk te Amsterdam," *Bouwbedrijf*, no. 3 (September 1924): 97–103. Relevant here is Bourdieu's discussion of the difficulty of understanding culture across class lines (Pierre Bourdieu, *Distinction: A Social Critique of the Judgement of Taste* (Cambridge: Harvard University Press, 1984), 372–75.

57. On the origins and development of the Amsterdam School, see Ellinoor Bergvelt et al., *Amsterdamse School, 1910–1930* (Amsterdam, 1975), exhibition catalog, Stedelijk Museum; Wim de Wit, ed., *The Amsterdam School: Dutch Expressionist Architecture, 1915–1930* (Cambridge: MIT Press, 1983), exhibition catalog, Cooper Hewitt Museum; Maristella Casciato, *La scuola di Amsterdam* (Bologna: Zanicelli Editore, 1987).

58. For a critical biography of De Klerk, see Suzanne Frank, *Michel de Klerk, 1884–1923: An Architect of the Amsterdam School* (Ann Arbor: UMI Research Press, 1984), and Manfred Bock et al., *Michel de Klerk: Bouwmeester en tekenaar van de Amsterdamse School, 1884–1923* (Rotterdam: NAi, 1997). On P. L. Kramer, see Bernhard Kohlenbach, *Pieter Lodewijk Kramer, 1881–1961: Architect van de Amsterdamse School* (Naarden: V and K Publishing, 1994).

59. Jan Gratama identified Michel de Klerk, J. M. van der Mey, and P. L. Kramer as part of an Amsterdam School in "Het werk van Berlage," in *Dr. H. P. Berlage en zijn werk* (Rotterdam: W. L. and J. Brusse, 1916), 24–51.

60. J. T. J. Cuypers, son of the rationalist P. J. H. Cuypers, resigned from the Committee of Aesthetics over De Klerk facades proposed in 1915 for the Spaaarndammerplantsoen. See Searing, "Housing in Holland," 183.

61. Jan Gratama, "Kroniek," part 70, *Bouwkundig Weekblad* 36, no. 33 (11 December 1915): 244.

62. Mayor and aldermen to Arie Keppler, 24 January 1919, 155 VH 1919, archive 5187, GAA.

63. Housing Committee meeting of 20 March 1920, Notulen van de Commissie van bijstand in het beheer der zaken van Volkshuisvesting (1920), archive 5102, GAA. The project was defended by Gulden, Wibaut, and Keppler, who said it was not more costly. Actually, the committee's objections began with complaints from the director of the Building and Housing Inspection Office, H. van der Kaa, about the increased costs of housing society housing and a nasty letter from the minister of labor. This led to the detailed comparison of the costs of public and private construction in 1913 and 1919 (2729 VH 1920).

64. Johanna ter Meulen to Johanna Han van Vlissingen, 20 December 1914, no. 29, archive 492, GAA.

65. Housing Committee discussion of Nachtegaalstraat housing in Spreeuwpark, 18 May 1915, Notulen van de Commissie van bijstand in het beheer der zaken van Volkshuisvesting [1915], archive 5102, GAA.

66. David Harvey, *The Condition of Postmodernity: An Enquiry into the Origins of Cultural Change* (Oxford: Basil Blackwell, 1989), 265–78.

67. Arie Keppler to mayor, 12 July 1918, 3788 WD 1918, in 1987 VH 1918, archive 5187, GAA: "Een goed resultaat is door mij bereikt, door bij den bouw aan het Spaarndammerplantsoen den eisch te stellen, dat die bouw door een bepaald architect moest geschieden." Kep-

pler also complained to the Committee of Aesthetics about failures in the Zaanbuurt, Nieuwendammerham, and in Amsterdam South at the meeting of 15 May 1919 (Notulen vergaderingen der stemgerechtigde leden der Schoonheidscommissie, archive 458/14, GAA). The most famous housing complexes in Amsterdam, De Klerk's projects for Eigen Haard in the Spaarndammerbuurt have been extensively studied: Helen Searing, "Eigen Haard: Worker's Housing and the Amsterdam School," *Architectura*, no. 2 (1971): 148–75, and "Michel de Klerk's Designs for Amsterdam's Spaarndammerbuurt, 1914–1920: A Contribution to Architectural Lyricism," *Nederlands Kunsthistorisch Jaarboek* 22 (1971): 175–213; Maristella Casciato and Wim de Wit, *Le case Eigen Haard di De Klerk, 1913–1921* (Rome: Officina Edizioni, 1984); Vladimir Stissi, "De Woningblokken van De Klerk, in Bock et al., *Michel de Klerk*, 56–93, 180–85, 194–205, 239–48.

68. Arie Keppler to mayor, 13 October 1919, 8764 WD 1919, in 4656 VH 1919, archive 5187, GAA.

69. Dirk Hudig and H. C. A. Henny, *Handleiding voor woningbouwvereenigingen* (Zwolle: De Erven J. J. Tijl, 1911), 23.

70. Keppler and Tellegen presented the Handwerkers Vriendenkring with the names of eight architects at a meeting on 29 October 1912. At the meeting of 12 November 1912, the society selected Leliman, saying that certain of the names were out of the question, presumably for ideological reasons (*De Handwerksman* 22, no. 8 [December 1912]).

71. Eigen Haard to CBSA, 28 September 1901, CBSA 234, RA 152, IISG.

72. Theo Rueter, "Bouwvereenigingen en architecten," *Bouwkundig Weekblad* 42, no. 14 (2 April 1921): 83.

73. For instance, these societies kept the same architect for all their projects between 1909 and 1919: HIJSM, Greve (2 projects); Het Oosten, Moolenschot, Lippits, Scholte (5); Patrimonium, Kuipers and Ingwersen (8); Dr. Schaepman, Rijnja (4); Het Westen, Walenkamp (3); Amsterdamsch Bouwfonds, Van der Pek (2); Amsterdam-Zuid, Gulden and Geldmaker (5); ACOB, Van Epen (3); Bouwmaatschappij tot Verkrijging van Eigen Woningen, Weissman (7).

74. For a summary of Calvinist attitudes toward art, see Abraham Kuyper, *Het Calvinisme en de kunst* (Amsterdam: J. A. Wormser, 1888).

75. The cultural program of the Social Democrats is described in Jose van Dijk, *Het Socialisme spant zijn gouden net over de wereld: Het kunst- en cultuurbeleid van de SDAP* (Montfort: Uriah Heep, 1990).

76. Ad Bevers, *Oost-West thuis best: Gedenkschrift bij gelegenheid van het vijftigjarig bestaan der R.K. Wbv. "Het Oosten" te Amsterdam* [1962], 30; *Patrimonium's Bode* 4, no. 1 (1 July 1917), project behind Schinkel.

77. Algemeene Woningbouw Vereeniging, *Jaarverslag* (23 March 1910–31 December 1911), 7. At its founding the society had 32 members; after the meeting at which Berlage's commission was announced, membership climbed to 137.

78. Discussion at Architectura et Amicitia meeting, 10 January 1912 (*Architectura* 20, no. 47 [23 November 1912]: 400).

79. For instance, see reactions of all the main architectural societies to the mayor and aldermen on the controversial decision of the Committee of Aesthetics on the design of the Colonial Institute: "Hierbij zij er op gewezen dat de Schoonheidscommissie is een zuiver aesthetisch-

technische commissie, die bouwkundige ontwerpteekeningen te beoordelen heeft, waar omtrent de nietdeskundige uit den aard der zaak, zeer moeilijk het vereischte inzicht kon krijgen" (*Bouwkundig Weekblad* 34, no. 13 [28 March 1914]: 145). Note however, that the BNA later indicated that it favored lay members in the Committee of Aesthetics.

80. Committee of Aesthetics meeting of 2 November 1916, Notulen van de werkvergaderingen der Schoonheidscommissie, archive 458/16, GAA. This suggestion was vetoed on the grounds that if the Committee of Aesthetics made the appointment, it would be unable to judge the facade without prejudice.

81. J. F. Staal, "'De Bouwwereld' en de Schoonheidscommissie," *Architectura* 25, no. 6 (10 February 1917): 27.

82. The Committee of Aesthetics submitted a modified version of Staal's proposal to mayor and aldermen. Whenever a builder gave evidence through his submissions that he lacked the insight or will to select a competent designer, the committee would force him to choose a designer from a list of six architects of its own choosing. The list comprised young gifted architects rather than established ones. Once an architect had been chosen for a job, his name would be dropped from the list and replaced with new names so as to rotate the opportunities for work (Committee of Aesthetics meetings of 16 and 23 November 1916, Notulen van de werkvergaderingen der Schoonheidscommissie, archive 458/16, GAA; Committee of Aesthetics to mayor and aldermen, 29 December 1916, SC no. 48, and 8 January 1916, SC no. 53, archive 458/20, GAA). This proposal was soon rejected by the director of public works, who objected that the builder might start by spending time and money on an incompetent designer to no avail and then be forced to hire an inexperienced young architect. He preferred a system that allowed the builder free choice, but required him to submit his designer's name to the Committee of Aesthetics for approval upon applying to lease land from the city (A. W. Bos to alderman of public works, 23 April 1917, Dienst PW no. 248, doss. 247 G.E., archive 458/20, GAA; Committee of Aesthetics meeting, 30 August 1917, archive 458/14, GAA). Wibaut, as alderman of housing, also contributed to this discussion by suggesting that the Committee of Aesthetics apply two standards of competence when considering the builder's choice of architect. For ordinary sites, with no special aesthetic requirements, Wibaut proposed that the committee accept as competent any designer professionally qualified by a degree from Delft or membership in one of the architectural societies. But for a site where, in the opinion of the committee, high aesthetic requirements should be set, the committee assumed the authority to judge whether the designer, regardless of his professional qualifications, was an architect of recognized abilities, capable of handling the commission (24 September 1917, 1363 VH 1917, archive 5187, GAA). These proposals arose in reaction to construction of a historicist design for the office building of the insurance company Koninklijke Hollandse Lloyd episode despite the negative recommendation of the Committee of Aesthetics (see chapter 6, note 66).

83. J. H. Schaad, "Stedenschoon en woningbouw met steun volgens de Woningwet," *Bouwkundig Weekblad* 34, no. 44 (31 October 1914): 483.

84. One project proposed three- and four-story housing in Amsterdam South, the other laid out a neighborhood of low-rise housing in the northern tip of Nieuwendammerham.

85. J. Mol, *Gedenkboek uitgegeven ten gelegenheid van het 50-jarig bestaan der Vereeniging Bouw-*

maatschappij tot Veerkrijging van Eigen Woningen (Amsterdam, 1918), 81, 111–15. The same series of events occurred with their next project, in the Indische district. In 1918, when the society published a history in honor of its fiftieth anniversary, it proudly presented its two latest projects by Weissman, the projects for Amsterdam South and Nieuwendammerham.

86. Committee of Aesthetics meetings of 23 May 1919 and 6 June 1919, Notulen van de werkwergaderingen der Schoonheidscommissie, archive 458/16, GAA.

87. Committee of Aesthetics to mayor and aldermen, 19 June 1919, SC no. 110, archive 458/20, GAA.

88. For the history of the Committee of Aesthetics and its relation to the Amsterdam School, see Helen Searing, "Housing in Holland and the Amsterdam School" (Ph.D. diss., Yale University, 1971), 215–24. A number of A. W. Weissman's scathing satirical verses aimed at the proponents of the Amsterdam School are translated there.

89. Arie Keppler to mayor, 25 June 1919, 5214 WD 1919, in 2648 VH 1919, archive 5187, GAA.

90. Arie Keppler to mayor, 2 July 1919, 5412 WD 1919, in 2791 VH 1919, archive 5187, GAA: "Het goedkeuren der plannen zou mijnerzijds zeer betreurd worden. Amsterdam heeft, wat betreft de verzorging der nieuwe arbeiderswijken, een naam gekrijgen in Binnen- en Buitenland. De uitvoering der plannen van den architect Weissman zou dien naam ten zeerste schaden."

91. A. W. Weissman to mayor and aldermen, 17 July 1919, 3057 PW 1919, archive 5180, GAA.

92. Vereeniging Bouwmaatschappij tot Verkrijging van Eigen Woningen to mayor and aldermen, 17 July 1919, 3056 PW 1919, archive 5180, GAA.

93. See Amsterdam City Council discussion of proposal no. 796 *Gemeenteblad* 2 (1919), meeting of 30 July 1919, 1692–93.

94. Arie Keppler to Committee of Aesthetics, 5 May 1919, 3622 WD 1919, archive 458/20, GAA.

95. Committee of Aesthetics meetings of 15 May 1919 and 25 September 1919, Notulen vergaderingen der stemgerechtigde leden der Schoonheidscommissie, archive 458/14, GAA.

96. Committee of Aesthetics to director of the Housing Authority, 27 September 1919, SC no. 115, archive 458/20, GAA.

97. Arie Keppler to mayor, 13 October 1919, 8764 WD 1919, in 4656 VH 1919, archive 5187, GAA.

98. Handwritten note on Keppler's letter of 13 October 1919, 4656 VH 1919, archive 5187, GAA.

99. Ibid. A controversy ensued over a revolutionary memo Keppler prepared in 1918. He tried to organize a centralized architectural office for preparation of drawings for all housing societies, working with the Federation of Amsterdam Housing Societies (Federatie van Amsterdamsche Woningbouwvereenigingen) and the Club of Amsterdam Housing Architects (Club van Amsterdamsche Woningbouwarchitecten), but with little result. At the same time, Keppler was encouraging collective organization of the building trades, with worker self-management. On this topic, see Frans Becker and Johan Frieswijk, *Bedrijven in Eigen Beheer: Kolonies en productieve associaties in Nederland tussen 1901 en 1958* (Nijmegen: SUN, 1978).

100. J. F. Staal, "Gemeentelijk aesthetisch toezicht op het bouwen," *De Nieuwe Tijd* 25 (January 1920): 12–17.

101. Theo Rueter, "Inleiding tot een bespreking over de noodzakelijkheid van een moderne bedrijfsorganisatie van architecten," quoted in J. P. M[ieras], "Veranderingen in het architectenberoep," *Bouwkundig Weekblad* 40, no. 50 (13 December 1919): 310–15. See also his "Bouwvereenigingen en architecten," *Bouwkundig Weekblad* 42, no. 14 (2 April 1921): 82–84, and no. 17 (23 April 1921): 105–7, and his letter in *Bouwkundig Weekblad* 39, no. 31 (3 August 1918): 180–82.

102. A. W. Reinink, *Amsterdam en de Beurs van Berlage: Reacties van tijdgenoten* (The Hague: Staatsuitgeverij, 1975), 71.

103. R. N. Roland Holst, "Proletariaat en kunst," *De Nieuwe Tijd* 9 (1904): 787–90.

104. Z. D. J. W. Gulden, *Gemeenteblad* 2 (1917), meeting of 10 January 1917, 31.

CHAPTER EIGHT

1. The following discussion has been influenced by a reading of Jürgen Habermas, *The Structural Transformation of the Public Sphere: An Inquiry into a Category of Bourgeois Society* (Cambridge: MIT Press, 1991), and Craig Calhoun, ed., *Habermas and the Public Sphere* (Cambridge: MIT Press, 1992).

2. The Committee of Aesthetics conflicted with the mayor and aldermen over the design of new police headquarters. In a letter of 25 January 1911, the committee asked mayor and aldermen for the authority to review all designs for municipal buildings. For contemporary histories of the Committee of Aesthetics, see W. J. de Groot, "Het Instituut der Gemeentelijke Schoonheids Commissie," *Bouwkundig Weekblad* 34, no. 4 (27 May 1916): 46–47; Delprat speech, *Gemeenteblad* 2 (1914), meeting of 25 March 1914, 625–28.

3. *Gemeenteblad* 1 (1915), no. 93, 26 January 1915, 57–66.

4. Z. D. J. W. Gulden, *Gemeenteblad* 2 (1915), meeting of 25 February 1915, 235. Gulden's examples were Staringplein and the Transvaal district. Keppler claimed that the Committee of Aesthetics did not even exercise its right to review proposed buildings in the Transvaal district (Arie Keppler, "De architect en het woningvraagstuk," *Bouwkundig Weekblad* 20, no. 47 [23 November 1912]: 399).

5. Quoted from an address to the Verbond van Nederlandse Kunstenaars Vereenigingen in F. J. Kubatz, "Bauberatung," *Bouwkundig Weekblad* 33, no. 33 (16 August 1913): 408.

6. See chapter 2, note 75. For the development of Berlage's planning theory, see Vincent Rossem, "Berlage and the Culture of City Planning," in *Hendrik Petrus Berlage: Complete Works*, ed. Sergio Polano (New York: Rizzoli, 1988), 45–64.

7. Berlage, "Stedenbouw," *De Beweging* 10, no. 3 (March 1914): 234; cf. "Het aesthetisch gedeelte van stedenbouw," *Bouwkundig Weekblad* 34, no. 1 (3 January 1914): 7.

8. "Het aesthetisch gedeelte van stedenbouw," *Bouwkundig Weekblad* 34, no. 11 (4 March 1914): 126–27.

9. Berlage quotes Brinckmann's statement "Stadte bauen heisst mit dem Hausmaterial Raum gestalten" at the start of his explanation of the Hague plan, "Het uitbreidingsplan van 's Gravenhage," *Bouwkunst* 1 (July–October 1909): 97.

10. *Bouwkundig Weekblad* 34, no. 9 (28 February 1914): 98.

11. Berlage, "Stedenbouw," *De Beweging* 10, no. 3 (March 1914): 245. Cf. "Het aesthetisch gedeelte van stedenbouw," *Bouwkundig Weekblad* 34, no. 2 (10 January 1914): 11.

12. Berlage, "Stedenbouw," *De Beweging* 10, no. 5 (May 1914): 152. Cf. lecture of 2 March 1914 in *Bouwkundig Weekblad* 34, no. 12 (21 March 1914): 138.

13. Berlage, "Stedenbouw," *De Beweging* 10, no. 5 (May 1914): 127, 151. Cf. *Bouwkundig Weekblad* 34, no. 12 (21 March 1914): 138.

14. H. P. Berlage, "Memorie van toelichting behorende bij het Ontwerp van het uitbreidingsplan der Gemeente Amsterdam" (March 1915), *Gemeenteblad* 1 (1917), no. 854, 27 July 1917, 910–14, app. A. Berlage referred to the 1906 Serrurier-Falkenberg report, which had also concluded that housing would improve with the coming of large-scale development by financially secure developers. Berlage's *blokbouw* ("building block") prescription for Amsterdam unleashed economic controversy during council discussion of the plan. Would Amsterdam refuse to lease land to small builders? This was not a tenable position. W. H. Vliegen explained the intent of the mayor and aldermen to support *blokbouw* on the important streets, such as the avenue leading to the proposed (but never built) Academy of Fine Arts (*Gemeenteblad* 2 [1917], meeting of 26 October 1917, 2021).

15. A. W. Bos to alderman of public works, 18 October 1915, Dienst PW doss. 4548 G.E. 1915, archive 5213, GAA. Arie Keppler, director of the newly established Housing Authority and Jan van der Waerden, director of the Building and Housing Inspection Office, supported the idea of the designer of a plan giving direction to the building on it (director of the Housing Authority and director of the Building and Housing Inspection Office to alderman of housing, 31 March 1916, 46 VH 1915, archive 5187, GAA).

16. Public Works Committee meeting of 16 December 1915, Notulen van de Commissie van bijstand in zake Publieke Werken (1915), archive 5087, GAA, 249–50.

17. Keppler proposal, 19 July 1913, BWT no. 6^{36}, 9204 AZ 1913. Keppler sent the director of the Building and Housing Inspection Office a map of the Spaarndammer district with possible sites for the societies HIJSM, Patrimonium, Het Oosten, Amsterdamsch Bouwfonds, and Het Westen. Keppler's experiments in planning coordination are also discussed in Vincent Rossem, "Architectuur en stad in 1913: De overstap van bouwkunst naar stedebouw," in *Nederland 1913: Een reconstructie van het culturele leven*, ed. Jan de Vries (Amsterdam: Meulenhoff/Landshoff, 1988), 132–54.

18. Keppler, Tellegen, and the director of public works visited the Van Verschuer district in Arnhem to see if it offered any ideas for Amsterdam (*Gemeenteblad* 2 [1918], meeting of 2 October 1918, 2294). The *hof* was a solution first published in the Berlin Plan Competition of 1910.

19. In December 1913, Keppler designed a single block encompassing a *hof* to replace three blocks in the southwest corner of the Public Works plan for the Spaarndammerbuurt. He explained that "dit blok is gedacht als te worden bebouwd met eene harmonishe bebouwing" (Arie Keppler, "Gewijzigd plan Polanenbuurt," 30 December 1913, Dienst PW 2307 doss. 882, in Dienst PW 1616/1921, archive 5213, GAA). Tellegen then requested of the director of public works that the plan for the southwest portion of the Spaarndammerbuurt be changed in accordance with Keppler's proposal and provided a sketch plan by Keppler. Tellegen notes, "Het plan-van der Mey is daarvan een verbeterde editie" (J. W. C. Tellegen to alderman of

housing, 14 January 1915, 158[18] AZ 1910, in 3163 VH 1914, archive 5187, GAA). Van der Mey's plan of the *hof* accompanies the memo from the director of public works to the alderman of public works, 5 March 1914, Dienst PW 2037 doss. 882, in Dienst PW 1616/1921, archive 5213, GAA.

20. The Health Board, Public Works, and Housing Committees all praised it. The Health Board visited Arnhem and was impressed by the *hofs* there (Health Board to mayor and aldermen, 23 September 1915, 232 GC 1915, archive 5269, GAA). The Public Works plan for the Spaarndammer district (*Gemeenteblad* 1 [1915], no. 1084, 28 September 1915, 2390–92) was approved on 13 October 1915.

21. Jan Gratama, "Kroniek," part 62, *Bouwkundig Weekblad* 36, no. 13 (24 July 1915): 100–101.

22. Although De Klerk's design followed Berlage's call for *blokbouw*, Searing has pointed out that the lack of constructive expression in De Klerk's work ran against Berlage's rationalism. Cuypers resigned from the Committee of Aesthetics over the question of the separation of construction from aesthetic judgment in relation to the block by De Klerk across from this one (Searing, "Housing in Holland," 183–84).

23. Committee of Aesthetics meeting of 25 November 1915, Notulen van de werkvergaderingen der Schoonheidscommissie, archive 458/16, GAA. The existing block by De Klerk faced the Spaarndammerplantsoen and turned onto Krommeniestraat, adjacent to and across from the proposed housing for Het Oosten by Lippets, Scholten, and Moolenschot, which in turn connected to Leliman's housing for Eigen Haard. On the other side of Krommeniestraat, Gulden and Geldmaker planned a project for Amsterdam-Zuid that faced the Spaarndammerplantsoen.

24. Committee of Aesthetics meetings of 30 December 1915, 9 December 1915, 24 February 1916, Notulen vergaderingen der stemgerechtigde leden der Schoonheidscommissie, archive 458/14, GAA; Arie Keppler to Michel de Klerk, 12 January 1916, 144 WD 1916, archive 458/20, GAA. De Klerk wanted continuity, not a break with the adjacent housing as the Committee of Aesthetics suggested. He wanted a high continuous roofline (De Klerk to Keppler, 14 January 1916, archive 458/20, and Keppler to alderman of housing, 29 March 1916, 1439 WD 1916, in 170 VH 1916, archive 5187, GAA).

25. In a memo to the alderman of housing, when Keppler noted that Eigen Haard had requested the lease on the land originally reserved for Hille, he wrote: "Mijnerzijds zal getracht worden den bouw te doen ontwerpen door den Architect M. de Klerk" (Arie Keppler to alderman of housing, 21 March 1916, 1287 WD 1916, in 878 VH 1916, archive 5187, GAA). See also Keppler's letter to alderman of housing, 29 March 1916, 1439 WD 1916, in 170 VH 1916, archive 5187, GAA: "Bovendien is het mij gelukt de woningbouwvereeniging 'Eigen Haard' bereid to vinden de bebouwing aan het Spaarndammerplein te doen uitvoeren door den Architect M. de Klerk, zoodat ook rondom dit plein de eenheid van het stadsbeeld niet verbroken behoeft te worden. Wel zal de derde zijde van het plein voor een deel bebouwd worden naar plannen van de Architecten Gulden en Geldmaker, doch overleg met den Architect M. de Klerk acht ik niet buitengesloten te meer daar deze mij bereids verklaarde, dat de ontworpen bebouwing van de heeren G. en G. [Gulden en Geldmaker] naar zijne meening niet storend op het door hem ontworpen stadsbeeld zou werken."

26. Committee of Aesthetics meeting of 30 December 1915, Notulen vergaderingen der

stemgerechtigde leden der Schoonheidscommissie, archive 458/14, GAA. There was also some futile discussion of making private developers adhere to supervision (Committee of Aesthetics to mayor and aldermen, 14 January 1916, SC no. 12, 170 VH 1916, archive 5187, GAA). This issue once again split Public Works from the Building and Housing Inspection Office and the Housing Authority. The director of the Building and Housing Inspection Office shared the committee's point of view and hoped to coordinate private developers as well (see Jan van der Waerden to alderman of housing, 6 March 1916, 32^2 AZ 1916, in 170 VH 1916, archive 5187, GAA). In another letter, the Committee of Aesthetics complained to mayor and aldermen about developers who put their profit before all else and of the Public Works land policy, which worked against Berlage's plan (letter of 29 December 1916, SC no. 49, archive 458/20, GAA).

27. From the end of the nineteenth century, Amsterdam had been planning an extension into the polders north of the IJ. For the history of planning of Amsterdam North, see L. Jansen, "De geschiedenis van Amsterdam Noord," *Ons Amsterdam* 14, no. 12 (December 1962): 354–59, and 15, no. 2 (February 1963): 42–44; Arie Keppler, *Plan van uitbreiding van de overzijde van het IJ* (Amsterdam: Woningdienst, 1926). The plan produced by the IJ Committee of 1903 designated several residential districts surrounded by industrial development (IJ Committee plan of 27 April 1903, set by Raadsbesluit 20 January 1906, *Gemeenteblad* 1 (1905), no. 1024, 1 November 1905, 2357. A general extension plan for the IJ was set on 29 July 1914. Street plans drawn up by the Public Works Department in 1910 designed a low-rise neighborhood in Nieuwendammerham. The southern portion of the district, Spreeuwpark, was one of the first areas constructed by the housing societies. Low rise, two- and three-story projects surrounded the plain central square of this rather inept plan (*Gemeenteblad* 1 [1910], no. 706, 12 July 1910, 755–60, and no. 798, 24 July 1912). Building was limited to three stories on the recommendation of the Health Board (Health Board report, 27 December 1909, 438 GC 1909, arcive 5269, GAA). The Public Works plan changed the street pattern, but kept the land use suggested by the IJ Committee. The housing societies that built here were Dr. Schaepman, Het Oosten, and the Algemeene.

28. The individual architects—Noorlander, Leliman, and Kuipers and Ingwersen—also drew up plans. These were little improvement over the Public Works plan. The collaborative plan was the work of Keppler with Leliman, Walenkamp, and Kuipers and Ingwersen (director of the Building and Housing Inspection Office to alderman of housing, 21 January 1915, 1931 VH 1914).

29. Keppler also generally urged that schools be designed by the same architects as designed the housing rather than by the Public Works civil servants.

30. Director of public works to alderman of public works, 24 February 1915, 812 PW 1915, archive 5180, GAA. Keppler had submitted his plan to Public Works for comment fully expecting the ideas to influence the final decision. But Van der Mey made little use of the ideas. The director of the Public Works Department, A. W. Bos was even upset that Van der Mey had met with Keppler and the housing architects to plan the Zaanhof.

31. Director of the Building and Housing Inspection Office to alderman of housing, 21 January 1915, 1931 VH 1914, archive 5187; director of public works to alderman of public works, 27 July 1914, 4955 PW 1914, archive 5180.

32. Alderman of housing to alderman of public works, 5 May 1915, 704 VH 1915, archive 5187, GAA. Bos also disagreed on the cost of the land and the density of construction.

33. The plan (*Gemeenteblad* 1 [1916], no. 1113, 10 October 1916, 2577) was passed on 18 October 1916, .

34. Arie Keppler to alderman of housing, 29 March 1916, 1439 WD 1916, in 170 VH 1916, archive 5187, GAA.

35. Arie Keppler to director of public works, 29 February 1916, 952 WD 1916, and director of public works to alderman of public works, 13 June 1916, 2762 PW 1916, archive 5180, GAA.

36. Committee of Aesthetics meetings of 9 July 1917 and 8 November 1917, Notulen van de werkvergaderingen der Schoonheidscommissie, archive 458/16, GAA; Arie Keppler to Committee of Aesthetics, 31 May 1917 (*Verslag Schoonheidscommissie* [1917]).

37. *Gemeenteblad* 2 (1917), meeting of 26 October 1917, 2029.

38. Committee of Aesthetics meeting of 20 June 1918, Notulen van de werkvergaderingen der Schoonheidscommissie, archive 458/16, GAA. The Coöperatie district was on the site originally planned for an academic hospital.

39. For a close analysis of the project, see Helen Searing, "With Red Flags Flying: Housing in Amsterdam, 1915–1923," in *Art and Architecture in the Service of Politics*, ed. Linda Nochlin and Henry Millon (Cambridge: MIT Press, 1978), 254–64.

40. Z. D. J. W. Gulden, *Gemeenteblad* 2 (1915), meeting of 3 November 1915, 1664.

41. Committee of Aesthetics meetings of 12 August 1915 and 23 September 1915, Notulen vergaderingen der stemgerechtigde leden der Schoonheidscommissie, archive 458/14, GAA. The intent to judge the architects on the Building and Housing Inspection Office list was also clearly stated in the meeting of 26 August 1915.

42. J. N. Hendrix, Public Works Committee meeting of 10 October 1918, Notulen van de Commissie van bijstand in zake Publieke Werken (1918), archive 5087, GAA, 292.

43. For example, the works of De Klerk, Kramer, Gratama and Versteeg, Gulden and Geldmaker, and J. F. Staal. On the architectural shaping of the southern extension of Amsterdam, the role of the Committee of Aesthetics the application of the Amsterdam School its association with the Social Democratic Party, see Searing, "With Red Flags Flying," 230–69; Helen Searing, "Amsterdam South: Social Democracy's Elusive Housing Ideal," *VIA* 4 (1980): 59–77.

44. Van Epen did not sign the drawings for the society's architect Rijnja (Committee of Aesthetics meeting of 8 November 1917, Notulen van de werkvergaderingen der Schoonheidscommissie, archive 458/16, GAA).

45. Committee of Aesthetics meeting of 19 May 1920, Notulen van de werkvergaderingen der Schoonheidscommissie, archive 458/16, GAA. The assistant was Jan Kuyt.

46. Committee of Aesthetics meeting of 4 July 1919, Notulen van de werkvergaderingen der Schoonheidscommissie, archive 458/16, GAA.

47. It was his Zeeburgerdijk project in the Indische district (Committee of Aesthetics to director of the Housing Authority, 27 September 1919, SC no. 115, archive 458/20, GAA).

48. Committee of Aesthetics meeting of 29 August 1919, Notulen van de werkvergaderingen der Schoonheidscommissie, archive 458/16, GAA. The project was subjected to repeated rejections meeting after meeting until 15 October 1919 when they suggested that Moolenschot get an aesthetic assistant. The committee finally approved the design after numerous revisions on 22 March 1920.

49. Lippits's reputation was based on his 1912 designs for the middle-class housing society

Samenwerking (X., "Woningen der Amsterdamsche Coöp. Woningbouwvereeniging Samenwerking," *Bouwkundig Weekblad* 32, no. 30 [27 July 1912]: 358–59, and *Twintigjarig overzicht 1908–1928 Amsterdamsche Coöperatieve Woningvereeniging "Samenwerking"* [Amsterdam, 1929], 4–5).

50. Committee of Aesthetics meeting of 19 September 1919, Notulen van de werkvergaderingen der Schoonheidscommissie, archive 458/16, GAA.

51. This raised a question of authority resolved in a meeting of the Committee of Aesthetics with Berlage and Keppler present on 3 October 1919. Berlage's position as aesthetic adviser of the south plan was to coordinate the massing, building heights, and land use, not to oversee details as if he were a were a Committee of Aesthetics of his own. Berlage had been consulted by both Lippits and Scholte for Het Oosten and Jan Stuyt for Amsteldijk, who were building on neighboring sites (Committee of Aesthetics to mayor and aldermen, 9 October 1919, SC no. 118, archive 458/20; Lippits and Scholte to Committee of Aesthetics, 14 October 1919, archive 458/20, GAA. See also discussion of this in Francis F. Fraenkel, *Het plan Amsterdam-Zuid van H. P. Berlage* (Alphen aan den Rijn: Caneletto, 1976), 81–82.

52. Arie Keppler's obituary of J. H. W. Leliman noted his importance for introducing low-rise housing to Amsterdam with the Eigen Haard housing in the Indische district (*Tijdschrift voor Volkshuisvesting* 2, no. 5 [15 May 1921]: 123–24).

53. Committee of Aesthetics to mayor and aldermen, 6 June 1917, SC no. 62, archive 458/20, GAA; Committee of Aesthetics meeting of 13 December 1917, Notulen van de werkvergaderingen der Schoonheidscommissie, archive 458/16, GAA.

54. Keppler had previously arranged for Eigen Haard to take over De Klerk's project for the developer Klaas Hille on the side of the Spaarndammerplantsoen opposite to the block he had completed for Hille (see note 26 above). During the preparations for the second block, De Klerk stated that he could design something reasonable on the awkward triangular block between the Spaarndammerplantsoen and the Zaanhof. Keppler arranged for him to do so for the housing society Eigen Haard (Arie Keppler, obituary for Michel de Klerk, *Architectura* 27, no. 38 [29 December 1923]: 236).

55. Committee of Aesthetics meeting of 1 February 1917, Notulen van de werkvergaderingen der Schoonheidscommissie, archive 458/16, GAA. De Klerk in 1916 had commented that Berlage was not an artist.

56. Committee of Aesthetics meeting of 24 August 1920, Notulen van de werkvergaderingen der Schoonheidscommissie, archive 458/16, GAA. Van Epen ran into difficulties with the Committee of Aesthetics in 1919 and 1920 with his housing designs for Samenwerking, on the Amsteldijk for Algemeene, on Krusemanstraat for ACOB and Rochdale, and on Cronjestraat for Algemeene. This dispute was a precursor of the committee's objections to modernism in Amsterdam in the late 1920s. A critical but balanced discussion of Van Epen's work is J. P. M[ieras], "Woningcomplex Staatsliedenbuurt Amsterdam," *Bouwkundig Weekblad* 40, no. 37 (13 September 1919): 223–24. See also M. C. Kuipers, "Gezond en vrolijk wonen: Over het werk van J. C. Van Epen, 1860–1960" (master's thesis, University of Leiden, 1976). Van Epen's own account of the Amstelveenscheweg project is in *Bouwkundig Weekblad* 39, no. 49 (7 December 1918): 284–85; see also Wim van Beek, *Vroolijk-wonen: Geschiedenis van een heel klein stukje Amsterdam* (Amsterdam: Uitgeverij de Spieghel, 1996).

57. J. C. van Epen, "Schoonheid: Nadeelige gevolgen van Schoonheidscommissies, de dood der ware kunst," *Bouwkundig Weekblad* 43, no. 39 (30 September 1922): 377–78. He turned to J. E. van der Pek's idea that those with professional membership should have free passage through Committee of Aesthetics. See *Bouwkundig Weekblad* 44, no. 4 (27 January 1923): 51–52, and no. 5 (3 February 1923: 62–64.

58. I am grateful to Ed Taverne for suggesting this evocative description.

59. Searing, "Housing in Holland," ix.

60. J. F. Staal, "'De Bouwwereld' en de Schoonheidscommissie," *Architectura* 25, no. 6 (10 February 1917): 36. Staal also argued later against admittance of nonarchitects to the Committee of Aesthetics in 1924. He satirically suggested that if businessmen were admitted as M. J. Granpré Molière had suggested, then there would have to be a representative of the workers' unions, since these are democratic times ("De ideale Schoonheidscommissie," *Bouwkundig Weekblad* 44, no. 3 [20 January 1923]: 35–36).

61. *Gemeenteblad* 2 (1917), meeting of 25 October 1917, 1975. Earlier Loopuit had also stated that there was need in Amsterdam for many young architects, not just one, and that he supported the free competition of ideas (*Gemeenteblad* 2 [1915], meeting of 3 November 1915, 1670). W. H. Vliegen (Social Democrat), C. B. Posthumus Meyjes (Christelijk Historische), and J. N. Hendrix (Roman Catholic) agreed with his position.

62. Helen Searing analyses the "denouement" of the style as applied in Amsterdam West in "Housing in Holland," 318–19.

63. J. B. van Loghem, "Moderne bouwkunst en Schoonheidscommissie," *Bouwkundig Weekblad* 38, no.1 (6 January 1917): 6. "Al zal dan ook een schoonheidscommissie in haar kwaliteit geen kunstwerk kunnen doen ontstaan, zij kan zeker wanneer zij blijft afwijzen de dorre producten uit antiquarischen geest gesproten, of door domme behoudzucht van den lastgever ontstaan, veel bijdragen tot het zuivere begrip omtrent kunst."

64. Committee of Aesthetics meeting of 15 May 1919, Notulen vergaderingen der stemgerechtigde leden der Schoonheidscommissie, archive 458/14, GAA; Arie Keppler to mayor, 12 June 1918, 3788 WD 1918, in 1987 VH 1918, archive 5187, GAA.

65. Keppler had earlier asked the Committee of Aesthetics if it had preferences for architects in Amsterdam South, and it had said it was not authorized to chose architects and could not influence choice (Committee of Aesthetics meeting of 20 June 1918, Notulen van de werkvergaderingen der Schoonheidscommissie, archive 458/16, GAA).

66. Berlage at Committee of Aesthetics meeting of 15 May 1919, Notulen vergaderingen der stemgerechtigde leden der Schoonheidscommissie, archive 458/14, GAA. Attending: P. J. de Jongh, Jan de Meyer, D. F. Slothouwer, Pieter Vorkink, Jansen, H. T. Wijdeveld, J. F. Staal, De Rooij, with A. R. Hulshoff, H. P. Berlage, and Arie Keppler.

67. Committee of Aesthetics meeting of 18 November 1919, Notulen van de werkvergaderingen der Schoonheidscommissie, archive 458/16, GAA. Staal was also named a leader of building, in Watergraafsmeer.

68. Jan Gratama, "Complex arbeiderswoningen bij het Stadion te Amsterdam," *Bouwkundig Weekblad* 42, no. 47 (19 November 1921): 300.

69. The Bouwmaatschappij took on C. J. Blaauw. Dr. Schaepman hired Jan Kuyt Wzn. Patrimonium's architects Kuipers and Ingwersen took on E. A. C. Roest.

70. See *Nieuws van de Dag* of 11 November 1921 and Gratama, "Complex arbeiderswoningen."

71. The architects and societies were as follows: municipal housing, Public Works architect Nicolaas Lansdorp, Jr.; Ons Huis, L. Zwiers; De Dageraad, August M. J. Sevenhuysen; Onze Woning (Bouwmaatschappij), C. J. Blaauw; Patrimonium, Tjeerd Kuipers, A. U. Ingwersen, E. A. C. Roest; Algemeene, Jan Gratama and G. Versteeg; Rochdale, G. F. la Croix; Ons Belang, Willem Noorlander; Dr. Schaepman, Jan Kuyt Wzn.; Het Oosten, J. J. L. Moolenschoot.

72. Committee of Aesthetics to mayor and aldermen, 6 December 1915, archive 458/20, GAA; mayor and aldermen to Committee of Aesthetics, 10 July 1916, archive 458/20, GAA. The Public Works Committee argued that Public Works already had a first-class architect in Van der Mey and therefore its designs did not need to be reviewed (meeting of 2 March 1916, Notulen van de Commissie van bijstand in zake Publieke Werken [1916], archive 5087, GAA).

73. Van der Mey was soon joined by Piet Kramer in the service of Public Works; later P. L. Marnette, Nicolaas Lansdorp and A. R. Hulshoff joined. The sculptor Hildo Krop also played a role in developing the forms that typified public design in Amsterdam in the 1920s. An account of the changes in the design of street furniture throughout Amsterdam due to the change in aesthetic policy in the Public Works Department is given in Kasper van Ommen, *Straatmeubilair: Amsterdamse School, 1911–1940* (Amsterdam: Stadsuitgeverij, 1992).

74. Z. D. J. W. Gulden, *Gemeenteblad* 2 (1916), meeting of 4 November 1916, 1799.

75. A. R. Hulshoff, "De aesthetische leiding van den woningbouw van 'Amstel's Bouwvereeniging,' in de uitbreiding 'Zuid' te Amsterdam," *Bouwkundig Weekblad*, no. 17 (23 April 1921): 101–4; Searing, "Housing in Holland," 285–89; Fraenkel, *Het plan Amsterdam-Zuid*, 63–76. The architects were: Piet Kramer, D. E. Slothouwer, P. L. Marnette, Michel de Klerk, A. Kint, J. Zietsma, A. van Baalen, Jan Boterenbrood, Dick Greiner, G. F. La Croix, G. J. Rutgers, C. Kruyswijk, Nicolaas Lansdorp, H. Th. Wijdeveld, Barend van der Nieuwer-Amstel, A. J. Westerman, Margaret Kropholler. For an interesting account of the way this complex functioned when subletting as a result of the housing shortage led to overcrowding, see Gemeentelijke Woningdienst, *Verslag van het onderzoek naar de woningtoestanden in het z.g. Amstellaankwartier* (Amsterdam, 1923).

76. Searing, "Housing in Holland," 311–18; *Plan West* (Amsterdam, 1925). The architects on the committee were Gratama, Hulshoff, Versteeg.

77. Committee of Aesthetics meeting of 16 November 1922, Notulen vergaderingen der stemgerechtigde leden der Schoonheidscommissie, archive 458/14, GAA.

78. *Bouwverordening*, art. 95 bis, added 25 January 1922.

79. The Committee of Aesthetics also merged with the Committee for City Beauty (Commissie voor Stadsschoon, founded in 1908 by A. W. Weissman and A. L. Gendt), a committee composed of representatives of societies dedicated to the preservation of Amsterdam's beauty and largely concerned with issues of historic preservation. The fact that these representatives were not architects raised a commotion in architectural circles (*Gemeenteblad* 1 [1924], no. 85, 25 January 1924, 145, passed 26 March 1924). The proposed composition of the new Committee of Aesthetics was nine architects, one painter, one sculptor, one landscape architect, one archeologist, and four laymen interested in urban design. Originally, only architects were to have the vote. Later a decorative artist was added and nonarchitects were given the vote. The

lay presence was criticized in the architectural press, for instance by J. F. Staal, C. J. Blaauw, and by Architectura et Amicitia. But the BNA and NIVS were in favor of it and Granpré Molière defended it. Although lay members were given the vote, this was largely obviated by the division of tasks whereby district commissions, rather than the whole Committee of Aesthetics, would judge facades. The issue of lay participation was raised earlier in the council by Social Democrat Vliegen during the Janus affair, when the Committee of Aesthetics was accused of forcing "hypermodernism" on an office building. Vliegen and others accused the architects of behaving like a monopoly and stated that they had no trust in the committee without a lay voice. See *Gemeenteblad* 2 (1921), meeting of 9 March 1921, 522–32. In the *Bouwkundig Weekblad*, the controversy can be followed in articles by M. J. Granpré Molière, C. B. Posthumus Meyjes, and J. F. Staal (*Bouwkundig Weekblad* 44, no. 1 [6 January 1923]: 4–7; no. 2 [13 January 1923]: 22–23: and no. 3 [20 January 1923]: 35–36).

80. They also were asked to list buildings of architectural and historical interest to be preserved; to plan for the change and restoration of monuments, canals, and planting plans; and to take up anything necessary to carry out the new ordinance.

81. *Gemeenteblad* 1 (1926), no. 374, 7 May 1926, 690.

82. Public Works Committee meeting of 2 April 1925, Notulen van de Commissie van bijstand in zake Publieke Werken (1925), archive 5087, GAA.

83. *Gemeenteblad* 1 (1926), no. 374, 7 May 1926, 690–91.

84. Director of public works, chairman; director of the Building and Housing Inspection Office, director of the Housing Authority, city architect, chief of land management, the designer of the south plan, and an architect to be appointed.

85. *Gemeenteblad* 1 (1926), no. 374, 7 May 1926, 692–97.

86. Ibid., 687–88.

87. Ibid., 698.

88. H. L. de Jong, open letter to mayor, aldermen, and Amsterdam City Council, October 1925, AA 276.006, GAA. De Jong preferred a state exam for architects similar to those for doctors, lawyers, and engineers.

89. On this issue of the difficulty of government in taking a position on questions of aesthetic quality, see Adorno: "The demand made by administration upon culture is essentially heteronomous: culture—no matter what form it takes—is to be measured by norms not inherent to it and which have nothing to do with the quality of the object, but rather with some type of abstract standards imposed from without, while at the same time the administrative instance—according to its own prescriptions and nature—must for the most part refuse to become involved in questions of immanent quality which regard the truth of the thing itself or its objective bases in general" (Theodor W. Adorno, "Culture and Administration," *The Culture Industry: Selected Essays on Mass Culture* [London: Routledge, 1991], 98).

90. David Harvey, *The Condition of Postmodernity: An Enquiry into the Origins of Cultural Change* (Oxford: Basil Blackwell, 1989), 273, 276, 278 and passim.

CONCLUSION

1. "Snarepijperij," *De Kroniek* 3, no. 115 (7 March 1897): 78.

2. Ibid.

3. E. Kuipers, “Arbeiderswoning-complexen van M. de Klerk,” *Woningbouw* 3, no. 4 (October 1919): 31.

4. Theodor W. Adorno, “Culture and Administration,” in *The Culture Industry: Selected Essays on Mass Culture* (London: Routledge, 1991), 112.

5. Paul Rabinow, *French Modern: Norms and Forms of the Social Environment* (Cambridge: MIT Press, 1989), 12.

6. See David Harvey, *The Condition of Postmodernity: An Enquiry into the Origins of Cultural Change* (Oxford: Basil Blackwell, 1989), 108, on the formation of the state.

7. Other examples of this synthesis can be found in the Netherlands, for instance in Willem Dudok’s Hilversum, M. J. Granpré Molière’s Vreewijk, J. B. van Loghem’s Tuinwijk Zuid and Jan Wils’s Papaverhof.

8. The most striking example of such a neighborhood comprised the projects of the housing society Samenwerking, a middle-class rather than working-class district.

9. A comparison between the urbanism of Berlage and Otto Wagner would be illuminating. See, however, Iain Boyd Whyte, “Modernist Dioscuri? Otto Wagner and Hendrik Petrus Berlage,” in *Otto Wagner: Reflections on the Raiment of Modernity*, ed. Harry Francis Mallgrave (Santa Monica: Getty Center for the History of Art and the Humanities, 1993), 157–97.

10. Noud de Vreeze, *Woningbouw, inspiratie en ambities: Kwalitatieve grondslagen van de sociale woningbouw in Nederland* (Almere: Nationale Woningraad, 1993), 15.

INDEX